HEALTH CARE
ETHICS
AND THE LAW

Donna K. Hammaker

Director, National Institute Health Care Management & Law
MGA, Wharton School of the University of Pennsylvania; JD, Temple University School of Law
Hebrew University Faculty of Law and London School of Economics
Former Adjunct Professor of Health Law, MBA Program in Biotechnology &
Health Industry Management, Pennsylvania State University
Formerly President & CEO, Collegiate Health Care Corp.

Thomas M. Knadig

Hospice Chaplain, Hospital of the University of Pennsylvania Health Care System
MDiv, St. Mary's Seminary & University; MA, Notre Dame University; EdD, Widener University
Oxford University, Massachusetts Institute of Technology, and University of California-Berkeley
Adjunct Professor of Humanities, Widener University
Formerly Board Chairman, Collegiate Health Care Corp.

with Sarah J. Tomlinson

Office of the General Counsel, Fox Rothschild LLP
Health Policy Doctoral Student, Temple University College of Public Health;
JD, Villanova University School of Law; MBA, Pennsylvania State University
Adjunct Professor of Health Law, Immaculata University

JONES & BARTLETT
LEARNING

World Headquarters
Jones & Bartlett Learning
5 Wall Street
Burlington, MA 01803
978-443-5000
info@jblearning.com
www.jblearning.com

Jones & Bartlett Learning books and products are available through most bookstores and online booksellers. To contact Jones & Bartlett Learning directly, call 800-832-0034, fax 978-443-8000, or visit our website, www.jblearning.com.

10167-6

Production Credits

VP, Executive Publisher: David D. Cella
Publisher: Michael Brown
Associate Editor: Lindsey Mawhiney Sousa
Associate Editor: Nicholas Alakel
Senior Vendor Manager: Tracey McCrea
Senior Marketing Manager: Sophie Fleck Teague
Manufacturing and Inventory Control Supervisor: Amy Bacus
Composition: S4Carlisle Publishing Services
Project Management: S4Carlisle Publishing Services
Cover Design: Kristin E. Parker
Cover Image and Section Headers: © Photology1971/Shutterstock
Rights & Media Specialist: Merideth Tumasz
Media Development Editor: Shannon Sheehan
Printing and Binding: Edwards Brothers Malloy
Cover Printing: Edwards Brothers Malloy

Library of Congress Cataloging-in-Publication Data
Hammaker, Donna K., author.
   Health care ethics and the law / Donna Hammaker.
      pages cm
   Includes bibliographical references and index.
   ISBN 978-1-284-10160-7 (pbk.)
1. Medical laws and legislation—Moral and ethical aspects—United States. 2. Public health laws—United States.
3. Medical ethics—United States. I. Title.
   KF3821.H365 2016
   174.2—dc23
                                                                          20150332916048

Printed in the United States of America
20 19 18 17 16   10 9 8 7 6 5 4 3 2 1

Contents

2. Values and Principles Confronting Our Health Care System   39

PART II. THE ETHICS OF ACCESS TO HEALTH CARE — 89

3. Access to Affordable Health Insurance — 91

PART III. THE ETHICAL DEVELOPMENT OF HUMAN CAPITAL — 175

6. Employers' Health Care Costs — 177

7. Management and Labor Relations — 197

PART IV. IMPROVING THE QUALITY AND EQUALITY OF HEALTH CARE   215

8. Evidence-Based Medicine   217

11. The HIV/AIDS Pandemic   293

PART VII. OUR FUTURE HEALTH CARE SYSTEM   431

16. Our Future: A New Kind of Health Care Ethics   433

Preface

"A long habit of not thinking a thing is wrong, gives it a superficial appearance of being right."

— **Thomas Paine** (1737–1809), one of the Founding Fathers of the United States, from *Common Sense* (1776)

© Courtesy: Everett Collection/Everett Collection Inc./age fotostock

Authors' Vision

This text will engage students with the ethical decisions faced by health care professionals every day. Based on principles and their applications in health care ethics and the law, this text extends beyond areas that are often included in discussions of political philosophy and the principles of justice. While aware of the intimate interplay between morality and ethics, no distinction is made between the two in this text, as they can be united in a consistent manner. Far from overlooking the separation of ethics and the law, it is assumed, as U.S. Supreme Court Justice Oliver Wendell Holmes (1841–1935) articulated, that ethics and the law should not be separable; therefore, all materials addressed in the text encompass both health care ethics and the law. At the same time, what is lawful may not always be ethical, but what is ethical should always be lawful.

For many people, the fundamental questions of ethics are: "what should I do?" and "how should I act?" However, ethics seeks to provide principles in addition to standards or rules of conduct. Such principles can guide people in identifying ethical issues and making ethical decisions in those not infrequent situations that may be outside the purview of the standards and rules. In this text, the law can be understood in light of organizing principles or consideration of social policy. This approach excludes theoretical puzzles not based on observation and data analysis.

Many people are passionate adherents of the principle of utilitarianism: "Everyone is obligated to do whatever will achieve the greatest good for the greatest number." Others are just as devoted to the basic principle of libertarianism: "Everyone is obligated to act only in ways that respect the human dignity and moral rights of all persons."

Ethical principles like these provide guidance for our actions; they balance stakeholder interests and personal motivations. People apply these principles by asking what is required of them when considering, for instance, whether to:

- Accept hospice care or begin a new invasive experimental treatment regime that lacks clinical evidence of its curative efficacy and may not be covered by health insurance
- Have an abortion or take to term a child that will be severely disabled, whether physically or intellectually or both

Health care professionals also apply ethical principles when they ask what is required of themselves or what is required of health care policies and organizations when considering, for instance, whether to:

- Provide affordable access to health insurance coverage to all members of society
- Limit health insurance coverage of medications and medical treatments to those that are determined to be effective based on evidence-based medicine
- Provide equal access to health care without regard to the ability to pay for such services

Ethical principles, though more general and requiring intelligent application, prevent health care ethics from being a mere list of rules and regulations. Many ethicists, in an effort to be helpful in the maximum number of cases, focus on principles so as to broaden the considerations beyond health laws and regulations, thereby preventing ethics from becoming a matter of checking whether actions are in compliance with carefully crafted rules of do's and don'ts. This focus on principles also enables the discussion to include a very fundamental component of ethics: values. The traditional values of compassion, equality of opportunity, and justice are referred to throughout this text. These same ethicists point out that by focusing only on what people should do or how they should act ignores the more important issue of what human beings should be and what their health care systems should stand for. In other words, the fundamental questions of ethics are not what people should do, but what kind of person should they be; what social responsibilities should health care systems have as a result of their corporate existence (an existence that is derived from the people through their representative state governments)?

According to value ethics (or virtue ethics), there are certain ideals, such as a commitment to excellence, toward which everyone should strive and which allow the full development of humanity. These common ideals are discovered through reflection on what human beings have the potential to become. With this approach to ethics, one strives to grasp the core values of common ideals and then bring them to bear on everyday decision-making. The essential elements in these ideals, once identified, could hold the key to addressing true reform of the U. S. health care system.

Values are attitudes and character traits that enable people to be and to act in ways that develop their human potential. They enable the nation to pursue the ideals its people have adopted. How does a person, and then society, develop values? Values are developed through learning and through practice. People can improve their character by practicing self-discipline, while a good character can be corrupted by repeated self-indulgence. Just as the ability to run a marathon develops through disciplined training and practice, so too does the capacity to be fair or to be compassionate develop through daily effort.

Values become habits. That is, once values are acquired, they become characteristic of a person. For instance, people who develop the value of fairness are often referred to as being fair-minded because they tend to be fair in all circumstances. Moreover, people who develop values are more disposed to act in ways that are consistent with their principles. The person who has values is the ethical person.

Habits create systems. At the heart of the value approach to ethics is the idea of systems. Ethical attitudes and character traits are not developed in isolation, but within and by the communities in which people choose to place themselves (including employers for which health care professionals choose to work). Individual personalities are affected by the ideals and values to which their communities attach importance and by the role models their communities present for imitation. This value approach urges health care professionals to pay attention to the contours of the health care systems in which they work and the habits of character that their employers encourage and instill.

Health care systems are only as ethical as the health care professionals who work within them, and vice versa. An ethical health care system will not tolerate unethical behavior by anyone associated with it, however far removed the person might be from the center. Ethics, then, is not simply a matter of having ethical principles and learning to apply them to specific situations. Health care ethics is a matter of trying to determine the kind of health care professional one should be and subsequently attending to the development of character within the health care system where one chooses to work.

Throughout this text are two strong, recurring themes: namely, that health care professionals have an obligation to be ethical and that the nation's laws should be reformed to help create health care systems that improve the quality and equality of health care for all stakeholders and members of society. A premise related to the imperative to create ethical health care systems is that the convergence of many health care sectors is rapidly changing the principles governing provider competition and regulation. These changes require the American legal system to expand the boundaries of health care ethics as it recognizes what is best and what is essential in the U.S. health care system.

While the health care industry faces unique ethical challenges, health care systems are increasingly shifting strategies to stay ahead of the curve of emerging ethical issues and government laws and regulations. Providers are constructing new breakthroughs in health care delivery and seeking to return to the common ideals of reason through modern science. All of this active change is taking place amid innovative U.S. reform initiatives. Health care ethics should challenge these dynamic changes with a stern but fair message about moral limits.

Text Approach

Real-World Knowledge

This text explores ethical dilemmas in which there are two or more valid decisions to choose from. Real-world issues are explored that are often decided based on personal ethics, such as abortion and end-of-life care. This text bridges research and practice, reflecting current issues facing the health care industry and government agencies. The ethics concepts in this text are old-fashioned practical questions of life: right and wrong and how to treat other people justly and fairly. The application of justice and compassion seeks to provide health care professionals with sufficient knowledge of ethics to become intelligent, critical thinkers in professional practice.

This is a practical ethics text relevant to undergraduate students seeking the basic management skills required to work in health care organizations, as well as graduate students currently working in health care organizations as health care industry administrators, physicians, nurses, pharmacists, therapists, scientists, and other administrative and clinical managers. This text is also relevant to consumers of health care who are simply attempting to navigate the complex U.S. health care system. Every attempt is made within the text to support health care ethics with practical applications of ethical decisions that health care professionals face in their everyday lives.

Depth and Breadth

This text does not overwhelm students with technical language and logic; instead, it covers basic principles of ethics and then focuses on practical applications of ethics in the real world of health care delivery and practice. Challenging court decisions and current health care actions are presented. Learning experiences can be customized by selecting from 16 topical chapters or by studying a specific topic in-depth using the multiple online resources provided.

Ethical Principles

There is a focus on interpretation, insight into ideas of ethics, and the methodologies for ethical decision-making. Principles underlying the ethics of health care are woven throughout this text as reference points. Students can develop and strengthen their skills in ethical decision-making through examination of the difficult ethical considerations presented in each chapter. Traditional principles will, however, only serve as a reference. Students do not have to be confined to any one normative model or framework for making ethical decisions. Rather, students are encouraged to be disciplined and independent in their decision-making and discover new models for arriving at ethical decisions. Students can build new models that will assist them in thinking through the implications of ethical issues.

Normative Law Standards

What sets this text apart from other texts on health care ethics is its focus on the normative standards of the law in supporting the foundation for ethics. In contrast to the philosophical standards used in most traditional texts on health care ethics, in this text, the prescribed standards of conduct in almost every recent court decision of first impression are examined; cases of first impression set forth completely original issues of law for decision by the courts. This unique method of selecting court decisions to ascertain ethical underpinnings highlights the changing nature of ethics and its current effect on the health care industry. Significant U.S. Supreme Court cases, as well as landmark cases from the U.S. Courts of Appeal and highest state courts will also be examined where the decisions are still good law and relevant. Each of the selected court decisions in this text, and the accompanying Student Manual, addresses new, important, and substantive issues involving health care ethics.

Court decisions are examined with a focus on how ethical principles underlying the law are currently being applied, the correctness of traditional assumptions and choices, and what might be done differently in future similar situations. Although the role of the courts is to interpret and apply existing law, their decisions often prompt legislators to write new laws in response to new thinking and changes in society. Additionally, although it is not the role of the courts to make judgments about what is ethical or unethical, their decisions certainly contain assumptions about ethics. Therefore, in an effort to provide some help to the reader in making ethical decisions, this textbook employs a methodology of examining recent U.S. court decisions for ideas about ethics. The courts are in no way dictating ethics, but their decisions may indicate the direction a society is moving in terms of its accepting or rejecting certain actions and whether those actions are tolerable or desirable from an ethical point of view. It should be emphasized again that legal does not equal ethical, but it provides some indications about what is considered ethical.

Models for Decision-Making

This text seeks to apply the best ethical practices to the health care industry. Students are exposed to decision-making models and their application in a health care context, whether in seeking new models to overcome the failure of markets and governments to provide health care to millions of people, or when searching for ways to better understand the nation's complex health care reforms. Students learn about key elements of ethics that allow the U.S. health care culture to operate.

State-of-the-Art Research on Health Care Ethics and the Law

This text is traditional legal scholarship written with state-of-the-art research methods, using online databases that are revolutionizing research on health care ethics and the law, including foremost:

- Knowledge@Wharton (Wharton School of the University of Pennsylvania)
- NLM (National Library of Medicine)
- Westlaw and LexisNexis
- OVRC (Opposing Viewpoints Research Center)
- ProQuest

The text reviews the philosophies of ethics and seeks common themes in the law as well as conflicts. Knowledge of the ethical considerations that arise as innovations transform global health care industry practices and public policy are clearly explained so that students can be open to new possibilities for applying what they learn when the ethical imperatives are not clear or are contradictory.

Primary Research with Health Care Professionals

Background information was obtained from a comprehensive search of published literature and reports obtained from various business, law, and medical trade journals. Secondary research of peer-reviewed journals is all-inclusive in a bibliography for each chapter; some reference is made to government reports and policy papers. This research, in turn, was supplemented with reviews by a panel of more than 30 health care professionals from all aspects of the health care industry. Their shared opinions and insights helped supplement the online databases with first-hand knowledge on current and future trends in health care ethics. They identified ethical matters that have the most social significance to them as leaders in the health care industry. This review process resulted in chapters having importance for real-world issues, present-day events, and the current state of the nation's health care reforms.

Organization of This Text

The text is divided into six general parts:

Part I, "Introduction to Health Care Ethics," provides an overview of the ethical issues facing the U.S. health care system.

> Chapter 1, *The Ethics of Health Care*, describes the ethical principles underlying the U.S. health care system; eight models for decision-making are provided to help health care professionals identify ethical issues and make the right decisions.

> Chapter 2, *Values and Principles Confronting Our Health Care System*, explains how the health care industry seeks to develop systems to help it make ethical decisions; the focus of this chapter is on ten near-universal values that often govern and guide decisions when ethical dilemmas are reviewed.

Part II, "The Ethics of Access to Health Care," addresses Americans' resolve to obtain the best health care system for as little investment as possible; the focus is on what is fair and just.

> Chapter 3, *Access to Affordable Health Insurance*, draws attention to the ethical obligation and challenge of finding a way to provide access to essential health care for all U.S. residents, especially vulnerable members of our society.

> Chapter 4, *Patients' Rights and Responsibilities*, looks at the ethical issues involved in health care reform legislation, patient rights, and universal basic coverage.

> Chapter 5, *Charitable Care and Tax-Exempt Hospitals*, examines whether non-profit hospitals are required to provide mutually affordable health care in return for the substantial tax exemptions they receive; the focus of this chapter is on what is a fair health care bill.

Part III, "The Ethical Development of Human Capital," concentrates on equality of opportunity in staffing U.S. health care organizations and the ethical issues of fairness affecting the management of employees.

> Chapter 6, *Employers' Health Care Costs*, deals with growing efforts to trim employers' health care costs in an ethical manner. Particular attention is devoted to smoking- and weight-related behaviors and adherence to medication and treatment regimens, areas that are linked to preventable health conditions and health care cost savings.

> Chapter 7, *Management and Labor Relations*, covers the ethical principles underlying the unionization of physicians and nurses, as well as newer concerns surrounding wage disparity in the health care industry.

Part IV, "Improving the Quality and Equality of Health Care," explores areas that could combat rising health care costs and improve the quality and equality of health care.

> Chapter 8, *Evidence-Based Medicine*, reviews the ethical issues confronting a discipline that has been around for a little more than a decade and is at the top of the list of improvements for improving patient safety, avoiding unnecessary medical procedures, and helping to provide more reliable and higher-quality health care.

> Chapter 9, *Medical Malpractice*, considers the ethical dilemmas facing health care professionals when malpractice occurs, as well as medical standards of care and malpractice reform.

Part V, "Our Health Care System's Ethical Response to Vulnerable Members of Society," takes a systematic look at the intellectually disabled, people suffering from the effects of Human Immunodeficiency Virus and Acquired Immune Deficiency Syndrome (HIV/AIDS), and victims of gun violence. The emphasis is on the costs of health care for the most vulnerable members of our society.

Chapter 10, *Mental Health*, focuses on the ethical issues involved in the health care system's response to mental illness. It seeks to address who should be responsible for the costs of living with a chronic mental disease or dangerous, severe mental disorder.

Chapter 11, *The HIV/AIDS Pandemic,* discusses the devastating HIV/AIDS epidemic; attention is focused on providing equal access to antiretroviral medications, which slow the progression of HIV/AIDS.

Chapter 12, *Environmental Safety and Gun Injury Prevention*, sets forth the ethical issues underlying the quandary of the modern U.S. health care system: while it is the most expensive in the world, Americans are neither healthier nor longer-lived than residents in other similarly situated countries.

Part VI, "Pressing Issues Facing Our Health Care System," comprises of chapters describing pivotal ethical issues and real-world pitfalls the United States is confronting.

Chapter 13, *Women's Reproductive Health*, spotlights the disparate provision of health care for procreation concerns. It addresses the ethical principles underlying reproductive issues against the backdrop of how abortion, the newer forms of contraception, and maternity care coverage are falling out of reach for more women in the United States.

Chapter 14, *Nutrition and Food Safety*, investigates ethical issues underlying the debate between the food industry and public health advocates over junk food, advertising, and obesity.

Chapter 15, *End-of-Life Care*, poses the ethical question of whether human beings have a right to die at a time and place of their own choosing.

Part VII, "Our Future Health Care System," briefly overviews health care ethics within the context of health care reforms in the United States.

Chapter 16, *Our Future: A New Kind of Health Care Ethics*, offers a framework for ethical reform of the current health care system.

How to Use This Text

One of the strengths of this text is the consistent approach to topics in each chapter. Each chapter has been methodically developed so students have the opportunity to understand what the law is, as well as the ethical principles that act as a foundation for the law. This text can be used at both introductory and advanced levels by merely changing the amount of guidance provided in each chapter. The same format is used in each chapter:
- "Learning Objectives" provide an overview of what is to be learned in each chapter.
- "Key Terms" list the terminology and specialized terms used in the health care industry and its relevant law.
- "Ethical or Unethical Decision" sections at the beginning of each chapter are short vignettes pulled from in-depth articles or drawn from actual court decisions pertinent to the chapter, demonstrating that society cannot always separate right from wrong or always know what the most ethical course of action is.

- The heart of each chapter explains the basics of ethical decision-making for those with little or no training in ethics; namely, the importance of health care ethics, its basic principles, and how it applies to practical management applications. Specific court decisions illustrate how ethical issues are currently being identified and how ethical principles are being applied to decisions in the real world. Understanding the legal reasoning of these court decisions will assist in reaching the most ethical decisions, particularly when such decisions may involve transforming the current legal order.
- "Ethical Dilemmas" dispersed throughout each chapter offer students the opportunity to apply their decision-making skills on both sides of an ethical issue to rationally arrive at ethical decisions.
- The "Ethical or Unethical Decision" that introduces every chapter is revisited at the end, and applies what has been put forth in the chapter and what has been decided by the courts thus far.
- "Chapter Summary" summarizes the most important ethical issues and principles covered in each chapter. The Chapter Summary pulls together practical knowledge and insight on emerging trends in reform of the U.S. health care industry.
- "References" sections list the extensive body of research that provides the foundation of this text.

Teaching Materials

Dramatic changes in the health care industry have pushed forward new questions about value creation. Because the health care industry is a highly regulated environment, and there are genuine ethical issues that place individuals at risk, the integrity of this text is very important. This text will help students prepare for real-world challenges. The technology-enhanced learning tools accompanying this text are available in multiple formats to fit students' learning preferences, and a range of instructional tools will meet virtually every instructor's needs.

Study Guide

Students are provided with an online study guide as a resource to help them apply the ethical principles and concepts and to master the terminology. This guide, which will be updated periodically as the law evolves, includes:

- **Chapter Outlines**.
- **Review Questions** assess students' knowledge.
- **Ethical Dilemmas** as they are presented in the text's chapters, with additional thought-provoking questions intended to ask students to analyze the selected ethical issues by reference to the eight decision-making models. This is where students can reach reasoned and ethical conclusions based on ethical principles presented and discussed in each chapter.
- **Related Ethical Issues** reinforce practical insights gained in the chapter to assess or improve the outcome of ethical issues facing the U.S. health care system. These questions include emerging ethical issues addressed in recent law review articles and symposia.
- **Analysis of New Court Decisions** outlines the legal standards of conduct from emerging cases on the topics covered in each chapter.
- **You Decide** presents competing statements and counterstatements about the issues covered in each chapter. This section enables students to reach their own rational decisions on the basis of ethical principles and personal reflection on the issues.

- **Further Your Knowledge** provides detailed material citing the research supporting the chapter narrative in the main text. At times, this section expands upon the ideas described in the main text, explains important caveats, or offers additional examples of a compelling fact. This section will help students if they want to investigate certain topics in more depth, such as the relationship of a health care topic to Jodi Picoult's bestselling novels.
- **Web Links** provide the opportunity to do further research on the topics presented in each chapter.

Instructor's Resources

The Instructor's Resources are computerized tools for instructional needs. These comprehensive and convenient online materials are designed to enhance class discussion and measure student progress. They provide a wide variety of valuable items to help instructors plan their courses and implement activities by chapter. The availability of these resources in an electronic format increases their value as teaching resources. They include:

- Suggested talking points for the Ethical Dilemmas from the study guide with a focus on how the eight decision-making models could be applied, the correctness of traditional ethical principles and choices, and what different ethical principles might be used in future, similar situations
- Additional short vignettes of actual court decisions pertinent to each chapter
- Additional group and individual activities, including summaries of film and television documentaries
- Links to websites providing additional materials to research cited in the chapter References in both the text and the student guide
- **PowerPoint Presentations** are available to visually enhance lectures and aid students in note-taking.
- **Computerized Testbank** contains short-answer, multiple-choice, and true/false questions from each chapter. This versatile program enables instructors to create their own tests and to write additional questions.
- **Comprehensive Syllabus Templates** have been developed to help instructors customize specific course titles.

About the Authors

Donna K. Hammaker, a health law attorney, earned graduate degrees in law and government administration from Temple University School of Law and the Wharton School at the University of Pennsylvania, and completed graduate studies at the Hebrew University Faculty of Law and the London School of Economics. Before entering academia, Hammaker was a member of the Pennsylvania Bar, admitted to practice before the U.S. District Court for the Eastern District of Pennsylvania, and the U.S. Court of Appeals for the Third Circuit. Hammaker was also president and chief executive officer of Collegiate Health Care, the nation's first inter-university managed care organization. She has served on the adjunct faculty and taught graduate management and health law at Immaculata University, Pennsylvania State University, Rutgers University, Saint Joseph's University, and Widener University. Hammaker recently authored the textbook, *Health Care Management and the Law* with Sarah J. Tomlinson (Delmar-Cengage Learning, 2011).

Thomas M. Knadig, a Templeton scholar in science and religion, is a hospice chaplain with the University of Pennsylvania Health Care System and holds a faculty appointment at Widener University. He earned graduate degrees in education administration, philosophy, and theology from Widener University, University of Notre Dame, and Saint Mary's Seminary and University. Knadig completed post doctoral studies at Oxford University in England, Massachusetts Institute of Technology, and the University of California-Berkeley. A former ordained Jesuit priest, Knadig was board chairman of Collegiate Health Care and executive director of the College Consortium on Drugs and Alcohol, a preferred provider organization with an education and training institute that served colleges and universities in North America. He has served on the adjunct faculty and taught core undergraduate ethics and religion courses at Immaculata University, LaSalle University, Saint Joseph's University, and Wheeling College.

Sarah J. Tomlinson is an attorney with the Office of the General Counsel of Fox Rothschild, LLP, a national law firm with over 600 attorneys in 21 offices nationwide. The firm has extensive experience as counsel to health care facilities and organizations and advises hundreds of physicians, medical groups, and health care institutions and provides representation in litigation, corporate, regulatory, and transactional matters. Tomlinson, a member of the Pennsylvania Bar, is a doctoral student in public health with a focus on health policy at Temple University's College of Public Health, and has earned graduate degrees in law and business administration from Villanova University School of Law and Pennsylvania State University. She is also a member of the adjunct faculty at Immaculata University, where she teaches legal and social aspects of health care administration and nursing law. This is Tomlinson's second textbook publication involving health law.

Interaction with the Authors

The standard for this text on health care ethics is excellence. Our goal is for every instructor adopting this text to have an excellent experience with it, along with its ancillary teaching materials. Adopters of this text may contact the authors to ask questions regarding materials in this text, to offer suggestions, to share teaching concerns, or to seek resolution of health law and ethics disputes. If the next generation of health care managers can reclaim a supple awareness of the challenging standards of ethics, the U.S. health care system may regain some of its earlier prestige. As Tocqueville maintained in his 1840 influential text about American law and society, *Democracy in America*, the greatest task of each generation is not to erase the past and reconstruct the present, but to recognize what was best in the past, what was essential, and to carry it forward.

The U.S. health care system will thrive again when the nation learns to acknowledge the force of this insight. However, if health care ethics is seen as nothing but a collection of arbitrary rules and regulations, and social forces are treated as obstacles to be overcome, rather than as shared boundaries to be reckoned with, the U.S. health care system will stay in its current crisis mode. Health care ethics should not be a wholly owned subsidiary of any one ideology. Instead, health care ethics should challenge all ideologies, with a firm understanding of the limits of law in a democracy based on notions of ethics and morality.

Donna K. Hammaker
Thomas M. Knadig
with Sarah J. Tomlinson

Acknowledgments

This text has been reviewed by individuals chosen for their diverse perspectives of the health industry and technical expertise. Joseph L. Fink, III, health law attorney and pharmacist, who is Professor of Pharmacy Law and Policy at the University of Kentucky College of Pharmacy, with joint faculty appointments as Professor of Health Services Management in the UK College of Public Health, Professor of Health Administration in the Martin School of Public Policy and Administration, and as Professor of Clinical Leadership and Management in the UK College of Health Sciences, reviewed and provided clear perspective on every chapter in the text. Gleb Epelbaum of Temple University Beasley School of Law and Emma Hopkins, a research intern, reviewed every chapter and provided student perspectives on ethical issues within the U.S. health care system. The purpose of this independent review was to provide critical comments that would assist in making this text as sound as possible and to ensure objectivity. Research support for this text was provided by the Penn State University-Great Valley MBA program in Biotechnology and Health Industry Management. The authors are also indebted to the following individuals for their review:

Anderson, Brent: Siemens Medical Services
Arujuna, Vinod: Boston Scientific
Benning, Shawn: Johnson & Johnson
Bezio, Timothy: Teva Pharmaceuticals
Bilo, Michael: Pfizer
Burhams, Sara Baumler: Shire Pharmaceutical
Caranfa, Justin: Precision Biotech
Choper, Jessica: Pfizer
Crowland, Keith: Kaiser Permanente
Enright, Patty: ROI Performance Solutions
Fischer, Carol: AstraZeneca
Hammaker, Jessica: Penn State Milton S. Hershey Medical Center
Hammaker, Krista E.: Bastyr University School of Naturopathic Medicine
Hardy, Chris: Pfizer
Hopkins, Patrick: JP Morgan (formerly with Genzyme and Johnson & Johnson)
Jordan, William: Sanofi-Aventis
Kaymak, Yilmaz C.: Novocure
Klein, Jordan: University of Pennsylvania Health Care System-Pennsylvania Hospital
Liu, Jeffrey: Johnson & Johnson
MacGregor, John: Perelman School of Medicine & University of Pennsylvania Health Care System-Hospital of the University of Pennsylvania
McHale, Wendy Wesoloskie: Merck
Mennor, Robert: Siemens Medical Services
Mullen, Eliose: United Food & Commercial Workers Union (Ret.)
Nelson, Ginny: AmeriHealth
Pentz, William: Cancer Treatment Centers of America
Sacco, Carolyn: Mpathy Medical
Spinks, Scott: Johnson & Johnson
Turnbull, Kathy: Independence Blue Cross
Weber, Michael: Merck
Wright, Peter: ReMed
Wu, Jason (Jisheng): Frontage Clinical Services

© marekuliasz/Shutterstock

Learning Objectives

Describes what readers should be able to do after completing each chapter.

Key Terms

Lists important terms that are defined and used in each chapter.

Ethical or Unethical Decision

Helps readers reach a judgment on the basis of ethical principles and personal reflection. The greater societal context of decisions should be considered, as opposed to yielding to more selfish drives or incremental changes that merely support maintenance of the status quo. The decisions are often derived from current headlines. Ethics should be integrated with the law instead of distinguishing between the law and ethics.

Ethical Dilemmas

Expands upon the ethical issues presented in each chapter. While Congress, state legislatures, and lower trial courts are debating these dilemmas, they have not been satisfactorily dealt with by the highest federal and state appellate courts or the U.S. Supreme Court.

Although the nation's highest courts can provide hints and inklings about ethics, it is ultimately each individual's responsibility to make rational decisions about ethics based on fair and just criteria. Thus, while there is a lack of widely accepted agreement for or against any of the choices possible relating to the ethical dilemmas in this text, reasoned and ethical conclusions should be based on ethical principles, as well as other common standards essential for a civil society built upon just law. To avoid emotion and prejudice, it is important that decisions be made in honest consultation with others who also seek just and reasoned resolutions of ethical dilemmas.

Law and Ethics Analysis: Court Decisions

Summarizes the legal assumptions and ethical choices used by the courts (U.S. Supreme Court, U.S. Courts of Appeal, highest state courts) in their analysis of the issues presented in this text. The law necessarily involves ethical reasoning in judicial decision-making. Material in these sections presents the legal reasoning of these court decisions, many of first impression, involving questions of law which have been presented for the first time and which have never been decided before in any reported court decisions. The case summaries will assist reflections on how to reach the most ethical decisions, particularly when such decisions may involve transforming the current legal order. References, where available, at the end of each case summary provide additional commentary on the court decisions; law review articles that simply cite the court decisions (but do not make any type of analysis of the decisions) are not listed.

Chapter Summary

Provides an overview of each chapter.

References

Helps readers investigate topics in more depth. Each citation expands upon the ideas described in each chapter, explains important caveats, or offers additional examples of a compelling fact.

Foreword

Human judgment and perceptions are malleable. For instance, in one research study by Christopher Chabris and Daniel Simons, two cognitive psychologists at the University of Illinois, subjects were asked to watch a video and count the number of times players with white shirts passed a basketball (Simons & Chabris, 1999). Most of the subjects achieved a fairly accurate count of the passes, but less than half saw something more important: a person in a black gorilla costume walking right into the center of the action and then moving off. More than half the subjects were so involved in the counting task that they did not perceive the gorilla—an entire gorilla—right in front of their eyes! *See generally* Chabris & Simons, 2010; Wind & Crook, 2006.

It is sobering to consider: Focused attention creates blinders that limit what our mind perceives overall. The question to keep in mind when thinking of health care ethics is this: What parts of the U.S. health care system are blindly driven by our narrow perceptions and failure to perceive the gorilla moving through our entire field of vision?

Health care ethics is often defined in terms of rules, principles, values, and decision processes. Ethical issues are a product of what our minds determine to be ethical. A simple idea indeed: what is acted upon is more a product of shared perceptions than reality. This idea, however, has far-reaching implications, as the decisions reached and actions taken in the ongoing reform of the U.S. health care system are directly affected by our perceptions.

Different Perceptions But Shared Values

The focus of this text is how best to cultivate ethics in health care. The goal is to embark on a journey toward a higher quality and more equitable U.S. health care system by considering the nation's shared values. As the nation reforms its health care system, four questions arise:

- What wisdom is found in writings from previous centuries to the present time that helps guide us in making ethical decisions?
- What fresh perceptions can be discovered by exploring the ethics of new and different systems of delivering health care?
- What are the sources of the principles that are the foundation for the nation's collective thinking about ethics in health care?
- Which ethical principles should be retained in order to make sense of new ones?

Different perceptions about ethics in health care may be the biggest obstacle to realization of the concept of what constitutes an effective, efficient, high-quality health care system. The rightness or wrongness of the U.S. health care system is judged by generally accepted ethical principles; for instance, how right or wrong is the measure of providing affordable access to health insurance coverage to nearly all members of American society? To transform the U.S. health care system to achieve and equitably deliver quality health care may require a transformation of the American idea of what is ethical.

New Approach to the Ethics in Health Care

Changing the nation's thinking about health care ethics creates powerful opportunities for action. The health care industry plays a major role in the U.S. economy and, according to almost any objective account, a highly positive role. Admitting the current inability to identify a common public ethic could be the beginning of newfound wisdom with regard to health care reform. In other words, any reform of health care will first require acknowledging the gorilla in the room. The debates about the right to access health care, efficiency, and quality, not to mention the many debates surrounding such discrete health care issues as contraception, guns, and HIV/AIDS, among many others, are the players in the white shirts. The gorilla is what constitutes fairness in the allocation of the nation's limited resources.

Values Driven

We often think the world is how we perceive it and that everyone else's values are as we know them for ourselves. The principles of ethics, as illustrated in Feature Box F-1, that underlie most American values, are explained in this text along with explanations as to what they mean in a health care setting.

FEATURE BOX F-1

What is the meaning of these seven principles of ethics?

1. Ethical issues arise when actions or situations involve actual or potential harm to someone or something.
2. The action that provides the greatest benefit is the most ethical.
3. All actions should strive for the highest quality outcomes (not just high-quality outcomes).
4. Everyone must be accorded respect as human beings.
5. Individuals must always be treated as an end, not merely as a means. To treat anyone as a means is to use them to advance self-interests, but to treat everyone as an end is to respect their human dignity by allowing them the freedom to choose for themselves.
6. Individuals should be treated the same, unless they differ in ways that are relevant to the situation in which they are involved.
7. Whenever anyone is treated unequally on the basis of arbitrary characteristics, their fundamental human dignity is violated.

Motivated by Decision-Making Models

Although most Americans are driven by ethical principles, we are also driven by decision-making models, or the cognitive patterns we use to determine whether an action or situation is ethical or unethical. Consider the underlying values behind these decision-making models that could help the nation recognize and resolve the most pressing ethical issues in health care.

What do most Americans think about once they read the seven ethical principles listed in Feature Box F-1?

- What are the assumptions underlying these ethical principles and what should be investigated further to determine which situations would logically follow if the assumptions were accepted?

- Could a single, coherent principle make sense of all these assorted principles?
- Which principles underlying these values should be reexamined, and which would be simply reinventing the wheel?
- What role do the values of compassion, justice, and equality of opportunity play in the U.S. health care system?
- To what extent are the the nation's leaders mindful of the decision-making process behind transforming the U.S. health care system?

Mind Barriers

We must continually examine the principles that shape the nation's thinking about ethics in health care. Americans may think health care reform is too complex or that established interests are too entrenched to change, but these barriers may simply be in the nation's mindset or collective consciousness. The nation's sense of ethics could be preventing some of the best elements of the U.S. health care system from reclaiming the ideals of reason through rational decision-making.

Today, there are three attitudes very prevalent in the nation's mindset that make it difficult to perceive ethical issues in the health care space.

- *Pluralism*: Differences in what is valued in health care make it difficult to perceive what represents an ethical issue.
- *Relativism*: Even when everyone perceives an ethical issue, there are disagreements about the relative values of competing interests.
- *Individualism*: Historical tradition in the United States places a high value on allowing individuals to act independently. In our individualistic culture, it is difficult to convince Americans that they are not, ethically speaking, completely free to pursue their own personal ends without regard to the harm their actions may cause others.

The combined attitudes of pluralism, relativism, and individualism make it difficult to perceive harm or to recognize ethical issues generally.

Testing Reality

Instead of accepting the nation's mindset as it is, extensive use of various decision-making models is needed to determine what is working best in U.S. health care and why. Some areas to explore include:

- What incentives can be created to insure the uninsured and provide affordable access to health insurance coverage to as many members of society as possible?
- How can the U.S. health care system be changed to motivate everyone to adopt behaviors that prevent or delay the onset of most chronic diseases and illnesses?
- What will induce health care providers to use evidence-based medicine that is based on the best available scientific evidence, as opposed to making decisions based on clinical experience?

Perhaps new ethical principles should be developed to achieve high-quality, equitable health care with:

- Government-funded subsidies to ensure affordability
- Mechanisms to ensure health insurance availability
- Management of risks that can prove profitable (rather than managing avoidance of risks)

Is this vision part of the nation's new collective consciousness, or is it just the tip of the iceberg on a sea of possibilities that are yet to be discovered ?

Cognitive Patterns in Our Decision-Making

Neuroscience can be helpful in understanding how our minds work to create and preserve old decision-making models and how to change the framework for decision-making in order to develop new decision-making models. We think we perceive the real world, but we actually perceive the cognitive patterns, or structured relationships and concepts stored in our minds, evoked by new external situations. We only partially perceive the new sensory stimuli we take in; we actually perceive the relationships evoked by our neural activity. *See generally* Freeman, 2000, 2001; Wind & Crook, 2006.

In other words, neuroscience has shown that we do not really perceive what we take in. As stimulation flows into our brains, it evokes a pattern that the mind uses to represent the external situation, so we are not aware that what we are actually thinking is what is already in our own minds (Chabris & Simons, 2010; Wind & Crook, 2006). Walter Freeman, a biologist, theoretical neuroscientist, and philosopher at the University of California at Berkeley, has conducted pioneering research on how the mind generates meaning. Freeman discovered that the neural activity due to sensory stimuli disappears in the brain's cortex. It disappears! We do not really perceive what we take in (Wharton, 2005). With this situation in mind, we may ask:

- How can this text be used to come up with different mindsets to view the ethics of health care?
- What ethical issues are overwhelming, and is it possible to zoom out to look at the broader social context?
- What ethical issues are limited by an overly broad perspective, and is it possible to zoom in to examine the details and their effects on individuals affected?

Once again, it is sobering to consider: we think we perceive real ethical issues, but we actually only perceive the cognitive patterns that are already in our minds (Wind & Crook, 2006).

The Neuroscience of Cognitive Patterns

If we are not aware of the power of the cognitive patterns in our minds that are used to generate new thoughts, we may just accept what we think we perceive as reality. This misunderstanding of reality can be limiting, and sometimes even dangerous, because we tend to be comfortable with and dependent upon our cognition, the actual thinking process that produces our perceptions (Wharton, 2005). When we perceive new information, we form new cognitive patterns, or modify or extend old ones. New thoughts arise from combinations of cognitive patterns that already exist in our minds. These new thoughts, in turn, shape and filter our future perceptions. This added functioning is the foundation of our thinking process. In other words, we begin with what we have in our minds and expand upon it.

Because our minds tend to resist changes in cognitive patterns, the process of generating new ideas and creating new cognitive patterns can be difficult. One instance of this conceptual inertia is health care reform; we have a hard time moving away from what we know and what we already do. This is why changing the U.S. health care system opens everyone up to uncertainty and risk, along with perhaps our jobs, or our employers' ways of doing business. Most of us are risk averse, staying within our comfort zones, even if it causes increasing problems. *See generally* Wind & Crook, 2006.

Filtered Thinking

Once we acknowledge that our views are shaped and filtered by our own sometimes out-of-date thinking, we understand why many health care professionals choose to travel down well-worn pathways. A conscious effort is required to think about health care reforms on less traveled pathways in a way that the dominant status quo does not drown out reform ideas originating on weaker neural pathways. We must recognize the need to constantly compare the health care system the nation has against the health care system the nation should have.

In allowing a wider range of health care reforms to be brought to resolving the problems in U.S. health care, the usual filtered thinking that would otherwise be perceived as irrelevant by the dominant pathway does not occur. A wider range of views becomes available that makes possible a creative combination of existing ideas to address various questions.

- Do the medical products and health care services most Americans have meet the expectations of what they want and need?
- Does the U.S. health care system meet the needs of most Americans, and do most Americans think it will continue to do so?
- Is the continued enhancement of the U.S. health care system worth the costs, and how might the health care system look without this cost limitation?
- How can the federal government help design new experiments so the states can test the limits of shared values or gain new insights that might suggest new values and new ethical principles?

Test Decision-Making Models

There is a real need for a systematic way to approach the process of making ethical decisions in health care. Fortunately, normative standards of conduct have developed over time and across cultures as rational people of goodwill have considered human relationships and how human beings act when they are at their best. The first chapter of this text explains eight decision-making models based on the insights of major philosophers of ethics from ancient times to the present (Social Media Model, Utility Model, Rights Model, Exceptions Model, Choices Model, Justice Model, Common Good Model, and Virtue Model). These decision-making models, while rational, must still be constantly tested instead of simply relied upon as accepted frameworks to decide what is ethical or unethical. This modeling and re-modeling will help determine what the ethical principles are today and what will work best tomorrow.

As the nation decides what to do next, now that comprehensive reform of the U.S. health care system is both economically necessary and legally feasible, one decision-making model that could be used in making decisions is the Choices Model. Under this model, respect for every member of society is a priority, with a focus on how decisions are made.

- Everyone is given the freedom to choose what they value. We are not free to make our own choices if we are forced to choose something we do not value. For instance, existing health insurance laws and regulations may limit our freedom to choose the health care we want and value most.
- The Choices Model gives everyone the information necessary to know what they value most in the situation being considered. For instance, no longer is the starting point in health care reform about whether to expand insurance coverage of essential health care. The debate going forward is how to do it and how to make it affordable for everyone.
- Make an ethical decision and decide whether the new situation gives everyone the freedom and the information to choose what they value. For instance, while nearly all members of society have a right to purchase adequate health insurance, everyone must also have the freedom to decide what is adequate.

Putting the Decision-Making Models Together

While each of the eight decision-making models helps determine what standards of conduct can be considered ethical, several issues remain.

- Not everyone agrees on the content of some of the specific approaches presented in this text, especially some of the more controversial issues.
- There is a lack of national consensus on what constitutes human rights and the common good.
- There are few, if any, generally held ideas regarding the ethics in health care and proper conduct that everyone would agree are morally justified all the time.
- Implementation of the advantages and benefits of health care reform are being constantly challenged, with little national agreement on what is a benefit and what is a harm.

It is disheartening that, for all the nation's talk of reform, it appears that many stakeholders in health care still devote themselves to perpetuating their own interests, not to advancing the nation's common good, despite the health care system's formidible power to do so.

Making Ethical Decisions

Making ethical decisions requires a trained sensitivity to ethical issues and a practiced method for exploring the ethical aspects of a decision and weighing the considerations that should affect the choice of a course of action. Having a portfolio of decision-making models to call upon in any given challenging situation is absolutely essential for anyone working in the health care industry. When used regularly, the models become habitual; we can automatically work through them without consulting the specific steps.

Power of Rational Thinking

Debates in neuroscience focus on our minds as computers versus evolutionary-based biological systems subject to human error, and on the influence of nature versus nurture in shaping our thinking. Our minds constantly change and evolve over time; their architecture is not static, like machines. Over one billion neurons continually die and regenerate. Several trillion synapses are continually destroyed and re-created. Our minds select and reinforce or weaken certain synapses to forge the complex neural structures that determine our thinking. *See generally* Wind & Crook, 2006.

Practical steps to understanding, and perhaps changing, thinking about the ethics in health care include:

- Becoming explicitly aware of why we perceive, or fail to perceive, ethical issues and what that implies
- Understanding the relevance of ethical principles and deciding if they still fit or whether the principles should change and new principles ought to be generated
- Developing a portfolio of decision-making models that:
  - Minimize the risk of not following ethical principles
  - Allow the use of the decision-making models that work best for particular actions and situations
  - Prevent ethical principles from becoming dogma, an absolute transformation, or revolution
- Overcoming the inhibitors of change and reform by reshaping the decision-making infrastructure and helping others change their own thinking

- Experimenting with and continually assessing and strengthening our deci-sion-making models

See generally, Wind & Crook, 2006.

Inattentional Blindness

Inattentional blindness, also known as *perceptual blindness*, occurs when the collective thinking of individuals is adapted at different rates (Chabris & Simons, 2010). It is the term applied to the gorilla study described earlier, where participants were so focused on the counting task at hand that they missed a glaringly obvious, unexpected, object in plain sight. Variations between what is considered ethical and unethical, right and wrong, legal and illegal are shaped by the:

- Differences in values and perceptions
- Distinction between the goals and priorities of regulators and the regulated
- Divergent views within health care delivery systems between administrative and clinical staff, and among health care professionals and consumers of health care
- Dissimilar requirements of the health insurance industry and the insured
- Differences in ethical principles and opinions as to what health care reforms are needed or not needed

The invisibility of the gorilla is a reminder that looking at something is not necessar-ily the same as seeing it. Paying attention to one thing often comes at the cost of missing something else altogether. It is not enough to simply change one's thinking about ethics in health care, however. The practical infrastructures and routines that support ethical deci-sion-making must also be addressed.

- What ethical principles does the U.S. health care system currently use?
- How does the choice of decision-making models shape each health care sector's position on ethical issues and their decisions about them?

Zooming In and Zooming Out

In light of this immense complexity, we must learn to both zoom in and zoom out. When examined in detail, parts of a system, like almost any phenomenon, will seem to be unsta-ble, even fluctuating wildly. It is important for us, as stakeholders in the U.S. health care system, to develop the ability to zoom in and zoom out our thinking. For instance, zooming in may focus on details underlying core medical technologies. Zooming out focuses on how those technologies will impact the larger health care space, such as questioning how society will pay for the advanced medical technologies being developed.

New Approach to Ethical Decision-Making

We must focus on what to do with the principles of ethics and understand the process of making ethical or unethical decisions. Health care systems, like individuals, must focus on the forces that shape and reshape their ethical principles. There are several ways to change the nation's decision-making about health care.

- The process for making sense of the ethics in health care should be understood in terms of ethical principles
- The difficulties in setting cost limits and perceiving things differently must be recognized

- The neuroscience of cognitive patterns involved in everyday decision-making must be implicitly understood and acknowledged

Only then can the national framework for decision-making be transformed.

Practical Implications of This New Approach to Ethics

The practical implications are limitless for this new approach to ethics in health care. There is great risk in changing old views about the ethics in health care, according to which health care was available based largely on the ability to pay for such care. At the same time, there are great possibilities in the unprecedented opportunities to blend the best of the old and the new so that nearly all members of society will have access to affordable health insurance coverage. In this text, always ask:

- What principles of ethics underlie the court decisions and health care actions reported?
- What are some different decision-making models for looking at the situations outlined in each chapter?
- How do different ethical principles change the options available?

The possibilities for creative thinking in reform of the U.S. health care system are endless. Once we consider what we are attempting to do—create new pathways in our minds—and how we might do it, the road seems less formidable (Weinstein & Morton, 2003). Pay particular attention to how different ethical principles often define the battle lines on ethical issues. Throughout this text, readers should consider whether the nation's shared principles of ethics in health care are promoting or limiting individual and societal interests.

By Colin Crook, Senior fellow of The Wharton School of the University of Pennsylvania and former Chief Technology Officer for Citicorp, co-author, The Power of Impossible Thinking: Transform the Business of Your Life and the Life of your Business, *with Yoram (Jerry) R. Wind, also of The Wharton School.*

Bibliography

Chabris, C. F., & Simons, D. J. (2010). *The invisible gorilla: And other ways our intuitions deceive us.* New York, NY: Crown Publishing Group.

Freeman, W. (2001). *How brains make up their minds.* New York, NY: Columbia University Press.

___. (2000). *Neurodynamics: An exploration in mesoscopic brain dynamics (Perspectives in Neural Computing).* Philadelphia, PA: Springer (overview of Freeman's published works).

___. (1995). *Societies of brains. A study in the neuroscience of love and hate (The International Neural Networks Society).* New York, NY: Routledge's Lawrence Erlbaum Taylor & Francis Group.

Simons, D. J., & Chabris, C. F. (1999). Gorillas in our midst: Sustained inattentional blindness for dynamic events. *Perception, 28,* 1059–1074.

Weinstein, J., & Morton, L. (2003). Stuck in a rut: The role of creative thinking in problem solving and legal education. *Clinical Law Review, 9,* 835–875.

Wharton School at the University of Pennsylvania. (2005). What's behind the 4-minute mile, Starbucks and the moon landing? The power of impossible thinking. *Knowledge@Wharton.*

Wind, J., & Crook, C. (2006). *The power of impossible thinking: Transform the business of your life and the life of your business.* Philadelphia, PA: Wharton School Publishing.

Introduction

If you think that our country is just as confused about our national ethical perspective on health care since the Affordable Care Act as it was before its passage, then you are about to find that you are not alone. Neither are you incorrect. That is because there is no one national ethical perspective on health care. As Americans, we are fiercely tied to and proud of our individual values and morals. How will we ever combine over 318 million viewpoints into one mindset?

As a co-author of the Affordable Care Act, this was the challenge we faced in trying to write a law that both sides of the congressional aisle would find acceptable enough to enact, and what a challenge that was! This Act finally aligns Americans with the rest of the developed world in believing that health care is a human right, not a privilege. But as everyone is already aware, we still have a long way to go.

Health Care Ethics and the Law presents readers with over 150 ethical dilemmas that have no clear resolution in either the courts of law or the court of public opinion, from macro issue questions, such as "what is holding back decisions on implementing U.S. health care reforms?" to micro issue questions, such as "is obesity, and with it diabetes, an individual and family responsibility, or do governments and public health agencies have a role in preventing diet- and weight-related diseases?" But instead of leaving readers hanging with the present state of uncertainty, this text provides readers with a framework of eight decision-making models, ten universal values, and eight principles in the American Ethic to draw upon when deciding these issues for themselves, both personally as health care consumers and professionally as health care providers. Do I ever wish I had such a roadmap when I was grappling with these issues as General Counsel at Keller Army Community Hospital!

My special friends, Donna, Thomas, and Sarah, have made a significant contribution toward helping us clarify our thinking on health care reform and its underlying ethics. As an educator myself, I value this book for its role in encouraging readers to become principled humanitarians, which is precisely the sort of health care professionals that we need to continue working toward our goal of ensuring that all Americans have the right and the means to pursue the American dream. I hope you will join me in the national conversation aimed at improving our individual health and our health care system.

Sincerely,

Honorable Patrick J. Murphy
Former Congressman, Pennsylvania 8th District

List of Abbreviations

ACA: Affordable Care Act of 2010

ADA: Americans with Disabilities Act of 1990

AIDS: Acquired Immune Deficiency Syndrome

ARVs: anti-retroviral medications

CHIP: Children's Health Insurance Program

CNA: California Nurses Association

CPR: cardiopulmonary resuscitation

CSA: Controlled Substances Act of 1970

DERP: Drug Effectiveness Review Project

DNR: do-not-resuscitate

DOJ: U.S. Department of Justice

D&E: dilation and evacuation

D&X: intact dilation and extraction

EBM: evidence-based medicine

ECs: emergency contraceptives

ERISA: Employee Retirement Income Security Act of 1974

FLSA: National Fair Labor Standards Act of 1938

FDA: U.S. Food and Drug Administration

GRAS: generally recognized as safe

GM: genetically modified

HFCS: high-fructose corn syrup

HHS: U.S. Department of Health and Human Services

HIV: Human Immunodeficiency Virus

LSMT: life-sustaining medical treatment

MEC: medical ethics committee

NEISS: National Electronic Injury Surveillance System

NICBCS: National Instant Criminal Background Check System

NLRA: National Labor Relations Act of 1935

NLRB: National Labor Relations Board

NVSS: National Vital Statistics System

OTC: over-the-counter

PDA: Pregnancy Discrimination Act of 1978

PLCAA: Protection of Lawful Commerce in Arms Act of 2005

PCORI: Patient-Centered Outcome Research Institute

PTSD: post-traumatic stress disorder

PVS: permanent vegetative state

STD: sexually transmitted disease

TB: tuberculosis

USDA: U.S. Department of Agriculture

VA: U.S. Department of Veteran Affairs

List of Court Decisions

Abigail Alliance v. von Eschenbach, 495 F.3d 695 (U.S. Court of Appeals for the District of Columbia Circuit 2007), *cert. denied*, 128 S. Ct. 1069 (U.S. Supreme Court 2008) (patients' right to lifesaving experimental medications; see Chapter 4).

Acuna v. Turkish, 930 A.2d 416 (Supreme Court of New Jersey 2007), *cert. denied*, 555 U.S. 813 (U.S. Supreme Court 2008) (informed consent for abortions; see Chapter 13).

Aetna Health Inc. v. Davila, 542 U.S. 200 (U.S. Supreme Court 2004) (new protections for current and near-term prospective retirees with employer-provided health insurance; see Chapter 4).

AT&T Corp. v. Hulteen, 129 S. Ct. 1962 (U.S. Supreme Court 2009) (workplace accommodations for pregnant employees; see Chapter 2).

Ayotte v. Planned Parenthood of Northern New England, 546 U.S. 320 (U.S. Supreme Court 2006) (parental notification for abortions; see Chapter 13).

Betancourt v. Trinitas Hospital, 415 N.J. Super. 301 (Superior Court of New Jersey, Appellate Division 2010) (patients' right to life or death; see Chapter 2).

Burwell, et al. v. Hobby Lobby Stores, Inc., et al., 134 S. Ct. 2751 (U.S. Supreme Court 2014) (restricting women's access to contraceptives; see Chapter 13).

Carey v. Population Services International, 431 U.S. 678 (U.S. Supreme Court 1977) (*per se* medical exceptions for abortions; see Chapter 13).

Cigna Corp. v. Amara, 131 S. Ct. 1866 (U.S. Supreme Court 2011) (new protections for current and near-term prospective retirees with employer-provided health insurance; see Chapter 4).

Cincinnati Women's Services, Inc. v. Taft, 468 F.3d 361 (U.S. Court of Appeals for the 6th Circuit 2006) (judicial bypass of parental consent requirement and mandatory in-person, informed consent meetings; see Chapter 13).

City of Akron v. Akron Center for Reproductive Health, Inc., 462 U.S. 416 (U.S. Supreme Court 1983), *overruled*, *Planned Parenthood v. Casey*, 505 U.S. 833 (U.S. Supreme Court 1992) (permissible state regulation of abortions; see Chapter 13).

City of New York v. A-1 Jewelry & Pawn, Inc. (A-1 Jewelry III), 252 F.R.D. 130 (U.S. District Court for the Eastern District of New York 2008), *vacated and remanded*, *City of New York v. Mickalis Pawn Shop, LLC, et al.*, 645 F.3d 114 (U.S. Court of Appeals for the 2nd Circuit 2011) (holding that injunction granted in *City of New York v. A-1 Jewelry & Pawn, Inc.* was insufficiently specific and overbroad), *dismissed*, *City of New York v. Adventure Outdoors*, 2015 U.S. Dist. LEXIS 75447 (U.S. Dist. Court for the Eastern Dist. of NY 2015) (parties reached settlement) (illegal gun sales; see Chapter 12).

Commonwealth of Virginia ex rel. Cuccinelli v. Sebelius, 656 F.3d 253 (U.S. Court of Appeals for the 4th Circuit 2011), *cert. denied*, 133 S. Ct. 59 (U.S. Supreme Court 2012) (fidelity or infidelity to the law; see Chapter 16).

Consumers' Checkbook v. U.S. Department of Health and Human Services, 554 F.3d 1046 (U.S. Court of Appeals for the District of Columbia Circuit 2009), *cert. denied*, 559 U.S. 1067 (U.S. Supreme Court 2010) (access to the Medicare database; see Chapter 8).

Long Island Care at Home, Ltd. v. Coke, 551 U.S. 158 (U.S. Supreme Court 2007) (minimum wages and overtime coverage; see Chapter 7).

McDonald v. City of Chicago, 130 S. Ct. 3020 (U.S. Supreme Court 2010) (right to bear arms; see Chapter 12).

Mead v. Holder, 766 F. Supp. 2d 16 (U.S. District Court for the District of Columbia 2011), *affirmed, Seven-Sky v. Holder*, 661 F.3d 1 (U.S. Court of Appeals for the D.C. Circuit 2011), *cert. denied*, 133 S. Ct. 63 (U.S. Supreme Court 2012) (individual health insurance mandate [seeChapter 1]; comprehensive reform of health care [see Chapter 16]).

Morales v. Sociedad Espanola de Auxilio Mutuo y Beneficencia, 524 F.3d 54 (U.S. Court of Appeals for the 1st Circuit 2008), *cert. denied*, 555 U.S. 1097 (U.S. Supreme Court 2009) (EMTALA denial of treatment).

National Federation of Independent Business, et al. v. Sebelius, et al., together with, Florida, et al. v. U.S. Department of Health and Human Services, et al., 132 S. Ct. 2566 (U.S. Supreme Court 2012) (access to affordable health insurance [see Chapter 2]; access to essential health care [see Chapter 3]).

Planned Parenthood Cincinnati Region v. Taft, 444 F.3d 502 (U.S. Court of Appeals for the 6th Circuit 2006) (*per se* medical exceptions; see Chapter 13).

Planned Parenthood of Southeastern Pennsylvania. v. Casey, 505 U.S. 833 (U.S. Supreme Court 1992) (right to and permissible abortion regulations; see Chapter 13).

Regents of the University of Colorado, et al. v. Students for Concealed Carry on Campus, LLC, 271 P.3d 496 (Colorado Supreme Court 2012) (right to firearms on college campuses; see Chapter 12).

Riegel v. Medtronic, Inc., 552 U.S. 312 (U.S. Supreme Court 2008) (patients' right to sue manufacturers of innovative medical products; see Chapter 4).

Roe v. Wade, 410 U.S. 113 (U.S. Supreme Court 1973), *rehearing denied*, 410 U.S. 959 (U.S. Supreme Court 1973) (right to and permissible abortion regulations; see Chapter 13)

Schiavo ex rel. Schindler v. Schiavo, 403 F.3d 1289 (U.S. Court of Appeals for the 11th Circuit 2005), *rehearing denied*, 404 F.3d 1223 (U.S. Court of Appeals for the 11th Circuit 2005) (discontinuance of life-sustaining treatment; see Chapter 15).

Seven-Sky, et al. v. Holder, et al., 661 F.3d 1 (U.S. Court of Appeals for the District of Columbia Circuit 2011), *cert. denied*, 133 S. Ct. 63 (U.S. Supreme Court 2012) (fidelity or infidelity to the law; see Chapter 16).

Sorrell v. IMS Health Inc., 131 S. Ct. 2653 (U.S. Supreme Court 2011) (protecting patient privacy and confidentiality [see Chapter 2]; patients' right to access off-label medications [see Chapter 4]).

Standridge v. Union Pacific Railroad Company, 479 F.3d 936 (U.S. Court of Appeals for the 8th Circuit 2007) (inclusion or exclusion of contraception coverage; see Chapter 13).

State v. Musser, 721 N.W.2d 734 (Iowa Supreme Court 2006) (criminalization of exposure to HIV; see Chapter 11).

Thomas More Law Center, et al. v. Barack Hussein Obama, et al., 651 F.3d 529 (U.S. Court of Appeals for the 6th Circuit 2011), *cert. denied*, 133 S. Ct. 61 (U.S. Supreme Court 2012) (individual health insurance mandate [see Chapter 1]; fidelity or infidelity to the law [see Chapter 16]).

Torres-Lazarini v. United States, 523 F.3d 69 (U.S. Court of Appeals for the 1st Circuit 2008) (opportunity to sue for medical malpractice; see Chapter 9).

Tummino v. Torti, 603 F. Supp. 2d 519 (U.S. District Court for the Eastern District of New York 2009), *reconsideration denied*, *Tummino v. Hamburg*, 260 F.R.D. 27 (U.S. District Court for the Eastern District of New York 2009) (emergency contraception; see Chapter 13).

United States v. Franklin, 435 F.3d 885 (U.S. Court of Appeals for the 8th Circuit 2006), *rehearing denied* (U.S. Court of Appeals for the 8th Circuit 2006) (conditional release from involuntary commitment; see Chapter 10).

United States Citizens Association, et al. v. Sebelius, et al., 754 F. Supp. 2d 903 (U.S. District Court for the Northern District of Ohio 2010), as amended 2011 (access to health care; see Chapter 3).

Virginia ex rel. Cuccinelli v. Sebelius, et al., 656 F.3d 253 (U.S. Court of Appeals for the 4th Circuit 2011), *cert. denied*, 133 S. Ct. 59 (U.S. Supreme Court 2012) (the ethics of individual health insurance mandates [see Chapter 1]; access to health care [see Chapter 3]).

Virginia Mason Medical Center v. National Labor Relations Board, 558 F.3d 891 (U.S. Court of Appeals for the 9th Circuit 2009) (refusal to bargain; see Chapter 7).

Virginia Office for Protection and Advocacy v. Stewart, 131 S. Ct. 1632 (U.S. Supreme Court 2011) (abuse and neglect of mentally disabled patients; see Chapter 10).

Waddell v. Valley Forge Dental Associates, Inc., 276 F.3d 1275 (U.S. Court of Appeals for the 11th Circuit 2001), *cert. denied*, 535 U.S. 1096 (U.S. Supreme Court 2002) (HIV infection as a disability; see Chapter 11).

PART I

Introduction to Health Care Ethics

Part I provides an overview of the ethical issues facing the U.S. health care system.

CHAPTER 1

© Jannis Tobias Werner/Shutterstock

The Ethics of Health Care

"Personal or individual conscience, personal or individual integrity, personal or individual moral autonomy, or any other individualized philosophical values, are not firm foundations upon which to construct a policy regarding professional health care ethics."

— **Frank H. Knight** (1885–1972), neo-classical economist at the University of Chicago, from *Ethics and Economic Reform* (1935)

LEARNING OBJECTIVES

After completing this chapter, the reader should be able to:

1. Explain how to arrive at the desired or intended result when making decisions that are ethical.
2. Understand and evaluate eight decision-making models based on the insights of major philosophers of ethics.
3. Apply decision-making models when making ethical judgments within the health care industry.

KEY TERMS

Affordable Care Act
  of 2010
Common good
Compensatory justice
Distributive justice
Duties
Ethical
Ethical health care
  system
Ethical judgment
Exception
Existentialist
Extrinsic value
Fair value

Fairness
Free-riders
Idealist
Inattentional blindness
Intrinsic value
Justice
Justification
Legal rights
Liberty
Marginal utility
Medicaid
Moral rights
Negative moral rights
Pluralism

Pluralistic society
Positive moral rights
Privilege
Risk pool
Shared values
Smell test
Stakeholder society
Stakeholders
Unethical
Utilitarianism
Virtues
Vulnerable populations

ETHICAL OR UNETHICAL DECISION

Individual Health Insurance Mandates

Ethics Issue: *Should everyone share broadly in the risks and costs of poor health? And if so, what decision-making models could help reach this conclusion?*

In Brief: The State of Virginia has asked the federal courts to decide whether individual health insurance mandates should be imposed on its citizens under the **Affordable Care Act of 2010** (ACA), the most comprehensive reform of the U.S. health care system and private health insurance industry in almost a century. Virginia contends that if the individual health insurance mandate is constitutional, then there is no limit to the federal government's power; the government could force people to do almost anything for the common good of the nation. This really is a dispute over how much power Congress has to move Americans from their focus on individualism into a **stakeholder society**, where any legal rights enjoyed are integrally linked to moral responsibilities. In this case, the moral responsibility to maintain one's health and prevent poor health or injury is an essential part of any moral right to access health care. The ethical issue is how much power should be used by the federal government to help create a health care system that works properly for everyone—healthy people and people in poor health.

— *Commonwealth of Virginia ex rel. Cuccinelli v. Sebelius,* 656 F.3d 253 (U.S. Court of Appeals for the 4th Circuit 2011), *cert. denied,* 133 S.Ct. 59 (U.S. Supreme Court 2012). (*See Ethical or Unethical Decision* at the end of the chapter for discussion of this ethics issue.)

Introduction

This chapter is designed as an introduction to thinking ethically. Most health care professionals have an image of how they perceive themselves and how they are when they act ethically or are at their best. Almost everyone also has an image of what an **ethical health care system** should be: where medicine's ethical foundations of honesty, competence, and compassion are married to commerce in the delivery of high-quality care and where respect for patient needs has the highest priority. Nearly everyone also has images of what an ethical government and society should be: where every member of society has access to affordable health insurance, and where basic coverage is established through an ethical process. Health care ethics deals with all three of these levels, as illustrated in **FEATURE BOX 1-1**. The goal of this textbook is to embark on a journey to discover the nation's **shared values**, or the accepted ethical principles which constitute justice and fairness in the United States when it comes to health care.

Ethical Decision-Making

How does one make an ethical decision and what is the decision based on? Are there agreed-upon ethical principles or values in the health care industry to guide health care professionals so that they do not simply choose what is most convenient or advantageous

Three Levels of Health Care Ethics

- Acting ethically as individuals by assuming clear responsibilities for which everyone is held accountable
- Creating ethical health care systems that are sustainable
- Making government and the society it represents become more ethical in the ways it treats every member of society

— Sources: Beauchamp & Childress, 2012; Levine, et al., 2007.

rather than what is most ethical? Is there a process one can follow to be sure decisions are made thoughtfully and properly? Fortunately, many philosophers of ethics, from ancient times to the present, have addressed these very questions.

Administrative and judicial decisions throughout this text show how judgments are being made about whether actions and situations are **ethical** or **unethical**, right or wrong, in conformance with accepted ethical principles or not. One indication that an action calls for an ethical decision, as opposed to simply a legal or business decision, is that the action involves an actual or a potential burden or harm to individuals or to the health care system itself (*see, e.g.,* Hamilton, 2009a). Another indication that an action calls for an ethical decision is if it violates what society generally considers ethical behavior or what the law defines as a lawful act. Philosophical models for decision-making can assist in ensuring that the best **ethical judgments** are being made when actions involve an actual or a potential burden or harm to an individual or individuals, or to the health care system itself, or when there is a violation of the law or breach in ethical behavior. Variations between what is considered ethical and unethical, right and wrong, legal and illegal are shaped by **inattentional blindness**, also known as perceptual blindness. Inattentional blindness occurs when the collective thinking of individuals is adapted at different rates (Chabris & Simons, 2010).

A Process for Ethical Decision-Making

There is a recognized process that can facilitate decisions about what should be done. This process contains decision-making models which, when used as part of this larger

1. Ethically speaking, what makes the need for comprehensive reform of the U.S. health care system so difficult to recognize? Clearly, there is inattentional blindness between those who favor a major revamping of the U.S. health care system and those who oppose comprehensive reforms. How can this unwillingness to understand each side's viewpoints be overcome?

decision-making process, can be very helpful in managing health care actions and situations. The steps in this larger process are illustrated in **FEATURE BOX 1-2** and **FIGURE 1-1**.

Models for Ethical Decision-Making

Eight different decision-making models have been identified by leading philosophers of ethics, all of which are listed in **FEATURE BOX 1-3**, and described in full afterward.

In most situations, all eight models are not needed. One or two models can be selected to explain why the action being considered is ethical or unethical. With knowledge of all eight models, the most appropriate ones can be chosen, and the appeals others are making can be identified and countered in situations in which there is no clear ethical choice. It is not necessary to go through each of the eight steps in Feature Box 1-2 for each of the decision-making models presented in this chapter. The process for ethical decision-making is one illustration of how arguments evolve to a decision. As health care reforms are being implemented, the nation is encountering ethical decisions that will be examined throughout this text and are outlined in **FEATURE BOX 1-4**.

The U.S. medical model is based primarily on treating and managing diseases. There is lip service given to prevention, but virtually the entire health care system is based on procedures linked to treating disease as opposed to preventing it. Health insurance plans, including Medicare, direct very few resources to prevention. Medicare itself provides coverage for a comprehensive physical examination only one time, when an individual enters the system. After that, comprehensive physicals have to be paid out of pocket, perhaps aided by Medicare supplemental private insurance. Prevention, in contrast, emphasizes not only early detection of disease that, if ignored, would become serious and expensive, but also behavior interventions to eliminate the potential for disease in the first place or, if disease occurs, to lessen its severity. Health care reforms shift the emphasis on treatment of disease to prevention of disease.

FEATURE BOX 1-2

Eight-Step Process for Ethical Decision-Making

- Recognize the ethical issues
- Gather all relevant facts
- Put *all* decision-making models on the table
- Evaluate why the different models are a valid way to decide whether an action or situation is ethical or unethical from various perspectives
- Apply the appropriate models
- Make decisions based on the models
- Monitor the results of those decisions
- Repeat the process again as changes occur

— Sources: Chabris & Simons, 2010; Freeman, 2001, 2000, and 1995; Markkula, 2009; Simons & Chabris, 1999; Wharton, 2005; Wind & Crook, 2006.

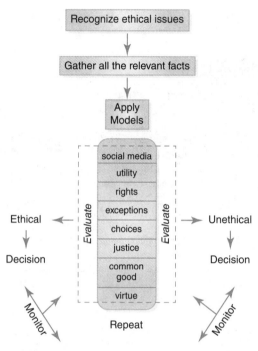

FIGURE 1-1 Process for Ethical Decision-Making

Sources: Markkula, 2009; Wind & Crook, 2006.

Social Media Model

The most common form of decision-making is the Social Media Model. This model was known as the **smell test** (does the situation reek of dishonesty, or is there a whiff of impropriety in the air?) or "the front page [of the newspaper] test" in the days before the social networking phenomenon. Mainly the Social Media Model asks how one would feel having one's actions go viral; if that level of public scrutiny is undesirable, the action is probably unethical. The Social Media Model is where most discussion of ethical issues begins.

Application of the Social Media Model

As illustrated in **FIGURE 1-2**, the Social Media Model entails two steps:

Step 1: Define what the reaction would be, based on popular opinion, if the action or situation being considered was publicized on a social network.

Step 2: Make an ethical decision. Decide whether the situation should continue. To determine why a situation should continue, inquiry must move beyond the Social Media Model to one or more of the seven other decision-making models.

Step 3: Monitor the results of the decision and repeat the process as changes occur.

Would most people be comfortable blogging about the action or situation in question, or letting it continue? Knowing whether most people would find that some actions or situations may be wrong can assist in modifying the actions or situations to help make them more ethical. For instance, states generally require people to manifest the symptoms of Acquired Immune Deficiency Syndrome (AIDS) before providing **Medicaid** insurance

FEATURE BOX 1-3

Eight Decision-Making Models

- *Social Media Model* is based on a combination of philosophies from Kant to Rawls and Dworkin, all introduced further below (Dworkin, 1996/2010 and 2008a-c; Kant, 1781/2009; Rawls, 2005 and 1999). This model has also been informally known as "the smell test" or "the front page test."
- The ideas of Jeremy Bentham (1746–1832), a British jurist and social philosopher; John Stuart Mill (1806–1873), a British social philosopher; and the modern principles of Ronald Dworkin (1931–2013), a New York University scholar of philosophy and constitutional law, combined to develop the philosophy of utilitarianism (Bentham, 1789/2015; Dworkin, 2011/2013, 2013, 2010, 1996/2010, and 1977; Mill, 1863/2011).
- Immanuel Kant (1724–1804), a German philosopher, developed the ethical principles for the *Rights Model* (Kant, 1788/2009 and 1790/2009), which was expanded by F.H. Bradley (1846–1924), a British **idealist** philosopher who believed people need to aspire to goodness and high ethical principles (Bradley, 1988/1927), and Dworkin (2013, et al., 1996/2010, and 1991).
- The *Exceptions Model* is based on the ancient principles developed by Confucius (551 BC-479 BC), a Chinese social philosopher, up to the contemporary ideology of John Rawls (1921–2002), a Harvard professor and social philosopher, and Dworkin (Dobbin, 2008; Dworkin 1998/2013, 1994, and 1985; Rawls, 1971/2005 and 2001; Van Norden, 2001).
- Three classical Greek philosophers: Socrates (469 BC-399 BC) and his student, Plato (427–347 BC), and Plato's student, Aristotle (384–322 BC), laid the foundations for the *Choices Model* (Aristotle, 322 BC/2012; Plato, 380 BC/2007).
- Plato, Aristotle, and Bradley, along with the modern principles of Rawls and Dworkin, who put human dignity at the center of the ethical systems, are the leading proponents of the *Justice Model* (Aristotle, 322 BC/2012; Bradley, 1935, 1927/1988, and 1893/1916; Dworkin, 1998/2010, 2008b, 1986, and 1978; Plato, 380 BC/2007; Rawls, 1971/2005, 2001, 1999, and 1974).
- Writings from Epictetus (55-135), the stoic Greek philosopher, Aristotle, and Plato serve as the basis of the *Common Good Model* (Aristotle, 322 BC/2012; Dobbin, 2008; Plato, 380 BC/2007; Van Norden, 2001).
- The leading philosophers of the *Virtue Model* are Jean-Paul Sartre (1905–1980), a French **existentialist** who believed people must take responsibility for their own actions and shape their own destinies (Sartre, 2000, and 1990/1983), and Dworkin (1996/2010, 2002a, 2002b, and 1978).

— Sources: Beauchamp & Childress, 2012; Markkula, 2009a and 2009b; O'Neill, 2014.

— Note: This list only includes philosophies and works of philosophers that have been recognized and recurrently cited by the U.S. Supreme Court, the U.S. Court of Appeals, and state Supreme Courts since 2010; Rawls is the most cited and Dworkin the second.

FEATURE BOX 1-4

Selected Ethical Decisions to Think About

- Will implementation of the nation's health care reform legislation withstand public scrutiny (*Social Media Model*)?
- Are the benefits of the reform being maximized and the burdens or harms minimized (*Utility Model*)?
- Are legal rights being respected (*Rights Model*)?
- What if everyone were entitled to receive health care (*Exceptions Model*)?
- Are people able to make their own choices (*Choices Model*)?
- Are the benefits and burdens being fairly distributed (*Justice Model*)?
- Are the common benefits of the nation being considered (*Common Benefit Model*)?
- Do the health care reforms improve the best elements of the nation's health care system (*Virtue Model*)?

— Sources: Beauchamp & Childress, 2012; Markkula, 2009.

ETHICAL DILEMMAS 1-2

2. What is holding back decisions on implementing U.S. health care reforms? Ethically speaking, what interests are supporting the focus on medical treatments and thwarting the shift in priorities to prevention of illness and disease?

---

to purchase the antiretroviral medications (ARVs) that prevent the development of those symptoms (*see, e.g.,* Bolin, 2014; Underhill, 2012). Medicaid is the need-based state-federal health coverage program for those who are poor and financially distressed or who have high out-of-pocket medical expenses. Blogging about this policy may indicate whether this presents an ethical issue but not why this government policy may be unethical. Discussions about indigent Americans facing early deaths from AIDS because of their lack of access to early intervention and care is a quick way of deciding whether this state of affairs is ethical or not.

Strengths and Limitations of the Social Media Model

The strength of the Social Media Model is its focus on public scrutiny and the common consensus on what is ethical. With this model, ethics is as much about what a group thinks as it is about what an individual thinks. The Social Media Model enlists the emotions of

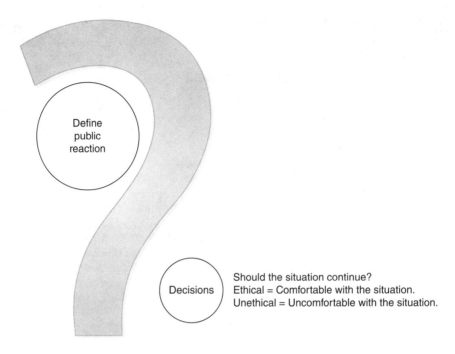

Social Media Decision-Making Model

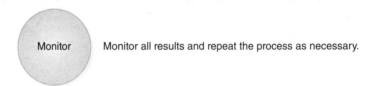

FIGURE 1-2 Social Media Decision-Making Model
Sources: Beauchamp & Childress, 2012; Markkula, 2009a.

personal or organizational shame and embarrassment, two powerful motivators to help ensure that actions are ethical.

The weakness of the Social Media Model is that it only benefits the society or the space in which health care professionals choose to work. Americans are often blind to the ethical dimensions of government policies, or they accept unethical policies as ethical, or the nation is divided on whether policies are ethical or unethical. Living with unethical conduct dulls the ability to notice the wrongfulness of some policies. In this instance, the health care reform's expansion of Medicaid coverage to uninsured Americans who are HIV-positive, who would otherwise not be eligible for Medicaid, has been criticized as being an unnecessary financial burden on states. This demand to consider financial cost is met by pleas to consider the human cost of denying access to ARVs while an uninsured person's immune system is still strong. In this instance, personal ethics cloud sound fiscal judgment. The government pays more to care for someone with full-blown AIDS than they would pay to give the same person ARVs to prevent the onset of AIDS and keep them functioning as a contributing member of society. Early access to Medicaid coverage to purchase ARVs to suppress the HIV retrovirus transforms HIV into a treatable, non-fatal health condition (Purcell, 2010). Ethically speaking, the issue is whether suffering and premature deaths from AIDS need occur, or whether 18,000 Americans should die from HIV/AIDS every year because of unmet medical needs (*see* CDC, 2013).

Utility Model

Utilitarianism, a philosophy of ethics which asserts that the ends justify the means, is a straightforward model for determining ethical courses of action. To discover what should be done in any situation, the various courses of action that could be performed are identified. All of the foreseeable benefits and burdens that could result are then determined. The action that provides the greatest benefit to the most people becomes the most ethical course of action.

For the Utility Model, outcomes or consequences determine what is ethical or unethical. Actions are ethical if they result in the best overall outcome. Outcomes in the health care industry can be measured by such indicators as health versus illness, quality of life, life expectancies, and burdens (current and future costs).

The Utility Model is a valid way to decide which actions are ethical or unethical because everyone counts the same; everyone wants to be healthy or avoid being ill. An ethical decision is based upon what results in healthy lifestyles or the lowest level of unhealthy behaviors, regardless of who is affected. For instance, employers cannot ethically regulate the consequences of weight status for overweight and obese employees unless all employees are sanctioned for their unhealthy behaviors. A policy could monitor the health status of all employees regardless of weight and sanction those with high risk for heart attack, stroke, or diseases such as diabetes. Using the Utility Model, everyone affected by lifestyle discrimination policies has equal standing when a decision is reached.

Balancing Benefits over Burdens

Health care ethics depends on balancing the consequences of conduct. Utilitarianism holds that the right course of action in any situation is the one that produces the greatest balance of benefits over burdens for everyone affected. As long as maximum benefits are produced for everyone, utilitarianism does not focus on how the benefits were created. **Duties** or ethical obligations are justified by reference to the benefits that come from a situation or the burden that is prevented. In this instance, employers are constantly weighing the resulting benefits and burdens of their employees' health care costs.

The principle of utilitarianism can be traced to Jeremy Bentham and John Stuart Mill, eighteenth- and nineteenth-century philosophers who sought an objective basis for determining what laws should be enacted by governments. Bentham and Mill believed that laws that would bring about the greatest net benefits to society once the burdens had been taken into account were the most ethical. Bentham's motto was 'the greatest benefit for the greatest number' (Bentham, 1789/2015). Today, utilitarianism often describes benefits and burdens in purely economic terms (Knight, 2000; *see also* Rawls, 1971/2005).

Application of the Utility Model

The Utility Model, as illustrated in **FIGURE 1-3**, involves a six-step framework that focuses on how a decision is made and on outcomes.

Step 1: Identify the alternative actions that are possible and determine who would be affected by any decision. For instance, employers and employees would be the most affected by lifestyle discrimination policies that were enacted to help reduce and fairly allocate health care costs.

Step 2: For each of the alternatives, determine the costs and the benefits for each of the groups affected. This prediction of short-term and long-term outcomes considers the relative value, or **marginal utility**, of the outcomes for different people. In this instance, particular attention could be directed to smoking and the growing prevalence of obesity; that is to say, preventable behaviors and conditions that are both recognized as serious health issues that can no longer be ignored, as well as problems that can often be addressed through environmental interventions.

Step 3: Select the action in the current situation that produces the greatest benefits over burdens for everyone affected. If the burdens outweigh the benefits, the action with the least burden relative to the benefits is the best alternative; this alternative has the greatest net benefits for this one situation.

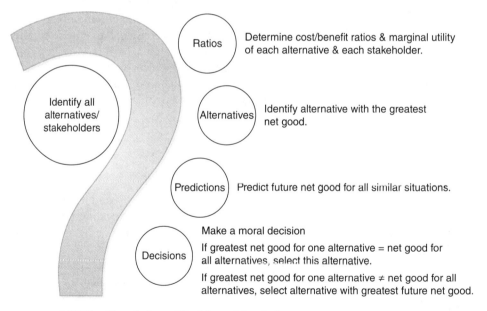

Utility Decision-Making Model

FIGURE 1-3 Utility Decision-Making Model

Sources: Beauchamp & Childress, 2012; Markkula, 2009a.

Step 4: Predict the consequences of the action for all similar situations. Because what is done in one situation often becomes a policy for future actions, the best alternative is the one that maximizes benefits for this and all future situations.

Step 5: Make an ethical decision. If the same action is selected in steps three and four, then this is the most ethical action. If different actions are selected, then decide which individual action will produce the greatest long-term benefits and cause the least burden to everyone affected; this is the most ethical action.

Step 6: Monitor the results of the decision and repeat the process as changes occur.

Strengths and Limitations of the Utility Model

The strength of the Utility Model is that outcomes matter in the health care industry. If the outcomes of a particular decision are not good, it is obvious that the ethical principles being used are not good. Therefore, factual data and assessing the probability of potential outcomes are important when deciding what actions are the most ethical. Similarly, the welfare of health care systems must be included in decisions involving the Utility Model; health care systems are affected by individual outcomes. This emphasis on rational calculation and on including everyone that is affected by a decision reinforces the principle that relying upon intuition is often an unreliable method of ethical decision-making.

The weakness of the Utility Model is that it requires accurate probability assessments of likely outcomes. Outcomes may be difficult or impossible to predict because of the complexity of the health care industry and the rapidly changing laws and regulations affecting health care. Moreover, when the U.S. health care system attempts to measure national outcomes on a short-term basis, it becomes nearly impossible to focus on the long-term outcomes of any reform efforts. In addition, while utilitarianism is a popular ethical theory, there are some difficulties in relying on it as a sole method for ethical decision-making. First, utilitarian calculations require that the values assigned to the benefits and burdens resulting from one situation be compared to the benefits and burdens from other situations. But it is often impossible to measure and compare values in health care, as the value of a person's life and respect for human dignity are completely incalculable. Nevertheless, even with this unqualified commitment to respecting life and human dignity, the consequences of actions are often difficult and imprecise to calculate.

One of the greatest difficulties with utilitarianism is its failure to consider principles of justice or whether individuals are treated fairly when decisions are made. If ethical decisions are to take into account considerations of justice and give people their appropriate due or what they are properly owed, then utilitarianism cannot be the sole principle guiding decisions. It can, however, play a role in these decisions. Utilitarianism considers the immediate and the less immediate consequences of actions (*see* Rawls, 1971/2005). Given its insistence on summing the benefits and burdens in any given situation, utilitarianism looks beyond self-interests to consider impartially the interests of everyone affected. The utilitarian standard of ethical conduct is that of everyone affected by the result of a decision (Mill, 1863/2011).

Rights Model

Moral rights are essential to the respect of everyone's human dignity and self-determination. **Legal rights**, in contrast, are human constructs created by society, enforced by governments, and subject to change. **Moral rights** are perennial rights that are not easily subject to change. Everyone possesses moral rights and these moral rights empower people to engage in conduct that does not violate the rights of others, generally as understood and explained by the law (Spiropoulos, 2010).

For instance, under this model, in the United States, **vulnerable populations** that experience health disparities as a result of lack of access to health care and increased exposure to health risks are morally entitled to something from society; they are generally protected by law from actions that benefit society at their expense. Diverse vulnerable groups are most often comprised of minorities, underprivileged people, and people who are marginalized by societal norms, such as sexual orientation or immigrant status (AHRQ, 2012). Vulnerable groups also include high-risk mothers (defined as unmarried, low-income women), children, people with HIV/AIDS, and homeless families. A significant difference in the overall disease incidence, morbidity, mortality, and survival rates among vulnerable populations in the United States exists compared to the health status of the general society (IOM, 2001).

Yet human beings are recognized as valuable in and of themselves (referred to as the **intrinsic value** or the essential parts of a person), regardless of vulnerabilities arising from their health attributes or health insurance status (referred to as the **extrinsic value** or the inessential parts of a person) (*see* Roberts, 2011). Legal rights point to the social conditions required for expression of these values. That is, without access to health care, people cannot live in a way that expresses their intrinsic value.

ETHICS CASE
Disparities in Access to Health Care

Korab, et al. v. Fink, et al.
[Non-Immigrant Resident of the United States v. Governor of Hawaii]
748 F.3d 875 (U.S. Court of Appeals for the 9th Circuit 2014),
cert. denied, 135 S.Ct. 472 (U.S. Supreme Court 2014)

Facts: Tony Korab, a dialysis patient who had been seeking a kidney transplant, sued to stop the reduction of his Medicaid benefits, asserting that it was unconstitutional to deprive him of a kidney transplant. The reduction in his Medicaid benefits occurred because Korab was a foreign citizen who had been granted legal resident status as a non-immigrant (includes people who enter the United States on a temporary basis for business or study). By passing welfare reform, Congress made non-immigrants a category of residents that no longer qualified for federal reimbursement. Consequently, Korab became ineligible for the federal Medicaid subsidy. For the purpose of state Medicaid, Congress created three categories of eligibility: one category is eligible for state benefits; another is denied benefits; and a third may be eligible at the discretion of state governments. Korab fell into the third category. Congress justified its refusal to provide access to health care by insisting that self-sufficiency was always a basic principle of U.S. immigration law; immigrants should not depend on American society to meet their medical needs, but rather rely on their own capabilities and the resources of their families, their sponsors, and private organizations.

Legal Analysis: There is considerable debate over immigrants' rights to Medicaid and access to health care. The approaches adopted by different courts diverge significantly based on the different state schemes involved as well as distinct approaches to immigrants.

After federal welfare reform, Hawaii initially continued providing non-immigrant residents with Medicaid. Hawaii did so using state funds and pursuant to the discretion that Congress gave states regarding eligibility for Medicaid. In 2010, following the 2008 economic crisis, Hawaii reduced funding for comprehensive Medicaid benefits because of state budget constraints. Non-immigrant residents were offered less comprehensive Medicaid benefits that did not cover organ and tissue transplants or long-term care services. Korab challenged the constitutionality of this reduction in Medicaid coverage, claiming that it violated the U.S. Constitution by failing to provide him kidney transplant coverage on par with that offered to U.S. citizens.

The court ruled that the state of Hawaii did not violate the U.S. Constitution by offering non-immigrant residents less inclusive Medicaid coverage. Because Congress gave states the authority to decide state-benefit eligibility criteria, the court found that Hawaii's course of action was merely following the direction established by Congress. The court further found that Hawaii had no obligation to fill the gap left by Congress's withdrawal of federal funding for non-immigrant residents.

The U.S. Supreme Court declined to consider the policy and equity issues behind access to Medicaid.

Rule of Law: State budget constraints are a legitimate reason for restricting access to Medicaid.

Ethics Issue: Should foreign citizens who have been granted legal non-immigrant resident status in the United States be eligible to receive access to Medicaid?

Ethics Analysis: This case highlights the disparity in access to health care that arises between non-immigrants, immigrants, and other alien residents in this country. Although undocumented immigrants are unlikely to receive comprehensive health care, disparities in access to health care do not exist only between illegal and legal residents; foreign citizens who have been granted legal resident status in the United States are also subject to disparate determinations for Medicaid coverage.

The situation in this case raises several ethical concerns. Budget constraints always reflect values and, therefore, the matter of ethics must be extended to the process whereby the priorities in state budgets are determined. Because access to Medicaid depends on state budget constraints unrelated to a population's need for access to health care, the right to reduce access highlights the equity concerns that arise when immigrant populations are categorized in the United States. The ethical solution may not be to divest the states of their budgetary power to make autonomous judgments about whether to provide state benefits to immigrant populations; rather, the federal government should issue guidelines to states on how to make fair and equitable decisions in apportioning access to Medicaid. The U.S. Supreme Court's attention to this issue could have been an important step in determining whether, and if so when, disparity in access to health care can be justified, but that opportunity was not realized since it declined to review this case.

Court's Holding and Decision: States may restrict access to Medicaid for foreign citizens who have been granted legal resident status in the United States.

See Cousins, 2014 (discussing this court decision).

Application of the Rights Model

The Rights Model, as illustrated in **FIGURE 1-4**, involves a five-step framework that focuses on respecting life and human dignity.

Step 1: Identify the moral right being upheld or violated and explain why it deserves the status of a legal right. Moral rights are best understood by considering the

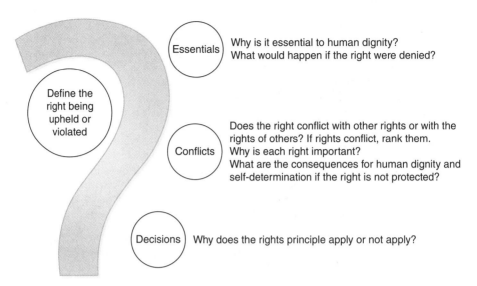

Essentials
Why is it essential to human dignity?
What would happen if the right were denied?

Define the right being upheld or violated

Conflicts
Does the right conflict with other rights or with the rights of others? If rights conflict, rank them.
Why is each right important?
What are the consequences for human dignity and self-determination if the right is not protected?

Decisions
Why does the rights principle apply or not apply?

Rights Decision-Making Model

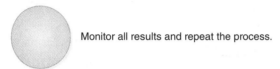

Monitor all results and repeat the process.

FIGURE 1-4 Rights Decision-Making Model

Sources: Beauchamp & Childress, 2012; Markkula, 2009a.

consequences of people being denied their legal rights. For instance, the health insurance industry is now banned from denying coverage for preexisting health conditions, imposing lifetime caps, or rescinding existing coverage after a person becomes ill. Everyone will now have the benefit of affordable health insurance. Access to health care is no longer a **privilege**, defined as a restricted right or benefit that is not available to everyone. Everyone now has the obligation to purchase health insurance and will have the right to health care.

Step 2: Determine whether the legal right conflicts with the moral rights of others. For instance, does the legal right to affordable health insurance conflict with the nation's ability to assist the least advantaged in purchasing this insurance? Specifically, how will this insurance mandate, along with the entitlement to health care, affect the nation's federal debt? If the federal debt is left unregulated and allowed to freely increase, it will create major financial and fiscal crises in the future, while overburdening U.S. taxpayers tremendously (*see* Wharton, 2010). The moral right to health care is in conflict with the financial cost of care without comprehensive health care reform. In other words, the legal right to affordable coverage conflicts with the tax burden imposed upon everyone, unless patient-centered care and other new forms of health care delivery result in savings as all of the reforms are put into place (CBO, 2011).

Step 3: If the rights conflict, decide which right has precedence. Explain why each right is important and show the consequences for human dignity and self-determination if the right is not protected. People can disagree about which right is more important, as no ranking principle is universally accepted. For instance, the right to have access to affordable health insurance has precedence over the right of the insurance industry to maximize the utility of insurance **risk pools**, which group together individuals with similar health risks to help allocate costs for health care expenses. Because of the intrinsic value of every human being, the well-being of the nation's residents and their right to health care has greater weight than the financial cost of the care for the government subsidies that are required to voluntarily pool dissimilar health risks in order to more evenly share the burden. Likewise, the ability to pay a reasonable cost, or **fair value**, for health care has priority over the assistance provided to access the needed care. *See generally* Rawls, 1971/2005.

Step 4: Make an ethical decision. Decide whether the rights principle does or does not apply and why. If the rights principle applies in this instance, not every U.S. resident will have access to exactly the same health insurance. Although access to basic health insurance will be ensured, there will always be freedom to pursue additional health care based on the ability to pay fair value for that care.

Step 5: Monitor the results of the decision and repeat the process as changes occur.

Strengths and Limitations of the Rights Model

The strength of the Rights Model is that moral rights are a powerful tool for showing respect for life and human dignity. Moral rights have no legal validity, however, unless the intrinsic value in human beings is recognized and enshrined in the law. While most people recognize their own value, not everyone recognizes that others are equal to themselves. Because vulnerable populations have few resources to improve their health care, they are at greater risk for developing health issues and suffering poor health conditions. *See generally* Beauchamp & Childress, 2012. The weakness of the Rights Model is that it is not helpful in most ordinary situations in which people disagree over whether an action is ethical or unethical.

Legal rights, however, sometimes conflict with societal benefits, as well as with other social liberties and privileges. For instance, the absolute natural right of humans to the uninterrupted enjoyment of their health (*see, e.g.,* Blackstone, 1753/2010) sometimes conflicts with the delivery of affordable, high-quality health care, as well as with the **liberty**, or freedom, to pursue one's own dictates in maintaining health insurance coverage. In this case, restrictions on liberty may be ethically justified on the grounds that health insurance coverage is in people's best interests. Solving these conflicts means that some moral rights are sometimes subordinated.

Because there are few universally recognized legal rights (such as the right to access affordable, high-quality health care), people must be vigilant in defending their claims to such rights (*see* Restatement, 1987). Moreover, because of its persuasive power, the Rights Model is regularly applied to situations that are not really serious enough to qualify as a threat to legal rights. *See generally* Beauchamp & Childress, 2012. For instance, while there may be a right to access affordable health insurance for women's reproductive care with mandated coverage for comprehensive prenatal care, should there be a corresponding legal right to mandate access to free contraceptive coverage to prevent unintended pregnancies? A mandate on employers who object to contraception for religious reasons is among the most restrictive means the government could choose to increase access (Rivkin & Whelan, 2012).

Exceptions Model

The Rights Model is often used before the Exceptions Model (Markkula, 2009a). An **exception** claims that in a given situation, an action may be ethical if done by one person but unethical if done by a different person. This is the opposite of claiming that it must be ethical because everyone else is doing it. The Exceptions Model asks what would happen if the individual exception became the ethical principle for everyone.

Application of the Exceptions Model

The Exceptions Model, as illustrated in **FIGURE 1-5**, involves a six-step framework that focuses on how a decision is made.

Step 1: Describe the general and specific ethical issues of the situation. For instance, whether a particular lifesaving treatment protocol would be covered by an insurance plan for a terminally ill patient who has exhausted all other traditional treatment options is a specific ethical issue. Expanded access for patients with a life-threatening or serious disease, but who do not qualify for a clinical trial because of other health problems, age, or other factors, is another specific ethical issue.

Step 2: Determine what would happen if the exception was adopted by others in similar situations. If the exception was adopted by others in similar situations, the exception might become unacceptable for anyone to do because everyone was trying to do it. For instance, current government regulations insist that the public's interest in filtering safe and efficacious medications through clinical trials has a higher priority than the lives of individual patients who are denied access before medications are approved.

Step 3: Decide which exceptions are unacceptable if they became the rule for everyone. For instance, if it is unacceptable to deny investigational medications to patients who have no alternative treatment for life-threatening or serious disease, then

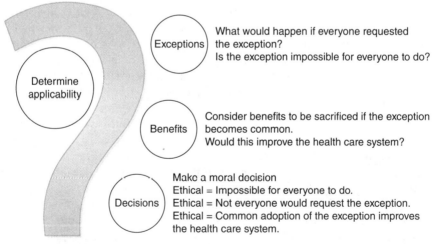

Exceptions Decision-Making Model

FIGURE 1-5 Exceptions Decision-Making Model

Sources: Beauchamp & Childress, 2012; Markkula, 2009a.

Congress must decide upon a better balance between the risks and benefits of bringing new medications to market.

Step 4:   Consider what will have to be sacrificed if the exception becomes common. Determine if this is the kind of health care system that should be created. If this is not the kind of health care system that should be created, in which the exception becomes common, then the exception is not ethical because it is unacceptable for others. For instance, not to follow current government regulations on access to investigational medications would be to make an exception for some patients who do not deserve open access to unapproved medications, since everyone would be considered to have equal access rights. In other words, if access for some patients were allowed before the investigational medications were approved as safe and efficacious, the government would have to allow open access for everyone.

Step 5:   Make an ethical decision. If the exception is not practical because everyone would be doing it, then the exception is unethical. Similarly, if common adoption of the exception would create an unacceptable result, then the exception is unethical. The reverse is also true. The exception is ethical if not everyone would be requesting exceptions or if common adoption of the exception is acceptable. For instance, if open access to investigational medications would place unapproved medications in the market that have not been proven to be safe and efficacious, then open access to unapproved medications is unethical. Likewise, if open access to investigational medication would create an unacceptable result, then the exception for patients who have no alternative treatment for life-threatening or serious disease is unethical. On the contrary, to provide investigational medications to patients with no other alternative treatments would be ethical if not everyone would be requesting the unapproved medications.

Step 6:   Monitor the results of the decision and repeat the process as changes occur.

Strengths and Limitations of the Exceptions Model

While everyone is equal in regard to certain courses of action, the strength of the Exceptions Model is that it addresses the issue of **free-riders**. Individuals and institutions who take the benefits the ethic of the common good provides, but refuse to do their part to support the common good of their community, are free-riders. The term *free-riders* also refers to the economic problem of people taking advantage of health insurance programs and exploiting the U.S. health care system without due compensation. Certain benefits or exclusions simply cannot be justified for some people, even when no burden is caused, unless the people affected can justify why they deserve to be the exception (Purdy & Siegel, 2012). For instance, why should people over 65 and the disabled be entitled to receive government health insurance if they have the financial resources to purchase affordable private health insurance?

The weakness of the Exceptions Model is that when courses of action are described, ethical issues can be missed, depending on how the situation is being portrayed. Some may portray unacceptable situations differently and give a picture of what may not be the actual situation. For instance, when debating implementation of the individual health insurance mandate (or a requirement that people demonstrate they are covered so they will not be a burden on society if they become seriously ill or injured), the alternative for people who refuse to obtain affordable coverage is for them to choose to die in their own circumstances. In this instance, society lets the uninsured die on their own if they refuse to use their own financial resources to secure affordable coverage and they face a time and situation when and where they choose not to pay for their own health care.

Choices Model

Many controversies center on choosing among moral rights. A moral right flows from human dignity; moral rights are universally accepted by society to be legitimate, and they are near-universal in that they apply to everyone in similar situations. For instance, if society agrees there is a moral right to access health care, then people may be justified in their claim to the right to be provided with affordable health insurance. The **justification** of a claim is dependent on some ethical principle acknowledged and accepted not just by the claimant, but also by society in general. These ethical principles may be as specific as the Universal Declaration of Human Rights (United Nations, 1949) or as general as the legal right to access affordable health insurance. Moral rights are justified by acknowledged ethical principles which are not necessarily clearly codified in law, such as the moral right to access health care.

Negative and Positive Moral Rights

One of the most influential interpretations of moral rights is based on the work of Immanuel Kant, who maintained that everyone has a human dignity that must be respected (Kant, 1781/2009). This human dignity makes it wrong to harm others, such as the denial of health insurance for preexisting health conditions that are outside one's direct control with no modifiable risk factors.

Ethical principles are often used to justify both a moral right to access health care and the privileges related to this right to care. These related privileges are grouped into negative and positive moral rights. A positive moral right is to permit or oblige action; for instance, it is the right to be treated in an emergency situation. A negative moral right is to permit or oblige inaction; for instance, it is the right not to be treated without one's consent.

Negative moral rights, such as the moral right not to be denied access to health care, are moral rights that protect the legal right to choose what health insurance coverage to purchase. These moral rights are called negative rights because such moral rights are claims that impose a negative duty. For instance, the moral right to access health care imposes a duty on the health insurance industry to provide affordable insurance plans. Consumers of health care have a negative right against the health insurance industry in that the health insurance industry is prohibited from acting in a manner that hinders participation in the market.

A moral right to access health care, however, is worthless if people are unable to afford health insurance coverage for their care. A moral right to access health care, then, implies that everyone has a fundamental right to what is necessary to secure a minimum level of health and well-being. **Positive moral rights**, therefore, are rights that provide something that people need to secure their well-being, such as a right to access medical treatments to treat their illnesses. Positive moral rights impose duties on society, such as the ethical obligation to actively assist people to have or to do something. The moral right to access health care, therefore, imposes a social duty to provide people with health insurance to purchase health care. Respecting positive moral rights thus requires more than merely not acting against people's rights or interfering with them. Positive moral rights impose the ethical obligation to assist the welfare of vulnerable populations who are in need of assistance. *See generally* Beauchamp & Childress, 2012.

Conflicts between Moral and Legal Rights

Whenever there is a conflict between moral rights and legal rights, life and human dignity must be respected (Keyes, 2011). Ethical actions must enhance people's basic well-being (Dolan & Peasgood, 2008). How an action might affect legal rights must be considered.

Actions are unethical to the extent that they violate people's moral rights (Peery, 2008). For instance, manipulation of information about implementation of health care reform efforts undermines the moral right to truth and honesty (*see* Wharton, 2010).

When moral and legal rights come into conflict, decisions must be made about which right has priority (Keyes, 2011). While everyone may be entitled to access health care, the moral right to access may have to be balanced against the rights of vulnerable populations and the rights of the nation's taxpayers. How are federal and state governments going to pay for the health care of the uninsured and underinsured? The competing interests at stake have to be examined to answer this question. A judgment should be reached as to whether the interests of society or the interests of vulnerable populations are more vital for ensuring that life and human dignity are respected. For instance, economic costs are mutually exclusive to equality of access to health care (*see* Zamir & Medina, 2008).

Moral rights have a central role in health care ethics. Attention to moral rights ensures that the well-being of vulnerable populations is protected when society threatens that well-being (Rawls, 1971/2005). If vulnerable populations have a moral right, then it is wrong to interfere with that moral right even if society benefits by lower health care costs from such interference.

But moral rights are not the sole consideration in health care ethics. In some situations, the social burdens or the injustices that would result from respecting a moral right are too great to be lawful, and that moral right may have to be limited by the law (*see* Calnan, 2010). Moreover, an emphasis on moral rights is not just a matter of not interfering with others. Relying exclusively on a moral rights model tends to favor vulnerable people at the expense of society.

Things have value because people value them. All people deserve equal respect (Keyes, 2011). What one person values has no claim to be more valuable than what others may value (Zamir & Medina, 2008). People must be free; their choices cannot be obstructed when making their own choices based on what they value. Government can only choose for people in special circumstances that are justified (Keyes, 2011), such as when national health care reform is the law or health insurance contracts are forced to provide basic coverage by regulation. Then traditional limitations and business conventions may have to change because of this new set of legal commitments.

Application of the Choices Model

The Choices Model, as illustrated in **FIGURE 1-6**, involves four steps with a focus on how a decision is made. Respect for the individual is a priority when the Choices Model is used.

Step 1: Give everyone the freedom to choose what they value. People are not free to make their own choices if they are being forced to choose something they do not value. For instance, prior choices, such as existing insurance laws and regulations or health insurance contracts, may limit people's freedom to choose what they value most in health care.

Step 2: Give everyone the information necessary to know what they value in the situation being considered. For instance, no longer is the starting point in health care reform about whether to expand coverage of health care services. The debate going forward is how to do it and how to make it affordable. People must have access to all the information necessary to evaluate the ways in which the nation can deliver health care to all U.S. residents. Then they can determine which alternative is most in line with their values. Practical determinations must be made about whether the information is adequate or whether some people would choose differently if they had additional information. *See generally* Wharton, 2010.

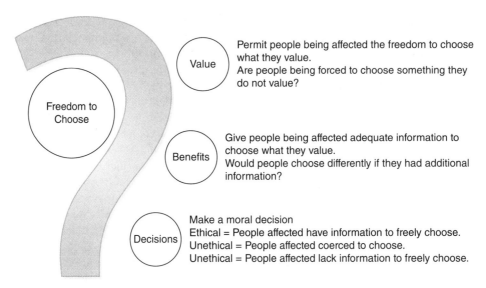

Choices Decision-Making Model

Monitor all results and repeat the process.

FIGURE 1-6 Choices Model for Decision-Making

Sources: Beauchamp & Childress, 2012; Markkula, 2009a.

Step 3: Make an ethical decision. Decide whether the action or situation gives everyone the freedom and the information to choose what they value. For instance, while all U.S. residents have a legal right to purchase basic coverage (public and private), everyone must have the freedom to decide what health risks they are financially willing to assume themselves as well as what level of additional health insurance coverage they wish to purchase to insure that they have access to advanced care or access to highly specialized physicians.

Step 4: Monitor the results of the decision and repeat the process as changes occur.

Strengths and Limitations of the Choices Model

The Choices Model reflects one of the fundamental ways of showing respect for the equality of other humans and respecting everyone's ability to determine the course of their own lives by making choices based on what they think is valuable. Many ethical violations involve denying people information or limiting their freedom to choose. For instance, one of the most controversial aspects of health care reform is the mandate that everyone be required to obtain a basic health insurance plan as defined by the federal government. While there is no uniform definition of what basic coverage should be required, one side views the minimum coverage provision (also known as the individual mandate or the minimum essential coverage requirement) as a denial of the freedom to choose whether to purchase an economic product. The other side claims that the minimum coverage provision is essential to creating effective health insurance markets. The counterargument, however, is that in the absence of a mandate,

33 million people have already made an economic decision to forgo health insurance coverage and attempt to self-insure, which decreases the freedom of choice of society and the insured by forcing them to pay for free-riders, since health care is a service that nearly everyone will utilize at some point in their lifetime, whether or not they are insured, and sometimes whether or not they choose to. Access to health care is a major national problem that requires a national solution, and the solution can work only under conditions in which everyone has health insurance (Baker, 2011).

At the same time, this model can reinforce a simplistic view of decision-making, implying that people are clear about what they value and make rational choices based on those values. In this instance, most people cannot rationally determine their health risks when choosing health insurance coverage, since they cannot accurately predict or calculate their future health care expenses. The concept of freedom is the subject of much disagreement. If someone chooses to obtain health insurance coverage, but cannot afford the comprehensive insurance that they need, their freedom to choose may be limited. Moreover, the line between persuasion and coercion can be difficult to draw. When does a tax for being uninsured become coercive? When does making something look attractive take away from a person's freedom to reject it? For instance, when do government mandates take away the freedom to reject coverage for specified health care services?

Justice Model

No concept has been more consistently linked to health care ethics than the concept of justice. From Plato to Rawls, every major philosopher has held that justice is the core of ethics (Madsen, 2008). Justice means giving people their appropriate due, or what they are properly owed. Although the terms *justice* and *fairness* are closely related and often used interchangeably, they are distinct. **Justice** is used with reference to principles of rightness (Lanshe, 2009); **fairness** refers to objective judgments of the decision-making process that are not specific to particular situations or individuals (Rawls, 1971/2005). For instance, justice mandates that all U.S. residents are entitled to a minimum level of primary health care (including medications) to treat the most common injuries and diseases. This level of care should be universally accessible and affordable to all U.S. residents so they have the unfettered opportunity to achieve and maintain high levels of health which are necessary for a lifetime of well-being and human dignity. Fairness does not, however, entitle everyone to the most technologically advanced care or unfettered access to highly specialized physicians.

Both terms encompass notions of what is morally right or what is expected. When differences arise over what or how benefits and burdens should be distributed, questions of justice inevitably arise. Justice derives its relevance from the conflicts of moral and legal rights that are created when resources are limited and differences exist over who should get what. When such conflicts arise, reasonable principles of ethics are needed so that everyone can accept judgments for determining what people deserve.

Foundations of Justice

The foundations of justice can be traced to the notions of social stability, equality, interdependence, and human dignity (*see* Cohn, 2011). The stability of society depends upon the extent to which the members of that society feel that they are being treated justly (Rawls, 1971/2005). When some members of society are subject to unequal treatment, the foundation has been laid for public unrest, disturbances, and social strife. Members of society are interdependent, and they will retain their voluntary social unity only to the extent that their institutions and their laws are just.

Principles of Justice

The most fundamental principle of justice was defined by Aristotle more than 2,000 years ago: namely, the principle that equals should be treated equally and like things treated alike (Aristotle, 322 BC/2012). For instance, it is necessary to distinguish women from men when addressing health care issues that affect women. While it has been almost 50 years since the U.S. Supreme Court stated that women have the right to access contraception as easily as men have the right to access condoms, many American women, half a century later, still do not have easy or affordable access to birth control. In a just society, the reproductive needs of women would be met and women would have comprehensive access to reproductive care. Principles of justice may require that the root causes of gender health disparities be effectively addressed.

If everyone is equal, that is, has equal value as a human being, then everyone has an equal claim to share the nation's health care resources. By default, equal resources may be distributed to everyone since everyone has equal claims. But, as illustrated in **FEATURE BOX 1-5**, there are circumstances in which everyone does not have an equal claim when resources are limited; a fair distribution in such situations depends on the reasons for their equality or inequality.

FEATURE BOX 1-5

Some Justifiable Reasons for Inequality

- *Accomplishments*: some people simply achieve more than others, so it is just when someone who attains impressive achievements and success is given resources that are not distributed to others who accomplish little; some people can pay for innovative medical products or services that others cannot.
- *Contracts*: prior agreements may exist about how distribution of resources should occur (for instance, tax and welfare legislation), so it is just when the government gives benefits to those who are poor or financially distressed that it does not provide to those at the top of the economic pyramid.
- *Contributions*: some people plainly contribute more to society than others, so it is just when those who make a greater contribution receive more benefits than others.
- *Effort*: some people just work more efficiently or their work products are deemed more valuable by society, so it is just when those who exert more effort receive more benefits.
- *Need*: some vulnerable populations have a justifiable need to receive more resources than others, so it is just when those who have more need for services receive more assistance in securing them.
- *Vulnerability status*: some people may have claims because they are part of a vulnerable population (such as sick children and the disabled), so it is just when they receive more medical products or services than are given to healthy people.
- *Seniority*: some may have applied first for distribution of resources, so it is just when the transplant recipient who is first on the wait list is given first choice over another subsequent patient with a similar level of need when an organ is procured.

— Sources: Beauchamp & Childress, 2012; Markkula, 2009a.

While some criteria justify differential treatment, there are also criteria that are not justifiable grounds for giving people different treatment. For instance, is it fair for adults with preventable health conditions, attributable to smoking and being overweight, to be charged the same health insurance premiums as adults with healthy lifestyles? There are also criteria that do justify treating people differently. For instance, what is a fair level of compensation for patients who are harmed by medical errors, unneeded medical treatments, or defective medical products, versus patients who are harmed because they did not follow their recommended courses of treatment?

Different Kinds of Justice

There are different philosophies of justice. **Distributive justice** refers to the extent to which society's institutions ensure that benefits and burdens are distributed among society's members in ways that are fair and just. When the institutions of a society distribute benefits or burdens in unjust ways, there is a strong presumption that those institutions should be changed. A second kind of justice is compensatory justice. **Compensatory justice** refers to the extent to which people are fairly compensated for their injuries by those who have injured them; just compensation is proportional to the loss inflicted on a person. This is precisely the kind of justice that is at stake in trying to hold gun manufacturers, distributors, and dealers liable for health care burdens arising from crimes involving illegal guns (*see, e.g.*, LCAV, 2011).

Application of the Justice Model

The Justice Model, as illustrated in **FIGURE 1-7**, involves a five-step framework that is used in almost all decisions involving distribution of limited resources.

Step 1:   Define the distribution of resources by determining who is getting the benefits and burdens in the situation. Should those who get benefits also share burdens?

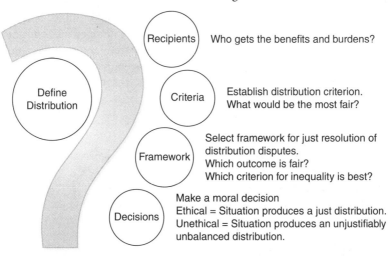

Recipients — Who gets the benefits and burdens?

Define Distribution

Criteria — Establish distribution criterion. What would be the most fair?

Framework — Select framework for just resolution of distribution disputes. Which outcome is fair? Which criterion for inequality is best?

Decisions — Make a moral decision. Ethical = Situation produces a just distribution. Unethical = Situation produces an unjustifiably unbalanced distribution.

Justice Decision-Making Model

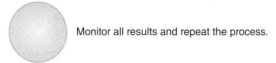

Monitor all results and repeat the process.

FIGURE 1-7 Justice Decision-Making Model

Sources: Beauchamp & Childress, 2012; Markkula, 2009.

Step 2: Once the distribution is known, establish which criterion for distribution would be the most fair and justify why it would be most fair in the situation.

Step 3: Select a framework to decide what is fair if disagreement persists over which outcome is fair or over which criterion for inequality is best in the situation, then choose a framework to decide what is fair.

Step 4: Make an ethical decision. Decide whether an action will produce a fair distribution and why.

Step 5: Monitor the results of the decision and repeat the process all over again as changes occur.

Strengths and Limitations of the Justice Model

The greatest strength of the Justice Model is its broad focus on the wide-ranging problem of adapting health care decisions to respond to the needs and interests of all **stakeholders** affected. This approach to health care asks everyone affected—government, academics, patients, and the health care industry—to address and balance the multiple claims of shared interests and concerns.

While research shows justice to be one of the most fundamental ethical instincts in humans, the weakness of the model is that there is no single criterion for a fair distribution, so the Justice Model is always open to disagreement among ethically minded people. That is, although the Justice Model provides assurances that its distribution of resources is necessary to protect the human rights of vulnerable populations, at the same time, distributions that are fair can improperly violate the human rights of those upon whom such decisions are imposed (*see* Rawls, 2001).

For instance, when half the pregnancies in the United States are unintended, the nation's policies on reproductive care are not responding to women's needs or the interests of many of the children born in the United States. Because there is no single criterion for defining when human life begins, there is no agreement upon the ethics of contraception. Mandates to provide basic contraception coverage can improperly violate the religious rights of those upon whom such decisions are imposed, even though at the same time, the Justice Model provides that affordable access to contraception is necessary to protect the reproductive rights of women, and arguably those of men as well.

Common Good Model

Being able to live together in society involves common burdens and benefits that are important to the welfare of everyone. For a society to be sustainable, the burdens and benefits must function together to achieve the **common good**. In other words, the common good is achieved when the burdens and benefits of life function together to achieve a sustainable society. In this instance, it includes the things Americans commit to do as a society that benefit everyone.

Although the common good is often associated with the philosophy of utilitarianism, the Utility Model focuses on benefits for the people affected by a decision, whereas the Common Good Model considers more than just those affected. Since everyone has access to the common benefits, society has the ethical obligation to accept the burdens of establishing and maintaining the common benefits.

While the common good has a critical place in current discussions of health care reform, the ethic originated more than 2,500 years ago in the writings of Confucius, Epictetus, Plato, and Aristotle. They defined the *common good* as certain general conditions that exist equally to everyone's advantage. The common good ethic, then, is having a U.S. health care system work in a manner that benefits everyone. Because such a health care system could have a powerful impact on the well-being of all members of American society, it is no surprise that its reform is linked to how well the system functions.

The ethic of the common good in health care does not just happen by coincidence. Establishing and maintaining common benefits and burdens requires the cooperative efforts of many people. But these efforts pay off, for the common resources of the nation are greater than the individual resources of any one provider or health care system. When all members of society have access to health care, no one can be easily excluded.

Societal Obstacles to Acceptance of the Common Good

Although everyone could benefit from the ethic of the common good, not everyone willingly responds to the need to cooperate to establish and maintain common benefits; a number of obstacles hinder American society from successfully doing so.

Pluralism

The very idea of the common good is hard to define in a **pluralistic society** like the United States, where cultural differences are encouraged and political and economic powers are shared by different nationalities and minorities. The inscription on U.S. coins, *e pluribus unum* (out of many, one), reflects the nation's pride in being a melting pot of different nationalities and minorities; the United States has always had an underlying and unifying national consensus about standards of justice and what constitutes right and wrong.

Pluralism, that underlying and unifying national consensus about standards of fairness and justice, has itself, however, come under attack in the recent health care reforms. Different people have different ideas about what is worthwhile in health care or what constitutes the benefits needed. Others disagree about how the burdens should be distributed across society. Given these differences in values and what constitutes right and wrong, it is almost impossible, but not out of the question, to agree on health care system reforms that everyone will support.

Relative Values

Even if everyone agreed upon what was valued, there would be disagreements about the relative values of health care reform. While everyone might agree, for instance, that access to affordable health care should be part of the common benefits, some want to focus on the nation's investment in health information technology, others want to focus on evidence-based medicine, and still others will claim that any major reform is unnecessary. Such disagreements undercut the nation's ability to evoke a sustained and widespread commitment to the ethic of the common good. In the face of such pluralism, efforts to bring about the common good lead to adopting or promoting the views of some, while excluding others, violating the principle of treating people equally. Moreover, any reform efforts force everyone to support some specific notion of the common good, violating the freedom of those who do not share in this ideal.

Free-Riders

Another obstacle encountered by proponents of the ethic of the common good is the free-rider issue. The common benefits are available to everyone, including those who choose not to do their part to maintain the common good. Individuals can become free-riders by taking the benefits the ethic of the common good provides while refusing to do their part to support the common benefits. Government health insurance, for instance, is one of the common benefits to which everyone over age 65 is entitled. Many, however, are reluctant to do their share in managing this consumption of health care. When up to one-half of the medical treatments received are not evidence-based and do not improve health (*see, e.g.,* IOM, 2009), the free-riders are destroying the common good, including that of patients and the health care providers and health insurers who pay for the treatments (*see* Purdy & Siegel, 2012; Todd, 2011). The national reluctance to support efforts to control government health insurance costs has helped lead to the system's near collapse.

Individualism

Attempts to promote the ethic of the common good are affected by individualism (Berman, 2011). Historical traditions place a high value on individual freedom, on personal rights, and on allowing people to act independently (*see* Mariner, 2009). American culture views society as comprised of separate independent individuals who are free to pursue their own individual goals and interests without interference from others. In this individualistic culture it is difficult to convince people that they should sacrifice some of their freedom and some of their self-interest for the sake of the common good.

Unequal Sharing of Burdens

Appeals to the ethic of the common good confront the problem of an unequal sharing of burdens. Maintaining the common good often requires that some people bear burdens that are much greater than those borne by others. For instance, making the health care system more affordable and equitable may require mandating that everyone purchase health insurance. The health insurance industry may be forced to change its approach to doing business from one of mitigating risk to that of attempting to eliminate risk. It may be unjust to force people and whole industries to carry unequal burdens for the sake of the ethic of the common good. The prospect of having to carry unequal burdens leads some individuals and industries to resist any attempts to secure the common good.

Application of the Common Good Model

Whereas the Utility Model focuses on the total benefits and burdens produced, the Common Good Model focuses on whether the action or situation contributes to or burdens a particular aspect of the common good. The Common Good Model, as illustrated in **FIGURE 1-8**, involves six steps with a focus on how decisions benefit everyone. Whether applied to a defined group or applied in general, society is the priority when the Common Good Model is used.

Step 1: Identify what specific aspects of the common good are involved by zooming in and then zooming out. For instance, it is important for the biotechnology industry to zoom in on the details underlying its core medical technologies. The industry also needs to zoom out, to define how society will pay for the advanced medical technologies that biotechnology is developing.

Step 2: Define which specific parts of the common good that depend on the current situation for their functioning could move forward or backward by a change. Some actions will strengthen the common good and others will weaken it. In this instance, the common benefits serve among other things, the biotechnology industry, the health care delivery systems and providers who use the products of biotechnology, the legal and the regulatory systems that are necessary for

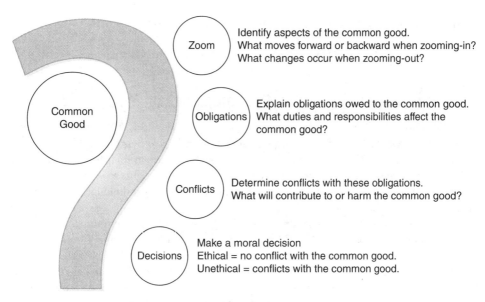

Common Good Decision-Making Model

Monitor all results and repeat the process.

FIGURE 1-8 Common Good Decision-Making Model
Sources: Beauchamp & Childress, 2012; Markkula, 2009.

the production and marketing of biotech products, as well as the technology that makes all these activities possible. The common benefits ethic also includes the ideologies used to maintain different aspects of the common good.

Step 3: Explain the ethical obligation to promote and protect particular aspects of the common good. For instance, define the ethical obligations that the biotechnology industry or parts of it have to maintain because they benefit from them. In this case, if the biotechnology industry benefits from its commercial models and regulatory framework, there is an ethical obligation to promote these particular aspects of the common benefits or at least not to burden them. The best elements of the U.S. biotechnology industry should be protected, especially its scientifically advanced institutions with their elaborate systems of specialized knowledge, advanced technologies, and rules of conduct.

Step 4: Determine whether the proposed action or situation conflicts with this ethical obligation. Laws and regulations must strengthen the common benefits and protect aspects of them from risks. For instance, biotechnology executives might recognize that even though they may charge hundreds of thousands of dollars for their patented products, maintaining trust in the biotechnology industry may require that they modify their pricing structure. Maximizing the effects of the law means that lobbying for their interest group has to be more restrained; or that maintaining the courts as an efficient problem resolution mechanism requires that, even though the deep pockets of biotechnology companies enable them to litigate patent lawsuits indefinitely, they should not do so.

Step 5: Make an ethical decision. Determine whether the action or situation conflicts with the ethical obligation to contribute to the common good.

Step 6: Monitor the results of the decision and repeat the process as changes occur.

Strengths and Limitations of the Common Good Model

The Common Good Model provides an important reality check. No matter how much someone contributes to their own success, the model reminds them that society also contributes and that existing institutions and ideologies enable them to carry on their activities. The ethic of the common good is a challenge for all Americans to view themselves as members of the same society, while respecting and valuing their individual right to choose the type of health care they want.

There is a great deal of disagreement over what constitutes the common good and over relative values when ideals conflict. Moreover, the Common Good Model runs contrary to a long-standing American tradition of individualism and the pursuit of self-interest, so it may stir up immediate resistance that could distract from the ethical issues to be resolved. Obstacles to the ethic of the common good highlight the broader question concerning the kind of health care system the nation wants and how this can be best achieved.

Virtue Model

The kind of person health care professionals choose to be and the kind of health care system they decide to work for are as important as their actions on the job. Character and work culture are represented and influenced both by how health care professionals act and by what they aspire to be. To focus only, as the other decision-making models do, on how to judge whether actions and situations are ethical or unethical overlooks an important aspect of health care ethics. Most people in the health care industry aspire to have **virtues**, or habits of acting in certain ways that correspond to their core values. Compassion, courage, diligence, education, fairness, generosity, honesty, integrity, self-control, and tolerance are virtues that health care professionals, and the health care industry in general, aspire to acquire. If someone knows who they are and who they aspire to be, they can decide how to act by considering whether an action is something that would be done by the kind of person they want to be. People's futures are often shaped by their actions. The same can be said for organizations. *See generally* Beauchamp & Childress, 2012; Markkula, 2009a.

Application of the Virtue Model

The Virtue Model, as illustrated in **FIGURE 1-9**, is comprised of a five-step framework that focuses primarily on the kind of person someone aspires to be and secondarily on judging their individual actions.

Step 1: Determine whether the situation helps you to or hinders you from becoming the type of professional you most want to be.

Step 2: Establish whether the situation corresponds to the industry's reputation or vision of what it would like to be. This image is explained in health care providers' mission and vision statements, the core values, and the ethics code.

Step 3: Ascertain whether the situation improves the delivery of high-quality, equitable health care.

Determine the value of personal virtue.
Does the situation cultivate development of personal virtue?

Determine the value of organizational virtue.
Does the situation correspond to the organization's best values and ideals?

Review organizational values.
Does the situation improve high-quality, equitable health care?

Make a moral decision
Ethical = actions correspond to virtues.
Unethical = actions do not correspond to virtues.

Virtue Decision-Making Model

Monitor all results and repeat the process.

FIGURE 1-9 Virtue Decision-Making Model

Sources: Beauchamp & Childress, 2012; Markkula, 2009.

Step 4: Make an ethical decision. Actions that correspond to the virtues most people in the health care industry want to be associated with are ethical.

Step 5: Monitor the results of the decision and repeat the process as changes occur.

Strengths and Limitations of the Virtue Model

The Virtue Model focuses not only on individual actions but also on the larger questions of what kind of health care professional it is beneficial to be and on the role that one's environment plays in setting ideals. The Virtue Model emphasizes that being an ethical person is not just a matter of following ethical principles, but also involves developing habits of acting in ways that society thinks people should act. Most people do not act in a consistent manner across different situations (*see* Mitchell, 2006). This does not mean that people do not have dispositions to act a certain way; rather, it suggests that consistent virtue may be very hard to develop because situational factors greatly affect people's decisions and conduct. *See generally* Moffit, 2002.

Comparing Conclusions from the Different Decision-Making Models

The immense complexity of the U.S. health care system requires that portfolios of decision-making models be available for making ethical decisions. Use of multiple models increases the level of confidence in the rightness of decisions, especially when a situation is complicated, or a decision makes a significant difference to people or an organization.

In health care ethics, it is important to be confident but never certain. Using several models increases the chance of generating new insights into why some actions are unethical or wrong. Having different perspectives on why something is wrong can be helpful in designing alternatives that produce the benefits that made the action attractive in the first place but without the qualities that made it wrong (Beauchamp & Childress, 2012).

Balancing Options Using Several Decision-Making Models

Different models highlight the limitations of other decision-making models, as illustrated in **FEATURE BOX 1-6**. Often, the use of multiple models in making controversial or complicated decisions balances their strengths against their limitations.

Resolving Conflicts in Judgment

For most situations involving ethical issues, the decision-making models yield the same judgment (*see, e.g.*, Hamilton, 2009); the only difference is their rationale as to why certain actions are unethical. In some situations, however, the models result in different ethical judgments. As illustrated in **FEATURE BOX 1-7**, when this happens and the conflicts cannot be resolved, one might ask what the correct course of action is.

FEATURE BOX 1-6

Contrast of Different Models for Decision-Making

- *Social Media Model* helps determine whether the application of any other models is necessary.
- *Choices* and *Rights Models* focus attention on the importance of respect for the human dignity of individual patients and health care professionals, whereas the *Exceptions* and *Utility Models* focus more on outcomes.
- *Exceptions* and *Choices Models* focus on how decisions are made, whereas the *Utility Model* is concerned with results as opposed to the conditions or rules the action can meet.
- *Virtue Model* focuses primarily on the kind of health care professional someone aspires to be and secondarily on judging individual actions.
- *Utility Model* focuses on the benefits or total net effects for the people affected by a decision, whereas the *Common Good Model* considers more than just those affected.

— Sources: Beauchamp & Childress, 2012; Hamilton, 2009.

FEATURE BOX 1-7

When Ethical Conflicts Cannot Be Resolved

- If the actions being considered are ethical according to some of the decision-making models and unethical according to others, a judgment must be made. The best course of action should minimize ethical conflicts; in other words, it should pass the challenge that the Social Media Model presents.
- Health care professionals sometimes disagree about the ethical thing to do. These disagreements can be expected. At least, however, the ethics of the actions or situation are being questioned and pondered so as to determine how best to act and to ensure that a particular course of action is not entirely unethical.
- Balancing the various decision-making models is part of developing the practical management skills health care professionals need to cultivate. Sometimes, however, a judgment must simply be made. Maintaining the common good may require moderating or even foregoing the exceptions, choices, rights, justice, or virtue claims. Alternatively, strong considerations that are raised by the Exceptions, Choices, Rights, Justice, Utility, or Virtue Models may override the claims of the Common Good Model.

— Source: Beauchamp & Childress, 2012.

Conflicts in ethical judgments are at the apex of a steep and slippery slope in health care ethics. When making these controversial decisions, intuition does not always guarantee that the judgments reached are the most ethical. Judgments often become clouded in these situations. To overcome this limitation, discussions should be held until consensus is reached about the best balance among the models for the situation.

Problematic Moral Clarity—Universal Values and Principles

This text seeks moral clarity on universal values and principles as they pertain to the *American ethic of health care*. Decisions should not and cannot be divorced from values. This aim will not result in a definitive statement, but rather, a question: What actions will best reflect the universal values and principles that have served America so well for the past two centuries? Above all, everyone must become more fully aware of what they say they believe in and put a priority not on projecting their values and principles, but upon reflecting them more deeply, accurately, and consistently.

ETHICAL OR UNETHICAL DECISION

Individual Health Insurance Mandate

Ethics Issues: *Should everyone share broadly in the risks and costs of poor health? And if so, what decision-making models could help reach this conclusion?*

Ethics Analysis: Yes, everyone has an ethical obligation to share in the risks and costs of poor health under the Rights and Justice Models. Everyone should be required to participate in and become a member of one of the nation's risk pools, where the risks and costs of poor health are pooled broadly and where access to care is provided on the basis of medical need. People may be required to contribute toward financing the nation's health care costs based on their ability to pay. Everyone may freely select which risk pool to participate in to cover their risks of poor health by entering into a contract relationship with a health insurer; public insurance plans (Medicaid) and individual subsidies will be available for anyone unable to pay for private insurance.

Ethics Analysis: No, people should not be required to share the risks and costs of poor health under the Common Good Model. Health insurance is not like social insurance; society has no ethical obligation to cover everyone's risks of poor health. People should not be required to engage in economic activity by being required to enter into a contract relationship with a health insurer. Congress should not require people, who are not doing anything to help finance the nation's health care costs, to do something. Access to health care should be tied to the ability to pay.

Court's Holding and Decision: Case dismissed. While Virginia claimed that Congress lacked authority to enact the minimum coverage provision to maintain health insurance, the federal court of appeals held that Virginia lacked standing to litigate this issue. Virginia lacked the sovereign authority to nullify federal law. Virginia could not litigate in federal court to protect its citizens from operation of the nation's health care reform.

— *Commonwealth of Virginia ex rel. Cuccinelli v. Sebelius*, 656 F.3d 253 (U.S. Court of Appeals for the 4th Circuit 2011), *cert. denied*, 133 S.Ct. 59 (U.S. Supreme Court 2012). *See* Adler & Cannon, 2013; Ben-Asher, 2012; Howard, 2012; Huberfeld, 2011; Kapp, 2012; Leonard, 2012; McCullough, 2013; Morgan & Hale, 2012; Record, 2012; Sachs, 2012; Siegel, 2012; Somin, 2012; Thomson, 2012; Willis & Chung, 2012 (discussing this court decision). *See also Mead v. Holder*, 766 F.Supp.2d 16 (U.S. District Court for the District of Columbia 2011), *affirmed, Seven-Sky v. Holder*, 661 F.3d 1 (U.S. Court of Appeals for the D.C. Circuit 2011), *cert. denied*, 133 S.Ct. 63 (U.S. Supreme Court 2012); *Florida, et al. v. U.S. Department of Health and Human Services*, 648 F.3d 1235 (U.S. Court of Appeals for the 11th Circuit 2011), *affirmed in part and reversed in part*, 132 S.Ct. 2566 (U.S. Supreme Court 2012); *Liberty University, et al. v. Geithner, et al.*, 671 F.3d 391 (U.S. Court of Appeals for the 4th Circuit 2011), *cert. denied*, 133 S.Ct. 60 (U.S. Supreme Court 2012); *Thomas More Law Center v. Obama*, 651 F.3d 529 (U.S. Court of Appeals for the 6th Circuit 2011), *cert. denied*, 133 S.Ct. 61 (U.S. Supreme Court 2012).

CHAPTER SUMMARY

- The health care industry is seeking firm foundations, reasoned principles of ethics, and helpful guidelines to assist it in making ethical decisions.
- Ethical decision-making generally uses an eight-step framework: recognize the ethical issues; gather all the relevant facts; survey decision-making models; evaluate the relevance of each model for the situation; apply the appropriate model(s) to the situation; make decisions based on the model(s); monitor the results of those decisions; monitor progress and repeat the process as changes occur.
- The Social Media Model holds that a decision is ethical if it withstands public scrutiny.
- The Utility Model indicates that a decision is ethical when it maximizes good and minimizes harm to the greatest number.
- The Rights Model states that a decision is ethical if it respects and guarantees the human rights of the people affected.
- The Exceptions Model asserts that a decision is ethical when a benefit given to one person can become a normative standard of conduct toward all people.
- The Choices Model requires that people make their own free and independent choices.
- The Justice Model maintains that a decision is ethical when the various benefits and burdens associated with the decision are fairly distributed.
- The Common Good Model finds that a decision is ethical when the common benefits and burdens are balanced with the common good.
- The Virtue Model deems that a decision is ethical if it manifests essential human virtues and thereby enables health care professionals and providers to be noble and humane.
- Use of multiple models increases the level of confidence in the rightness of decisions by balancing the models' strengths against their limitations.

REFERENCES

Adler, J. H., & Cannon, M. F. (2013). Taxation without representation: The illegal IRS rule to expand tax credits under the PPACA. *Health Matrix: The Journal of Law-Medicine, 23*, 119–195.

AHRQ (Agency for Health Research and Quality). (2012). *National health care disparities.* Rockville, MD: AHRQ.

Aristotle. (2012). *Ethics.* London, England: Pearson's Penguin Classics (Original work published 322 BC).

Baker, A. J. R. (2011). Fundamental mismatch: The improper integration of individual liberty rights into commerce clause analysis of the Patient Protection and Affordable Care Act. *University of Miami Law Review, 66*, 259–312.

Beauchamp, T. L., & Childress, J. F. (2012). *Principles of biomedical ethics* (7th ed.). New York, NY: Oxford University Press.

Ben-Asher, N. (2012). Obligatory health. *Yale Human Rights and Development Law Journal, 15*, 1–18.

Bentham, J. (2015). *Introduction to principles of morals and legislation.* Rochester, NY: The Scholar's Choice (Original work published 1789).

Berman, M. L. (2011). A public health perspective on health care reform. *Health Matrix: The Journal of Law-Medicine, 21*, 353–383.

Blackstone, W. (2010). *Commentaries on the laws of England.* Renton, WA: Forgotten Books (Original work published 1753).

Bolin, M. (2014). The Affordable Care Act and people living with HIV/AIDS: A roadmap to better health outcomes. *Annals of Health Law, 23*, 28–60.

Bradley, F. H. (1988). *Ethical studies.* Oxford, England: Clarendon Press (Original work published 1927).

____. (1935). *Collected essays.* Vols. 1-2. Oxford, England: Clarendon Press.

____. (1916). *Appearance and reality.* New York, NY: Macmillan (Original work published 1893).

Calnan, A. (2010). The instrumental justice of private law. *University of Missouri-Kansas City Law Review, 78,* 559–615.

CBO (Congressional Budget Office). (2011, February 18). Letter from D. L. Elmendorf, Director of the CBO to P. Ryan, Chairman, House Committee on the Budget, U.S. House of Representatives, Washington DC.

CDC (Centers for Disease Control and Prevention). (2013). *HIV surveillance report: Diagnoses of HIV infection and AIDS in the United States and dependent areas.* Atlanta, GA: CDC.

Chabris, C. F., & Simons, D. (2010). *The invisible gorilla: And other ways our intuitions deceive us.* New York, NY: Crown Publishing Group.

Cohn, M. (2011). Form, formula and constitutional ethos: The political question and justiciability doctrine in three common law systems. *American Journal of Comparative Law, 59,* 675–713.

Cousins, M. (2014). Equal protection: Immigrants' access to healthcare and welfare benefits. *Hastings Race and Poverty Law Journal, 12*(1), 21–56.

Dobbin, R. (2008). *Discourses and selected writings.* London, England: Pearson's Penguin Classics (Original work of Epictetus published 108 AD).

Dolan, P., & Peasgood, T. (2008). Measuring well-being for public policy: Preferences or experiences? *Journal of Legal Studies, 37,* 5–26.

Dworkin, R. M. (2013). *Justice for hedgehogs.* Cambridge, MA: Belknap Press (Original work published 2011).

___. (2013). *Religion without god.* Cambridge, MA: Harvard University Press.

___. (2013). *Taking rights seriously (Bloomsbury revelations).* New York, NY: Bloomsbury Academic (Original work published 1996).

___. (2010). *Freedom's law: The moral reading of the American Constitution.* Cambridge, MA: Harvard University Press (Original work published 1996).

___. (2008a). *Democracy possible here? Principles for a new political debate.* Princeton, NJ: Princeton University Press.

___. (2008b). *Justice in robes.* Cambridge, MA: Belknap Press.

___. (2008c). *The Supreme Court phalanx: The Court's new right-wing bloc.* New York, NY: New York Review Books.

___. (2002a). *A badly flawed election: Debating* Bush v. Gore, *the Supreme Court, and American democracy.* New York, NY: New Press.

___. (2002b). *Sovereign virtue: The theory and practice of equality.* Cambridge, MA: Harvard University Press.

___. (1994). *Life's dominion: An argument about abortion, euthanasia, and individual freedom.* New York, NY: Vintage/Random House.

___. (1991). *Bill of rights for Britain: Why British liberty needs protection.* London, England: Chatto & Windus of Random House.

___. (1986). *Law's empire.* Cambridge, MA: Belknap Press.

___. (1985). *A matter of principle.* Cambridge, MA: Harvard University Press.

___. (1978). *Taking rights seriously.* (5th Edition). Cambridge, MA: Harvard University Press.

___. (Ed.). (1977). *The philosophy of law (Oxford readings in philosophy).* New York, NY: Oxford University Press.

___. (2013). *Taryn Simon: An American index of the hidden and unfamiliar.* Ostfildern, Germany: Hatje Cantz (Original work published 2008).

Freeman, W. (2001). *How brains make up their minds.* New York, NY: Columbia University Press.

___. (2000). *Neurodynamics: An exploration in mesoscopic brain dynamics (perspectives in neural computing).* Philadelphia, PA: Springer (overview of Freeman's published works).

___. (1995). *Societies of brains. A study in the neuroscience of love and hate (The International Neural Networks Society).* New York, NY: Lawrence Erlbaum/Taylor & Francis Group.

Hamilton, III, J. B., at Markkula Center for Applied Ethics. (2009). *Identify ethical issues.* Santa Clara, CA: Santa Clara University.

___. (2009a). *How to compare conclusions from the different tests.* Markkula Center for Applied Ethics. Santa Clara, CA: Santa Clara University.

Howard, A. E. D. (2012). The Constitution and the role of government. *Charleston Law Review, 6,* 449–510.

Huberfeld, N. (2011). Federalizing Medicaid. *University of Pennsylvania Journal of Constitutional Law, 14,* 431–484.

IOM (Institute of Medicine). (2009). *Initial national priorities for comparative effectiveness research.* Washington, DC: National Academies of Sciences.

___. (2001). *Crossing the quality chasm: A new health system for the 21st century.* Washington, DC: National Academies Press.

Kaiser Family Foundation. (2014). *The global HIV/AIDS epidemic.* Washington, DC & Menlo Park, CA: Kaiser.

Kant, I. (2009). *The critique of pure reason.* London, England: Pearson's Penguin Classics (Original work published 1781 and also referred to as Kant's "First Critique").

___. (2009). *The critique of practical reason.* London, England: Pearson's Penguin Classics (Original work published 1788 and also referred to as Kant's "Second Critique").

___. (2009). *The critique of judgment.* London, England: Pearson's Penguin Classics (Original work published 1790 and also referred to as Kant's "Third Critique").

Kapp, M. B. (2012). If we can force people to purchase health insurance, then let's force them to be treated too. *American Journal of Law and Medicine, 38*, 397–409.

Keyes, E. (2011). The just society and the liberal state: Classical and contemporary liberalism and the problem of consent. *Georgetown Journal of Law and Public Policy, 9*, 1–65.

Knight, F. H. (2000). *Selected essays by Frank H. Knight.* Vol. 1-2 (ed. by Ross B. Emmett). Chicago, IL: University of Chicago Press.

___. (1935). *Ethics and economic reform.* Edison, NJ: Transaction Publishers.

Lanshe, J. (2009). Morality and the rule of law in American jurisprudence. *Rutgers Journal of Law and Religion, 11*, 1–60.

LCAV (Legal Community Against Violence). (2011). *Gun violence statistics.* San Francisco, CA.

Leonard, E. W. (2012). Affordable Care Act litigation: The standing paradox. *American Journal of Law and Medicine, 38*, 410–444.

Levine, M. A., et al. for the American Medical Association Ethical Force Program. (2007). Improving access to health care: A consensus ethical framework to guide proposals for reform. *Hastings Center Report, 37*(5), 14–19.

Madsen, P. (2008). Professionals, business practitioners, and prudential justice. *McGeorge Law Review, 39*, 835–849.

Mariner, W. K. (2009). Toward an architecture of health law. *American Journal of Law and Medicine, 35*, 67–87.

Markkula Center for Applied Ethics. (2009). *Making an ethical decision.* Santa Clara, CA: Santa Clara University.

___. (2009a). *A framework for thinking ethically.* Santa Clara, CA: Santa Clara University.

___. (2009b). *Ethics operationalized: Effective ethics for the workplace.* Santa Clara, CA: Santa Clara University.

McCullough, R. L. (2013). What is all the fuss about?: The United States Congress may impose a tax (it's called the "individual mandate"). *Southern California Interdisciplinary Law Journal, 22*, 729-780.

Mill, J. S. (2011). *Utilitarianism, liberty, and representative government.* Toronto, Canada: University of Toronto Libraries (Original work published 1863).

Mitchell, J. B. (2006). My father, John Locke, and assisted suicide: The real constitutional right. *Indiana Law Review, 3*, 43–101.

Moffit, R. E. (2002). The economic and ethical dimensions of health policy. *Journal of Contemporary Health Law and Policy, 18*, 663–672.

Morgan, E., & Hale, S. T. (2012). Health care access: Access after health care reform. *The Georgetown Journal of Gender and the Law, 13*, 307–332.

O'Neill, O. (2014). *Acting on principle: An essay on Kantian ethics.* (2nd ed.). New York, NY: Cambridge University Press.

Peery, Jr., N. S. (2008). Corporate social performance: Ethics and corporate culture. *McGeorge Law Review, 39*, 813–834.

Plato. (2007). *The republic.* London, England: Pearson's Penguin Classics (Original work published 380 BC).

Purcell, J. (2010). Adverse clinical and public health consequences of limited anti-retroviral licensing. *Berkeley Technology Law Journal, 25*, 103–134.

Purdy, J., & Siegel, N. S. (2012). The liberty of free riders: The minimum coverage provision, Mill's "harm principle," and American social morality. *American Journal of Law and Medicine, 38*, 374–396.

Rawls, J. (2005). *A theory of justice.* Boston, MA: Belknap Press (Original work published 1971).

___. (2005). *Political liberalism.* New York, NY: Columbia University Press.

___. (2001). *Justice as fairness: A restatement.* Cambridge, MA: Harvard University Press.

___. (1999). *Collected papers.* S. Freeman (Ed.). Cambridge, MA: Harvard University Press.

___. (1974). The independence of moral theory. *Proceedings and Addresses of the American Philosophical Association, 48*, 5–22.

Record, K. L. (2012). Litigating the ACA: Securing the right to health within a framework of negative rights. *American Journal of Law and Medicine, 38*, 537–547.

Restatement (Third) of Foreign Relations Law of the United States. (1987). Philadelphia, PA: American Law Institute.

Rivkin, Jr., D. B., & Whelan, E. (2012, February 15). Birth-control mandate: Unconstitutional and illegal. *Wall Street Journal*, p. A13.

Roberts, J. R. (2011). The Genetic Information Nondiscrimination Act as an antidiscrimination law. *Notre Dame Law Review, 86*, 597–648.

Sachs, S. E. (2012). The constitutionality of the Affordable Care Act: Ideas from the academy: The uneasy case for the Affordable Care Act. *Law and Contemporary Problems, 75*, 17–27.

Sartre, J.-P. (2000). *Existentialism and human emotions.* New York, NY: Citadel.

____. (1990). *Notebooks for an ethics [cahiers pour une morale].* Chicago, IL: University of Chicago Press (Original work published 1983).

Siegel, N. S. (2012). The constitutionality of the Affordable Care Act: Ideas from the academy: Free riding on benevolence: Collective action federalism and the minimum coverage provision. *Law and Contemporary Problems, 75,* 29–74.

Simons, D. J., & Chabris, C. F. (1999). Gorillas in our midst: Sustained inattentional blindness for dynamic events. *Perception, 28,* 1059–1074.

Somin, I. (2012). The constitutionality of the Affordable Care Act: Ideas from the academy: A mandate for mandates: Is the individual health insurance case a slippery slope? *Law and Contemporary Problems, 75,* 75–106.

Spiropoulos, A. C. (2010). Rights done right: A critique of libertarian originalism. *University of Missouri-Kansas City Law Review, 78,* 661–704.

Thomson, K. (2012). State-run insurance exchanges in federal healthcare reform: A case study in dysfunctional federalism. *American Journal of Law and Medicine, 38,* 548–569.

Todd, A. E. (2011). No need for more regulation: Payors and their role in balancing the cost and safety considerations of off-label prescriptions. *American Journal of Law and Medicine, 37,* 422–443.

Underhill, K. (2012). Paying for prevention: Challenges to health insurance coverage for biomedical HIV prevention in the United States. *American Journal of Law and Medicine, 38,* 607–666.

United Nations. (1949). *Universal declaration of human rights.* New York, NY: UN.

Van Norden, B. W. (Ed.). (2001). *Confucius and the analects: New essays.* New York, NY: Oxford University Press.

Wharton School at the University of Pennsylvania. (2010). Health care reform: Not ready to be discharged yet. *Knowledge@Wharton.*

____. (2005). What's behind the 4-minute mile, Starbucks and the moon landing? The power of impossible thinking. *Knowledge@Wharton.*

Willis, S. J., & Chung, N. (2012). No healthcare penalty? No problem: No due process. *American Journal of Law and Medicine, 38,* 516–536.

Wind, J., & Crook, C. (2006). *The power of impossible thinking. Transform the business of your life and the life of your business.* Philadelphia, PA: Wharton School Publishing.

Zamir, E., & Medina, B. (2008). Law, morality, and economics: Integrating moral constraints with economic analysis of law. *California Law Review, 96,* 323–391.

CHAPTER 2

© Mary Evans Picture Library/Mary Evans Picture Library Ltd/age fotostock

Values and Principles Confronting Our Health Care System

"Only ignorance! Only ignorance! How can you talk about only ignorance? Don't you know that it is the worst thing in the world, next to wickedness?—and which does the most mischief heaven only knows. If people can say, 'Oh! I did not know, I did not mean any harm,' they think it is all right."

— **Anna Sewell** (1820–1878), English author of *Black Beauty* (1877)

LEARNING OBJECTIVES

After completing this chapter, the reader should be able to:

1. Understand the role, responsibilities, and decision-making process of medical ethics committees in health care organizations.
2. Explain the difference between medical ethics committee decisions that are legal and those that are ethical.
3. Describe the values and principles that often govern and guide the decisions of medical ethics committees when ethical dilemmas are reviewed.

KEY TERMS

Adverse selection	Chronic pain	Corrective justice
American ethic	Compassion	Economic utility
Autonomy	Competency	Emergency care
Autonomy from government	Corporate autonomy	Enterprise liability
Beneficence	Corporate practice of medicine doctrine	Entitlement spending
Best interests standard	Corporate well-being	Equality of opportunity

Equitable access to health care	Medical futility	Public ethic
Ethical dilemmas	Medicare	Reasonable and necessary care
Fairness	Minimum coverage provision	Responsible corporate officer doctrine
Human dignity	Moral preferences	
Hyde Amendment	Negative law	Risk pooling
Individual responsibility	Negative moral rights	Social contract
Informed consent	New federalism	Social determinants of health
Joint Commission	No-fault insurance	
Justice	Non-malfeasance	Social justice
Life-sustaining medical treatment	Personal autonomy	Social risks
	Positive law	Truthfulness
Mature minor	Positive moral rights	Universal values
Medicaid	Potentially avoidable events	Vulnerable populations
Medical ethics committees	Principles	

ETHICAL OR UNETHICAL DECISION

Balancing Values in Treatment Decisions by Medical Ethics Committees

Ethics Issue: *Should medical ethics committees balance their values with the values of patients and their families when treatment decisions must be made?*

In Brief: Marie-Eve Laurendeau and Stephane Mantha, parents of a severely disabled infant daughter, filed a $3.5 million lawsuit against Montreal Children's Hospital for keeping their daughter on life support without their consent. Phebe Mantha was born in November 2007 at another Montreal hospital, where she suffered complications during birth. Phebe was transferred to Montreal Children's Hospital, where physicians told her parents she would never be able to breathe or feed on her own. The parents were told Phebe would be blind and deaf, and would never talk or walk. They were also told Phebe would have very little consciousness of life. The physicians recommended that Phebe's feeding tubes and ventilator support be withdrawn. Based on this prognosis, the parents agreed to withdrawal of Phebe's life support, believing this would avoid unbearable suffering for their daughter.

But the unexpected occurred: after Phebe was disconnected from the ventilator, she breathed on her own. The parents thought their decision meant that Phebe was to have her feeding tube removed. The hospital's medical ethics committee, without consulting either parent, ordered Phebe's feeding to continue. Phebe's physicians and her parents believed Phebe would die within hours after being disconnected from the ventilator even with a feeding tube.

Ten weeks passed before the hospital told the parents Phebe had to go home. The parents were trained and provided the equipment needed to keep Phebe alive. They had to attend to Phebe 10 to 20 times a day, feeding her and suctioning her airways and stomach. More than three years later, Phebe is in constant danger of catching a life-threatening illness and requires round-the-clock attention to survive; she is in constant pain, cannot walk or sit, cannot hold her head up all the time, and does not talk. No one knows how long Phebe will live.

— *Laurendeau v. LaSalle Hospital*, No. 500-17-048988-094 (Quebec Superior Court 2009). (*See Ethical or Unethical Decision* at the end of the chapter for discussion of this ethics issue.)

Introduction

Complex ethical situations occur on a regular basis in health care. Life and death decisions often involve **ethical dilemmas** where there are two or more valid positions being debated by the medical community and patients. **Medical ethics committees** (MECs) are the forum where many ethical dilemmas are resolved by multidisciplinary teams (**FIGURE 2-1**). These teams are commonly comprised of health care professionals from medicine, nursing, law, chaplaincy, and social work. MECs support and advise patients, families, and caregivers as everyone works together to reach the most ethical decisions possible.

Although many ethical issues in health care have gradually been redefined as legal issues (Weinberg, 2012), MECs often address the differences between what is legal and what is ethical when such differences arise. Sometimes it is not easy to tell them apart; sometimes they conflict; sometimes it is difficult to discern whether the differences even exist. What is legal is sometimes unethical; what is ethical sometimes is not legal; what is legal or illegal or ethical or unethical is sometimes not explicitly so. The effort of this text is to help provide deeper understanding of the topics where there is no clear consensus on what is legal and what is ethical. Although both the law and ethics come into play when ethical decisions are at stake, they are not the same. While the common law, and eventually statutory law, evolves from the common ethic, laws can be applied for good or to effectuate evil without regard to the implied ethics of situations; ethics, by definition, are directed toward the common good (Marcus, 2010; Smith, 2009a).

History of Medical Ethics Committees

In 1976, the New Jersey Supreme Court endorsed the creation of MECs as an alternative venue for resolution of **medical futility** disputes, which occur when medical treatment fails to end total dependence on intensive care, fails to result in any detectable improvement in or benefit to patient health, or only preserves permanent unconsciousness (Nachman, 2011). In one case, a New Jersey father was authorized, as guardian of his permanently unconscious daughter Karen Quinlan, to request termination of the **life-sustaining medical treatment** (LSMT) that was mechanically forestalling the moment of her death. LSMT refers to advanced medical technologies such as dialysis, feeding tubes to provide artificial nutrition and hydration, intravenous medications that maintain blood pressure, and mechanical

FIGURE 2-1 Multidisciplinary Medical Ethics Committee
© Derek Latta/E+/Getty Images

ventilators and respirators, that sustain life when the body is unable to do so by itself. The court suggested that the hospital MEC confirm Karen's prognosis before LSMT was withdrawn. In addition, the court granted immunity for the health care providers who honored LSMT refusals after the involvement of MECs. With this ruling, MECs were created as an alternative to the judicial system to help clarify ethical actions for health care providers. *See In re Quinlan*, 355 A.2d 647 (New Jersey Supreme Court 1976), *cert. denied*, 429 U.S. 922 (U.S. Supreme Court 1976).

Maryland followed New Jersey's lead in recognizing a role for MECs. Then in 1983, a presidential commission recommended that all hospitals create MECs to help resolve questions about foregoing LSMT (President's Commission, 1983). Following this development, other states mandated that hospitals establish MECs.

The most significant event in the history of MECs occurred in 1992, however, when having a MEC became a necessary condition for hospitals, nursing homes, and home care agencies seeking approval by the Joint Commission. An independent, not-for-profit organization, the **Joint Commission** is the nation's predominant standards-setting and accrediting body in health care. Joint Commission accreditation is required for Medicare and Medicaid certification and licensing in many states. Consequently, most health care organizations took action when the Joint Commission mandated that organizational policies had to be in place to address ethical issues. The creation of MECs was the most common response to this Joint Commission mandate. *See generally* Hester & Bjarnadottir, 2007.

ETHICS CASE
The Role of MECs in Deciding Patients' Right to Live v. Patients' Right to Die Disputes

Betancourt v. Trinitas Hospital
[Patient v. Hospital]
415 N.J.Super. 301 (Superior Court of New Jersey, Appellate Division 2010)

Facts: Rueben Betancourt, a 72-year-old patient at Trinitas Hospital, underwent surgery to remove a malignant tumor from his thymus gland. The surgery went well, but while Betancourt was recovering in the postoperative intensive care unit, the ventilation tube that was supplying him with oxygen became dislodged. As a result, his brain was deprived of oxygen, and he was left in a persistent vegetative state with no mental functioning. Ultimately, he required dialysis three times per week, was maintained on a ventilator, developed a staph infection, and was fed with a feeding tube. After various unsuccessful attempts to resolve the issue of LSMT with Betancourt's family, his physicians claimed that continued medical treatment would be futile and would violate the standard of care.

The hospital's MEC was consulted concerning the efficacy of continuing Betancourt's LSMT and it concluded that further medical treatment was futile. Continued LSMT would not end Betancourt's total dependence on intensive care; it would only mechanically preserve his permanent state of unconsciousness. Yet, Betancourt's family refused to cease LSMT. No other health care facility would accept Betancourt. Ultimately, the hospital acted unilaterally and placed a Do Not Resuscitate (DNR) order in Betancourt's chart and declined to provide further dialysis treatment because, in the hospital's opinion, it only mechanically prolonged Betancourt's dying process.

Betancourt's family filed a lawsuit to stop the hospital from withholding LSMT based on their religious beliefs that their God should be permitted to decide the time of death. Within three months of reinstating LSMT, Betancourt died. Before his surgery, Betancourt had not executed an advance directive and had not designated a health care representative, nor had he memorialized specific wishes regarding the withholding or withdrawal of LSMT. By the time Betancourt died, his outstanding hospital bill was $1.6 million.

Legal Analysis: At the onset, the court noted that while advanced medical technology to mechanically sustain human life has existed for more than 30 years, disputes about continuing LSMT that has no medical benefit do not frequently occur. The court distinguished between what constitutes medical futility for mentally incapacitated, yet medically stable patients, and mentally incapacitated patients facing imminent death. While there is no universal agreement about futile treatment for medically stable patients, the legislature defined medical futility for patients who are dying as any LSMT that fails to end total dependence on intensive care or that mechanically preserves permanent unconsciousness.

Defining what constitutes medical futility for mentally incapacitated, yet stable, patients is a profound and universal ethical issue; it warrants debate not in the context of litigation but rather by legislatures, as well as the executive branch of government, that both have responsibility for developing policies that impact the lives of everyone in society. Court-appointed guardians should presume that mentally incapacitated patients would choose the preservation of their lives; the exception to this presumption is when continued LSMT would merely artificially prolong the dying process.

Rule of Law: Although court-appointed guardians have the authority to make treatment decisions on behalf of patients legally incapable of making health care decisions, the parameters of what constitutes medically futile care for patients who are mentally incapacitated, yet stable, is a legislative, not judicial, issue when disputes arise.

Ethics Issue: What is the propriety of courts appointing guardians for patients who are legally incapable of making health care decisions when the issue of whether continued LSMT is medically futile is disputed?

Ethics Analysis: What constitutes medical futility is an ethical issue. Consistent with the terms of an advance directive, LSMT may be withheld or withdrawn from patients when continued treatment is likely to be ineffective or futile in prolonging life, or is likely to merely prolong an imminent dying process.

One side of this debate holds that patients' right to forego LSMT is not absolute, but instead is subject to certain interests of society. The most significant of these societal interests is the preservation of life, understood to embrace both an interest in preserving patients' lives and a related but distinct interest in preserving the sanctity of all human life as an enduring social value. Decisions to maintain medically appropriate LSMT must take precedence over other societal interests.

The other side of this debate acknowledges that setting limits fairly is a requirement of an ethical health care system. In this instance, medically futile care for patients on the verge of death cannot be justified. Justice demands a fair allocation of resources toward vital needs (Levine et al., 2007). At the same time, it would be unethical to forego LSMT for patients who are mentally incapacitated, yet stable.

Court's Holding and Decision: Near-universal rules to resolve medical futility disputes for patients who are mentally incapacitated, yet stable, are legislative decisions; such decisions should not be unilaterally decided by the courts or MECs.

See Pope, 2014 and 2014a (discussing this court decision).

Policy and Treatment Decisions Facing Medical Ethics Committees

While MECs serve as decision-makers for health care organizations, they also play an advisory role in ethics consultations for patients and their families. MECs also make decisions on behalf of incapacitated patients with no family or friends. Other times MECs adjudicate disputes and conflicts between providers and patients' families. Both in law and in practice, MECs have significant authority and responsibility to make decisions involving patients. State law generally defers to MECs to determine the course of treatment if there is a conflict; the exception is where the law is not clear. For instance, in the *Betancourt v. Trinitas Hospital* decision, state law failed to define what constituted medically futile care for a patient who was mentally incapacitated, yet medically stable.

When there are conflicts between providers and patients' families, MECs may adjudicate the disputes, but only the courts have the power to make decisions where competing interests cannot be reconciled to accept a MEC's advisory decision. MECs should not act unilaterally when family disputes arise. In every instance involving MECs, a fundamental value is patient self-determination, or the right of competent patients (or their legal representatives) to exercise control over their own medical futures (Maron, 2012). This value permeates the role of MECs.

Dealing with Ethical Dilemmas

The primary role of MECs is to work through ethical dilemmas. In many of these situations, the law is often not clear and the courts may be considering competing positions for the first time. The hope is that this text will help everyone, especially health care professionals serving on MECs, to make the most ethical decisions possible. When dealing with ethical dilemmas, it is best to determine and understand the factors, as illustrated in **FEATURE BOX 2-1**, that impact almost all decision-making and actions.

Decisions Confronting Medical Ethics Committees

The ethical dilemmas in this text, as illustrated in **FEATURE BOX 2-2**, are unresolved legal cases taken from the news headlines; they deal with topics that are part of the national debate on issues arising from circumstances in which the legal answers are not clear or are unknown. This occurs because there is simply not enough law to determine what course of conduct is clearly permitted or prohibited under every circumstance.

This text examines how to respond when situations are encountered for which the law fails to offer clear and precise solutions. The only thing that is clear is just how unclear and imprecise health care laws are. Given the increasingly complex medical and political environment of 21st-century health care in the United States, coupled with the potential life-or-death implications for specific patients, ethical discretion and personal values take on increased importance in decision-making. In addition, there is the complexity of choosing

---

FEATURE BOX 2-1

Factors Impacting Ethical Decision-Making

- Potentially competing sources of guidance in the law
- Rules of professional responsibility
- The complex dynamics of personal motivations
- The ethics of individual responsibilities and social obligations
- The primacy of universal and personal values

— Sources: AMA, 2012a; ASBH, 2010; Beauchamp & Childress, 2012; Moore, 1903/1998; Moulton & King, 2010; Percival, 1803/2002.

FEATURE BOX 2-2

Ethical Dilemmas

- Should lifestyle behaviors be taken into account in determining whether patients could be eligible for organ transplants?
- Under what circumstances should terminally ill patients have access to experimental medical technologies?
- How should health care professionals define medically unnecessary care and futile care for patients with terminal prognoses or seriously degenerative chronic conditions?
- Is it appropriate to withhold oral contraceptive prescriptions from women who have been informed of the risks involved and choose to forgo screening for unrelated health conditions?
- Should the administration of life-shortening analgesia be lawful in hospitals and hospice care?
- Does inappropriate use of curative treatment that fails to end total dependence on intensive care or that preserves permanent unconsciousness deprive patients of their fundamental rights to dignity and humane treatment?
- How should the interests of patients who refuse life-saving hydration and nutrition be balanced alongside their right to self-determination at the end of life?
- What could justify a medical team to withhold prognosis or treatment plan information from a **mature minor**, an adolescent who has the mental competence and intellectual capacity to make health care decisions?
- What is the proper balance between the rights of parents and the rights of minors to choose or refuse lifesaving medical treatment?

— Sources: AMA, 2012a; ASBH, 2010; Beauchamp & Childress, 2012; Moore, 1903/1998; Moulton & King, 2010; Percival, 1803/2002.

---

between two or more valid choices in many situations. The dynamic interplay with patients' lives and deaths has the potential to make various decisions highly subjective and resistant to codification, meaning no law could adequately address all such decisions, but the law at least has the potential to guide the making of ethical decisions.

Universal Values in Ethical Decision-Making

One responsibility of MECs is to help health care providers apply ethical principles to their actions (AMA, 2012). There are ten **universal values**, as illustrated in FEATURE BOX 2-3, which often govern and guide decisions when ethical dilemmas are reviewed. *Universal values are personal* **principles** that define what is ethical and right to do, or principles of a group (such as the universal values of physicians or nurses), or the principles of a nation (such as the fundamental principle of American democracy, and the principle that members of American society are valued and rewarded on the basis of their merit).

FEATURE BOX 2-3

Ten Universal Values in the American Ethic

- **Personal autonomy:** ensures that individuals have the right to make independent decisions about their own health care based on their own value systems. Burdens all stakeholders (patients and health care providers alike) to be well-informed regarding treatment decisions; involves more than simply protecting individuals' freedom to decide within the existing health care system. Presumably, such freedom in self-governance is always informed by moral preferences that are relevant considerations as opposed to transient arguments.
- **Beneficence:** promotes the well-being of others in ways that serve their best interests and are beneficial to them, all the while seeking to achieve the highest quality (not just high-quality) results on their behalf. Implies that one does not inflict harm but rather seeks to prevent harm.
- **Compassion:** one of the foundational principles of the emerging ethics of health care; requires health care professionals to respond to those suffering from disease or injuries with a deep awareness of patients' human dignity. Arises from the common humanity of everyone, especially the relationship between providers of health care and their patients. This ethical obligation is supported by economic and social considerations.
- **Equality of opportunity:** another foundational principle of the emerging ethics of health care; ensures that nearly all members of society have an equal claim to health care. Requires society to provide subsidies to help cover the health insurance costs of anyone who faces disproportionate health burdens from unavoidable ill health.
- **Fairness:** promotes giving to others what they are due or what they are properly owed. Requires that there be freedom from bias and injustice in the U.S. health care system so that patients in distress may receive the essential care they medically need while requiring those entrusted with governance of limited health resources act in a trustworthy and ethical manner.
- **Human dignity:** respects the inherent worth of everyone; requires a commitment to respond to everyone with mutual affinity, respect, and stateliness.
- **Individual responsibility:** emphasizes personal accountability for healthy lifestyles and preventable ill health. This ethical obligation is both a free choice and a personal and shared duty; assumes that avoidance of unhealthy day-to-day choices will help avoid preventable ill health from occurring or delay the onset of and the severity of symptoms from unpreventable aging and illness.

(continued)

- **Justice:** a foundational principle of health care ethics; fairness and equality in the way everyone is treated and decisions are made. Ensures access to affordable health insurance and the kinds of essential care that is owed. Depends on society's notion of what is right and fair and the allocation of shared societal resources for health care (which should incorporate precise measures of the total societal costs of preventable ill health and total societal benefits from health care).
- **Non-malfeasance:** avoidance of harm; the opposite side of the coin of beneficence. Requires health care professionals to first do no harm, or if no good can be done without causing harm, then actions that have no curative effect or result should not be undertaken.
- **Truthfulness:** an overriding component at all levels of the U.S. health care system; takes an ongoing commitment to build and maintain with all stakeholders. Requires the medical products industry and other health care professionals to honestly and accurately report health information to patients; recognizes patients' right to know the truth of their health status. Trust and personal autonomy are compromised by withholding truth from patients.

— Sources: AMA, 2012a; Beauchamp & Childress, 2012; Kenny, et al., 2010; Levine, et al., 2007; Nuttfield Council, 2007; Percival, 1803/2002; Petrini & Gainotti, 2008; Post, et al., 2006; Thayer, 2011; Thompson, et al., 2006; Wiley, 2012.

When the subjective spiritual and emotional preferences of each member of society (defined here as **moral preferences**) are given social significance and made relevant, each person is connected to every other person in their community and together they are given human dignity that befits them to make decisions (Katz, 2010).

The American Ethic: An Evolving Public Ethic

The American ethic of health care has shared purposes and problems that are different from individual purposes and problems (Lee, 2012). A **public ethic** is often synonymous with universal values and refers to the state, its government, and its policies. In this instance, the American ethic is more than simply a collection of Americans with personal values (Lee, 2012). The **American ethic** is a combination of Americans' characters, their customs, norms, and traditions.

Universal principles cascade from universal values. This text, for instance, offers not a single theoretical approach to health care ethics; rather, it is an acceptance of pieces of numerous important philosophies of ethics and a theory of how they might be reconciled or utilized in a complementary manner when possible. Universal values and their cascading universal principles are put forth from this combination of ideas. This approach to ethics offers to knowledgeable and invested physicians, nurses, and other health care professionals (and students studying to become members of the health care profession) a set of guiding ethical principles that in turn provide consistency in ethical decision-making where there is currently great need and little concurrence (Baylis & Sherwin, 2008; Kenny, et al., 2010). This approach also acknowledges a democratic and respectful pluralism (Jennings, 2009). It is a Rawlsian approach to accepting numerous distinct and seemingly incompatible comprehensive doctrines (Rawls, 1971/2005 and 1993/2005). This approach to ethics also fits well in the U.S. political system, a system that prides itself on balancing respect for individuals with maintaining a society designed to advance the best in everyone (Lee, 2012).

Alignment of the American Ethic with Medical Decision-Making

Universal values and principles transcend and are embodied in the law; they do not give answers as to how to handle particular situations, but provide a useful framework for understanding conflicts and ethical dilemmas. When reviewing the topics in each chapter, four questions, as outlined in **FEATURE BOX 2-4**, should be considered.

Autonomy

Autonomy is the hallmark of health care ethics. As such, respect for autonomy is recognized in more health care situations than any other ethical principle (Beauchamp & Childress, 2012). The value of autonomy applies to individuals as well as to institutions.

Principles of Autonomy

There are three types of autonomy: personal, corporate, and governmental. Though often used interchangeably, their definitions are distinct. It is this principle which most hinders the pursuit of the common good.

Personal Autonomy: The Right to Self-Determination

Personal autonomy is significant in two respects: patient autonomy and the professional autonomy of physicians. Patient autonomy is rooted in respect for the right of patients to make independent decisions about their health care. Respect for patient autonomy incorporates at least two ethical principles: first, patients should be treated as autonomous agents; and second, patients with diminished personal autonomy are equally entitled to protection.

FEATURE BOX 2-4

Framework for Medical Decision-Making: Four Necessary Questions

- Which values and ethical principles apply?
- Which values should be applied for the most ethical decision?
- Are there other values and ethical principles that should be in place and, if so, what should they be?
- Which decision-making model(s) would best serve the applicable values and ethical principles?

— Sources: ASBH, 2010; Jaffe & Hope, 2010; Jennings, 2009; Kenny, et al., 2010; Moulton & King, 2010; Nuttfield Council, 2007; Percival, 1803/2002; Petrini & Gainotti, 2008.

Patient autonomy thus divides into two separate ethical requirements: the requirement to acknowledge personal autonomy, and the requirement to also protect those with diminished personal autonomy. *See generally* Carnahan, 2011.

In addition to patient autonomy, physicians have always maintained their personal autonomy from corporations. This professional autonomy, however, is increasingly threatened by the rise of organized economic enterprises in the health care industry (Ameringer, 2011). Physicians are now accountable to the health insurance industry and to the government, and that external scrutiny has become the norm (Starr, 2013). The corporatization of medical services has led to closer scrutiny of physicians in order to mitigate against malpractice; this scrutiny is facilitated by gathering information about physician performance (Starr, 2013).

Corporate Autonomy: An Autonomous Economic Person

Corporate autonomy is about the right to self-governance of the health care industry; in other words, the right to be free from unwarranted interference by the government (Mansbach, 2011). Corporate autonomy extends to the right of the health care industry to freely make business decisions. Whereas personal autonomy generally encompasses the idea that patients should remain free from coercion, corporate autonomy means that organized economic enterprises should have autonomous corporate management. After all, health care corporations are but the formal organization of activities by physicians and other providers of health care.

Because corporations owe their existence to government as creatures of **positive law**, this means corporations only have the rights and privileges granted to them by the government. Therefore, the health care industry is subject to legitimate regulation of its corporate self-interests by the government. As such, corporations are autonomous, self-directed beings that are subject to regulation by the government against harmful activities (Goforth, 2010). For instance, when health care systems fail to meet their societal obligations, such as failing to provide health care to the sick and vulnerable, they may be regulated to do so as a condition of their corporate survival, particularly when they receive government funds or tax exemptions. Positive law can be compared to **negative law**, or what corporations cannot do. For instance, tax-exempt health care systems cannot neglect their charitable obligations and still maintain their exempt status.

Autonomy from Government

Autonomy from government assures that patients and the health care industry have the right to make decisions and act on them as free and independent moral agents. At the same time, there is a need for the federal government to have sufficient powers to promote the general welfare of all members of society, balanced against autonomous state and individual interests (Madison, 1788/1982). In health care reform, the role of the federal government depends as much on federalism as it does on the autonomy of its citizens and the states.

Application of the Value of Personal Autonomy and Self-Determination

Personal autonomy is a general indicator of health. Respect for the autonomous choices of patients upholds the ability of patients to make informed choices, and to take actions based on their personal values and beliefs (Fry-Revere, et al., 2010).

Providing Women Their Rights to Reproductive Care

The right to women's reproductive care is subject to continuous challenge because positive moral rights are generally not recognized under the U.S. Constitution (Kinney, 2008). By definition, **positive moral rights** require action; one must act or others are obliged to act. Women's right to reproductive care is generally a negative moral right in the United States (*Harris v. McRae, et al.*, 448 U.S. 297 (U.S. Supreme Court 1980) (upholding the **Hyde Amendment** denying federal funding for abortions), *rehearing denied*, 448 U.S. 917 (U.S. Supreme Court 1980)). **Negative moral rights** permit inaction; one may refrain from acting or others may refrain from acting.

In other words, while the U.S. Supreme Court has told the government to let women alone and not interfere with their autonomous reproductive choices, the U.S. Constitution does not require the government to provide reproductive care or assist women to exercise their personal autonomy. For instance, Congress and state legislatures may not prohibit women from obtaining an abortion before their fetuses are viable, but the government does not have to provide funding for women who cannot afford the cost of an abortion. *See generally* Orentlicher, 2012.

Insuring Access to Health Care

Arguments for the right to health care parallel the arguments for women's right to reproductive care. Similar to the arguments for abortion, Congress and state legislatures may not prevent patients from receiving treatment for their illnesses or injuries, but nothing in the U.S. Constitution imposes a duty on government to ensure that patients can in fact obtain health care. In other words, a refusal to provide government health insurance coverage for a particular medical treatment can effectively mean a denial of health care. For instance, if Medicare decides not to reimburse hospitals for a particular treatment, the treatment will not be available for most patients with Medicare coverage unless they also have supplemental insurance policies. *See generally* Orentlicher, 2012.

Managing Medically Futile Care

Personal autonomy relates to the right of patients to choose their care and treatment, but many illnesses are characterized by the loss of personal autonomy. When physicians question whether to keep treating a patient, or nurses feel moral distress over a patient's unrelenting pain, or medical opinion is split, or a family wants to pursue medically futile care, MECs often become involved in care decisions (Adamy & McGinty, 2012). Treatment in these situations is arguably not preserving or respecting human life; it is delaying the natural process of death (Standley & Liang, 2011). MECs and physicians may determine, and then advise patients and their families, whether their choice of treatment requested or being provided is ethically appropriate.

Protecting Patients' Right to Informed Consent

Informed consent in this context is the voluntary, knowing, and competent decision of patients to accept or reject certain medical treatment. The requirement of informed consent functions as recognition of the right to protection of personal autonomy and integrity, yet it does not imply a waiver of patients' right to compensation in the event of injury from **potentially avoidable events** (or avoidable hospital acquired-conditions, including foreign objects retained after surgery, air embolisms, blood incompatibilities, stage III and IV pressure ulcers, falls and traumas, vascular catheter-associated infections, catheter-associated urinary tract infections, and manifestations of poor glycemic control)

(Beauchamp & Childress, 2012). Informed consent is based on respect for personal autonomy, self-determination, and fairness; consent embodies the need to respect the human dignity of patients and their autonomous decisions (Pike, 2012).

Application of the Value of Corporate Autonomy

A principle-based approach to decision-making as opposed to prescriptive rule setting is lacking within the U.S. regulatory space (Davis, 2009a). If it does not evolve, a bureaucratic mindset will likely usurp corporate autonomy to the ultimate disadvantage of patient safety and health care reform (Greenwood, 2012). The only purpose of government regulation is to assure that health care business decisions are ethical, especially because so many of them are government-funded; the health care industry (as all businesses) must seek to serve the common good of society and the best interests of everyone, ethically speaking. Because of the health care industry's unique relationship with its consumers, however, it must be held to the highest standards of fairness and justice.

Protecting the Well-Being of Health Care Institutions

Corporate autonomy is an indicator for the well-being of health care institutions that physicians, nurses, and other health care professionals are a part of (Tauber, 2005). Well-being, or corporate long-term financial health and stability, has implications for the personal ethics of individuals. While the aim of all health care decisions is to care for individual patients who will benefit from the care provided, at the same time, the health care facility providing the care must be cared for (Singer, 2010). The goal is to have everyone who requests care benefit from the facility's services. For instance, the principle of corporate autonomy could justify the admission policies of hospitals for upfront payments for care, such as payment of health insurance deductibles and co-payments, before care is received, or the requirement that patients make payment arrangements to pay for care before non-emergency care is received.

Regulating the Health Care Industry

Based on the principle of corporate autonomy, it is important that the United States have a sensible regulatory process that bases decisions on rational cost-benefit analysis, does not allow excessive delays in the time to make decisions, and lightens compliance burdens as much as possible (Goolsbee, 2010). Regulations with high costs relative to their benefits should be modified or eliminated. It is in everyone's interest to find ways to reduce compliance costs, and to eliminate or reconcile out-of-date and conflicting rules and regulations.

Application of the Value of Autonomy from Government

Autonomy from government, beneficence, fairness, justice, and non-malfeasance are interrelated values (Fry-Revere, et al., 2010; Karako-Eyal, 2011; Mansbach, 2011); all five arise out of the ethical principle of respect for human dignity (Carnahan, 2011). Respect for human dignity defines the framework for defining autonomy from government.

Accepting the New Federalism

A promising constitutional paradigm is emerging. Two competing visions of the value of autonomy from government are converging into a new federalism (Ryan, 2011). Under this **new federalism**, Congress is empowered to address any problem that the states are unable to address separately (Lash, 2011). For instance, with the U.S. health care system suffering from adverse selection and cost-shifting in state health insurance markets, Congress has an ethical obligation to intervene to correct the interstate problem (Koppelman, 2011). At the same time, whenever a federal intervention imposes on personal autonomy, the states should retain primary regulatory authority, because state power better preserves individual liberty (Hills, 2006).

The new federalism balances two visions of personal autonomy with the mandate that nearly everyone have access to affordable health insurance; in this instance, the efficiency of national health care reforms converges with the liberties of state regulation of insurance. Under this new approach to federalism, the federal government has the best structures for regulatory efficiency, while state governments have the best structures to preserve individual liberty. In turn, efficiency and liberty serve as mutual constraints for one another. The goal of the U.S. federal system of government is to optimize the balance between the two visions of personal autonomy while preserving state and federal powers. *See generally* Moncrieff, 2012.

Safeguarding Federal and State Outlays for Health Care

With access to and the cost of care the subjects of considerable debate, a primary goal of health care reform is to slow the growth of health care costs. Even so, 10 percent of the patients with Medicare insurance coverage account for 64 percent of the federal government's hospital spending (CBO, 2008). A disproportionate share of health care costs occurs in the final year of life (CEA, 2009; Dartmouth, 2011). For instance, while nearly 7 percent of all hospital patients die every year, those 1.6 million patients account for almost one-fourth of total hospital costs (Adamy & McGinty, 2012). Clearly, to rein in cost growth, basic coverage for medical treatment for severe illness, especially near the end of life, must be expanded, regardless of whether it is someone who is actively dying or just eventually dying; namely, for everyone (Pope, et al., 2011).

There are few processes for dealing with personal autonomy in end-of-life care decision-making. Informed consent to withhold or withdraw treatment is conditioned upon the requirement of predicting death, which is notoriously difficult, particularly when expensive LSMT holds out the promise of dying another day (Pope, et al., 2011). Just because medical technology permits extending life, or prolonging death, does not necessarily mean that life should be extended at any cost (Fleck, 2011 and 2009).

Providing Access to Essential Health Care

In providing health care, physicians and MECs often advise boards of directors regarding treatment policies that involve modest sacrifices in the health care provided to individual patients for the common good of everyone served by their health care facility. Although health care providers will always have patients who need a disproportionate amount of resources, it is debatable whether such patients with bleak prospects should be kept alive without objective consideration of their survival chances or even the health benefit, if any, of consumption of such voluminous resources (Adamy & McGinty, 2012). If rising health care costs are ever to be controlled, the realities of terminal illness must be confronted (Pope, et al., 2011). For instance, a recent heart transplant case that resulted in a spiral of non-preventable infections at Johns Hopkins Hospital cost the public insurance programs more than $4 million over a two-year period before the patient died; $800,000 remained unpaid to Johns Hopkins Hospital (Adamy & McGinty, 2012). In this case, the issue was that the medical team could not agree whether treatment was futile, and the family wanted to pursue every possible treatment option.

ETHICAL DILEMMAS 2-1

1. Should the individual needs and desires of patients be the only consideration affecting the treatment decisions of MECs, or are there circumstances in which professional resources and the economic impact on the health care facility providing the care may be considered?

Although treatment decisions can be based on financial and professional resources of the health care facility they are made in, such as not performing any organ transplants, from an ethical perspective, financial considerations should not affect LSMT decisions. Decisions about LSMT should always be based on clinical judgment and the autonomous right of patients, or their families or legal representatives when appropriate, to choose their care and treatment (Standley & Liang, 2011). At the same time, there is no ethical obligation to continue treatment when the medical team is unanimous about a patient's survival and no objective benefit will be had from continued care (Pope, et al., 2011). Controversies arise when the medical teams, patients, or the family, as in the case at Johns Hopkins Hospital, disagree about the futility of continued care (Adamy & McGinty, 2012). If MECs cannot amiably resolve the competing interests, such controversies must be decided by the courts before any LSMT can be withdrawn. While respect for personal autonomy must be balanced with beneficence to prevent unnecessary and untimely deaths, a competent person's refusal of treatment must be respected even when the proposed treatment would probably be beneficial (Fenigsen, 2011). From an ethical perspective, truly informed consent helps to satisfy the dual goals of personal autonomy and beneficence (Conley, et al., 2010).

Beneficence

Beneficence refers to actions that promote the well-being of others; it is one of the core values of health care ethics (Beauchamp & Childress, 2012). Personal autonomy and beneficence serve as the framework for medical decision-making and play a prominent role in assuring that everyone has access to health care (Noah, 2012). Beneficence is the value driving the United States' push toward universal health care.

Principles of Beneficence

The principle of beneficence holds that actions are moral, correct, and proper insofar as they are capable of achieving good results that are beneficial to individual or **corporate well-being** (Karako-Eyal, 2011). The American College of Physicians maintains that beneficence, promoting the medical good of patients, is indeed the only fundamental principle of health care ethics (Moulton & King, 2010). Possible benefits must be maximized and possible harms minimized under the principle of beneficence.

Application of the Value of Beneficence

Beneficence is about acting in ways that are beneficial to others. It involves the legal principles of providing competent health care, respecting the human rights of patients, protecting patient information, and maintaining the centrality of the physician's responsibility to patients (Mansbach, 2011). This principle parallels the Hippocratic Oath by requiring providers of health care not only to refrain from injuring patients at all times, but also to advance the interests of their patients. Beneficence requires that treatments must be of the highest quality in order to serve the best interests of patients as defined by each patient.

Providing Access to Affordable Health Insurance

Although beneficence underlies the right to health care, beneficence also prompts considerations about economic utility. By definition, **economic utility** seeks to ensure that benefits are worth more than the harms caused. In other words, the benefits of providing access to affordable health insurance to nearly all members of society should be worth more than the costs of subsidizing insurance premiums for those unable to afford basic coverage for their health care.

Affording Access to Essential Health Care

The ethical obligation of beneficence justifies the part of the health care reform known as the **minimum coverage provision**, which requires nearly everyone to purchase basic coverage to help fund care for the sick, which is called risk pooling. **Risk pooling** involves a shifting of health care resources from the healthy to the sick. Risk pooling is a means to enable nearly all members of society to more equitably access health care on the basis of medical need, as opposed to on the basis of ability or willingness to pay (Hoffman, 2011).

The absence of a clear and robust consideration of beneficence undermines affordable access to quality care and the aims of health care reform (Clark, 2011). One example of beneficence can be seen in reforms linked to health insurers (public and private), and the providers that focus on reducing costly medication errors and potentially avoidable events in hospitals. In this instance, self-disclosure reforms are in the best interest of insurers, as they will not be required to reimburse hospitals for potentially avoidable events.

Balancing the Risks and Benefits of Medical Treatments

Beneficence requires physicians to provide a direct benefit to their patients while simultaneously balancing the benefits with the risks of producing the best overall outcome (Fry-Revere, et al., 2010). Regrettably, there is often no consensus on what may always best help patients. Clinical evidence suggests that the number of patients undergoing surgeries would decline if more patients were fully informed; such failure to communicate the relevant risks, benefits, and alternatives of a medical procedure, including the option of doing nothing, violates the principal of beneficence (Moulton & King, 2010). Beneficence is violated whenever the potential harms exceed the potential benefits. In the instance of surgeries, although surgery may correct a medical condition, it may not always be necessary when medications or lifestyle changes may manage symptoms.

Physician recommendations and communication with patients are major driving forces of geographic variations in medical procedure rates for a wide range of health conditions in the United States, as opposed to clinical need or patient preference (Dartmouth, 2008). For instance, the variation in rates of intensive care unit use in the last month of life, chemotherapy in the last 14 days of life, deaths occurring in the hospital, and the use of hospice care (Dartmouth, 2012) all frequently reflect the tension between the traditional values of patient autonomy and the values of beneficence. It is important to recognize the difference between an ethical stance that views the role of physicians as non-directive and respectful of patient values, and the stance that accepts the active intervention of physicians in the decision-making of their patients for their greater good.

Protecting Human Research Subjects

Beneficence is also one of the pillars of clinical trials and the protection of human research subjects which requires researchers to minimize possible harms (Conley, et al., 2010). This tension is most evident in the current controversy surrounding access to investigational medications by the terminally ill. Advanced medical technologies are arriving rapidly and with each innovation there are great promises for improvements to human health. Nevertheless, an ethical framework must be designed to promote the continued development of medical innovations while simultaneously providing early access to patients who would benefit from medical products or services in early clinical trials. To do nothing for the terminally ill who have no other treatment options jeopardizes medical innovations for patient care (Stein & Savulescu, 2011).

Preserving the Lives of Mature Minors

The legal principles surrounding mature minors emphasize beneficence above all other considerations. Mature minors' capacity to make autonomous treatment decisions is based on a **best interests standard** that is based on beneficence. In this instance, this standard refers to the highest quality care that will be administered to terminally ill and suffering minors at the end of their lives, not necessarily for the purpose of extending their biological lives for the longest time, but to offer compassion and pain control. Often, the best interests standard conflicts with the mature minors' personal autonomy. This conflict acknowledges that rational choice and competence exist in varying degrees in minors of the same or varying ages. As such, ethical decisions must ensure that when mature minors reject LSMT, they do so based on rational and defensible grounds. *See generally* Iyioha & Akorede, 2010.

Justifying Vaccinations

The principal justification for vaccination laws is to protect individuals against infections. Vaccinations are also justified by compelling societal interests: upholding herd immunity and protecting vulnerable members of society from vaccine-preventable illnesses (Parkins, 2012). While vaccines prevent harm to others by reducing the burden of health care costs caused by the infectious diseases prevented, the principal rationale for vaccination laws is beneficence: the avoidance of disease in vaccinated individuals outweighs the infringement upon personal autonomy (Shapiro, 2012).

Making Restitution for Gun Injuries

Ethically speaking, because manufacturers of firearms are the beneficiary of firearms sales, the firearms industry should arguably bear the burden of gun injuries as well (Ruttenberg, et al., 2011). Restitution for the costs of environmental safety and gun injury prevention is justified by the duties of beneficence. Moreover, restitution reaffirms that individual interests matter, not just societal interests such as concerns about public safety (Goldberg, 2011).

Some states take a corrective justice approach to gun violence by providing gun injury victims with a legal right to restitution (Caldwell, 2011). **Corrective justice** in this instance is defined in terms of undoing a wrong or as giving rise to specific reasons for rectifying wrongs. Although state restitution laws would cover victims' losses from gun injuries, the federal Protection of Lawful Commerce in Arms Act of 2006 protects firearms manufacturers from civil actions seeking restitution for criminal acts of gun violence involving their products. All the same, when manufacturers purposefully design firearms with more harmful uses than beneficial ones and engage in distribution practices that encourage sales to those who should not possess guns, they arguably cross the ethical line (Rutkow & Teret, 2011; Wagman, 2010). While beneficence is a cultural as well as ethical ideal, the nation needs to come to terms with the value of gun injury prevention in deciding what level of environmental safety is acceptable for everyone.

Compassion

The Hippocratic Oath requires members of the medical profession to adhere to the values of beneficence and compassion (Tames, et al., 2011). Compassion is often part of individual healing in health care (Fichter, 2009). Defined as empathy for others and a truly humane attitude of caring or "being with the patient," compassion enables physicians, nurses, and other health care professionals to respond to individual health needs.

Principles of Compassion

While physicians, nurses, and other health care professionals should treat patients with compassion, mercy, and respect for human dignity and rights, this is a subjective determination (Hethcoat, 2011). What is not subjective is the ethical and legal obligation to provide essential health care with some level of compassion to everyone (Baker, 2010). Neglect of the uninsured and underinsured must end if the United States is to live up to its own purported standards of compassion and human dignity and achieve the maximum use of its work force (Mauldin, 2011).

Application of the Value of Compassion

Compassion and benevolence for patients are often equated with treatment of illness and injuries, especially in medical or public emergencies (Sutton, 2010). Compassion and justice are also relevant to reducing the risk of malpractice as well as to the physician-patient relationship when medical errors occur. Compassion is one of the core values driving the nation's health care reforms (AMA, 2012).

Administering Health Insurance Benefits

The principle of compassion lays an ethical framework for administration of health insurance benefits and provision of best practices for designing an ethical benefits program (AMA, 2012a). Compassion requires that health care benefits be flexible, responsive to individual values and priorities, and attentive to those with critical needs and special vulnerabilities. Above all, ethical decisions regarding benefit coverage should look toward the individual and not just the population base (Levine, et al., 2007).

ETHICAL DILEMMAS 2-2

2. Should health care reform be spurred by limitless compassion, or should the compassion of human nature be checked as the values and ethical principles of compassion flow into national policies and opposing interests are balanced until a stable equilibrium emerges?

Designing Government Insurance Programs

Compassion was the normative principle underlying enactment of **Medicare** as a government health insurance program for people over 65 years of age and the disabled, along with **Medicaid**. Principles of compassion in Medicare and Medicaid health insurance were meant to focus on attentiveness, responsiveness to medical needs, and trust, as illustrated in **FEATURE BOX 2-5**. While government insurance programs are intended to show reasonable compassion for the truly needy, they are also designed to encourage self-reliance without impoverishing the federal and state governments or providing services beyond that affordable by the average taxpayer (Thayer, 2011).

Allocating Finite Health Care Resources to Preventable Disabilities and Health Conditions

American society is divided about compassion for others. While empathy and concern about injustice become more intense when people develop personal connections with those who have experienced hardship or injustice (Land, 2011), there is little compassion for individuals and families with preventable disabilities and ill health. For instance, Down syndrome (or Down's syndrome) is not a mysterious force but a prenatally diagnosable chromosomal abnormality detectable by a blood test during the first trimester; it evokes compassion in some and indifference in others (Caruso, 2010; WHO, 1994). Compassion often does not extend to families with children with Down syndrome who need shared societal resources to cover the costs of intensive therapeutic services and care of significantly burdensome concurrent health conditions (Odibo, et al., 2005; Tyler, 2012). One reason for this divide in compassion is that the average cost of care for Down syndrome disease over a lifetime is $57.5 million (Boulet, et al., 2008; McGrath, et al., 2011). In other words, when it comes to distributing finite health care resources, disabilities that are the result of a choice to carry a known abnormal pregnancy to term do not carry much weight compared to non-preventable health conditions, such as major birth defects that are non-detectable with current prenatal testing or that were not tested for because there was no personal or family

---

FEATURE BOX 2-5

Principles of Compassion in Medicare and Medicaid Insurance

- **Attentiveness:** Medicare and Medicaid were meant to be responsive to the special needs of everyone with government health insurance coverage.
- **Responsiveness to medical needs:** Preventive care was to be provided and where acute care was needed, it was supposed to be provided in response to what was deemed to be medically necessary.
- **Trust:** The federal government was to assume responsibility for paying for the health care of all members of society with government health insurance coverage without regard to the ability of the states or the willingness of American society to pay for government health insurance on a continuing basis.

— Sources: AMA, 2012a; NICE, 2008; President's Council on Bioethics, 2015.

history of a particular condition (*see* Farrell, 2013). In this instance, the abortion rate for prenatally diagnosed Down syndrome is more than half of such pregnancies (Dixon, 2008).

Authorizing Physician-Assisted Dying

Compassion and respect for patients' autonomous right to rationally decide if and how they will receive medical treatment at the end of their lives are the bases for physician-assisted dying legislation. It is often compassionate to terminate or refuse LSMT that merely prolongs the dying process of terminally ill patients; in many such instances, life is not being prolonged; rather, the process of dying with intractable pain and unnecessary human suffering is mechanically extended.

Each stage of the physician-patient interaction should be compassionate in physician-assisted dying. Physicians and terminally ill patients work together to create a means by which patients can control the time and manner of their deaths (Bostrom, 2010). Death can be a painless transition; it need not be faced with uncertainty and intractable suffering (Fenigsen, 2011). Analgesic medications can be compassionately administered to alleviate intractable pain.

Consenting to Non-Treatment of Chronically Irreversibly Comatose Children

There is a line of reasoning that would deny LSMT to severely disabled children as an act of compassion that is done in the child's best interests, thereby declaring that the value of human life can sometimes be superseded by other values (Fenigsen, 2010; Muller, 2011). For instance, when children have progressive degenerative diseases of the brain or severe chromosome disorders or suffer severe brain trauma and possess only the most basic form of consciousness or perception, treatment may be withheld. It is difficult to distinguish such cases from patients in a persistent vegetative state where treatment only prolongs their dying, except that rudimentary consciousness in children may be accompanied by the potential for pain and suffering, which is all the more reason for compassionate non-treatment (Fulginiti, 2010). Each and every medical problem requiring the exercise of medical judgment varies in complexity and severity, but what all cases have in common are patients who have a medical condition, the treatment or non-treatment of which must be evaluated with compassion (Summerhill & Chandler, 2009).

Equality of Opportunity

In the United States, the intersection between health and equality of opportunity is most often framed around access to essential health care (Tyler, 2012). Equality of opportunity recognizes that individuals must have the unfettered opportunity to achieve and maintain high levels of health. Health is necessary for a lifetime of well-being and human dignity, not to mention supporting oneself and one's family. Equality is essential for every U.S. resident to fulfill the American promise of life and the pursuit of happiness, and personal health is an essential ingredient to ensure equal opportunity (Levine, et al., 2007).

Principles of Equality of Opportunity

Equality of opportunity does not equate with equality of results in the United States (Marshall, 2012). While access to health care does not necessarily include unfettered access to advanced care or to highly specialized physicians, it does provide access to medically necessary care covered by basic health insurance. Whenever Americans do not have access to health care, equality of opportunity is compromised. Not receiving essential health care consistently leads to poor health outcomes and reduced ability to meaningfully contribute to society (Gratzer, 2008; Hyman, 2009).

Application of the Value of Equality of Opportunity

Physicians, nurses, and other health care professionals see firsthand the effects of inequalities and the social determinants of health on their patients' bodies and thus may be the first to detect the unmet needs and policy failures that harm health (Tyler, 2012). Despite increasingly complex laws, inequality has proved remarkably resilient, especially for the most marginalized groups, or **vulnerable populations**, in American society (poor and financially distressed people, children, the disabled, minorities, and the elderly). These social groups experience health disparities as a result of lack of access to health care and therefore face increased exposure to health risks (Landers, 2010).

Ensuring Universal Access to Affordable Health Insurance Coverage

Equality of opportunity does not easily permit other ethical values to be ignored, such as fairness and justice (Hart, 2012). For instance, just distribution of health care resources is made on the basis of fairness to everyone. Distributive justice allots health care benefits and burdens among all U.S. residents; such distribution is determined by the aggregate health risks, costs, and potential gains of everyone in society. This means some individuals may not be able to afford as comprehensive a health insurance plan as they desire because the cost is too great for them and they do not qualify for insurance subsidies. Injustice may involve unequal access to advanced care and highly trained specialists, as opposed to a lack of access to some extremely costly and at times futile health care with no proven evidence-based value (Beauchamp & Childress, 2012).

Providing Equitable Access to Reasonable and Necessary Care

The principle of equality of opportunity provides that **equitable access to health care** is more than simply access to **emergency care** in situations that pose an immediate threat to health; it is access to care that is reasonable and necessary based on medical need that might have serious implications for continued health and well-being. What constitutes **reasonable and necessary care** should be a socially determined allocation of health risks and insurance principles that pragmatically conforms to the values of compassion, fairness, and justice (Hoffman, 2011). Reasonable and necessary care does not mean that what is done for one person is owed to all others in similar circumstances. Rather, everyone has a legitimate expectation for appropriate diagnosis and treatment to improve their health outcomes, including the best that modern medicine has to offer when appropriate (AMA, 2012a; Pagan, 2007).

Implementing Lifestyle Employment Discrimination Practices

The idea of holding individuals responsible for their choices can be compatible with beneficence; after all, equality is respect for the inherent worth of every human. Giving each individual equal human respect means providing essential health care to everyone, even if some people bear some responsibility for health conditions that are preventable (Fleischer, 2011). Although distinguishing choice from chance is complex and controversial, future health insurance might seek to promote health and financial security only with respect to health needs resulting from unavoidable harms (Hoffman, 2011). In other words, holding individuals responsible for their own poor choices serves the interests of others.

Providing for Pregnant Employees

The principle of equality of opportunity requires that reasonable accommodations be made for women who are pregnant; ethically speaking, women are entitled to the same workplace opportunities that employees who are not pregnant automatically enjoy (Weber, 2010). In this instance, what is ethically required is more than what current law requires. The law requires employers to provide necessary accommodations if they have chosen to provide them for other temporarily disabled workers with similar levels of incapacity. This legal principle is particularly deleterious for women in traditionally male-dominated occupations that are physically strenuous or hazardous, like emergency medical services (Grossman, 2010). Partially in response to these shortcomings, health care reform looks at health care as necessary to achieve fairness in the form of equality of opportunity (Satz, 2008).

Fairness

Fundamental fairness is included in the concept of justice and encompasses concepts of liberty, equality, and efficiency (Beauchamp & Childress, 2012). Fairness promotes giving to others what they are due (AMA, 2012a). Costs, as opposed to principles of fairness, have their limits in deciding what is right and what is wrong. Society is looking for fundamental fairness, but fairness is not always amenable to precise measurement of costs and benefits or even to measurement at all (Burleson, 2011).

Principles of Fairness

Criticism of health care reform is often centered on the argument that costs unfairly outweigh benefits, but this economic argument can be countered with assurances that the costs of reform are generally low and will decrease over time as there is a paradigm shift to preventive care (Hoffman, 2011). In other words, costs are for the most part being redistributed as opposed to increased. Although economic arguments are constructive and significant, they cannot be the only indicator of how the U.S. health care system should be reformed to meet the social obligations owed to Americans (Rosenbaum, 2011).

Economic arguments alone cannot fully protect patient rights or uphold patient responsibilities. It is important to protect individuals in ways that go beyond economic efficiency. It is not sufficient to measure the success or failure of reform by financial terms only, to the exclusion of the American public ethic and its underlying values. It is ethical principles, not economic data, that will determine what is ethical or unethical. It is the ideals of fairness, compassion, equality of opportunity, and justice that the U.S. health care system values.

Moreover, there are costs for which society is willing to pay that can be extremely high. Yet, the fact that cost effectiveness does not ensure patients' right to health care indicates that economic reasoning is not the only basis for making health care decisions. This is not to say that fairness and economic efficiency are mutually exclusive goals. Health care resources are allocated based upon a combination of need and ability to pay. In the context of fairness, equality of opportunity can be established by balancing efficiency and equity. *See generally* Burleson, 2011; Rawls, 1971/2005.

Application of the Value of Fairness

Objective judgment of what is fair comes into play when attending to the human rights and interests of stakeholders in the health care industry. Economic utility is not always the best justification for health care decisions because individuals place a significant value on fairness in deciding whether or not to accept health outcomes (Hollander-Blumoff, 2010). The difference between what people are willing to pay and the price they actually pay must be fair; in this instance, health insurance coverage must be worth more than the cost of the insurance (Kopson, 2010).

In addition, there are some economically rational health outcomes that sectors of the health care industry will not accept. The outcomes are rejected outright on the grounds that they are unfair. For instance, the health care reform measure limiting the administrative expenses of private health insurers is generally opposed by the insurance industry as being unfair (Bayly, 2012). Private health insurers want to pay executive salaries and returns to shareholders without limitation, as illustrated in **TABLE 2-1**. The principle of fairness, however, requires that insured patients in medical distress receive the care they need (Sage, 2014). Fairness requires that health insurance executives, who are entrusted with governance of limited health resources, act in a trustworthy and ethical manner and allocate resources to the insured in a fair manner, as opposed to serving their self-interests with extraordinary compensation to the detriment of what insured patients are due (*see, e.g.,* Bayly, 2012; Osborn & Schoen, 2013). *See generally* Wharton, 2007a.

Reforming Regulation of Private Health Insurance

The private health insurance industry is questioning its need to comply with all the health outcomes metrics in the Affordable Care Act of 2010 (ACA). The industry maintains that some health outcomes are economically unfair to their business definition of value and their goals of solvency and fairness (Bayly, 2012). In particular, many private health insurers question the metrics requirements that limit their business's administrative costs as compared to their care costs, an outcome measure that is economically favorable to the U.S. health care system and the nation's need to ensure fair insurance pricing (NAIC, 2010).

Private health insurers maintain that limits to their administrative costs are not consistent with their business perceptions of fairness; insurers oppose the federal mandate

TABLE 2-1 Annual Compensation for Health Insurance CEOs

Aetna	$30.7 million
Wellpoint	$17.0 million
Centene	$14.5 million
Cigna	$13.5 million
United Health	$12.1 million
Humana	$8.8 million

Data from the 2013 Annual Proxy Statements submitted to the U.S. Securities and Exchange Commission.

— Source: SEC, 2014.

requiring that at least 80 percent of the health insurance premiums collected be used to pay for claims (Bayly, 2012). Compared to this new 20 percent federal mandate, for every dollar consumers of health care spent on private health insurance before the Affordable Care Act, 30 to 40 cents went toward administrative costs; profit and investment returns to shareholders were approaching $90 billion annually before the health care reforms took place (SEC, 2011). Current debate is centered on the principle of fairness: is it fair to compare government health insurance with private market participation in health insurance in terms of administrative costs? An estimated 97 cents of each government health insurance dollar is put toward actual health care, compared to 60 to 70 cents of each private insurance dollar (Wharton, 2007).

Redistributing the Risk of Poor Health

One of the justifications for the minimum coverage provision is redistributive on of risk. The risk of poor health should arguably be shouldered fairly and more equally by everyone (Hoffman, 2011). Yet, the fairness of compelling the young and healthy to share responsibility for financing the health care of the not so young and perhaps not so healthy is a red herring used by both sides in the debate about health care reform (*e.g.*, Majerol, et al., 2015).

On the one hand, opponents' fairness argument diverts attention from insurers' need to protect their self-interests and maintain the status quo of fragmented insurance markets. Market fragmentation, in turn, serves to protect the inefficiencies of insurers' **adverse selection** practices. Adverse selection occurs when price increases or reduced benefits make health insurance no longer price-effective; those who make fewer and less expensive claims are taken out of the risk pool, leaving only higher-risk individuals. The result is that adverse selection prevents Americans from sharing broadly in the risk of poor health and, in doing so, entrenches a system where access to care remains tied to ability to pay and often mainly only benefits those who need it least, that is, those in good health (Hoffman, 2010).

On the other hand, health care reforms that move too far beyond underwriting risk undermining actuarial fairness, threatening the very idea of insurance (Bodaken, 2008). Supporters of health care reform, in contrast, view health insurance as simply a mechanism for financing health care; affordable health insurance should be available to nearly everyone because access to essential health care should be universally available (Mariner, 2010), perhaps even a human right (Daniels, et al., 2009). Again, fairness and economic efficiency are not mutually exclusive goals. The argument has been persuasively made that providing a basic level of universal health care will improve the nation's economic prospects and ability to compete (Johnson, 2012).

Improving Fairness in Coverage Decisions by Health Insurers

Although difficult decisions regarding health insurance coverage will always have to be made, health care benefits should be administered with economic fairness and compassion. An ethical framework for the fair and consistent administration of health care benefits could markedly improve quality health care, while improving regulation of the insurance industry's self-interests (Levine, et al., 2007). While costs and cost control must be considered in order to have a sustainable administration of insurance benefits, increased incorporation of principles of fairness in the business practices of private insurers could advance consumer satisfaction (Westfall, 2011).

Reorienting Insurance Incentives to Encourage Healthy Lifestyles

Traditional health insurance had no direct interest in favoring individual enrollees who assumed personal responsibility for maintaining their health and were committed to healthy lifestyles versus those who were not, such as smokers, the obese, and those who fail to adhere to their prescribed and agreed-upon treatment regimens (Marciarille & DeLong, 2012). Today, the issue is whether this impartial approach to health insurance coverage is fair to those who maintain healthy lifestyles.

Managing Hospital Readmissions

Hospital readmissions are prevalent and costly, with almost one-fifth of hospitalized government health insurance patients being readmitted within 30 days of their initial stay due to uncoordinated care following their discharge (Jencks, et al., 2009). Hospitals have had little financial incentive to ensure that patients get the care they need once they leave, and in fact they benefited financially when patients did not recover and returned for more treatment (Rau, 2012). As part of health care reform, the amount government health insurance pays to hospitals with excess readmissions of patients will be reduced. Supporters of this reform maintain that it will save billions of dollars (CBO, 2010). Opponents maintain that the measure may unfairly decrease the quality of patient care and increase the financial distress of hospitals, including increased bankruptcies (Swider, 2012).

Responding to Selective Non-Treatment and Selective Abortion

Debate centers on a basic question about fairness and whether it is acceptable for prospective parents to choose death for their nascent offspring as opposed to life with a disability (Samaha, 2007). With regard to selective non-treatment, discrimination on the basis of disability, regardless of severity, is viewed as morally indefensible from birth; an infant's medical condition should arguably be the sole focus of treatment decisions (Muller, 2011). While there are parallels between selective non-treatment of neonates and selective abortion of fetuses, the focus has been on informed consent during prenatal testing when deciding whether it is acceptable to choose abortion (Dixon, 2008).

Improving the Fairness of Malpractice Compensation

Damages caps do not address the shortcomings of the current malpractice system regarding deterrence and fair compensation. A link has been demonstrated, however, between patient safety and malpractice claims (Greenberg, et al., 2011). As patient safety outcomes improve, malpractice claims decrease. While damage caps could arguably decrease health care costs, with the priority health care systems placed on patient safety, malpractice claims have declined by half nationwide in the past 20 years (Kaiser, 2011). In turn, malpractice payouts have declined nationwide from $8 billion to $4 billion per year during the past decade (NPDB, 2012).

Proponents of a federal cap on non-economic damages of $250,000, meant to compensate the patient for non-quantifiable harm such as pain and suffering, maintain that such a cap could significantly reduce total health care costs (CBO, 2009). These cost savings are separate from compensatory damage payouts, meant to reimburse actual costs to the patient, and punitive damage payouts, meant to deter future neglectful conduct. These savings result primarily from a reduction in defensive medicine and avoidance of diagnostic procedures that are lacking in any benefit (or not likely to result in any further information that would contribute to an accurate diagnosis) (CBO, 2009a; Nelson, et al., 2011). In contrast, opposition to damages caps is based on the view that caps unfairly penalize the most severely injured patients and are unlikely to reduce health care costs significantly ($5.4 billion is less than 1 percent of the total health care costs). Moreover, medical accountability could be reduced and deterrence weakened by damage caps, resulting in an additional 4,800 patient deaths per year (Kaiser, 2011). In other words, it appears that damage caps disadvantage the most severely injured patients in return for the promise of only slightly lower health care costs for all (Nelson, et al., 2011).

Compensating Participants Injured in Medical Research

The requirement of informed consent is based on fairness and respect for the personal autonomy of participants who volunteer to participate in medical research; consent embodies the need to respect participants and their autonomous decisions (Pike, 2012). Given the difficulties of compensating every injured research participant, along with the difficulty of recovering damages through the U.S. judicial system, plus the prevention of recovery altogether by research participants outside the United States, the result is substantial unfairness in the nation's clinical research sector. Moreover, the United States is a moral outlier in not mandating equitable and effective compensation to injured participants in medical research (Macklin, 2010). A fair and ethical medical research system would make injured participants whole in return for their contribution to the advancement of science (Pike, 2012).

Holding the Food Industry Responsible for Unsafe Food Products

With a general notion that the food industry is not doing enough to ensure safety of the nation's food supply, there is debate about the fairness or unfairness of holding individual executives responsible for food-borne illness, especially outbreaks resulting in deaths. Under the **responsible corporate officer doctrine**, there is no need to prove that executives actually knew that certain manufacturing activity violated the law; rather, the test is whether the executives were aware of the activity (Steinzor, 2010). One side of this debate maintains that the complexity of U.S. food regulations might result in inadequate food safety from honest mistake or confusion (Johnson, 2014). The other side maintains that food manufacturers' safety practices are not adequate to avoid unsafe food products that poison consumers (Cohoon, 2010), such as salmonella poisoning from improper testing and inspection at the manufacturing site (Pagnattaro & Peirce, 2010).

Neglect of food safety harms the nation by eroding public trust in the food industry as well as government regulatory agencies. It signals to those affected by unsafe, contaminated food products that the basic human needs of consumers matter less than the economic benefit of food manufacturers (Gostin, et al., 2011). Society as a whole clearly has a stake in food safety.

Human Dignity

The U.S. Constitution seeks to enshrine human dignity as a national ideal; consequently, the worth and human dignity of everyone must be respected (Gerwint, 2011; President's Council, 2015). This focus on human dignity is premised on a belief that individuals are capable of exercising control over decisions that directly affect their lives and morally deserve to do so, as opposed to being subject to the whims of government (Shaub, 2012).

Debate often centers on how to respect human dignity involving end-of-life choices in a pluralistic society. There are at least two distinct approaches: let patients decide for themselves at what point their life is no longer worth preserving, or clarify the point after which there is no longer a social obligation to provide treatment, including LSMT (Fry-Revere, et al., 2010). Ideally, the two approaches to decision-making should converge and be balanced against one another.

Principles of Respect for Human Dignity

The principle of human dignity means a variety of things to different people, especially for end-of-life care that too often results in demeaning or humiliating care that reduces the sense of self-respect that is important to the integrity of everyone (Brownsword, 2007). While human dignity refers to respect for the inherent worth of others, it also involves shared decision-making. Respecting people's human dignity means respecting their competent decisions; disrespecting people's choices means showing disrespect to their human dignity and disrespecting their capacity to make decisions (Miola, 2006). In this instance and by definition, **competency** means someone has sufficient mental capacity to understand and voluntarily make knowing and informed decisions about his or her care, whether or not expedient.

Application of the Value of Respect for Human Dignity

Respect for human dignity is important in the interrelated legal doctrines of informed consent and the right to access high-quality health care (Fry-Revere, et al., 2010; Karako-Eyal, 2011; Mansbach, 2011). These doctrines influence decisions about physicians' ethical obligations to their patients as well as patients' responsibilities in maintaining healthy lifestyles.

Honoring Patients' Consent to Non-Treatment

Human dignity has a much broader meaning than simply respecting individual patient autonomy. When patients lose their capacity to make decisions about their treatment, as in the case of Parkinson's or Alzheimer's diseases, the question of what constitutes essential human dignity arises. Forcing medical treatments on objecting people, even if they lack capacity, disregards their human dignity (Pleschberge, 2007). Providing life-prolonging treatments to individuals with borderline capacity, but who have always stated they did not want to live in a diminished state, shows a profound lack of respect for their inherent dignity as human people and their right to pursue a dignified death (Herring, 2008).

Consenting to Physician-Assisted Dying

The rights of human dignity and individual privacy, together, encompass the right of competent, terminally ill patients to consent to physician-assisted dying (Bostrom, 2010). Using the assistance of a physician to obtain a prescription for a lethal dose of medication that a patient may then decide to self-administer is ethical and legal in at least five states (Montana, Oregon, Vermont, and Washington, and one county in New Mexico). Although patients' right to die with human dignity is increasingly recognized, most states refuse to protect patients' physicians from sanctions (Tobler, 2010), maintaining that it is against public policy to permit physician conduct that results in harm. Yet, the unnecessary **chronic pain** of terminally ill patients, defined as pain lasting longer than three to six months, should be able to be treated by physicians for the sake of human dignity; intractable pain blocks the aspiration of almost all other human values (Linares, 2012). Such treatment includes physician-assisted death under appropriate conditions.

Providing Incentives for Donation of the Human Body or Its Body Parts

The new legality of being able to donate bone marrow in return for compenation may begin to free the nation from the ethical fiction that donating human body parts for free is noble while accepting compensation is undignified (Schwark, 2011). While any attempt to assign a monetary value to the human body or its body parts, even in the hope of increasing organ supply, diminishes human dignity, the opposite is also true (Clark, 2006; Schwark, 2011). Allowing the donation of the human body and its parts increases human dignity and encompasses the value of human life. When donors give up a part of themselves in order to save the life of another, whom they may not even know, this is the very essence of valuing human life (Derco, 2010). Donors, in other words, should have the ultimate power to control what becomes of their body and its parts. To hold otherwise would be a conflict between medical progress and human dignity and privacy (Gatter, 2012).

Meeting the Need for Forcible Medication of Prison Inmates

Individuals should always have the right to protect their essential human dignity, including most instances in which criminal defendants are involuntarily subjected to antipsychotic medications for trial competence and prison safety. There is no agreement, however, on whether it is constitutional or ethical to forcibly medicate condemned death row inmates to restore their competence for execution (Sewall, 2010). The difficulty is that physicians are not actually harming criminal defendants physically, and may even be helping them under a narrow understanding of the meaning of beneficence. While the personal autonomy of criminal defendants is certainly being overridden, since the government has apparently carved out a specific exception to generally held notions of personal autonomy, much as it does with minors or the incompetent, it is not entirely clear that physicians who offer such care operate beyond the bounds of ethical medical practice and the principles of nonmalfeasance. *See generally* Appel, 2011. This is an instance in which the ethical values of physicians and prison inmates may differ from the ethical values of the government and the public, and may therefore differ from what is deemed ethical according to law.

Protecting the Human Rights of HIV/AIDS Patients

Health care reform measures are effective only within a human rights framework that respects human dignity and fundamental human rights (Wojcik, 2010). As a society, the question is whether, after the collection of personal health information reveals individual differences in health status, such as a positive test result for HIV, everyone should still continue to be treated the same. Some people, by virtue of their disabilities or illness, may have greater or lesser claims on society for support. Every effort should be made to ensure that HIV status information is not used for purposes that discriminate, or has the effect of infringing human rights, fundamental freedoms, or the human dignity of individuals that could lead to their stigmatization (Pompeo, 2011). All the while, there is vigorous debate over balancing human rights and individual responsibility and the right to the highest attainable standard of health, especially for people who are infected with HIV/AIDS (Kirby, 2009).

Individual Responsibility

Albert Einstein observed that the problems most individuals face cannot be solved at the same level of thinking they employed when they created them (Einstein, 1923/2015). Today, under the Affordable Care Act, a paradigm shift or change in U.S. health care is rapidly evolving. Nearly everyone now has to accept responsibility for obtaining and maintaining basic coverage.

While health has always been an individual responsibility in the United States (compared to other advanced economies where individual health is a shared ethical obligation), there is now a significant focus on prevention of disease as opposed to treatment of disease. Although individual responsibility for one's health has always been viewed as an unrestricted choice, the focus has recently shifted to emphasizing the ethical obligation to manage one's health, while stressing personal accountability for maintaining a healthy lifestyle and avoiding preventable ill health. With the newest health care reforms, the greatest power U.S. consumers of health care possess is their ability to choose healthy lifestyles (Kelly, et al., 2007). At the same time, everyone is individually responsible for using preventive care services to prevent diseases from ever occurring or to delay their onset or reduce their severity (Berman, 2011).

Principles of Individual Responsibility and Self-Reliance

It is human nature to act and not be acted upon; by choosing how to respond to life, individuals can create the conditions of their lives (Covey, 1990/2014). In regard to health care, everyone has an individual and shared responsibility to make healthy decisions. Everyone is responsible for their health via their lifestyle choices, and often also responsible for their illnesses, suffering, and death. The vision of autonomous individuals is deeply ingrained in American culture; consequently, health care policies are generally framed around this individualistic archetype that anyone can do whatever they want regardless of the consequences to one's health (Berman, 2011).

Application of the Value of Individual Responsibility

The U.S. health care system defines itself in terms of health, individual responsibility, fairness, and equality (Copp, 2012). With 55 percent of health status determined by lifestyle choices, there is debate over whether health care costs should be imposed proportionately, based on one's health risks and day-to-day lifestyle choices (Davis, 2007; Solar & Irwin, 2007). Ethically speaking, the nation will be closer to achieving moral and economic fairness in health care when health status is more closely aligned with health care costs (Copp, 2012; Marmont & Wilkenson, 2005). The principles of fairness and justice require that individuals who are not compliant with their treatment regimes, who have casual sex with multiple partners, smoke tobacco, abuse medications and alcohol, refuse vaccinations, partake in dangerous activities such as extreme sports, and fail to maintain healthy weights must accept responsibility for the consequences of their day-to-day choices. These concepts of fairness and justice as they relate to health stem from notions of individual as opposed to social responsibility for individual, community, and population health.

Adopting Comprehensive Paradigms of Prevention

Health care in the United States is generally understood through the lens of American individualism. By contrast, other developed countries focus more on the **social determinants of health**, or the living conditions people experience: access to health care, early childhood development, education, employment and working conditions, food security, housing, income and income distribution, social exclusion, social safety network, unemployment and job security, gender, race, and disability status. Social determinants are the primary factors that shape people's health, not medical treatments (IOM, 2011).

Although each individual bears personal responsibility for his or her own health, two different, but non-exclusive, paradigms of preventive health prevail in the United States. The public health paradigm focuses on population-based primary prevention by focusing on social determinants of health (Berman, 2011). Such interventions seek to prevent illness or injury from ever occurring by preventing public exposure to risk factors. For instance, food security is addressed by regulating the manufacturing of foods.

By contrast, the individual responsibility paradigm focuses on secondary and tertiary preventive health once an individual is ill (Tyler, 2012). Secondary prevention focuses on expanding access to health care by screening, testing, and detection of early risk factors in individuals before disease becomes symptomatic (such as hypertension), and early treatment (such as adherence to blood pressure treatment regimens). Tertiary prevention seeks to prevent a worsening of symptoms in individuals already suffering from a disease by encouraging healthy lifestyle choices and aggressive symptom management.

Choosing Healthy Lifestyles

The consensus holds that it is ethical to impose extra health care costs on individuals who choose unhealthy lifestyles that result in otherwise preventable health conditions (Marmont & Wilkenson, 2005). Nicotine addiction, obesity, and medication noncompliance are important societal issues that justify surcharges on anyone who smokes, or is obese, or refuses to adhere to their evidence-based treatment regimens. The roles of individual responsibility in sexually transmitted disease (STD) and immunization coverage are rapidly becoming lifestyle issues (Fan, 2012; Shapiro, 2012). When individuals make unhealthy choices that expose themselves and others to significant risk and then expect everyone else to pay for their lifestyle decisions, an expectation that is often met, this behavior creates incentives for others to act irresponsibly, or at least does not encourage others to act responsibly. It also violates the ethical standard of individual responsibility (Katz, 2010).

At the same time, and while the burden of preventable disease and illness brought on by poor lifestyle choices should be borne by the individual (Tyler, 2012), no one knows with certainty how much illness is due to a breach of individual responsibility and how much is unavoidable. For instance, no one knows how much obesity is due to a breach of individual responsibility and how much is due to or the result of blameworthy food industry practices, such as overeating of non-nutritious food, or even to biological or environmental factors, as science is beginning to investigate (Katz, 2010).

Considering Personal Responsibility Legislation

Maintaining good health is primarily an individual responsibility. Consistent with this principle is the perspective of today's health care reforms that Americans need to take increased personal responsibility for their health (Berman, 2011). At least 23 states have adopted personal responsibility laws forbidding lawsuits against the food industry, including the fast-food and the junk/snack sectors, for obesity-related harms attributed to overconsumption of food (Steinzor, 2010).

Regulating Non-Nutritious Foods

Debate over regulation of non-nutritious food is split. There is no consensus over the proper delegation of responsibility between individuals and society in general (Liu, 2012).

The issue is whether government intervention interferes with individual choice and informed decision-making.

On one side, the food industry ostensibly promotes public health solutions to obesity-related health conditions; such solutions focus attention on the choices of individual consumers and minimize the role of the food industry (Berman, 2011). The food industry maintains that restrictions on non-nutritious foods undermine individual responsibility while diminishing individual choice (Steinzor, 2010). The other side, while acknowledging the importance of individuals' responsibility for their own health, maintains that non-nutritious food advertising geared toward children is an appropriate target of regulation because of the predictable, negative impact it has on health at that population level (Berman, 2011; Liu, 2012). Today, there is a growing movement that emphasizes individual responsibility's role in the principle of justice, especially when safeguarding food products consumed by children.

Justice

This ethical value as it relates to health stems from notions of individual responsibility (as opposed to social responsibility) for individual or even population health (Tyler, 2012). The concept of justice requires that social benefits and social burdens be distributed in accordance with the demands of integrity. Justice details, at least in part, the means by which resources that are paid for are allocated (Fry-Revere, et al., 2010). Justice usually involves respecting patient rights and acting fairly in the distribution of limited resources to individual patients (Mansbach, 2011).

Principles of Justice

The justice principle concerns the distribution of health care resources as well as policy decisions regarding who has access to health care. Efforts to reduce the federal deficit that could result in cuts to health care spending at the state level are not properly considering the principles of justice and compassion (Ravitch & Volcker, 2012). In this instance, many who oppose health care reform and express opposition to expansion of government health insurance because of its cost seem to be comfortable with the government's spending comparable, and often much larger, sums of money for other purposes (Dolgin, 2010).

Competing Interests: Justice and Compassion in State Medicaid Spending

Justice and compassion balance competing economic interests. On one side there is a health care system that demands fair compensation for the care it renders. On the other side are the human rights of patients who are demanding access to the U.S. health care system. Justice and compassion see the intertwined interests of the U.S. health care system and the cared-for patients as closely linked with each other. The principles of justice seek a fair resolution between these competing interests. Principles of compassion see the interests as importantly intertwined as opposed to simply competing. *See generally* Held, 2006.

The nation's failure to honor the historical enactment of Medicaid, where public health insurance was to assure equal access to high-quality care to everyone in need of it, has caused a degenerative effect in social justice. Many point to institutional failures as the problem with the U.S. health care system (Foster, 2010). One side cites a failure to understand public perceptions of justice and the other side cites the lack of commonly accepted principles of the ethics of compassion. Both sides are partially right. For instance, the states' growing gaps between entitlement spending for government health insurance and tax revenue are becoming unsustainable (Ravitch & Volcker, 2012). Note, however, that **entitlement spending**, by definition, includes all tax expenditures, such as student loans and scholarship grants, home mortgage interest deductions, and failure to tax the earnings of qualified pension plans, not simply spending for government health insurance (Adamy & McGinty, 2012).

Nevertheless, the challenges of spending on health care are squeezing spending on education, infrastructure, and other government services (Corkery, 2012). While the principles of justice and compassion consider the limits that may be appropriate for government health insurance spending, neither principle can answer the question of whether taxes should be raised or cut, nor can propose specific spending cuts for the states (Ravitch & Volcker, 2012). Both ethical principles are ideal for a perfect world, but neither principle provides precise guidelines for living in an imperfect world in which the choices and decisions that must be made are seldom clear-cut (Held, 2006). Neither ethical principle provides clear answers on whether simply fixing taxes to raise more revenue can fix the government health insurance problem, nor whether there is a need for deep cuts to public benefits and entitlements (Corkery, 2012).

Intertwined Interests: Justice and Compassion in Malpractice

The principles of justice and compassion assume responsibility for reducing the risk of malpractice (Raper, 2011). Principles of justice extend compassion to patients harmed by medical errors, especially vulnerable populations. Principles of justice are used as a backdrop to consider questions about the law and its impact on patient compassion. Justice and compassion are both recognized as the foundation for remediation of malpractice claims (Pike, 2012).

Defining Malpractice in Terms of Compensatory, Distributive, and Social Justice

Social risks, the economic and societal conditions that affect everyone's health, such as the ability to access affordable health insurance, are shared by everyone. Under the principles of justice, compensating victims of medical errors is constrained by the requirements of distributive justice, which mandates that the needs and resources of society be taken into account when compensating malpractice claims (Smith, 2009).

At the same time, when medical errors are caused by fault-based conduct, victims who seek compensation through malpractice claims are constrained by the requirements of compensatory justice, which mandates that the resources of the culpable party be taken into account for compensation purposes, in contrast to the resources of society (Culhane, 2007). *Compensatory justice* is the form of justice that seeks to redress injury even when no fault or blame is associated with the injury (Pike, 2012). By definition, compensatory justice refers to the extent to which victims are compassionately, fairly, and justly compensated for their injuries. Just compensation is proportional to the harm inflicted.

The ethical principle of **social justice** seeks to redress medical errors that result in malpractice claims by focusing on systems-oriented solutions to patient safety (Raper, 2011). By definition, social justice refers to the idea of creating a society based on the principles of equality and social solidarity, that understands and values human rights, and that recognizes the dignity of every human being. The health care industry and the professionals who work in the U.S. health care system, by and large, strive to be an expression of this ideal.

Application of the Value of Justice

Justice is more than neutral application of the law. Comprehension of the law must be subservient to real life, rather than real life being subservient to the law (Crowe, 2010). In this instance, the animating principles of three of the kinds of justice are distinct, for while corrective justice applies only where a particular individual and action are identified, the principles of distributive and social justice apply in every circumstance (Culhane, 2007).

Providing Universal Access to Affordable Health Insurance

The nation's **social contract** is the U.S. Constitution, which binds American society together in the interests of not only justice but also compassion, equality of opportunity, and fairness (Rawls, 1993/2005). The submission of unbridled self-interests to "government of the people, by the people, for the people" informs the heart of American democracy (Lincoln, 1863/1953). The idea of this nation's social contract of "we the people" in the Preamble of the U.S. Constitution is that everyone places their interests under the direction of the general will, and the group receives each individual as an indivisible part of the whole (Rousseau, 1762/2012). The whole of American society is greater than any individual, and the whole has a social responsibility to each individual part.

The scope of this social contract was reexamined by the U.S. Supreme Court when the constitutional validity of the Affordable Care Act was initially decided. The validity of the health care reform law rested on whether Congress possessed the right to mandate that nearly everyone purchase and maintain health insurance. In 2012, the U.S. Supreme Court recognized the right of Congress to expand the role of the federal government in health care and to mandate that nearly everyone obtain health insurance. *See National Federation of Independent Business, et al. v. Sebelius, et al.*, 132 S.Ct. 2566 (U.S. Supreme Court 2012). In other words, Congress and the U.S. Supreme Court both recognized that improvement of the enduring and complex problems of the U.S. health care system is virtually impossible without a federal response (Gostin, 2008).

Almost half a century earlier, in 1965, the social contract was also examined when the constitutional validity of government health insurance was questioned by opponents of those programs. Then, the issue was whether Congress possessed the right to expand its Social Security legislation to include government health insurance coverage for the nation's most vulnerable populations. Since 1965, government focused on the consistent application of the ethical principles of justice in government health insurance (Held, 2006).

The principle of justice has always sought to focus on questions of equality of opportunity and fairness. Equality of opportunity means always asking whether patients with government health insurance have equal rights and equal access to the same level of care that is equal in scope to patients with private health insurance. Fairness, in contrast, means asking whether the provision of care is always impartial; are patients with private insurance favored over patients with government coverage? *See generally* Herring, 2008.

Today, health care laws and reform are changing the focus of health insurance. While accepting the relative rights arising from government insurance programs, the focus is now on social obligations that are undertaken for ethical reasons (Rawls, 1993/2005), ostensibly for the nation's common good. In other words, the right to access affordable health insurance is an entitlement that arose from the concept of human dignity and was freely granted by expansion of the nation's Social Security legislation. The principles of ethics surrounding what is owed to Americans are based on the values of justice that have been accepted by society to be legitimate for the past half-century. Health care laws and reform are not neutral;

both are directed toward justice. Today, health insurers are being forced to return to their role as social protectors (McKoy, et al., 2005).

Setting Treatment Priorities

Issues regarding setting treatment priorities and allocating medical products and services fall under the justice principle (Katz, 2010). For instance, deciding whether to add newer medications in addition to older less expensive medications, as well as brand-name versus generic products to a hospital's formulary list for dispensing medications to patients, is influenced by the justice principle (Kesselheim, 2011). In addition, the justice principle is implicated when health insurers make decisions based on cost efficiency, such as requiring patients to try generic medications before agreeing to cover brand-name products. Like medication decisions, patients may not always be given the necessary information to decide whether they should select a more expensive medical device with a higher level of long-term safety versus a less expensive device with short-term benefits (Cornell, 2012).

While the justice principle is used in prioritizing patients in an emergency or in trauma settings or those on organ transplant wait lists, it also affects patients seeking preventive care, including the allocation of vaccines and the time of physicians (Wolfson, 2007). The justice principle also applies to patients who are not dying or comatose but who live with intractable pain, sometimes from the medications and technologies that are keeping them alive. In such cases, there may be a higher ethical obligation to provide end-of-life comfort care; the provision of such palliative care may often be more ethical than life-prolonging treatments.

Redressing Medical Errors

What the health care industry owes to patients who are the victims of medical errors is a controversial issue (Raper, 2011). Perhaps because the issue of malpractice seems too difficult to answer, most answers concerning the ethical obligation to assist injured patients focus on specific events, such as medication errors, misdiagnoses, or surgical blunders. Thus, debate surrounding this issue is often constrained or does not take into account the

---

ETHICAL DILEMMAS 2-3

3. Do MECs have the right to debate the merits of treatment decisions, or is this debate solely within the purview of individual patients and their families?

4. Should MECs develop information and guidelines, and offer support to physicians who are assisting individual patients and their families in deciding what probability of success determines whether a treatment is worth undertaking (a question of odds), and what quality of outcome is worth undertaking a treatment (a question of ends), or should MECs comment on such matters only after they are presented by medical professionals?

5. Should MECs be involved in decisions between physicians and individual patients and their families about when the benefits of treating terminal illnesses, such as end-stage cancer, with chemotherapy and radiation may outweigh the risks to quality of life, or should MECs comment on such matters only after they are presented by medical professionals?

broader social issues of justice and fairness to the needs and resources of society. Although this is understandable and perhaps even politically necessary, the question is whether the health care industry should settle for the results of a narrow approach to malpractice. *See generally* Culhane, 2007.

Using Alternatives to Litigation: No-Fault Malpractice Insurance

All three principles of justice would use a collaborative model to resolve successful malpractice claims, such as no-fault insurance as an alternative to the current litigation system. The central premise of the **no-fault insurance** model is that patients need not prove negligence to access compensation; they must prove only that they have suffered an injury, that it was caused by their medical treatment, and that it meets whatever severity or other threshold criteria apply, much like the workers compensation system. Compensation to injured patients is justified by all three principles of justice by positing consent to pay those harmed. Even though consents to compensation for medical errors might affect the financial interests of the government (through its government health insurance programs) and the health insurance sector (through its private health insurance), it would avoid requiring the malpractice insurance sector to resort to the legal system (Culhane, 2007). No-fault insurance may, however, be less able to satisfy the principles of non-malfeasance.

Non-Malfeasance

Non-malfeasance or *primum non nocere* ("first of all, do no harm") imposes an ethical obligation not to inflict harm on others. Non-malfeasance designates the obligation of not doing harm to other people, whether deliberately or through negligence (Karako-Eyal, 2011). The principle of non-malfeasance may be combined with the principle of beneficence into a single principle where the principle of non-malfeasance is one of the components of beneficence. Although beneficence and non-malfeasance are similar and closely related, they are distinguished from each other and presented as two different principles so as not to obscure distinctions between the two (Beauchamp & Childress, 2012).

Principles of Non-Malfeasance

Non-malfeasance refers to the principle of doing no harm. Harmful care should never be prescribed; conversely, only care unlikely to be harmful should ever be prescribed (Beauchamp & Childress, 2012). At the very least, patients should understand the risks and benefits of any care; the likely benefits should outweigh the likely risks. In practice, however, most medical treatments carry some risk of harm. In some situations where the outcomes without treatment are life-threatening, risky treatments with a high chance of harm are justified, as the risk of not treating is also very likely to do harm (Ausiello, 2012). Clearly, non-malfeasance is not an absolute principle; it balances against the principle of beneficence (Beauchamp & Childress, 2012). In other words, the principle of beneficence declares that what is best for each person should be accomplished; the principle incorporates both the negative ethical obligation of non-malfeasance as well as the positive ethical obligation of beneficence, to do that which is good (Wright, 2006).

Application of the Value of Non-Malfeasance

It is widely believed that anything done in the public interest is good for society and good for the individual members of society; when the "anything" involves people's health, this belief is rapidly converted to law (Cooper, 1979). While the extent to which non-malfeasance should be followed is often debatable because there is no agreement on what constitutes harm, the ethical principle generally accords with the traditional roles assigned to physicians.

Mandating Vaccinations against Infectious Disease

Non-malfeasance is one of the cornerstones of individual health care decisions. For every individual right, there is, however, a corresponding responsibility to consider the needs of the common good. Often, the benefits and harms between rights and responsibilities are balanced when deciding what the most ethical decision should be. In the United States, this balancing of interests is often done within the framework of utilitarianism, where the ends justify the means. In this instance, the principle of non-malfeasance requires compulsory vaccination in order to advance society's common good and secure the public-at-large from exposure to the spread of infectious disease (Smith, 2009a).

Determining Best Courses of Treatment

The task of physicians, in conjunction with their patients, is to decide upon the best course of treatment for a specific medical need, using the principle of non-malfeasance, as well as the principles of respect for personal autonomy, beneficence, and justice as guideposts as opposed to hard-and-fast rules (Fry-Revere, et al., 2010). For instance, chemotherapy inhibits the growth of and ultimately kills cancerous tumors, but it also harms or kills healthy cells; the administration of oncology medications markedly harms (in the relative sense) patients. While the intended outcome of medical treatment is in the best interest of halting the growth of cancer, the action itself defies the ethical obligation to do no harm, because the effects of chemotherapy on the human body are devastating.

Protecting Patient Privacy and Confidentiality

Health care institutions and individual physicians, nurses, and other health care professionals who fail to protect patient privacy and confidentiality violate the principles of non-malfeasance (Bauer, 2009). Violations of the principle of non-malfeasance are especially problematic in the context of women's reproductive choices, especially for women undergoing abortions in states requiring parental consent (Laufer-Ukeles, 2011). A second controversial area is the extent to which physicians may speak to patients about firearms and enter any solicited information into medical records (Hethcoat, 2011). Non-malfeasance and preservation of personal autonomy support the need to protect patient health and welfare in both these instances.

Although unauthorized use of personal health information erodes public trust in the U.S. health care system, disclosure of individual patient information must be balanced against the principles of beneficence (the negative ethical obligation of non-malfeasance) to protect the public's health. For instance, states are authorized to review computerized databases to track prescription medications for controlled substances in an effort to identify and control drug abuse (Orentlicher, 2011) and conduct surveillance on STDs and HIV/AIDS (Fan, 2012).

In a U.S. Supreme Court decision reviewed in Chapter 4 of this text, the Court determined that the pharmaceutical industry may purchase certain physician-identifiable prescription data without the consent of physician-prescribers for the purpose of marketing medications; the Court determined that this data-mining neither violates patient privacy and confidentiality nor harms individual patients (Boumil, et al., 2012; *Sorrell, et al. v. IMS Health Inc., et al.*, 131 S.Ct. 2653 (U.S. Supreme Court 2011)). Thus, the principle of non-malfeasance is not mutually exclusive from other ethical principles; rather, the challenge is figuring out what insight non-malfeasance provides.

Truthfulness

Truthfulness, honesty, and transparency are key attributes of health care ethics. Truthfulness in this context includes honestly representing medical products, health care services, and health insurance coverage, including clear and adequate disclosure of all material terms. Health care providers and insurers must clearly disclose all that influences patients' treatment decisions with integrity and transparency.

Principles of Truthfulness

Consensus for health care reform need not be unanimous for it to be legitimate, although the higher the level of agreement the better. Each of the stakeholders in reform of the U.S. health care system should consider their respective interests and values. Health care industry leaders must develop a greater degree of genuine respect for government regulators and operate their organizations with integrity (Osborn, 2010).

To sustain an always fragile consensus on health care reform, supporters of reform, as well as opponents to reform, cannot obfuscate or manipulate the truth, lest either side find itself in opposition to the people upon whom they rely for legitimacy (Goolsbee, 2010). For instance, opponents of health care reform claim the law would add $701 billion to the deficit, while supporters claim the law will save society $1.3 billion (Annenberg, 2011). In this case, both sides are misrepresenting the fiscal effect of the Affordable Care Act (Foster, 2010); meanwhile, repealing the law would worsen the federal deficit over the next 10 years by $230 billion (CBO, 2010a).

Application of the Value of Truthfulness

Benjamin Franklin explained his approach to making truthful decisions by describing what he did when he had a difficult decision to make. "To get over [any uncertainty] . . . my way is to divide half a sheet of paper by a line into two columns; writing over the one Pro, and the other Con. Then . . . I put down under the different heads short hints of the different motives . . . for and against the measure . . ." (Franklin, 1772/2012).

The U.S. health care system came under siege for its truthfulness and integrity when it was discovered that up to one-half of the nation's health care was devoted to medical treatments that did not improve health (IOM, 2011, 2011a, and 2009; Todd, 2011), was ineffective (Commonwealth Fund, 2011), and often made patients worse (Kimbuende, et al., 2010). For instance, physicians are more likely to order diagnostic tests when they conduct the testing in their offices or have an ownership interest in the testing facility. Using the Franklin decision-making technique, some physicians are clearly more likely to take particular actions once they see how well they benefit from self-referrals. At the same time, threats to veracity and truthfulness can be occasions to define industry standards and regulations. Responsible behavior by individuals can be reinforced by the fair application of clear regulatory rules and prohibitions (Osborn, 2010).

Preventing Conflicts of Interest

Physicians should not allow conflicts of interest or bias to influence their decision-making (Sax, 2012). Above all, they must act with the highest levels of truthfulness and integrity in their relationships with patients so as to avoid even the appearance of impropriety (Osborn, 2010). While some conflicts are difficult to avoid, physicians have a responsibility to avoid entering such situations whenever possible. For instance, physicians are prohibited from referring patients for certain services to entities in which the physicians have a financial interest without self-disclosure to their patients (*see* CMS, 2011). Kickbacks and conflicts of interest affect the integrity of treatment decisions.

Another instance, based on current scientific data, is the removal of amalgam restorations from non-allergic patients for the claimed purpose of removing toxic substances from the body, when such treatment is performed solely at the recommendation or suggestion of a dentist. Such recommendations are unethical, because they stand to benefit only the dentist who is paid for the unnecessary care (Sfikas, 2005).

Licensing Physicians, Nurses, and Other Health Care Professionals

In addition to biological factors, illness can result from the loss of intrinsic values of any of the defining characteristics of humans, such as conscience and the instinct for truthfulness (Maslow, 1962/2011). Consequently, state boards may order medical evaluations when they have probable cause to believe that a licensed professional poses a risk to patient safety and well-being. When a conflict arises between a professional right to pursue a medical profession and the government's right to protect its citizenry, the professional right must yield to the state's power to prescribe reasonable rules and regulations in order to protect the state's people from unfit and dishonest physicians.

Eliminating the Corporate Practice of Medicine Doctrine

Good moral character, including simple honesty and truthfulness, is a requirement for licensed health care professionals. The **corporate practice of medicine doctrine** seeks to keep the economic and business incentives of corporations from interfering with the duties of licensed physicians (Hoffmann, 2010). Corporate enterprises cannot, under this doctrine, properly protect truthfulness because of their overriding concern with financial success. This predilection allegedly operates to slant conduct in favor of the corporation. Consequently, physicians maintain that it is inappropriate for corporations to attempt to practice medicine, a profession involving personal trust, truthfulness, and confidential relations (Sparks, 2012).

Nevertheless, as the retail clinic model for delivery of health care expands, like the walk-up clinics in CVS and Wal-Mart, the way Americans receive care is rapidly changing. While all business decisions affecting patients medically must still be made by licensed physicians in retail clinics, the professional autonomy of physicians from corporations that is framed around the value of truthfulness is quickly becoming obsolete (Ameringer, 2011). As retail clinics are more fully integrated into the medical community to help address the medical needs of all, the time is fast arriving to eliminate the corporate practice of medicine doctrine and adopt enterprise liability to better promote the efficiency and quality of U.S. health care (Ballerini, 2010). **Enterprise liability**, in this instance, is defined as the shifting of liability away from individual physicians, nurses, and other health care professionals and onto the corporate owners of retail clinics. *See generally* Hoffmann, 2010.

Reporting in Incentive-Payment Systems

Health care policy should create incentives for self-reform such as self-reporting of medication compliance, activity levels, and individual dietary regimes, as well as corporate reform, such as self-reporting of preventable or potentially avoidable events in hospitals. Yet, such individually reported conduct is dependent upon the truthfulness of individuals' self-reporting. Truthfulness and responsible behavior must be reinforced by the fair application of clear rules of reporting if incentive-payment systems are to succeed (Osborn, 2010).

How individuals and health care organizations should be allowed to reform themselves for incentive payments alone is debatable, as there are limits to the willingness of humans to credibly self-report discretionary behavior (Marciarille, 2011). The value of truthfulness and the human tendency to dissemble facts are important considerations in premium-oriented approaches to care, such as in care coordination of chronic diseases and in self-reporting of recidivism for hospital-acquired infections and other potentially avoidable events.

Prescribing Off-Label Medications and Other Medical Products

The value of truthfulness is related to other values such as professional competence and diligence in prescribing. Off-label prescribing, in particular, goes directly to the relevance of the truthfulness of medical and scientific information (Osborn, 2010). For instance, the medical products and services industry is prohibited from promoting off-label uses in any way, and physicians and other health care prescribers are increasingly being required to use evidence-based medicine in their treatment and prescribing decisions. This is so even where the accuracy and truthfulness of off-label use appears to be beneficial to patients. *Contra* Klasmeier & Redish, 2011 (advocating off-label prescribing).

Advertising Non-Nutritious Foods to Children

American consumers of health care have the right to demand safety and truthfulness in product labeling from the food industry. Ethically and by law, the food industry should truthfully label food products, lead efforts to recall unsafe foods, as well as restrict (or ban) non-nutritious food, especially food targeted to children (Zacher, 2011). Marketing directed at children, whether for foods purchased or purchasable by children, is analyzed from the perspective of children; truthfulness is measured by the impact on children, not others to whom the advertising is not primarily directed (Liu, 2012). When the food industry does not support healthy choices and induces children to request and think they prefer non-nutritious foods because of the use of cartoon characters and other promotions on packaging, this practice violates the value of truthfulness (Pomeranz, 2011).

Universal Principles of Ethics

People mistakenly think the world is how they perceive it and that universal values are, or should be, as they know them personally. Certain principles of ethics, as illustrated in **FEATURE BOX 2-6**, underlie most American values. With any principle, it is important to identify its core underlying values; when expressions of a principle are linked to universal values, the principle is more likely to gain acceptance (Noyes, 2012).

Each of these universal principles has underpinnings in the natural law. For instance, all societies emphasize the importance of compassion, and of sharing wealth with the most

FEATURE BOX 2-6

Eight Universal Principles in the American Ethic

- Ethical issues arise when actions or situations involve actual or potential harm to someone or something. Often these issues are also dilemmas that present two or more alternative solutions. An established and agreed-upon set of values and principles is needed to guide those who are charged with deciding so they can be confident in the ethical quality of their decision.
- The action that provides the greatest benefit is the most ethical. This principle prevents partiality and narrowness when deciding on a course of action. The greatest benefit also includes the *to the greatest number* principle, which further ensures an inclusive quality to decisions.
- All actions should strive for the highest quality outcomes, not just high-quality outcomes. Only the highest quality outcome can include the greatest benefit to the greatest number of stakeholders. It is the best course of action given the knowledge and resources available. For instance, a less than *highest quality outcome* decision will generally deprive patients from receiving appropriate and ethical care.
- Everyone must be accorded equal respect with regard to their status as human beings. Ethical courses of action may not intentionally harm one person while seeking to help another. Respect must embrace everyone, or it is not respect.
- Everyone must always be treated as an end, not merely as a means. To treat anyone as a means is to use them to advance self-interests, but to treat everyone as an end is to respect their human dignity by allowing them the freedom to choose for themselves.
- Everyone should be treated the same, unless they differ in substantive ways that are relevant to the situation in which they are involved. Each person and his or her health needs are different. However, respect for the value of each person must be equal, and the maximum good for each person must be included in ethical decisions.
- Whenever any member of society is treated unequally on the basis of arbitrary or material characteristics, his or her fundamental and innate human dignity is violated. The complexity of health care decisions is often overwhelming; the temptation is to take the most expedient course of action. Although practical decisions can appear to resolve the burden of the dilemma and relieve troublesome concerns, more fundamental values are needed to ensure ethical as opposed to inappropriate arbitrary decisions.
- All individuals, institutions, and the government have a responsibility to be compassionate. There exists an inherent ethical obligation to share wealth with the most vulnerable members of society, even if the less fortunate members have not always earned the wealth that is being shared. The inherent worth and human dignity of everyone must be respected; to respect some members but not others, is not human respect.

— Sources: AMA, 2012a; Beauchamp & Childress, 2012; Moore, 1903/1998; Percival, 1803/2002.

vulnerable populations of society, even if the less fortunate members have not always earned the wealth that is being shared. Only an American ethic of health care, a relatively specific set of shared ethical values such as personal autonomy, compassion, fairness, justice, and truthfulness, will in time be sufficient to support the positive and unifying forces operating to reform the U.S. health care system (Musumeci, 2011). While individuals have moral responsibilities, the government also has moral responsibilities with respect to everyone (Noyes, 2012). Furthermore, the perceived benefit of universal principles also makes such principles human rights principles.

Difference between Legal and Ethical Decisions

Health care law and ethics, though distinct, are partners when MECs make difficult decisions and decide ethical dilemmas; neither is truly effective without the other. Both are grounded in the shared values of committee members serving on the MEC. Without grounding in generally accepted ethical principles, decisions by the MEC will ultimately be ineffective. Ethics, however, is not just important to effective decision-making; ethics is also the central intelligence for all decisions by the MEC. Ethics directs the MEC toward the common good. Ethics gives the MEC purpose and direction. Without ethics, MEC decisions would be without significance and lack meaning for the patients, families, and caregivers who work together with everyone to reach the best decisions possible. *See generally* AMA, 2012; Weinberg, 2012.

A number of issues in health care illustrate ethical dilemmas. As Tocqueville observed in his classic study of the United States, the law regularly resolves ethical differences (Tocqueville, 1835/2011). Yet, many legal issues that seem to be settled are not actually settled ethically. The continuing debates over women's reproductive rights and decisions about end-of-life care are instances where both the law and the ethics are unsettled. Although the law views the definition of conception as settled science, many ethicists accept philosophical and theological definitions of conception, not the scientific understandings of reproductive biology. Similarly, the law views the withdrawal of LSMT the same as the withholding of such treatment, and holds that withdrawing artificial nutrition and hydration is no different than withdrawing artificial ventilation; many ethicists find an ethical distinction between these actions (Orentlicher, 2010). An important goal of this text is to understand the nature of the distinctions between health care law and ethics, and to figure out how to recognize and possibly reconcile some of the differences that exist.

The Future: Socially Responsible Decisions

Although there is no commonly accepted definition of social responsibility for MECs, the expectation is that committee decisions will be socially responsible (ASBH, 2010). At its most basic level, social responsibility ensures that the policies governing MECs, as well as the decision-making processes behind the decisions they implement, are effectuated in a way that avoids harm.

Social responsibility is a key ethical obligation of MECs. If, however, notwithstanding the best of intentions, there are organizational constraints on the MEC's ability to always achieve sociably responsible actions, then the definition of responsibility will have to be expanded. Social responsibility must always be about more than compliance with the law; it must also include efforts to improve the quality and equitable delivery of the health care being provided. In fact, the most critical dimension of social responsibility for MECs may well be the committee members' impact on policies affecting the organization's implementation of health care reforms. *See generally* Vogel, 2006.

ETHICAL OR UNETHICAL DECISION

Balancing Values in Treatment Decisions by Medical Ethics Committees

Ethics Issue: *Should medical ethics committees balance their values with the values of patients and their families when treatment decisions must be made?*

Ethics Analysis: No, MECs cannot impose their values on patients and their families; only courts have the power to overturn treatment decisions made by patients and their families when there is a conflict with what a MEC recommends. The MEC had no right to order life-sustaining feeding to continue after the ventilator was disconnected unless there was a treatment dispute with the parents of the infant; the committee overstepped its bounds by not allowing the infant to die.

Ethics Analysis: Yes, treatment decisions affecting infants are not about the values of families; they are about the human value of this particular infant and what was best for this particular infant. The MEC placed paramount value on the life of this particular infant and ordered life-sustaining feeding once the infant began to breathe on her own after being disconnected from a ventilator.

Settlement and Statutory Law: While none of the allegations in this case were proven in court before a settlement was reached, MECs are generally only consulted in situations where there is no agreement about a treatment decision. When the MEC overturned the parents' decision to withdraw life support, the MEC violated the law because only the courts have the power to do that.

— *Laurendeau v. LaSalle Hospital*, No. 500-17-048988-094 (Quebec Superior Court 2009).

CHAPTER SUMMARY

- MECs are the forum where many ethical dilemmas are reviewed and resolved by multidisciplinary teams comprised of health care professionals from medicine, nursing, law, chaplaincy, and social work.
- MECs often address the difference between what is legal and what is ethical and attempt to reconcile the two when possible.
- Laws can be applied for good or can effectuate evil. Ethics, by definition, is directed toward the common good.
- While MECs generally play an advisory role in ethics consultation for patients and their families, MECs are increasingly serving as decision-makers for health care organizations.
- MECs help health care providers develop the decision-making capacity to determine how ethical principles should be applied.
- There are ten values that often govern and guide the decision-making process of MECs when ethical dilemmas are reviewed: personal autonomy, beneficence,

compassion, equality of opportunity, fairness, human dignity, individual responsibility, justice, non-malfeasance, and truthfulness.
- The expectation is that MEC decisions will be socially responsible, although there is no commonly accepted definition of social responsibility applicable to them.

REFERENCES

Adamy, J., & McGinty, T. (2012, July 7–8). The crushing cost of care. *Wall Street Journal*, p. C1-C2.

AMA (American Medical Association). (2012). *The ethical force program: Advancing ethics in health care*. Chicago, IL: AMA.

___. (2012a). *Code of medical ethics, Opinion 9.11: Ethics committees in health care institutions*. Chicago, IL: AMA.

Ameringer, C. F. (2011). State-based licensure of telemedicine: The need for uniformity but not a national scheme. *Journal of Health Care Law and Policy, 14*, 55–85.

Appel, J. M. (2011). Capital punishment, psychiatrists and the potential "bottleneck" of competence. *Journal of Law and Health, 24*, 45–77.

ASBH (American Society for Bioethics and Humanities). (2010). *Core competencies for health care ethics consultation*. Glenview, IL: ASBH.

Ausiello, D., Chairman, Department of Medicine, Massachusetts General Hospital. (2012, February 17). Remarks at the panel discussion on Innovations in Pharma and Biotech: Challenges and Solutions to Innovation in the Pharma/Biotech Industry at the 2012 Wharton Health Care Business Conference, Philadelphia, PA.

Baker, J. R. (2010). Whom would Jesus cover? A biblical, ethical lens for the contemporary American health care debate. *Journal of Law and Health, 23*, 1–28.

Ballerini, J. E. (2010). The apparent agency doctrine in Connecticut's medical malpractice jurisprudence: Using legal doctrine as a platform for change. *Quinnipiac Health Law Journal, 13*, 317–376.

Bauer, K. A. (2009). Ethics of health care law reform: Privacy and confidentiality in the age of e-medicine. *Journal of Health Care Law and Policy, 12*, 47–62.

Baylis, F. K., & Sherwin, S. A. (2008). Relational account of public health ethics. *Public Health Ethics, 1*(3), 196–209.

Bayly, E. (2012). American health benefit exchanges: State regulators must encourage private market participation. *Journal of Health Care Law and Policy, 15*, 197–226.

Beauchamp, T. L., & Childress, J. F. (2012). *Principles of biomedical ethics* (7th ed.). New York, NY: Oxford University Press.

Berman, M. L. (2011). A public health perspective on health care reform. *Health Matrix: The Journal of Law-Medicine, 21*, 353–383.

Bodaken, B. G. (2008). Where does the insurance industry stand on health reform today? *Health Affairs, 27*, 667–674.

Bostrom, B. A. (2010). *Baxter v. State of Montana. Issues in Law and Medicine, 26*, 79–82.

Boulet, S. L., et al. (2008). Health care expenditures for infants and young children with Down syndrome in a privately insured population. *Journal of Pediatrics, 153*, 241–246.

Boumil, M. M., et al. (2012). Prescription data mining, medical privacy and the First Amendment: The U.S. Supreme Court in *Sorrell v. IMS Health Inc. Annals of Health Law, 21*, 447–491.

Brownsword, R. (2007). Human rights-what hope? Human dignity-what scope? In J. Gunning & S. Soren Holm, (Eds.), *Ethics, law and society*, 1–189. Williston, VT: Ashgate.

Burleson, E. (2011). Perspective on economic critiques of disability law: The multifaceted federal role in balancing equity and efficiency. *Indiana Health Law Review, 8*, 335–364.

Caldwell, B. (2011). Punishment v. restoration: A comparative analysis of juvenile delinquency law in the United States and Mexico. *Cardozo Journal of International and Comparative Law, 20*, 105–141.

Carnahan, S. J. (2011). Biobanking newborn bloodspots for genetic research without consent. *Journal of Health Care Law and Policy, 14*, 299–330.

Caruso, D. (2010). Autism in the United States: Social movement and legal change. *American Journal of Law and Medicine, 36*, 483–539.

CBO (Congressional Budget Office). (2010, March 20). Letter from Douglas W. Elmendorf, Director, CBO to Nancy Pelosi, Speaker, U.S. House of Representatives (D-California). Providing a final cost estimate of the direct spending and revenue effects of the Patient Protection and Affordable Care Act. Washington, DC: CBO.

___. (2010a). *Selected CBO publications related to health care legislation*. Washington, DC: CBO.

___. (2009, December 10). Letter from Douglas W. Elmendorf, Director, CBO, to Senator John D. Rockefeller, IV (D-West Virginia). Additional information on the effects of tort reform. Washington, DC: CBO.

___. (2009a, October 9). Letter from Douglas W. Elmendorf, Director, CBO, to Senator Orrin G. Hatch (R-Utah). CBO's analysis of the effects of proposals to limit costs related to medical malpractice (tort reform). Washington, DC: CBO.

___. (2008). *Technological change and the growth of health care spending*. Washington, DC: CBO.

CEA (Council of Economic Advisers). (2009). *The economic case for health care reform: Update*. Washington, DC: The White House, Executive Office of the President.

Clark, B. (2011). Using law to fight a silent epidemic: The role of health literacy in health care access, quality, and cost. *Annals of Health Law, 20*, 253–327.

Clark, P. J. (2006). Financial incentives for cadaveric organ donation: An ethical analysis. *The Internet Journal on Law, Healthcare and Ethics, 4*(1).

CMS (Centers for Medicare and Medicaid Services). (2011, May 6). Voluntary self-referral disclosure protocol. Washington, DC: CMS.

Cohoon, L. (2010). New food regulations: Safer products or more red tape? *Journal of Health and Biomedical Law, 6*, 343–375.

Commonwealth Fund. (2011). *National scorecard on U.S. health care system performance*. New York, NY: Commonwealth Fund.

Conley, J. M., et al. (2010). Enabling responsible public genomics. *Health Matrix: The Journal of Law-Medicine, 20*, 325–385.

Cooper, T. (1979). Shattuck lecture: The challenge to the medical profession. *New England Journal of Medicine, 300*(21), 1185–1188.

Copp, A. (2012). The ethics and efficacy of a "fat tax" in the form of an insurance surcharge on obese state employees. *Quinnipiac Health Law Journal, 15*, 1–31.

Corkery, M. (2012, July 18). Report details threats to states' fiscal health. *Wall Street Journal*, p. A3.

Cornell, C., Vice President of Corporate Development, Medtronic. (2012, February 17). Remarks at the panel discussion on Innovations in Medtech at the 2012 Wharton Health Care Business Conference, Philadelphia, PA.

Covey, S. R. (2013). *The 7 habits of highly effective people: Powerful lessons in personal change*. New York, NY: Simon and Schuster-Free Press (Original work published 1990).

Crowe, C. (2010). Videri quam esse [to seem, rather than to be]: The role of empathy in judicial discourse. *Law and Psychology Review, 34*, 121–133.

Culhane, J. G. (2007). An international debate on culture, disaster, biotechnology and public health: What does justice require for the victims of Katrina and September 11? *DePaul Journal of Health Care Law, 10*, 177–211.

Daniels, N., et al. (2009). Access, cost, and financing: Achieving an ethical health reform. *Health Affairs, 28*, 909–916.

Dartmouth Institute for Health Policy and Clinical Practice. (2012). *Care for dying Medicare patients at elite cancer centers differs little from community hospitals*. Hanover, NH: Dartmouth Medical School.

___. (2011). *Trends and variation in end-of-life care for Medicare beneficiaries with severe chronic illness*. Hanover, NH: Dartmouth Medical School.

___. (2008). *The Dartmouth atlas of health care*. Hanover, NH: Dartmouth Medical School.

Davis, K. U. (2007). *Slowing the growth of U.S. health care expenditures. What are the options?* Prepared for the Commonwealth Fund & Alliance for Health Reform 2007 Bipartisan Congressional Health Policy Conference. New York, NY: Commonwealth Fund.

Davis, P. (2009). *Economist intelligence unit: Beyond box-ticking: A new era for risk governance*. Philadelphia, PA: ACE Group and KPMG.

Derco, L. M. (2010). America's organ donation crisis: How current legislation must be shaped by successes abroad. *Journal of Contemporary Health Law and Policy, 27*, 154–182.

Dixon, D. P. (2008). Informed consent or institutionalized eugenics? How the medical profession encourages abortion of fetuses with Down Syndrome. *Issues in Law and Medicine, 24*, 3–61.

Dolgin, J. L. (2010). Class competition and American health care: Debating the State Children's Health Insurance Program. *Louisiana Law Review, 70*, 683–748.

Einstein, A. (2015). *Relativity, the special and the general theory*. Princeton, NJ: Princeton University Press (Original work published 1923).

Fan, M. D. (2012). Decentralizing STD surveillance: Toward better informed sexual consent. *Yale Journal of Health Policy, Law and Ethics, 12*, 1–38.

Farrell, R. M. (2013). Women and prenatal genetic testing in the 21st century. *Health Matrix: The Journal of Law-Medicine, 23*, 1–13.

Fenigsen, R. (2011). Verbatim: Other people's lives: Reflections on medicine, ethics, and euthanasia. *Issues in Law and Medicine, 27*, 51–70.

___. (2010). Verbatim: Other people's lives: Reflections on medicine, ethics, and euthanasia. *Issues in Law and Medicine, 25*, 33–76.

Fichter, A. (2009). The law of physicianing: A study of the codification of medical professionalism. *Health Matrix: The Journal of Law-Medicine, 19*, 317–385.

Fleck, L. M. (2011). Just caring: Health care rationing, terminal illness, and the medically least well off. *Journal of Law, Medicine and Ethics, 39*, 156–167.

___. (2009*). Just caring: Health care rationing and democratic deliberation.* New York, NY: Oxford University Press.

Fleischer, M. P. (2011). Equality of opportunity and the charitable tax subsidies. *Boston University Law Review, 91*, 601–663.

Foster, R. S. (2010). Estimated financial effects of the Patient Protection and Affordable Care Act, as amended. Baltimore, MD: U.S. Department of Health and Human Services, Centers for Medicare and Medicaid Services.

Fry-Revere, S., et al. (2010). Death: A new legal perspective. *Contemporary Health Law and Policy, 27*, 1–75.

Fulginiti, A. (2010). The soul and its impact on life and death choices: A constitutional study of abortion, the right to die, and other bioethical dilemmas. *Rutgers Journal of Law and Religion, 11*, 459–494.

Gatter, K. (2012). Biobanks as a tissue and information semi-commons: Balancing interests for personalized medicine, tissue donors and the public health. *Journal of Health Care Law and Policy, 15*, 303–346.

Gerwint, L. E. (2011). Planning for pandemic: A new model for governing public health emergencies. *American Journal of Law and Medicine, 37*, 128–171.

Goforth, C. R. (2010). A corporation has no soul: Modern corporations, corporate governance, and involvement in the political process. *Houston Law Review, 47*, 617–661.

Goldberg, J. C. P. (2011). Tort in three dimensions. *Pepperdine Law Review, 38*, 321–335.

Goolsbee, A., Chief Economist, President Obama's Council of Economic Advisors. (2010). Second public meeting of the President's Economic Recovery Advisory Board at the U.S. Treasury, Washington, DC.

Gostin, L. O. (2008). Meeting basic survival needs of the world's least healthy people: Toward a framework convention on global health. *Georgetown Law Journal, 96*, 331–392.

Gostin, L. O., et al. (2011). Restoring health to health reform: Integrating medicine and public health to advance the population's well-being. *University of Pennsylvania Law Review, 159*, 1777–1822.

Gratzer, D. (2008). *The cure: How capitalism can save American health care.* Jackson, TN: Encounter Books.

Greenberg, M. D., et al. (2011). *Is better patient safety associated with less malpractice activity?* Santa Monica, CA: RAND Corp.

Greenwood, J., President, Biotechnology Industry Organization. (2012, February 16). Keynote speaker at the 18th Annual Wharton Health Care Business Conference: Innovation in a changing health care environment. Philadelphia, PA.

Grossman, J. L. (2010). Pregnancy, work, and the promise of equal citizenship. *Georgetown Law Journal, 98*, 567–628.

Hart, D. K. (2012). Exploring power, agency and action in a world of moving frontiers: In a word. *Southwestern Law Review, 41*, 215–230.

Held, D. (2006). *Models of democracy* (3rd ed.). Stanford, CA: Stanford University Press.

Herring, J. (2008). Entering the fog: On the borderlines of mental capacity. *Indiana Law Journal, 83*, 1619–1649.

Hester, D. H., & Bjarnadottir, D. (2007). *Ethics by committee: A text on consultation, organization, and education for hospital ethics committees.* Lanham, MD: Rowman & Littlefield.

Hethcoat, II, G. O. (2011). In the crosshairs: Legislative restrictions on patient-physician speech about firearms. *DePaul Journal of Health Care Law, 14*, 1–34.

Hills, Jr., R. M. (2006). The individual right to federalism in the Rehnquist court. *George Washington Law Review, 74*, 888–905.

Hoffman, A. K. (2011). Three models of health insurance: The conceptual pluralism of the Patient Protection and Affordable Care Act. *University of Pennsylvania Law Review, 159*, 1873–1954.

___. (2010). Oil and water: Mixing individual mandates, fragmented markets, and health reform. *American Journal of Law and Medicine, 36*, 7–77.

Hoffmann, A. (2010). Minute medicine: Examining retail clinic legal issues and legislative challenges. *Health Matrix: The Journal of Law-Medicine, 20*, 467–497.

Hollander-Blumoff, R. (2010). Just negotiation. *Washington University Law Review, 88*, 381–432.

Hyman, D. A. (2009). Employment-based health insurance and universal coverage: Four things people know that aren't so. *Yale Journal of Health Policy, Law, and Ethics, 9*, 435–451.

IOM (Institute of Medicine). (2011). *Clinical practice guidelines we can trust.* Washington, DC: National Academies of Sciences.

___. (2011a). *Standards for developing trustworthy clinical practice guidelines.* Washington, DC: National Academies of Sciences.

___. (2009). *Initial national priorities for comparative effectiveness research.* Washington, DC: National Academies of Sciences.

Iyioha, I., & Akorede, Y. A. O. (2010). You give me welfare but take my freedom: Understanding the mature minor's autonomy in the face of the court's parens patriae jurisdiction. *Quinnipiac Health Law Journal, 13*, 279–315.

Jackson, B. (2011). A budget-busting law: Republicans and Democrats both misrepresent the fiscal effect of the health care law. Philadelphia, PA: Annenberg Public Policy Center.

Jaffe, H. W., & Hope, T. (2010). Treating for the common good: A proposed ethical framework. *Public Health Ethics, 3*(3), 193–198.

Jencks, S. F., et al. (2009). Rehospitalizations among patients in the Medicare fee-for-service program. *New England Journal of Medicine, 360*, 1418–1428.

Jennings, B. (2009). Public health and civic republicanism: Toward an alternative framework for public health ethics. In A. Dawson & M. Verweij (Eds.), *Ethics, prevention, and public health (Issues in Biomedical Ethics)*, 424–440. New York, NY: Oxford University Press.

Johnson, R. (2014). *The federal food safety system: A primer.* Washington, DC: Congressional Research Service.

Johnson, T. (2012). Backgrounder: Healthcare costs and U.S. competitiveness. New York, NY: Council on Foreign Relations.

Kaiser Family Foundation. (2011). *Number of paid medical malpractice claims.* Washington, DC: Kaiser Commission on Medicaid and the Uninsured.

Karako-Eyal, N. (2011). Physicians' duty of disclosure: A deontological and consequential analysis. *Quinnipiac Health Law Journal, 14*, 1–47.

Katz, M. (2010). Towards a new moral paradigm in health care delivery: Accounting for individuals. *American Journal of Law and Medicine, 36*, 78–135.

Kelly, M. P., et al. (2007). *The social determinants of health: Developing an evidence base for political action. Final Report to the World Health Organization, Commission on the Social Determinants of Health from the Measurement and Evidence Network [MEKN].* London, England: National Institute for Health and Clinical Excellence and Santiago, Chile: Universidad del Desarrollo.

Kenny, N. P., et al. (2010). Re-visioning public health ethics: A relational perspective. *Canadian Journal of Public Health, 1–2*, 9–11.

Kesselheim, A. S. (2011). Off-label drug use and promotion: Balancing public health goals and commercial speech. *American Journal of Law and Medicine, 37*, 225–257.

Kimbuende, E., et al. (2010). *U.S. health care costs.* Washington, DC: Kaiser Family Foundation.

Kinney, E. D. (2008). Health care financing and delivery in the United States, Mexico, and Canada: Establishing intentional principles for sound integration. *Wisconsin International Law Journal, 26*, 934–964.

Kirby, M. (2009). Human rights and bioethics: The Universal Declaration of Human Rights and UNESCO Universal Declaration of Bioethics and Human Rights. *Journal of Contemporary Health Law and Policy, 25*, 309–331.

Klasmeier, C., & Redish, M. H. (2011). Off-label prescription advertising, the FDA and the First Amendment: A study in the values of commercial speech protection. *American Journal of Law and Medicine, 37*, 315–357.

Koppelman, A. (2011). Bad news for mail robbers: The obvious constitutionality of health care reform. *Yale Law Journal, 121*, 515–528.

Kopson, M. S. (2010). Medical tourism: Implications for providers and plans. *Journal of Health and Life Sciences Law, 3*(2), 147–172.

Land, A. (2011). Lawyering beyond without leaving individual clients behind. *Clinical Law Review, 18*, 47–74.

Landers, R. M. (2010). Tomorrow may finally have arrived, the Patient Protection and Affordable Care Act: A necessary first step toward health care equity in the United States. *Journal of Health and Biomedical Law, 6*, 65–77.

Lash, K. T. (2011). "Resolution VI" [of the U.S. Constitution]: National authority to resolve collective action problems under Article 1, Section 8. *Notre Dame Law Review, 87*(5) 2123–2164.

Laufer-Ukeles, P. (2011). Reproductive choices and informed consent: Fetal interests, women's identity, and relational autonomy. *American Journal of Law and Medicine, 37*, 567–622.

Lee, L. M. (2012). Public health ethics theory: Review and path to convergence. *Journal of Law, Medicine and Ethics, 40*, 85–97.

Levine, M. A., et al. (2007). Improving access to health care: A consensus ethical framework to guide proposals for reform. *Hastings Center Report, 9/10*, 14–19.

Linares, A. D. (2012). Opioid pseudoaddiction: A casualty of the war on drugs, racism, sexism, and opiophobia. *Quinnipiac Health Law Journal, 15*, 89–125.

Lincoln, A. Gettysburg address. (1953). In R. P. Basler, et al. (Eds.), *Collected works of Abraham Lincoln:* (1809–1865) (Vol. 4). New Brunswick, NJ: Rutgers University Press (Original work published 1863).

Liu, L. (2012). Reshaping the American concept of consumer interest in the food policy debate. *Yale Journal of Health Policy, Law and Ethics, 12*, 171–207.

Macklin, R. (2010). Fair benefits in developing countries: Maximin as a good start. *American Journal of Bioethics, 10*(6), 36–37.

Madison, J. (1788). The federalist #44. In J. E. Cooke (Ed.). (1982). *The federalist.* Middletown, CT: Wesleyan University Press.

Majerol, M., et al. (2015). *The uninsured: A primer: Key facts about health insurance and the uninsured in America.* Washington, DC: Kaiser Commission on Medicaid and the Uninsured.

Mansbach, R. (2011). Altered standards of care: Needed reform for when the next disaster strikes. *Journal of Health Care Law and Policy, 14*, 209–239.

Marciarille, A. M. (2011). Healing Medicare hospital recidivism: Causes and cures. *American Journal of Law and Medicine, 37*, 41–80.

Marciarille, A. M., & DeLong, J. B. (2012). Bending the health cost curve: The promise and peril of the Independent Payment Advisory Board. *Health Matrix: The Journal of Law-Medicine, 22*, 75–121.

Marcus, D. (2010). The Federal Rules of Civil Procedure and legal realism as a jurisprudence of law reform. *Georgia Law Review, 44*, 433–509.

Mariner, W. K. (2010). Health reform: What's insurance got to do with it? Recognizing health insurance as a separate species of insurance. *American Journal of Law and Medicine, 36*, 436–451.

Marmont, M., & Wilkenson, R. (2005). *Social determinants of health*. New York, NY: Oxford University Press.

Maron, R. F. (2012). Who has a will to live? Why state requirements for advance directives should be uniformly revised. *Regent University Law Review, 24*, 169–199.

Marshall, W. P. (2012). The welfare state and American exceptionalism: National healthcare and American constitutional culture. *Harvard Journal of Law and Public Policy, 35*, 131–152.

Maslow, A. H. (2011). *Toward a psychology of being: Reprint of 1962 first edition*. Eastford, CT: Martino Fine Books (Original work published 1962).

Mauldin, J. A. (2011). All smoke and no fire? Analyzing the potential effects of the Mental Health Parity and Addiction Equity Act of 2008. *Law and Psychology Review, 35*, 193–207.

McGrath, R. J., et al. (2011). National profile of children with Down syndrome: Disease burden, access to care, and family impact. *The Journal of Pediatrics, 159*, 535–541.

McKoy, J. M., et al. (2005). Is ethics for sale? . . . Juggling law and ethics in managed care. *DePaul Journal of Health Care Law, 8*, 559–613.

Miola, J. (2006). The need for informed consent: Lessons from the ancient Greeks. *Cambridge Quarterly: Healthcare Ethics, 15*, 152–160.

Moncrieff, A. R. (2012). Cost-benefit federalism: Reconciling collective action federalism and libertarian federalism in the Obamacare litigation and beyond. *American Journal of Law and Medicine, 38*, 288–325.

Moore, G. E. (1998). *Principia ethica*. Paris, France: Presses Universitaires de France (Original work published 1903).

Moulton, B., & King, J. S. (2010). Aligning ethics with medical decision-making: The quest for informed patient choice. *Journal of Law, Medicine, and Ethics, 38*, 85–94.

Muller, J. F. (2011). Disability, ambivalence, and the law. *American Journal of Law and Medicine, 37*, 469–521.

Musumeci, M. (2011). Modernizing Medicaid eligibility criteria for children with significant disabilities: Moving from a disabling to an enabling paradigm. *American Journal of Law and Medicine, 37*, 81–124.

Nachman, D. D. (2011). Living wills: Is it time to pull the plug? *Elder Law Journal, 18*, 289–333.

NAIC (National Association of Insurance Commissioners). (2010). *Draft: American Health Benefit Exchange Model Act*. Washington, DC: NAIC.

Nelson, III, L. J., et al. (2011). Medical liability and health care reform. *Health Matrix: The Journal of Law-Medicine, 21*, 443–516.

NICE (National Institute for Health and Clinical Excellence). (2008). *Social value judgments*. London, England: NICE.

Noah, B. A. (2012). The role of race in end-of-life care. *Journal of Health Care Law and Policy, 15*, 349–377.

Noyes, J. E. (2012). The common heritage of mankind: Past, present, and future. *Denver Journal of International Law and Policy, 40*, 447–471.

NPDB (National Practitioner Data Bank). (2012). *National summaries*. Rockville, MD: U.S. Department of Health and Human Services, Health Resources and Services Administration, Bureau of Health Professions, Division of Practitioner Data Banks.

Nuttfield Council on Bioethics. (2007). *Public health: Ethical issues*. London, England: Nuttfield Council.

Odibo, A., et al. (2005). A cost-effectiveness analysis of prenatal screening strategies for Down syndrome. *Obstetrics and Gynecology, 106*, 562–568.

Orentlicher, D. (2012). Rights to healthcare in the United States: Inherently unstable. *American Journal of Law and Medicine, 38*, 326–347.

___. (2011). The commercial speech doctrine in health regulation: The clash between the public interest in a robust First Amendment and the public interest in effective protection from harm. *American Journal of Law and Medicine, 37*, 299–314.

___. (2010). Health care law: A field of gaps. *Annals of Health Law, 19*, 1–4.

Osborn, J. E. (2010). Can I tell you the truth? A comparative perspective on regulating off-label scientific and medical information. *Yale Journal of Health Policy, Law and Ethics, 10*, 299–355.

Osborn, R., & Schoen, C. (2013). *The Commonwealth Fund International Health Policy survey in eleven countries*. New York, NY: The Commonwealth Fund.

Pagan, J. A., Professor of Economics at the University of Texas and Senior Fellow at the Leonard Davis Institute of Health Economics at the University of Pennsylvania. (2007, February 7). Beazley Symposium on *Access to essential health care: Immigration from the Mayflower to border patrols: Who should have access to essential health care in the U.S.* at Loyola University Chicago School Law, Beazley Institute for Health Law and Policy. Chicago, IL.

Pagnattaro, M. A., & Peirce, E. R. (2010). From China to your plate: An analysis of new regulatory efforts and stakeholder responsibility to ensure food safety. *George Washington International Law Review, 42,* 1–56.

Parkins, C. (2012). Protecting the herd: A public health, economics, and legal argument for taxing parents who opt-out of mandatory childhood vaccinations. *Southern California Interdisciplinary Law Journal, 21,* 437–490.

Percival, T. (2002). *Medical ethics: A code of institutes and precepts, adapted to the professional conduct of physicians and surgeons.* Woodcliff Lake, NJ: Eisai, Inc. & Janssen Pharmaceutica, Inc. (Original work published 1803).

Petrini, C., & Gainotti, S. (2008). A personalist approach to public health ethics. *Bulletin of the World Health Organization, 86*(8), 624–629.

Pike, E. R. (2012). Recovering from research: A no-fault proposal to compensate injured research participants. *American Journal of Law and Medicine, 38,* 7–62.

Pleschberge, S. (2007). Dignity and the challenge of dying in nursing homes: The residents' view. *Age & Ageing, 36,* 197–202.

Pomeranz, J. L. (2011). Extending the fantasy in the supermarket: Where unhealthy food promotions meet children and how the government can intervene. *Indiana Health Law Review, 9,* 117–185.

Pompeo, N. (2011). Major League Baseball's use of DNA testing on Central and South American prospects in the age of the Genetic Information Nondiscrimination Act of 2008. *Health Matrix: The Journal of Law-Medicine, 21,* 627–653.

Pope, T. M. (2014). Freedom of choice at the end of life: Patients' rights in a shifting legal and political landscape: Dispute resolution mechanisms for intractable medical futility disputes. *New York Law School Law Review, 58,* 347–368.

____. (2014a). The growing power of healthcare ethics committees heightens due process concerns. *Cardozo Journal of Conflict Resolution, 15,* 425–447.

____. (2010). Health law and bioethics: Pressing issues and changing times: Surrogate selection: An increasingly viable, but limited, solution to intractable futility disputes. *Saint Louis University Journal of Health Law and Policy, 3,* 183–252.

Pope, T. M., et al. (2011). Caring for the seriously ill: Cost and public policy. *Journal of Law, Medicine and Ethics, 39,* 111–113.

Post, L. F., et al. (2006). *Handbook for health care ethics committees.* Baltimore, MD: Johns Hopkins University Press.

President's Commission for the Study of Ethical Problems in Medicine and Biomedical and Behavioral Research. (1983). *Deciding to forego life-sustaining treatment: A report on the ethical, medical, and legal issues in treatment decisions.* Washington, DC: President's Commission.

President's Council on Bioethics. (2015). *Human dignity and bioethics.* Washington, DC: President's Council on Bioethics.

Raper, S. E. (2011). No role for apology: Remedial work and the problem of medical injury. *Yale Journal of Health Policy, Law and Ethics, 11,* 267–318.

Rau, J. (2012, August 13). Medicare to penalize 2,211 hospitals for excess readmissions. *Kaiser Health News.*

Ravitch, R., & Volcker, P. (2012). *Report of the State Budget Task Force.* New York, NY: State Budget Task Force.

Rawls, J. (2005). *A theory of justice.* Boston, MA: Belknap Press of Harvard University Press (Original work published 1971).

____. (2005). *Political liberalism.* New York, NY: Columbia University Press (Original work published 1993).

Rosenbaum, S. (2011). Realigning the social order: The Patient Protection and Affordable Care Act and the U.S. health insurance system. *Health and Biomedical Law Society, 7,* 1–31.

Rousseau, J.-J. (2014). *The major political writings of Jean-Jacques Rousseau: The two "Discourses" and the "Social Contract".* Chicago, IL: University of Chicago Press (Original work published 1762). (Social contract discussed in this chapter.)

Rutkow, L., & Teret, S. P. (2011). The potential for state attorneys general to promote the public's health: Theory, evidence, and practice. *Saint Louis University Public Law Review, 30,* 267–300.

Ruttenberg, R., et al. (2011). The taxpayers' burden from product-related harm. *Kansas Journal of Law and Public Policy, 21,* 121–193.

Ryan, E. (2011). Negotiating federalism. *Boston College Law Review, 52*(1), 1–136.

Sage, W. M. (2014). Putting insurance reform in the ACA's rear-view mirror. *Houston Law Review, 51,* 1081–1113.

Samaha, A. M. (2007). What good is the social model of disability? *University of Chicago Law Review, 74,* 1251–1308.

Satz, A. B. (2008). Toward solving the health care crisis: The paradoxical case for universal access to high technology. *Yale Journal of Health Policy, Law, and Ethics, 8,* 93–142.

Sax, J. K. (2012). Financial conflicts-of-interest in science. *Annals of Health Law, 21,* 291–327.

Schwark, D. (2011). Organ conscription: How the dead can save the living. *Journal of Law and Health, 24*, 323–352.

SEC (U.S. Securities & Exchange Commission). (2014). Corporate annual proxy statements from *Aetna, Centene, Cigna, Humana, United Health, and WellPoint.* Washington, DC: SEC.

___. (2011). *Corporate annual income statements for 2010 from Aetna, Amerigroup, Centene, Cigna, Conventry Health Corp., Health Net, Humana, United Health, United American, and WellPoint.* Washington, DC: SEC.

Sewall, M. P. (2010). Pushing execution over the constitutional line: Forcible medication of condemned inmates and the Eighth and Fourteenth Amendments. *Boston College Law Review, 51*, 1279–1322.

Sewell, A. (2015). *Black beauty.* London, England: Faber & Faber Childrens Books (Original work published 1877).

Sfikas, P. M. (2005). Letter from the Chief Counsel and Associate Executive Director, American Dental Association to the Editors of Health Matrix. *Health Matrix: The Journal of Law-Medicine, 15*, 459–464.

Shapiro, M. H. (2012). Updating constitutional doctrine: An extended response to the critique of compulsory vaccination. *Yale Journal of Health Policy, Law, and Ethics, 12*, 87–169.

Shaub, J. D. (2012). Children's freedom of speech and expressive maturity. *Law and Psychology Review, 36*, 191–242.

Singer, L. E. (2010). The aftermath of federal health care reform: The challenge for states and the private sector. *Annals of Health Law, 19*, 67–71.

Smith, II, G. P. (2009). Re-shaping the common good in times of public health emergencies: Validating medical triage. *Annals of Health Law, 18*, 1–34.

___. (2009a). *Distributive justice and the new medicine.* Northampton, MA: Edward Elgar Publishing.

Solar, O., & Irwin, A. (2007). *Towards a conceptual framework for analysis and action on the social determinants of health.* Geneva, Switzerland: World Health Organization, Commission on Social Determinants of Health.

Sparks, K. B. (2012). Medication adherence technology: Medicine of the future, emerging privacy concern. *Journal of Contemporary Health Law and Policy, 28*, 324–349.

Standley, S. C., & Liang, B. A. (2011). Addressing inappropriate care provision at the end-of-life: A policy proposal for hospitals. *Michigan State Journal of Medicine and Law, 15*, 137–176.

Starr, P. (2013). *Remedy and reaction: The peculiar American struggle over health care reform.* New Haven, CT: Yale University Press.

Stein, M. S., & Savulescu, J. (2011). Welfare versus autonomy in human subjects research. *Florida State University Law Review, 38*, 303–344.

Steinzor, R. (2010). The future of food regulation: High crimes, not misdemeanors: Deterring the production of unsafe food. *Health Matrix: The Journal of Law-Medicine, 20*, 175–201.

Summerhill, M. J., & Chandler, A. M. (2009). Company representatives in the operating and treatment room: How to navigate the ever-expanding theories of liability for medical device and pharmaceutical companies. *DePaul Journal of Health Care Law, 12*, 253–276.

Sutton, V. (2010). Is there a doctor (and a lawyer) in the house? Why our good Samaritan laws are doing more harm than good for a national public health security strategy: A fifty-state survey. *Journal of Health and Biomedical Law, 6*, 261–300.

Swider, J. D. (2012). A dose of reality: Unintended consequences of penalizing hospital readmissions in the PPACA [Patient Protection and Affordable Care Act]. *Indiana Health Law Review, 9*, 361–388.

Tames, P. C., et al. (2011). Medical-legal partnership: Evolution or revolution. *Clearinghouse Review: Journal of Poverty Law and Policy, 45*, 124–145.

Tauber, A. I. (2005). *Patient autonomy and the ethics of responsibility.* Cambridge, MA: Massachusetts Institute of Technology Press.

Thayer, L. (2011). In determining whether a patient is medically indigent, county boards can impute a patient's potential income and future tax returns - *St. Luke's Magic Valley Regional Medical Center. v. Board of County Commissioners of Gooding County*, 237 P.3d 1210 (Idaho 2010). *Journal of Health and Biomedical Law, 7*, 115–131.

Thompson, A. K., et al. (2006). Pandemic influenza preparedness: An ethical framework to guide decision-making. *BioMed Central: Medical Ethics, 7*, 12.

Tobler, L. (2010). Planning for end-of-life care. Washington, DC: National Conference of State Legislatures.

Tocqueville, A. de (2011). *Democracy in America.* Chicago, IL: University of Chicago Press (Original work published 1835).

Todd, A. E. (2011). No need for more regulation: Payors and their role in balancing the cost and safety considerations of off-label prescriptions. *American Journal of Law and Medicine, 37*, 422–443.

Tyler, E. T. (2012). Aligning public health, health care, law and policy: Medical-legal partnership as a multilevel response to the social determinants of health. *Health and Biomedical Law Society, 8*, 211–247.

Vogel, D. (2006). *The market for virtue: The potential and limits of corporate social responsibility.* Washington, DC: Brookings Institution Press.

Wagman, S. (2010). No one ever died from copyright infringement: The inducement doctrine's applicability to firearms manufacturer liability. *Cardozo Law Review, 32*, 689–721.

Weber, M. C. (2010). Unreasonable accommodation and due hardship. *Florida Law Review, 62*, 1119–1178.

Weinberg, J. K. (2012). Institutional ethics committees: Should we kill all the lawyers? The role of lawyers on hospital ethics committees. *Annals of Health Law: American Society of Law, Medicine and Ethics Special Edition, 21*, 181–190.

Westfall, P. (2011). The Affordable Care Act's impact on the administration of health benefits. *DePaul Journal of Health Care Law, 14*, 99–131.

Wharton School at the University of Pennsylvania. (2007). Harry and Louise, the sequel? The universal health care debate is back. *Knowledge@Wharton.*

WHO (World Health Organization). (1994). *Bulletin of the World Health Organization, 72*(1), 145.

Wiley, L. F. (2012). Rethinking the new public health. *Washington and Lee Law Review, 69*, 207–272.

Wojcik, M. E. (2010). Some lessons learned from the AIDS pandemic. *Annals of Health Law, 19*, 63–66.

Wolfson, S. A. (2007). Screening for violence and abuse through the lens of medical ethics. *De Paul Journal of Health Care Law, 11*, 1–21.

Wright, B. A. (2006). Process: The best medicine for seriously ill infants. *Journal of Health and Biomedical Law, 2*, 69–107.

Wright Veilleux, J. (2012) in Catching flies with vinegar: A critique of the centers for Medicare and Medicaid self-disclosure program in *Health Matrix: The Journal of Law-Medicine, 22*, 169–225, 171 (quoting Franklin, B. (1772, September 19). Letter to Joseph Priestly.).

Zacher, A. (2011). False hope and toxic effects: Proposed changes to the FDA drug approval process would fail to benefit the terminally ill. *Quinnipiac Health Law Journal, 14*, 251–282.

PART II

The Ethics of Access to Health Care

Part II addresses Americans' resolve to obtain the best health care system for as little investment as possible; the focus is on what is fair and just.

CHAPTER 3

Access to Affordable Health Insurance

"To me our country is a living, breathing presence, unimpressed by what others say is impossible, proud of its own success, generous, yes, and naive, sometimes wrong, never mean, and always impatient to provide a better life for its people in a framework of a basic fairness and freedom."

— **Ronald Reagan** (1911–2004), 40th President of the United States

LEARNING OBJECTIVES

After completing this chapter, the reader should be able to:

1. Describe the parameters of the American social contract and understand the importance of basic fairness and human equality in the provision of health care.
2. Understand the ethical principles underlying the challenge of finding a way to provide affordable access to health insurance for all U.S. residents, but especially for vulnerable populations at the bottom of the socioeconomic pyramid.
3. Explain the risk pooling programs being developed to provide effective and affordable health insurance coverage to millions of uninsured and underinsured Americans.
4. Summarize the different ethical principles motivating the federal mandate to provide universal health care by requiring almost all U.S. residents to maintain health insurance.
5. Evaluate the ethical issues surrounding tax subsidies to offset much of the cost of buying private health insurance.

KEY TERMS

Actuarial fairness	Common good	Economic fairness
Adverse selection	Cost-sharing	Egalitarianism
Affordable Care Act of 2010 (ACA)	Cost-shifting	Emergency care
	Distributive justice	Federal preemption

Fee-for-service
Guaranteed issue
Health insurance exchanges
Health risks
Indemnity health insurance
Insurance risk pools
Limited-benefit health
   insurance

Managed care
Minimum coverage
   provision
Moral imperative
Public legitimacy
Reasonable and
   necessary care
Risk spreading

Shared responsibility
   payment
Social contract
Social solidarity
Uncompensated
   care

ETHICAL OR UNETHICAL DECISION

Access to Health Care

Ethics Issue: *Should most Americans be required to maintain health insurance as a moral and economic imperative of national health care reform based upon the ethical principles of human equality and social solidarity?*

In Brief: Four uninsured Michigan residents, along with Thomas More Law Center, a public interest law firm that provides health insurance to its employees, claimed that the **minimum coverage provision** of the **Affordable Care Act of 2010 (ACA)** unconstitutionally compels them to purchase health insurance. Each of them objects to being compelled by the federal government to purchase medical coverage or to pay a **shared responsibility payment** for failure to maintain basic coverage based on household income. This annual penalty is assessed on anyone who does not purchase or maintain a certain level of coverage.

In reviewing the minimum coverage provision, the court noted how Congress determined that this provision was an essential part of the ACA. The court then provided background on the ACA and explained the five interrelated parts of the law that were designed to improve affordable access to health care and minimize the **cost-shifting** that occurs whenever insurers charge more for certain medical products or services in order to subsidize services and products that are provided at or below cost.

First, the ACA expands **insurance risk pools**, the pooling of similar health risks by health insurers to help pay for health care expenses, by building upon the existing nationwide system of employer-based health insurance to spread the costs of illness and disease across U.S. society. Tax incentives for employer-provided health insurance for small businesses were established and large employers are now required to offer health insurance coverage to expand the pooling of health risks by insurers to help pay for the costs of their employees' health care. **Health risks**, in this instance, are defined as the likelihood of illness or injury adversely affecting an employer's workforce, as well as the health of individual employees. Second, the ACA provides for the creation of **health insurance exchanges** that allow individuals and small businesses to leverage their collective buying power to obtain competitively priced health insurance. Third, the ACA expands eligibility for Medicaid and offers federal tax credits for payment of health insurance premiums. Fourth, the ACA provides for **guaranteed issue** of health insurance by prohibiting insurers from denying basic coverage to individuals with preexisting conditions and bars them from charging higher rates to individuals based on their medical history. Lastly, the ACA requires almost all individuals to obtain minimum essential health insurance coverage, the so-called minimum coverage provision.

The court further explained the congressional findings accompanying the minimum coverage provision that requires almost all U.S. residents to maintain health insurance (thereby automatically enrolling virtually everyone in the United States into an insurance risk pool for medical coverage financed through broad-based premiums and tax subsidies for those unable to pay the premium costs). Ideally, under the ACA, the costs of illness and disease will be spread across an entire society as government and private health insurers pool the nation's health risks to help pay for everyone's health care expenses, especially for the increasing number of uninsured adults who are adversely affected by serious illness or injury.

The principle of **social solidarity** is key to reform of the nation's health insurance system, whereby health care is financed by individuals on the basis of their ability to pay, but is available to all who need health care on more or less equal terms. Social solidarity suggests that most Americans have a harmony of interests and responsibilities that are integral to living as a citizen of the United States, as opposed to alone as individuals with no interest in or ethical obligation to anyone other than themselves. In other words, Americans as a society have implicitly agreed to give up some personal autonomy in favor of the benefits to society at large.

—
— *Thomas More Law Center v. Obama*, 651 F.3d 529 (U.S. Court of Appeals for the 6th Circuit 2011) (holding the minimum coverage provision constitutional), *cert. denied*, 133 S.Ct. 61 (U.S. Supreme Court 2012), *related proceeding at United States Citizens Association, et al. v. Sebelius, et al.*, 754 F.Supp.2d 903 (U.S. District Court for the Northern District of Ohio 2010), *as amended* 2011 (holding that the Association's challenge was not barred). (*See Ethical or Unethical Decision* at the end of the chapter for discussion of this ethics issue.)

Introduction

Health care access is at the forefront of public concern. Despite the broad parameters of the ACA, consensus on how to move ahead with reforms remains elusive, and the landscape for health care in the United States continues to shift (Blumenthal, 2015; Wharton, 2011). Several questions remain unanswered, including how to expand access to affordable health insurance, what the potential minefields for doing so are, and what the best ways to ensure that the U.S. health care system performs well are (Lavizzo-Mourey, 2011). Meanwhile, Americans are becoming increasingly unhealthy, despite the fact that the United States spends more on health care per capita and in toto than any other nation.

Cost as Barrier to Accessible Health Care

The ethical principles that currently prevail for accessing health care in the United States do not provide for consistency in the way everyone is treated, as is required by most ethical theories. One challenge facing the nation is how much inequality in health care access a just society should tolerate (Powers & Faden, 2008). There is near-unanimous agreement that the lack of access to affordable health insurance is one of the principle shortcomings of the U.S. health system relative to health systems in other similar high-income, developed countries. Lack of universal access to medical coverage is believed to be the most significant contributor to the underperformance of the U.S. health care system in terms of broad population health measures, such as life expectancy (Schneider & Ohsfeldt, 2007).

Americans are simply not as healthy as they could and should be (Lavizzo-Mourey, 2011). As illustrated in **FIGURE 3-1**, about 39 million working-age Americans report cost as a barrier to receiving needed health care, a number that has been growing by an average of 1 million people annually over the past decade (DeNavas-Walt, et al., 2008; Kaiser Family Foundation, 2014). The uninsured of limited means experience the most consistent erosion in access, resulting in a widening gap in access to care between the insured and uninsured (Hoffman & Schwartz, 2008).

Basic Coverage for the Uninsured or Underinsured

One of the most intractable problems that has faced public policy makers for decades is how to provide health insurance to the millions of uninsured and underinsured in a way that is both effective and affordable. For more than half a century, there has been discussion about the fundamental question of how many households are uninsured and whether the uninsured are actually harmed due to lack of basic coverage (IOM, 2004). As illustrated in **FEATURE BOX 3-1**, today there appears to be a general consensus about who the uninsured are and why they are uninsured (Majerol, et al., 2015; Martinez & Cohen, 2015). What happens to the uninsured of limited means when they need health care or when the medical

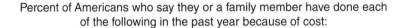

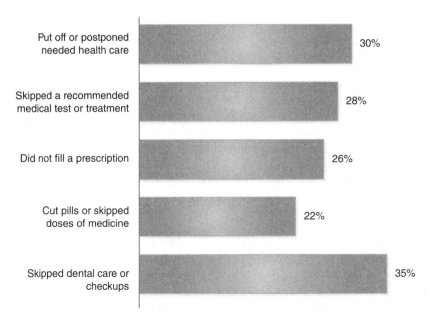

FIGURE 3-1 Lack of Access to Health Care

Sources: Commonwealth Fund, 2015; Kaiser & HRET, 2010.

FEATURE BOX 3-1

Facts About the Uninsured

- 7 in 10 uninsured adults cite unemployment or high costs as a major barrier to purchasing health insurance coverage, compared to 2 in 10 uninsured adults who say they are uninsured because they do not need basic coverage.
- Most of the uninsured are in a working family with low or moderate middle-class incomes (meaning a family of four earning less than $88,000/year) and cannot afford family premiums without employer contributions.
- 6 in 10 of the uninsured have at least one full-time worker in their family, while 2 in 10 have only part-time workers.
- Nearly three-quarters of the uninsured have been unemployed and uninsured for more than a year.
- Children are the least likely to be uninsured because they are more likely to qualify for government coverage through Medicaid or the Children's Health Insurance Program.

— Sources: AHRQ, 2015; CDC/NCHS 2015; Cohen, et al., 2011; Collins, et al., 2011; Kaiser, 2014 and 2015; Majerol, et al., 2015; Martinez & Cohen, 2015; SHADAC, 2011. Note: Includes adults under age 65 who are not eligible for Medicare insurance coverage.

---

expenses of the underinsured exceed their basic coverage and ability to pay for care is well documented (Kaiser Commission, 2011). Individuals who lack basic coverage decline or delay care, resulting in worse health outcomes (HHS, 2015; Levine, et al., 2007). Moreover, medical debt from being uninsured or underinsured continues to be the leading reason for personal bankruptcy (Kaiser Commission, 2011).

About 33 million Americans, or 1 in 10 people in the United States, have no health insurance (Carman, et al., 2015), and most of them have middle-class incomes (Kaiser, 2014; Singh, 2011). The uninsured population is not static; Americans fall into and out of medical coverage for various periods of time (Martinez & Cohen, 2015). The effect of having millions of uninsured people, however, is considerable (Ouellette, 2013). For instance, the uninsured risk serious illness or death by delaying necessary care. Lack of health insurance causes more than 45,000 unnecessary deaths every year (Wilper, et al., 2009).

Economics of the Uninsured

The purpose of health insurance is to pool risks in order to provide access to affordable health care for all insured. The insured pay into the insurance risk pool hoping they will never have to use their insurance. Everyone who pays into insurance risk pools is forced to pay higher health insurance premiums into the pools than they otherwise would because of cost-shifting and **adverse selection** in the health care and insurance markets (Siegel, 2011). Adverse selection occurs whenever price increases or reduced benefits make health insurance no longer price-effective, causing people with higher health risks to seek insurance to a greater extent than healthier people who are lower health risks.

For instance, it costs more to treat the uninsured when they become seriously ill as a result of a lack of routine, preventive care (Calvo, 2008; Majerol, et al., 2015). The uninsured usually postpone medical treatments until they are very ill. Once their medical needs can no longer be unattended, the uninsured often seek care from hospitals, because emergency departments are obligated by law to provide care regardless of ability to pay. Their **uncompensated care**, the sum of charitable care and bad debts, is then shifted from the uninsured to the insured. Thus, as the number of uninsured increases (Singh, 2011), so does the cost of health insurance to the insured, as providers shift costs to the insured for recoupment of uncompensated care. *See generally* CEA, 2009; Singleton, 2010.

As illustrated in **FIGURE 3-2**, as the costs of health care increase, health insurance premiums also increase, leading to the insured being underinsured (Russo, et al., 2007). As the costs of health insurance and health care increase, fewer employers continue to provide health insurance coverage to their employees, and those that do shift more of the cost to the employees themselves, without a corresponding increase in wages (Cancelosi, 2011). The end result of this cost-shifting is that the insured do not always have adequate medical coverage when a catastrophic injury or major illness hits, because they have lowered their level of coverage to what they can afford (Russo, et al., 2007).

Societal costs, in addition to the cost-shifting of uncompensated care for the uninsured, may take noneconomic forms such as a less productive workforce. Whether individual insurance mandates are effective in reducing societal costs is not always clear (Hoffman, 2010). What is clear is that the long-term uninsured of sufficient means who can afford health insurance but choose not to purchase medical coverage are shifting their share of the insurance risk pools to everyone else (AHIP, 2008). Estimates suggest that young adults comprised a large part of the voluntary opt-outs and numbered over 13 million before the ACA permitted them to remain on their parents' health insurance policies until they are 26 (CAHI, 2007). As illustrated in **FEATURE BOX 3-2**, less than 14 percent of young adults are now uninsured (Kovach & Gielau, 2012).

Spillover Effect of the Uninsured

While the health care costs of the uninsured, in terms of uncompensated care, are helping drive up overall costs, the spillover effect of not being insured is more disturbing (Collins, et al., 2006). The uninsured with chronic illnesses are less likely to receive appropriate care to manage their health conditions and have consistently worse clinical outcomes than do comparable insured patients (IOM, 2009). As illustrated in **FIGURE 3-3**, 1 percent of the U.S.

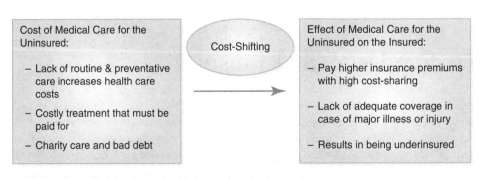

FIGURE 3-2 Cost-Shifting from the Uninsured to the Insured
Sources: Commonwealth Fund, 2015; Majerol, et al., 2015.

FEATURE BOX 3-2

Facts about Young Adults

- 1 in 5 young adults were uninsured before 2010, the highest rate of uninsured of any age group; today, about 1.8 million remain uninsured.
- Young adults have the lowest rate of access to employer-based insurance; the uninsured rate among employed young adults is one-third higher than older employed adults.
- 1 in 6 young adults suffers from a chronic illness like cancer, diabetes, or asthma.
- Nearly half of the uninsured young adults experience difficulties paying off their medical bills.

— Sources: DeCastro, 2011; DOL, 2012; Kenney & Pelletier, 2008. Note: As the young adult population under age 26 transitions into the job market, they often have entry-level jobs, part-time jobs, jobs in small businesses, or other employment that typically comes without employer-sponsored health insurance.

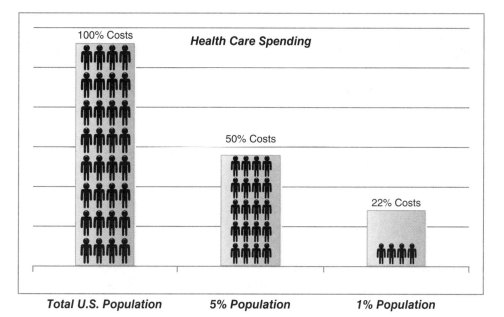

FIGURE 3-3 Disproportionate Health Care Spending
Sources: Majerol, et al., 2015; Martinez & Cohen, 2015; Zuvekas & Cohen, 2007.

population is responsible for about one-fourth of the nation's health care spending, and the top 5 percent accounted for half the spending (Zuvekas & Cohen, 2007). One widespread characteristic of this patient population is the seriousness and chronic nature of their illnesses. Moreover, their health conditions often arise from a general failure to receive preventive medical products or services and seek timely health care, two common attributes of being uninsured (Halpern, et al., 2008). As illustrated in **FEATURE BOX 3-3**, these hidden costs must be made more visible and better controlled.

Reframing Choices about Health Insurance

In seeking to address the challenge of insuring the uninsured, a multitude of different scenarios have been examined and tried over the past half-century (Bodenheimer & Grumbach, 2012). No matter what solutions are considered to address the uninsured, however, health risks always occupy center stage (Maher, 2011). The ethical controversy surrounding health risks is choosing which preferences should be used in designing medical interventions: who should decide what course of treatment is more desirable than another or who has the right to make the decision for others based upon such a view?

The Allocation of Health Risks

The allocation of health risks is a dominant force in the U.S. health care system (Hunter, 2008). Distribution of health care costs and access to affordable health insurance come up whenever health care is discussed. Most people do not necessarily use the term *health risks*

FEATURE BOX 3-3

Spillover Effect of Being Uninsured

- Mainly because of delayed diagnoses, uninsured cancer patients die sooner, on average, than comparable insured patients with breast, cervical, colorectal, or prostate cancer.
- Uninsured patients with diabetes are less likely to receive the recommended standard of care, which, over time, places them at risk for additional chronic disease and disability.
- Uninsured patients with hypertension or high cholesterol have less access to care, are unlikely to take medications, and experience worse health than those with health insurance.
- Uninsured HIV patients are more likely to forgo needed care, face greater delays in accessing appropriate care, are less likely to receive highly effective medications, and are less likely to be able to maintain a recommended treatment regimen over time.
- The uninsured with depression and anxiety disorders are less likely to receive mental health care consistent with clinical practice guidelines.
- Compared to insured patients, hospitalized individuals without insurance receive fewer needed services, worse quality care, and have a greater risk of resultant injuries or of dying in the hospital or shortly after discharge.

— Sources: CDC/NCHS, 2015; IOM Committee, 2009; Kaiser, 2014; Majerol, et al., 2015; Martinez & Cohen, 2015; SHADAC, 2011.

in the same way health insurance experts do, which is a fact that can potentially lead to less than optimal political decisions about health care (Wharton, 2007). The language that describes access to health insurance gets in the way of clear thinking and sometimes obscures quite different ways of thinking (Pauly, 2007).

There is no better example of this language confusion than discussion about the allocation of health risks. Debates about health risks often occur as if there were consensus on the allocation of health risks. But in reality, everyone in the room wants to distribute costs in a variety of ways, from giving priority to clinical decisions about the care needed to pooling health risks through insurance. Still others refer to trade-offs between the health risks and benefits of medical interventions, as illustrated in **FEATURE BOX 3-4**.

Philosophies Underlying the Affordable Care Act

Embedded in the controversy surrounding health care reform is the question of what ethical principles should guide the allocation of health risks in the U.S. health care system. In this instance, *health risks* are defined as the pooling of health care costs through the nation's insurance system (government and private insurers). While the most reasonable ethical principles are those that everyone accepts and agrees to from a position of fairness, there is no public consensus on what constitutes fairness. There is no disagreement that everyone should receive what is just and what will benefit them, it is just that there is no agreement on the details (Powers & Faden, 2008).

In attempting to identify the principles that give to others what they are due, no one has been more influential in this century than John Rawls (1921–2002) of Harvard University. Rawls is one of the leading contemporary figures in American legal philosophy. Frequently cited by the U.S. judiciary and in law review articles (more than 3,000 times according to the Westlaw research service), Rawls received the National Humanities Medal for his work, as illustrated in **FEATURE BOX 3-5**.

FEATURE BOX 3-4

Health Risks: Allocating the "What Ifs" of Human Health

- What future health care costs might arise?
- What will anyone's health be in the future?
- What are the odds of needing health insurance if healthy?
- What is the possibility that a serious injury from an accident might occur?
- What are the chances of being diagnosed with a serious illness?
- What are the possible health outcomes of medications or other medical treatments?
- What adverse side effects could occur from a complication of surgery or medical procedure?

— Sources: Pauly, 2007; Wharton, 2007.

FEATURE BOX 3-5

National Humanities Medal to John Rawls

"John Rawls is perhaps the greatest political philosopher of the 20th century . . . he wrote A Theory of Justice, *that placed our rights to liberty and justice upon a strong and brilliant new foundation of reason. Almost singlehandedly, John Rawls revived the disciplines of political and ethical philosophy with his argument that a society in which the most fortunate helped the least fortunate is not a moral society, but a logical one. Just as impressively, he has helped a whole generation of learned Americans revive their faith in democracy itself."*

— **William J. Clinton** (1946–), 42nd President of the United States

— Source: Clinton, 1999.

Distributive Justice

Distributive justice is concerned with what is fair and just with respect to the allocation of health risks (Rawls, 1971/2005 and 2001). Under this theory, if all U.S. residents were provided equal access to affordable health insurance, the U.S. health care system would be considered guided by the principles of distributive justice. Allocation of health risks would be a means to the desired goals of a fair and just health care system for everyone, as opposed to an end in itself. In other words, health insurance is not an appropriate and legitimate end in itself; it is simply the best means of affordable access to care (Hall, 2011). The focus on making access to affordable health insurance available for nearly everyone would require insurers to make a paradigm shift; their attention would shift to the welfare of discrete individuals. As opposed to focusing on managing groups contained within risk pools, insurers could focus their attention on managing individual health risks.

The medical needs of almost everyone are identical at the outset; hence, the allocation of health risks in terms of how risks are allocated to individuals is the same. As individual needs arise, however, fairness diverts from that of the highest welfare of all individuals. Fair and just distribution of health care resources is made on the basis of fairness to everyone. Distributive justice would allot health benefits and burdens among all U.S. residents; such distribution would be determined by the aggregate health risks, costs, and potential gains of everyone in society. This means that some individuals may not receive all the health care they require or desire because the cost would be too great to society as a whole. Injustice under this approach would involve unequal access to health care, as opposed to a lack of access to some extremely costly, and at times futile, health care, as well as decisions that would deny care to which individuals are entitled, but which fails to apportion burdens justly. *See generally* Beauchamp & Childress, 2012.

In this instance, equitable access to health care would be more than simply access to **emergency care** in situations that pose an immediate threat to health; it would also be access to care that is reasonable and necessary based on medical need that might have serious implications for continued health and well-being. In this case, what constitutes **reasonable and necessary care** is a socially determined allocation of health risks and insurance principles

ETHICAL DILEMMAS 3-1

1. While individuals are largely responsible for their own health, what is the most ethical way to efficiently promote social solidarity and the equitable distribution of health risks?

that pragmatically conforms to society's values. Reasonable and necessary care would not, therefore, be a utilitarian abstraction calling for across-the-board equity in the sense that what is done for one person is owed to all others in similar circumstances. Everyone should have a legitimate expectation for appropriate diagnoses and treatment to improve their health outcomes, which may at times include the best that modern medicine has to offer, but these decisions are part medical and part economic because they are predicated upon what necessary care is reasonable for society or members of an insurance risk pool to pay (AMA, 2012; Pagan, 2007).

Ethical Principle of Fairness to Everyone

The theoretical approach to health care reform is based on the ethical principle that inequalities should work to the benefit of everyone in society. A fair health care system provides access to health care to the healthiest people at the top of the socioeconomic pyramid as well as to people who are suffering the most from disease and illness and are poor and financially distressed. The question that must be asked of any reform is whether it benefits everyone. If it does, then it meets the test for fairness; otherwise, it does not. This policy approach is framed around two theories: the theory of social contracts and the theory of economic fairness.

Theory of Social Contracts

The preamble to the U.S. Declaration of Independence, as stated in **FEATURE BOX 3-6**, reflects a concise understanding of the social contract theory that underpinned the foundation of the original American government (Khan, 2010).

FEATURE BOX 3-6

The Nation's Social Contract

"We hold these truths to be self-evident, that all men are created equal, that they are endowed by their Creator with certain unalienable Rights, which among these are Life, Liberty and the pursuit of Happiness. That to secure these rights, Governments are instituted among Men, deriving their just powers from the consent of the governed."

— The Declaration of Independence, preamble (July 4, 1776).

In a just society, there is an unstated **social contract** between the governed and their government, implicit within which is the agreement that the governed have consented to be governed. The American social contract defines the scope of the U.S. Constitution. In 1965, the constitutional validity of government health insurance rested on whether Congress possessed the right to expand its Social Security legislation to include Medicare and Medicaid. In 2010, the constitutionality of the ACA rested on whether Congress possessed the right to further expand Medicaid and mandate that most individuals obtain health insurance.

A social contract implies that Americans give up some rights to their government in order to receive and jointly preserve social order, which is the theoretical groundwork of democracy (*see generally* Locke, 1689/2008; Rousseau, 1762/2009). For John Locke, the purpose of government is to serve and benefit the people; government must be controlled by the people for which the government was made. For Jean-Jacques Rousseau, citizens of a nation place themselves and their authority under the supreme direction of the general will, and the group receives each individual as an indivisible part of the whole. Rousseau conceived the public interest as a norm about the collective good that is distinct from the sum of individual interests. Self-interest uniting for a nation's common good, and the submission of the individual to government by social contract, inform the heart of democracy and stand as the most contentious component of health care reform today. The **common good** is achieved when the burdens and benefits of life function together to achieve a sustainable society; it includes the things Americans commit to do as a society that benefit all U.S. residents.

Governments have an egalitarian socially contracted obligation to provide access to health care (Rawls, 1971/2005), a belief that is shared by the majority of the citizens in every democracy in the world (Sage, 2008). **Egalitarianism**, in this instance, is based on equality, human dignity, and a belief that everyone is, in principle, equal and should enjoy equal access to health care. Through the advent of modern medicine, universal access to health care is vital to ensuring that all U.S. residents have equal opportunity to achieve "Life, Liberty, and the Pursuit of Happiness" (Starr, 1983). Today, access to health care is considered by many to be a right of citizenship (Hoffman, 2010). This text is about the parameters of this social contract and how it is developing in the United States.

Ethics of the Minimum Coverage Provision

By the logic of the theory of **economic fairness**, which is integral to the theory of social contracts, the minimum coverage provision requiring that everyone obtain and maintain health insurance, if successful at redistribution of the costs of health risks, might affirm a conception of insurance as a social institution where everyone shares collectively in the economic burden of health risks (Fehr & Schmidt, 2006). Thus, by collectivizing risk among nearly all U.S. residents and providing, in return, affordable access for everyone when in need of care, it is possible to conceive that the minimum coverage provision might catalyze a more solidarity-focused approach to health insurance (AHIP, 2008). Over time, the combined interests and responsibilities in health care, especially support for universal access to care, might increase public confidence in and legitimacy for health insurance laws that are dependent on the fair redistribution of the costs associated with health risks (Hoffman, 2010).

Public legitimacy is an important requirement for the minimum coverage provision to work. In this instance, **public legitimacy** is defined as public confidence in and support for the minimum coverage provision law that can arise from the way the mandate is to be implemented, the extent to which the law responds to public wishes, whether it succeeds in satisfying public expectations for access to affordable health care, and whether the health reforms related to the minimum coverage provision respect human rights (Katz, 2010). With public legitimacy, reform of the U.S. health care system is enhanced; without it, there is public resistance to getting things done, if they get done at all.

Theory of Economic Fairness

Considerations of economic fairness have not been prominent in the making of health insurance policies. The explanations are numerous and include the difficulty of tracking the costs and benefits of insuring against health risks and the inability of health economists to make regulatory recommendations regarding fairness. Moreover, Congress and state legislatures generally ignore or mask the insurance consequences of distribution policies related to health risks. The history of health care reform shows that it would be unusual, and confusing, to regulate health insurance solely on considerations of distributive justice or economic fairness considerations (Kleinbard, 2008). For instance, the debate about permitting health insurers to take genetic information into account or to ignore genetic information does not address the issue of how to allocate the costs for purely genetically determined diseases (Logue & Avraham, 2003). There are, nevertheless, numerous opportunities in which distributive justice can be combined with the goals of economic fairness.

In making any ethical decision, the essential question must always be whether this is fair and whether it makes economic sense (Rawls, 2001). In this instance, in ensuring that all U.S. residents are able to access affordable health insurance, the theory of economic fairness is that there can be no fairness if something does not make economic sense. Wherever one ends up in society, one wants the transactions that affect one's life to be reasonably just and comprehensible. The activities in one's life should be conducted according to fair and socially acceptable rules that are in accordance with what is expected.

A Theoretical Framework Based on John Rawls's Political Philosophy

Health care decisions should be supported by a set of principled rationales that can be generalized to the reform process (Berkman, 2009). In addressing access to affordable health insurance, one ethical framework, based on John Rawls's political philosophy, is illustrated in **FEATURE BOX 3-7.**

Equality of Health Opportunities

While Americans have decided to act collectively so that everyone can access health care when in need, regardless of income or health status, adoption of the equality of opportunity principle is not the same as mandating that every U.S. resident have access to exactly the same health care. Achieving this level of equality would offend American notions of individual autonomy and responsibility. Nonetheless, access to affordable health insurance coverage will be guaranteed wherever an individual is on the socioeconomic pyramid, but there will always be freedom to pursue additional health care based on the ability to pay fair value for that care. *See generally* Rawls, 1971/2005.

Theoretical Framework for Health Care Reform Based on John Rawls's Political Philosophy

First Principle: Universal Health Insurance

- All U.S. residents have an equal claim to access affordable health insurance.
- The means to access this health care must be the same for everyone.
- Each person is free to select the health care system and providers for their health care.
- Health care providers are guaranteed to receive fair value for services provided.

Second Principle: Pooled Health Risks

- Inequalities brought about by the inability to pay fair value for health care are permissible if the following two conditions are met:
  - Affordable health insurance must be accessible to all U.S. residents based on fairness; in other words, access to health care must be based on medical need and equality of opportunity.
  - The greatest assistance to access affordable health insurance must be given to the least advantaged.

— Source: Rawls, 1971/2005.

ETHICAL DILEMMAS 3-2

2. Although 9 out of 10 Americans are able to maintain health insurance (HHS, 2015), should *all* lives have equal value when allocating the distribution of health risks?
3. Should the ability to pay, as opposed to medical need, be the predominant criterion for access to health care?
4. Should all Americans be entitled to access affordable health insurance because they are a part of the nation, or should they only be entitled to the level of health insurance corresponding to their work and contributions to the nation?

Hierarchy of Ethical Principles

The fox knows many things, a Greek poet said, but the hedgehog knows one big thing (Dworkin, 2011). The fox, the analogy goes, views the world through many lenses of experience, while the hedgehog views the world through a single defining lens. The one big thing, when it comes to ethical principles, is how people are treated. Ethical principles have a fairly definite hierarchy on the basis of their relative strength and effectiveness in protecting human or fundamental rights, as well as individual rights (Beck, 2007). Most Americans accept certain fundamental principles, the most important of which is the belief that each human life has a special kind of objective value (Dworkin, 2008). In the United States, it is a given that the value of human equality and dignity should not change as long as the U.S. Constitution is in place.

In addressing access to and payment for health care, the hierarchy of ethical principles developed by Rawls is one theoretical framework underlying the ACA (Rubin, 2012). The first principle, of equal access to affordable health insurance, is the ground layer of the hierarchy upon which all other principles are based. Access to health insurance has priority over the second principle of pooling health risks. In other words, the right to health care has a greater weight than the cost of the care. The ability to pay fair value for health care has priority over the subsidies provided to access the needed care. *See generally* Rawls, 1971/2005.

The Relationship between Ethical Principles and Their Application

Ethical principles and their application are two distinct but related issues. The ethical principles underlying universal access to health insurance are not validated or invalidated by the nation's ability or inability to apply them. Just because the U.S. health care system cannot equally apply all the ethical principles does not mean the ethical principles are not valid (Beauchamp & Childress, 2012).

If all the ethical principles were applied perfectly and if the United States could find a way to pay for health care without any limitations, there would be no inequalities. If the United States had the ability to pay for every medical technology and every medication needed by every U.S. resident, inequalities of access to health care would not exist (CBO, 2008a). Essentially, if the United States had unlimited resources, there would be no inequalities.

However, the United States does not have the financial resources to pay for everything. The scarcity of resources for health care mandates that available financial resources be maximized (Levine, et al., 2007). Thus, the nation must decide what type of health risks should be covered by basic health insurance so that nearly everyone in society can access some level of health care (AMA, 2012). For instance, should everyone with prescription drug coverage be entitled to access the newest branded medications without **cost-sharing**, or payment of deductibles and co-payments, if generic alternatives or older branded medications are available at a fraction of the cost? Or should all branded medications be available only with higher cost-sharing by patients with basic coverage?

While there is no public consensus as to the ethicality of setting a limit on the total amount basic coverage insurance will pay, whether ethical or unethical, limits are an economic and political necessity arising out of reality. No society can devote unlimited resources to health care; therefore, restraining costs is also an ethical obligation (Levine, et al., 2007). Some health experts maintain that $1.4 trillion in funding could open up if the overused, underused, misused, and ineffective treatments could be monitored and reduced with adherence to evidence-based medicine (*e.g.*, Todd, 2011; RAND, 2006). Others maintain that cost savings could reach $1.8 trillion if unhealthy behavioral practices, safety and quality errors, and needless administrative and regulatory costs were also reduced (*e.g.*, Fisher, et al., 2009; Harris, 2011; Skinner, et al., 2011).

ETHICAL DILEMMAS 3-3

5. Should the decision to provide universal access to affordable health insurance be based on an ethical obligation to the nation's most vulnerable members (the principles of distributive justice) and on the nation's character, or should the nation simply base its policies on a self-interest rationale?

The Ethics of Managing Health Risks

The ethics of risk pooling practices by the health insurance industry raise more controversial questions than any other subject in this chapter. The ethical controversy surrounding health risk pooling arises out of the determination of which preferences to use in designing medical interventions (Wharton, 2007). By definition, health risks involve uncertainty. Uncertainty makes people uneasy. It is not simply that people do not like bad health outcomes; rather, they do not like not knowing what the outcome will be (Pauly, 2007). In the achievement of health and the use of health care, health risks seem to be everywhere at once. To complicate matters, consumers of health care often inaccurately predict health risks when selecting a health insurance plan or when they are deciding among various medications or treatment options (Wharton, 2007). For instance, consumers of health care may purchase a high-deductible health insurance plan to reduce premium costs, but then find they are unable to meet their deductible and co-payment costs when faced with a catastrophic illness or accident.

Spectrum from Actuarial Fairness to Social Solidarity

As debate about health insurance continues to center on how to allocate health care resources, the apexes of this debate swing from social solidarity to actuarial fairness principles (Hurwitz, 2009). These two principles represent two opposing endpoints along the spectrum of possible approaches to the allocation of health risks (Ericson & Doyle, 2003). The solution to more equitable allocation of health risks is likely somewhere between these two endpoints: one that embraces both principles of social solidarity and actuarial fairness.

At one end of the spectrum is the social solidarity approach, which would spread health risks across the population of almost all U.S. residents, also known as *community rating* (Kaiser, 2011). Everyone would have the same access to affordable health insurance. Under the solidarity principle, almost all U.S. residents would be entitled to health insurance on equal terms, no matter their health status or ability to pay, with allocation of health resources based on medical needs (Hurwitz, 2009). Opponents maintain that social solidarity is unfair because the healthy would be subsidizing the not-so-healthy (Stone, 2008).

At the other end of the spectrum is the actuarial fairness approach, an endpoint that is banned under the ACA. **Actuarial fairness** creates segmented risk pools based on the health risks generalized to specific individuals. Enrollment rules and premiums are adjusted according to the individual's projected health care costs (Kaiser, 2011). Some individuals may be considered uninsurable (with no guaranteed-issue insurance available at any cost due to preexisting health conditions), whereas others are underinsured with disproportionately high premiums based on their health status, and still others are charged disproportionately high premiums based on presumptive health risks that are not accurate as to those individuals. Actuarial fairness does not consider the social consequences of health insurance or the allocation of health resources; instead it sets premiums in proportion to expected future costs (Hurwitz, 2009). Opponents maintain that actuarial fairness results in untenable avoidance of health risks as opposed to management of risks. Moreover, the insurance industry selectively segmented or avoided certain health conditions and treatments through basic coverage limitations, exclusions, and high cost-sharing. *See generally* Goldberg & Camic, 2009.

The ACA is based on the premise that Americans have the right to have their health risks properly managed (CBO, 2008a; Ericson & Doyle, 2003). Government and the private insurance industry have a **moral imperative** to deliver an equitable risk pooling system because it is the right and ethical thing to do (*see, e.g.,* Fehr & Schmidt, 2006; Lavizzo-Mourey, 2011; Levine, et al., 2007). While it is debatable how this imperative will be accomplished, an equitable risk system must be established to share societal resources, regardless of opposition or difficulty (Powers & Faden, 2008; Dworkin, 2011). An equitable insurance risk pooling system covering all U.S. residents is an unavoidable ethical obligation that should be in the nation's best self-interest (Khan, 2010). Ethical management of health risks would act collectively for both the public's own self-interest as well as social solidarity (Buhay, 2010; Hunter, 2008). Health insurance premiums would be indexed to one's efforts to maintain one's health (evidenced by healthy lifestyles with a focus on non-smoking and weight management, adherence to treatment plans, and active self-management focused on preventive care) as opposed to their actual health status (Hurwitz, 2009). In other words, premiums would depend upon how responsible a consumer of health care the insured is. *See generally* Rawls, 1971/2005.

Before the ACA, the nation's approach to risk pooling for the non-Medicare insured effectively increased the odds that those who were in poor health status would be uninsured or underinsured (Goldberg & Camic, 2009), a situation that is increasingly indefensible and unsustainably expensive. Preexisting conditions were not always covered by health insurance if there was a change in employment status; rather, preexisting conditions were only covered following a year or more of continuous coverage following a change in employers or a period of unemployment. In the interim, out-of-pocket costs for medical expenses could be prohibitively expensive (IOM, 2009). In other instances, when people became sick, they would suddenly find substantial increases in their health insurance premiums, leading many Americans to become underinsured as they sought more affordable coverage when they most needed access to quality health care (Collins, et al., 2011; Majerol, et al., 2015).

In exchange for near-universal compulsory enrollment in insurance plans under the ACA, the health insurance industry agreed to address how to best differentiate among virtually the entire U.S. population in exposing individuals to financial risks associated with health care (Stone, 2008). This approach is compatible with the solidarity principle's understanding that all U.S. residents should have reasonable access to health care no matter their ability to pay; at the same time, it is responsive to the principle of actuarial fairness that health care costs be allocated to those expected to cause them (Hurwitz, 2009).

ETHICAL DILEMMAS 3-4

6. From an ethical point of view, should tax subsidies to maintain access to basic insurance coverage vary according to economic status or health risks?

The Ethics of Limited-Benefit Health Insurance Plans

Although most health insurance plans offer basic coverage for inpatient hospitalization, some insurers offer low-premium plans that cover some outpatient services, which are more likely to be needed, while leaving less likely but far more expensive hospital costs uncovered or only partially covered, known as **limited-benefit health insurance**. Although this type of health insurance plan could reduce treatments of minimal value, consumers of health care face higher cost-sharing or tighter control of their health care (CBO, 2008). While perhaps appealing, this approach is problematic from an ethical, as well as an economic, standpoint (Wharton, 2007). Even though the risk of requiring a hospitalization is less likely than requiring a physician's visit, everyone should be protected against hospital costs because of their much higher consequences to an individual's or family's economic health (Pauly, 2007).

Though consumers of health care with less extensive coverage may be treated fairly from an economic perspective with low premiums, they are not being treated fairly in terms of access to basic coverage. Banned under the ACA, limited-benefit health insurance is described as a perfect storm: a term describing what happens when a certain confluence of health risks occurs that causes a financial disaster or bankruptcy for the insured as a result of being underinsured (Wharton, 2007). Consumer advocates call limited-benefit plans junk because of all their exclusions and limitations (Oechsner & Schaler-Haynes, 2011).

Clearly, there is consensus that limited-benefit plans, with large holes in the health insurance safety net and inadequate basic coverage, are not optimal insurance products. At the same time, employers who are struggling to shoulder the high costs of health insurance for their employees are in a quandary when they shift the health insurance burden to their employees by offering them limited-benefit plans. With limited-benefit plans now banned under the ACA, employers are forced to pay more for employer-provided health insurance that covers health care, and some may have to shift the increased costs to their employees.

The Unfortunate Realities of Health Risks

Misperceptions about health risks affect the debate about how to best provide basic coverage for the uninsured and underinsured. In the United States, it is hard to override public misperceptions, especially misperceptions about health risks (Pauly, 2007). For instance, there is debate on whether the young and the healthy, nicknamed "the invincibles," should subsidize the old and the not-so-healthy. Yet it is time to acknowledge that traditional **indemnity health insurance** that is **fee-for-service** (paying for whatever health care a physician recommends) and allows unlimited choice of providers has transformed itself from a **risk-spreading** product, where the insurance provider assumes the risk-taking for all costs, to a **managed care** product that administers health care. Managed care applies utilization review

---

ETHICAL DILEMMAS 3-5

7. Should the federal government help ensure that consumers of health care do not seriously underestimate their health risks, or should everyone maintain the liberty and individual freedom to purchase the health insurance coverage they themselves determine they may need?

8. With the consequences of being underinsured well documented, should limited-benefit plans continue to be outlawed because they shift costs away from the insurance industry to the underinsured and society?

techniques to control the risks and losses for the health care it covers. As such, cost-sharing for health care costs is rapidly becoming the norm (Morreim, 2008).

High-Risk Individuals with Chronic Conditions

Although states are debating whether to place limitations upon enrollment in Medicaid, such as maintenance of a healthy weight, not smoking, and not misusing medications, there is little relationship between individual health risks and health insurance premiums in the private insurance market (Wharton, 2007). The insurance industry attempts to segment health risks, and some high-risk individuals may pay more than their healthy counterparts, although the segmentation has never worked when applied to the total insured population (Jost, 2007). People whose anticipated health expenses are twice the average person's pay premiums only about 20 to 40 percent higher than other, healthier people (Wharton, 2007). The result of these market forces is that the health insurance premiums paid by those with chronic conditions are not consistently greater than those paid by healthy people.

Administration Costs and Industry Profits (Net Revenue)

Before the ACA, for every dollar spent on private health insurance, 30 to 40 cents went toward administration costs and investment return to shareholders. For Medicare, an estimated 97 cents of each dollar is put toward actual health care (Wharton, 2007a; *cf.* Shorter, 2010 (citing a survey of insurance and medical executives which revealed that administration expenses alone constituted 30 percent of costs)). Private health insurance is too expensive, not because the insurance industry increases premiums for high risks, but because of the steep administrative costs and demand for billions of dollars in profits, approaching $90 billion annually (SEC, 2011).

Individuals at all health risk levels are being charged premiums that are too high relative to the benefits they get back in actual care (Pauly, 2007). The industry maintains that its high administrative costs arise because their risk pools are expensive to administer (Wharton, 2007). Others point to the insurance industry's profit margins (Shorter, 2010) and the millions spent each year in executive salaries (SEC, 2011). Unfortunately, faced with high premium prices, people with the greatest need of insurance are the ones who are the most often unable to afford it.

Wasteful Health Insurance Regulation

The debate confronting health care reform revolves around individual rights and the proper role of government in the health insurance market (*compare* Donatucci, 2010 (proponent of comprehensive federal reform), *with* Leonard, 2010 (proponent of incremental state-based reforms)). An overriding issue is whether federal and state insurance regulators can regulate how government funds are being spent by insurance companies, that is, private, for-profit enterprises that are unable, or unwilling, to provide health insurance at an affordable rate

ETHICAL DILEMMAS 3-6

9. Ethically speaking, should the federal government mandate that the health insurance industry reduce its administration costs and standardize its underwriting procedures, or should market forces be relied upon to self-regulate the insurance industry?

(Kinney, 2010). The United States spends a greater percentage of its gross domestic product (GDP) on health care than any other industrialized country (Angrisano, et al., 2007), and its system of insurance regulation is partly to blame for this high level of spending (Hoffman, 2010). As illustrated in **FIGURE 3-4**, more than three-fifths of the nation's health care spending is misallocated.

While the federal government regulates nearly all employer-sponsored insurance coverage, states retain the power to regulate insurance contracts issued to their residents. As a result, employers who purchase insurance to cover their health plan benefits are subject to both federal and state regulation, whereas employers who self-insure are exempt from all state insurance regulations and subject to only minimal federal regulations. Although the American federal system allows for (if not encourages) variation among the states, market inefficiencies skew the quality and pricing of health insurance when employers are subject to 50 different state-based regulatory systems (Oechsner & Schaler-Haynes, 2011). This division of regulatory authority greatly inhibits efforts to reform and expand health insurance (Kinney, 2010).

For instance, while all states regulate health insurance, most states do not have standardized benefit choices, and before the ACA, there were no national minimum standards. States weighed benefit flexibility and choice, on the one hand, and benefit standardization and uniformity, on the other hand. Before the ACA, markets in most states reflected an assortment of confusing benefit choices that contributed to market inefficiencies and consumer underinsurance. *See generally* Oechsner & Schaler-Haynes, 2011.

Individual and Employer Mandates to Provide Health Insurance

A growing number of state and local governments are experimenting with universal health insurance, a feature that was adopted by the ACA. The similarity is that most of these states have mandates requiring individuals to maintain basic coverage and employers to provide

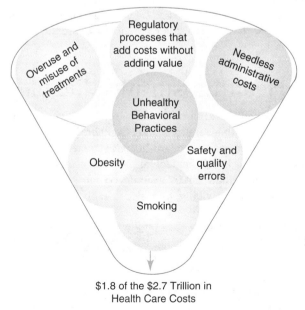

$1.8 of the $2.7 Trillion in Health Care Costs

FIGURE 3-4 $1.8 Trillion Bucket of Misallocated Spending

Sources: Harris, 2011; IOM, 2004; PricewaterhouseCoopers, 2008; Skinner, et al., 2011.

adequate levels of health insurance for their employees. Individual and employer mandates, based on the principle of social solidarity, are now a staple of all comprehensive health care reform discussions (Young, 2010). In a recent reform, the mayor of San Francisco and the city's Board of Supervisors asked everyone to act together to provide access to affordable health insurance to an estimated 80,000 residents who were previously uninsured, roughly half of whom worked.

ETHICS CASE
Fair Share Health Care Reform Measures

Golden Gate Restaurant Association v. City and County of San Francisco, et al.
[Employers v. Local Municipality]
546 F.3d 639 (U.S. Court of Appeals for the 9th Circuit 2008),
cert. denied, 130 S.Ct. 3497 (U.S. Supreme Court 2010)

Facts: In San Francisco, where 10 percent of the city's residents had no health insurance and 15 percent of businesses provided no health insurance coverage for their employees, the Board of Supervisors passed the San Francisco Health Care Security Ordinance to fund a network of primary care services for uninsured residents. While the ordinance met with general approval, its provision mandating contributions from local businesses that did not meet minimum health spending requirements was the subject of litigation.

The ordinance created a Health Access Program designed to make health care available to the city's more than 80,000 uninsured residents. Funding for the program, which provides primary care for the uninsured at both public and private facilities throughout the city, comes from mandatory contributions from businesses that do not meet designated health care contribution levels for their employees; municipal, state, and federal government grants; and payments from individual enrollees.

Employers can meet the required contribution levels in a variety of ways: contributing to employee health savings accounts; donating to the city's new health access program; paying a third party for health care delivery for their employees; or reimbursing their employees directly for their health care expenses. Such provisions are often called "Fair Share" because employers must either help pay for public health care programs or pay by providing their employees with health insurance themselves. Golden Gate Restaurant Association, representing the interests of more than 800 San Francisco restaurants, brought an action challenging the ordinance. The Association claimed that federal law preempted the ordinance.

Legal Analysis: The court concluded that the public interest would be best served by allowing the ordinance to go forward in its entirety. The court emphasized that there was a presumption against **federal preemption** when laws fall within the state's traditional police power to regulate health and safety. In addition, while employers would face an administrative burden in the form of required record maintenance, the court noted this burden fell equally on employers who had plans regulated by ERISA and those who did not.

Rule of Law: The spending requirements of San Francisco's Fair Share ordinance do not establish employer-sponsored health insurance plans, nor do they conflict with employer-sponsored health insurance plans regulated by ERISA.

Ethics Issue: Should federal law preempt a local Fair Share ordinance unanimously supported by the City of San Francisco based on the principle of social solidarity?

Ethics Analysis: The court focused on what would best serve the public interest and concluded that the public would be best served by allowing the ordinance to go forward in its entirety. While the value of social solidarity was regularly invoked in support of the ordinance, the court expressed confidence in the ordinance's political legitimacy, since the San Francisco Board of Supervisors passed the ordinance unanimously with support of the mayor. The court further concluded that federal courts should exercise their power with proper regard for the rightful independence of local governments in carrying out their domestic policies to help create security for everyone.

Court's Holding and Decision: No, federal law does not preempt San Francisco's Fair Share ordinance.

See, e.g., Diller, 2012; Hermer & Lenihan, 2014; Hoffman, 2014; Sanford, 2014 (discussing this court decision).

ETHICAL DILEMMAS 3-7

10. Can individual and employer mandates (if able to achieve broad health risk redistribution and provide nearly everyone affordable access to health insurance) expand legitimacy for the notion of collectivizing health risks in the name of more equitable access to health care, or should government take a less proactive but more incremental role to achieve the same goal?

Challenges of Access to Health Care

Economically speaking, the United States could no longer afford to maintain its fragmented delivery of health care or entertain reforms that sought to patch, as opposed to cure, a fractured system that denied access to 1 in 6 Americans (Emanuel & Fuchs, 2008; Emanuel, 2014). Arguments against health care reform present the uninsured and underinsured as being responsible for their own lack of health insurance, emphasizing self-interest more than economic arguments about market conditions that make basic coverage less available to anyone with serious or chronic illnesses. As stated in FEATURE BOX 3-8, however, the moral case for health care reform is far easier to understand (Lynch & Gollust, 2010 (citing Obama)).

FEATURE BOX 3-8

Ethical Justification for Health Care Reform

"While the explicit ethical justification is that health reform is decisive for the nation's future prosperity, health care is above all an ethical issue; at stake are not just the details of policy, but fundamental principles of social justice and the nation's character . . . ."

— **Edward M. Kennedy** (1932–2009), U.S. Senator from Massachusetts

— Sources: Lynch & Gollust, 2010; Obama, 2009.

ETHICAL OR UNETHICAL DECISION

Access to Health Care:

Ethics Issue: *Should most Americans be required to maintain health insurance (and thereby participate in a health insurance risk pool), as an imperative of national health care reform based upon the ethical principles of human equality and social solidarity?*

Ethics Analysis: Yes, Congress found that uncompensated health care for the uninsured cost over $43 billion/year, costs that are shifted to others through higher health insurance premiums; this cost-shifting increases family premiums by an average of more than $1,000/year (ACA, 42 U.S.C. §18001 et seq. (2010)).

Ethics Analysis: No, if some Americans never access the health care market or are fully capable of paying for any health care they consume, they should not be compelled to purchase health insurance. Congress has no power to regulate inactivity.

Court's Holding and Decision: The ACA's requirement that most Americans maintain health insurance falls within Congress's constitutional authority over interstate commerce. Everyone will access health care at some point, whether voluntary or not, and therefore the question is how to pay for it.

— *Thomas More Law Center v. Obama*, 651 F.3d 529 (U.S. Court of Appeals for the 6th Circuit 2011) (holding the minimum coverage provision constitutional), *cert. denied*, 133 S.Ct. 61 (U.S. Supreme Court 2012), *related proceeding at United States Citizens Association, et al. v. Sebelius, et al.*, 754 F.Supp.2d 903 (U.S. District Court for the Northern District of Ohio 2010), *as amended* 2011 (holding that the Association's challenge was not barred). *Compare Mead, et al. v. Holder, et al.*, 766 F.Supp.2d 16 (U.S. District Court for the District of Columbia 2011) (holding the minimum coverage provision constitutional), *affirmed*, 661 F.3d 1 (U.S. Court of Appeals for the D.C. Circuit 2011), *with Virginia ex rel. Cuccinelli v. Sebelius, et al.*, 656 F.3d 253 (U.S. Court of Appeals for the 4th Circuit 2011) (dismissing Virginia's challenge to the minimum coverage provision for lack of standing), *cert. denied*, 133 S.Ct. 59 (U.S. Supreme Court 2012). *See also National Federation of Independent Business, et al. v. Sebelius, et al.* and *Florida, et al. v. U.S. Department of Health and Human Services, et al.*, 648 F.3d 1235 (U.S. Court of Appeals for the 11th Circuit 2011), *affirmed in part and reversed in part*, 132 S.Ct. 2566 (U.S. Supreme Court 2012) (holding the minimum coverage provision and the entire legislation constitutional, except the mandated expansion of the Medicaid program).

See also Blumstein, 2014; Grover, 2011; Kahn, 2014; Leonard, 2012; Maher, 2011; Pratt, 2011; Moncrieff, 2013; Record, 2012; Somin, 2014; Willis & Chung, 2012 (discussing this court decision). *Compare* Barnett, 2010 (arguing that the minimum coverage provision is unconstitutional), *with* Tribe, 2011 (arguing that the minimum coverage provision is constitutional).

CHAPTER SUMMARY

- While access to health care is at the forefront of public concern, especially the matter of how much inequality in care a just society can tolerate, one of the most intractable problems facing the U.S. health care system is how to provide affordable health insurance to the millions of uninsured and underinsured in a way that is fair and equitable to everyone.
- The economics of the uninsured are unfair, since everyone who pays into insurance risk pools is forced to pay higher health insurance premiums because it costs more to treat the uninsured and underinsured when they face catastrophic injuries or become seriously ill.

- Health providers and the insurance industry do not necessarily use the term *health risks* in the same way, which can lead to less than optimally ethical decisions about patient care.
- Distributive justice is concerned with what is fair and just with respect to the allocation of health risks and is based on the ethical principle that inequalities should work to the benefit of everyone in society.
- In a just society, there is an unstated social contract between the governed and their government which implies that Americans give up some rights to their government in order to receive and jointly preserve social order; in this instance, the government has a social contract to provide access to affordable health insurance, an egalitarian belief that is shared by the majority of the citizens in every democracy in the world.
- In making any ethical decision, the essential questions must always be whether it is fair and whether it makes economic sense.
- Adoption of the equality of opportunity principle is not mandating that every U.S. resident have access to exactly the same health care; it is mandating that everyone have the opportunity to access essential care so they can achieve and maintain high levels of health, which are necessary for a lifetime of well-being and human dignity, as well as continuing contribution to society.
- Most Americans accept certain fundamental principles, the most important of which is the belief that each human life has a special kind of objective value.
- Actuarial fairness and social solidarity are two principles representing two opposing endpoints along the spectrum of possible approaches to the allocation of health risks.
- While consumers of health care with limited-benefit health insurance plans may be treated fairly from an economic perspective with low premiums, they are not being treated fairly in terms of access to basic coverage.

REFERENCES

AHIP (America's Health Insurance Plans). (2008). *Press release: Health plans propose guaranteed coverage for pre-existing conditions and individual coverage mandate.* Washington, DC: AHIP.

AHRQ (Agency for Healthcare Research and Quality). (2015). *Healthcare cost and utilization project.* Rockville, MD: Department of Health and Human Services, AHRQ.

AMA (American Medical Association). (2012). *The ethical force program: Advancing ethics in health care.* Chicago, IL: AMA.

Angrisano, C., et al. (2007). *A framework to guide health care system reform.* San Francisco, CA: McKinsey Global Institute.

Barnett, R. (2010, April 29). Editorial: The insurance mandate in peril. *Wall Street Journal*, p. A19.

Beauchamp, T. L., & Childress, J. F. (2012). *Principles of biomedical ethics* (7th ed.). New York, NY: Oxford University Press.

Beck, G. (2007). The idea of human rights between value pluralism and conceptual vagueness. *Penn State International Law Review, 25*, 615–657.

Berkman, B. E. (2009). Incorporating explicit ethical reasoning into pandemic influenza policies. *Journal of Contemporary Health Law and Policy, 26*, 1–19.

Blumenthal, D., et al. (2015). The Affordable Care Act at five. *New England Journal of Medicine, 372*(25), 2451–2458.

Blumstein, J. F. (2014). Understanding the faulty predictions regarding the challenges to health reform. *University of Illinois Law Review, 2014*, 1251–1263.

Bodenheimer, T., & Grumbach, K. (2012). *Understanding health policy: A clinical approach* (6th ed.). New York, NY: McGraw-Hill Medical.

Buhay, M. (2010). A prescription for a public health approach to regulating the pharmaceutical industry's right to market and sell its products. *Journal of Health Care Law and Policy, 13*, 459–493.

CAHI (Council for Affordable Health Insurance). (2007). *Understanding the uninsured and what to do about them.* Washington, DC: CAHI.

Calvo, J. M. (2008). The consequences of restricted health care access for immigrants: Lessons from Medicaid and SCHIP. *Annals of Health Law, 17*, 175–212.

Cancelosi, S. E. (2011). The bell is tolling: Retiree health benefits post-health reform. *Elder Law Journal, 19*, 49–118.

Carman, K. G., et al. (2015). Trends in health insurance enrollment. *Health Affairs, 34*, 2013–2015.

CBO (Congressional Budget Office). (2008). *Technological change and the growth of health care spending.* Washington, DC: CBO.

___. (2008a). *Key issues in analyzing major health insurance proposals.* Washington, DC: CBO.

CDC/NCHS (Centers for Disease Control and National Center for Health Statistics). (2015). *National health interview survey.* Atlanta: GA: CDC/NCHS.

CEA (Council of Economic Advisers). (2009). *The economic case for health care reform.* Washington, DC: The White House, Executive Office of the President.

Clinton, W. J. (1999, September 29). Remarks at the September 29, 1999, presentation of the National Humanities Medal to John Rawls at The White House, Washington, DC.

Cohen, R. A., et al. (2011). *Health insurance coverage: Early release of estimates from the National Health Interview Survey.* Hyattsville, MD: Centers for Disease Control, National Center for Health Statistics.

Collins, S. R., et al. (2011). *Help on the horizon: How the recession has left millions of workers without health insurance, and how health reform will bring relief.* New York, NY: Commonwealth Fund.

___. (2006). *Squeezed: Why rising exposure to health costs threatens the health and financial well-being of American families.* New York, NY: Commonwealth Fund.

DeCastro, P. J. (2011). Health coverage for young adults: Tax incentives for extending health coverage to children under age 27 as amended by the Affordable Care Act. *Journal of Contemporary Health Law and Policy, 28*, 86–110.

DeNavas-Walt, C., et al. (20). *Income, poverty and health insurance coverage in the United States.* Washington, DC: U.S. Census Bureau.

Diller, P. A. (2012). The city and the private right of action. *Stanford Law Review, 64*, 1109–1172.

DOL (U.S. Department of Labor). (2012). *Fact sheet: Young adults and the Affordable Care Act: Protecting young adults and eliminating burdens on families and businesses.* Washington, DC: DOL, Employee Benefits Service Administration.

Donatucci, L. (2010). Current issues in public policy: Federal regulation of the insurance industry: One for all and all for who? How federal regulation would help the industry into the new millennia. *Rutgers Journal of Law and Public Policy, 7*, 398–441.

Dworkin, R. (2011). *Justice for hedgehogs.* Cambridge, MA: Harvard University Press.

___. (2008). *Is democracy possible here? Principles for a new political debate.* Princeton, NJ: Princeton University Press.

Emanuel, E. J. (2014). *Reinventing American health care.* New York, NY: Perseus Books Group, Public Affairs.

Emanuel, E. J., & Fuchs, V. (2008). *Healthcare, guaranteed: A simple, secure solution for America.*

Ericson, R. V., & Doyle, A. (2003). *Risk and morality.* Toronto, Canada: University of Toronto Press.

Fehr, E., & Schmidt, K. M. (2006). The economics of fairness, reciprocity and altruism: Experimental evidence and new theories. In S.-G. Kolm & J. M. Ythier (Eds.). *Handbook of the economics of giving, altruism and reciprocity* (Vol. 1, pp. 616–691). Amsterdam, Holland: Elsevier-North Holland.

Fisher, E., et al. (2009). *Dartmouth Atlas Project topic brief: Health care spending, quality, and outcomes: More isn't always better.* Lebanon, NH: Dartmouth Institute for Health Policy and Clinical Practice.

Goldberg, Jr., F. T., & Camic, S. (2009). Legal solutions in health reform: Tax credits for health insurance. *Journal of Law, Medicine and Ethics, 37*, 73–83.

Grover, S. T. (2011). Religious exemptions to the PPACA's [Patient Protection and Affordable Care Act] health insurance mandate. *American Journal of Law and Medicine, 37*, 624–651.

Hall, M. A. (2011). Focus on health care reform: Approaching universal coverage with better safety-net programs for the uninsured. *Yale Journal of Health Policy, Law, and Ethics, 11*, 9–19.

Halpern, M. T., et al. (2008). Association of insurance status and ethnicity with cancer stage at diagnosis for twelve cancer sites: A retrospective analysis. *Lancet Oncology, 9*(3), 222–231.

Harris, M. (2011, February 25). Chief Information Officer, Information Technology Division, Cleveland Clinic, Capstone speaker on Leadership in an Evolving Global Market at the 2011 Wharton Health Care Business Conference, Philadelphia, PA.

Hermer, L. D., & Lenihan, M. (2014). Medicaid matters: The future of Medicaid supplemental payments: Can they promote patient-centered care? *Kentucky Law Journal, 102*, 287–326.

HHS (U.S. Department of Health and Human Services). (2015). *Health insurance coverage and the Affordable Care Act.* Washington, DC: HHS.

Hoffman, A. K. (2010). Oil and water: Mixing individual mandates, fragmented markets, and health reform. *American Journal of Law and Medicine, 36*, 7–77.

Hoffman, C., & Schwartz, K. (2008). *Trends in access to care among working-age adults.* Washington, DC: Kaiser Commission on Medicaid & the Uninsured.

Hoffman, J. (2014). Preemption and the MLR provision of the Affordable Care Act. *American Journal of Law and Medicine, 40*, 280–297.

Hunter, N. D. (2008). Risk governance and deliberative democracy in health care. *Georgetown Law Journal, 97*, 1–59.

Hurwitz, J. G. (2009). Indexing health insurance to marginal health status: A spoonful of economics helps the premiums go down. *DePaul Journal of Health Care Law, 12*, 43–66.

IOM (Institute of Medicine). (2010). *Bridging the evidence gap in obesity prevention: A framework to inform decision making.* Washington, DC: National Academies Press.

___. (2004). *Insuring America's health: Principles and recommendations.* Washington, DC: National Academies Press.

___. (2001). *Crossing the quality chasm: A new health system for the 21st century.*

IOM Committee on the Consequences of Uninsurance. (2009). America's uninsured crisis: Consequences for health and health care. Washington, DC: National Academies Press.

Jost, T. S. (2007). *Health care at risk.* Durham, NC: Duke University Press.

Kahn, J. H. (2014). The individual mandate tax penalty. *University of Michigan Journal of Law Reform, 47*, 319–358.

Kaiser Commission on Medicaid and the Uninsured. (2011). *Issue brief: Five basic facts on the uninsured.* Washington, DC: Kaiser.

Kaiser Family Foundation. (2015). *Survey of low-income Americans and the Affordable Care Act.* Menlo Park, CA: Kaiser.

___. (2014). *Key facts about the uninsured population.*

___. (2011). *How private health insurance coverage works: A primer.*

Kaiser & HRET (Health Research and Educational Trust). (2010). *Employer health benefits 2010 annual survey.* Washington, DC: HRET.

Katz, M. (2010). Towards a new moral paradigm in health care delivery: Accounting for individuals. *American Journal of Law and Medicine, 36*, 78–135.

Keehan, S., et al. (2008). Health spending projections through 2017. *Health Affairs, 27*(2), 146–155.

Kennedy, E. M. (2009, May). Letter to President Barack Obama, read to a Joint Session of Congress on September 9, 2009. Washington, DC: U.S. Congress.

Kenney, G., & Pelletier, J. (2008). *Spotlight on low income uninsured young adults: Causes and consequences.* Washington, DC: Kaiser Commission on Medicaid and the Uninsured.

Khan, F. (2010). Towards achieving lasting healthcare reform: Rethinking the American social contract. *Annals of Health Law, 19*, 73–78.

Kinney, E. D. (2010). For profit enterprise in health care: Can it contribute to health reform? *American Journal of Law and Medicine, 36*, 405–435.

Kleinbard, E. (2008, July 31). *Tax expenditures for health care.* Chief Economist for the Joint Tax Committee in Congress, Testimony before the U.S. Senate Committee on Finance. Washington, DC.

Kovach, A., & Gielau, R. (2012). The great Medicaid expansion of 2014: What it is and how to make it succeed. *Journal of Poverty Law and Policy, 45*, 388–397.

Lavizzo-Mourey, R. (2011, June 21). President & Chief Executive Officer, Robert Wood Johnson Foundation, Speaker at the 15th Annual Wharton Leadership Conference: Leading in a reset economy and uncertain world. Philadelphia, PA.

Leonard, E. W. (2012). Rhetorical federalism: The value of state-based dissent to federal health reform. *Hofstra Law Review, 39*, 111–168.

___. (2010). Affordable Care Act litigation: The standing paradox. *American Journal of Law and Medicine, 38*, 410–442.

Levine, M. A., et al. (2007). Improving access to health care: A consensus ethical framework to guide proposals for reform. *Hastings Center Report, 9/10*, 14–19.

Locke, J. (2008). *Two treatises of government.* Birmingham, AL: Palladium Press (Original work published 1689).

Logue, K., & Avraham, R. (2003). Redistributing optimally: Of tax rules, legal rules, and insurance. *Tax Law Review, 56*, 157–257.

Lynch, J., & Gollust, S. E. (2010). *Working paper: Playing fair: Fairness beliefs and health policy preferences in the United States* (Robert Wood Johnson Foundation Scholars in Health Policy Research Program). Philadelphia, PA: University of Pennsylvania, Wharton Business School.

Maher, B. S. (2011). The benefits of opt-in federalism. *Boston College Law Review, 52*, 1733–1793.

Majerol, M., et al. (2015). *The uninsured: A primer—key facts about health insurance and the uninsured in America.* Menlo, CA: Kaiser Family Foundation.

Martinez, M. E., & Cohen, R. A. (2015). *Health insurance coverage: Early release of estimates from the National Health Interview Survey.* Atlanta, GA: Centers for Disease Control and Prevention's National Center for Health Statistics.

Moncrieff, A. R. (2013). The individual mandate as healthcare regulation: What the Obama administration should have said in *NFIB v. Sebelius. American Journal of Law and Medicine, 39*, 539–572.

Morreim, E. H. (2008). High-deductible health plans: Litigation hazards for health insurers. *Health Matrix: The Journal of Law-Medicine, 18*, 1–64.

Oechsner, T. J., & Schaler-Haynes, M. (2011). Keeping it simple: Health plan benefit standardization and regulatory choice under the Affordable Care Act. *Albany Law Review, 74*, 241–311.

Ouellette, A. (2013). Health reform and the Supreme Court: The ACA survives the battle of the broccoli and fortifies itself against future fatal attack. *Albany Law Review, 6*, 87–119.

Pagan, J. A. (2007, February 7). Professor of economics at the University of Texas and senior fellow at the Leonard Davis Institute of Health Economics at the University of Pennsylvania, speaker at Beazley Symposium, *Access to essential health care: Immigration from the Mayflower to border patrols: Who should have access to essential health care in the U.S.?* Loyola University Chicago School Law, Beazley Institute Health Law and Policy, Chicago, IL.

Pauly, M. V. (2007). Health risks and benefits in health care: The view from economics. *Health Affairs, 26*, 653–662.

Powers, M., & Faden, R. (2008). *Social justice: The moral foundations of public health and health policy (Issues in Biomedical Ethics)*. New York, NY: Oxford University Press.

Pratt, D. (2011). Health care reform: Will it succeed? *Albany Law Journal of Science and Technology, 21*, 493–589.

PricewaterhouseCoopers. (2008). *The price of excess: Identifying waste in healthcare spending*. New York, NY: PricewaterhouseCoopers.

RAND Corp. (2006). *First national report card on quality of health care in America (the Community Quality Index Study)*. Santa Monica, CA: RAND.

Rawls, J. (2005). *A theory of justice*. Boston, MA: Belknap Press (Original work published 1971).

____. (2001). *Justice as fairness: A restatement*. Cambridge, MA: Harvard University Press.

Reagan, R. (1999, September 29). Remarks at his announcement for presidential candidacy at the University of Texas at Austin, Austin, TX.

Record, K. L. (2012). Litigating the ACA: Securing the right to health within a framework of negative rights. *American Journal of Law and Medicine, 38*, 537–546.

Rousseau, J.-J. (2009). *Discourse on political economy and the social contract* (Oxford World's Classics). New York: Oxford University Press (Original work published 1762).

Rubin, E. (2012). The Affordable Care Act, the constitutional meaning of statutes, and the emerging doctrine of positive constitutional rights. *William and Mary Law Review, 53*, 1639–1715.

Russo, A., et al. (2007). *Healthcare Cost and Utilization Project: Trends in potentially preventable hospitalizations among adults and children*. Rockville, MD: Agency for Healthcare Research and Quality.

Sage, W. (2008). Health regulation and governance: Relational duties, regulatory duties, and the widening gap between individual health law and collective health policy. *Georgetown Law Journal, 96*, 497–522.

Sanford, S. T. (2014). Health care reform symposium: The state of the states roundtable. *Journal of Health Care Law and Policy, 17*(1), 101–127.

Schneider, J. E., & Ohsfeldt, R. L. (2007). The role of markets and competition in health care reform initiatives to improve efficiency and enhance access to care. *Cumberland Law Review, 37*, 479–511.

SEC (U.S. Securities & Exchange Commission). (2011). *Corporate annual income statements for 2010 from Aetna, Amerigroup, Centene, Cigna, Conventry Health Corp., Health Net, Humana, United Health, United American, and WellPoint*. Washington, DC: SEC.

SHADAC (State Health Access Data Assistance Center). (2011). *State level trends in employer sponsored health insurance: A state-by-state analysis*. Minneapolis, MN: SHADAC.

Shorter, J. B. (2010). Final-offer arbitration for health care billing disputes: Analyzing one state's proposed dispute resolution process. *Appalachian Journal of Law, 9*, 191–215.

Siegel, N. S. (2011). Four constitutional limits that the minimum coverage provision respects. *Constitutional Commentary, 27*, 591–619.

Singh, I. (2011, February 25). Executive Vice President of the Clinton Foundation, Capstone speaker at the 17th Annual Wharton Health Care Business Conference: Leadership in an evolving global market. Philadelphia, PA.

Singleton, J. P. (2010). Can you really have too much of a good thing? How benevolent tax policies have contributed to the explosion of health care costs and how new policies threaten to do more of the same. *DePaul Business and Commercial Law Journal, 8*, 305–338.

Skinner, J. S., et al. (2011). *Report of the Dartmouth Atlas Project: A new series of Medicare expenditure measures by hospital referral region*. Lebanon, NH: Dartmouth Institute for Health Policy and Clinical Practice.

Somin, I. (2014). *NFIB v. Sebelius* and the constitutional debate over federalism. *Oklahoma City University Law Review, 39*, 415–440.

Starr, P. (1983). *The social transformation of American medicine: The rise of a sovereign profession and the making of a vast industry*. New York, NY: Basic Books.

Stone, D. (2008). Protect the sick: Health insurance reform in one easy lesson. *Journal of Law, Medicine and Ethics, 36*(4), 652–659.

Todd, A. E. (2011). No need for more regulation: Payors and their role in balancing the cost and safety considerations of off-label prescriptions. *American Journal of Law and Medicine, 37*, 422–443.

Tribe, L. (2011, February 8). Op-Ed: On health care, justice will prevail. *New York Times*, p. A27.

Wharton School at the University of Pennsylvania. (2011). Robert Wood Johnson Foundation's Risa Lavizzo-Mourey: The challenges facing health care reform. *Knowledge@Wharton.*

___. (2007). A prescription for healthier medical care decisions: Begin by defining health risks. *Knowledge@Wharton.*

___. (2007a). Harry and Louise, the sequel? The universal health care debate is back. *Knowledge@Wharton.*

Willis, S. J., & Chung, N. (2012). No healthcare penalty? No problem: No due process. *American Journal of Law and Medicine, 38*, 516–536.

Wilper, A. P., et al. (2009). Health insurance and mortality in U.S. adults. *American Journal of Public Health, 99*, 2289–2295.

Young, C. L. (2010). Pay or play programs and ERISA section 514: Proposals for amending the statutory scheme. *Yale Journal of Health Policy, Law and Ethics, 10*, 197–237.

Zuvekas, S. H., & Cohen, J. W. (2007). Prescription drugs and the changing concentration of health care expenditures. *Health Affairs, 26*(1), 249–257.

© Frank Capri/Archive Photos/Getty Images

CHAPTER 4

Patients' Rights and Responsibilities

"The assault on the national government is represented as a disinterested movement to 'return' power to the people. . . . It transfers power to the historical rival of the national government and the prime cause of its enlargement—the great corporate interests."

— **Arthur Schlesinger, Jr.** (1917–2007), Pulitzer Prize-winning historian and American social critic

LEARNING OBJECTIVES

After completing this chapter, the reader should be able to:

1. Understand the ethical principles underlying patient rights and the political choices confronting the nation as it attempts to fairly allocate responsibility to pay for medically needed care.
2. Describe how patients can and cannot protect themselves when seeking available health care in today's managed care marketplace.
3. Explain the factors that affect patient rights and influence the ability of patients to make their own responsible decisions with regard to their health care.
4. Summarize the ethical issues that underscore the difficult job of trying to hold down costs while giving patients more say in the kind of medical treatments they can obtain.

KEY TERMS

Acute care	Health-based comparative effectiveness	Rationing
Basic health insurance		Reasonable and necessary care
Charitable care	Health-related well-being	
Consent	Human solidarity	Risk pools
Detailing	Informed consent	Safety net hospitals
Experimental treatments	Insurance analysis	Social loafers
Free-rider	Medical triage	Supplemental health insurance
Fundamental right	Medically needed care	
General well-being	Moral imperative	Universal coverage
Health capital	Off-label	Unmet medical need

Patients' Right to Sue Manufacturers of Innovative Medical Products

---

Ethics Issue: *Should patients have the right to sue manufacturers of innovative medical devices in state courts under consumer safety laws for injuries resulting from use of experimental treatments involving high-risk devices?*

In Brief: Charles Riegel underwent heart surgery to improve his life-threatening heart condition after his heavily calcified right coronary artery was found to have a 95 percent blockage. Because of the diffuseness of his heart disease and heavy arterial calcification, a rotablator was used to open the artery. Riegel's physician then decided to perform a balloon angioplasty. After several inflations were made without any change in the artery, the artery was stented and several traditional catheters were tried without success. When a new high-risk catheter was stented as a last resort, it also ruptured, and Riegel rapidly deteriorated and sustained serious personal injuries.

Riegel and his wife brought suit against Medtronic, the manufacturer of the last catheter that ruptured in Riegel's coronary artery. The experimental catheter was a high-risk medical device that had received fast-track approval from the U.S. Food and Drug Administration (FDA) based on limited but promising clinical data in animal testing, prior to the start of human clinical trials to prove its safety and effectiveness for human use. The Riegels claimed that the device was designed, labeled, and manufactured in a manner that violated New York consumer protection regulations. Medtronic claimed their lawsuit was preempted by federal law.

— *Riegel v. Medtronic, Inc.*, 552 U.S. 312 (U.S. Supreme Court 2008). (*See Ethical or Unethical Decision* at the end of the chapter for discussion of this ethics issue.)

Introduction

The patient rights debate is about what health care is owed to patients, or, what they are entitled to. The debate is underscored by the difficulty of trying to minimize costs while giving patients greater freedom of choice in the kind of care available. Defining the principles of patient entitlement largely affects the middle class as opposed to people who are covered by government health insurance, such as Medicare and Medicaid (Dubay, et al., 2007). While the uninsured may be eligible for **charitable care**, or discounted or free care, the middle-class insured lack a real safety net for catastrophic events when their health insurance coverage needs exceed their ability to pay for their health care or the requisite level of insurance.

The Ideal: Universally Accessible and Affordable Health Insurance

Health insurance should ideally be universally accessible and affordable to everyone so they can achieve and maintain high levels of health, which are necessary for a lifetime of well-being, human dignity, and meaningful contribution to society. Many Americans have come to favor a system of universal coverage as an alternative option to decrease the current burden of personal health care costs (Dartmouth, 2011). **Universal coverage** is a payment system that provides access to affordable health insurance for everyone, with the option of buying **supplemental health insurance** coverage for unrestricted access to advanced care and highly specialized physicians (Singh, 2011).

Health insurance should provide coverage for prevention, traditional diagnosis, and treatment of diseases and health conditions. A fundamental issue in the patient rights debate concerns how patients protect themselves when confronted by serious illness or a catastrophic trauma. In other words, should patients be entitled to access the highest quality health care at the nation's leading medical centers based on medical need alone, without regard to their ability to pay, or should access be based on the health insurance coverage they selected and the lifestyle choices they freely made?

Paying for Medically Needed Care

At this time, there is no agreement on what specific level of health care is required or who is entitled to access highly specialized physicians and the latest medical technologies based on medical need alone. **Medically needed care** refers to the highest attainable standard of necessary health care and medical treatments, including advanced medications and medical devices that are needed but not received because they are unaffordable or delayed because of costs. For instance, should a hospital use less expensive medical devices that may have to be replaced in a shorter period of time or comparable but more expensive and more durable devices that generally last longer, if the hospital's insurance payment is the same? Who should determine whether more is necessarily better, or when something is good enough from a medical standpoint? In other words, the United States has not addressed the question of whether everyone should be entitled to access the latest medical technologies and obtain the highest level of care without regard to their ability to pay or whether everyone should be entitled to such services and medical products only either through cash payments or supplemental health insurance purchased for this very purpose.

Today, the middle class is the only patient group in America that is unprotected with no entitlement to medically needed care. Although caps on health insurance were removed under provisions of the Affordable Care Act of 2010 (ACA), until then, middle-class Americans had nowhere to turn for assistance when their legitimate claims for care exceeded their insurance caps. Similarly, today the middle class has nowhere to turn when they cannot afford to pay deductibles and co-payments for medically needed care.

ETHICAL DILEMMAS 4-1

1. Are annual and lifetime limits on health insurance the most ethical way for the insurance industry to allocate losses, or should limits on health insurance coverage for medically needed health care be banned by law as a matter of ethics?
2. Are there better and more ethical cost containment frameworks available to the health insurance industry than shifting the costs onto individual policy holders when they are faced with catastrophic accidents or serious illness?

Conflicting Interests: Insured Patients vs. Health Insurers

The health care system is comprised of parties with conflicting interests that are legally and socially protected (Matthew, 2010). For instance, while most hospitals proclaim that their primary concern is patient care, this assertion does not address how prices are set or the ethical obligations hospitals have to their board of trustees, religious order, or governing foundation (Tyrell, 2010). Moreover, hospitals always face two interests when health insurance is involved. On one side are the patients and on the other side are the payers: the government (Medicare and Medicaid) and the private health insurance industry. Payers generally attempt to realign the interests of hospitals with their cost-minimizing priorities for payment (Tyrell, 2010), and patient interests do not always align with insurance interests (Matthew, 2011). Reform of health care costs must focus on fixing the relationship between these conflicting economic interests (Reinhardt, 2006).

The U.S. political system has taken a comprehensive look at this pressing issue and its answer seems to be a comprehensive system of payment where everyone has health insurance coverage that is fairly broad. The most divisive issue in this health care reform debate is the proper role of the federal government in balancing competing interests within the U.S. health care system, especially between patient rights to medically needed care and patient responsibilities to obtain health insurance that funds the level of care they may someday need. The unique American values of liberty and **consent**, defined here as the freedom to think and act without being constrained by government, complicate health care reform. The entire subject of health insurance coverage is so complex, however, that the issue of patient rights and responsibilities does not lend itself to easy analysis. In particular, the political power of patients and their advocacy organizations has affected this debate.

Economic Imperative for Implementation of Health Care Reforms

Although most people do not completely understand, and many are not even aware of, the relationship between health care and U.S. economic competiveness (Posner, 1981/1983), there is no disagreement that there is a relationship (TFAH & RWJF, 2014). Common sense economics demands that the United States address affordable health insurance coverage for one simple reason: it is cost effective to do so. It is generally less costly to provide comprehensive health insurance that covers preventive and regularly administered health care than it is to provide delayed charitable care on an as-needed, often emergency, basis (Kaiser Family Foundation, 2006). It simply costs less to provide regular, basic preventive health care than it costs to provide delayed **acute care** for serious diseases, as every other developed economy in the world has discovered (TFAH & TWJF, 2011). In stark terms, the nation's priority must be given to the protection of human health in order to ensure its economic growth and competitiveness (Parisi, 2010). Health care costs and economic productivity and competiveness are so inextricably linked that one cannot be separated from the other (Posner, 1981/1983). Examples of this principle are universal testing and treatment for tuberculosis before the disease becomes active and provision of access to antiretroviral medications to people who test positive for HIV before AIDS symptoms develop.

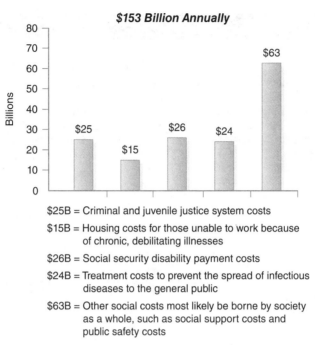

FIGURE 4-1 Costs of Maintaining People Outside the Health Care System
Sources: Allen, 2010; CDC/NCHS, 2015; Singh, 2011; TFAH & RWJF, 2014.

Moreover, the nation's social welfare costs will not be increased (shifted to different players, but not increased) by mandating that everyone have health insurance to assist in providing access to affordable health care (Singh, 2011). What makes this economic fact controversial is Americans' ambivalence over using government interventions to assist others who are sick (Stone, 2008). In other words, the myth of American self-reliance is at times divorced from the reality of and ethical obligation toward those in need of this reform.

The nation is already paying for everyone to have some level of health care. It is simply paying when people show up in the nation's emergency rooms with acute health conditions that could have been prevented if they had had (less costly) access to care earlier. The nation is also paying when hospitals must raise their rates to cover uncompensated care costs attributable to charitable care and bad debt from the uninsured. Besides, other areas of society are offset by the provision of care to those previously unable to pay for medically needed care and who then become able to work and support themselves. **FIGURE 4-1** illustrates the cost of maintaining people outside the health care system (CDC/NCHS, 2009 and 2008).

Health Insurers' Problem with Free-Riders and Social Loafers

While there is always the problem of **free-riders**, or the uninsured who are exploiting the U.S. health care system without due compensation, a far greater problem is **social loafers**, or the people who do have health insurance but who fail to avail themselves of the preventive measures they could take which have been shown to reduce the risks of bad health (Billauer, 2007). The medical phenomenon of social loafers is often the result of family and other environmental factors that do not support healthy lifestyles (Johnson, 1758/2009). For

ETHICAL DILEMMAS 4-2

3. While the fear of free-riders drives some of the opposition to health care reforms, should individuals be forced to purchase health insurance, and if so, why?
4. Does the minimum coverage provision violate the American principles of liberty and freedom to choose not to purchase economic products?
5. Are not the true free-riders those people who decide not to procure health insurance when they can afford it but prefer to purchase other consumer goods instead?

instance, overweight and obese people often exert less effort to achieve weight goals when they are around other overweight people, just as smokers exert less effort to stop smoking when they are around other people who smoke.

Although there are reasons why people can fall temporarily into the health insurance gap, such as divorce, unemployment, financial stresses, and mental health issues, people have a constant ethical obligation to plan for life's uncertainties, including maintaining health insurance coverage. Moreover, while uninsured free-riders are real problems, the social loafers who do have health insurance, but freely choose not to avail themselves of it, are arguably more of an ethical problem (Wharton, 2011). Social loafers who refuse to afford themselves the benefits of preventive care increase the national burden of health care costs and force it upon other members of society. Hence, social loafers who do not utilize screening diagnostics inflate the cost of health care just as free-riders do (Billauer, 2007). Free-riders and social loafers both reap the benefits that the ethics of the common good provide, but refuse to do their part to support the common good of their communities.

Whether health care reform will generate enough savings to offset its cost remains to be seen. The majority of health care experts believe it will (Wharton, 2011). A wide range of changes could occur: in people's health, in the sources and extent of health insurance coverage, in the delivery of health care, and in emergence of new advanced medical technologies that are difficult to predict, but that could have a significant effect on health care spending.

Ethical Imperative for Health Care Reform

The nation already decided there was no ethical justification for more than 37 million Americans to have unmet medical needs (CDC/NCHS, 2009); five years after the ACA was adopted, that number has dropped by half (CDC/NCHS, 2015). Yet, millions still have **unmet medical needs** and need health care but do not get it because they cannot afford it or delay care because of the cost (Kenney, et al., 2012). Today's children are becoming the first generation in American history predicted to live shorter, less healthy lives than their parents (TFAH & RWJF, 2014). While critics may say the United States cannot afford to provide universal access to medically needed health care to its population, most Americans cannot identify an ethical reason for over 10 percent of the population to have unmet medical needs in the United States (CDC/NCHS, 2015; Kenney, et al., 2012). In other words, the United States cannot afford not to, either financially or morally.

ETHICAL DILEMMAS 4-3

6. What ethical principles justify the world's leading economic power agreeing, or not agreeing, to expand its government health insurance programs, while mandating that the nation's private health insurance industry provide access to affordable health insurance coverage so everyone can access care based on medical need?

At the same time, it is not fair for the federal government to promise a wide range of benefits through its insurance programs, and then try to economize on those promises by lowering its payment rates to those who provide those benefits. For instance, health care providers should not be required to engage in the practice of cost-shifting to subsidize medical products and treatment services that are reimbursed at or below cost to patients with government health insurance. Ethically speaking, when the repeated reduction of provider payment rates is a source of considerable aggravation to providers serving the Medicaid and Medicare insured populations, the federal government becomes the biggest free-rider in the U.S. health care system (Harris, 2011).

The New Patient's Bill of Rights

Part of the ACA is a new Patient's Bill of Rights, which sets forth consumer protections patients to which are entitled. The Patient's Bill of Rights, as illustrated in **FEATURE BOX 4-1**, does not address the issue of whether health care is a right or a privilege. There is no public consensus on whether health care is a moral entitlement arising from the humanity of people or a legal entitlement freely granted by law. A right is the inverse of a privilege. If society decides that health care is a privilege, then health care is conditioned on the ability to pay or otherwise purchase health insurance that will provide coverage for the highest attainable standard of medically needed care, including advanced medications and medical devices. In this instance, medically needed care may be delayed or not received at all if someone is underinsured and the necessary care is unaffordable because of costs. In contrast, if society decides that health care is a right, then everyone will be provided access to affordable health insurance coverage to obtain medically needed care, with subsidies available to people at the lower end of the socioeconomic pyramid.

The Patient's Bill of Rights does not address how to find a way to provide health insurance coverage to everyone who needs life-sustaining, advanced care, nor does it address Medicare reform. The level of personal financial ethical obligation required to obtain access to the latest medical technologies and medications remains an unresolved issue in reform of the U.S. health care system.

Patients' Right to Access Affordable Health Insurance

Patients' right to access affordable health insurance is confusing and immersed in exceptions. While coverage may exceed what is currently covered as deemed medically needed by different insurers, limitations are crucial to defining health insurance. By definition, **basic health insurance** does not extend coverage to long-term critical care or extensive hospitalizations for acute care (Satz, 2008a). Although the right to health insurance is necessarily

FEATURE BOX 4-1

Patient's Bill of Rights

- Allows young adults under 26 to stay on their parent's family health insurance policy or be added to it
- Bans insurers from imposing preexisting condition exclusions on children under 19
- Enables women to see an OB-GYN without a referral
- Ensures patients can choose the primary care physician or pediatrician they want from their plan's provider network
- Guarantees renewability of health insurance regardless of health status
- Limits rating variation of health insurance based only on age, geographic area, family composition, or tobacco use
- Mandates access to affordable basic health insurance
- Presumes eligibility for Medicaid insurance
- Prevents insurers from requiring prior approvals before seeking emergency care at a hospital outside a plan's provider network
- Prohibits insurers from rescinding or taking away health insurance coverage based on technicalities and unintentional mistakes on an application
- Provides access to essential health care
- Requires insurers to spend 80–85 percent of their premium dollars on health care
- Restricts the use of annual caps on coverage
- Stops insurers from setting lifetime limits on coverage
- Allows coverage for individuals participating in clinical trials

— Source: 45 C.F.R. §§144, 146–47 (2010).

interpreted relative to traditional diagnostics and short-term acute care of serious disease or trauma (generally less than 25 days of inpatient care), as illustrated in **FEATURE BOX 4-2**, future coverage will most likely be driven by prevention.

Prior to health care reform, the focus of health insurance was acute care. Medicaid provided coverage for only a narrow set of primary care services, while Medicare expressly excluded preventive services (Satz, 2008). New and emerging predictive technologies that further prevention by enhancing diagnostic and screening options were generally not covered by government health insurance (Satz, 2008a). Patients were unwittingly overlooked and sometimes even harmed by this policy, as well as by physicians and others in the current health care system that often focused on limited as opposed to long-term treatment. No one purposely wanted to do harm to others, but in the course of events, patients did end up hurt because they did not receive all the treatment that was clinically effective and needed (Watson, 2007).

Patients' Right to Emergency Care

The principle of **human solidarity**—the recognition that human interests and responsibilities are mutually shared—guides the federal government in how health care providers and the health insurance industry should develop policies to define what constitutes coverage for

---

FEATURE BOX 4-2

Patients' Rights to Basic Health Insurance Coverage

- Traditional diagnostics, including diagnostic imaging (computed or positron emission tomography [CT or PET] scans or magnetic resonance imaging [MRI])
- Traditional therapies
- Accepted genetic testing
- Conventional medical devices
- Customary tissue and organ repair and replacement
- Established pharmaceuticals
- General surgical procedures
- Predictive tests, such as cholesterol tests

— Sources: Dartmouth, 2011; Satz, 2008 and 2008a.

---

medically needed care. While Americans always had a moral and more recently a legal right to emergency care, the health insurance industry placed barriers on this right (Iserson & Moskop, 2007). Some insurers would only pay for emergency care provided by a limited network of providers. Other insurers required prior approval before receiving emergency care at hospitals outside of their networks. This meant financial hardship when patients got sick or injured when they were away from home or not near a network hospital.

The ACA removed these barriers to make emergency care more accessible to patients. Insurers can no longer charge higher cost-sharing (co-payments or coinsurance) for emergency care obtained out of a health plan's network. The rules also set requirements on how health insurers must reimburse out-of-network providers. Hospitals must provide for appropriate medical screening to determine whether an emergency health condition exists. While complete or continuous care is not required beyond stabilization of emergency conditions, insurers must still implement policies whereby they will not deny payment for emergency care, even when it is determined that no medical emergency existed.

At the same time, this moral and legal right is of no consequence for people without access to emergency care at all. A third of the urban acute-care hospitals, which served higher shares of poor and financially distressed populations, have shut their emergency departments or closed altogether since 1990 (Hsia, et al., 2011). One side of the debate about patient rights to emergency care asserts that this is an expression of a healthy marketplace (Schumpeter, 1942/2014). The other side dismisses this assertion, since a large number of people without health insurance or with government insurance could not support the full costs of these hospitals. The populations served by the closed emergency departments can no longer obtain immediate medical assistance; no reforms have emerged to replace the bankrupt systems that faced economic destruction. The question of whether this loss is defensible when it makes emergency care less accessible, both by increasing the distance that must be traveled or by increasing loads and wait times at accessible hospitals, remains unanswered. One thing is certain: **safety net hospitals** that serve poor and financially distressed patients and that deliver a significant level of uncompensated care to the uninsured require particular attention if emergency care access is to be sustained, as lack of access to primary care in the same areas drives up emergency room visits to those hospitals (Dobson, et al., 2006). The nation has an ethical obligation to ensure that access to emergency trauma care is equitably distributed in the United States when facilities are not always available to patients needing urgent medical treatments, such as for cardiopulmonary arrest. *See generally* Hsia, et al., 2011.

Employees' Right to Sue Employers

Employees cannot sue their employers for denial of employer-provided health insurance coverage, unless the employer played a direct role in deciding whether care should be provided. Generally, the courts favor allowing employees the right to sue employers directly involved in coverage decisions (Kim, 2005). If physicians are employed at corporate clinics or in an employer-provided onsite preventive health services program and play a significant role in making treatment decisions with regard to employees, that employer will probably be sued if employees are actually harmed. For instance, harm could arise by denial of urgent care or rejection of requests for referrals to specialists (Suk, 2011).

There is a potential for conflicts of interest when administrators of insurers and self-insured medical coverage plans both determine and pay benefit claims. In other words, conflicts of interest should be taken into account when employers pay health insurance claims out of their own pockets while able to profit by denying claims for coverage from their employees. A controversial part of health care reform, that failed to become part of the new Patient's Bill of Rights, was a proposal to expand employee rights to sue employers (Garden, 2014). Employers providing health insurance coverage to their employees were alarmed because they saw scenarios in which they could be sued when employees were harmed by denial of coverage. A recent U.S. Supreme Court decision has broad repercussions for employer-provided health insurance. Employees with employer-provided health insurance may now have the legal protections that were resisted by employers when the ACA was enacted.

ETHICS CASE
Protections for Prospective Retirees with Employer-Provided Health Insurance

Cigna Corp., et al. v. Amara, et al.
[Health Services Employer v. Employees]
131 S.Ct. 1866 (U.S. Supreme Court 2011)

Facts: Commentators have characterized this ruling as one of the most significant changes governing health insurance coverage in two decades. Although the facts of this case involve employee retirement plans at one of the nation's largest health insurers, the decision has broad repercussions for any employees covered by employer-provided health insurance plans. Since a 2004 U.S. Supreme Court decision involving employees insured by Aetna and Cigna (*Aetna Health, Inc., et al. v. Juan Davila, et al.*, 542 U.S. 200 (U.S. Supreme Court 2004)), if employer-provided health insurers negligently denied or delayed employees' medical treatment, employees could not sue the employer-insurers for injuries. Rather, employees could only recover the cost of the denied coverage. These restrictions led to numerous cases in which courts found that health insurers and employers had behaved deceitfully in providing incorrect information about their employer-provided health insurance plans, resulting in injuries and death to thousands of insured employees. Yet, heretofore, the insurance industry and employers faced no consequences for their willful misrepresentations.

In this case, employees complained that Cigna deceived them when it amended its $3.2 billion pension plan in 1998. Cigna told its employees in handouts and meetings that the new plan was an overall improvement in their retirement benefits, when in fact it froze the pensions of 25,000 older, long-tenured employees, in many cases for years, without their knowledge.

Rule of Law: If employers provide misleading information to their employees about their benefits, employers may be required to amend the terms of their benefit plans to conform to the terms in the plan summary, as opposed to the less generous benefits described by formal plan documents.

Legal Analysis: When there is a conflict between summary plan documents given to employees and the detailed plan documents, which employees rarely see, employees can take legal action to get their plans amended to their benefit. Although courts cannot award benefits that are not in a benefits plan, when employers breach their fiduciary ethical obligation to their employees, courts can order plans to be amended to conform to the terms in the summary plan documents given to employees. This is a significant change in the law, since courts had previously refused to restore benefits lost as a result of violations of disclosure rules and fiduciary duties.

Before this U.S. Supreme Court decision restored employee protections, remedies had been severely curtailed for nearly two decades. Three earlier U.S. Supreme Court decisions harshly reduced the remedies available to current and near-term prospective retirees with employer-provided retirement plans who had their benefits curtailed or eliminated outright. Previously, employers faced no consequences for behaving unlawfully or deceitfully, even when their actions resulted in catastrophic financial losses to their employees.

Ethics Issue: When employees are harmed after being unlawfully denied coverage they were led to believe they had from summary documents in their employer-provided health insurance plans, do fairness and justice demand that they be provided a remedy?

Ethics Analysis: The era of rights without any remedy for violations may be over for employers who deliberately provide misleading information to employees about their health insurance benefits. For nearly two decades, employees had rights through disclosure as opposed to by regulation. If an employer told its employees they could not sue it, then employees were told they could make a decision about whether they wanted to accept their employer's health insurance coverage. If current and near-term prospective retirees with employer-provided health insurance had their health insurance curtailed or eliminated outright, they had no remedy. This U.S. Supreme Court decision may have finally restored basic fairness to employer-provided health insurance and employer-promised retirement benefits.

Court's Holding and Decision: Yes, when employers provide misleading summary information to their employees, employers are required to provide all employees the benefits the employer led them to believe they had.

See, e.g., Lewis, 2014; Maher, 2013; Muir & Stein, 2015; Pratt, 2012; Wiggins, 2012 (discussing this court decision).

Many Americans believed their future health care costs would be covered by their employers, yet a generation of current and near-term prospective retirees has had their health insurance curtailed or eliminated outright. Ethically speaking, government has an obligation to provide affordable access to coverage since it failed to previously protect reasonable employee expectations (DiSarro, 2011; Valenza, 2011).

Patients' Right to Accountability by Health Insurers

There is ongoing controversy about whether coverage should be regulated by the free market system or whether government should impose regulations to protect the common welfare of patients. One of the most contentious issues in health care deals with when and where patients can take legal action if they feel a health insurer wrongly denies them coverage and, as a result, causes them harm (Wharton, 2008). One side of this debate maintains that insurers should be accountable when they deny medical treatments recommended by physicians. The other side argues that increased liability on insurers will lead to increased costs, which will make health insurance even more costly.

The ACA provides protection in health insurance plans via a straightforward way for consumers to appeal to their health insurers and to an independent appeals process if their insurer denies coverage or a claim. Prior to the right to demand accountability by health insurers, a patient harmed as a direct result of an improper denial of treatment could recover only the value of that treatment, and nothing for the injuries that were a foreseeable consequence of such denial. *See Aetna Health, Inc., et al. v. Juan Davila, et al.*, 542 U.S. 200 (U.S. Supreme Court 2004).

Restricted Access to the Newest Medical Technologies

While access to health care is arguably a moral right, there is no public consensus whether medically needed care should be a legal right or a privilege. Yet it is not necessary to define this distinction between a legal right and a privilege before the nation begins to define the minimum core obligations of health insurance (Garden, 2014). Although the ACA provided for a legal right to access affordable health insurance, a number of treatment procedures and medical products are not reimbursable with health insurance, either government or private. Nevertheless, the ethical principles of fairness and justice should underlie any decisions as

ETHICAL DILEMMAS 4-4

7. What ethical principles—in addition to the universal values of compassion, fairness and justice—should determine the right degree of health insurance coverage?
8. Who should determine this right degree of health insurance coverage: government, the health insurance industry, or an independent third-party organization comprised of all the stakeholders affected, including physicians, hospitals, the government, private insurers, and patients?

to which services and products should be eligible for the health insurance coverage to which everyone is now entitled under the ACA regardless of ability to pay (Levine, et al., 2007).

When patients have the necessary financial resources, access to the newest cutting-edge medical technologies is readily available (Drummond & Sorenson, 2009). For instance, health insurers cover cataract surgeries, but for patients who want intraocular lenses implanted for permanent correction of their vision, there is an additional cost of about $4,000 per eye. Cataract surgery will correct clouded vision, but for a return to vision with 20/20 correction approximation, intraocular lenses are needed. Until there is a national consensus on how the government and the health insurance industry should deal with the rapidly rising use and costs of the newest cutting-edge medical technologies, access to the newest medical technologies and the most advanced care will remain controversial (Sisko, et al., 2009).

The new Patient's Bill of Rights did not help decide what medical technologies everyone should be able to obtain. Moreover, neither Congress nor any state legislature has determined any particular level of aggregate health care spending or otherwise made the trade-off between health care and other social goods. In addition, no one appears ready to decide how to allocate spending among health care needs, other than foreclosing criteria based on the ability to pay. In other words, while everyone agrees that access to affordable health insurance should be available to anyone who requires medically needed care, there is no national consensus on how to accomplish this **moral imperative** (*see* Bernstein, 2012). While a moral imperative, by definition, is the right and ethical thing to do, regardless of opposition or difficulty, providing medically needed care to everyone based on need as opposed to the ability to pay is above all an ethical issue (Associated Press, 2009). As stated by Senator Edward Kennedy in Chapter 3, at stake are not just the details of policy, but fundamental principles of social justice and the nation's character.

Patients' Right to Access Medical Treatments

Patients have the moral right to control their medical treatment consistent with their values and personal preferences (Wennberg, 2010). The right to access what may be either ineffective or harmful off-label treatments or lifesaving experimental treatments is often an open issue. Judgments about the rational basis of informed consent must often be balanced with scientific evidence when deciding who has the right to specific medical treatments.

Informed Consent

Here, **informed consent** refers to the shared decision-making process between physicians and patients when scientific evidence alone does not identify a favored course of medical treatment (McAneny, 2011). Informed consent extends to the physician-patient dialogue involving the provision of information needed for patients to make knowledgeable decisions about their health care (Sawicki, 2012). While there is no ethical distinction between requiring informed consent of patients who participate in clinical trials of **experimental treatments** and requiring informed consent for **off-label** treatments outside the clinical trial context (both of which by definition mean the treatments are not yet proven to be safe or effective for the indicated use), the law makes a distinction between these types of actions. The first treatment practice is lawful, but the latter, while common practice, is generally prohibited.

Patients' Right to Off-Label Treatments

Terminally ill patients, especially those with cancer, are regularly treated with approved medications off-label. For instance, cancer medications are ordinarily approved for very narrowly defined diseases; the more narrow the disease population for approved use, the easier it is to obtain FDA approval. The wider the defined disease for approved use, the more likely it is that side effects will appear to obstruct regulatory approval. The FDA generally approves such medications for specific types of cancer and particular clinical indications. However, physicians frequently prescribe cancer medications for unapproved or off-label use outside of the narrowly defined indications for which a remedy has been shown to be effective (Kesselheim, 2011).

This right to off-label use of approved medications is based on the previously mentioned doctrine of informed consent, under which patients can choose any treatments if given sufficient information to understand the consequences, risks and benefits, and alternatives to such chosen treatments (NIH, 2007). The information provided must not only enable patients to make an evaluation of the nature of their chosen treatment and of any substantial risks, but also ensure that alternative options are clearly understood by patients, including the option to do nothing.

ETHICS CASE
Patients' Right to Access Off-Label Medications

Sorrell, et al. v. IMS Health Inc., et al.
[Attorney General of Vermont v. Data Miner]
131 S.Ct. 2653 (U.S. Supreme Court 2011)

Facts: The FDA requires pharmacies to record patient prescription data, including the identity of prescribers. This patient-prescriber data is then sold to third parties who use the data to produce prescribing reports that are sold to the pharmaceutical industry for use in their marketing. Pharmaceutical sales representatives, in turn, use the data in the prescribing reports to tailor their face-to-face conversations with individual prescribers, known in the industry as **detailing**.

In 2007, the Vermont State legislature enacted its Prescription Confidentiality Law to address the use of prescriber-identifying data to enhance prescriber detailing. Vermont was concerned that industry sales tactics were influencing prescribers to prescribe newer brand-name medications over generics. Vermont was also concerned that industry sales tactics were contributing to rising Medicaid costs. Vermont additionally expressed concern about the protection of patient privacy. The Vermont law mandating the collection of prescriber data provided state funding for counter-detailing to educate physicians on the uses of generic medication.

The Vermont law applied only to pharmacies, health insurers, and the pharmaceutical industry, limited only pharmaceutical marketing, and was designed to impact detailers whose speech conflicted with the goals of the government in reducing health care costs. Vermont prohibited the sale of prescriber-identifying data and the use of that information for industry marketing. In so doing, Vermont sought to foster more neutral and scientific detailing discussions centered on the safety, effectiveness, and costs of medications. IMS Health, the medical products industry's leading data miner (former employer of Hammaker, one of the co-authors of this textbook), challenged the Vermont law as an affront to free speech under the First Amendment.

Rule of Law: Although the First Amendment right to free speech restricts the government's ability to limit the use of patient-prescriber data, commercial speech may be restricted to protect patient privacy and serve a state's interest of reducing health care costs.

Legal Analysis: The Court held that the Vermont law contained both content- and speaker-based restrictions that were designed to restrict the effectiveness of marketing tactics by the pharmaceutical industry. Indeed, the legislative findings acknowledged that the law's express purpose was to lessen the effectiveness with which detailers could market their brand-name medications. The Court saw Vermont's opposition to the industry's targeted marketing as nothing less than viewpoint discrimination aimed at suppressing the industry's commercial messages in favor of Vermont's message of cost effectiveness.

By restricting the use of the patient-prescriber identifying data, Vermont tried to indirectly influence the pharmaceutical industry's promotion of more expensive brand-name medications over less expensive generics. The effect of detailing on physician prescribing, however, cannot justify restrictions on commercial speech. The fear that patients might make bad decisions if given data about using brand-name medications as opposed to generics cannot justify content-based burdens on speech. First Amendment jurisprudence is especially skeptical of regulations that appear to keep patients in the dark for what the government perceives to be their own good, such as using less expensive generics. Persuasive information alone does not permit the government to quiet the speech or to burden its messengers.

The Court concluded that the debate over detailing and the prescription of brand-name medications must be settled by free and uninhibited speech, not by restricting the pharmaceutical industry's ability to promote its pro-brand messages. Accordingly, the Vermont law was struck down. The Court was not persuaded by Vermont's cost justifications for the law.

Ethics Issue: Should the government be able to limit the use of patient-prescriber data that was gathered in accordance with state regulations, if this data was subsequently used by the pharmaceutical industry in a way that violated patient privacy rights or failed to serve the government's interests in controlling health care costs?

Ethics Analysis: The Vermont law was viewed as a content-based prohibition because it allowed the patient-prescriber data to be used for educational purposes but not for the disfavored purpose of pharmaceutical marketing. The Court also characterized the prohibition as a speaker-based restriction because everyone but the pharmaceutical industry could use the patient-prescriber data. The Court concluded that the Vermont law impermissibly burdened disfavored speech by disfavored speakers. Whenever the government restricts speech because of a disagreement with the content of the message, then strict judicial scrutiny of a law is compelled by the First Amendment, meaning that the law must pass the highest legal standards in order to be upheld. In this instance, the Vermont law did not directly advance the stated goals of achieving the government's policy objectives or reducing costs and protecting patient privacy. If it had advanced the government's interests, the law would have been upheld by the Court.

There are two prevailing positions about regulating commercial speech. One side holds that restrictions should be subject to a strict standard of judicial review. While the First Amendment is not necessarily less protective of commercial speech, the free flow of information is vitally important in health care where information can save lives.

The other side rejects the reasoning that regulations on commercial speech must be reviewed with the highest scrutiny (Jacobs, 2011). This side maintains that government restrictions on the content of commercial data are widespread and well accepted, such as the FDA regulations on the content of pharmaceutical labels and marketing materials. This side warns that heightened barriers to regulatory rules might affect the content of commercial messages. If this happens, they warn that the judiciary could widely interfere with accepted regulatory activities. This side of the debate fears that if strict scrutiny were to be applied to commercial speech, the legislative/judicial balance could change in a way that could significantly weaken regulation of the pharmaceutical industry.

Court's Holding and Decision: No, the Vermont law was a violation of the First Amendment. Although the government may place incidental burdens on commercial speech (for instance to protect patient privacy and control costs), the Vermont law was more than a mere incidental burden and thus was subject to strict scrutiny, which the law did not survive.

See, e.g., Baron, 2012; Bhagwat, 2012; Blackman, 2014; Blitz, 2014; Brandon, 2012; Dhooge, 2014; Gooch, et al., 2013; Hethcoat, 2012; Jacobs, 2014; Janssen, 2014; Joseph, et al., 2012; Mermin & Graff, 2013; Pasquale & Ragone, 2014; Schindler & Brame, 2013; Shinar, 2013; Spacapan & Hutchison, 2013; Spears, et al., 2015; Swartz, 2012 and 2015; Thomson, 2013; Wolf, 2013; Young, 2012 (discussing this court decision).

To be clear, nothing in the *Sorrell* decision allows use of off-label treatments. The data at issue in *Sorrell* involved only patient-prescriber data that had little, if anything, to do with promotion of off-label uses for otherwise FDA-approved medications. Vermont did not state that its marketing prohibition was designed, even in part, to prohibit off-label treatments. Notwithstanding these distinctions, the parallels between the FDA's prohibition of off-label marketing and the impediments to physician detailing struck down as unconstitutional in *Sorrell* are difficult to ignore. *See generally* Joseph, et al., 2012. While pharmacies continue to sell their patient information to data miners like IMS Health, which analyze and report on this information, and pharmaceutical companies continue to pay for access to these reports so their marketing efforts can be more closely tailored to a particular prescriber's habits and preferences, the *Sorrell* decision recognized that physician detailing is proven to affect physician decision-making. Post-*Sorrell* research finds that physician detailing may indeed result in the prescribing of medications that may not be appropriate for patients, may not be the most cost-effective option, or may be downright dangerous for particular patients (Vukadin, 2014).

Patients' Right to Lifesaving Experimental Treatments

The FDA can grant accelerated approval to medical treatments based on limited but promising clinical data, as it did in the *Riegel* case in the *Ethical or Unethical Decision* section at the start of this chapter, but that it refused to do in *Abigail Alliance, infra.* Proponents of access maintain the FDA should use fast-track regulations to give terminally ill patients the right to choose potentially lifesaving medical treatments while more lengthy and definitive clinical trials are undertaken (O'Reilly, 2008). The medical products industry, however, is concerned about accelerated deaths or harm to patients beyond the harm from their disease or illness. The law is uncertain about whether patients have the right to sue for deaths or injuries caused by experimental medical products; sometimes they do and sometimes they do not (*see* Jacobson & Parmet, 2007).

Currently, many lawsuits against the medical products industry are based on state consumer safety regulations that are stronger than federal FDA standards (Mundy & Wang, 2008; Chemerinsky, et al., 2011). Use of experimental treatments raises the issue of whether seriously and terminally ill patients should be free to choose experimental treatments that have passed limited safety trials, often conducted with groups of only 25–30 people, but have not been proven effective in larger patient populations. The values of personal dignity, individual autonomy, self-preservation, and the unconstrained right to choose one's course of treatment should underlie any just decision (Beauchamp & Childress, 2012).

ETHICS CASE
Patients' Right to Access Lifesaving Experimental Medications

Abigail Alliance v. Von Eschenbach, et al.
[Patients v. FDA]
495 F.3d 695 (U.S. Court of Appeals for the District of Columbia Circuit 2007),
certiorari denied, 552 U.S. 1159 (U.S. Supreme Court 2008)

Facts: The Abigail Alliance for Better Access to Developmental Drugs, an advocacy group dedicated to terminally ill patients, appeared to have won a victory when a trial court ruled that terminally ill, mentally competent adult patients had a legal right to access experimental medications that had been deemed safe enough for human testing in Phase I clinical trials but had not reached Phase II to evaluate both the effectiveness of the medication for a particular indication and its short-term side effects. Victory was short-lived, however. The decision was reversed on appeal, marking a setback in the drive for removal of the regulatory barriers that prevent terminally ill patients from gaining early access to experimental medications.

The reversal represented the latest act in a drama that began when Abigail Burroughs, a 21-year-old college student, ran out of conventional treatment options in her battle against head and neck cancer at Johns Hopkins Hospital. The Alliance filed a citizen petition with the FDA for access to cetuximab (Erbitus), an experimental medication only available to patients participating in clinical trials for colon cancer. The Alliance's petition proposed adding an early approval regime that would allow terminally ill patients to gain earlier access to experimental medications. The FDA failed to respond to the proposal, thus prompting the Alliance to proceed to this judicial challenge. Although cetuximab was approved as a treatment for head and neck cancer shortly after Abigail Burroughs died, this case was not resolved until seven years after her death, when the U.S. Supreme Court declined to hear the appeal.

Legal Analysis: Whether an asserted right constitutes a **fundamental right** and liberty interest is extremely important. Fundamental rights are human entitlements that are deeply rooted in the nation's history and traditions, and implicit in the principles of justice and liberty, such as the right to personal autonomy. If the government wishes to restrict a fundamental right, then the government must prove that it has a compelling interest justifying the restriction and that the restriction is narrowly tailored to serve that interest. However, if the restricted right is not a fundamental right, then the government can justify its intervention by showing instead that there is a rational basis for the restriction, an easier standard to meet than the test for restricting fundamental rights.

Because fundamental rights are not explicitly stated in the U.S. Constitution, the U.S. Supreme Court has established a two-pronged test to determine if the asserted right is a fundamental one. This analysis requires proponents of a proposed fundamental right to describe the asserted fundamental liberty interest and show that the asserted right is deeply rooted in the nation's history and tradition, such that neither liberty nor justice would exist if it were sacrificed. The first part of the test is very important: too broad, and a right becomes too comprehensive and impossible to evaluate; too narrow, and a right appears inconsequential.

Rule of Law: The majority opinion described the right of terminally ill patients to access experimental medications and found no fundamental right to potentially toxic medications with no proven therapeutic benefit. The dissenting opinion cast the patients' right to experimental medications in terms of the right of the terminally ill to preserve their lives and found a fundamental right.

Ethics Issue: Should terminally ill patients have access to potentially lifesaving, but also potentially life-threatening, experimental medications?

Ethics Analysis: The key question is how patients' right to lifesaving experimental medications is described. If future cases choose to define this right narrowly, courts could infer a narrow right from a broader, established fundamental right. This has been done in the past; for instance, the right to abortions from the broader right to privacy and the right to use contraception from the right to be free from government intrusion as well as the right to plan one's family.

The issue of access to potentially lifesaving experimental medications continues to be controversial. If Congress were to permit terminally ill patients to access experimental medications, then the FDA would have to create a system to allow that access. The Alliance's proposal represents one legislative possibility for addressing this problem. The proposal would involve granting terminally ill patients who have exhausted all FDA-approved therapies the personal autonomy of selecting post-Phase I experimental medications with their physicians and would lift the current prohibition of charging any price higher than the cost for experimental medications.

The second feature of the Alliance's proposal, allowing commercialization, or charging a price higher than the cost of experimental products, would safeguard clinical trials. The intention of this feature is to create incentives to actively distribute experimental medications, as opposed to merely recover costs under the current FDA regulation. The ethics of high prices could, however, act as a barrier to some patients seeking access to experimental medications, thus forcing them to participate in free clinical trials, which would create disparities in access based on economics.

Court's Holding and Decision: No, terminally ill patients do not have a legal right to access experimental medications.

See, e.g., Hill, 2012; Janssen, 2014; Mathes, 2012; Pivarnik, 2014 (discussing this court decision).

Even if patients have a right to experimental treatments, this right has always been restricted by financial considerations. The ability to pay determined whether patients had access to experimental treatments because health insurance would only cover the costs of medical products approved by the FDA. The new Patient's Bill of Rights changes this

ETHICAL DILEMMAS 4-5

9. Should government and private health insurance coverage be extended to include the costs of experimental treatments?

dynamic by ensuring health insurance coverage for anyone participating in clinical trials. Insurers are now prohibited from dropping or limiting coverage because patients choose to participate in clinical trials. This mandate applies to all clinical trials that treat cancer or other life-threatening diseases.

The Ethics of Managing Access to Patient Care

As health care spending continues to rise, the government is continuously forced to make hard decisions about the distribution of its limited resources (Syrett, 2007). In addressing this situation, some commentators distinguish between rationing the allocation of health resources and medical triage (Rothstein, 2010; Schulman, et al., 2008). **Rationing** refers to the transparent withholding of limited resources from specific groups of patients so the resources will be available for others. Rationing decisions that withhold medical treatments clearly rest upon resource constraints (Syrett, 2007). **Medical triage**, in contrast, refers to the screening of individual patient needs on a case-by-case basis (Smith, 2009).

As the possibility of turning to rationing strategies to manage the mismatch between demand for and supply of medical treatments, the ethics of making rationing decisions is questioned (Syrett, 2007). This, in turn, leads to growing involvement of the law, because the ability of patients to sue helps ensure a level playing field if explicit rationing decisions are ever made. Yet anyone who thinks lawsuits are a solution to managing costs and the demand and supply of health care is wrong. Lawsuits cannot possibly address the fundamental ethical question of how much a human life is worth (Wharton, 2008).

There is a near-universal agreement that most patients' desire for health care exceeds their willingness, or ability, to pay for it. There is also a widespread but largely untested perception that patients are unwilling to accept even reasonable limits on health care (Gold, et al., 2007). But are they?

Managing the Allocation of Limited Health Resources

The entire issue of access to affordable health insurance coverage has become so complex that it does not lend itself to easy analysis or cost-containment solutions. The health insurance industry and employers paying premiums for health insurance coverage are in a tough position. Everyone wants to cut costs, which inevitably involves rationing care, but they are outraged at the manner in which care is rationed (Wharton, 2008). For instance, there is outrage when the leading U.S. health care systems require significant upfront payments to access their services. Everyone is content to purchase less expensive high-deductible health insurance, until the moment they realize they cannot afford the

---

ETHICAL DILEMMAS 4-6

10. Should health insurance help preserve social solidarity by pooling and sharing the risk of health care costs among all Americans, or should health insurance be a mechanism for identifying each person's expected health risks and enabling people to prepay for their expected expenditures?

high co-payments before receiving care. At the same time, most health insurers have gone to excess in cost containment by restricting access to medically needed care (Wharton, 2008). To analogize, if a system contains excess fat, and if a scalpel is carefully used, the fat can be trimmed without harming the muscle or the nerves. But some health insurers have used a hatchet to cut out the fat in health care and have harmed patients and the U.S. health care system as a result.

Misunderstanding Health-Based Comparative Effectiveness

Health-based comparative effectiveness compares two or more medical treatments to determine which interventions are most effective for which patients and under what circumstances. This research has the potential to be applied to a broad range of health care services, yet it has met with criticism because of its potential to restrict access to care (Satz, 2008). This disapproval fails to understand that comparative effectiveness is a benchmark strategy meant to carefully guide clinical decision-making. As such, comparative effectiveness informs, as opposed to suggests, the best way to manage the health of patients.

Critics often confuse this approach with health decisions on general well-being and the many other factors that are prioritized in the broader insurance analysis of whether to provide coverage (Miller, 2010). In **insurance analysis**, the health of the individual insured is not the principle that guides decision-making. Health insurers safeguard the **general well-being** of insured patient populations by minimizing health risks; at the same time the goal of health insurance is the management of those risks. As illustrated in **FIGURE 4-2**, diseases and injuries are managed, rather than patients' health.

As such, general well-being differs from **health-related well-being**. Decision-making on health-related well-being is based on the medical needs of individual patients; decision-making on general well-being provides health insurance coverage for treatment of specific diseases or injuries of patient populations (Posner, 1983/1981). In other words,

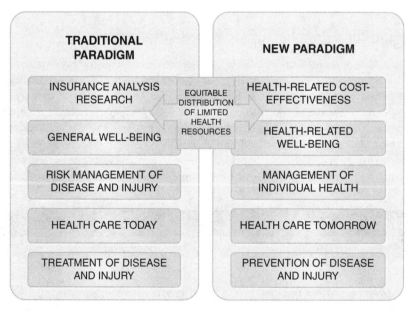

FIGURE 4-2 Fair and Just Administration of Health Resources
Sources: Miller, 2010; Posner, 1981/1983.

the objective of health insurance analysis is to equitably shift health risks from individuals to the community through **risk pools** in exchange for payment of insurance premiums. Risk pools focus on the spreading of similar health risks by individuals with that of similar patient populations. In contrast, the objective of comparative effectiveness research is to equitably distribute health resources based on the medical needs of individuals.

In clinical trials, the health-related well-being of individual patients is not the intention guiding decisions. While all investigators must safeguard patients' welfare by minimizing risks, the goal of clinical trials is not the promotion of the well-being of individual patients, but general well-being by increasing scientific knowledge and future social benefits (Parker, 2008).

Trade-offs can be made between health care and other goods, as well as between individual patients and insured patient populations if decisions are focused on general well-being; such trade-offs are not possible if the focus is on health-related well-being of individual patients (Satz, 2008). Some economists would say the difference between the two approaches is about the kind of world we live in, and the kind we want to create (Sowell, 2010).

Patient-Centered Outcomes Research Institute

The Patient-Centered Outcomes Research Institute, established by the ACA, is responsible for evaluating existing studies and conducting its own research to recommend what type of medical interventions are most effective. The objective of the Institute is not to develop a single national standard of care, but rather to develop a variety of best practices with the objective of improving the quality and efficiency of care.

When it comes to health care, placing a value on costs often leads to qualified health insurance coverage (Blake, 2015). Using rankings of comparative effectiveness of medical interventions to make coverage decisions is a clear and obvious way to allocate costs (Basu & Philipson, 2010). Without definite rankings of which medical interventions are the most effective, rationing is implicit; everyone knows health insurance will only cover a fixed and limited amount for specific medical interventions. At the same time, health insurers cannot be expected to provide coverage for everything. In the end, patients cannot expect to get everything they might want (Mantel, 2015).

The mechanism for rationing is performed in the name of what is **reasonable and necessary care**, defined as the legitimate expectation for appropriate diagnosis and treatment to improve patient outcomes. Reasonable and necessary care at times includes the best that modern medicine has to offer. Yet this term, which involves part medical and part economic decisions, is rarely defined. What constitutes *reasonable and necessary care* is largely unexamined and generally misunderstood (*see* Tassel, 2013). In addition, the term is idiosyncratically applied by the government and the health insurance industry.

In this text, *reasonable and necessary care* entails the evaluation and assessment of a patient's unique health conditions and needs to determine that person's care and health insurance coverage. Ethically speaking, everyone has a legitimate expectation for appropriate diagnosis and treatment. Coverage is based on receiving medical treatments that are reasonable and necessary, which may include the best that modern medicine has to offer. By the definition of what is reasonable and necessary, this involves decisions that are part medical and part economic (AAMC, 2010). Insurers make judgments about what necessary care is reasonable for members of risk pools to pay.

Human health is just too unpredictable at the individual level for explicit rationing of health care. Yet it is not feasible to continue basing coverage decisions on clinical evidence alone without consideration for effectiveness. Most health research maintains that coverage decisions should be based on comparative effectiveness criteria (Donnelly, 2010; Kupersmith, 2009). Health insurance is expensive partly because of the degree of coverage; there are many medical procedures with high prices and minimal medical benefits (Chernew, et al., 2010). At some point coverage produces too little benefit for the costs demanded. There is no national consensus, however, on what level of health risk patients must face in order to warrant the use of the latest medical technologies (Basu & Philipson, 2010).

The Growing Cost of Health Care

If past trends had continued without comprehensive reform, total health care spending would have claimed more than 30 percent of gross domestic product (the value of everything produced in the United States) not long after 2030 (Kogan & Fiedler, 2007). As spending on health care continues to rise, the United States is coming to a point where compromises are inevitable (Cutler, 2005). Before the ACA, spending on health care was growing at twice the rate of inflation and accounting for 1 dollar out of every 6 dollars earned (CMS, 2009). Either other forms of spending had to be cut back to make room, or health care dollars had to be spent more wisely (Aaron, 2008; Keehan, et al., 2008). Health care has improved exponentially since Medicare and Medicaid were established; these successes suggest ways in which all health care can be improved, the system made easier to deal with, and coverage extended to all U.S. residents (Cutler, 2005).

If the nation's health care costs will be increased by mandating that everyone have health insurance coverage, the costs of maintaining people outside the health care system must be offset against the costs of other areas of society (such as the costs of unnecessary disability and unemployment due to illness). If the indirect costs of providing access to health care are not an offset consideration, the mandate for individual health insurance could be called into question.

These decisions are hard because they involve social values where there is no clear right or wrong. Members of the public are appropriate parties to weigh in on the ethical issues surrounding comparative effectiveness (Gold, et al., 2007). Ideally, public debate should continue on health care values and the ethical difficulties involved until a public consensus is reached; yet a consensus will probably never be reached when ethics and values differ so greatly.

The Subjective Nature of Medical Necessity

The term *reasonable and necessary* has been the benchmark by which health insurance coverage decisions are made. However, this term is subject to multiple interpretations and, because of this subjectivity, insurance decisions are not always based on objective notions of medical benefit (Wharton, 2008). For instance, insurers discourage the use of brand-name medications, yet they often pay out more money over the long term when patients do not respond as well to lower-cost generics or develop side effects requiring additional medical interventions that could have been avoided by the use of more expensive brand-name medications (Murray, 2006; Noah, 2011).

The ethical principle of fairness should determine coverage by health insurers. While what constitutes medically needed care should be based upon the unique health condition and particular needs of each patient, evidence-based findings of expected health benefits should be incorporated into coverage determinations (Basu & Philipson, 2010).

Patients' Right of Access to Health Information

Regulation intended to improve the flow of health information to patients is unequivocally desirable in terms of equity and efficiency. Patients need to be able to compare their treatment options with the treatment of others when deciding which health providers achieve the best outcomes. Patients also need health information in determining what amount of health care coverage they need and how much is reasonable to pay for it.

Health care costs could be contained if information measuring the relative quality of providers were available (Aaron, 2008). While the nation's spending on health care is well worth it, much of the spending is unnecessary or could be reduced by changing the way in which care is provided (Cutler, 2005). Millions of patients with often easily manageable chronic diseases, from hypertension to depression to diabetes, are overtreated, undertreated, or untreated because of inefficiencies in the way the system reimburses care, resulting in poor health and in some cases premature death and even serious harm to others (Longo, et al., 2015).

The need to rate the effectiveness of individual physicians is another key battle in the effort to reshape the U.S. health care system. Consumer advocates, employers, and the health insurance industry maintain that access to Medicare and private insurance claims filed by physicians could help independent groups monitor quality and wasteful health care spending (CBO, 2006). The ethical concern is whether access to the Medicare and private insurance databases would result in a significant gain in public understanding of health care, and if so, whether the financial information of physicians implicates privacy issues that require balancing against any public interest in disclosure (Pearson & Bach, 2010). The answer to the first concern is undisputable: there are important public interests in disclosure of the claims data. The availability of the claims databases could be the beginning of an important patient choice movement that could help contribute to higher quality health care and lower costs (Sox & Greenfield, 2009).

Patients could benefit from a deeper understanding of the risks and benefits of a number of medical treatments provided by different providers. Patients could be further empowered to make the best treatment choices based on consideration of all the relevant factors, including which physicians have the best track records in treating their particular illness or disease. Access to this health information could affect everything from elective procedures for non-serious conditions to complex medical treatments such as open-heart surgery and cancer therapy (Tunis, 2009). Patients need information to compare outcome and cost data in the context of their individual needs and health goals.

Defining Medically Needed Care

Just as there is a moral and legal right to emergency care, there is now a moral and legal right to medically needed care (Annas, 2008). Yet there is no public consensus on what the total level of health care spending should be for the nation, nor has there been discussion on whether economic trade-offs are required between health care and other social goods such as higher education. There is no consensus on how to allocate the nation's total spending among health needs (Wilensky, 2008).

One challenge is to define exactly what constitutes this moral right to medically needed care. Generally, a moral right based on effective citizenship and fair equality of opportunity does not require that everyone receive the same benefit. In this instance, there is no agreement that everyone is entitled to the most technologically advanced health care. Thus, the moral right to medically needed care imposes an ethical obligation on society to provide medically needed care to all, but it does not create an unlimited right for individuals to access medical interventions without regard for effectiveness and limited resources (Sandhu, 2007).

Preventive Care

In addition to the moral appeal of mandating health insurance coverage for medically needed care, strong economic arguments can be made for eliminating the ability to remain uninsured (Falit, 2006). It usually costs less to provide preventive and regularly administered health care than it does to provide delayed charitable care (Kaiser Commission, 2004). This is especially true when the cost of lost productivity or unemployment as a result of health conditions is taken into account. There is a financial burden associated with the loss of income and quality of life that the uninsured experience because of poorer health and shorter life spans. The aggregate annual amount of this lost **health capital** (the cost of missed work, unemployment, poor health, and early death) is between $65 billion and $130 billion (IOM, 2002 and 2010). This loss represents 2 to 4 percent of the total $2.8 trillion that the United States spends on health care each year (Keehan, et al., 2008). The annual cost of preventable health conditions is $298 billion to $1.3 trillion (Harris, 2011; IOM, 2010).

If more money is spent on preventive care, then health care professionals who treat preventable health conditions will lose a share of their income (Keehan, et al., 2008). Physicians, nurses, and other health care professionals working and delivering health care services fear the changes required to switch from a focus on medical treatments to a focus on prevention of disease. Hospitals, nursing homes, and other institutional facilities are concerned how the community-based approach to health care will affect them (Somerville, et al., 2015). Everyone fears the process of apportioning health care resources differently. There is anxiety whenever the status quo is changed (Block, 2014).

Given the billions of dollars lost in health capital because of poorer health and shorter life spans, ethically speaking, Americans should be made more accountable for their own lifestyle choices, as illustrated in FEATURE BOX 4-3. At the same time, accountability options must acknowledge that not all preventable conditions are actually preventable. For instance, some people get lung cancer even if they never smoked; others are overweight due

---

FEATURE BOX 4-3

Fair and Just Options for Personal Accountability

Society need not pay for health conditions that could have had their onset delayed or been prevented altogether:
- Link voluntary lifestyle choices to health insurance coverage
- Connect the price of health insurance premiums to lifestyle choices
- Compel individuals who fail to monitor their health with routine checkups to pay higher premiums for health insurance

Sources: Harris, 2011; IOM, 2010; Keehan, et al., 2008.

to a medical condition or a medication, or maybe even genetics, rather than poor diet and exercise choices.

Patients' Rights and Responsibilities

President Franklin D. Roosevelt encouraged the United States to embrace the global recognition of a right to health in his State of the Union address in 1944 while advancing his idea of a Patient's Bill of Rights, including the right to adequate health care and the opportunity to achieve and enjoy good health (Roosevelt, 1944). Although it took 66 years, the nation finally followed through with Roosevelt's overall vision with the passage of the Patient's Bill of Rights in 2010. The new Patient's Bill of Rights goes a long way toward enacting basic fairness measures. When patients are unlawfully injured by the health care industry, justice demands that they have the opportunity to seek a remedy. Patients' hope is that the law may make a difference.

ETHICAL OR UNETHICAL DECISION

Patients' Right to Sue Manufacturers of Innovative Medical Devices

Ethics Issue: *Should patients have the right to sue manufacturers of innovative medical devices in state courts under consumer safety laws for injuries resulting from use of experimental treatments involving high-risk devices?*

Ethics Analysis: Yes, patients should have the right to sue manufacturers of approved medical devices in state courts. Patient safety should prevail, even if the outcome might result in more stringent state-level regulation of cutting-edge medical devices. State consumer safety laws should have priority over federal laws for approving the safety of medical devices. States should have the capacity to make independent ethical decisions and act on them; this is particularly true for new medical innovations.

Ethics Analysis: No, patients should not have the right to sue manufacturers of new and innovative medical devices. FDA premarket approval of medical devices should preempt state consumer safety laws for injuries caused by the devices. There is a need for consistent and uniform regulation by the federal government so as to protect the nation's need to support medical innovations.

Court's Holding and Decision: Patients cannot sue manufacturers of defective medical devices in state courts when the devices have received premarket approval from the FDA. State law is preempted from challenging the safety and effectiveness of FDA-approved medical devices; patients must sue in federal courts.

— *Riegel v. Medtronic, Inc.*, 552 U.S. 312 (U.S. Supreme Court 2008). *See, e.g.*, Conko, 2011; Conroy, 2010; Freeman, 2014; Gifford, 2012; Glover, 2012; Hart, 2010; Herrmann, et al., 2010; Kolodin, 2015; Leske & Schweitzer, 2011; Mota, 2010; Rosman, 2010; Seidenfeld, 2010; Sharkey, 2014; Sharpe, 2011; Smirniotopoulos, 2011; Smith, 2015; Valoir &, Ghosh, 2011; von Biela, 2010; Watkins, 2010; Wellington, 2014; Whitney, 2010; Zieve, 2010 (discussing this court decision).

CHAPTER SUMMARY

- Patients' right to health insurance coverage is based on the ethical principle of distributive justice.
- Historically, while Americans have a right to emergency care, the health insurance industry has placed controversial limitations on this right.
- One of the most contentious ethical issues in health care deals with when and where patients can take action if they feel that a health insurer wrongly denies them coverage and, as a result, causes them harm.
- When patients have the necessary financial resources, the newest cutting-edge medical technologies are readily available; however, there is no public consensus on what ethical principles should guide decisions about what care should be covered by basic health insurance and when additional coverage for unrestricted access to advanced care or access to highly specialized physicians should be required.
- As health care spending continues to rise, governments are continuously forced to make ethical decisions about the just distribution of their limited resources.
- Just as there is a right to emergency care, more energy and imagination are being directed to expanding the right to care that is medically needed.

REFERENCES

AAMC (Association of American Medical Colleges). (2010). *Summary of patient-centered outcomes research provisions.* Washington, DC: AAMC.

Aaron, H. J. (2008). Health care rationing: Inevitable, but impossible? *Georgetown Law Review, 96,* 539–558.

Annas, G. J. (2008). Health care reform in America: Beyond ideology. *Indiana Health Law Review, 5,* 441–461.

Associated Press. (2009, September 9). Kennedy is gone, but health care still his issue. New York, NY: MSNBC.

Baron, J. B. (2012). Property as control: The case of information. *Michigan Telecommunications and Technology Law Review, 18,* 367–418.

Basu, A., & Philipson, T. J. (2010). The impact of comparative effectiveness research on health and health care spending (NBER Working Paper 16633). Cambridge, MA: National Bureau of Economic Research.

Beauchamp, T. L., & Childress, J. F. (2012). *Principles of biomedical ethics* (7th ed.). New York, NY: Oxford University Press.

Bernstein, D. E. (2012). *Rehabilitating Lochner: Defending individual rights against progressive reform.* Chicago, IL: University of Chicago Press.

Bhagwat, A. (2012). Details: Specific facts and the First Amendment. *Southern California Law Review, 86,* 1–61.

Billauer, B. P. (2007). Current issues in public policy: The right to health—A holistic health plan for the next administration. *Rutgers Journal of Law and Public Policy, 5,* 234–281.

Blackman, J. (2014). What happens if data is speech? *University of Pennsylvania Journal of Constitutional Law Heightened Scrutiny, 16,* 25–36.

Blake, V. (2015). Narrow networks, the very sick, and the Patient Protection and Affordable Care Act: Recalling the purpose of health insurance and reform. *Minnesota Journal of Law, Science and Technology, 16,* 63–142.

Blitz, M. J. (2014). The Pandora's box of 21st century commercial speech doctrine: *Sorrell, R.A.V.,* and purpose-constrained scrutiny. *Nexus: Chapman's Journal of Law & Policy, 19,* 19–49.

Block, W. E. (2014). A collection of essays on libertarian jurisprudence. *Saint Louis University Law Journal, 58,* 541–563.

Brandon, S. C. (2012). What's mine is yours: Targeting privacy issues and determining the best solutions for behavioral advertising. *The John Marshall Journal of Computer and Information Law, 29,* 637–672.

CBO (Congressional Budget Office). (2006). *Designing a premium support system for Medicare.* Washington, DC: Congressional Budget Office.

CDC/NCHS (Centers for Disease Control/National Center for Health Statistics). (2015). *Failure to obtain needed medical care: National Health Interview Survey.* Washington, DC: CDC/NCHS.

___. (2009). *Limitations in activities of daily living (ADLs) and instrumental activities of daily living (IDALs): National Health Interview Survey.* Washington, DC: CDC.

___. (2008). *Percent of U.S. adults 55 and over with chronic conditions: National Health Interview Survey.* Washington, DC: CDC.

Chemerinsky, E., et al. (2011). Twenty-second annual Supreme Court review: October 2009 term: The Supreme Court 2009 term overview and 2010 term preview. *Touro Law Review, 27*, 33–61.

Chernew, M. E., et al. (2010). Evidence that value-based insurance can be effective. *Health Affairs (Project Hope), 29*(3), 530–536.

CMS (Centers for Medicare and Medicaid Services). (2009). *National health expenditure data: Historical and projections, 1965–2017.* Washington, DC: CMS.

Conko, G. (2011). Hidden truth: The perils and protection of off-label drug and medical device promotion. *Health Matrix: The Journal of Law-Medicine, 21*, 149–187.

Conroy, A. (2010). FDA approval and federal preemption after *Riegel* and *Levine. Quinnipiac Health Law Journal, 14*, 285–313.

Cutler, D. (2005). *Your money or your life.* New York, NY: Oxford University Press.

Dartmouth Institute for Health Policy and Clinical Practice. (2011). *Dartmouth atlas of health care: Improving patient decision-making in health care.* Lebanon, NH: Dartmouth College.

Dhooge, L. J. (2014). The First Amendment and disclosure regulations: Compelled speech or corporate opportunism? *American Business Law Journal, 51*, 559–659.

DiSarro, A. (2011). Freeze frame: The Supreme Court's reaffirmation of the substantive principles of preliminary injunctions. *Gonzaga Law Review, 47*, 51–98.

Dobson, A., et al. (2006). Mission vs. market: The cost-shift payment "hydraulic": Foundation, history, and implications. *Health Affairs, 25*(1), 22–33.

Donnelly, J. (2010). *Comparative effectiveness research* (Health Affairs/Robert Wood Johnson Foundation Health Policy Brief). Princeton, NJ: Robert Wood Johnson Foundation.

Drummond, M., & Sorenson, C. (2009). Nasty or nice? A perspective on the use of health technology assessment in the United Kingdom. *Value in Health: The Journal of the International Society for Pharmacoeconomics and Outcomes Research, 12*(2), 8–13.

Dubay, L., et al. (2007). The uninsured and the affordability of health insurance coverage. *Health Affairs, 26*(1), 22–30.

Falit, B. P. (2006). The Bush administration's health care proposal: The proper establishment of a consumer-driven health care regime. *Journal of Law, Medicine and Ethics, 34*, 632–636.

Freeman, A. (2014). Predicate creep: The danger of multiple predicate devices. *Annals of Health Law Advanced Directive, 23*, 127–139.

Garden, C. (2014). Meta rights. *Fordham Law Review, 83*, 855–906.

Gifford, D. G. (2012). The constitutional bounding of adjudication: A Fuller(ian) explanation for the Supreme Court's mass tort jurisprudence. *Arizona State Law Journal, 44*, 1109–1164.

Glover, J. M. (2012). The structural role of private enforcement mechanisms in public law. *William & Mary Law Review, 53*, 1137–1217.

Gold, M. R., et al. (2007). Medicare and cost-effectiveness analysis: Time to ask the taxpayers. *Health Affairs, 26*(5), 1399–1406.

Gooch, G. R., et al. (2013). The moral from *Sorrell*: Educate, don't legislate. *Health Matrix: The Journal of Law-Medicine, 23*, 237–277.

Harris, M. (2011, February 25). Chief Information Officer, Information Technology Division, Cleveland Clinic, Capstone speaker on Leadership in an Evolving Global Market at the 2011 Wharton Health Care Business Conference, Philadelphia, PA.

Hart, A. N. (2010). Products liability: Federal preemption of state-law failure-to-warn claims: Has the presumption against preemption gone too far? *The Seventh Circuit Review, 6*, 308–336.

Herrmann, M., et al. (2010). The meaning of the parallel requirements exception under *Lohr* and *Riegel. New York University Annual Survey of American Law, 65*, 545–583.

Hethcoat, III, G. O. (2012). Regulating pharmaceutical marketing after *Sorrell v. IMS Health Inc. Quinnipiac Health Law Journal, 15*, 187–208.

Hill, B. J. (2012). What is the meaning of health? Constitutional implications of defining "medical necessity" and "essential health benefits" under the Affordable Care Act. *American Journal of Law and Medicine, 38*, 445–470.

Hsia, R., et al. (2011). Factors associated with closures of emergency departments in the United States. *Journal of the American Medical Association, 305*, 1978–1985.

IOM (Institute of Medicine). (2010). *Bridging the evidence gap in obesity prevention: A framework to inform decision making.* Washington, DC: National Academies Press.

___. (2002). *Crossing the quality chasm: A new health system for the 21st century.* Washington, DC: National Academies Press.

Iserson, K. V., & Moskop, J. C. (2007). Triage in medicine, part I: Concept, history, and types. *Annals of Emergency Medicine, 49*(3), 282–287.

Jacobs, A. J. (2011). Is state power to protect health compatible with substantive due process rights? *Annals of Health Law, 20*, 113–149.

Jacobs, L. G. (2014). Compelled commercial speech as compelled consent speech. *The Journal of Law and Politics, 29*, 517–533.

Jacobson, P., & Parmet, W. (2007). A new era of unapproved drugs: The case of *Abigail Alliance v. Von Eschenbach*. *Journal of the American Medical Association, 297*(2), 205–208.

Janssen, W. M. (2014). A "duty" to continue selling medicines. *American Journal of Law and Medicine, 40*, 330–392.

Johnson, S. (2009). The idler. In D. Greene (Ed.). *The major works* (Oxford World's Classics). New York, NY: Oxford University Press (Original work published in 1758).

Joseph, J. H., et al. (2012). Is *Sorrell* the death knell for FDA's off-label marketing restrictions? *Journal of Health and Life Sciences Law, 5*(2), 1–33.

Kaiser Commission on Medicaid and the Uninsured. (2004). *The cost of care for the uninsured: What do we spend, who pays, and what would full coverage add to medical spending? Issue update.* Washington, DC: Kaiser Family Foundation.

Kaiser Family Foundation. (2006). *Kaiser public opinion spotlight: The public, managed care and consumer protections.* Menlo, CA: Kaiser Family Foundation.

Keehan, S., et al. (2008). Trends: Health spending projections through 2017: The baby-boom generation is coming to Medicare. *Health Affairs, 27*(2), 145–155.

Kenney, G. M., et al. (2012). A decade of health care access declines for adults holds implications for changes in the Affordable Care Act. *Health Affairs, 21*(5), 899–908.

Kesselheim, A. S. (2011). Off-label drug use and promotion: Balancing public health goals and commercial speech. *American Journal of Law and Medicine, 37*, 225–257.

Kim, J. W. (2005). Managed care liability, ERISA preemption, state "right to sue" legislation in *Aetna Health, Inc. v. Davila*. *Loyola University of Chicago Law Journal, 36*, 651–702.

Kogan, R., & Fiedler, M. (2007). *CBPP (Center on Budget and Policy Priorities): The technical methodology underlying CBPP's long-term budget projections.* Washington, DC: CBPP.

Kolodin, Z. J. F. (2015). Standing to challenge regulatory failure in the age of preemption. *New York University Environmental Law Journal, 22*, 157–180.

Kupersmith, M. J. (2009). Director of the Neuro-Ophthalmology Division, Mt. Sinai Roosevelt Hospital, paper presented at the U.S. Department of Veterans Affairs Symposium: *What can the health care system learn from 30 years of comparative effectiveness research at the Veterans Administration?* Washington, DC: U.S. Department of Veterans Affairs.

Leske, K. O., & Schweitzer, D. (2011). Frustrated with preemption: Why courts should rarely displace state law under the doctrine of frustration preemption. *New York University Annual Survey of American Law, 65*, 585–610.

Levine, M. A., et al. (2007). Improving access to health care: A consensus ethical framework to guide proposals for reform. *Hastings Center Report, 9/10*, 14–19.

Lewis, J. A. (2014). At the intersection of insurance and tax: Equitable remedies under the Affordable Care Act. *John Marshall Law Review, 47*, 1–17.

Longo, D., et al. (2015). *Harrison's principles of internal medicine* (19th ed.). New York, NY: McGraw-Hill Professional.

Maher, B. S. (2013). Thoughts on the latest battles over ERISA's remedies. *Hofstra Labor and Employment Law Journal, 30*, 339–353.

Mantel, J. (2015). A defense of physicians' gatekeeping role: Balancing patients' needs with society's interests. *Pepperdine Law Review, 42*, 633–726.

Mathes, M. (2012). The next civil rights movement? Health care and the aged: Arguing equality in the absence of a right. *Temple Political & Civil Rights Law Review, 21*, 337–347.

Matthew, D. B. (2011). Implementing American health care reform: The fiduciary imperative. *Buffalo Law Review, 59*, 715–807.

____. (2010). Health care in America: Defeating health disparities: A property interest under the Patient Protection and Affordable Care Act of 2010. *West Virginia Law Review, 113*, 31–47.

McAneny, B. L. (2011). *Report of the AMA Counsel on Medical Service, CMS Report 7-A-10, Shared decision-making.* Chicago, IL: American Medical Association.

Mermin, S. E., & Graff, S. K. (2013). The First Amendment and public health, at odds. *American Journal of Law and Medicine, 39*, 298–307.

Miller, J. D. (2010). The Patient-Centered Outcomes Research Institute. *Journal of Health and Life Sciences Law, 4*(1), 4–25.

Mota, S. A. (2010). Federal preemption after Medtronic, Altria Group, and Wyeth. *Oklahoma City University Law Review, 35*, 147–167.

Muir, D., & Stein, N. (2015). Two hats, one head, no heart: The anatomy of the ERISA settlor/fiduciary distinction. *North Carolina Law Review, 93*, 459–549.

Mundy, A., & Wang, S. S. (2008, October 27). In drug case, justices weigh right to sue. *Wall Street Journal*, p. B1.

Murray, A. (2006, February 1). Health-care fixes should focus on quality. *Wall Street Journal*, p. A2.

NIH (National Institutes of Health). (2007). *Understanding clinical trials*. Bethesda, MD: NIH.

Noah, L. (2011). Commercial free speech vs. public health promotion (at the FDA). *Health Matrix: The Journal of Law-Medicine, 21*, 31–95.

O'Reilly, J. T. (2008). Losing deference in the FDA's second century: Judicial review, politics, and a diminished legacy of expertise. *Cornell Law Review, 93*, 939–979.

Parisi, T. J. (2010). The onus is on you: Wellness plans and other strategies being employed for patients to take ownership of their health. *Quinnipiac Health Law Journal, 13*, 243–278.

Parker, L. S. (2008). From imaging to genomics: The future of incidental findings: Should they be viewed as benefits? *Journal of Law, Medicine and Ethics, 36*, 341–350.

Pasquale, F., & Ragone, T. A. (2014). Protecting health privacy in an era of big data processing and cloud computing. *Stanford Technology Law Review, 17*, 595–653.

Pearson, S., & Bach, P. (2010). How Medicare could use comparative effectiveness research in deciding on new coverage and reimbursement. *Health Affairs, 29*(10), 1796–1804.

Pivarnik, G. (2014). Cells as drugs? Regulating the future of medicine. *American Journal of Law and Medicine, 40*, 298–321.

Posner, R. A. (1983). *The economics of justice*. Boston, MA: Harvard University Press (Original work published 1981).

Pratt, D. (2012). Summary plan descriptions after *Amara*. *John Marshall Law Review, 45*, 811–860.

Reinhardt, U. E. (2006). Pricing and payment: The pricing of U.S. hospital services: Chaos behind a veil of secrecy. *Health Affairs, 25*(1), 57–69.

Roosevelt, F. D. (1944, January 11). President's message to the 79th Congress on the State of the Union. *Published Papers, 12*, p. 41.

Rosman, M. E. (2010). Challenges to state anti-preference laws and the role of federal courts. *William and Mary Bill of Rights Journal, 18*, 709–766.

Rothstein, M. A. (2010). Currents in contemporary ethics. *Journal of Law, Medicine and Ethics, 38*, 412–418.

Sandhu, P. K. (2007). A legal right to health care: What can the U.S. learn from foreign models of health rights jurisprudence? *California Law Review, 95*, 1151–1192.

Satz, A. B. (2008). The limits of health care reform. *Alabama Law Review, 59*, 1451–1499.

____. (2008a). Towards solving the health care crisis: A paradoxical case for universal access to high technology. *Yale Journal of Health Policy, Law, and Ethics, 8*(1), 93–143.

Sawicki, N. N. (2012). Informed consent beyond the physician-patient encounter: Tort law implications of extra-clinical decision support tools. *Annals of Health Law, 21*, 1–10.

Schindler, D. S., & Brame, T. (2013). This medication may kill you: Cognitive overload and forced commercial speech. *Whittier Law Review, 35*, 27–78.

Schlesinger, Jr., A. (2003). *The crisis of the old order*. New York, NY: Houghton Mifflin/Harcourt-Mariner Books (Original work published 1957).

Schulman, D. I., et al. (2008). Public health legal services: A new vision. *Georgetown Journal on Poverty Law and Policy, 15*, 729–779.

Schumpeter, J. (2014). Capitalism, socialism, and democracy (2nd ed.). Impact Books: Manassas Park, VA (Original work published 1942).

Seidenfeld, M. (2010). Who decides who decides: Federal regulatory preemption of state tort law. *New York University Annual Survey of American Law, 65*, 611–659.

Sharkey, C. M. (2014). Tort-agency partnerships in an age of preemption. *Theoretical Inquiries in Law, 13*, 359–386.

Sharpe, J. C. (2011). Toward (a) faithful agency in the Supreme Court's preemption jurisprudence. *George Mason Law Review, 18*, 367–437.

Shinar, A. (2013). Public employee speech and the privatization of the First Amendment. *Connecticut Law Review, 46*, 1–71.

Singh, I. (2011, February 25). Executive Vice President of the Clinton Foundation, Capstone speaker at the 17th Annual Wharton Health Care Business Conference: Leadership in an evolving global market. Philadelphia, PA.

Sisko, A., et al. (2009, February 24). Health spending projections through 2018: Recession effects add uncertainty to the outlook. *Health Affairs*, 346–356.

Smirniotopoulos, A. (2011). Bad medicine: Prescription drugs, preemption, and the potential for a no-fault fix. *New York University Review of Law and Social Change, 35*, 793–862.

Smith, C. (2015). Scouting for approval: Lessons on medical device regulation in an era of crowdfunding from Scanadu's "Scout." *Food and Drug Law Journal, 70*, 209–238.

Smith, II, G. P. (2009). Re-shaping the common good in times of public health emergencies: Validating medical triage. *Annals of Health Law, 18*, 1–34.

Somerville, M. H., et al. (2015). Intersection of law, policy and prevention: Hospitals, collaboration, and community health improvement. *Journal of Law, Medicine and Ethics, 43*, 56–59.

Sowell, T. (2010). *Basic economics: A common sense guide to the economy* (4th ed.). New York, NY: Basic Books.

Sox, H. C., & Greenfield, S. (2009). Comparative effectiveness research: A report from the Institute of Medicine. *Annals of Internal Medicine, 151*(3), 203–244.

Spacapan, L. T., & Hutchison, J. M. (2013). Prosecutions of pharmaceutical companies for off-label marketing: Fueled by government's desire to modify corporate conduct or pursuit of a lucrative revenue stream? *Annals of Health Law, 22*, 407–444.

Spears, J. M., et al. (2015). Embracing 21st century information sharing: Defining a new paradigm for the Food and Drug Administration's regulation of biopharmaceutical company communications with healthcare professionals. *Food and Drug Law Journal, 70*, 143–160.

Stone, D. (2008). *The Samaritan's dilemma: Should government help your neighbor?* New York, NY: Perseus Book Group-Nation Books.

Suk, J. C. (2011). Preventive health at work: A comparative approach. *American Journal of Comparative Law, 59*, 1089–1134.

Swartz, M. (2015). Are physician-patient communications protected by the First Amendment? *Cardozo Law Review de novo, 2015*, 92–104.

___. (2012). Physician-patient communication and the First Amendment after *Sorrell*. *Michigan State University Journal of Medicine and Law, 17*, 101–125.

Syrett, K. (2007). *Law, legitimacy and the rationing of healthcare: A contextual and comparative perspective.* New York, NY: Cambridge University Press.

Tassel, K. V. (2013). Using clinical practice guidelines and knowledge translation theory to cure the negative impact of the national hospital peer review hearing system on healthcare quality, cost, and access. *Pepperdine Law Review, 40*, 911–974.

TFAH & RWJF (Trust for America's Health & Robert Wood Johnson Foundation). (2014). *Investing in America's health: A state-by-state look at public health funding and key health facts.* Washington, DC: TFAH & Princeton, NJ: RWJF.

___. (2011). *The new prevention fund: An investment in the future health of America.*

Thomson, H. B. (2013). Whither *Central Hudson*? Commercial speech in the wake of *Sorrell v. IMS Health*. *Columbia Journal of Law and Social Problems, 47*, 171–207.

Tunis, S. R., Office of Clinical Standards and Quality, Centers for Medicare and Medicaid. (2009). Strategies to improve comparative effectiveness research methods and data infrastructure. Discussion paper presented at the Engelberg Center for Health Care Reform and The Hamilton Project Forum on Implementing Comparative Effectiveness Research: Priorities, Methods and Impact. Washington, DC.

Tyrell, III, J. E. (2010). Non-profits under fire: The effects of minimal charity requirements legislation on not-for-profit hospitals. *The Journal of Contemporary Health Law and Policy, 26*, 373–402.

Valenza, M. A. (2011). *Cigna v. Amara*: Supreme Court resolves several ERISA claim issues while leaving others for the lower courts. *Transactions: The Tennessee Journal of Business Law, 13*, 139–164.

Valoir, T., & Ghosh, S. (2011). FDA preemption of drug and device labeling: Who should decide what goes on a drug label? *Health Matrix: Journal of Law-Medicine, 21*, 555–598.

Viscusi, W. K., & Born, P. (2005). Medical malpractice insurance in the wake of liability reform. *The Journal of Legal Studies, 25*, 463–490.

von Biela, L. M. (2010). A disclosure dilemma: What you don't know can kill you, but so can what you do know. *Food and Drug Law Journal, 65*, 317–346.

Vukadin, K. T. (2014). Failure-to-warn: Facing up to the real impact of pharmaceutical marketing on the physician's decision to prescribe. *Tulsa Law Review, 50*, 75–113.

Watkins, L. (2010). How states can protect their policies in federal class actions. *Campbell Law Review, 32*, 285–309.

Watson, S. D. (2007). Consumer-directed Medicaid and cost-shifting to patients. *Saint Louis University Law Journal, 51*, 403–432.

Wellington, K. B. (2014). Cyberattacks on medical devices and hospital networks: Legal gaps and regulatory solutions. *Santa Clara High Technology Law Journal, 30*, 139–200.

Wennberg, J. E. (2010). *Tracking medicine: A researcher's quest to understand health care.* New York, NY: Oxford University Press.

Wharton School at the University of Pennsylvania. (2011). In the health care sector, who should choose which treatment is best? *Knowledge@Wharton.*

___. (2008). Cost-effective medical treatment: Putting an updated dollar value on human life.

Whitney, D. W. (2010). Guide to preemption of state-law claims against class III PMA medical devices. *Food and Drug Law Journal, 65*, 113–139.

Wilensky, G. R. (2008). Cost-effectiveness information: Yes, it's important, but keep it separate, please! *Annals of Internal Medicine, 148*, 967–968.

Wiggins, K. (2012). Medical provider claims: Standing, assignments, and ERISA preemption. *John Marshall Law Review, 45*, 861–891.

Wolf, A. J. (2013). Detailing commercial speech: What pharmaceutical marketing reveals about bans on commercial speech. *William and Mary Bill of Rights Journal, 21*, 1291–1323.

Young, E. A. (2012). The constitutionality of the Affordable Care Act: Ideas from the academy: Popular constitutionalism and the underenforcement problem: The case of the national healthcare law. *Law and Contemporary Problems, 75*, 157–201.

Zieve, A. M. (2010). Thoughts on the rise and decline of the implied preemption theory for state law damages claims. *New York University Annual Survey of American Law, 65*, 661–680.

CHAPTER 5

Charitable Care and Tax-Exempt Hospitals

"When health is absent, wisdom cannot reveal itself, art cannot become manifest, strength cannot be exerted, wealth is useless, and reason is powerless."

— **Herophilus** (335-280 BC), ancient Greek physician

LEARNING OBJECTIVES

After completing this chapter, the reader should be able to:

1. Summarize the ethical principles underlying policies that require tax-exempt hospitals to provide fair and reasonable charges for health care services in return for substantial federal, state, and local tax exemptions.
2. Explain whether tax-exempt hospitals are doing enough to justify their tax exemptions in terms of their charitable care policies.
3. Understand the complexity of policies that allocate costs and seek payment for health care services in tax-exempt hospitals.

KEY TERMS

Actual price
Bad debt
Chargemaster
Charitable care
Charitable care
  standard
Class action lawsuits

Community benefit standard
Cost-shifting
Cross-subsidization
Emergency Medical
  Treatment and Active
  Labor Act of 1986
  (EMTALA)

For-profit subsidiaries
List price
Means-tested discount
Medically necessary care
Price discrimination
Tax-exempt
Uncompensated care

Charitable Obligations of Tax-Exempt Hospitals

Ethics Issue: *Do tax-exempt, not-for-profit hospitals deserve the tax exemptions they have historically received?*

In Brief: Provena Covenant Medical Center, one of two regional full-service non-profit hospitals serving the Midwest college town of Champaign-Urbana, Illinois, is part of a health care system with six hospitals and a host of **for-profit subsidiaries** that are managed and owned by the tax-exempt hospitals to fulfill key hospital functions, including emergency physicians, the hospital pharmacies, and cafeterias. Provena's **charitable care** program for free or discounted services was typical of many hospitals: charitable care was limited to patients at or below the federal poverty level with discounts for care based on income. Few people with hospital debt knew of the program. If patients failed to respond quickly to bills, their cases were referred to aggressive collection agencies; at that point it was too late to apply for charitable care or discounts.

If a patient did hear about the hospital charitable care program, the application was confusing, the deadline was short, and the processing time was long. Every application had to be approved by a committee in the corporate office, and, even for seniors on fixed incomes, approval only lasted six months. Often patients did not know they owed Provena money until a collection agency contacted them or they were sued. Predatory collection agencies harassed patients with phone calls and letters, sued financially distressed patients, garnished wages and bank accounts, obtained liens on homes, and asked for arrest warrants when patients failed to keep up with any follow-up enforcement proceedings.

For the tax year in question, Provena had patient revenues of $714 million; of approximately 110,000 admissions, 302 patients received free or discounted care, at a cost to the hospital of $2.5 million, which was $1.268 million less than Provena's local property tax exemption. In other words, the hospital's $2.5 million charitable care program was $1.268 million less than the $3.768 million Provena would have had to pay in local property taxes, but for its exemption from the local taxes other comparable companies paid. **Tax-exempt** status exempts health care systems like Provena from payment of federal, state, and local taxes, while enabling them to solicit charitable donations. Nearly 25,000 people in the surrounding county had incomes below the federal poverty level and an estimated 20,000 were uninsured. Provena claimed $7.1 million of **bad debt**, defined as accounts written off as unpaid even though patients had the ability to pay. Provena always maintained that its operations were like every other tax-exempt hospital. Following initial denial of its 2004 property exemption by the local county board of review, Provena hung posters in its public restrooms advising of its charitable care program.

— *Provena Covenant Medical Center, et al. v. Department of Revenue, et al.*, 925 N.E.2d 1131 (Supreme Court of Illinois 2010). (*See Ethical or Unethical Decision* at the end of the chapter for discussion of this ethics issue.)

Introduction

Concerns over the cost of health care, as well as concerns about who pays for it and how, go back as far as the second millennium B.C. and the ancient Code of Hammurabi (Martin, 2011). At issue in this chapter is how tax-exempt hospitals carry out their charitable mission when attempting to allocate scarce health resources in the most effective way possible. In return for their tax-exempt status, hospitals seek to provide a substantial amount of charitable care even though there is no protocol for how much should be put toward such care (McWilliams & Alop, 2010). While long-term care facilities and other types of care present similar ethical issues for tax-exempt health care systems, the focus of this chapter is on the 31 cents of every health care dollar that is spent on hospitals, as opposed to all other health care costs such as outpatient care and medications (Kaiser Family Foundation, 2012).

There is no public consensus on how to define charitable care so that it does not distort the health care market. As the nation reforms its health care systems, there are questions about whether and under what circumstances hospitals deserve tax exemption, and if certain hospitals are granted tax exemption, what society should demand in exchange. While some may question the ethicality of running hospitals as business enterprises, whether or not hospitals should be run this way is not addressed in this chapter. There is no need to discuss whether generating revenue is fundamental to every aspect of hospital care when the health care industry accounts for nearly 17 percent of the nation's gross domestic product (Channick, 2012); health care is a large and growing business enterprise that is the largest employer in many communities (AHA, 2013). Determining who controls the nation's health resources usually explains who the dominant players are, and how they are able to organize and change the U.S. health care system. Unquestionably, the most straightforward way to understand how the system functions, where ethical vulnerabilities lie, and why it is so difficult to institute comprehensive reforms is to identify who controls the resources. *See generally* Jacobson & Mathur, 2010.

Lack of Access to Medically Necessary Health Care

More than 1 in 10 Americans, or 35 million people, are being denied access to **medically necessary care** due to costs (Kaiser Family Foundation, 2014a). *Medically necessary care* refers to medical treatments that are needed but not received or are delayed because they are unaffordable. Private health insurance no longer guarantees that people will be able to access affordable health care. Moreover, access is declining more for people in fair or poor health than for healthier people (Hoffman, 2010).

ETHICAL DILEMMAS 5-1

1. Are tax policies for tax exemptions of health care systems ethical when more than one in ten Americans are forced to delay or are denied access to medically necessary health care and medications due to costs?
2. If tax exemption policies for hospitals are unethical, are the government and the health insurance and health care industries obligated to seek more just and egalitarian regulatory structures to make access to health care more affordable?

Uninsured and Underinsured Patients: Two Challenging Patient Groups

Although the United States is in the midst of the most significant health insurance expansion since Medicare and Medicaid were enacted in 1965, 79 million Americans are uninsured or underinsured (Schoen, et al., 2014). The tax-exempt hospitals that provide **uncompensated care** (the sum of charitable care and bad debt) to this patient population are stretched to the breaking point (Felland, et al., 2010). The cost of charitable care or discounted care to the uninsured, plus the bad debt from the underinsured, is not sustainable. Major teaching hospitals lose more than $6 billion a year from providing care to uninsured and underinsured patients (Kirch, 2008; *see also* Maher, 2014).

Underinsured Patients

Today, the average annual cost of health insurance of $16,800 for family coverage exceeds the equivalent of a minimum-wage worker's annual wages, at $15,000 (NCSL, 2015; U.S. Census Bureau, 2014). Given this state of affairs, the government and the health insurance industry have an ethical obligation to ensure that premiums do not continue increasing to the point where people have little left to cover the access fees required to obtain preventive, routine health care (Fowler & Jost, 2008).

Health insurance is the most important determinant of access to health care (Collins, 2007). People without adequate coverage risk financial disaster if they find themselves in need of expensive health care. Complete lack of health insurance, however, is only one part of the problem, as even the insured have serious gaps in coverage. A growing number of the underinsured are finding themselves on shaky financial ground because of the cost of health care not covered by their insurance plans (Commonwealth, 2013).

One in 10 working-age adults faces potential financial hardship from being underinsured (Kaiser Commission, 2010). Much of the growth in the underinsured market comes from the middle class. While low-income people remain vulnerable, middle-income families are being hit the hardest because they do not qualify for charitable care or government health insurance programs (Schoen, et al., 2011).

Uninsured Patients

The law and all ethical theories require consistency in the way people are treated, yet no consistent ethical standards prevail for accessing health care in the United States (Bloche, 2009). People who spend any time without health insurance report significantly higher rates of cost-related access problems, are significantly less likely to have a regular family physician, and are less likely to report that they always or often receive the health care they need when they need it (Collins, 2007). As the cost of health insurance continues to increase, fewer employers, particularly small business enterprises, are able to provide comprehensive health insurance to their employees. Although government health insurance fills some of this gap, this assistance is mostly for children from financially distressed families (Kaiser Commission, 2015), as illustrated in **FEATURE BOXES 5-1** and **5-2**.

FEATURE BOX 5-1

The Ethics of Forgetting the Middle Class: Who Are the Uninsured and Underinsured?

- For the working middle class with annual incomes of $50,000 to $140,000, the underinsured percentage rate has reached double digits.
- Nearly 62 million Americans lack affordable health insurance, which represents almost 13 percent of the population under 65 years of age.
- The lack of health insurance coverage directly contributes to three deaths every hour.

— Sources: Schoen, et al., 2014; U.S. Census Bureau & BLS, 2012; Wilper, et al., 2009.

FEATURE BOX 5-2

The Forgotten Working Poor: America's Dichotomy Between Access to Health Care and Equality of Opportunity

- Employer-provided health insurance has decreased to 6 in 10 working-age Americans.
- Most American families still obtain their health insurance through their employers, but that is not a guaranteed benefit for approximately 160 million employees and their dependents.
- More than three-fourths of the uninsured come from working families.

— Sources: Collins, 2007; Kaiser Commission, 2010; Smith & Medalia, 2014.

The Social Compact with Tax-Exempt Health Care Systems

Whether charitable care provided by hospitals is a viable standard for tax exemption is debatable, especially for the uninsured or underinsured. Even so, after Medicare and Medicaid were established in 1969, centuries' worth of legal precedent as to what defined charitable purposes was no longer applicable. The hospital industry contended there would not be enough demand for charitable care to satisfy tax exemption standards because government health insurance now reimbursed hospitals for care previously provided free of charge (Becker, 2007). The hospital industry maintained that most Americans would be covered either by the new government insurance programs or by private health insurance, and pushed for a more flexible tax exemption standard (Carreyrou & Martinez, 2008).

As illustrated in **FEATURE BOX 5-3**, as opposed to the provision of charitable care, this new standard for determining tax-exempt status became known as the **community benefit standard**. Since then, hospitals have qualified for tax-exempt status by providing emergency care, health education, and community-building activities that directly address social determinants of health. For the first time since 1751, when the nation's first hospital was established in Philadelphia by Dr. Thomas Bond (known as the father of clinical medicine in America) and Benjamin Franklin, tax-exempt hospitals were no longer required to offer charitable care directly to the poor and financially distressed (Cohen, 2006). While the community benefit standard does not require tax-exempt hospitals to offer charitable care, many hospitals continue to do so. For instance, Pennsylvania Hospital, the nation's first hospital, is now part of the University of Pennsylvania Health System, a $3 billion health care system that provides about one dollar in charitable care for every $400 in revenue (University of Pennsylvania, 2014).

Heightened Scrutiny of the Community Benefit Standard

There is a national debate about what charitable care means and whether tax-exempt health care systems deserve their exemption status. While Congress is questioning the debt-collection policies of tax-exempt hospitals, **class action lawsuits**, which are brought by a large group of plaintiffs or in which a large number of defendants are sued, are being brought by groups of uninsured patients against numerous tax-exempt health care systems (Berg, 2010). These lawsuits allege that hospitals have charged uninsured patients fees well in excess of those charged to insured patients. It may be worth noting that these cases are being litigated by some of the same plaintiff attorneys who successfully initiated class action suits against the tobacco industry (Nie, 2007).

Hospital Charges for the Uninsured

Whether tax-exempt hospitals are overcharging uninsured patients is under scrutiny (Olson, 2005). Specifically, uninsured patients are charged more for the same care than

---

FEATURE BOX 5-3

The Underinsured: A Rapidly Increasing Socioeconomic Challenge

- More than 31 million working-age adults were underinsured in 2014, nearly double those found to have had inadequate coverage in 2003.
- Over the past decade, the rate of underinsured tripled among middle- and high-income families, or those with at least $40,000 in income.
- The health and financial security of American families are at risk: premiums for health insurance coverage for a typical family of 4 with employer-based coverage almost doubled since 1999 (from $805 to $1,420/month), while wages rose only 19 percent.

— Sources: Auerbach & Kellermann, 2011; Commonwealth Fund, 2013; Schoen, et al., 2011.

insured patients (Kuntze, 2008). While the exact rate of discount that insured patients receive is unknown, the typical range of discounts is between 45 and 50 percent (Anderson, 2007). One nationwide study found that the uninsured pay 2.5 times what the insured pay for the same medical treatments (Saar, 2008). In other words, the insurance industry negotiates price discounts for patients with health insurance; patients without insurance pay the undiscounted price. This results in hospitals billing insurance companies 45 to 50 percent less for insured patients than they bill uninsured patients for the same medical treatments. While it is the high fee billings and unrelenting collection procedures together that raise ethical concerns (Berg, 2010), the inescapable fact is that the insured generally cannot afford to pay their undiscounted hospital charges (Jacoby & Holman, 2010).

ETHICS CASE
Hospital Charges for the Uninsured

DiCarlo v. St. Mary's Hospital, et al.
[Uninsured Patient v. Tax-Exempt Hospital]
530 F.3d 255 (U.S. Court of Appeals for the 3rd Circuit 2008)

Facts: DiCarlo brought a class action lawsuit against an acute care medical/surgical hospital and the tax-exempt health care system operating the hospital, alleging breach of contract, breach of the obligation of good faith and fair dealing, unjust enrichment, breach of fiduciary obligation, and fraud. The hospital accepted discounted payments from health insurance plans that negotiated discounts with the hospital, and provided free or discounted care to patients eligible for charitable care.

DiCarlo was admitted to the hospital after experiencing an increased heart rate. At the time he was admitted, DiCarlo was uninsured and did not qualify for government health insurance or charitable care. Upon his arrival at the hospital, DiCarlo consented to whatever medical treatment was deemed medically necessary and guaranteed payment of all charges for services rendered. Following his treatment, the hospital charged DiCarlo $3,483 excluding separately billed physician fees.

Legal Analysis: The court discussed the policy concerns about health care costs and found that the judiciary was ill-equipped to determine what fair and reasonable hospital costs were, or to make legislative determinations as to what constituted medically necessary care.

First, DiCarlo contended he only agreed to pay a reasonable price, which he defined as the government health insurance or charitable care rates, not the undiscounted rates charged to the uninsured. This breach-of-contract claim goes directly to the issue of how to charge uninsured hospital patients for health care. All the same, the court dismissed this claim, finding that it did not reflect how hospital charges are actually set.

Hospitals have a uniform set of charges, known as the **chargemaster**, which applies to all patients. Discounted charges and computations apply in different situations. Discounts are negotiated with various private health insurance plans; another discount is accepted if patients are covered by government insurance plans that mandate discounts; still other discounts are given to patients eligible for charitable care programs; and free care is available to patients who demonstrate financial need but are ineligible for any government programs.

Second, the court dismissed the claim relating to breach of the duty of good faith and fair dealing. DiCarlo might have been entitled to relief under the covenant of good faith and fair dealing if his reasonable expectations of what he was obligated to pay were destroyed after signing the consent form agreeing to pay for medical treatment. DiCarlo may also have had a case if the hospital acted with ill motives or without any legitimate purpose. In signing the consent form, however, DiCarlo promised to pay in full the definite price terms set by the hospital; his obligations were clear.

Third, in order to state a claim for unjust enrichment, the hospital must have received and retained a benefit from DiCarlo that would be unjust. However, DiCarlo did not give anything at all to the hospital. Therefore, the court dismissed this claim against the hospital.

Fourth, the court refused to expand the fiduciary duty of hospitals to act on patients' behalf with regard to their billing practices. Analogizing the practice to the debtor-creditor relationship, the breach of fiduciary duty claim was dismissed. There was no duty to act on behalf of or for the benefit of uninsured patients when the hospital set its price terms. In other words, when a hospital sets its prices for a medical treatment, its only duty is to seek adequate payment for the hospital; the court determined that hospitals are under no obligation to make medical treatments affordable.

Finally, in dismissing the fraud claim, the court found that the hospital's pricing and billing practices were not covered by state fraud laws prohibiting deliberate deception for financial gain. Hospital debt collectors are usually not covered by state consumer fraud statutes, so long as they are operating in their professional capacities.

Rule of Law: Tax-exempt hospitals are not required to provide free or reduced rates for medical treatments to uninsured patients; moreover, it is not unreasonable to charge uninsured patients higher rates merely because various insurers have negotiated lower rates.

Ethics Issue: Is discriminatory pricing for health care an ethical policy?

Ethics Analysis: The court refused to address the ethical issues at hand. This approach to the law is based on formal logic prevalent at the beginning of the 20th century. In this instance, while the severe economic hardship faced by the uninsured was acknowledged, the court declined to determine what fair and reasonable should be for tax-exempt hospitals, or to decide what should constitute charitable care. Nor would the court examine the underlying issue of this case as to whether it is fundamentally fair to charge the uninsured greater amounts than those paid by the insured or patients eligible for charitable care.

A more current but competing approach replaces this formalism with a pragmatic attitude toward law generally. This attitude treats law as made, not found. Law therefore is based on human experience and ethics, as opposed to formal logic. Legal principles are not inherent in some universal, timeless logical system; they are social constructs designed by people in specific social contexts for specific purposes to achieve specific ends. In this instance, the courts could explain what fair and reasonable prices should be and what should constitute charitable care for tax-exempt hospitals. But this is not the approach this court took in deciding this case.

Court's Holding and Decision: Yes, tax-exempt hospitals may establish discriminatory pricing for their health care services.

See Markey, 2010 (discussing this court decision); *see also* Koppel, 2011.

ETHICAL DILEMMAS 5-2

3. Should the uninsured have the same human right to access hospital care as the privately insured and those covered by government insurance?

Charitable Care Standard

The traditional **charitable care standard** of tax exemption considered the conventional role of public hospitals as health care facilities catering to the financially distressed who could not be treated and cared for in their homes (Schirra, 2011). Traditionally, most patients were treated in their homes rather than in public hospitals. As patients started receiving most of their care in hospitals, the traditional charitable care standard evolved accordingly.

Today, hospitals are generally organized as nonprofit entities whose main purpose is providing access to medically needed care. Tax-exempt, nonprofit hospitals have an obligation to provide health care to anyone, regardless of ability to pay (Tyrrell, 2010). The standard does not deny tax-exempt hospitals the right to charge uninsured and underinsured patients who have the ability to pay; rather, it provides an obligation to provide charitable care to persons unable to pay. In addition, hospitals may charge patients a **means-tested discount** and thereby render charitable care. Means-tested discounts, the reduced price for health care based on the income and other resources patients have to pay their medical bills, could greatly assist uninsured or underinsured patients to meet their financial obligations. The charitable care standard assumes that hospitals could attain tax exemption even if their primary function is providing health care to patients able to pay, as long as they provide free or reduced rates to those with no ability to pay (Schirra, 2011).

Community Benefit Standard

The charitable care standard evolved from a requirement to provide charitable care to a community benefit standard that considers the general promotion of health as sufficient justification for tax-exempt status (Nie, 2007). In return for not paying taxes, tax-exempt hospitals are expected to provide a community benefit, a loosely defined federal requirement whose most important component is charitable care.

Many tax-exempt hospitals, however, include other costs in their community benefit accounting, including development costs, community education, and research expenditures (Lagnado, 2004; Lenihan & Hermer, 2014). Other tax-exempt hospitals include the salaries of their employees as a community benefit, further obscuring the issue of charitable care (Carreyrou & Martinez, 2008). At the same time, others maintain that the impact of job production is a benefit that should be seen as promoting the community's well-being (CBO, 2006). Often, hospitals also include unpaid patient bills, plus the difference between the list prices of health care they provide and what they are paid by insurers (Carreyrou & Martinez, 2008). Excluding all these community benefit costs, many tax-exempt hospitals spend less on actual charitable care than they receive in tax breaks (CBO, 2006).

Bad Debt as a Contribution to Charitable Care

Given the complexity of the health care payment system, controversy ensues when tax-exempt hospitals write off bad debt and classify that write-off as a charitable care contribution to the community. The only distinction between charitable care and bad debt is that hospitals make no attempt to collect bills for charitable care (Lenihan & Hermer, 2014). This complexity appears as a theme in many of the class action lawsuits on charitable care, which often arise out of the intersection of charitable care, uncompensated care, and bad debt, and how hospitals report these relative costs for payment.

Nearly all hospitals that bill patients and collect after care is delivered incur a certain amount of bad debt. Hospitals make allowances for bad debt and consider the financial implications in their fiscal budgets and forecasts. On average, tax-exempt hospitals charge patients 20 percent extra in order to make up for bad debt (Courtney, 2011). With bad debt increasing health care costs, this is one of the factors justifying the minimum coverage provision requiring nearly everyone to purchase health insurance coverage. With near-universal medical coverage, health care costs could decrease by the amount historically generally allocated to bad debt, thus making access to health care more affordable for everyone. At the same time, hospitals will be required to provide that much less in charitable care, since more patients will be able to afford lower-priced care.

Discriminatory Pricing for Health Care

Although some may debate the discriminatory prices hospitals charge for similar individual treatments and medical supplies under similar circumstances, price discrimination is really an unsuitable way to describe how hospital prices are determined, because it is based on an incomplete picture of the pricing system. Hospital pricing can be divided into two kinds of pricing. First, there is the **list price**, which is the undiscounted real cost for health care services rendered. From these list prices, insurers and other groups negotiate discounts with hospitals to arrive at so-called **actual prices**. By definition, actual prices are one of two charges used by hospitals for payment; in fact, it is a term of art (meaning its industry definition is different from what the commonly accepted definition of those words would be), in that insurers negotiate this discounted charge from the list price for health care services rendered (Purdy & Siegel, 2012). Although list prices vary widely from hospital to hospital, the actual prices paid are relatively static (Reinhardt, 2006). The difference between the list prices and the actual prices falls on uninsured patients who pay full price for the care they receive.

Price discrimination, the practice of charging different prices to different patients for identical health care even when the actual costs are identical, is common practice (Lenihan & Hermer, 2014; Lagnado, 2004a). To further complicate matters, half of the revenue of most tax-exempt hospitals comes from government insurance at levels that do not cover the costs incurred by hospitals. In fact, hospitals are paid about one-third of their list prices by Medicare and Medicaid (Reinhardt, 2006). Hospitals would operate at a loss if they were only paid by government health insurance programs. **Cost-shifting** to private health insurance companies makes up the other remaining real costs for care rendered to patients with government-financed health insurance (Nussbaum, 2012). In other words, a cost-shift occurs whenever the insurance industry charges more for certain medical products and health care services in order to subsidize products and services that are provided at or below cost (Dobson, et al., 2006). Given this pricing complexity, along with the additional losses for uncompensated care, the rationale behind hospitals seeking to maximize payments from the remaining segments of their private markets suddenly becomes much more understandable, if not logical (Moncrieff, 2012; Purdy & Siegel, 2012).

Hospitals' For-Profit Approach to Charitable Care

By the 20th century, the U.S. hospital system was largely tax-exempt with a for-profit approach to providing hospital care (Kinney, 2010); few public hospitals remained. In other words, tax-exempt hospitals did not operate as public institutions but rather as parts of complex private, not-for-profit health care systems with financial support coming from a few limited private sources. Charity is the sole master of the nonprofit approach, whereas profits are the master of the for-profit approach. Until recently, generous payment rates from health insurance permitted tax-exempt hospitals to provide significant levels of charitable care by cross-subsidizing that care with charges paid by insured patients. In **cross-subsidization**, one patient group subsidizes an other. In this instance, *cross-subsidization* is defined as the misattribution of costs incurred from charitable care to the care of the uninsured. Today, the result is that the uninsured bear the costs of charitable care; the uninsured are the only payer group receiving undiscounted care (Dobson, et al., 2006; Lenihan & Hermer, 2014).

As insurance payments have become more strict and discriminating about paying for high-priced advanced care, most tax-exempt hospitals have become increasingly focused on financial performance and survival. Support for charitable care was the first casualty at all but the best-managed health care systems. In other words, private health insurance costs have risen, and coverage under private insurance became less comprehensive, with higher deductibles and co-payments (Kaiser Family Foundation, 2009). Health insurance premiums are increasing to the point where more and more insured patients are becoming underinsured, which means that more hospital care is becoming uncompensated care, which in turn gets written off as charitable care and bad debt (Kinney, 2010). This is one reason charitable care is suffering. With the demands for charitable care intensifying, the billions in tax dollars saved by tax-exempt hospitals and meant to be directed toward the community's health are being scrutinized across the United States (Rosenbaum & Margulies, 2011), as illustrated in **FIGURE 5-1**. There is a general consensus that under no circumstances should the hospital industry that is so heavily subsidized by tax dollars be allowed to become a cash cow for anyone unable to provide high-quality care at an affordable rate (Kinney, 2010).

Obligation of Tax-Exempt Hospitals to Provide Charitable Care

The obligation of providing universal access to comprehensive and continuous medical coverage is something that must be done; it is not a charitable ideal (Miller-Wilson, 2009). Many lawmakers are concerned about the plight of patients who are labeled as self-pay, which includes the uninsured, in the wake of reports that more and more Americans are being bankrupted by medical debts (Kaiser Commission, 2014; Pratt, 2011). At the same time, there is no consensus about whether tax-exempt hospitals are obligated to provide charitable care if they are not provided fair and mutually reasonable payments for the costs

ETHICAL DILEMMAS 5-3

4. What ethical principles should federal, state, and local governments use to determine their obligation to society when deciding whether to forgo tax revenue from tax-exempt hospitals?

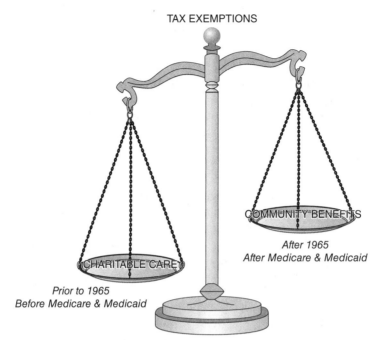

TAX EXEMPTIONS

COMMUNITY BENEFITS

After 1965
After Medicare & Medicaid

CHARITABLE CARE

Prior to 1965
Before Medicare & Medicaid

Do community benefits outweigh $50 BILLION in forgone taxes?

FIGURE 5-1 Evolution of the Nation's Social Contract: Tax-Exempt Health Care Systems
Sources: CBO, 2006; Hackney, 2013; NCCS, 2012; Rosenbaum & Margulies, 2011; Weisblatt, 2014.

of health care by the government. When hospitals are paid only one-third of their real costs of treating patients with government insurance (Reinhardt, 2006), there is no reason the two-thirds discount should not be viewed as a form of charitable care.

Heightened Scrutiny of Charitable Care Practices

Many tax-exempt health care systems are under scrutiny, and some tax-exempt hospitals have already been singled out for their charitable care practices, as illustrated in **FEATURE BOX 5-4**. Several tax-exempt hospitals across the country have been charged with billing uninsured patients significantly more than insured patients for the same health care (like Provena Covenant Medical Center at the beginning of this chapter), and then using overly aggressive collection practices to collect the resultant medical debt. While it may appear that hospitals are billing insured patients too much so that they can write off even more care provided to the uninsured and underinsured as uncompensated care, bad debt, or charitable care, the fact remains that the uninsured are subsidizing such care through cost-shifting (Moncrieff, 2012; Nussbaum, 2012; Purdy & Siegel, 2012). In other words, systematically higher prices (above cost) are paid by the uninsured to offset lower prices (below-cost discounted prices) paid by private and public insurance payers.

Legal proceedings and class action lawsuits brought against tax-exempt health care systems highlight the contradictory views about the rising cost of health care and the increasing number of underinsured patients (Moskowitz, 2005). Some hospitals are choosing to enter settlement agreements as opposed to litigating the myriad of unresolved issues as to what constitutes charitable care. Regardless, this litigation has made hospital pricing, billing, and collection practices issues of public concern and serves as a signal to tax-exempt

FEATURE BOX 5-4

The Ethics of Charitable Care Practices

- Discriminatory pricing:
  - Charging uninsured patients with the undiscounted cost for care without regard to ability to pay, while discounting costs for patients with health insurance
- Misuse of tax-exempt assets and revenue:
  - Allowing for-profit entities to derive a profit from use of their tax-exempt facilities (e.g., food services, anesthesiology practices, physician practices, and parking)
  - Failing to use their tax-exempt surpluses to provide affordable health care
- Focusing on expensive procedures
- Overly aggressive collection practices:
  - Securitizing and then selling patients' debts to aggressive third-party debt collectors
- Price gouging:
  - Charging patients more than the cost of care rendered in order to cover the cost of unreimbursed care
- Refusing to provide emergency services without regard to the ability to pay, in violation of laws that require emergency care to be rendered regardless of ability to pay

— Sources: Berg, 2010; Carreyrou & Martinez, 2008 and 2008a; Fleischer, 2011; Lenihan & Hermer, 2014; Martinez, 2008; Matthew, 2011; Schirra, 2011.

hospitals that they should expect closer scrutiny as the number of financially distressed patients continues to grow (Batchis, 2005). Aggressive patient billing and collection practices by the entire hospital industry helped blur the distinction between for-profit and tax-exempt hospitals; the for-profit focus on profits and the nonprofit focus on charitable care is no longer distinct (Horwitz, 2007). The distinction between for-profit and tax-exempt activities is further blurred by non-charitable, for-profit entities (especially physician group practices and pharmacies) deriving profits from the use of tax-exempt hospital facilities. Now, the various levels of government are examining this widespread discontent as state and local governments are squeezed by revenue shortfalls and are eyeing the revenue bases of tax-exempt hospitals and challenging their tax-exempt status (Maples, 2007).

Evolving Tax-Exempt Health Care Delivery Systems

Propelling this conflicted situation is the changing business structure of tax-exempt hospitals. One-third of the nation's hospitals are losing money because government health insurance is often not enough to cover the hospitals' costs of treating patients (Ahle, 2007), and most of these hospitals are in communities handling large numbers of uninsured and underinsured patients, particularly those located in cities (AHA, 2013).

The traditional foundation of the remaining hospitals as compassionate caregivers is being transformed as they increasingly evolve into comprehensive health care delivery systems with significant revenues. The size of their tax exemptions is increasingly criticized, in part because their revenues have risen so sharply in recent years, and also because they represent such a big portion of the nation's health care spending. How tax-exempt surpluses are spent is increasingly being questioned. Tax-exempt hospitals are expected to channel the surpluses they generate back into their operations. As illustrated in **FEATURE BOX 5-5**, many tax-exempt hospitals do not.

As a result of the way tax-exempt hospitals have used their surpluses for non-essentials, some health care economists maintain that all hospitals should pay taxes (Reinhardt, 2006). One claim is that the hospital industry has an ethical obligation to help avoid corruption of government. Some government officials question the claim of hospitals to be exempt from taxes; meanwhile, the same government officials attempt to exact political donations for themselves in the form of re-election contributions or donations to other tax-exempt charities the government officials or their families control, as well as pork-barrel payments for special interest projects in lieu of property, income, sales, and franchise taxes (Galle, 2012). In addition, some claim that tax-exempt hospitals differ little from for-profits in the provision of charitable care and, therefore, should either lose their tax-exempt status or adhere to new strict and specific requirements to provide charitable care (Horwitz, 2007). **FEATURE BOX 5-6** answers the question of who is benefiting from the $718 billion private-based, for-profit approach to hospital care.

Many tax-exempt hospitals saw earnings soar in recent years; the combined annual net revenue of the 50 largest tax-exempt hospitals jumped nearly eightfold to more than $4.0 billion in the past decade (Carreyrou & Martinez, 2008). One reason for hospitals' soaring profits is the increase in mergers (Reeves & Stucke, 2011; Walker, 2012). By merging and gaining scale, many tax-exempt hospitals also gained leverage in price negotiations with health insurers. No fewer than 25 hospital systems now have revenues of more than $250 million a year (Carreyrou & Martinez, 2008).

Federal, State, and Local Governments at Odds over Hospital Tax Exemptions

While the argument over hospital tax exemption is ongoing at the federal level, the real battle is waged at the state and local levels. Although tax-exempt status is defined by the

---

FEATURE BOX 5-5

Ethical (Unethical) Use of Tax-Exempt Surpluses

- Accumulating large cash reserves
- Providing luxury facilities
- Building expensive new facilities
- Purchasing the latest medical equipment and technologies
- Rewarding hospital executives with excessive multimillion-dollar salaries

— Source: Carreyrou & Martinez, 2008.

FEATURE BOX 5-6

Who is Benefiting from the $718 Billion Private-Based For-Profit Approach to Hospital Care?

When 85+ cents of every dollar comes from American taxpayers:

- $492 billion in Medicare benefit payments (including hospital outpatient services)
- $398 billion in Medicaid spending
- $44 billion in tax exemptions
- $32 billion in government subsidies
- $23 billion in charitable contributions (cash)

— Sources: AHA, 2013; Giving Institute, 2011; IOM, 2011; Kaiser Commission, 2015; Kaiser Family Foundation, 2014. Note: All hospital revenue is annual.

federal government, tax-exempt hospitals are also eligible to seek exemption from paying state and local taxes (Schirra, 2011). State and local governments have historically waived taxes for nonprofits such as hospitals, citing the beneficial work they provide for the community (Sataline, 2010). The state and local exemptions pre-date federal exemptions by 200 years, back to when the first hospitals were founded in the mid-1700s, and when public hospitals functioned exclusively for the financially distressed members of the community. Beginning in the middle part of the 20th century, tax-exempt hospitals relieved state and local governments from operating public hospitals and the burden of caring for those unable to afford health care, which offset the loss in state and local tax revenue. *See generally* Mayo, 2010.

Over time, tax-exempt hospitals evolved into huge business enterprises (Greaney & Boozang, 2005). Therefore, state and local governments have a vested interest when it comes to determining tax exemption status for hospitals, and they actively join in the debate as to what constitutes charitable care (Burns, 2004). In fact, the theories concerning charitable care are sharpened by states and localities and are used to attack or support the federal tax-exempt status of hospitals (Berg, 2010; McWilliams & Alop, 2010). Many government entities in recent years have taken a harder position, taxing part of some hospitals' income when their work is deemed to be mainly commercial or not a public benefit (Sataline, 2010).

It is clear that the federal approach to this debate differs from state and local approaches because of two opposing viewpoints. On the one hand, the federal government has a strong incentive to support tax exemption to foster competition between for-profits and non-profits, thereby improving quality and innovation in health care delivery. On the other hand, states and localities have noted the surpluses that these tax-exempt hospitals accumulate and question whether community benefits from these hospitals really outweigh the benefit governments would receive from federal, state, and local taxes. The most important benefit tax-exempt hospitals provide to governments is absorbing the difference between the cost of care as opposed to the reimbursed costs from patients with government health insurance (Bush, 2007).

Ethical Difficulties Confronting Tax-Exempt Hospitals

Uninsured patients and providing charitable care are ethical issues for hospitals and the U.S. health care system as a whole. Charitable care, however defined, challenges hospitals to bear a large part of the responsibility for providing that care (Mayo, 2010). Tax-exempt hospitals need to rethink their overall role in the communities they serve (Tahk, 2014). Their for-profit approach to pricing and charitable care raises serious questions about the billions of dollars in tax exemptions they receive (Carreyrou & Martinez, 2008).

Balancing Financial Viability and Mission

The lawsuits brought against tax-exempt hospitals due to their billing and collection activities have resulted in some modifications as to how patients are billed and bad debts are collected (Berg, 2010). In fact, most hospitals have clarified their pricing and charitable care programs (Courtney, 2011). However, with more than 64 million Americans uninsured or underinsured, tax-exempt hospitals are under tremendous pressure to correctly determine when patients are eligible for charitable care and when patients can afford to pay.

While health care should ideally never be compromised due to the ability or inability to pay, hospitals have an ethical obligation to all of their patients to attempt to obtain payment from those who can afford to pay. These critical distinctions between the most vulnerable patients and those with critical needs are a constant challenge to tax-exempt hospitals, which strive to balance their charitable missions with running a fiscally responsible business enterprise. Although a distributive justice approach should guide the allocation of health resources so that everyone has an opportunity to receive health care, it would be naive to argue that money is not the driving force motivating health care delivery (Jacobson & Mathur, 2010).

Aggressive pressure on uninsured patients to pay more than their insured counterparts is not the ethical way to obtain fiscal health, even though some costs are shifted to the insured to offset uncompensated care. When these debts cannot be collected, these non-cash collection situations should be seen as a clear signal that something is fundamentally wrong with patient access to hospital care. To find the proper balance between a hospital's charitable mission and financial viability, operational principles should be applied to the entire hospital business enterprise. Payment processes should result in similar decisions under similar circumstances (Levine, et al., 2007)

The Ethics of Upfront Billing Practices

Tax-exempt health care systems are constructing barriers to access by shifting health insurance restrictions and limitations to patients, such as demanding upfront payments before medical treatments are rendered (Jacoby & Holman, 2010). This is an evolving shift in health care ethics from sharing health risks to assuming individual responsibility for one's health. This shift in ethics also means not only that patients will be required to be more responsible for their own preventive care, but also that they will become obligated to make lifestyle changes to avoid preventable diseases, delay their onset, or at least reduce the severity of their effects. In the near future, patients will increasingly be forced to accept financial responsibility for their unhealthy lifestyle choices, such as upfront payments for their care not covered by basic health insurance. Creating ethical health care systems requires setting explicit goals for how much of the nation's shared resources should be devoted to health care and how these limited resources should be spent (Fleck, 2011); in turn, these goals should recognize the many costs of preventable ill health to society (Wharton, 2012).

Many hospitals are adopting this new policy to improve their finances instead of billing patients after they receive care (Carreyrou & Martinez, 2008). Pointing to their rising bad debt and charitable care costs, hospitals are asking patients for money before they receive treatment. Hospitals say they have turned to the practice because of a spike in patients who do not pay their medical bills (Kinney, 2010).

Uncompensated care cost the hospital industry $49 billion (*Florida, et al. v. U.S. Department of Health and Human Services, et al.*, 648 F.3d 1235 (U.S. Court of Appeals for the 11th Circuit 2011), *affirmed in part and reversed in part*, 132 S.Ct. 2566 (U.S. Supreme Court 2012)), more than double the cost of $21.6 billion in 2000 (AHA, 2015). This bad debt is driven by a larger number of Americans who do not have enough insurance to cover their health care costs when catastrophe strikes. Even among those with adequate insurance, deductibles and co-payments are growing so large that insured patients have trouble paying hospitals as well (Martinez, 2008).

Life-Threatening Medical Emergencies

Although the **Emergency Medical Treatment and Active Labor Act of 1986** (EMTALA) requires hospitals to screen, treat, and stabilize anyone who seeks emergency treatment, hospital emergency departments are not required to cover the cost of that treatment or any poststabilization treatment (Lucas & Williams, 2009; CMS, 2015). Hospitals are required to treat medical emergencies such as heart attacks or serious injuries from accidents, but they are not required to treat health conditions that are not immediately life-threatening (Zoellner, 2010); the only exception is pregnant women who are in active labor, they must be treated until delivery is complete. Additional treatment can be conditioned, however, on a determination of the ability to pay for such care and contracts agreeing to pay incurred charges. Moreover, hospitals may transfer patients to other hospitals for care as long as the patients are in stable condition (Lucas & Williams, 2009).

Regulatory Environment

There are several confusing policies intended to prevent discriminatory billing that instead result in overly aggressive collection actions. For instance, there are bad debt rules and regulations requiring hospitals to make all reasonable attempts to collect payment from a patient before discharging the uncollected debt as uncompensated care or bad debt (McGrath, 2007). Hospitals nationwide choose to interpret this to mean that they are precluded from offering discounts to the uninsured (OIG, 2004). Combine this complexity with special fraud alerts and anti-kickback laws outlining when hospitals can and cannot waive co-payments and deductibles or confer benefits, and the confusion about billing practices expands.

While these policies do not and never have prohibited hospitals from providing discounts to patients, they have often been used to require the uninsured to pay full price for

ETHICAL DILEMMAS 5-4

5. When, under what circumstances, or why, should tax-exempt hospitals be required to provide medically necessary health care to patients?

their health care. These regulations that were never clarified by regulators made it easier for hospitals to refuse to use discounts or other means of financial assistance for patients (OIG, 2004). It is doubtful that hospitals were genuinely confused or misinterpreted the law; just as it is debatable whether it is ethical for hospitals to interpret regulations to mean that they cannot offer discounted care (Nie, 2007).

Transparent Provision of Price Information before Treatments

Tax-exempt hospitals could model their business practices after those of retail medical clinics (Schleiter, 2010), or cosmetic and other elective medical surgery clinics that are self-pay. One ethical practice is having documentation to support medical bills (Peters, 2007). Patients should have an idea in advance of what amount they will be billed (in non-emergency situations) and be able to understand the bill when it arrives (Chittick, 2011). The bill should detail what treatments and medical products it encompasses and should set forth the expectation of prompt payment by a specified due date, in addition to providing information on how to enter into an affordable payment plan if necessary.

Hospitals should be obligated to notify prospective patients what the hospital plans to provide them in terms of health care and, at the very least, a reasonable estimate of the total price for the anticipated care. While handing patients detailed charges for each and every conceivable service is unreasonable, patients should have an understanding of the nature of their financial obligations before any non-emergency treatment is accepted (Schleiter, 2010). Simply put, hospitals should provide patients with complete and accurate price information.

While hospitals cannot be expected specify an exact amount to be paid when emergency treatments are rendered or when unexpected health conditions arise, general payment obligations of patients can be set forth for most hospital treatments (Peters, 2007). With emergency care, nobody usually knows just what particular condition the patient has, or what treatments will be necessary to remedy the disease, sickness, or injury presented. It is incongruous to expect hospitals to fully perform their obligation to provide emergency care to patients and then not send patients invoices for charges (including charges not covered by health insurance) (McGrath, 2007). This would not be a realistic expectation. However, patients should know what is not covered by their health insurance before agreeing to non-emergency treatments (Chittick, 2011). It bears repeating: price information should be provided before treatment is accepted.

Ethical Vulnerabilities of Tax-Exempt Health Care Systems

While the United States has favored a market-based, for-profit health care model, that system has not been as successful as most would like. Perhaps it is time to revisit the ethical principles underlying this approach to health care, given today's comprehensive reforms with evidence-based medicine and health information technology now playing a prominent role in treatment decisions. Indeed, debate on charitable care suggests that continuing on the path where treatment decisions are based on clinical evidence alone, without consideration of costs, may no longer be feasible, especially when half of the care provided is medically unnecessary (Berwick & Hackbarth, 2012; Wharton, 2012). The obligation to provide charitable care in lieu of taxes is uncertain. Determining who should be charged and how much to charge for health care is a complicated issue.

What has occurred in the past several years, through scandal, insider transactions, and private equity mergers and acquisitions, has been a sustained challenge to the long-standing way in which tax-exempt hospitals are perceived and, ultimately, regulated (Colinvaux, 2011; Piraino, 2008). In some ways, hospitals lack motivation to evolve or there are impediments to doing so that effectively perpetuate the status quo of treating disease, essentially imposing an institutional bias against disease prevention (Brody & Tyler, 2010). Everyone knows they are medically vulnerable because no one is going to live forever, but as more Americans realize they are also financially vulnerable, changes and solutions that work financially, medically, ethically, and politically will be in order (Commonwealth, 2013).

ETHICAL OR UNETHICAL DECISION

Charitable Obligations of Tax-Exempt Hospitals

Ethics Issue: *Do tax-exempt, not-for-profit hospitals deserve the tax exemptions they have historically received?*

Ethics Analysis: No, charitable care is seriously insufficient at most tax-exempt hospitals. Hospitals do not dispense charitable care to all who ask for it and obstacles are routinely placed in the way of uninsured and underinsured patients seeking charitable care. Those with the greatest need for health care often have the greatest difficulty obtaining care, which is blatantly unethical (Levine, et al., 2007).

Ethics Analysis: Yes, denial of property tax exemptions challenges the charitable care of most tax-exempt hospitals serving vulnerable populations, such as uninsured and underinsured patients. While the incremental provision of health care for such populations is ethical, it risks diverting attention from the larger ethical obligation of providing access to every member of society requiring medically necessary care.

Court's Holding and Decision: Provena was not entitled to $8.8 million in property tax exemptions. Provena failed to demonstrate that it was a public charity or that its properties were used for charitable or beneficent purposes, in part because of the way it treated poor and financially distressed patients and in part because most of its revenue was derived from providing services for a fee.

— *Provena Covenant Medical Center, et al. v. Department of Revenue, et al.*, 925 N.E.2d 1131 (Supreme Court of Illinois 2010). *See* Basanta, et al., 2010; Brody, 2010; Colinvaux, 2011; Sataline, 2010 (discussing this court decision). *See also* Lagnado, 2004.

CHAPTER SUMMARY

- One of the most controversial ethical issues faced by nonprofit health care systems is the amount of charitable care offered by their tax-exempt hospitals as they attempt to allocate scarce health resources in the most effective way possible.
- The upward trend in the underinsured rate reflects how much rising health care costs for workers have outpaced wage increases, thereby leading to questions about the ethical underpinnings of the very system that perpetuates this trend.

- With the demands for charitable care intensifying across the United States, the billions in tax dollars received by tax-exempt hospitals for the community's health are being scrutinized to see if there is an ethical exchange.
- The ethical obligation of tax-exempt hospitals to provide charitable care is at the center of health care reform and the policy debate about how the nation might provide reasonably priced, comprehensive, and continuous medical coverage to almost everyone.
- The traditional foundation of health care delivery systems as compassionate care-givers is being transformed as they increasingly evolve into multibillion-dollar enterprises.
- One-third of the nation's hospitals are losing money because government insurance is often not enough to cover their costs of treating patients; most of the hospitals under financial strain are in communities handling large numbers of uninsured and under-insured patients.
- Price discrimination, the practice of charging different prices to different patients for identical health care even when the costs are identical, is standard despite an apparent lack of ethical justification.
- In return for not paying taxes, tax-exempt hospitals are expected to provide a community benefit, a loosely defined federal requirement whose most important component is charitable care.
- Given the complexity of the health care payment system, legal and ethical controversy ensues when tax-exempt hospitals write off bad debt and then classify that write-off as a charitable care contribution to the community.
- Many tax-exempt hospitals are adopting new policies to improve their finances: providing transparent medical bills so patients have an idea in advance of what amount they will owe (in non-emergency situations) and making health care contingent on upfront payments, as opposed to billing patients after they receive care.

REFERENCES

AHA (American Hospital Association). (2015). *Uncompensated hospital care cost fact sheet*. Chicago, IL: AHA.
___. (2013). *Beyond health care: The economic contribution of hospitals*.
Ahle, H. R. (2007). Shaping a new direction for law and medicine, an international debate on culture, disaster, biotechnology and public health: Anticipating pandemic avian influenza: Why the federal and state preparedness plans are for the birds. *DePaul Journal of Health Care Law, 10*, 213–250.
Anderson, G. F. (2007). From "soak the rich" to "soak the poor": Recent trends in hospital pricing. *Health Affairs, 26*(3), 780–789.
Auerbach, D. I., & Kellermann, A. L. (2011). A decade of health care cost growth has wiped out real income gains for an average U.S. family. *Health Affairs, 30*(9), 1630–1636.
Basanta, W. E., et al. (2010). Survey of Illinois law: Healthcare law. *Southern Illinois University Law Journal, 34*, 1033–1075.
Batchis, L. S. (2005). Can lawsuits help the uninsured access affordable hospital care?: Potential theories for uninsured patient plaintiffs. *Temple Law Review, 78*, 493–541.
Becker, C. (2007). Community center of attention: IRS, finance poised to pounce on tax-exempt status. *Modern Healthcare, 37*(29), 8–9.
Berg, J. (2010). Putting the community back into the "community benefit" standard. *Georgia Law Review, 44*, 375–431.
Berwick, D. M., & Hackbarth, A. (2012). Eliminating waste in U.S. health care. *Journal of the American Medical Association, 10*(1001), 362–366.
Bloche, M. G. (2009).The emergent logic of health law. *Southern California Law Review, 82*, 389–480.
Brody, E. (2010). All charities are property-tax exempt, but some charities are more exempt than others. *New England Law Review, 44*, 621–732.
Brody, E., & Tyler, J. (2010). Governance: Respecting foundation and charity autonomy: How public is private philanthropy? *Chicago-Kent Law Review, 85*, 571–617.

Burns, J. (2004). Are nonprofit health care systems really charitable? Taking the question to the state and local level. *Journal of Corporate Law, 29*, 665–683.

Bush, H. (2007, October). Regulations: Court ruling, IRS initiative highlight issues in debate over tax-exempt status. *Hospital Health Network, 81*(10), 24–25.

Carreyrou, J., & Martinez, B. (2008, April 4). Tax-exempt hospitals, once for the poor, strike it rich with tax-breaks, they outperform for-profit rivals. *Wall Street Journal*, p. A1.

____. (2008a, April 4). Charitable vs. nonprofit: Hospitals' exemption. *Wall Street Journal*, p. A10.

CBO (Congressional Budget Office). (2008). *Budget options: Health care*. Washington, DC: CBO.

____. (2006). *Tax-exempt hospitals and the provisions of community-benefits*.

Channick, S. A. (2012). Taming the beast of health care costs: Why Medicare reform alone is not enough. *Annals of Health Law, American Society of Law, Medicine and Ethics Special Edition, 21*, 63–78.

Chittick, N. V. (2011). Hidden charges: The need for transparency in Kentucky health-care markets. *University of Louisville Law Review, 49*, 415–443.

CMS (Centers for Medicare and Medicaid Services). (2015). *Medicare program: Clarifying policies related to the responsibilities of Medicare-participating hospitals in treating individuals with emergency medical conditions*. Baltimore, MD: U.S. Department of Health and Human Services, CMS.

Cohen, B. (2006). The controversy over hospital charges to the uninsured. No villains, no heroes. *Villanova Law Review, 51*, 95–148.

Colinvaux, R. (2011). Charity in the 21st century: Trending toward decay. *Florida Tax Review, 11*, 1–71.

Collins, S. R. (2007, November 4). *Widening gaps in health insurance coverage in the U.S: The need for universal coverage*. Invited testimony on Income Security and Family Support, Committee on Ways and Means, U.S. House of Representatives, Hearing on Impact of Gaps in Health Coverage on Income Security.

Commonwealth Fund. (2013). *Health insurance survey*. New York, NY: Commonwealth Fund.

Courtney, B. A. (2011). Hospital tax-exemption and the community benefit standard: Considerations for future policymaking. *Indiana Health Law Review, 8*, 365–397.

Dobson, A., DaVanzo, J., & Sen, N. (2006). The cost-shift payment 'hydraulic': Foundation, history, and Implications. *Health Affairs, 25*(1), 22–33.

Felland, L. E., et al. (2010). *The economic recession: Early impacts on health care safety net providers*. Washington, DC: Center for Studying Health System Change.

Fleck, L. M. (2011). Health care rationing, terminal illness, and the medically least well off. *Journal of Law, Medicine and Ethics, 39*, 156–168.

Fleischer, M. P. (2011). Equality of opportunity and the charitable tax subsidies. *Boston University Law Review, 91*, 601–663.

Fowler, E. J., & Jost, T. S. (2008). Why public programs matter, and will continue to matter, even after health reform. *Journal of Law, Medicine and Ethics, 36*, 670–675.

Galle, B. (2012). The role of charity in a federal system. *William and Mary Law Review, 53*, 777–851.

Giving Institute. (2011). *Annual report*. Chicago, IL: American Association of Fundraising Counsel.

Greaney, T. L., & Boozang, K. M. (2005). Mission, margin, and trust in the nonprofit health care enterprise. *Yale Journal of Health Policy, Law and Ethics, 5*, 1–87.

Herophilus. (2007). *Herophilus: The art of medicine in early Alexandria*: Edition, translation and essays by von Staden, H. New York, NY: Cambridge University Press.

Hoffman, A. K. (2010). Oil and water: Mixing individual mandates, fragmented markets, and health reform. *American Journal of Law and Medicine, 36*, 7–77.

Horwitz, J. R. (2007). Does nonprofit ownership matter? *Yale Journal of Regulation, 24*, 139–204.

IOM (Institute of Medicine). (2011). *Geographic adjustment in Medicare payments*. Washington, DC: National Academies Press.

Jacobson, P. D., & Mathur, S. K. (2010). It's not all about the money. *American Journal of Law and Medicine, 36*, 389–404.

Jacoby, M. B., & Holman, M. (2010). Managing medical bills on the brink of bankruptcy. *Yale Journal of Health Policy, Law, and Ethics, 10*, 239–297.

Kaiser Commission on Medicaid and the Uninsured. (2015). *Medicaid moving forward*. Washington, DC: Kaiser Family Foundation.

____. (2014). *Key facts about the uninsured population*.

____. (2010). *Kaiser health tracking poll*.

Kaiser Family Foundation. (2014). *The facts on Medicare spending and financing*. Menlo Park, CA: Kaiser Family Foundation.

____. (2014a). *How does cost affect access to care?*

____. (2012). *Health care costs: A primer*.

____. (2009). *Health care and the middle class: More costs and less coverage*.

Kinney, E. D. (2010). For profit enterprise in health care: Can it contribute to health reform? *American Journal of Law and Medicine, 36*, 405–435.

Kirch, D. (2008). *Reform is no "either or": We must fix the payment system along with access.* New York, NY: Modern Access & Commonwealth Fund.

Koppel, G. S. (2011). Seeing the forest for the trees. *Akron Law Review, 44,* 999–1066.

Kuntze, C. (2008). The fight for equal pricing in health care. *Journal of Legal Medicine, 29*(4), 537–552.

Lagnado, L. (2004, December 27). California hospitals open books, showing huge price differences. *Wall Street Journal,* p. A1.

___. (2004a, September 21). Anatomy of a hospital bill; Uninsured patients often face big markups on small items; "Rules are completely crazy." *Wall Street Journal,* p. B1.

Lenihan, M., & Hermer, L. D. (2014). On the uneasy relationship between Medicaid and charity care. *Notre Dame Journal of Law, Ethics and Public Policy, 28,* 165–208.

Levine, M. A., et al. (2007). Improving access to health care: A consensus ethical framework to guide proposals for reform. *Hastings Center Report, 9/10,* 14–19.

Lucas, C. K., & Williams, M. A. (2009). The rights of nonparticipating providers in a managed care world: Navigating the minefields of balance billing and reasonable and customary payments. *Journal of Health and Life Sciences Law, 3*(1), 132–152.

Maher, K. (2014). Reforming Medicare-financed graduate medical education. *Journal of Contemporary Health Law and Policy, 30,* 336–362.

Maples, A. M. (2007). State attorney general oversight of nonprofit healthcare entities: Have we reached an ideological impasse? *Cumberland Law Review, 37,* 235–261.

Markey, M. (2010). Health law. *Wayne Law Review, 56,* 1251–1263.

Martin, T. D. (2011). The impact of healthcare reform on revenue-cycle management and claim coding. *Journal of Health and Life Sciences Law, 4*(3), 159–180.

Martinez, B. (2008, April 28). Cash before chemo: Hospitals get tough, bad-debts prompt change in billing: $45,000 to come in. *Wall Street Journal,* p. A1.

Matthew, D. B. (2011). Implementing American health care reform: The fiduciary imperative. *Buffalo Law Review, 59,* 715–807.

Mayo, T. W. (2010). Tax-exempt hospitals: Renewed focus on indigent care. *Journal of Health and Life Sciences Law, 4*(1), 140–152.

McGrath, J. (2007). Overcharging the uninsured in hospitals: Shifting a greater share of uncompensated medical care costs to the federal government. *Quinnipiac Law Review, 26,* 173–211.

McWilliams, V., & Alop, A. A. (2010). The dearth of charity care: Do nonprofit hospitals deserve their tax exemptions? *Clearinghouse Review: Journal of Poverty Law and Policy, 44,* 110–121.

Miller-Wilson, C. (2009). Becoming poor: Stories of the real "safety net" and the consequences for middle America. *Quinnipiac Health Law Journal, 13,* 1–37.

Moncrieff, A. R. (2012). Cost-benefit federalism: Reconciling collective action federalism and libertarian federalism in the Obamacare litigation and beyond. *American Journal of Law and Medicine, 38,* 288–324.

Moskowitz, E. (2005). Recent developments in health law: Class-action suits allege improper charitable care practices. *Journal of Law, Medicine and Ethics, 33,* 168–170.

NCSL (National Conference of State Legislatures). (2015). *Health insurance: Premiums and increases.* Washington, DC: NCLS.

Nie, D. L. (2007). Nonprofit hospital billing of uninsured patients. Consumer-based class actions move to state courts. *Indiana Law Review, 4,* 173–204.

Nussbaum, A. (2012). Can Congress make you buy health insurance? The Affordable Care Act, national health care reform, and the constitutionality of the individual mandate. *Duquesne Law Review, 50,* 411–466.

OIG (Office of the Inspector General). (2004). *Hospital discounts offered to patients who cannot afford to pay their hospital bills.* Washington, DC: U.S. Department of Health & Human Services.

Olson, M. D. (2005). Defending the next round of nonprofit hospital class-action lawsuits. *Journal of Healthcare Finance, 31,* 75–89.

Peters, K. T. (2007). What have we here? The need for transparent pricing and quality information in health care: Creation of an SEC [Securities and Exchange Commission] for health care. *Journal of Health Care Law and Policy, 10,* 363–390.

Piraino, Jr., T. A. (2008). The antitrust implications of "going private" and other changes of corporate control. *Boston College Law Review, 49,* 971–1035.

Pratt, D. (2011). Health care reform: Will it succeed? *Albany Law Journal of Science and Technology, 21,* 493–589.

Purdy, J., & Siegel, N. S. (2012). The liberty of free riders: The minimum coverage provision, Mill's "harm principle," and American social morality. *American Journal of Law and Medicine, 38,* 374–396.

Reeves, A. P., & Stucke, M. E. (2011). Behavioral antitrust. *Indiana Law Journal, 86,* 1527–1586.

Reinhardt, U. E. (2006). The pricing of U.S. hospital services: Chaos behind a veil of secrecy. *Health Affairs, 25,* 57–69.

Rosenbaum, S., & Margulies, R. (2011). Tax-exempt hospitals and the Patient Protection and Affordable Care Act: Implications for public health policy and practice. *Public Health Reports, 126*(2), 283–289.

Saar, D. L. (2008). Blindsided (again): Iowa hospitals' abuse of the hospital lien statute and what has been done to correct it. *Drake Law Review, 56,* 463–501.

Sataline, S. (2010, March 19). Illinois high court rules nonprofit hospital can be taxed. *Wall Street Journal,* p. B4.

Schirra, J. J. (2011). A veil of tax exemption? A proposal for the continuation of federal tax-exempt status for "non-profit" hospitals. *Health Matrix: The Journal of Law-Medicine, 21,* 231–277.

Schleiter, K. E. (2010). Retail medical clinics: Increasing access to low cost medical care amongst a developing legal environment. *Annals of Health Law, 19,* 527–575.

Schoen, C., et al. (2014). *America's underinsured: A state-by-state look at health insurance affordability prior to the new coverage expansions.* New York, NY: Commonwealth Fund.

___. (2011). Affordable Care Act reforms could reduce the number of underinsured U.S. adults by 70 percent. *Health Affairs, 30*(9), 1762–1771.

Smith, J. C., & Medalia, C. (2014). *Income, poverty, and health insurance coverage in the United States.* Washington, DC: U.S. Census Bureau.

Tahk, S. C. (2014). Tax-exempt hospitals and their communities. *Columbia Journal of Tax Law, 6,* 33.

Tyrrell, III, J. E. (2010). Non-profits under fire: The effects of minimal charity care requirements legislation on not-for-profit hospitals. *Journal of Contemporary Health Law and Policy, 26,* 373–402.

University of Pennsylvania. (2014). *2012/13 Annual financial report.* Philadelphia, PA: University of Pennsylvania.

U.S. Census Bureau. (2014). *Poverty thresholds.* Suitland, MD: U.S. Census Bureau, Housing and Economic Statistics Division.

U.S. Census Bureau, & BLS (Bureau of Labor Statistics). (2012). *Current population survey.* Suitland, MD: U.S. Census Bureau and Washington, DC: BLS.

Walker, D. S. (2012). Business organizations: When "business purpose" disappears: A consideration of an LLC for a 501(c)(3) nonprofit organization. *William Mitchell Law Review, 38,* 627–672.

Wharton School at the University of Pennsylvania. (2012). Looking for solutions in a rapidly changing health care environment. *Knowledge@Wharton.*

Wilper, A. P., et al. (2009). Health insurance and mortality in U.S. adults. *American Journal of Public Health, 99*(12), 2289–2295.

Zoellner, E. R. (2010), Medical repatriation: Examining the legal and ethical implications of an emerging practice. *Washington University Journal of Law and Policy, 32,* 515–538.

PART III

The Ethical Development of Human Capital

Part III concentrates on equality of opportunity in staffing U.S. health care organizations and the ethical issues of fairness affecting the management of employees.

© Michael Milken (1946–), Chairman of FasterCures, a Washington-based center of the Milken Institute

CHAPTER 6

Employers' Health Care Costs

"Improved public health translates directly into greater national productivity, which underpins all economic growth. So let's get our priorities straight. America's economy used to be the sun—the gravitational center—in the 'solar system' of leading nations. In the future, we will no longer be the sun. But by investing in our own health we can help solidify our position as Jupiter, the largest planet."

— **Michael Milken** (1946–), Chairman of FasterCures, a Washington-based center of the Milken Institute (2011)

LEARNING OBJECTIVES

After completing this chapter, the reader should be able to:

1. Summarize the ethical principles underlying the growing efforts to reduce and fairly allocate employers' health care costs.
2. Understand the existing forces that inadvertently support the present status quos of smoking, obesity, and diabetes.
3. Explain how employers decide what types of medical interventions to implement, when addressing preventable behaviors that comprise the daily lifestyle choices of employees.
4. Describe the factors behind tolerating employee behaviors that cost employers money and affect employee work performance, but which can be effectively addressed through environmental interventions.
5. Assess ways in which the health care industry could work with employers to develop frameworks for employee preventive self-care, such as developing work spaces that encourage healthy lifestyles.

KEY TERMS

Americans with Disabilities Act of 2006	Diabetes	Health status
	Dynamic pricing	Lifestyle discrimination
Civil Rights Act of 1964	Geographic rating	Obese

Overweight   Preventive care   Treatment adherence
Personalized prevention   Prospective medicine   Unhealthy behaviors
Preventable behaviors   Risk classification   Wellness rules
Preventable diseases   Self-insured

ETHICAL OR UNETHICAL DECISION

Employees' Voluntary Lifestyle Choices: Smoking Tobacco

Ethics Issue: *Should employees be fired for smoking in the workplace?*

In Brief: Jay Dubbs was employed by Mountain View Thoroughbred Racing as a full-time public attendant. The employer has a policy prohibiting smoking or use of tobacco in the work space except in specifically designated areas. Dubbs was aware of this smoking policy and knew where the designated smoking areas were located, but he chose to smoke in a nonsmoking men's bathroom during working hours. Dubbs claimed he was struggling with anxiety and that smoking a cigarette calmed his nerves. His employer terminated him.

— *Dubbs v. Unemployment Compensation Board of Review,* 2010 Pa. Commw. Unpub. LEXIS 484 (Commonwealth Court of Pennsylvania 2010).

Introduction

Each year, more than 40 percent of premature deaths in the United States result from **unhealthy behaviors**, such as smoking, overeating, or failure to take medications as pre-scribed (Wharton, 2009). While these unhealthy behaviors often result in increased health care costs, **preventive care** that prevents disease and illness from ever arising has not been as widely implemented as hoped for. One reason for failure to implement preventive care is that the institutionalized models of the health care industry are far more focused on treating than on preventing disease (Hardcastle, et al., 2011). As a consequence, employees have not always been motivated to maintain healthy lifestyles beyond their general aware-ness that fitness equates with feeling well about oneself and life in general (Majette, 2011). Furthermore, the health insurance industry had always been reluctant to pay for preventive care before the Affordable Care Act (Marks, 2011).

As employers are trying to reduce the cost of employer-provided health insurance, the ep-idemics of depression, diabetes, cardiovascular disease, and other chronic, expensive ailments are bringing new urgency to the concept of preventive care (Landro, 2004). Consequently, employers are taking a much more aggressive look at **preventable diseases**, or diseases the onset of which can often be avoided by living a healthful lifestyle. Tobacco-related illnesses, obesity, and diabetes, as well as other chronic conditions such as arthritis and circulatory disorders, are all receiving renewed attention, for all these diseases are generally preventable or can be delayed from occurring or decreased in severity by changes in behavior.

The Ethics of Current Health Care Quality and Cost-Shifting Trends

Though there is no certainty about whether employees avoid preventive care for financial reasons, two current trends suggest that employers are inconsistent about how they want health insurance to work. One trend is investing in improving the quality of employee health care; the other trend is shifting the costs of this improvement to employees (Wharton, 2008). In other words, employers see the value of investing in improving employees' health, but they do not value it highly enough to shoulder the cost themselves. Taken together, the two trends illustrate that employers are struggling to accurately assess how decisions about employee health affect their bottom lines. The cost-sharing trend particularly comes at a time when information is lacking about whether short-term savings will lead to long-term health problems and added costs.

Cost-Shifting to Employees

More employers are shifting the cost of health insurance to employees partly because costs have more than doubled during the past decade (Callahan, 2012). In theory, employers should be able to pay higher wages if health insurance benefits continue to be reduced, but this is not always an accurate statement of economic theory (Eigen & Sherwyn, 2012). Research shows that the cost of health insurance is fully shifted out of the wages employees receive (Channick, 2010); as the costs for employer-provided health insurance increase, wages decrease.

Today, the costs for employer-provided health insurance are increasing at the same time that the cost-sharing by employees is increasing (Altman, 2015; Kaiser, 2012; Oechsner & Haynes, 2011). When measuring the true cost of employer-provided health insurance, employers must be able to accurately measure and consider the payoffs that come from improving the health of their employees.

Employers Neglect Employee Health Data Promoting Preventive Care

Most debates about health care costs avoid identifying practical and accurate employer-based mechanisms designed to encourage appropriate delivery and use of health care (Wharton, 2009). Yet, this is what employer-provided health insurance is all about. In other words, it is an instance of different mindsets looking at costs but not necessarily seeing the complete reality of what is being looked at (Wind & Crook, 2006).

Federal privacy legislation governs the collection of health information about individual employees, as employees may be vulnerable to subtle forms of exploitation by their employers (Plass, 2010). When dealing with controlling the costs of employer-provided health insurance, it is important for employees not to conjure up images of their employer

---

ETHICAL DILEMMAS 6-1

1. What ethical considerations affect how much employers should invest in the health of their employees, if at all?

as "Big Brother" doing things to take advantage of them. Even though employers have access to broad-based information about the health of their employees, most employers do not use it effectively and others do not analyze it at all (Wharton, 2009).

The assumption is that larger employers that insure themselves are very effective at understanding all of the different employer-benefit practices; in fact, they are not (Wharton, 2008). For instance, despite the acknowledged benefits of wellness programs, employers continue to challenge their value (Suk, 2011). While most wellness programs require initial health screenings to develop a baseline for metrics (such as cholesterol levels, blood pressure, weight, and nicotine use), this anonymous, aggregate baseline data is not always analyzed or evaluated by employers. Employers are not always aware that initial screenings catch potentially serious (and costly) health problems in their employees. Moreover, aggregate data is seldom analyzed to detect systemic changes in health insurance that could be made by employers.

Preventable Diseases and Chronic Health Conditions

If employers focused on how they spend their health care costs, they would discover that half of **health status**, or what makes employees healthy or unhealthy, is determined by their lifestyles (Solar & Irwin, 2010). This supports the research findings that most chronic diseases are preventable by changes in behavior (WHA, 2012). Of the $1.9 trillion employers spend annually on health care, less than 4 percent is devoted to improving employees' lifestyles (Davis, 2007), as illustrated in **FIGURE 6-1**. Although 80 percent of employers' health care costs are devoted to medical treatments, medical treatments affect only 10 percent of individuals' health status.

At issue in this chapter is whether employers' priorities should be realigned so that more of their spending is directed to what determines health status. The focus of employers' health

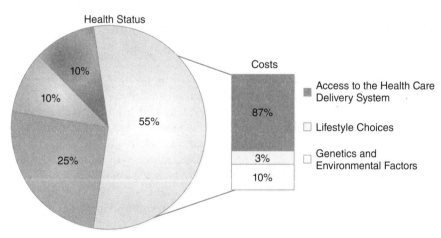

Lifestyle Choices (smoking, overweight/obesity, and medication adherence)

Environmental Factors (clean air and clean drinking water)

Genetics

Access to the Health Care Delivery System (treatment of disease and illness)

FIGURE 6-1 Attributes of Employee Health Status Compared to Employers' Health Care Costs

Sources: Schoen, et al., 2015; Solar & Irwin, 2010.

care costs could change to take into consideration some of the preventive issues illustrated in **FEATURE BOX 6-1**. Decisions to help modify employees' unhealthy behaviors in order to prevent disease and chronic health conditions from ever occurring are very different from the decisions to access the health care delivery system to treat these same diseases and conditions.

Prospective Medicine: The New Ethics of Health Insurance

Employers provide health insurance for 160 million employees (SAHIE, 2013). With the average cost of an employer-provided family insurance plan having risen to more than $15,700 per year, the need to trim employers' health care costs is undisputed (Kaiser, 2012). The key to cutting the costs of employer-provided health insurance is getting employees involved in their own health care while diseases can still be prevented, also known as **personalized prevention**. This includes smoking cessation, weight reduction, and **treatment adherence** programs that regularly remind and encourage employees to take advantage of diagnostic procedures; take prescribed medications; and modify their lifestyle choices as directed, such as by not smoking, eating a healthy diet, regularly exercising, and managing their weight.

Employers are also increasingly making health risk assessments and personalized health insurance available to their employees in hopes they will develop healthier lifestyles, or at least avoid unhealthy lifestyles (Parisi, 2010). The focus is shifting from treating preventable diseases, to tailoring treatments to individual needs so employees can develop healthy lifestyles and block preventable diseases from arising. Although the United States is one of the most advanced economies in the world, the overall health of Americans lags behind other similarly situated countries. For instance, the United States ranks 42nd in life expectancy and preventable chronic diseases affect half of all Americans, the highest rate of any other advanced country (Ward, et al., 2014; CIA, 2014).

This new approach to health care is called **prospective medicine**, which also includes tailoring medications and other medical treatments to individual needs. This approach uses individual medical histories to identify employees at the greatest risk of developing preventable diseases, and takes steps to intervene early to prevent their onset. The issue for employers is how the value of self-care can be raised so that employees will set priorities for their own health (Kinney, 2012). This is the leading issue surrounding the changes in how healthy and unhealthy lifestyles will be managed in the future. Health insurance in

---

FEATURE BOX 6-1

Changing the Focus of Employers' Health Care Costs

- What diseases and chronic health conditions are preventable?
- When are they preventable?
- How can employer-provided health insurance be restructured so as to provide a financial incentive for employees to adopt healthy lifestyles?

— Sources: Solar & Irwin, 2010; WHA, 2012.

ETHICAL DILEMMAS 6-2

2. Good health is an obvious asset to both individuals and employers, but what ethical issues affect how the burden of health care costs should be shared?

the future will provide care aimed at preventing disease and chronic health conditions from ever arising, so as to provide a financial incentive for employees to change their behaviors to prevent or delay illnesses from occurring in the first place (Westfall, 2011). For instance, employees with unhealthy lifestyles will pay higher health insurance premiums, as well as having higher deductibles and co-payments if they refuse to take advantage of preventive care.

Behavioral Determinants of Health

National business advocacy groups and associations now describe smoking, overeating, and the failure to take medications and follow prescribed treatment regimens as **preventable behaviors**, a word choice which recognizes that these day-to-day behaviors are necessary to avoid in order to preserve health. Recently, employers have declared war on these preventable behaviors for one simple reason: they are recognized as three avoidable, major drains on health care costs, as illustrated in **FEATURE BOX 6-2**. It is not the health of employees that is driving employers to take this seriously. The big driver is really the cost of health care, which employers either have to cover or pass on to their employees.

The business reason for doing something to diminish these predictors is that expenses related to employer-provided health insurance would be less. The general trend for most employers is that, sooner or later, the cost of health insurance depends on how expensive the medical needs of their employers are (Hoffman, 2010). Smoking and obesity in particular have come under attack because both conditions are directly related to rapidly rising

FEATURE BOX 6-2

Preventable Health Care Costs

Employers spend $1.9 trillion on health care costs:

- $1.5 trillion are costs from preventable behaviors
- $289 billion to $1.2 trillion for smoking-related diseases and chronic health conditions
- $129 to $147 billion for obesity
- $6 billion to $37 billion for overweight
- $134 billion for treatment non-adherence

— Sources: CDC, 2015 and 2015a; Harris, 2011; HHS, 2014; IOM, 2010; Solar & Irwin, 2010.

ETHICAL DILEMMAS 6-3

3. Should employees with healthy lifestyles subsidize the unhealthy choices of their counterparts on a day-to-day basis, or should employees with unhealthy lifestyles assume the cost of their freely made decisions?
4. Is it ethical for the healthy to pay more than the cost of the health care they expect to use, while the unhealthy pay less than the cost of the care they expect to use?

health care costs (Parisi, 2010). Employees' adherence to prescribed treatment regimens is just beginning to come under attack by employers (Wharton, 2009). Nevertheless, some employees claim they have a compelling interest to pursue their own health as they see fit, and therefore any intervention by employers is an unwarranted intrusion into privacy and their freedom to smoke tobacco, eat, exercise, and adhere to professional medical treatment advice as much or as little as they want (Yang & Nichols, 2011).

Smoking Tobacco

In 1964, the government first released a report stating that smoking tobacco is a health hazard and a primary contributor to lung disease (HHS, 2014), facts known at least as far back as the 1800s (Maxeiner, 2013). Since then, substantial research has established that smoking dramatically increases the risk of death from a plethora of diseases and chronic health conditions and is the leading risk factor for disability (Sokol, 2010; WHO, 2009). Despite widespread awareness and acceptance of the risks of smoking, 1 in 6 Americans still smokes (HHS, 2014). Employers spend an estimated $1.9 trillion on health care costs each year, much of which goes toward tobacco-related illnesses (Russell, 2007). In addition to this direct cost, smokers miss work more often due to illness, take longer to recover from common illnesses, and take more breaks throughout the average workday than their nonsmoking coworkers (Wharton, 2009). As illustrated in **FEATURE BOX 6-3**, many of the employment costs attributable to smokers, including increased health insurance costs and productivity losses due to absenteeism, are ultimately shared by nonsmoking employees.

Obesity

According to weight standards from the Centers for Disease Control, among developed countries the United States has the most obese people. Seven out of 10 adults in the United States aged 20 years or older are **overweight** or **obese**, as defined in **FIGURE 6-2**.

The effects of being overweight are comparable to having diabetes or high blood pressure; it is a true diagnosable disease that affects life expectancy (U.S. Surgeon General, 2010). As such, weight-related chronic health conditions account for approximately 9 percent of the nation's health care costs each year (Darling, 2012). As illustrated in **FEATURE BOX 6-4**, obesity is now considered a trigger for health problems and increased health care spending fast becoming comparable to smoking (NBGH, 2012). As obesity rises in the United States, the chronic health conditions associated with it drive more than one-fourth of the increased costs

Smoking Tobacco: The $200 Billion to $1.2 Trillion Annual Cost Burden

- Smokers cost employers an extra $100,000 to $5 million over a lifetime.
- Smokers cost the U.S. economy $289 billion a year.
- Employers pay as much as 40 percent more in health care costs than that paid for nonsmokers.
- Adverse health effects from smoking account for 440,000 deaths annually or nearly 1 of every 5 deaths.
- 8.6 million smokers suffer from serious illnesses attributable to smoking, including 90 percent of the lung cancer, coronary heart disease, and chronic obstructive lung disease.

— Sources: BLS, 2015; CDC, 2015; Harris, 2011; HHS, 2014; Wharton, 2006.

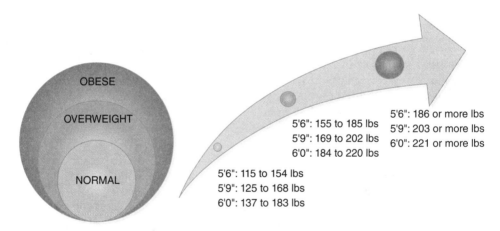

FIGURE 6-2 Defining Overweight and Obesity
Source: CDC, 2012.

of health care (Russell, 2007). It is estimated that by 2018, the annual cost burden of obesity on public and private health insurance will be as high as $344 billion per year (Browne, 2011).

Diabetes

Diabetes is a chronic metabolic disorder characterized by high blood sugar, either because the body does not produce enough insulin or because cells do not respond to the insulin that is produced. Most cases of diabetes can be prevented, delayed from occurring, or decreased in severity by weight management (Davis, 2011), for people become more resistant to insulin as they become more overweight (Yang & Nichols, 2011). The link between obesity

---

FEATURE BOX 6-4

Obesity: The $129 to $175 Billion Annual Cost Burden

- Cancers
- Type 2 diabetes
- Dyslipidemia (high blood cholesterol levels)
- Gallbladder disease
- Heart disease
- Hypertension
- Osteoarthritis
- Respiratory problems
- Sleep apnea
- Stroke

— Sources: CDC, 2012; Goizueta, 2011.

---

and diabetes is so strong that the term "obesity and with it diabetes" is becoming common (Browne, 2011; Cogan, 2011; Hardcastle, et al., 2011; Mitgang, 2011). While debate often revolves around whether diabetes is a private or public responsibility, in reality it must be both (Yang & Nichols, 2011). Although individuals are largely responsible for managing their weight and controlling their susceptibility to diabetes, at the same time, successful long-term weight management is in part influenced by environmental factors (Parker-Pope, 2011) and genetic factors. There are overlapping employee and employer interests in avoiding obesity and its myriad costs, especially when employer-provided health insurance benefits extend employment relationships beyond the workplace walls (Sonne, 2008).

Treatment Adherence

Smoking tobacco and overeating often advance the onset and increase the severity of preventable chronic diseases such as diabetes, arthritis, and circulatory disorders—diseases that are responsible for the most direct health care costs among employees. Many employees also repeat unhealthy personal behavioral choices by failing to take their prescribed medications or adhere to other forms of medical advice (Yang & Nichols, 2011). Nearly one-third to one-half of Americans fail to take medications as prescribed, which then increases the severity of their chronic diseases (Bailey, 2011; Schneider & Hall, 2009).

Health Laws Supporting Lifestyle Discrimination

Although the law protects disabled people who have experienced historical unfairness and recognizes the harmful effects of discrimination, lifestyle choices are voluntary. Though personal responsibility is complex, daily individual choices ultimately play the most prominent role in smoking, obesity, and treatment adherence.

ETHICAL DILEMMAS 6-4

5. Since treating early manifestations of disease is far less expensive than treating the chronic health conditions that result from long-term smoking of tobacco and obesity, how can the value of preventive self-care be raised so that employees will set priorities for their own health and see healthy lifestyles as a moral obligation?

Disability Legislation: Americans with Disabilities Act

Although some federal laws are specifically aimed at barring discrimination, none reach so far as to regulate employer scrutiny of employee lifestyle behaviors (Bosch, 2006). For instance, the federal **Americans with Disabilities Act of 2006** (ADA) prohibits employers from discriminating against disabled people on the basis of their disability with regard to employment (application, hiring, advancement, or discharge), compensation, or job training. The ADA also prohibits employers from requiring medical examinations or making other disability-related inquiries to determine whether an employee is disabled (or the extent of any such disability) unless the examination or inquiry is job-related and consistent with business necessity (Noyce, 2011).

The ADA, with its focus on preventing discrimination against those with a significant physical or mental impairment, is inapplicable to claims brought by employees or job applicants who are not restricted in major daily life activities. Although unhealthy lifestyle behaviors may lead to eventual disability, they are not considered a disability because they do not limit such life activities as required under the ADA (Tolle, 2007). Accordingly, while obese employees or job applicants may have recourse under the ADA, their legal protections are narrow and quite specific (Yang & Nichols, 2011). Smokers have no such recourse, nor would people who fail to take their medications as prescribed.

Civil Rights Legislation

The federal **Civil Rights Act of 1964** prohibits discrimination in employment based on race, color, national origin, sex, or religion. Because **dynamic pricing** of health insurance, which sets premiums based on lifestyle choices such as smoking and weight status, does not implicate race, color, national origin, sex, or religion, employees who are forced to pay higher insurance premiums based on lifestyle behaviors would have no recourse under the Civil Rights Act or similar state enactments (Strahilevitz, 2008; Ross & Yinger, 2006).

Invasion of Privacy

Employers' considerations of smoking and obesity do not usually violate privacy interests (Sonne, 2008). Because there is no recognized federal or state constitutional right to be free from non-arbitrary employment considerations, absent specific lifestyle legislation otherwise prohibiting such considerations, employers can implement **lifestyle discrimination** policies (Roche, 2011). Such policies protect the employer from employees attempting to pursue legal action related to their engaging in lawful, private off-duty conduct which the employer prohibits (Hong, 2007).

Privacy claims, like the right to be free from intrusion upon seclusion, require that an employer's intrusion be unreasonable and intrusive upon private affairs (Levinson, 2009). The mere fact that smoking or treatment adherence, or lack thereof, may take place in private is insufficient to subject the activity to privacy protection. The same reasoning would apply to overeating and/or not exercising.

Courts that have considered whether smoking is a private affair that implicates a legitimate privacy interest have concluded that it is not (Rutkow, et al., 2007). No courts have considered whether overeating and/or not exercising until excess weight or obesity occurs are subject to privacy protection. Nor has treatment adherence been litigated. However, claims for intrusion upon seclusion cannot be maintained where activities are by default disclosed, such as obesity, or undertaken in public, such as smoking.

Incentives Offered for Voluntary Choices

There is no doubt that rising health care costs increase the cost of health insurance. In an effort to counter this statistic and to help employees adopt healthier lifestyles, employers are offering a variety of programs and benefits (Wharton, 2006). While every state permits employers to penalize employees for smoking in the workplace or during working hours (Rutkow, et al., 2007), most states restrict employers from considering off-duty smoking (CDC, 2015). Crucially, if a penalty is imposed on employees for smoking, reasonable alternatives must be available by law to employees who cannot quit smoking. For instance, a smoker addicted to nicotine, a medical condition, could avoid being penalized by participating in a smoking-cessation program (Termini, 2010). Thus, employers with no-smoking-on-company-property policies may lawfully discipline or terminate employees who violate their smoking ban.

In many states, an increasing number of employers have enacted policies precluding the employment of smokers (Chadwick, 2006). The only protection from employment discrimination that smokers can rely on exists in the form of state laws prohibiting employment discrimination based on tobacco use, which exist in half the states, almost all of which are under challenge (Wall, 2013). For instance, the World Health Organization rejects all applicants who smoke, as do an increasing number of employers from health care organizations to airlines (Parisi, 2010). In contrast to this no-smoking approach by employers in states that tolerate lifestyle discrimination, other employers in those states have adopted a middle-of-the-road approach to employee smoking. Those employers, as opposed to prohibiting employment of smokers, have passed on the additional costs attributable to smoking to the employees who smoke by charging them more for health insurance (Wharton, 2009). Alternatively, employers may offer nonsmoking employees a financial reward for not smoking, such as a credit toward their health insurance.

Smoking opened the door for employers to also think about obesity, another leading preventable cost to the U.S. health care system. While obesity and treatment adherence have not been examined critically in the same way as smoking has, most employers see anti-obesity and treatment adherence initiatives as beneficial (Parisi, 2010).

Lifestyle Ratings for Health Insurance

Before health care reform, dynamic pricing of health insurance premiums based on lifestyle choices was restrained by federal law. Employers had to follow strict regulations whenever the cost of health insurance was based on unhealthy lifestyle choices. Opponents of health care reform claim that dynamic pricing for lifestyle choices involves reasoning that is little more than medical speculation. *See generally* Roskelley & Keene, 2011.

Wellness Rules

Federal so-called **wellness rules** require all employees covered under the same employer-sponsored health insurance plan to pay the same insurance premiums regardless of their health, with certain wellness programs being the exception (Hendrix & Buck, 2009). Employers can offer financial incentives of as much as 50 percent off the cost of insurance premiums covering an employee for participating in wellness programs. Prior to health care reform, this was narrowly restricted to 20 percent. One of the most popular incentives has become health insurance discounts to nonsmokers and those willing to submit to health risk assessments, including level of treatment adherence and monitoring of blood pressure, cholesterol levels, nicotine use, and weight. *See generally* Jesson, 2008.

This incentive for employer-sponsored health insurance plans is expanding. Under the wellness rule, health insurers cannot discriminate among individuals in eligibility, benefits, or premiums based on any health factor of an individual (health status and genetic information are all considered health factors) (Chancey, 2009). For instance, employers cannot charge smokers higher health care premiums without offering those with a nicotine addiction access to supplemental wellness programs, such as smoking cessation activities.

Unregulated Classification of Health Risks

Before the Affordable Care Act of 2010, only larger employers had health insurance where costs were based on actual employee claims (Westfall, 2011). The cost of health insurance for large employers was determined by risk classification systems based on actual health insurance claims (Lee, 2011). **Risk classification** is the system insurers use to underwrite health insurance in accordance with the risk factors known to affect the health of the insured (actual claims or demographics). Large employers are generally **self-insured**; they carry their own risks for health care costs rather than purchasing health insurance from an insurer.

In contrast, small employers had to generally purchase health insurance from the insurance industry based on gender and age (Camozzi, 2010). In states with unregulated markets, small employers paid as much as nine times more for the same health insurance coverage if they employed women and/or older employees (Corlette, 2015; Ross & Yinger, 2006). Their claims history had no relationship to the cost of their health insurance. In other words, the costs of health insurance for small employers was determined by **geographic rating**, also known as *community rating;* when one or more members in their geographic community developed a costly medical condition, all the small employers in that community had to pay higher premiums. Small employers could not effectively manage their health risks; their risks were based on the demographics of their geographic community, not on the actual claims of their employees. Without health care reform, health insurance costs for large employers would have continued to be based on actual claims; for small employers, costs would be based on demographics in general (Epstein & Stannard, 2012). Large employers could effectively manage their employee claims; small employers could not.

Regulated Classification of Health Risks

The Affordable Care Act limits the extent to which the health insurance industry can impose premium surcharges on small employers based on such factors as health status, age, tobacco use, and gender. Traditionally, risk classification practices were regulated by the states, with wide variations in how much insurers could adjust rates (Corlette, 2015).

ETHICAL DILEMMAS 6-5

6. Is there a principled limit to the scope of personal responsibility for one's health, or should health be a totally private matter?

Although states retain the authority to determine geographic rating (Ross & Yinger, 2006), the federal government can now review such determinations to ensure that they are adequate. Risks are now spread more broadly and insurers are not allowed to adjust rates based on the health status of individuals.

Lifestyle Discrimination

Although employees have used the courts to challenge employment policies that consider lifestyle behavior, such challenges have met with little success (Madison, et al., 2011). Unless a state prohibits employers from considering specific behaviors, employers have been successful in protecting their right to hire and fire employees as they please, meaning that employers can take an employee's health care costs into consideration in a decision to hire or fire that employee (Chadwick, 2006). To be sure, not all policies precluding the employment of smokers are ethically permissible. For instance, the use of race or gender to somehow target smokers or other such discriminatory treatment is not ethical. However, dynamic pricing of health insurance premiums is ever more common. Even if employers are prohibited, either by law or their own policies, from discriminating against those with higher than average health care costs, it is very difficult to prove that this is what the employer has done in any given case. Especially with the high level of applicants for every available job, it would be quite easy for an employer during the interview process to select an applicant of healthy weight over an overweight or obese applicant and justify it by simply saying that the healthy-weight applicant was better qualified or interviewed better.

While Santa Cruz and San Francisco in California, Michigan, and Washington, DC, have passed laws barring employment discrimination because of weight (Capell, 2007), outside these areas it remains very difficult for employees and job applicants to bring a successful case against employers for lifestyle discrimination based on weight. Weight, however, is much more of a dilemma for employers than smoking because often employers cannot practically refuse to hire overweight employees when 7 out of 10 adults in the United States aged 20 years or older are overweight or obese (Wharton, 2008). Employers are in a quandary; they want employees to lose weight to decrease potential health care costs, but they can not or do not want to fire them for being overweight.

Disclosure Requirement of Lifestyle Choices

Most employers who prohibit unhealthy behaviors require that employees agree to disclose their smoking, weight, or treatment adherence status. No intrusion into privacy occurs when employers have permission to commit the intrusive act or when the employee is on notice of the employment policy (Roche, 2011). Thus, for instance, when an employer has given notice of a no-smoking policy, the lifestyle smoker is caught between disclosing the smoking and being fired, or refusing disclosure and being found out and fired. The same logic would apply to treatment adherence. Weight is readily apparent, so it is difficult to claim a privacy intrusion (Desir, 2010).

Even if employees could establish that they had a reasonable expectation of privacy, employer scrutiny into employee lifestyle behaviors is reasonable. A balancing test is generally used in determining whether an employer's intrusion into an area the employee deems private is unreasonable (Swartz, 2010). Thus, the significance of employee privacy interests is balanced against employer business interests. Assuming that employers have a legitimate business interest in reducing the costs of employer-provided health insurance, such as the increased health care costs incurred due to employees' unhealthy behaviors, employer policies requiring employee self-disclosure are not inherently unreasonable, legally speaking (Parisi, 2010).

Lifestyle Choices in the Workplace

It is undisputed that employers incur certain costs as a result of hiring and retaining employees with unhealthy lifestyles (Wharton, 2009). If employers do not impose a surcharge for health insurance on such employees, then those additional costs are passed on to, or shared with, all employees (Lawrence, 2012). There is no doubt that the greatest harm caused by unhealthy behaviors is self-inflicted (Parisi, 2010). Nonetheless, such lifestyle consequences have a ripple effect resulting in employer consequences. From the employer's perspective, given a choice between a nonsmoker and a smoker or between someone who has a healthy weight or someone who is overweight, with all other things being equal, it would be an irrational business decision to choose the lifestyle smoker or overweight employee. In dollars and cents, the employer who chooses to hire the lifestyle smoker or employee with an unhealthy weight has opted to pay more for services that can be purchased for less. In other words, it is good business to hire nonsmokers and people with healthy weights.

Nonetheless, employers who opt to promote healthy lifestyles make a business decision to forego hiring from a segment of the available labor market (Wharton, 2009). In certain industries, a ban on employment of employees with unhealthy lifestyles may be impracticable. For instance, because the highest incidence of smoking is young unskilled employees, those businesses seeking a significant pool of unskilled laborers, such as home health aides, could ultimately limit their applicant pool to a point that any savings in health insurance costs would be offset by the increased wages necessary to broaden the applicant pool (Blanpain, 2005).

At the same time, lifestyle discrimination policies provide incentives for employees to adopt healthy behaviors (Wharton, 2009). In fact, there is some, albeit anecdotal, evidence supporting the proposition that lifestyle policies provide incentives for some employees to quit smoking, lose weight, or take their medications as prescribed. When cast in these terms, employers' concerns for employees' health sounds noble; numerous research studies quote employees testifying that without incentives from employers, they would have unhealthier lifestyles (Liskov & Mastroianni, 2010). Moreover, evidence is beginning to emerge showing that incentivizing employees may be effective (Wharton, 2009), such as providing financial incentives for making better lifestyle choices (Yang & Nichols, 2011). For instance, a smoking-cessation study at General Electric found that smokers who were offered financial incentives to quit smoking were almost 3 times as likely to remain smoke-free, compared with smokers who tried to quit without financial incentives (Volpp, 2009). Another study found that dieters who earned financial incentives lost weight more quickly than those who did not (Volpp, 2008).

Paying Your Way: Your Lifestyle Choice

Studies confirm that employers believe employees should be responsible for their own health; at the same time, employers believe employees are not held accountable (Watson Wyatt, 2015). There are two sides to the lifestyle debate. On the one hand, there is reluctance to allow employers to intrude into the health of employees (Bosch, 2006). In reality, however, employers have a right to make hiring decisions based on the predicted efficiency of job applicants. Inevitably, employees with unhealthy lifestyles will likely cost more in employer-provided health insurance and likely be less productive in general due to poor health (Wharton, 2009).

Many employers have opted to pass on health care costs attributable to unhealthy lifestyles to those employees who smoke, or are overweight or obese. Of course, this middle position is available only in those jurisdictions adhering to the premise that employment is at will. The middle approach of passing on employer costs attributable to preventable behaviors and conditions has two benefits. First, supplemental amounts paid by employees with preventable behaviors and conditions are intended to, and by all accounts do, offset at least some of the employer costs inherent in hiring these employees. Accordingly, to the extent that increased health care costs attributable to unhealthy lifestyles are passed on to employees, the increased costs are borne by those who create the risk of the increased costs as opposed to those who do not pose the same economic risk to employers (Parisi, 2010). Second, because it operates as a surcharge, it provides an incentive to employees to adopt healthier lifestyles. One of the advantages of the benefits surcharge is that it forces employees to be responsible for the additional costs incumbent in their lifestyles, while at the same time relieving employees from bearing health insurance costs not attributable to their own behavior. In short, it makes employees accountable for their behavior (Wharton, 2009).

Fairness in Balancing Health Care Costs

If health care resources are finite, healthy lifestyles constitute a legitimate employment consideration. Employers need to be able to manage the nature of the health risks they face, the likelihood of disease occurrence from unhealthy lifestyle choices, and the health care costs that may result from tobacco-related and weight-related diseases, as well as the failure to take medications as prescribed. Self-insured large employers and insurers that provide health insurance to small employers are interested because they need to know how to set premiums for different types of risk within the context of their overall risk portfolio.

Although some states proscribe employment consideration of off-duty smoking and weight, a significant number of states continue the at-will tradition of employment, allowing

ETHICAL DILEMMAS 6-6

7. Is it ethical for employers to penalize employees for smoking behaviors and weight conditions that increase employers' health care costs, or should employers bear these costs to attract good employees?

ETHICAL DILEMMAS 6-7

8. What types of medical interventions, if any, are ethically permissible for employers to require or encourage against preventable diseases triggered by voluntary lifestyle choices made on a day-to-day basis?

employers to fire or refuse to hire employees at their discretion (Browne, et al., 2010). In the middle are those employers that opt to hire smokers and obese employees, but only on the condition that those who smoke or who are obese pay at least some of the benefit costs attributable to their lifestyle choices. The prevailing view of employers is that policies covering unhealthy lifestyles at the expense of all employees are not fair (Baker, 2008).

No one seriously disputes that employee lifestyle choices affect health and impose significant health and productivity costs on employers (Thompson, et al., 2015). Employers are increasingly being called upon to fight chronic diseases, many of which are related to preventable behavior, not only to cut direct and indirect costs, but as a matter of social responsibility (World Economic Forum, 2007). There is considerable evidence that unhealthy lifestyles are directly related to increased employer costs (Wharton, 2009).

An equitable approach to managing health care costs should balance the concerns of employees with healthy lifestyles with those of employees who have unhealthy lifestyles and their accompanying preventable diseases and chronic health conditions. Attempts should be made to balance individual employee privacy concerns with the cost burdens imposed on employers who are forced to hire employees with unhealthy lifestyles. Under a balanced approach, if employers are proscribed from making hiring and firing decisions based on lifestyle behaviors, legislation could provide for employers to pass on the costs reasonably associated with their hiring and retention to the specific employees who choose unhealthy lifestyles (Copp, 2012). Under this scheme, it would be legitimate to charge a surcharge for employer-provided health insurance to those employees who smoke or are overweight or obese or refuse to adhere to their medication regimens.

Reducing and Fairly Allocating Employers' Health Care Costs

Ethically speaking, employees of equal lifestyle responsibility should pay health insurance premiums equal to other such employees, no matter their actual respective health status. Thus, employees with chronic and expensive health conditions, but who choose healthy lifestyles on a daily basis, would have lower health insurance premiums than healthy individuals with unhealthy lifestyles. Moreover, well-treated but chronically ill employees might have lower health insurance premiums than healthy employees who choose to smoke or be overweight or obese, or who are medically noncompliant. *See generally* Hurwitz, 2009.

Preventive medicine is compatible with recent health care reforms and the ethical principle that everyone should have access to affordable health insurance. At the same time, it is responsive to the fairness principle that health care costs be allocated more toward employees who voluntarily choose unhealthy lifestyles. Although this approach to health care is a fundamental change for the health care industry, it could help reduce and fairly allocate employers' health care costs.

Employees' Voluntary Lifestyle Choices: Smoking Tobacco

Ethics Issue: *Should employees be fired for smoking in the workplace?*

Ethics Analysis: Yes, smoking in a designated nonsmoking area does not violate an employee's constitutional right to privacy. Smoking is not a fundamental right superseding an employer's interest in maintaining a healthy work space as it relates to employment. Smoking is a willful act that may result in termination from employment.

Ethics Analysis: No, smoking is a private activity entitled to protection against employer consideration.

Court's Holding and Decision: Smoking in a non-designated smoking area in the workplace constitutes willful misconduct and employees may be fired for such conduct.

— *Dubbs v. Unemployment Compensation Board of Review*, 2010 Pa. Commw. Unpub. LEXIS 484 (Commonwealth Court of Pennsylvania 2010).

CHAPTER SUMMARY

- National business advocacy groups and associations now describe smoking, overeating, and the failure to take medications as prescribed as preventable behaviors, a word choice which recognizes that these harmful day-to-day behaviors are avoidable.
- With 7 out of 10 adults aged 20 years or older overweight or obese, weight-related chronic health conditions are a significant burden to the U.S. health care system, contributing as much as $129 to $175 billion to the nation's annual medical bill.
- Employers can offer financial incentives of as much as 50 percent off the cost of health insurance premiums covering an employee for participating in wellness programs and adopting healthy behaviors.
- While the law protects disabled people who have experienced historical unfairness and recognizes the harmful effects of discrimination, many lifestyle choices contributing to disabilities are voluntary and arguably not ethically deserving of protection.
- Because dynamic pricing of health insurance for unhealthy lifestyles does not implicate race, national origin, sex, or religion, employees who are forced to pay higher insurance premiums based on these characteristics have no recourse under the Civil Rights Act or similar state enactments.
- If health care resources are finite, healthy lifestyles constitute a legitimate employment consideration and lifestyle discrimination policies are ethical.
- Ethically speaking, equally responsible employees who choose healthy lifestyles should pay equal health insurance premiums, no matter their respective health status.

REFERENCES

Altman, D. (2015). *Public vs. private health insurance on controlling spending*. Menlo Park, CA: Kaiser Family Foundation.

Bailey, J. (2011, February 25). Senior Vice President, Private, Public and Institutional Customers, GlaxoSmithKline, Remarks at the panel discussion on Health Care Reform: Opportunities and Challenges Created through Health Care Reform at the 2011 Wharton Health Care Business Conference, Philadelphia, PA.

Baker, C. A. (2008). Bottom lines and waist lines: State governments weigh in on wellness. *Indiana Health Law Review, 5*, 185–199.

Blanpain, R. (2005). *Smoking and the workplace*. London, England: Kluwer Law International.

BLS (Bureau of Labor Statistics). (2015). *Current employment statistics highlights*. Washington, DC: U.S. Department of Labor.

Bosch, J. (2006). None of your business (interest): The argument for protecting all employee behavior with no business impact. *Southern California Law Review, 76*, 639–662.

Browne, M. N., et al. (2010). Overweight/obesity as a protected category: The complexity of personal responsibility for physical attributes. *Michigan State Journal of Medicine and Law, 14*, 1–69.

Browne, V. B. (2011). The rules of consumption: The promise and peril of federal emulation of the Big Apple's food laws. *Brooklyn Law Review, 76*, 1049–1092.

Callahan, D. (2012). The graying of America: Challenges and controversies: Must we ration health care for the elderly? *Journal of Law, Medicine and Ethics, 40*, 10–15.

Camozzi, B. D. (2010). Eleventh annual review of gender and sexuality law: Health care law chapter: Health care access. *The Georgetown Journal of Gender and the Law, 11*, 443–509.

Capell, P. (2007, October 2). Why weight-discrimination cases pose thorny legal tests. *Wall Street Journal*, p. B4.

CDC (Centers for Disease Control and Prevention). (2015). State-specific prevalence of current cigarette smoking among adults and secondhand smoke rules and policies in homes and workplaces. *U.S. Morbidity and Mortality Weekly Report, 64*(19), 532–536.

____. (2015a). *Chronic diseases: The leading causes of death and disability in the United States*. Atlanta, GA: U.S. Department of Health and Human Services.

____. (2012). *Defining weight and obesity*. Atlanta, GA: U.S. Department of Health and Human Services.

Chadwick, K. L. (2006). Is leisure-time smoking a valid employment consideration? *Albany Law Review, 70*, 117–141.

Chancey, A. K. (2009). Getting healthy: Issues to consider before implementing a wellness program. *Journal of Health and Life Sciences Law, 2*(3), 49–51.

Channick, S. A. (2010). Will Americans embrace single-payer health insurance: The intractable barriers of inertia, free market, and culture. *Journal of Theory and Practice: Law and Inequality, 28*, 1–50.

CIA (Central Intelligence Agency). (2014). *The world factbook*. Washington, DC: CIA.

Cogan, J. A. (2011). The Affordable Care Act's preventive services mandate: Breaking down the barriers to nationwide access to preventive services. *Journal of Law, Medicine and Ethics, 39*, 355–362.

Copp, A. (2012). The ethics and efficacy of a "fat tax" in the form of an insurance surcharge on obese state employees. *Quinnipiac Health Law Journal, 15*, 1–31.

Corlette, S. (2015). *New federal rating rules*. Philadelphia, PA: American Cancer Society.

Darling, H. (2012, January 26). President, National Business Group on Health, Remarks at the 2012 National Business Group Employers' Summit on Health Care Costs and Solutions: Tactics for Volatile Times, Washington, DC.

Davis, K. U. (2011). Racial disparities in childhood obesity: Causes, consequences, and solutions. *University of Pennsylvania Journal on Law and Social Change, 14*, 313–352.

____. (2007). *Slowing the growth of U.S. health care expenditures. What are the options?* Prepared for the Commonwealth Fund & Alliance for Health Reform 2007 Bipartisan Congressional Health Policy Conference, New York, NY: Commonwealth Fund.

Desir, J. (2010). Lookism: Pushing the frontier of equality by looking beyond the law. *University of Illinois Law Review, 2010*, 629–653.

Eigen, Z. J., & Sherwyn, D. (2012). A moral/contractual approach to labor law reform. *Hastings Law Journal, 63*, 695–746.

Epstein, R. A., & Stannard, P. M. (2012). Constitutional ratemaking and the Affordable Care Act: A new source of vulnerability. *American Journal of Law and Medicine, 38*, 243–268.

Goizueta Business School at Emory University. (2011). The impact of overweight/obesity on healthcare and the economy. *Knowledge@Emory* (Original work published 2004).

Hardcastle, L. E., et al. (2011). Improving the population's health: The Affordable Care Act and the importance of integration. *Journal of Law, Medicine and Ethics, 39*, 317–325.

Harris, M. (2011, February 25). Chief Information Officer, Information Technology Division, Cleveland Clinic, Capstone speaker on Leadership in an Evolving Global Market at the 2011 Wharton Health Care Business Conference, Philadelphia, PA.

Hendrix, A., & Buck, J. (2009). Employer-sponsored wellness programs: Should your employer be the boss of more than your work? *Southwestern Law Review, 38*, 465–499.

HHS (U.S. Department of Health and Human Services). (2014). *The health consequences of smoking—50 years of progress: A report of the surgeon general.* Washington, DC: HHS.

Hoffman, A. K. (2010). Oil and water: Mixing individual mandates, fragmented markets, and health reform. *American Journal of Law and Medicine, 36*, 7–77.

Hong, J. S. (2007). Can blogging and employment co-exist? *University of San Francisco Law Review, 41*, 445–476.

Hurwitz, J. (2009). Indexing health insurance to marginal health status: A spoonful of economics helps the premiums go down. *DePaul Journal of Health Care Law, 12*, 43–66.

IOM (Institute of Medicine). (2010). *Bridging the evidence gap in obesity prevention: A framework to inform decision making.* Washington, DC: National Academies Press.

Jesson, L. (2008). Weighing the wellness programs: The legal implications of imposing personal responsibility obligations. *Virginia Journal of Social Policy and the Law, 15*, 217–298.

Kaiser Family Foundation. (2012). *Family health premiums rise 4 percent to average of $15,745 in 2012, national benchmark employer survey finds.* Menlo Park, CA: Kaiser Family Foundation.

Kinney, E. D. (2012). Prospects for comparative effectiveness research under federal health reform. *Annals of Health Law, 21*, 79–86.

Landro, L. (2004, February 12). The informed patient: Preventive medicine gets more aggressive. *Wall Street Journal*, p. D1.

Lawrence, III, J. R. (2012). "Let us now try liberty": Freeing the private sector to tackle North Carolina's tobacco addiction by reinstating employment freedom of contract. *North Carolina Law Review, 90*, 510–550.

Lee, Jr., M. (2011). Adverse reactions: Structure, philosophy, and outcomes of the Affordable Care Act. *Yale Law and Policy Review, 29*, 559–602.

Levinson, A. R. (2009). Industrial justice: Privacy protection for the employed. *Cornell Journal of Law and Public Policy, 18*, 609–688.

Liskov, E. B., & Mastroianni, L. (2010). Team competition style worksite wellness program helps employees achieve meaningful weight loss. *Journal of the American Dietetic Association, 110*(9), A47.

Madison, K. M., et al. (2011). Public health reform: Patient Protection and Affordable Care Act implications for the public's health: The law, policy, and ethics of employers' use of financial incentives to improve health. *Journal of Law, Medicine and Ethics, 39*, 450–465.

Majette, G. R. (2011). Patient Protection and Affordable Care Act and public health: Creating a framework to focus on prevention and wellness and improve the public's health. *Journal of Law, Medicine and Ethics, 39*, 366–375.

Marks, A. (2011). Good health and low costs: Why the Patient Protection and Affordable Care Act's preventive care provisions may not produce expected outcomes. *Loyola Consumer Law Review, 23*, 486–504.

Maxeiner, J. R. (2013). Costs of no codes. *Mississippi Law Review, 31*, 363–380.

Milken, M. (2011, February 8). Commentary: Health-care investment—The hidden crisis: When the stock market values companies that make cosmetics and beer far above pharmaceutical companies, you know that incentives are out of whack. *Wall Street Journal*, p. A17.

Mitgang, M. (2011). Childhood obesity and state intervention: An examination of the health risks of pediatric obesity and when they justify state involvement. *Columbia Journal of Law and Social Problems, 44*, 553–587.

NBGH (National Business Group on Health). (2012). *Strategies for driving employee engagement in wellness, health care and job performance.* Washington, DC: National Business Group on Health.

Noyce, L. (2011). Private ordering of employee privacy: Protecting employees' expectations of privacy with implied-in-fact contract rights. *American University Labor and Employment Law Forum, 1*, 27–65.

Oechsner, T. J., & Haynes, M. S. (2011). Keeping it simple: Health plan benefit standardization and regulatory choice under the Affordable Care Act. *Albany Law Review, 74*, 241–311.

Parisi, T. J. (2010). The onus is on you: Wellness plans and other strategies being employed for patients to take ownership of their health. *Quinnipiac Health Law Journal, 13*, 243–278.

Parker-Pope, T. (2011, December 28). The fat trap. *New York Times*, p. C1.

Plass, S. (2010). Private dispute resolution and the future of institutional workplace discrimination. *Howard Law Journal, 54*, 45–81.

Roche, J. M. (2011). Why can't we be friends? Why California needs a lifestyle discrimination statute to protect employees from employment actions based on their off-duty behavior. *Hastings Business Law Journal, 7*, 187–204.

Roskelley, R. D., & Keene, II, D. R. (2011). Health care reform: Keeping abreast of oncoming obligations. *Nevada Lawyer, 19*, 6–13.

Ross, S. L., & Yinger, J. (2006). Uncovering discrimination: A comparison of the methods used by scholars and civil rights enforcement officials. *American Law and Economics Review, 8*, 562–614.

Russell, L. B. (2007). *Prevention's potential for slowing the growth of medical spending.* Washington, DC: National Coalition on Health Care (NCHC).

Rutkow, L., et al. (2007). Banning second-hand smoke in indoor public places under the Americans with Disabilities Act: A legal and public health imperative. *Connecticut Law Review, 40*, 409–458.

SAHIE (Small Area Health Insurance Estimates). (2013). *County and state health insurance estimates by demographic and income characteristics.* Washington, DC: U.S. Census Bureau.

Schneider, C. E., & Hall, M. A. (2009). The patient life: Can consumers direct health care? American Journal of Law and Medicine, *35*(1), 7–65.

Schoen, C., et al. (2015). *State trends in the cost of employer health insurance coverage.* New York, NY: The Commonwealth Fund.

Sokol, K. C. (2010). Smoking abroad and smokeless at home: Holding the tobacco industry accountable in a new era. *New York University Journal on Legislation and Public Policy, 13*, 81–136.

Solar, O., & Irwin, A. (2010). *A conceptual framework for analysis and action on the social determinants of health.* Geneva, Switzerland: World Health Organization, Commission on Social Determinants of Health.

Sonne, J. A. (2008). Monitoring for quality assurance: Employer regulation of off-duty behavior. *Georgia Law Review, 43*, 133–189.

Strahilevitz, L. J. (2008). Reputation nation: Law in an era of ubiquitous personal information. *Northwestern University Law Review, 102*, 1667–1738.

Suk, J. C. (2011). Preventive health at work: A comparative approach. *American Journal of Comparative Law, 59*, 1089–1134.

Swartz, J. (2010). The revivification of *in loco parentis* behavioral regulation in public institutions of higher education to combat the overweight/obesity epidemic. *New England Law Review, 45*, 101–137.

Termini, R. B. (2010). The Family Smoking Prevention and Tobacco Control Act and public health. *Pennsylvania Bar Association Quarterly, 81*, 147–162.

Thompson, M., et al. (2015). *Focusing on healthcare value.* New York, NY: PricewaterhouseCoopers' Health Research Institute.

Tolle, N. (2007, January). Non-physiologically caused overweight/obesity is not an impairment under ADA. *Employee Benefit Plan Review, 61*(7), 28.

U.S. Surgeon General. (2010). *The Surgeon General's vision for a healthy and fit nation.* Washington, DC: U.S. Surgeon General.

Volpp, K. G. (2009). A randomized, controlled trial of financial incentives for smoking cessation. *New England Journal of Medicine, 360*, 699–709.

____. (2008). Financial incentive–based approaches for weight loss: A randomized trial. *Journal of the American Medical Association, 300*(22), 2631–2637.

Wall, B. (2013). Lighten up: Should Massachusetts implement a smoking surcharge for state employees? *Suffolk University Law Review, 46*, 1223–1248.

Ward, B. W., et al. (2014). Multiple chronic conditions among U.S. adults: Estimates from the National Health Interview Survey. *Preventing Chronic Disease*, 11, E62–E65.

Watson Wyatt. (2015). *Employers expect changes to employee health care programs to retain competitiveness, according to new Towers Watson survey.* Arlington, VA: Watson Wyatt.

Westfall, P. (2011). Ethically economic: The Affordable Care Act's impact on the administration of health benefits. *DePaul Journal of Health Care Law, 14*, 99–133.

WHA (World Health Assembly). (2012). Outcome of the world conference on social determinants of health. Geneva, Switzerland: World Health Organization.

Wharton School of the University of Pennsylvania. (2009). One way to lower health costs: Pay people to be healthy. *Knowledge@Wharton.*

____. (2008). From incentives to penalties: How far should employers go to reduce workplace overweight/obesity?

____. (2006). Efforts are growing to trim the fat from employees and employers' health care costs.

WHO (World Health Organization). (2009). *Global health risks*: Mortality and burden of disease attributable to selected major risks. Geneva, Switzerland: WHO.

Wind, J., & Crook, C. (2006). *The power of impossible thinking: Transform the business of your life and the life of your business.* Philadelphia, PA: Wharton School Publishing.

World Economic Forum. (2007). *The global competitiveness report.* Geneva, Switzerland: World Economic Forum.

Yang, Y. T., & Nichols, L. M. (2011). Obesity and health system reform: Private vs. public responsibility. *Journal of Law, Medicine and Ethics, 39*, 380–385.

CHAPTER 7

© Leslie Banks/iStock/Getty Images Plus/
Thinkstock

Management and Labor Relations

"Upon the conduct of each depends the fate of all."

— **Alexander the Great** (356–323 BC), King of Macedon and founder of a new world order

LEARNING OBJECTIVES

After completing this chapter, the reader should be able to:

1. Describe why management and labor unions should work together to improve economic discontent and address the nation's growing wealth disparity.
2. Understand the issues involved in unionization of health care professionals in an emerging stakeholder society.
3. Explain how to effectively make ethical decisions regarding mandatory overtime.

KEY TERMS

Adverse events	Great Recession	National Labor Relations
Certification	Labor management	Board (NLRB)
Contingent employees	relations	Outsourced employees
Contingent work	Labor unions	Poverty wages
Decertification petition	Living wage	Service Employees
Ethics of care	Low-wage employees	International Union
Exempt employees	Management	Social contract
Fair Labor Standards Act	National Labor Relations	
of 1938 (FLSA)	Act of 1935 (NLRA)	

ETHICAL OR UNETHICAL DECISION

Refusal to Bargain in the Health Care Industry

Ethics Issue: *Can an employer refuse to bargain in good faith and then withdraw recognition from a certified labor union during the organizing process?*

In Brief: In 2000, the United Staff Nurses Union Local 141 won union **certification** and recognition that it would be the sole representative of employees in bargaining with their employer to protect their work interests at 1 of 20 medical clinics run by Virginia Mason Medical Center. When the Medical Center tested the certification by refusing to bargain with the union, the **National Labor Relations Board (NLRB)**, the federal agency that administers processes for designating labor unions as representatives of employees to protect their work interests, ordered the Medical Center to bargain in good faith.

The Medical Center's petition for review of that order to bargain was denied, and the labor union requested a meeting to begin negotiations. The parties met more than 20 times during the following months. However, within the year, the Medical Center obtained a union **decertification petition** from 8 of the 19 employees stating that the union no longer represented their work interests. The Medical Center immediately withdrew its recognition of the union, asserting that the union no longer had the support of its employees.

In response, the labor union filed an unfair labor practice charge, alleging that the Medical Center had encouraged a decertification campaign, failed to bargain with the union in good faith, and hired and fired employees based upon their relationship with the union. The union litigated the unfair labor charges against the Medical Center for the next 6 years.

— *Virginia Mason Medical Center v. National Labor Relations Board*, 558 F.3d 891 (U.S. Court of Appeals for the 9th Circuit 2009). (*See Ethical or Unethical Decision* at the end of the chapter for discussion of this ethics issue.)

Introduction

A new model for relations between **management** (the collective term for the senior executives who control managerial responsibilities and determine employee policies) and **labor unions** (the term for non-managerial employees who have collectively organized to protect and advance their interests in terms of wages, benefits, working hours, and conditions) is emerging. A model that is less focused on bottom lines, and more focused on science, medicine, and patient needs, is needed for the delivery of health care in the 21st century. Labor unions are stakeholders; they invest their human capital in the U.S. health care system and they have a moral right to consult with management (Wharton, 2011). There is the possibility that a reformed management and labor union model in the health care industry could arise if management partnered with labor unions to focus on managing the health care of patients as opposed to just managing costs. This change in focus from bottom-line attempts to get labor unions to cut costs the way management wants to, to an arrangement where both parties negotiate together to cut costs without losing the focus on patient care, could result in a reformed relationship between management and labor unions. This is a modernized cooperative model of union representation (Wharton, 2011).

Just as the **National Labor Relations Act of 1935 (NLRA)** was a new legal framework for management and labor relations created out of the distress, dislocation, and turmoil of the Great Depression, the Affordable Care Act of 2010 (ACA) is a new legal framework for health care created out of the financial suffering, confusion, and chaos of the **Great Recession**. As unemployment burgeoned during this recession, more than 50 million Americans found themselves uninsured (Kaiser Commission, 2010) and another 106 million found themselves underinsured (Felland, et al., 2010) and unable to access affordable health care (Jacobs & Graham-Squire, 2008).

The ACA, the most significant reform of the U.S. health care system in 70 years, was negotiated during this Great Recession. This new law affects the financing, delivery, quality, and availability of health care services for all Americans, not only by amending government health insurance programs, but also by substantially reforming the private insurance market to provide affordable coverage for almost all U.S. residents (Somers & Perkins, 2010). With the ACA's broad expansion of insurance coverage, new primary care physicians, nurses, and other health care professionals will be needed to ensure that more patients can get the quality care they need to stay healthy (HHS, 2010).

A new model of **labor management relations** that protects the shared interests of managers and employees could change the interactions and stances of management and labor unions as the ACA is implemented and more employees are added to the health care workforce. Just as management protects the interests of shareholders and owners of capital used in the health care industry, labor unions support employees and advance their interests in terms of wages, benefits, working hours, and work environment conditions (Runnels, et al., 2010).

Public Perceptions of Management and Labor Relations

The health care industry puts the **ethics of care** into quantifiable action by measuring success not simply by financial returns, but also by tracking investments that help people stay healthy and maintain a better quality of life, such as by preventing disease and helping to manage chronic conditions. Health care is a unique industry where the vulnerability of patients and the suffering caused by illness create an industry that is driven in part by an ethic of compassion. Yet, there is the need for a refined balance between management and labor unions in the care of patients (Runnels, et al., 2010).

The recent global economic downturn caused many to wonder whether the traditional model for management and labor relations is broken, with labor unions struggling to represent employees in their disputes with management. Whereas the traditional model is based on conflict caused by negotiations between management and labor and focused on controlling costs, the health care industry instead requires a model of collaboration focused on patient care (Wharton, 2011).

Nevertheless, a perception of ineffectiveness clouds the health care industry, while budget shortfalls generate debates over the role of labor unions in today's economy. For instance, tax-exempt hospitals have management processes to identify community needs and develop programs to meet those needs, but this does not translate to paying **low-wage employees** a **living wage**. *Low-wage employees* are defined as those earning $23,000 or less (Rosenbaum, 2011), or less than half of the $51,017 median U.S. wage (Noss, 2014). *Living wages* are wages above the poverty line and defined as $26,000 to $31,200 or more (Murray, 2012; Tung, et al., 2015), and ideally include access to affordable health insurance.

The U.S. health care system is at a crossroads, facing both challenges to its funding and opportunities for accelerating medical advancement. Americans are evenly divided about whether significant reform of the U.S. health care system would be helpful in their quest to access affordable, quality health care (Kaiser Family Foundation, 2011). As illustrated in **FEATURE BOX 7-1**, the only way to change perceptions about the ineffectiveness of management and the relevance of labor unions, however, is to change current reality (Maher, 2007). Management and labor unions must realize that there are ways in which a partnership, as opposed to contention, can catalyze change to add more value to the U.S. health care system.

The Role of Labor Unions in Today's Economy

A change in the agreed-upon role of labor unions in the health care industry is causing a deep divide in public opinion. For a considerable time, there has been no agreement on what labor unions' role should be. Public disagreement and division suggest that, at the very least, senior executives and labor leaders should engage in established rules of conduct (Gopalan, 2007). One side says that labor unions are an accepted part of American society, while another side questions what the role of labor unions should be in today's global economy (Wharton, 2011). Although Americans remain skeptical about how much confidence they can place in labor unions, the same skepticism can also be directed toward management (Secunda & Hirsch, 2008). Although labor unions' public support in disputes with management has remained steady over time (Maher & Belkin, 2011), these views run directly

---

FEATURE BOX 7-1

Management and Labor Need to Change Their Reality

Management and labor unions need to:
- *Better understand the ethics of care*: Values in the health care industry should come from the vulnerability of consumers of health care and the human suffering caused by illness. These conditions should ideally compel compassion in decision-making by management, employees, and labor unions (as opposed to decisions based primarily on financial returns, as in other industries).
- *Level the playing field*: Medicine is about quality health care and efficiency, and should not be about who can pay the least for staffing to provide patient care.
- *Benefit the common good*: Each side must appreciate where the other can be most helpful in reforming the U.S. health care system.

— Sources: Maher, 2007; Rawls, 1971/2005.

ETHICAL DILEMMAS 7-1

1. Given the ethics of care unique to the health care industry, how should management and labor unions collaborate to meet the conflicting demands of focusing on costs and bottom lines while also focusing on patient care?

counter to what might be expected for a labor movement in decline in recent years (Gould, 2012). The remainder of the chapter addresses this paradox: the contradiction between the desire for labor union representation and the reality of actual unionization.

Relevance of Labor Unions

There is tension over the idea that health care industry costs have to be cut, because it is unclear who will suffer the consequences of those cuts. Given this sense of conflict, there is a window of opportunity for strategic trade-offs between management and labor unions to engage in socially beneficial behavior that could address the wage stratification conditions in the health care industry's work space and expand employment opportunities for everyone.

The United States holds the dubious distinction of having the most unequal wage distribution of any advanced industrialized nation (Massey, 2008). While other developed countries face similar challenges, none rivals the singularly poor record of the United States for equitably distributing the benefits and burdens of recent economic shifts (Wharton, 2011a). Wage stratification is not simply inevitable; privileged groups systematically exploit and exclude low-wage employees who have few chances for earnings mobility (Massey, 2008). Although structural or systemic causes favor senior executives, this does not justify such extreme wage disparity (Wharton, 2011). The playing field must be leveled so that everyone has the opportunity to capture more benefits. The way to future prosperity, not to mention social cohesion, is through management and labor relations that forego income retention at the top of the socioeconomic pyramid in order for prosperity to touch those at the middle and bottom of the pyramid (Wharton, 2011). In particular, if this does not occur in the health care industry, those at the middle and bottom will likely leave for other opportunities, leaving the less qualified to deliver care to patients (Massey, 2008).

While labor unions' membership is flat overall in the United States (Trottman & Maher, 2011), the health care industry is becoming more unionized, as it is dominated by nurses and low-wage employees who are hoping for higher pay and benefits. Nurses, home health aides, maintenance staff, nurse aides, and security staff in hospitals, nursing homes, and other institutional health care facilities are successfully organizing. The **Service Employees International Union**, the largest labor organization in the health care industry, claims that labor unions represent more than one-third of the 11 million nurses, paramedics, and nurse aides in the health care industry (BLS, 2015). If management and labor unions would look into the root causes of why union wages and benefits are much better than non-union wages and benefits, a more equitable health care industry could be created (Wharton, 2011). For continued value creation, the health care industry must understand that wages and benefits are about more than pay; they are about equality (Saunders, 2012).

ETHICAL DILEMMAS 7-2

2. What justification is there for not addressing the income disparity problem as part of the nation's health care reform?
3. In other words, should the federal government subsidize the cost of health insurance, when the annual cost of health insurance coverage for a family exceeds the annual wages of a low-wage employee earning the minimum wage in the health care industry?
4. Does this situation reflect the ethics of care unique to the health care industry?

Issues Confronting Management and Labor

Not all jobs in the health care industry are well paid, respect the fundamental rights of employees, and ensure employees some security in case of job loss, personal or family illnesses, or other difficulties (Dahan, et al., 2011). As illustrated in **TABLE 7-1**, most low-wage jobs do not offer health insurance benefits, tend to have inflexible or unpredictable scheduling requirements, and provide little opportunity for career advancement (Boushey, et al., 2007; Tung, et al., 2015). All too often, low-wage jobs are replacing jobs that have traditionally supported a broad middle class. Remedying this condition in the health care industry's work space demands an ethical response from both management and labor unions (Dahan, et al., 2011). Yet, relatively little agreement exists about the policies, beyond raising the minimum wage, that can improve these low-wage jobs. While the problems facing low-wage employees are faced by every industry across the board, the health care industry employs nearly half the nation's low-wage employees (BLS, 2015b and 2015c). The well-being of these low-wage employees affects not only a significant portion of the nation's employees, but also patient safety, satisfaction, and the quality of care (Flood & Thomas, 2011).

Union Membership

With 7 percent of U.S. private-sector employees belonging to labor unions, the United States has one of the lowest percentages of private-sector employees covered by collective bargaining agreements as compared to other democracies around the world (BLS, 2015; Maher, 2007). There are tensions between those who are for and against restricting collective bargaining rights in the health care industry. Still, the public generally recognizes the need for labor unions to protect the rights of employees (Maher & Belkin, 2011). While a segment of Americans does not sympathize with labor unions, what is incongruous is that the public sympathizes with the average working person and is fearful that the U.S. workforce may be pulled down the socioeconomic pyramid (Wharton, 2011).

Research by the Economic Policy Institute (which receives about one-third of its funding from labor unions) estimates that the cost of adding 5 million non-unionized employees to the health care industry's unionized workforce would be approximately $34 billion

TABLE 7-1 One Out of Three Working-Age Americans Are Low-Wage Employees

Wage and Group Benefits	Low-Wage Employees	High-Wage Employees
Medical coverage with employer contribution: Individual worker and family	30–34%	100%
Paid time off for personal illness	39%	100%
Paid vacation days	51%	100%
Paid holidays	46%	100%
Job training or education	45%	100%

Data from the University of Berkeley Labor Center, 2012.
— Sources: Boushey, et al., 2007; Jacobs & Graham-Squire, 2008; Kaiser Family Foundation, 2008.

in new wages (Vidal, 2009). While this number would be offset by the economic benefits of poverty reduction when 900,000 families would be brought above the poverty level, no definitive study exists to explain how wage increases for low-wage employees would affect the nation's health care costs (Kochan & Shulman, 2007).

Income Disparities: Senior Executives versus Low-Wage Employees

There is debate around the increased costs to the health care system from unionization, and the resulting demands for higher wages and affordable health insurance benefits to unionized employees. Yet, it might be more appropriate to focus attention on the top of the socioeconomic pyramid as opposed to the bottom (Cahn & Carbone, 2015). The nation might begin by addressing the merits of the multimillion-dollar compensation packages in the health insurance industry and the hospital sector that relies on government insurance payments, especially at tax-exempt nonprofit entities and those entities that continually underperform and suffer losses. As illustrated in **TABLE 7-2**, the compensation disparity between the average employee and the average chief executive officer is wider than at any time in American history (Vidal, 2009; *see, e.g.*, Pfeffer, et al., 2013).

While senior executives no doubt contribute to the success of the health care industry, there is growing debate about their income disparity and how they get paid. The average total compensation of chief executive officers in the health insurance industry is $9.4 million compared to the 1.5 million health care aides who are working for **poverty wages**, or less than a living wage, as are 1 in 4 support staff in the health care industry (BLS, 2015; Vidal, 2009). Some senior executives are arguably compensated more than they can justify (Edmans, 2012), when total compensation of senior management executives across all industries has skyrocketed from 27 times more than the average employee in 1979 to 344 times higher today (Vidal, 2009). Although the structure of compensation is more important than its level, because it gets to the heart of how value is created in the U.S. health care system (Edmans, 2012), when one compares the importance of most health care aides for hospitalized patients to the compensation of some executives, the disparity cannot be justified.

Debate is ongoing over whether management and labor unions should address the differences in total compensation between senior executives and low-wage employees. This

TABLE 7-2 Comparable Economic Value

Average Minimum Wage Worker versus Average Wage of Chief Executive Officer	
Federal minimum wage: $7.25/hr.	CEO average wage: $3,220/hr.
HAS TO WORK	
2 minutes to earn a quarter	2 seconds to earn a quarter
444 hours to make $3,220	54 seconds to make $7.25
Work until death or retirement	Become a millionaire in less than 1 year

— Source: BLS, 2015a; Pfeffer, 2013.

Note: Some states and localities may have a higher minimum wage.

ETHICAL DILEMMAS 7-3

5. What ethical principles should underlie the health care industry's framework for protecting the human rights and interests of low-wage employees?
6. Are low-wage employees equally a part of the health care industry and as deserving of having their needs met as senior executives?
7. How has the status quo been institutionalized and wage inequality obfuscated in the health care industry?
8. Has this led to the health care industry becoming more unionized, and if so, could labor unions help address this economic stratification?

difference in total compensation, however, is the tip of the iceberg in seeking a balance between management and labor interests. For instance, on top of differences in wage compensation, everyone bears associated health care costs, such as higher health insurance premiums and reduced wages due to co-payments and co-insurance fees; these costs impose a greater burden on low-wage employees than on senior executives. Compensation packages should give everyone, senior executives and low-wage employees alike, strong incentives to do their jobs correctly (Edmans, 2012).

Current Labor Law

Modern union organizing campaigns are very sophisticated, yet labor law is biased in favor of employers (Boushey, et al., 2007). Current labor law has no enforcement powers to remedy management misconduct without legislative reforms. Remedial provisions in the NLRA pertain to violations committed by labor unions, not those perpetrated by management (Craver, 2010). Currently, federal court injunctions are required only for violations by labor unions; no such equitable remedy exists for unlawful acts committed by management. When management violates the law by refusing to bargain in good faith, the most common remedy issued by the NLRB is for management to promise to act correctly in the future; no penalty is imposed on management. Under current labor law, it is impossible to impose fines, imprisonment, or punitive damages on management.

Mandatory On-Call Policies in Health Care Settings

Most states do not have restrictions on mandatory overtime in health care settings, yet the most severe consequence of mandatory overtime is decreased patient safety with an increased rate of **adverse events** (Kugielska & Linker, 2008). Patient falls, medication administration errors, pressure ulcers, hospital infections, and mortality increase when mandatory overtime policies are in place (Scott, et al., 2006). Another consequence of equal severity is the detrimental health effects on affected employees (IOM, 2004).

ETHICS CASE
Mandatory On-Call Policies

Enloe Medical Center v. National Labor Relations Board
[Hospital v. Federal Government]
433 F.3d 834 (U.S. Court of Appeals for the District of Columbia Circuit 2005)

Facts: The California Nurses Association (CNA) is the collective bargaining representative of the nurses at Enloe Medical Center. The dispute in this case stemmed from management's unilateral adoption of a mandatory on-call policy that required nurses to work 1 4-hour on-call shift every 4 weeks, in addition to their regular 40-hour shifts. Nurses were permitted no more than 30 minutes to report when on call. Prior to this, on-call staffing was entirely voluntary. Management indicated that if nurses had a problem complying with the mandatory time requirement, nurses should contact their supervisors to make other arrangements. When the CNA learned of the on-call policy change, it told Enloe that it could not unilaterally make the proposed change without first negotiating with the labor union. The collective bargaining agreement included provisions spelling out management's unilateral rights to set the schedules of its employees, compensate nurses for on-call and call-back work, assign duties and hours to nurses, and establish standards related to patient care; the agreement did not require management to negotiate with the CNA on any of these provisions.

Legal Analysis: There is a fundamental and long-running disagreement as to the best approach to determine whether management has violated federal labor law when it refuses to bargain with its labor union over a subject covered in a collective bargaining agreement. Based on management's unilateral adoption of a mandatory on-call policy for nurses, the CNA filed a charge with the NLRB. The Board in turn issued a complaint against Enloe Medical Center.

Rule of Law: If a collective bargaining agreement gives management the right to adopt and implement on-call policies for when nurses must report to work, managers may amend or make individual exceptions to the policy without discussing these matters with the labor union.

Ethics Issue: Is it fair for management to make a unilateral decision about mandatory on-call shifts for unionized nurses, in addition to their regular 40-hour shifts, without consulting the union representing the nurses' interests, when on-call shifts had always been voluntary?

Ethics Analysis: Nursing has been particularly hard hit with shortages and requirements of mandatory on-call shifts, further contributing to the departure of nurses from their profession (AFL-CIO, 2005). The cyclical nature of this problem is evident: mandatory on-call time gives individual nurses heavier workloads, driving some to leave the profession; in turn, this reduces nursing staff levels and leads to more overtime, including in the form of mandatory on-call time, for remaining nurses (Hassmiller & Cozine, 2006). The management conflict is between choosing how to maintain adequate staffing levels: either through hiring additional staff or mandating that existing staff work overtime and on-call shifts (IOM, 2004).

Often nurses do not have advance notice of when they are required to work. While high costs discourage the use of overtime, it costs less to pay for overtime than to train and pay benefits to new nurses. The result is that nurses on average work about 8.5 weeks of overtime per year, with many nurses often working 16 hours per day. Regardless of the number of hours worked, nurses have an ethical obligation to consider their level of fatigue when deciding to accept any assignment extending beyond the regularly scheduled work day or week, including mandatory on-call assignments (Halm, et al., 2005).

Supporters of mandatory on-call policies maintain that costs compel management to rely on mandatory overtime in lieu of hiring more staff (Nelson & Kennedy, 2008). One concern is the cost of employee benefits. Using overtime to avoid hiring new staff allows hospitals to avoid paying the health insurance costs accompanying additional staff members. The fact that benefit costs have risen significantly faster than salaries makes reliance on mandatory on-call an attractive solution for management. The high cost of recruitment and training further underlies the use of mandatory on-call time. Using overtime allows a hospital to save money by minimizing the investment associated with recruiting and training new hires, and paying for their health insurance. Lastly, the unpredictable nature of the day-to-day hospital census provides an incentive for management to use mandatory on-call as another cost-saving measure. Since management cannot foresee the number of patients in the hospital at any given time, regular staff is employed to handle a low patient load and mandatory on-call time is used when the census increases. Hospitals can operate with lower labor costs by retaining only the exact number of nurses to accommodate demand.

Court's Holding and Decision: When there is a dichotomy between management rights and the effects of those rights, union employees have no recourse to compel bargaining unless the collective bargaining agreement specifies the particular discrete effects of a policy about which they seek to bargain.

See Albro, 2008; Kugielska & Linker, 2008 (discussing this court decision).

Other Work-Life Issues in the Health Care Industry

Ideally, there should be a healthy balance between life inside work and life outside work, yet many factors affect plummeting work-life balance in terms of sinking wage levels, increased working hours, and sparse health insurance benefits. The lopsided nature of the American at-will employment scheme also leaves health care industry employees with little to no job security (Coley, 2010). Together these issues contribute to the reality that employees are working longer and harder for less; in other words, the increased efforts and stress related to work have not translated to a higher quality of life, much less a higher quality of patient care (Lee, 2006). This raises ethical concerns about justice and fairness between management and labor unions.

This concern is especially controversial with regard to **exempt employees** who are salaried and **contingent employees** who do not have explicit or implicit contracts for long-term employment, including part-time and temporary employees, independent contractors, and **outsourced employees** of subcontracting employers. Exempt employees are not eligible for overtime wages, unlike hourly part-time and temporary workers who perform the same job functions.

Management of Exempt Employees

Ethical issues often arise with regard to whether employees are classified as exempt (salaried) or non-exempt (hourly) employees. While exempt employees may be paid overtime premiums, such as bonuses, flat amounts, paid time off, straight-time hourly amounts, time and one-half of a calculated hourly amount, or shift differentials, without invalidating their exempt status, most salaried employees in the health care industry get no extra compensation for putting in more than 40 hours per week (DOL, 2005). As exempt employees' share of workweeks over 40 hours is ever increasing, management claims they are in a bind. Even though the ethical principles of equality and fairness should objectively determine the overtime and exempt status of employees, whether management is treating employees equally and fairly is debatable (Pruitt, 2011).

In general, employees do not believe they are receiving what they are due from their employers (Coley, 2010). The health care industry perpetuates inequality by its increasing demands on exempt employees to work more than 40 hours per week (Rittich, 2010). Exempt employees, because they earn a set amount, end up earning lower hourly wages when they are not compensated for working overtime. In other words, the more salaried employees work per week, the lower their hourly wages.

The Nation's Home Care Sector

A long-term inequity was the health care industry's refusal to pay minimum wage and overtime to home health care aides, one of the most vulnerable employee groups in the health care industry (Spector, 2015). Home health care aides are likely to be female, black or Hispanic, foreign born, and single mothers (Smith & Baughman, 2007). Both the degree of inequality and the comparative absence of this situation's public status as an ethical issue are signs that ethnic, gender, and race discrimination are still a part of the American fabric (Umel, 2007). The inability of labor unions, which have always represented home health care aides and other low-wage employees, to exercise an effective voice for enforcement of government regulations evidences the intractability of underlying inequalities in the United States (*see* Rittich, 2010). It is also evidence of the inability of labor unions to exert countervailing economic pressure in the workplace (Nilliasca, 2011). The long-term care industry moved its business from nursing homes and institutions to home-based care because of the lower cost of care at patients' homes, which was the result of congressional exemptions from federal wage and hour laws (Spector, 2015).

ETHICS CASE
Minimum Wage and Overtime Coverage

Long Island Care at Home, et al., Ltd. v. Coke
[Home Care Agency v. Former Home Health Care Aides]
551 U.S. 158 (U.S. Supreme Court 2007)

Facts: Evelyn Coke worked for Long Island Care as a home health care aide providing caregiver services. Long Island Care at Home, a home care agency, provided home health care services to people who because of age or infirmity were unable to care for themselves. Coke claimed that Long Island Care failed to pay her and other home health care aides minimum wages and overtime wages to which they were entitled under federal and state laws.

Legal Analysis: The issue before the Court involved an interpretation of the **Fair Labor Standards Act of 1938 (FLSA)** and who is entitled to the protection of minimum wage and maximum hour rules. U.S. Department of Labor regulations state that caregivers who are employed by an agency other than a family or household are exempt. While the Department considered bringing caregivers within the scope of the FLSA over the years, the regulations were never changed. The regulations are entitled to administrative deference because the FLSA directed the Department of Labor to define *caregivers*. In this instance, the regulations are legally binding unless they are procedurally defective, arbitrary, capricious, or manifestly contrary to the FLSA. Applying these standards of law, the Court found that the regulations were enforceable on their face and upheld the regulations that home health care aides who provide caregiver services are exempt from overtime pay and minimum wage requirements.

Rule of Law: The FLSA exempts home health care aides from the wage and hour regulations.

Ethics Issue: Should overtime pay and minimum wage requirements apply to home health care aides?

Ethics Analysis: When Congress fails to define legislative terms, that task is delegated to the executive branch, as it was with the FLSA, and as it has been with many provisions in the ACA. When consequent regulations are determined by the appellate courts to be unjust, the courts either demand that the regulatory injustice be corrected by the executive branch or uphold the regulations with a directive that the dispute before them is a legislative matter that Congress or state legislatures should correct. In this decision, the U.S. Supreme Court did neither. The Court upheld the regulations as a matter of law without regard to the ethics and suffering of home health care aides as a result of unjust labor practices (Umel, 2007). The underlying purposes of maximum hours labor standards (workplace safety, and for society to work less, live more, and spread the wealth by employing more people working shorter hours, as opposed to employing fewer people working longer hours) were not acknowledged (Miller, 2008).

Although low-wage home health care aides provide essential and difficult services to the elderly and infirm, the lack of appropriate working conditions for some of the nation's most valuable members of the health care workforce poses serious problems for the provision of in-home and long-term care (IOM, 2015). Home health care aides are not fairly compensated, do not receive meal or rest breaks, endure racial discrimination and sexual harassment, and are subjected to job-related health hazards. Many of these violations go undetected and unresolved. Unfair working conditions are symptomatic of the underlying inequalities. Home health care aides are excluded from many protections afforded by state and federal law protecting workers in other industries. Moreover, existing legal protections that do protect home health caregivers remain underenforced. Many employers unknowingly violate laws that would otherwise protect home health care aides. In addition, home health care aides are uniquely susceptible to abuse due to vulnerabilities associated with their immigration status, financial position, and racial and gender stereotypes against females, blacks, and Hispanics (IOM, 2015). *See generally* Umel, 2007.

The U.S. Supreme Court did not focus on the immediate needs of home health care aides, nor the underlying inequities that produce them. In doing so, the Court failed to help put an end to abusive labor practices (Umel, 2007). The result is continuing high turnover rates and troubling consequences for the quality of care provided to consumers of home health care (Lippitt, 2011). Due to the nation's rapidly aging population over age 65, measures are necessary to ensure the improved retention rates of home health care aides and to attract the additional 800,000-plus aides that will be necessary to meet the future demand for in-home health care (DOL, 2009).

Ethically speaking, Congress should revise the FLSA and the federal government should correct the injustice of its regulations and require states to regulate home health care (Lippitt, 2011). In addition, government and private insurance rates should be equitably increased to ensure fair and just compensation for home health care aides (Lueck, et al., 2010). A quality home care workforce should be created to ensure that Americans are able to live out the last years of their lives with compassion, comfort, and human dignity.

Court's Holding and Decision: No, home health care workers are exempt from the wage and hour regulations of the FLSA requiring overtime pay and minimum wages.

See Leberstein & Christman, 2012; Levin, 2011; Lippitt, 2011; Nilliasca, 2011; Rosenbaum, 2010 (discussing this court decision).

A large number of courts were critical of this landmark decision. Most courts acknowledged the suffering of home health care aides, as well as the U.S. Supreme Court's refusal to help transform the home care sector of the long-term care industry; other courts recognized the costs of maximum hours labor standards.

Ethical Use of Contingent Employees

Contingent work, where there is no contract or expectation for long-term employment, has expanded rapidly since the mid-1990s (Snow, 2011). The number of part-time and temporary employees, independent contractors, and outsourced employees of subcontracting employers is reaching new heights. These contingent employees are in nontraditional employment relationships, as an increasing proportion of those working in the health care industry have no formal employment relationship with their employers or with employers' outside contractors (Mironi, 2010). The health care service delivery sector fills many of its low-wage jobs with contingent employees (Kaiser Family Foundation, 2008).

Contingent employees have weaker ties with their employers and less positive attitudes toward work, including lower job satisfaction, involvement, safety, loyalty, and commitment (Williamson, et al., 2009). Although there is a lack of research regarding the effects of employment status on patient outcomes, a critical question confronting management is whether weaker ties to employers correlate with higher rates of adverse events, including patient mortality.

Contingent employees are excluded from coverage under the NLRA and are beyond the reach of U.S. labor laws (Gould, 2007). They face continued downward pressure on their wages and generally receive no health insurance or pension benefits. With jobs that are often not well defined, few contingent employees are offered training or educational

ETHICAL DILEMMAS 7-4

9. Should home health care aides be entitled to more, less, or the same labor protections as other American workers?
10. What ethical obligations does the federal government have, if any, to protect elderly and infirm Americans, keep health care costs down, and effectuate the true congressional intent of the FLSA?

ETHICAL DILEMMAS 7-5

11. Eliminating contingent workers will cost the health care industry billions of dollars, and some of this burden will fall on privately insured patients as well as government insurance programs. Is it more important to have full-time salaried employees earning living wages with health insurance and pension benefits, or is it more important to keep health costs reasonable for patients?
12. Is there a way to achieve both ideals?
13. If low health costs are more important than properly compensated employees in the health care industry, are the management interests supporting the status quo of contingent employees not being covered by the NLRA, an ethical policy?
14. What ethical arguments could labor unions use to help change the status quo and bring contingent workers under the common employer strictures of the nation's labor laws?

benefits. While women's overall workforce participation has increased as a result of the nation's overhaul of the welfare system in the mid-1990s that forced welfare mothers into the workforce, low-wage women who are contingent employees are unlikely to have access to pregnancy-related benefits or family leave (Bornstein, 2012). Moreover, most contingent employees spend their careers with multiple employers with none of the employment advantages of traditional long-term employees in years past, such as pension plans or the option to carry health insurance into retirement.

Impact of Health Care Reform

Unionized employers are at a competitive disadvantage with companies abroad and sometimes with non-unionized domestic companies that do not provide as comprehensive a health insurance benefits package as unionized employers. Corporations outside the United States do not need to make the same substantial contributions for employer-provided health insurance benefits. Health insurance coverage outside the United States is mainly provided by governments, with all corporations, unionized and non-unionized, bearing the tax burden equally (Massey, 2008; Wharton, 2011). The impact of health care reform could level the health care costs playing field for unionized health care industry companies in the United States when almost everyone is required to have health insurance coverage.

Need for Comprehensive Labor Reforms

One of the difficulties facing the U.S. health care system is that consultation and cooperation between management and labor unions are foreclosed to both sides outside the context of their negotiated collective bargaining agreements. Cooperative management consultation with labor union representation is illegal unless it is conducted within the negotiation structure of collective bargaining agreements. Though counterproductive, this view of representation has been the basic framework for management and labor relations since the NLRA was adopted in 1935. Nevertheless, employees are stakeholders in the health care industry just as shareholders are. Employees invest their human capital; they should have rights to consult with management. If the NLRA were to change, more employees might be willing to opt for a more cooperative view of representation. The United States has not changed its labor laws since near the beginning of the last century, in 1935. The basic framework is antiquated. As is, management and labor unions are precluded by the NLRA from cooperating. *See generally* Wharton, 2011.

While law is the lowest common denominator of the **social contract** defining basic ethical principles, existing labor law no longer improves the plight of most U.S. employees or betters the American economy. Over the past 30 years, shareholder wealth and management compensation have grown steadily, while employee wages and benefits have barely kept pace with inflation, much less the actual rise in costs (Craver, 2010). Ethics must operate above this common denominator and inform the creation of new labor laws (Epstein, 2007).

When Manpower, Inc. is the nation's largest employer, with more than 4 million contingent employees having no long-term, stable employment relationships, there is a need for comprehensive reform of U.S. labor law (Craver, 2010). The common misconception is that the federal government or Wal-Mart are the nation's largest employers; however, Wal-Mart employs 1.4 million employees and 1 in 10 of the 2.7 million federal employees are contingent employees, often through Manpower (BLS, 2015a and 2015c). When the U.S. Treasury reports that almost half of the nation's tax filers are earning poverty wages, the reasons underlying the public's protests about the nation's growing wealth disparity are evident (Edmans, 2012). There is a need to think more deeply and critically about management and labor relations as part of the strategy for reform of the U.S. health care system and allow everyone working in the health care industry the opportunities to maximize their human capital.

ETHICAL OR UNETHICAL DECISION

Refusal to Bargain in the Health Care Industry

Ethics Issue: *Can an employer refuse to bargain in good faith and then withdraw recognition from a certified labor union during the organizing process?*

Ethics Analysis: Yes. While a number of legal challenges by an employer may arise related to labor union activity and bargaining, if an employer is able to obtain a decertification petition from some employees (not necessarily a majority), it may withdraw recognition from a union. This refusal to bargain is based on the belief that the union no longer has majority support.

Ethics Analysis: No. During a labor union organizing process, there are established steps in the process of union formation. When a union is established based solely on the number of authorization cards signed by employees, an employer is obligated to bargain with the union during the certification period.

Court's Holding and Decision: The Medical Center committed an unfair labor practice by withdrawing recognition from the labor union before the one-year certification period for bargaining expired.

— *Virginia Mason Medical Center v. National Labor Relations Board*, 558 F.3d 891 (U.S. Court of Appeals for the 9th Circuit 2009).

CHAPTER SUMMARY

- Evolving ethical principles are causing a deep divide in public opinion about the role of labor unions in today's service economy; one side says that labor unions are an accepted part of American society and the other side claims that labor unions are not necessary.
- There is public tension right now over the redistribution of health care costs, and who will benefit from or bear the consequences of any redistribution.
- Union organizing campaigns are very sophisticated today, yet labor law is biased in favor of employers. Comprehensive labor law reforms could help level the playing field between management and labor unions.
- Many factors, particularly the increase in two-income households, contribute to the perception of economic inequality, with employees in the health care industry working longer and harder for increasingly less compensation per hour and fewer non-monetary benefits.
- Ethical issues often arise when exempt (salaried) and non-exempt (hourly) employees perform the same work but receive different wages and benefits.
- Contingent work, where there is no contract, job security, or expectation for long-term employment, is rapidly expanding employee inequality in the health care industry.
- While law is the lowest common denominator of the social contract defining the most basic principles of ethics, existing labor law no longer improves the plight of employees or betters the American economy.

REFERENCES

AFL-CIO. (2005). *The costs and benefits of safe staffing ratios.* Washington, DC: AFL-CIO Department for Professional Employees.

Albro, A. (2008). Rubbing salt in the wound: As nurses battle with a nationwide staffing shortage, an NLRB decision threatens to limit the ability of nurses to unionize. *Northwestern Journal of Law and Social Policy, 3,* 103–130.

BLS (Bureau of Labor Statistics). (2015). *National industry-specific occupational employment and wage estimates: Health care and social assistance (including private, state, and local government hospitals).* Washington, DC: U.S. Department of Labor, BLS.

____. (2015a). *Overview of BLS wage data by area and occupation.*

____. (2015b). *National industry-specific occupational employment and wage estimates.*

____. (2015c). *Occupational outlook handbook: Registered nurses.*

Bornstein, S. (2012). Work, family, and discrimination at the bottom of the ladder. *Georgetown Journal on Poverty Law and Policy, 19,* 1–42.

Boushey, H., et al. (2007). *Understanding low wage work in the United States.* Washington, DC: Center for Economic Policy and Research.

Cahn, N., & Carbone, J. (2015). Growing inequality and children. *American University Journal of Gender, Social Policy and the Law, 23,* 283–317.

Cartledge, P. (2005). *Alexander the Great.* New York, NY: Vintage Publishing-Random House.

Coley, T. J. (2010). Getting noticed: Direct and indirect power-allocation in the contemporary American labor market. *Catholic University Law Review, 59,* 965–998.

Craver, C. B. (2010). The National Labor Relations Act at 75: In need of a heart transplant. *Hofstra Labor and Employment Law Journal, 27,* 311–356.

Dahan, Y., et al. (2011). Mapping the hard law/soft law terrain: Labor rights and environmental protection: Global justice, labor standards and responsibility. *Theoretical Inquiries in Law, 12,* 439–464.

DOL (U.S. Department of Labor). (2009). *Occupational outlook handbook: Home health aides and personal and home care aides.* Washington, DC: DOL, Bureau of Labor Statistics.

____. (2005). Exempt status of nurse practitioners. (FLSA Opinion Letter 2005-20). Washington, DC: DOL, Employment Standards Administration.

Edmans, A. (2012). How to fix executive compensation: For starters, don't link pay packages just to stock. Tie them to the company's debt as well. *Wall Street Journal*, p. R1.

Epstein, E. M. (2007). The good company: Rhetoric or reality? Corporate social responsibility and business ethics redux. *American Business Law Journal, 44*(2), 207–222.

Felland, L. E., et al. (2010). *The economic recession: Early impacts on health-care safety net providers*. Washington, DC: Center for Studying Health System Change.

Flood, C. M., & Thomas, B. (2011). Missing the mark on patient safety. *Chicago-Kent Law Review, 86*, 1053–1092.

Freeman, R. B. (2007). *Briefing paper: Do workers still want labor unions? More than ever*. Washington, DC: Economic Policy Institute.

Gopalan, S. (2007). Shame sanctions and excessive CEO pay. *The Delaware Journal of Corporate Law, 32*, 757–797.

Gould, IV, W. B. (2012). Beyond labor law: Private initiatives to promote employee freedom of association in the Obama era. *Indiana Law Journal, 87*, 69–103.

___. (2007). Independent adjudication, political process, and the state of labor-management relations: The role of the National Labor Relations Board. *Indiana Law Journal, 82*, 461–496.

Halm, M., et al. (2005). Hospital nurse staffing and patient mortality, emotional exhaustion, and job dissatisfaction. *Clinical Nurse Specialist, 19*(5), 241–251.

Hassmiller, S. B., & Cozine, M. (2006). Addressing the nurse shortage to improve the quality of patient care. *Health Affairs, 25*(1), 268–274.

HHS (U.S. Department of Health & Human Services). (2010). News release: Sebelius announces new $250 million investment to strengthen primary health care workforce. Washington, DC: HHS.

IOM (Institute of Medicine). (2015). *Future of home health care*. Washington, DC: National Academy of Sciences.

___. (2004). *Committee on the Work Environment for Nurses and Patient Safety-Keeping patients safe: Transforming the work environment of nurses*.

Jacobs, K., & Graham-Squire, D. (2008). *No recovery in sight: Health coverage for working-age adults in the United States and California*. Berkeley, CA: Center for Labor Research and Education.

Kaiser Commission on Medicaid and the Uninsured. (2010). *The uninsured: A primer: New facts about the uninsured*. Washington, DC: Kaiser.

Kaiser Family Foundation. (2011). *Kaiser health tracking poll: Public opinion on health care issues*. Menlo Park, CA: Kaiser.

___. (2008). *Kaiser Family Foundation/Harvard University/Washington Post survey of low wage workers*.

Kochan, T., & Shulman, B. (2007). *Briefing paper: A new social contract: Restoring dignity and balance to the economy*. Washington, DC: Economic Policy Institute.

Kugielska, L., & Linker, M. (2008). Balancing the Red Cross: An examination of hospital malpractice and the nursing shortage. *Hofstra Labor and Employment Law Journal, 25*, 563–599.

Leberstein, S., & Christman, A. (2012). Occupy our occupations: Why "we are the 99%" resonates with working people and what we can do to fix the American workplace. *Fordham Urban Law Journal, 39*, 1073–1105.

Lee, C. J. (2006). Federal regulation of hospital resident work hours: Enforcement with real teeth. *Journal of Health Care Law and Policy, 9*, 162–206.

Levin, R. M. (2011). Rulemaking under the 2010 Model State Administrative Procedure Act. *Widener Law Journal, 20*, 855–886.

Lippitt, J. (2011). Protecting the protectors: A call for fair working conditions for home health care workers. *Elder Law Journal, 19*, 219–255.

Lueck, S., et al. (2010). *Health reform package represents historic chance to expand coverage, improve insurance markets, slow cost growth, and reduce deficits*. Washington, DC: Center on Budget & Policy Priorities.

Maher, K. (2007, January 22). Are labor unions relevant? *Wall Street Journal*, p. R5.

Maher, K., & Belkin, D. (2011, March 11). Union fight heats up. *Wall Street Journal*, p. A1.

Massey, D. S. (2008). *Categorically unequal: The American stratification system*. New York, NY: Russell Sage Foundation.

Miller, S. D. (2008). Atrophied rights: Maximum hours labor standards under the FLSA and Illinois law. *Northern Illinois University Law Review, 28*, 261–346.

Mironi, M. (2010). Reframing the representation debate: Going beyond union and non-union options. *Industrial and Labor Relations Review, 63*, 367–383.

Murray, C. (2012). *Coming apart: The state of white America*. New York, NY: Random House-Crown Forum.

Nelson, R., & Kennedy, M. S. (2008). The other side of mandatory overtime. *American Journal of Nursing, 108*(4), 23.

Nilliasca, T. (2011). Some women's work: Domestic work, class, race, heteropatriarchy, and the limits of legal reform. *Journal of Race and Law, 16*, 377–410.

Noss, A. (2014). Household income. Washington, DC: U.S. Census Bureau.

Pfeffer, F. T., et al. (2013). Effects on employment, wealth, retirement security, and the social safety net: Wealth disparities before and after the great recession. *The Annals of the American Academy of Political and Social Science, 650,* 98–123.

Pruitt, L. R. (2011). Crowdsourcing the work-family debate: The geography of the class culture wars. *Seattle University Law Review, 34,* 767–813.

Rawls, J. (2005). *A theory of justice.* Boston, MA: Belknap Press (Original work published 1971).

Rittich, K. (2010). Competition in the global workplace: The role of law in economic markets: Between workers' rights and flexibility: Labor law in an uncertain world. *Saint Louis University Law Journal, 54,* 565–583.

Rosenbaum, J. A. (2010). Regrettably unfair: Brooke Astor and the other elderly in New York. *Pace Law Review, 30,* 1004–1059.

Rosenbaum, S. (2011). Realigning the social order: The Patient Protection and Affordable Care Act and the U.S. health insurance system. *Journal of Health and Biomedical Law, 7,* 1–31.

Runnels, M. B., et al. (2010). Corporate social responsibility and the new governance: In search of Epstein's good company in the employment context. *Akron Law Review, 43,* 501–535.

Saunders, L. (2012, July 8). President, American Federation of State, County and Municipal Employees, Newsmakers: C-Span, Washington, DC.

Scott, L. D., et al. (2006). Effects of critical care nurses' work hours on vigilance and patients' safety. *American Journal of Critical Care, 15,* 30–37.

Secunda, P. M., & Hirsch, J. M. (2008), Debate: Workplace federalism. *University of Pennsylvania Law Review, 34,* 28–52.

Smith, K. E., & Baughman, R. A. (2007). Caring for America's aging population: a profile of the direct-care workforce. Washington, DC: U.S. Department of Labor, Bureau of Labor Statistics-*Monthly Labor Review, 8,* 21–26.

Snow, T. (2011). Balancing the ERISA seesaw: A targeted approach to remedying the problem of worker misclassification in the employee benefits context. *George Washington Law Review, 79,* 1237–1275.

Somers, S., & Perkins, J. (2010). The Affordable Care Act: A giant step toward insurance coverage for all Americans. *Sargent Shriver National Center on Poverty Law Clearinghouse Review: Journal of Poverty Law and Policy, 44,* 330–341.

Spector, R. A. (2015). "Dignified jobs at decent wages": Reviving an economic equity model of employment discrimination law. *Berkeley Journal of Employment and Labor Law, 36,* 123–168.

Trottman, M., & Maher, K. (2011, February 24). Sparring unions now working as one. *Wall Street Journal,* p. A4.

Tung, I., et al. (2015). *The growing movement for $15.* New York, NY: National Employment Labor Project.

Umel, I. S. (2007). Cultivating strength: The role of the Filipino workers' center COURAGE campaign in addressing labor violations committed against Filipinos in the Los Angeles private home care industry. *UCLA Asian Pacific American Law Journal, 12,* 35–68.

Vidal, N. (2009). *Organizing prosperity: Union effects on job quality, community betterment, and industry standards.* Washington, DC: Economic Policy Institute.

Wharton School at the University of Pennsylvania. (2011). Union leaders vs. Republican legislators: What's at stake in the standoff. *Knowledge@Wharton.*

___. (2011a). Leadership, innovation and entrepreneurship in Eastern Europe, Russia and beyond. *Knowledge@ Wharton and Luiv Business School of the Ukranian Catholic University.*

Williamson, A., et al. (2009). Short trips and long days: Safety and health in short-haul trucking. *Cornell University Industrial and Labor Relations Review, 62,* 415–429.

PART IV

Improving the Quality and Equality of Health Care

Part IV explores areas that could combat rising health care costs and improve the quality and equality of health care.

© Ims Classic/NordicPhotos/age fotostock

CHAPTER 8

Evidence-Based Medicine

"The most incomprehensible thing about the universe is that it is comprehensible."

— **Albert Einstein** (1879–1955), theoretical physicist, philosopher, and Nobel Laureate

LEARNING OBJECTIVES

After completing this chapter, the reader should be able to:

1. Understand the ethical principles underlying evidence-based medicine.
2. Summarize the ethical issues facing physicians who support or oppose this evidence-based effort to provide more reliable medical treatment.
3. Describe the ethical principles justifying use of evidence-based guidelines to make decisions about the care individual patients should receive.
4. Explain the ethical controversy surrounding review of scientific studies with scientific improprieties—such as research bias, errors, and fraud—in peer-reviewed medical journals.
5. Evaluate current efforts to improve and implement evidence-based medicine more widely in mainstream health care delivery.

KEY TERMS

Authority-based medicine
Care coordination
Comparative effectiveness
Conflicts of interest
Evidence-based guidelines

Evidence-based medicine
Health outcomes
Medical monitoring
Off-label prescribing
Research bias

Research fraud
Retraction
Standards of care

ETHICAL OR UNETHICAL DECISION

Conflicts of Interest in Evidence-Based Guidelines

Ethics Issue: *Should conflicts of interest be banned in guideline-writing groups or just disclosed? Or, does this moralistic approach undermine the relationships between commercial interests and academic and research medicine that drives innovation and new advances?*

In Brief: Evidence-based guidelines are systematically developed statements to assist physician and patient decisions about appropriate care (IOM, 2011). Protecting the integrity and reliability of guidelines is essential to the U.S. health care system and fundamental to the practice of **evidence-based medicine** (EBM), which relies on reason, mathematics, and scientific evidence. Yet **conflicts of interest** often create a risk that the credibility of science will be unduly influenced by secondary (or sometimes arguably primary) commercial interests that are undisclosed (Beachy, et al., 2014; IOM, 2009). Most physicians writing guidelines have interests within the medical products industry that are secondary to their interest in writing guidelines, including owning industry stock and accepting multimillion-dollar industry royalties, honoraria, and consulting and speaking engagements (Mendelson, et al., 2011). The primary interest of these physicians is to protect the credibility of the guidelines issued by organizations such as the American Heart Association and American College of Cardiology that rank scientific evidence regarding the safety and effectiveness of various treatments for heart disease, stroke, and artery blockage (Burton, 2011). The secondary financial interests of these same physicians create a difficult situation, although this is not per se an ethical judgment about the character or actions of individual physicians.

   While it is assumed that physicians who confront conflicts of interest are equipped to deal with them rationally and even ethically, **research bias** is a factor sometimes outside the control of a purely conscientious, rational process (Korn, 2011). Research bias can occur when the research results are influenced or are analyzed in a certain way in order to support a predetermined conclusion; it can also occur more subconsciously through an inadvertent failure to account for all variables. Given the growth in the importance of being able to rely upon scientific studies, credible guidelines have become increasingly important to all stakeholders in the health care industry: physicians, hospitals, the government, insurers, and patients. Everyone has an interest in ensuring that the evidence upon which these guidelines are based is not biased.

See Ethical or Unethical Decision at the end of the chapter for discussion of this ethics issue.

Introduction

Ignorance of science led people in ancient times to rely upon myths in an effort to make sense of disease and illness. Eventually, people turned to philosophy, that is, to the use of reason and intuition to decipher science. Modern medical science is not just a collection of physicians each going their own way; rather, medicine today is based on the best available scientific evidence (Cochrane, 1972/1999). As is said, "everything in the universe follows laws, without exception" (Hawking & Mlodinow, 2012, p. 137).

Paradigm Shift in Medicine

A new decision-making model is evolving that is changing clinical decisions from one point of view to a new one (Friedland, 2009). As illustrated in **TABLE 8-1**, this change is from a model of **authority-based medicine**, where clinical decision-making was based on clinical experience and authority-based clinical training, to an EBM model based on scientific evidence.

This paradigm shift began to occur when it was discovered that up to one-third of the nation's health care was devoted to medical treatments that did not improve health (IOM, 2011b, 2010, and 2009; Landrigan, et al., 2010; Todd, 2011). Also, while more than one-third of the health care provided today is ineffective (IOM, 2009a and 2001; *see also* Binder, 2015; Commonwealth Fund, 2011; Radley, et al., 2014) or harmful (Levinson, 2010), there are further undeniable anomalies in medicine that actually make things worse (Kimbuende, et al., 2010).

Although there are different kinds of treatments for the same condition in different people, one role of EBM is to help sort out the effective from the ineffective, and the necessary from the unnecessary, in the practice of medicine. Recognizing the significance of human individuality and variability, the goal of EBM is to meet a higher scientific standard in medicine (Malinowski, et al., 2012). Contrary to popular misconceptions, the objective is not to have only one treatment per medical condition, as different people may need different treatments for the same condition; rather, the objective is to outline the treatment parameters for the unique diagnostic conditions of individual patients.

Definition of Evidence-Based Medicine

Best defined as a philosophy of care that assesses the risks and benefits of medical treatments, including lack of treatment, EBM promotes reliance on scientific studies, particularly randomized controlled clinical trials, in the practice of medicine

TABLE 8-1 Traditional Authority Based-Decisions versus Current Evidence-Based Decisions

Traditional Authority-Based Decisions	Current Evidence-Based Decisions
Knowledge of pathophysiology provides the foundation for clinical practice.	Knowledge of pathophysiology is necessary, but insufficient for clinical practice.
Clinical experience and expertise in a given subject area are sufficient to enable physicians to understand and apply clinical practice guidelines.	Physicians need to understand certain rules of research and scientific evidence to evaluate and apply medical literature and clinical practice guidelines.
Traditional medical training and common sense are sufficient to enable physicians to evaluate new tests and treatments.	When possible, physicians should use information derived from systematic, reproducible, and unbiased studies to increase their confidence in the true prognosis, efficacy of therapy, and usefulness of diagnostic tests.
Physicians rely on expert medical opinions.	Physicians rely on scientific evidence.
Individual clinical experience provides the basis for diagnosis, treatment, and prognosis of patients.	Clinical practice guidelines are the guiding principle for each patient's unique diagnosis, treatment, and prognosis.

— Sources: Freidland, 2009; Guzelian, 2005; Haynes, et al., 2005. Note: *Pathophysiology* refers to changes and disturbances in human organs caused by disease.

FEATURE BOX 8-1

Principles of Evidence-Based Medicine

- Clinical decisions should be based on the best available evidence.
- The clinical problem, as opposed to treatment protocols or clinical experi-ence, should determine the type of evidence to be sought.
- Identifying the best evidence means using epidemiological ways of thinking (searching for causes and patterns in the symptoms).
- Conclusions derived from identifying and critically appraising evidence are useful only if put into action in managing patients' health.
- Clinical outcomes should be constantly evaluated.

— Source: Davidoff, et al., 1995. Note: The 1995 *British Medical Journal* editorial announcing creation of the *Evidence-Based Medicine Journal* gave this comprehensive definition of EBM.

(Dolinar & Leininger, 2006). EBM began in the early 1990s in Canada and England when it was discovered that those countries' health care was effective only one-quarter of the time (Haynes, et al., 2005). EBM developed later in the United States as a key component of **care coordination**, or care continuum management, which was referred to as disease management before the focus of U.S. health care became prevention or delay of disease as opposed to treatment of already-developed disease. Care coordination programs co-ordinate clinical care for patients with chronic health conditions such as diabetes, heart disease, and asthma (Meir & Shaw, 2011).

At the same time, in order to evaluate the ethical limitations and understand the criticisms of EBM, it is useful to provide a specific definition of EBM. The definition in **FEATURE BOX 8-1** contains the core set of principles historically and currently underlying EBM.

Use of Evidence-Based Guidelines in Evidence-Based Medicine

Evidence-based guidelines are one embodiment of EBM; in practice, the two terms are often used interchangeably. The health care industry, medical schools, and the govern-ment are participating in the development of guidelines, not only for common ailments such as upper respiratory infections, but also for performing surgeries and tackling se-rious diseases such as cancer. It is difficult to ensure that the best care is provided to pa-tients unless physicians can keep abreast of hundreds of scientific studies with conflicting findings. Guidelines provide physicians a counterweight to this situation (Das, 2007). EBM entails incorporating key scientific findings into medical practice and measuring the associated **health outcomes**, or the effect of health care interventions (or lack thereof) on patient health status.

Malfunctions in the Practice of Medicine

Over the last few years, focus has been directed to costs and reliability in the U.S. health care system (Tollen, et al., 2011). Physicians and hospitals too often do not use the best scientific evidence available for treating even the most common health conditions (Good Stewardship Working Group, 2011). As illustrated in **FEATURE BOX 8-2**, there is a tremendous gap between what medical treatment is known to work and what treatment patients actually get, because some physicians simply are not aware of what the most effective treatments are, or else have their own reasons for not using them.

These statistics highlight a major shortcoming of the decentralized U.S. health care system: physicians treat common illnesses in a variety of ways, even though often only one treatment has shown the most success (Hack & Gwyer, 2013). One reason for this phenomenon is physicians' distrust of scientific evidence and awareness of the mistakes that occur in scientific studies (Anand, 2010). While some see this phenomenon simply as apathy, arrogance, or laziness (Farrow, 2010), the malfunctions in the practice of medicine may be more common than anyone will admit.

Unnecessary Care

The principles of *do no harm* (patient safety) and *the right treatment for the right patient* (effectiveness) are bedrock principles of medicine (Keckley & Frink, 2009). Although needless tests and procedures provide no real benefit to patients and often cannot do anything but harm patients (Landro, 2007), they do enrich the health care industry. As illustrated in **FIGURE 8-1**, Americans are not getting the care they need (Stremikis, et al., 2011).

FEATURE BOX 8-2

The Chasm Between Knowledge and Practice

- One in 3 surgeries performed on Medicare patients is unnecessary, including 1 in 5 pacemaker implant surgeries.
- More than half of all cataract surgeries involve unnecessary preoperative testing.
- Less than one-fourth of the people with hypertension have it under control with recommended medications.
- Less than half of heart attack patients are on beta blockers, which cut the risk of premature death.
- Most diabetics do not get routine hemoglobin screening, which is essential to detect complications such as kidney failure.
- Nearly half of the patients with brain cancer receive no chemotherapy despite evidence that it can boost survival; anti-seizure medications are widely used even though most brain cancer patients do not have seizures; and while depression is common in people with brain cancer, more than 90 percent are never given antidepressants.

— Sources: AHRQ, 2014 and 2014a; Al-Khatib, et al., 2011; ASA, 2015; Kadish & Goldberger, 2011; Piper, et al., 2014; Thompson, 2011; Van Tassel, 2013.

DIAGNOSTIC **T** **T** ESTS **THAT ARE REPEATED OR NOT NEEDED**

OFF-LABEL **U** SE **OF MEDICATIONS THAT DO NOT DO ANY GOOD**

MEDICAL **T** **T** REATMENT **WITH NO EVIDENCE OF BENEFIT**

$900 billion Misallocated
What scientific evidence can be <u>trusted</u> to distinguish what care is medically necessary?

FIGURE 8-1 One-Third of the Nation's Health Care Is Unnecessary

Sources: Avraham, 2014; Binder, 2015; IOM, 2009a and 2001; Radley, et al., 2014; Stremikis, et al., 2011.

Unfortunately, nothing has changed in the past two decades (*see, e.g.*, IOM, 2001; RAND, 2006). Patients are receiving the same level of unnecessary care today as they were more than 15 years ago despite all the advances in medicine over this time period (Berwick & Hackbarth, 2012).

Point, Counterpoint on Evidence-Based Medicine

Over the last 50 years, randomized clinical trials have produced relatively solid evidence, and their legitimacy and usefulness keep growing, yet critics claim that EBM is not what it purports to be. The chief criticism is that many evidence-based guidelines are based on small, nonrandomized trials with insufficient statistical power (Avraham, 2014). A second claim is that while guidelines are indisputable for many chronic conditions, such as controlling diabetics' blood sugar levels, for many other health conditions few reliable guidelines exist or the evidence is contradictory, or new scientific studies quickly emerge that undermine the original evidence (Landro, 2005).

Others claim that physicians simply do not want anyone advising them what is best for their patients and prefer instead to rely upon their own clinical experience (Mendelson & Carino, 2005). Some physicians claim that results of clinical trials do not apply to their patients. Other physicians wait to see if treating all their patients according

ETHICAL DILEMMAS 8-1

1. If physicians and hospitals are committed to their patients' well-being, what values underlie and support the resistance to consistently practicing EBM?

to guidelines produces better health outcomes in their practice (Hawryluck, et al., 2011). But the effects of medical treatment are often small; individual physicians typically have too few patients with any one illness or do not follow the guidelines long enough to detect such effects (Laakmann, 2015). Another obstacle to treating patients according to guidelines is that doing so takes time physicians claim they simply do not have. *See generally* Mehlman, 2012.

Medicine's Most Controversial Medical Procedure

While opposition to EBM could be tied to fears that evidence-based care might lead to curtailing the multimillion-dollar payments to physicians from the medical products industry, such payments could still be justified by legitimate consultation services and business arrangements (Zisk, 2013; Duffin, 2010). Yet one controversy makes proponents of EBM question how many physicians believe in and practice EBM.

When the federal Agency for Health Research and Quality (AHRQ) first issued a clinical practice guideline for lower back pain, which concluded that spinal fusion surgery usually does no good, and suggested that there were too many unnecessary back surgeries, orthopedic surgeons responded by lobbying Congress to punish the agency (Avraham, 2014). Congress cut the group's budget and stripped its authority to make Medicare payment recommendations, crippling for years the very idea of EBM. Two decades later, the overuse of spinal fusion surgery, as illustrated in **FEATURE BOX 8-3**, continues to be challenged (Epstein, 2011; Kallmes, et al., 2009). U.S. hospital costs exceeded $180 billion per year for spinal fusion surgeries for the latest year in which reliable information is available (Weiss, et al., 2014). While hospital costs are significantly increasing, the effectiveness of surgery for lower back pain (which is the most common indication of degenerative disk disease) continues to be questioned (Avraham, 2014; Freedman, 2010).

FEATURE BOX 8-3

The Perplexity of Evidence-Based Surgery: Spinal Fusion Surgeries

- Ethical conflicts of interest between surgeons and medical device manufacturers with multimillion-dollar payments to hundreds of surgeons
- Excessive rates of complications
- High rates of reoperation
- Questionable medical benefits in 4 out of 10 surgeries
- Rapidly rising rates of surgery: 400 percent increase in past decade
- Wide geographic variations in the rates of use

— Sources: Carreyrou, 2011; Carreyrou & McGinty, 2011; Whoriskey & Keating, 2013.

In 2011, the North American Spine Society acknowledged that surgeons who collectively received tens of millions of dollars from the medical-device manufacturer Medtronic failed to report serious complications in more than a dozen scientific studies about spinal fusion (Winslow & Carreyrou, 2011). This repudiation of spinal fusion surgery represents a watershed in the long-running debate over conflicts of interest in industry-sponsored scientific studies (Carreyrou, 2011). While it is extremely rare for the medical profession to publicly chastise its own colleagues, the risk of adverse events associated with spinal fusion is 10 to 50 times the original EBM estimates (Carragee, et al., 2011). Today, the consensus is that it harms patients to have biased scientific studies published (Korn, 2011); others maintain that it is criminal for surgeons to operate on patients when they know surgery is more likely than not to be harmful (Carreyrou & McGinty, 2011a). *See generally* Carreyrou, 2011; Freedman, 2010a.

Errors and Retractions in Scientific Studies Surge

Errors in scientific studies are increasing as more medical journals are using independent peer reviews (Steen, 2011). Although medical journals are becoming better at detecting errors and simple incompetence, they also reflect the competitive landscape of scientific research. Yet it could be an indicator of professional misconduct and **research fraud** where data has been intentionally fabricated, plagiarized, or falsified (Anand, 2010).

A **retraction** is a publicized withdrawal or correction of incorrect information, accompanied by termination of any further publishing of the incorrect information. Retractions are surging, with a 15-fold increase in the past decade (Naik, 2011; Markey, 2007). When a published scientific study is found to be unreliable, cannot be replicated, or is simply wrong, it is extremely difficult to make its effects go away because the published scientific study remains available with an accompanying retraction notice. This is one way researchers attempt to correct their published work while retaining credibility. The usefulness of scientific research is based on trust in its integrity, and the health care industry generally accepts findings published in peer-reviewed medical journals (Naik, 2011).

Co-Dependency between Medical Journals and Industry

Another possible explanation for the increase in retractions is that medical journals, instead of being independent arbiters of science, have ended up as co-dependent on the medical products industry. Medical journals are dependent on the industry because their authors and content are part of a social network where most of the key players are known by everyone else (Anand, 2010). A web of personal connections between the authors of scientific studies and the medical products industry cannot help but influence peer review (Jacobson, 2010). Without independence, it is unlikely there will be skepticism or a healthy system of checks and balances for confirming that evidence is objective.

Scientific studies published in peer-reviewed medical journals also encourage others to embark on related avenues of research, so if one scientific study is later found to be tainted, an entire research area comes into doubt. For instance, neither judicial decisions nor retractions could dissuade some physicians from believing the 1990s fraud that linked autism with vaccinations (Offit, 2010; Thomas, 2012). Millions of dollars' worth of private and government funding may go to waste and, in the case of EBM, patients can be put at risk (in this instance, by not receiving beneficial vaccinations) (Naik, 2011). Independent peer review of scientific studies is meant to assure patients that an unbiased set of eyes inspected the evidence.

Controversy Over Use of Evidence-Based Guidelines

Linking financial incentives with adherence to evidence-based guidelines is controversial (Avraham, 2011). Some question why physicians should be paid or incentivized to follow guidelines they should be adhering to already. Apart from the controversy, employers, health insurers, and the government are experimenting with programs that reward adherence to guidelines (Francis, 2012).

While few would argue against using scientific evidence to treat patients, some worry that going strictly by guidelines is akin to "cookbook" medicine and may interfere with physicians' intuition and experience when it comes to treating individual cases (Avraham, 2011). They also fear it could allow insurers to refuse to cover care that physicians might deem necessary for some patients if they do not follow guidelines exactly. Proponents insist, however, that guidelines do not exclude alternative treatments (Francis, 2012). They also stress that clinical trials of experimental treatment procedures will always be important methods of gathering new evidence for the ever-evolving practice of medicine (DeBoer, 2012). Moreover, guidelines help physicians stay on top of the explosion of new clinical trials and scientific studies.

Overused, Underused, Misused, and Ineffective Health Care

Longstanding physician resistance to use of evidence-based guidelines is often cited as a reason health care quality in the United States is not up to par with similar countries, especially considering how much is spent. Wide variations in how physicians treat patients with similar ailments are common in American medicine, reflecting a large gap between medical knowledge and clinical practice. For instance, scientific studies show that health care is often overused, underused, or misused (Todd, 2011).

Where there are more cardiac surgeons, for instance, there is greater use of their services; whether this is an overuse problem or simply the use of available resources is unclear. There is also an underuse problem, in that physicians do not treat some medical ailments as aggressively as best practices recommend. For instance, patients suffering myocardial infarctions (commonly known as heart attacks) that result from interruption of blood supply to part of the heart are reportedly put on beta blockers that relieve stress on the heart only half the time (McGlynn, et al., 2003; Piper, et al., 2014). In this situation, the use of EBM can reduce this variation in treatment of myocardial infarction by increasing access to appropriate medications, while decreasing access to inappropriate care and empowering patients to question the use of cardiac surgeries (Clark, 2011; Winslow, 2008).

Effectiveness and/or Ineffectiveness of Medical Treatments

Sound scientific evidence now exists regarding treatment(s) for about half of the most prevalent health conditions, but the gap between knowing what works best and the day-to-day provision of medical treatment is wide and continually expanding (Landro, 2007). One way to close this gap between knowledge and clinical practice is by insisting that physicians' choice of treatment be backed by current evidence of a treatment's effectiveness. Medical treatments that are overused, underused, misused, and ineffective highlight the consequences of using treatments that lack rigorous scientific scrutiny (Radley, et al., 2006). Billions of dollars are budgeted for scientific studies by the National Institutes of Health every year, but patients do not get the clinical benefits of what works best if physicians are not implementing the results of these studies in clinical practice. Ethically speaking, it is a huge and unnecessary waste of health care resources if physicians do not use EBM (Geetter, 2011).

Overtreatment

Less health care can result in better health (Grady & Redberg, 2010). For instance, the use of antibiotics is a serious instance of overtreatment. EBM could help decrease how antibiotics are used by preventing their use for viral infections, broadening treatment adherence for bacterial infections, and limiting use of antibiotics on animals used for human food.

There is strong evidence that most of the antibiotics prescribed for the treatment of ear infections, sore throats, and upper respiratory infections are medically unnecessary, as these common infections are largely due to viruses that are not susceptible to antibiotics (Pratt, 2011). The overuse of antibiotics causes microbes to become resistant, which makes the antibiotics ineffective. This, in turn, leads to more medical complications and additional costs.

Yet, the ethical obligation of physicians when it comes to antibiotic use is unclear. If physicians restrict access to antibiotics because of resistance concerns, ethical tensions occur between individual patients and society at large (Saver, 2008). Although patients want to take antibiotics to prevent and treat all bacterial infections, society's interests are better served if fewer people take antibiotics for minor infections because it will lead to less microbe resistance. EBM data suggests that up to 55 percent of antibiotic prescriptions are medically unnecessary and could be avoided, resulting in annual savings of $1.1 billion (Pratt, 2011). At the same time, there is the other side of the double-edged sword of overtreatment: inadequate antibiotic dosages also accelerate the development of microbe resistance (Kesselheim & Outterson, 2011). Not finishing antibiotic regimens leads to bacteria resistance.

Often ignored in this overtreatment debate is the high level of antibiotic use in animals, which contributes to microbe resistance in humans who ingest animals that were treated with antibiotics (Lessing, 2010). Until recently, EBM has focused on the overtreatment of humans, not the misuse of antibiotics in animal agriculture. Assertions are now being made by public health advocates that human health should not be jeopardized for the economic efficiency of industrialized livestock production (Schneider, 2011). Though Congress repeatedly attempted to curtail the use of antibiotics in livestock, there was little change for more than 30 years (GAO, 1999; Stathopoulos, 2010). Recently, the FDA issued an order banning the use of certain antibiotics in animal feed out of concern for rising resistance rates, some 30 years after EBM clearly showed that antibiotic use in animal feed contributed to microbe resistance in humans (Kesselheim & Outterson, 2011).

Undertreatment

An instance of undertreatment is the use of aspirin, beta blockers, and statins, all of which are medical treatments for heart disease, the leading cause of death in the United States (Kinney, 2010). Despite evidence-based guidelines calling for most patients with established heart disease to take aspirin as well as medications to lower cholesterol and blood pressure, only about one in four such patients are consistently being prescribed the recommended regimen (Winslow, 2007). Like overtreatment, undertreatment has another side to its double-edged sword: patient noncompliance.

ETHICAL DILEMMAS 8-2

2. What values are impeding physicians, the critical gatekeepers for entry into the U.S. health care system, from following evidence-based guidelines as opposed to relying solely on their clinical experience?

Misused Treatments

The U.S. health care system, as all social systems, requires a level of ethical behavior among its participants. Yet, these are tough times for trust in EBM. The pharmaceutical industry damaged EBM on a broad scale by its misuse of scientific evidence on antidepressants. A classic instance of misused treatment is the misinformation surrounding the safety and efficacy of antidepressants in the treatment of depressed children and adolescents. All the published scientific studies showed antidepressants to be safe and effective (Gibbons, et al., 2007), so physicians had good reason to believe that the treatment of children and adolescents with the new antidepressants was evidence-based care.

What they did not know is that the negative scientific studies were never published. The unpublished scientific studies had shown that the medications were neither effective nor safe, and that they doubled the rate of suicidal thoughts and behaviors in minors (Brent, et al., 2009). Once the unpublished studies became public knowledge, the FDA issued warnings that use of antidepressants posed a small but significant increased risk of suicidal thoughts for children and adolescents (FDA, 2010). As illustrated in **TABLE 8-2**, however, the damage was done; physicians no longer trusted antidepressants in the treatment of depressed minors (Burton, 2010).

Of course, not all scientific studies have tainted histories. Many uncover significant advances. Still, problems arise when studies pursued to achieve improper political or economic motivations intrude on the appropriate design and professional

TABLE 8-2 Misused Scientific Evidence: Clinical Reliability of Antidepressants Questioned

- Treatment with antidepressants decreased by one-third after suicidality warnings were placed on antidepressant prescriptions for children and adolescents.
- Annual suicide rate in children and adolescents increased by 10 percent.
- There are approximately 3,040 more U.S. suicides in children and adolescents each year as a direct result of clinical mistrust of antidepressants.

ETHICAL ISSUE: Made positive evidence public; never published negative evidence:
- Bristol-Myers Squibb
- Forest Pharmaceuticals
- GlaxoSmithKline
- Eli Lilly
- Organon Pharmaceuticals (subsequently acquired by Schering-Plough and then Merck)
- Pfizer
- Solvay Pharmaceuticals (subsequently acquired by Abbott)

Sources: Brent, et al., 2009; FDA, 2010; Forest Laboratories, 2011; Gibbons, et al., 2007.

conduct of clinical trials (Shapiro, 2012). This leads to bias in how results are interpreted and, more importantly, how they are reported. One criterion of the reliability of scientific evidence is whether the results of an entire study are published and thereby available to physicians, purchasers of health care, and policy makers for independent interpretation.

Ineffective Treatments

Off-label prescribing—the practice of using medications for an unapproved purpose, for an unapproved patient group, at an unapproved dosage, or by an unapproved form of administration—constitutes between 50 and 60 percent of U.S. prescriptions (Laakmann, 2011; Radley, et al., 2006). While there is continued variation in the use of medications and other medical products approved for usage by the FDA, this level of off-label prescribing is a troubling percentage, as off-label treatments carry an increased risk of ineffectiveness and harmful side effects (Cohen, et al., 2009). Although off-label use can be very beneficial to some patients, this common practice is often medically unnecessary (Todd, 2011) and borders on being medically experimental (Ausness, 2008; Laakmann, 2011).

The most recent instance of ineffective off-label medication use is Actimmune, which has been prescribed off-label to patients with a potentially fatal lung condition, pulmonary fibrosis. Actimmune was approved by the FDA to treat 2 other extremely rare diseases, but nearly all its sales (almost $100 million) came from off-label use for pulmonary fibrosis, which cost each patient about $50,000 per year and was not effective in treating the condition (Burroughs, et al., 2010). One reason this ineffective treatment was able to occur so widely is that the pharmaceutical industry seeks the FDA's approval to market its products only for the narrowest disease population upon which those products have been shown to demonstrate treatment efficacy, knowing that it can promote its products off-label to a wider population once its products are approved to enter the marketplace (Vertinsky, 2015).

Another recent example of ineffective off-label treatment is the prescribing of antipsychotic medications, which are approved to treat severe mental illnesses like schizophrenia, to patients suffering from depression or insomnia (Radley, et al., 2006). There is no scientific evidence supporting this ongoing off-label practice and there is no certainty about the benefits or safety of antipsychotic medications for use in depression and insomnia, especially when prescribed for children and young adults (Seida, et al., 2012).

Elimination of Geographic Variations

Another benefit of EBM would be to eliminate variations in health care from one geographic region of the nation to another. Research shows that physicians are not uniformly following evidence-based guidelines (IOM, 2011 and 2011a; Zhang, et al., 2010). The Institute of Medicine contends that even when there is a strong body of scientific evidence about new medications, medical devices, diagnostic tests, and surgical interventions, it can take 15 to 20 years for physicians and hospitals to incorporate them. Between the health care Americans have and the care they could have lies not just a gap, but a chasm (IOM, 2001). EBM could help close this abyss by demonstrating what works and does not work in health care (IOM, 2011a).

For instance, the rate of spine surgery has been reported to be 40 percent higher in the United States than in any other developed country (Carreyrou & McGinty, 2011). In addition, there is substantial variation in the rate of spine surgery between some regions of the United States and other regions (Whoriskey & Keating, 2013). Unbiased, easy-to-understand, comparative information evaluating health care services is currently lacking. Moreover, attempts to access the data to better understand how health care dollars are spent are met with stiff resistance from spinal surgeons and their professional medical associations.

ETHICS CASE
Access to the Medicare Database

Consumers' Checkbook v. U.S. Department of Health & Human Services, et al.
[Consumer Group v. Federal Government]
554 F.3d 1046 (U.S. Court of Appeals for the District of Columbia Circuit 2009),
cert. denied, 559 U.S. 1067 (U.S. Supreme Court 2010)

Facts: Consumers' Checkbook, a consumer group, requested access to the Medicare claims information of more than 40 million Medicare patients and 700,000 physicians for the purpose of identifying individual Medicare providers and determining each time a provider performed a particular service or procedure. No patient identifying information was requested.

The public's interest, it argued, was in obtaining information that would help the public make better informed health care decisions. Specifically, Consumers' contended that analysis of the requested data would allow the public to examine, among other things, whether the government was allowing payments to physicians whose practice patterns did not conform to existing evidence-based guidelines. In other words, it wanted to know whether the government was paying for the ineffective care and overuse, underuse, and misuse of treatments provided by physicians. To perform these types of analyses, Consumers' maintained that the Medicare claim information must include physician-identifying information linked to each service or procedure.

Legal Analysis: The court found that the requested information constituted an unwarranted invasion of the personal privacy of physicians. Four factors were considered in deciding whether the public had an interest in disclosure of the Medicare database, whether the data: (1) could advance the public's understanding, as distinguished from a narrow segment of interested people; (2) pertained to government activities; (3) revealed any meaningful information about Medicare not already part of public knowledge; (4) could significantly contribute to public understanding of Medicare.

With regard to the first factor, Consumers' stated that the benefit to the public would be significant because the Medicare database would allow for analysis of Medicare services not presently possible. For instance, scientific studies show that for some medical procedures, physicians performing a high volume of procedures produce superior quality outcomes. The Medicare data would allow analysis of this indicator of quality for Medicare providers. The government, however, contended that the Medicare data could not lead to quality analysis and the court agreed, stating that there was no consensus on which medical procedures performed by physicians correlated to the quality of those procedures. The court added that any analysis would be incomplete because it would not reflect procedures performed on non-Medicare patients.

The court rejected the argument that Medicare data would shed light on the government's transparency initiatives. The court found that the government was already in the process of comparing the quality and price of health outcomes so consumers of health care could make informed choices among physicians and hospitals. Once this data was compiled, regional health information alliances were to provide useful information for patients, which was exactly what was proposed by Consumers.'

Consumers' claimed that the Medicare data would enable the public to determine whether Medicare was paying physicians with insufficient certifications, disciplinary histories, or poor evaluations for a significant number of medical procedures. The court also rejected this factor, finding that the requested information was available through other publicly available sources.

Lastly, Consumers' claimed that the Medicare data could be analyzed in combination with other treatment records to determine whether individual physicians were following evidence-based guidelines. However, the court stated that Consumers' intended use of the data was irrelevant if it revealed little or nothing about the government's own conduct. The requested information must shed light on the government's performance of its duties versus providing information on physicians and their adherence to guidelines.

Rule of Law: Access to the Medicare database would result in an unwarranted invasion of the personal privacy of participating physicians without a significant gain in public understanding of Medicare.

Ethics Issue: Should data about physicians from the Medicare claims database be available for EBM research?

Ethics Analysis: Information sharing is an ethical imperative in health care. With access to impartial Medicare data, patients could be empowered to make decisions based on critical information that has been noticeably lacking in the health care marketplace. Heretofore, patients have been denied the right to information about the effectiveness of the U.S. health care system. With this Medicare data, patients could review data on everything from surgeries to treatments for high cholesterol and diabetes, and then determine which physicians and hospitals have the most experience, best outcomes, least complications, and lowest costs (Falit, 2006). Developing uniform sets of performance measures could provide benchmarks and promote the development of independent **standards of care**, which are the recognized degrees of care expected and required of health care professionals who have a duty to conduct themselves accordingly under like circumstances. Independent standards of care, as opposed to professional standards, could define the appropriate conduct of physicians, nurses, and other health care professionals in comparison to what reasonable professionals either do, or should do, in similar situations. In turn, this data could provide a limited but important set of measures of differences in the rates at which patients use key health care services.

Court's Holding and Decision: No; although the government has a responsibility to promote quality health care, the government is not authorized to exercise any supervision or control over the practice of medicine or the manner in which medical services are provided.

See Candeub, 2011; Madison, 2009 (discussing this court decision). *Contra*, CMS, 2014 (four years after this court decision, the federal government released the requested Medicare data on physicians with the express goal of making the U.S. health care system more transparent and accountable; Medicare's hospital data was released to the public three years after this decision).

Ethical Considerations in Shared Decision-Making between Physicians and Patients

There is an equally shared ethical obligation for physicians to follow evidence-based guidelines and for patients to follow treatment regimens and comply with physician recommendations (Matthew, 2011). One concern of EBM proponents is that patients waste valuable time and money on treatments that do not work. Patients must accept responsibility for being aware of the pros and cons of treatments so they can be involved in shared decision-making with their physicians. Importantly, this sometimes involves lifestyle changes as opposed to medical treatment. The traditional culture of paternalism and physician dominance in health care decision-making began to disappear as patients became more aware of the health risks of unnecessary or inappropriate treatment (Clark, 2011). One recent example of this trend can be seen in how compliance with evidence-based guidelines is increasingly important to insurers and employers eager to eliminate unnecessary diagnostic tests and ineffective treatment procedures, and to push patients to adopt healthier lifestyles, all of which help reduce health care costs in the long run.

Just as ethical standards of care for professionals have been reshaped to incorporate a conscious knowledge of financial as well as clinical risk, so too have the norms changed for responsible patients, who are now expected to do their part for the greater good by consuming health care prudently (Hunter, 2010). The ethical obligation of self-management has become a central part of health care reform, embedded in narratives that merge concepts of what is healthy, what is insurable, and what is ethical to purchase as consumers of health care (Kinney, 2011). For instance, patients are ethically obligated to be educated about self-management of their chronic health conditions (Hyman, 2010), adhere to their medication and treatment regimes, follow reasonable medical instructions, and timely respond to medical concerns (Clark, 2011).

Medical Technology Decisions

Controversial ethical issues surround the definition of what principles should underlie decisions to use high-priced medications or medical devices when less expensive alternatives are available (Pratt, 2011). Increasingly, EBM decisions are being used in every aspect of hospital operations, including questions such as whether it is necessary to use high-priced medical devices when less expensive ones are available. While EBM offers guidance on a wide range of medical technologies, clinical evidence must be distinguished from the financial ramifications of such decisions. The financial aspects of a decision are important and should not be disguised as science (Goossens, et al., 2008). For instance, some patients may be successfully treated with and able to tolerate the side effects of some lower-priced generics, in lieu of brand-name medications, but this does not mean that the therapeutic effectiveness of all generic and brand medications is always equivalent for every patient. Likewise, some orthopedic devices are more durable than less expensive devices; selecting a comparable lower-priced device is often a financial decision, not a medical decision.

Evolving Medical Advancements and Medical Efficacy

By definition, evidence-based guidelines are developed in good faith based on the best available scientific evidence. Unfortunately, this is not always the case, and this shortcoming of disregarding scientific evidence that is contrary to expectations must be acknowledged in any criticism of physician resistance to EBM. The history of bias in development of guidelines is a real problem. The trend is for the federal government either to conduct scientific studies itself or to independently commission and evaluate scientific studies from academic medical centers, as opposed to relying solely on information presented by the medical products industry. Federally funded clinical trials, however, show that it is unwise for anyone to develop guidelines in advance of or contrary to existing scientific evidence. Further scientific studies often reveal new information that requires changes in clinical practices. For instance, research shows that many prescribers ignore dose reductions for long-term medication treatments and fail to attempt to find the lowest effective dosage needed to control symptoms (Cassel & Guest, 2012).

Most importantly, scientific studies must be transparent. Sometimes, outcome data is subject to secrecy for years following completion of comparative studies of different treatments. Then, when the data is finally released, often the results cannot be replicated and the initial conclusions are directly contradicted by independent studies (Hershey, 2013; Houck, 2008). Such scenarios are not uncommon with respect to any medical product or service that is connected to new and rapidly evolving scientific developments. In other words, new findings usually have to be replicated three or four times before they become accepted (Greely, 2009). The historical lack of scientific transparency, however, does make physician resistance to so-called EBM understandable.

Hormone Replacement Therapy

Throughout the 1980s and 1990s, American physicians prescribed an unapproved combination of estrogen and progestin to postmenopausal women (Parker-Pope, 2007). The number of off-label prescriptions to treat the symptoms of menopause fell dramatically after interim results from a government study of hormone replacement therapy showed that the medications were causing breast cancer, heart attacks, strokes, and blood clots

ETHICAL DILEMMAS 8-5

5. What ethical lapses might have led to the follow-up studies finding that many of the initial conclusions about hormone replacement therapy were clearly incorrect, not clear, and not precisely defined, or premature and without any link to scientific evidence?

(Conko, 2011). While the $725 million Women's Health Initiative was well intended, it was surrounded by disputes over the cost of the therapy that influenced not only how the findings were computed but also how they were received (Lemmens & Telfer, 2012). When initial results appeared to confirm that hormone replacement therapy was associated with increased risks, the data was widely disseminated. Subsequent efforts that countered the initial conclusions were given little notice. Although the government initially said that the findings from the Women's Health Initiative applied to all women regardless of age or health status, subsequent meta-analysis by the Mayo Clinic using the same data showed that the age of women, the timing of hormone use, and the administration method (oral pill form, skin patch, spray, or vaginal suppository) dramatically changed the risks and benefits (Kahlenborn, et al., 2006). In fact, later studies directly contradicted the government's initial conclusions. While the type of hormones and the administration method are all associated with different risks, for women near the age of menopause, there is an increase in heart disease, dementia, and osteoporosis in those women who forego protective hormone replacement therapy (Faigman, 2012).

Necessity, or Lack Thereof, of Medical Monitoring of Tobacco Users

Massachusetts required the tobacco industry to pay for **medical monitoring**, or long-term public health surveillance, for asymptomatic smokers who were healthy (Harvard Law, 2010), after the National Cancer Institute determined that an annual CAT scan (computed tomography or CT scan) of smokers' lungs could reduce lung cancer mortality by 20 percent (NLST, 2011). Although these findings have broad implications for cancer treatment, controversy surrounds the need for the Institute's National Lung Screening Trial, a 9-year scientific study that is tracking 50,000 smokers at a cost of $200 million. At issue is why $200 million in government funds should be used to research the best EBM available

ETHICAL DILEMMAS 8-6

6. Ethically speaking, should regular CAT scans for the 90 million current and former smokers become a standard of care regardless of their actual individual risk of ever developing a medical condition, if such screening reduces the risk of death due to lung cancer by 20 percent?
7. If so, should the tobacco industry be forced to pay for the scans, or should the individuals with unhealthy lifestyles be forced to assume the costs of treating their preventable ailments because they caused the problems?

to treat preventable, self-inflicted ailments, such as those resulting from smoking, or why the tobacco industry should not be required to pay for the National Cancer Institute's research on lung screening just like the medical monitoring the industry is required to pay for in Massachusetts.

Despite charges of conflicts of interest and accusations that the study has design flaws that bias its outcome against screening (Armstrong, 2007), the ethical questions under consideration are complex. CT scanning is adept at detecting abnormalities that might be cancerous. Once they are detected, potentially risky lung biopsies are usually needed to confirm the presence of cancer in the lung. Usually, the biopsies turn up no cancer. Skeptics say patients may suffer health problems as a result of universal screening, such as complications from biopsies or needless surgery, offsetting any gains from enhanced detection (Armstrong, 2007; Bach, et al., 2007; NCI, 2011). Yet this misses the point: without this EBM research, there is no way to determine how preventable lung cancers should be treated, especially for the millions exposed to secondary smoke.

The Ethics of Comparative Effectiveness Research

Several organizations provide nonbiased comparative effectiveness research on medications, including The Independent Drug Information Service, the Alosa Foundation, the Drug Effectiveness Review Project (DERP), and the Pew Prescription Project. Their intention is to use systematic reviews of scientific studies to inform purchasing decisions in an effort to compare the effectiveness of medications (Francis, 2012). The logic behind these efforts is clear: to win the FDA's approval, a pharmaceutical company generally has to demonstrate that a new medication is safe and more effective than a placebo. The pharmaceutical industry does not, however, have to show how the new medication compares with other medications already on the market. This is useful information, particularly when the new medication might cost significantly more than alternatives with the same efficacy (Darrow, 2013).

The Ethics of Cost-Based Restrictions on Medical Products

One of the most controversial issues surrounding EBM is whether costs should be considered in making decisions about selection of medical products, or if clinical effectiveness should be the sole criterion. EBM could arguably create a veil behind which the government and insurers could justify restrictions on patients' access to more expensive products in order to reduce short-term costs (Darrow, 2014). For instance, while the DERP provides state purchasing agencies with findings of comparative effectiveness (which do not include cost considerations), the states retain total freedom with regard to how the information influences their policy decisions (Francis, 2012). The DERP does not take into account individual patient medical needs or ways to contain health care costs in the long term (Wechsler, 2008).

Independent or Industry-Supported Comparative Effectiveness Research

Although better information about the effectiveness of medications as well as their safety ought to be a starting point, supporters of DERP challenge the medical products industry to take the lead in coming up with alternatives to their efforts to control costs. At issue is whether the medical products industry should be expected and trusted to do **comparative effectiveness** research that honestly compares 2 or more products to measure their relative benefits and harms for prevention, diagnosis, treatment, and monitoring of health conditions. Others ask whether the United States needs a respected, independent organization, perhaps funded jointly by the health care industry and government, to study the available evidence and, when necessary, commission evidence-based analysis to determine which interventions are most effective for which patients, and under what circumstances. Moreover, it is equally critical to determine whether medical treatments are more meaningful than no efficacy at all (Darrow, 2013).

One Reform Measure: Patient-Centered Outcomes Research Institute

Congress created the Patient-Centered Outcomes Research Institute (PCORI) to conduct comparative effectiveness research. This research compares medical interventions to discern which treatments and medical products work best (Stopa, 2011). Comparative effectiveness data has the potential to narrow the gap between EBM and necessary and effective care in the practice of medicine by increasing the use of effective medical interventions (Keckley & Frink, 2009). Simultaneously, and for the first time, health outcome data is becoming publically available from health insurers and health care providers nationwide.

Similar to the Federal Reserve System, the PCORI is largely insulated from politics and industry conflicts of interest due to its funding, which is derived from fees charged to the health insurance industry (Beachy, et al., 2014; IOM, 2009). Like President Roosevelt did regarding monetary policy with the creation of the Federal Reserve System in 1913, decision-making on health care policy and health care delivery reform is delegated to a panel of experts and consumers of health care (Miller, 2010). The PCORI is structured with a central board in which all the health care industry stakeholders are closely aligned. Government, academics, patients, and the health care industry are represented on the PCORI board. As an independent body, the PCORI recommends coverage for only those medical treatments backed by EBM. The idea of creating the PCORI to regulate health care policy was to allow an impartial group of experts to improve health care at the federal policy level without research biases from political or industry influences (Miller, 2010; Parver, 2009).

ETHICAL DILEMMAS 8-7

8. Based on the ethical principle of the common good, should the federal government require the uniform disclosure of audited outcome data from all health insurers and health care providers nationwide?

9. Should the nation's needs—for controlling health care costs and guaranteeing that the quality of health care be improved by becoming more standardized—outweigh the traditional values of free enterprise and the unfettered freedom to practice medicine without government monitoring and evaluation?

Ethical Obligations of Care, Trust, and Evidence-Based Medicine

The traditional honor code in many private schools and our nation's military academies has a directness that is missing in the health care industry: "You will not lie, cheat, or steal, or tolerate those who do." Of the 12 words, the last 5 are most difficult to deal with because they require individuals in the health care industry to make judgments about whether the professional actions of their peers are right or wrong, ethical or unethical. The refusal to tolerate science and the practice of medicine that are not in conformity with reason and evidence should be at the core of EBM (Brody, 2010). Clearly, it is not enough for individuals in the health care industry to act professionally themselves; they also bear a duty of care for the U.S. health care system, which requires them to not tolerate unprofessional actions by anyone else.

When one-third of the nation's health care spending is devoted to ineffective and oftentimes harmful medical treatments simply because the medical profession does not trust EBM, there is an unwarranted tolerance of unprofessional actions (IOM, 2009; Todd, 2011). Now, as it turns out, the scientific studies underlying what is thought to be EBM are not always trustworthy because of conflicts of interest, research bias, scientific improprieties, and research fraud (Anand, 2010).

Yet, when one looks at the multiple professional codes of ethics in the health care industry, there is something different from the traditional honor code. There is no emphasis on not tolerating others who violate the codes (Carreyrou & McGinty, 2011b). The health care industry delegates the oversight of right and wrong in EBM to the government (Greaney, 2011). Everyone is an island in the health care industry; there is no concept that everyone is a related part of a complex system (Berg, 2010). For instance, there is little fear of the negative judgment of one's peers when the nation's top orthopedic surgeons think they can justify their receipt of multimillion-dollar payments from the medical device industry to recommend industry products to their fellow physicians (Carreyrou & McGinty, 2011). For EBM, the refusal of physicians and their professional associations to make negative judgments about acceptance of huge industry payments for scientific recommendations is critical. EBM must be practiced from the bottom up. This translates into trustworthy scientific studies that the medical profession can rely on and it means judgment against anyone who does not follow the higher ideals of EBM (Beachy, et al., 2014; IOM, 2011). The level of unnecessary and ineffective care in the U.S. health care system points to the impoverished sense of EBM in the health care industry and the recklessness of not caring whether health care is necessarily supported by genuine clinical evidence (IOM, 2011, 2009, and 2001).

The Future of Evidence-Based Medicine

As the debate on EBM continues, many agree that the current health care system covers too few people, costs too much, and does not deliver consistently high-quality health care. The question is how to ensure that patients receive quality, affordable health care. Without ensuring quality, access to health care may be meaningless. Without addressing costs, health care becomes inaccessible. By building true EBM into reform measures, Americans might all someday get quality, timely delivered, affordable health care.

ETHICAL OR UNETHICAL DECISION

Conflicts of Interest in Evidence-Based Guidelines

Ethics Issue: *Should conflicts of interest be banned in guideline-writing groups or just disclosed? Or, does this moralistic approach undermine the relationships between commercial interests and academic and research medicine that drives innovation and new advances?*

Ethics Analysis: Yes, physicians who write evidence-based guidelines should have no financial ties to the medical products industry that could lead to bias; such ties create potential conflicts-of-interest, even though they are disclosed (Burton, 2011). Improper bias in guidelines can have a potentially more widespread adverse effect on patient care than individual physicians' conflicts of interest (Mendelson, et al., 2011). While conflicts of interest are prevalent, there are a significant number of experienced experts without conflicts (AHA, 2014; CMSS, 2015).

Ethics Analysis: No, due to the complexity of their products, the medical products industry must rely on expert physicians to teach other physicians how to use some products; physicians are rightly paid consultation fees for this service and also royalties for inventing products. Moreover, ties to physicians are essential to ensuring that scientific advances truly improve the lives of patients. *See generally* Burton, 2011. The medical products industry is the engine of innovation, with advances in medicine dependent on the relationship between the industry and academic/research medicine (Stossel, 2015).

Statutory Law: In recognizing the reality of modern medicine, the Affordable Care Act of 2010 mandates disclosure of all physician payments, including all consultations and royalties, as opposed to banning conflicts of interest outright.

— Patient Protection and Affordable Care Act, 42 U.S.C. § 18001, *et seq.* (2010), *as amended by* Health Care and Education Reconciliation Act of 2010, Pub. L. No. 111-152, 124 Stat. 1029 through 124 Stat. 1084. *See also* AHA, 2014; Beachy, et al., 2014; CMSS, 2015; Stossel, 2015.

CHAPTER SUMMARY

- Ethics and modern medicine should be based on the full use of human reason and valid arguments along with the best available scientific evidence.
- Evidence-based guidelines are the embodiment of EBM and as such require ethical integrity.
- There is an unfortunate lapse in ethics and professionalism that accounts for the increased shortcomings in the practice of medicine wherein physicians and hospitals fail to use the best scientific evidence available for treating even the most common health conditions.

- U.S. health care has not been effective or ethical when there is no clear evidence of the effectiveness, or even the lack of harm, in more than half of the medical treatments delivered in the U.S. health care system.

- Linking financial incentives with EBM is controversial because it is ethically questionable whether physicians and hospitals should be paid to follow the evidence-based guidelines to which they should be adhering already.

- Overused, underused, misused, and ineffective health care is too often the unethical byproduct of the traditional practice of medicine, which focuses on the individual physician-patient relationship, and the longstanding physician resistance to using evidence-based guidelines.

- A benefit of EBM could be eliminating geographical, and ultimately unethical, variations in health care caused by physicians and hospitals not uniformly following evidence-based guidelines.

- One concern of EBM proponents is the injustice inflicted on patients who waste valuable time and money on medical treatments that do not work, and in the meantime may be foregoing more effective treatments; this waste could be minimized through evidence-based guidelines that give everyone access to the same best practice protocols.

- Increasingly, EBM decisions are being used in every aspect of hospital functions; one now-controversial practice is the use of less expensive medical devices when higher-priced, more durable devices that have better long-term effectiveness are available.

- The PCORI was created to evaluate comparative effectiveness on medical interventions for delivery of cost-effective EBM, thereby providing an ethical basis for the delivery of effective and efficient health care.

- It is not enough for individuals in the health care industry to act professionally themselves; they also bear a duty of care for the U.S. health care system and its stakeholders, which requires that they not tolerate unprofessional or unethical actions by anyone in the health care industry.

REFERENCES

AHA (American Heart Association). (2014). *Conflict of interest policy.* Dallas, TX: AHA.

AHRQ (Agency for Healthcare Research and Quality). (2014). *Comparative effectiveness review: Decision aids for cancer screening and treatment.* Rockville, MD: AHRQ.

___. (2014a). *Benefits and harms of routine preoperative testing: Comparative effectiveness.* Rockville, MD: AHRQ.

Al-Khatib, S. M., et al. (2011). Non-evidence based ICD implantations in the United States. *Journal of the American Medical Association, 305,* 43–49.

Anand, S. (2010). Using numerical statutory interpretation to improve conflict of interest waiver procedures at the FDA. *Southern California Law Review, 83,* 649–692.

Armstrong, D. (2007, October 8). Critics question objectivity of government lung-scan study; Tobacco companies paid key researchers as expert witnesses. *Wall Street Journal,* p. B1.

ASA (American Society of Anesthesiologists). (2015, April 16). *Press release: Medicare patients undergo unnecessary tests before cataract surgery, study finds.* Schaumburg, IL: ASA.

Ausness, R. C. (2008). "There's danger here, Cherie!" Liability for the promotion and marketing of drugs and medical devices for off-label uses. *Brooklyn Law Review, 73,* 1253–1326.

Avraham, R. (2014). Overlooked and underused: Clinical practice guidelines and malpractice liability for independent physicians. *Connecticut Insurance Law Journal, 20,* 273–332.

___. (2011). Clinical practice guidelines: The warped incentives in the U.S. healthcare system. *American Journal of Law and Medicine, 37,* 7–40.

Bach, P. B., et al. (2007). Computed tomography screening and lung cancer outcomes. *Journal of the American Medical Association, 297,* 953–961.

Beachy, S. H., et al. (2014). *Conflict of interest and medical innovation: Ensuring integrity while facilitating innovation in medical research: Workshop summary.* Washington, DC: Institute of Medicine.

Berg, J. (2010). Putting the community back into the "community benefit" standard. *Georgia Law Review, 44,* 375–431.

Berwick, D. M., & Hackbarth, A. (2012). Eliminating waste in U.S. health care. *Journal of the American Medical Association, 307*(14), 362–366.

Binder, L. (2015). Value-based purchasing versus consumerism: Navigating the riptide. *American Journal of Accountable Care, 3*(1), 11–14.

Brent, D. A., et al. (2009). Predictors of spontaneous and systematically assessed suicidal adverse events in the treatment of SSRI-resistant depression in adolescents (TORDIA) study. *American Journal of Psychiatry, 166*, 418–426.

Brody, H. (2010). Medicine's ethical responsibility for health care reform: The top five list. *New England Journal of Medicine, 362*(4), 283–285.

Burroughs, A. D., et al. (2010). Off-label promotion: Government theories of prosecution and facts that drive them. *Food and Drug Law Journal, 65*, 555–588.

Burton, A. O. (2010). "They use it like candy": How the prescription of psychotropic drugs to state-involved children violates international law. *Brooklyn Journal of International Law, 35*, 453–513.

Burton, T. M. (2011, March 29). Study cites cardiology conflicts. *Wall Street Journal*, p. A4.

Candeub, A. (2011). Contract, warranty, and the Patient Protection and Affordable Care Act. *Wake Forest Law Review, 46*, 45–93.

Carragee, E. J., et al. (2011). A critical review of recombinant human bone morphogenetic protein-2 trials in spinal surgery: Emerging safety concerns and lessons learned. *Spine Journal, 11*(6), 471–491.

Carreyrou, J. (2011, June 22). Senators look into Medtronic, doctors. *Wall Street Journal*, p. B1.

Carreyrou, J., & McGinty, J. (2011, April 13). Hospital bars surgeon from operating room: Medical board in Oregon separately investigates doctor who stood out for high rate of multiple spinal procedures. *Wall Street Journal*, p. A8.

___. (2011a, October 8). Taking double cut, surgeons implant their own devices. *Wall Street Journal*, p. A1.

___. (2011b, December 20). Secrets of the system: Top spine surgeons reap royalties, Medicare bounty. *Wall Street Journal*, p. A1.

Cassel, C. K., & Guest, J. A. (2012). Choosing wisely: Helping physicians and patients make smart decisions about their care. *Journal of the American Medical Association, 307*(17), 476–477.

Clark, B. (2011). Using law to fight a silent epidemic: The role of health literacy in health care access, quality, and cost. *Annals of Health Law, 20*, 253–327.

CMS (Centers for Medicare and Medicaid Services). (2014). *Press release: Historic release of data gives consumers unprecedented transparency on the medical services physicians provide and how much they are paid*. Washington, DC: CMS.

CMSS (Council of Medical Specialty Societies). (2015). *Code for interactions with companies*. Chicago, IL: CMSS.

Cochrane, A. L. (1999). *Effectiveness and efficiency: Random reflections on health services*. London, England: Royal Society of Medicine Press (Original work published 1972).

Cohen, J., et al. (2009). Off-label use reimbursement. *Food and Drug Law Journal, 64*, 391–403.

Commonwealth Fund. (2011). *Why not the best? Results from the national scorecard on U.S. health care system performance*. New York, NY: Commonwealth Fund.

Conko, G. (2011). The perils and protection of off-label drug and medical device promotion. *Health Matrix: The Journal of Law-Medicine, 21*, 149–187.

Darrow, J. J. (2014). Pharmaceutical gatekeepers. *Indiana Law Review, 47*, 363–420.

___. (2013). Pharmaceutical efficacy: The illusory legal standard. *Washington and Lee Law Review, 70*, 2073–2136.

Das, A. (2007). The asthma crisis in low-income communities of color: Using the law as a tool for promoting public health. *New York University Review of Law and Social Change, 31*, 273–314.

Davidoff, F., et al. (1995). Editorial: Evidence based medicine. *British Medical Journal, 310*, 1085.

DeBoer, M. J. (2012). Medicare coverage policy and decision making, preventive services, and comparative effectiveness research before and after the Affordable Care Act. *Journal of Health and Biomedical Law, 7*, 493–572.

Dolinar, R., & Leininger, S. L. (2006). Pay for performance or compliance? A second opinion on Medicare reimbursement. *Indiana Health Law Review, 3*, 391–420.

Duffin, J. (2010). *History of medicine* (2nd ed.). Toronto, Canada: University of Toronto Press.

Einstein, A. (1995). *Ideas and opinions*. New York, NY: Crown (Original work published 1936).

Epstein, N. E. (2011). Preoperative, intraoperative, and postoperative measures to further reduce spinal infections. *Surgical Neurology International, 2*(17), 1–7.

Faigman, D. L. (2012). The "M[enopause] word": An interdisciplinary adventure. *Hastings Women's Law Journal, 23*, 3–44.

Falit, B. P. (2006). Ancillary service and self-referral arrangements in the medical and legal professions: Do current ethical, legislative, and regulatory policies adequately serve the interests of patients and clients? *South Carolina Law Review, 58*, 371–413.

Farrow, F. L. (2010). The anti-patient psychology of health courts: Prescriptions from a lawyer-physician. *American Journal of Law and Medicine, 36*, 188–219.

FDA (Food and Drug Administration). (2010). *Public health advisory: Suicidality in children and adolescents being treated with anti-depressant medications.* Bethesda, MD: FDA.

Forest Laboratories. (2011). *Medication guide: Celexa.* New York, NY: Forest Laboratories.

Francis, M. H. (2012). Beyond safe and effective: The role of the federal government in supporting and disseminating comparative-effectiveness research. *Annals of Health Law, 21,* 329–381.

Freedman, D. H. (2010). Lies, damned lies, and medical science. *The Atlantic Monthly, 306*(4), 76–85.

____. (2010a). *Wrong: Why experts keep failing us and how to know when not to trust them.* New York, NY: Little, Brown.

Friedland, D. J. (2009). *Evidence based medicine: A framework for clinical practice.* New York, NY: Prentice-Hall Health.

GAO (U.S. General Accounting Office). (1999). *Food safety: The agricultural use of antibiotics and its implications for human health.* Washington, DC: GAO.

Geetter, J. S. (2011). Another man's treasure: The promise and pitfalls of leveraging existing biomedical assets for future use. *Journal of Health and Life Sciences Law, 4*(3), 1.

Gibbons, R. D., et al. (2007). Early evidence on the effects of regulators' suicidality warnings on SSRI prescriptions and suicide in children and adolescents. *American Journal of Psychiatry, 164,* 1356–1364.

Good Stewardship Working Group. (2011). The "top 5" lists in primary care: Meeting the responsibility of professionalism. *Archives of Internal Medicine, 171*(15), 1385–1390.

Goossens, A., et al. (2008). Physicians and nurses focus on different aspects of guidelines when deciding whether to adopt them: An application of conjoint analysis. *Medical Decision Making, 28,* 138–145.

Grady, D., & Redberg, R. F. (2010). Less is more: How less health care can result in better health. *Archives of Internal Medicine, 170*(9), 749–750.

Greaney, T. L. (2011). The Affordable Care Act and competition policy: Antidote or placebo? *Oregon Law Review, 89,* 811–845.

Greely, H. T. (2009). Law and the revolution in neuroscience: An early look at the field. *Akron Law Review, 42,* 687–715.

Guzelian, C. P. (2005). The kindynamic theory of tort. *Indiana Law Journal, 80,* 987–1036.

Hack, L., & Gwyer, J. (Eds.) (2013). *Evidence into practice: Integrating judgment, values, and research.* Philadelphia, PA: F.A. Davis.

Harvard Law. (2010). Supreme Judicial Court of Massachusetts recognizes cause of action for medical monitoring of tobacco users: *Donovan v. Philip Morris USA, Inc.*, 914 N.E.2d 891 (Mass. 2009). *Harvard Law Review, 123,* 1771–1778.

Hawking, S., & Mlodinow, L. (2012). *The grand design.* New York, NY: Random House.

Hawryluck, L. et al. (2011). Multi-professional recommendations for access and utilization of critical care services: Towards consistency in practice and ethical decision-making processes. *Journal of Law, Medicine and Ethics, 39,* 254-262.

Haynes, R. B., et al. (2005). *Clinical epidemiology: How to do clinical practice research (Clinical epidemiology)* (3rd ed.). Riverwoods, IL: Lippincott, Williams & Wilkins.

Hershey, J. C. (2013). Biases in clinical reasoning. In L. Hack & J. Gwyer (Eds.), *Evidence into practice: Integrating judgment, values, and research* (pp. 47–58). Philadelphia, PA: F.A. Davis.

Houck, J. A. (2008). *Hot and bothered: Women, medicine and menopause in modern America.* Cambridge, MA: Harvard University Press.

Hunter, N. D. (2010). Patient-centered law and ethics: Rights talk and patient subjectivity: The role of autonomy, equality, and participation norms. *Wake Forest Law Review, 45,* 1525–1549.

Hyman, D. A. (2010). Follow the money: Money matters in health care, just like in everything else. *American Journal of Law and Medicine, 36,* 370–388.

IOM (Institute of Medicine). (2011). *Clinical practice guidelines we can trust.* Washington, DC: National Academies of Sciences.

____. (2011a). *Standards for developing trustworthy clinical practice guidelines.*

____. (2011b). *Patients charting the course: Citizen engagement in the learning health system.*

____. (2010). *The healthcare imperative: Lowering costs and improving outcomes.*

____. (2009). *Conflict of interest in medical research, education, and practice.*

____. (2009a). *Initial national priorities for comparative effectiveness research.*

____. (2001). *Crossing the quality chasm: A new health system for the 21st century.*

Jacobson, P. D. (2010). Health law past and future: Looking for stability in all the wrong places. *Annals of Health Law, 19,* 25–30.

Kadish, A., & Goldberger, J. (2011). Selecting patients for ICD implantation: Are clinicians choosing appropriately? *Journal of the American Medical Association, 305,* 91–92.

Kahlenborn, C., et al. (2006). Oral contraceptive use as a risk factor for premenopausal breast cancer: A meta-analysis. *Mayo Clinic Proceedings, 81,* 1290–1302.

Kallmes, D. F., et al. (2009). A randomized trial of vertebroplasty for osteoporotic spinal fractures. *New England Journal of Medicine, 361*, 569–579.

Keckley, P. H., & Frink, B. B. (2009). Comparative effectiveness: A strategic perspective on what it is and what it may mean for the United States. *Journal of Health and Life Sciences Law, 3*(1), 53–90.

Kesselheim, A. S., & Outterson, K. (2011). Improving antibiotic markets for long term sustainability. *Yale Journal of Health Policy, Law, and Ethics, 11*, 101–167.

Kimbuende, E., et al. (2010). *Background brief: U.S. health care costs*. Menlo Park, CA: Kaiser Family Foundation.

Kinney, E. D. (2011). Comparative effectiveness research under the Patient Protection and Affordable Care Act: Can new bottles accommodate old wine? *American Journal of Law and Medicine, 37*, 522–566.

___. (2010). For profit enterprise in health care: Can it contribute to health reform? *American Journal of Law and Medicine, 36*, 405–435.

Korn, D. (2011). Financial conflicts of interest in academic medicine: Whence they came, where they went. *Indiana Health Law Review, 8*, 1–42.

Laakmann, A. B. (2015). When should physicians be liable for innovation? *Cardozo Law Review, 36*, 913–968.

___. (2011). Collapsing the distinction between experimentation and treatment in the regulation of new drugs. *Alabama Law Review, 62*, 305–348.

Landrigan, C. P., et al. (2010). Temporal trends in rates of patient harm resulting from medical care. *New England Journal of Medicine, 363*(22), 2124–2134.

Landro, L. (2007, May 16). Better ways to treat back pain: Insurers, employers target excessive scans and surgeries to improve patient outcomes. *Wall Street Journal*, p. D1.

___. (2005, January 26). Are treatment guidelines reliable? *Wall Street Journal*, p. D4.

Lemmens, T., & Telfer, C. (2012). Access to information and the right to health: The human rights case for clinical trials transparency. *American Journal of Law and Medicine, 38*, 63–112.

Lessing, A. (2010). Killing us softly: How sub-therapeutic dosing of livestock causes drug-resistant bacteria in humans. *Boston College Environmental Affairs Law Review, 37*, 463–491.

Levinson, D. R. (2010). *Adverse events in hospitals: National incidence among Medicare beneficiaries*. Washington, DC: U.S. Department of Health and Human Services, Office of Inspector General.

Madison, K. (2009). The law and policy of health care quality reporting. *Campbell Law Review, 11*, 215–255.

Malinowski, M. J., et al. (2012). Drug development, stuck in a state of puberty? Regulatory reform of human clinical research to raise responsiveness to the reality of human variability. *Saint Louis University Law Journal, 56*, 363–418.

Markey, M. L. (2007). Scientific misconduct in research. *American Health Lawyers Association, Journal of Health and Life Sciences Law, 1*(1), 63–92.

Matthew, D. B. (2011). Implementing American health care reform: The fiduciary imperative. *Buffalo Law Review, 59*, 715–807.

McGlynn, E., et al. (2003). The quality of health care delivered to adults in the U.S. *New England Journal of Medicine, 348*(26), 2635–2645.

Mehlman, M. J. (2012). Professional power and the standard of care in medicine. *Arizona State Law Journal, 44*, 1165–1235.

Meir, R., & Shaw, P. W. (2011). The link between quality and medical management: Physician tiering and other initiatives. *Journal of Health and Life Sciences Law, 4*(2), 36–64.

Mendelson, D., & Carino, T. (2005). Evidence-based medicine in the U.S.: De rigueur or dream preferred? *Health Affairs, 24*(1), 133–136.

Mendelson, T. B., et al. (2011). Health care reform: Conflicts of interest in cardiovascular clinical practice guidelines. *Archives of Internal Medicine, 171*(6), 577–584.

Miller, J. D. (2010). The Patient-Centered Outcomes Research Institute. *Journal of Health and Life Sciences Law, 4*(1), 26–39.

Naik, G. (2011, August 10). Mistakes in scientific studies surge. *Wall Street Journal*, pp. A1, A12.

NCI (National Cancer Institute). (2011, June 29). *NCI press release: NIH-funded study shows 20 percent reduction in lung cancer mortality with low-dose CT compared to chest X-ray*. Bethesda, MD: NCI.

NLST (National Lung Screening Trial) Research Team. (2011). Reduced lung-cancer mortality with low-dose computed tomographic screening. *New England Journal of Medicine, 365*(5), 395–409.

Offit, P. A. (2010). *Autism's false prophets: Bad science, risky medicine, and the search for a cure*. New York, NY: Columbia University Press.

Parker-Pope, T. (2007). *The hormone decision: Untangle the controversy—understand your options—make your own choices*. Emmaus, PA: Rodale.

Parver, C. P. (2009). Health care debate: National health care reform: Has its time finally arrived? *Journal of Health and Biomedical Law, 5*, 207–247.

Piper, M. A., et al. (2014). *Screening for high blood pressure in adults: A systematic evidence review for the U.S. Preventive Services Task Force*. Rockville: MD: U.S. Department of Health and Human Services, Agency for Healthcare Research and Quality.

Pratt, D. (2011). Health care reform: Will it succeed? *Albany Law Journal of Science and Technology, 21*, 493–589.

Radley, D. C., et al. (2014). *Aiming higher: Results from a scorecard on state health system performance*. New York, NY: The Commonwealth Fund.

___. (2006). Off-label prescribing among office-based physicians. *Archives of Internal Medicine, 166*, 1021–1026.

RAND Corp. (2006). *First national report card on quality of health care in America (the Community Quality Index study)*. Santa Monica, CA: RAND Corp.

Saver, R. S. (2008). In tepid defense of population health, physicians and antibiotic resistance. *American Journal of Law and Medicine, 34*(4), 431–491.

Schneider, S. A. (2011). Reconsidering the industrialization of agriculture. *Journal of Environmental Law and Litigation, 26*, 19–27.

Seida, J. C., et al. (2012). Antipsychotics for children and young adults: A comparative effectiveness review. *Pediatrics, 129*(3), 771–784.

Shapiro, M. H. (2012). Updating constitutional doctrine: An extended response to the critique of compulsory vaccination. *Yale Journal of Health Policy, Law and Ethics, 12*, 87–168.

Stathopoulos, A. S. (2010). You are what your food eats: How regulation of factory farm conditions could improve human health and animal welfare alike. *New York University Journal of Legislation and Public Policy, 13*, 407–444.

Steen, R. G. (2011). Misinformation in the medical literature: What role do error and fraud play? *Journal of Medical Ethics, 37*(8), 498–503.

Stopa, E. S. (2011). Harnessing comparative effectiveness research to bend the cost curve and achieve successful health reform: An assessment of constitutional barriers to limiting health care treatment options. *University of Pennsylvania Journal of Constitutional Law, 13*, 815–866.

Stossel, T. P. (2015). *Pharmaphobia: How the conflict of interest myth undermines American medical innovation*. Lanham, MD: Rowman & Littlefield.

Stremikis, K., et al. (2011). *A call for change: The 2011 Commonwealth Fund survey of public views of the U.S. health system*. New York, NY: Commonwealth Fund.

Thomas, J. (2012). Autism, medicine, and the poison of enthusiasm and superstition. *Journal of Health and Biomedical Law, 7*, 449–492.

Thompson, D. B. (2011). The next stage of health care reform: Controlling costs by paying health plans based on health outcomes. *Akron Law Review, 44*, 727–768.

Todd, A. E. (2011). No need for more regulation: Payors and their role in balancing the cost and safety considerations of off-label prescriptions. *American Journal of Law and Medicine, 37*, 422–443.

Tollen, L., et al. (2011). *Delivery system reform tracking: A framework for understanding change*. New York, NY: The Commonwealth Fund.

Van Tassel, K. (2013). Harmonizing the Affordable Care Act with the three main national systems for healthcare quality improvement: The tort, licensure, and hospital peer review hearing systems. *Brooklyn Law Review, 78*, 883–928.

Vertinsky, L. S. (2015). Patents, partnerships, and the pre-competitive collaboration myth in pharmaceutical innovation. *University of California Davis Law Review, 48*, 1509–1579.

Wechsler, J. (2008). Healthcare reform proposals challenge manufacturers. *Pharmaceutical Technology, 32*(6), 32–36.

Weiss, A. J., et al. (2014). *Characteristics of operating room procedures in U.S. hospitals*. Rockville, MD: Agency for Healthcare Research and Quality.

Whoriskey, P., & Keating, D. (2013, October 27). Spinal fusions serve as case study for debate over when certain surgeries are necessary. *Washington Post*, p. A1.

Winslow, R. (2008, November 10). Cholesterol drug cuts heart risk in healthy patients. *Wall Street Journal*, p. B1.

___. (2007, January 23). Opening arguments—the case against stents: New studies hint at overuse; Defenders say devices for heart disease give quick symptom relief. *Wall Street Journal*, p. A1.

Winslow, R., & Carreyrou, J. (2011, July 6). Heart treatment overused: Study finds doctors often too quick to try costly procedures to clear arteries. *Wall Street Journal*, p. B1.

Zhang, Y., et al. (2010). Geographic variation in the quality of prescribing. *New England Journal of Medicine, 363*(21), 1985–1988.

Zisk, M. A. (2013, February 17). Partner, Skadden, Arps, Slate, Meagher & Flom, remarks at the Panel Discussion on Partnerships in Innovation: Collaborating to Build a Productive Future, at the 2013 Wharton Health Care Business Conference: Innovation in a Changing Health Care Environment, Philadelphia, PA.

CHAPTER 9

Medical Malpractice

"The twin goals of patient safety and compensation for injury will only be achieved when physicians focus on medical safety and attorneys focus on reforms to the legal system to make it fairer, less costly, and less burdensome. Then, when catastrophic medical injury, preventable or not, does occur, patients . . . receive the compensation they need quickly."

— **Amos Grunebaum**, Director of Obstetrics and the Chief of Labor and Delivery at the New York Cornell Medical Center

LEARNING OBJECTIVES

After completing this chapter, the reader should be able to:

1. Understand the ethical principles of compassion and justice underlying the proposals to reduce the risk of malpractice.
2. Explain how to reach the most ethical decisions with regard to malpractice, standards of care, and malpractice insurance.
3. Evaluate the current ethical principles that are preventing adoption of enterprise liability that limits or eliminates the liability of physicians and other health care professionals for malpractice.

KEY TERMS

Benchmark	Economic damages	Preventable adverse events
Corporate practice prohibitions	Enterprise liability	Quality-adjusted life-year
	Joint Commission	Serious adverse events
Damages	Malpractice	Serious reportable events
Defensive medicine	Medical negligence	Standard of care
Disruptive innovation	Moral hazard	Treatment adherence
Drug cocktails	Non-economic damages	Vicarious liability

ETHICAL OR UNETHICAL DECISION

Medical Negligence

Ethics Issue: *Do pharmacies have a duty and ethical obligation to protect the public from customers who may be abusing prescription medications?*

In Brief: This is a malpractice lawsuit against a number of Nevada pharmacies for death and injury caused by Patricia Copening, a pharmacy customer who was abusing prescription medications with the pharmacies' knowledge. During a 12-month period, Copening received prescriptions for about 4,500 hydrocodone pills at 13 different pharmacies. Hydrocodone is a narcotic used for severe pain relief with a high potential for abuse that may impair one's ability to perform potentially hazardous tasks such as driving a vehicle.

While under the influence of hydrocodone, Copening struck Gregory Sanchez, Jr. and Robert Martinez with her vehicle while they were on the side of the road, killing Sanchez and leaving Martinez seriously injured. The incident resulted in Copening's arrest for driving under the influence of narcotics. Sanchez's daughters, his widow, the personal representatives of Sanchez's estate, and Martinez and his wife filed a wrongful death and personal injury complaint against Copening. During discovery, it was learned that the Nevada Prescription Controlled Substance Abuse Prevention Task Force, a state task force designed to protect the general public from unlawful distribution of controlled substances, had detected problems with Copening's prescription history. Following review of its computerized tracking program of prescriptions dispensed by pharmacies, the state task force sent a letter informing certain pharmacies about Copening's suspected abuse of narcotics.

State law provides that narcotic prescriptions should not be honored if a pharmacist deems a prescription to be fraudulent, not for a legitimate medical purpose, potentially harmful to the customer's health, or unlawful. Pharmacists are mandated to contact the prescribing physician or other prescriber before dispensing such prescriptions. If after the consultation, the pharmacist still reasonably believes that 1 of the 4 conditions exists, the narcotic prescription may not be dispensed. Upon discovering the letter about Copening to the pharmacies from the state task force, the original complaint was amended to include the pharmacy chains that dispensed narcotic prescriptions to Copening: Wal-Mart, Long's Drug Stores, Walgreen's, CVS Pharmacy, Rite Aid, Albertson's, and Lam's Pharmacy. All 7 pharmacy chains had knowledge of Copening's suspected abuse of narcotics when they dispensed her prescriptions.

— *Sanchez, et al. v. Wal-Mart Stores, et al.*, 221 P.3d 1276 (Supreme Court of Nevada 2009). (*See Ethical or Unethical Decision* at the end of the chapter for discussion of this ethics issue.)

Introduction

Malpractice, defined as improper and negligent conduct that causes injury to patients for which providers of health care may be sued, is one of the most controversial aspects of American health care law (Tenner & Ringel, 2014). One of the most contentious issues in malpractice is how the health care and legal systems handle medical errors of all types, ranging from medication errors to misdiagnoses and surgical blunders (MacCourt & Bernstein, 2009). In the field of malpractice, **medical negligence** is conduct that falls below the professional **standard of care** established by law for the protection of others against unreasonable risk of harm or injury. By definition, appropriate conduct is measured in comparison to what reasonable professionals either do or should do in similar circumstances, and is complicated with legal standards varying from state to state. Although there are competing ethical principles involved in malpractice, the principles of justice are often sacrificed in the legal system, both when assigning negligence, which by definition is fault-based, and when determining the standard of care (Dworkin, 2013).

To avoid giving up on ethical principles, the legal and health care systems, as well as patients, must make some difficult trade-offs and policy choices. The cost of malpractice insurance, for instance, has driven specialists out of certain geographic areas, making health care less accessible. Health care is also so expensive in the United States in part due to the cost of the **defensive medicine** that is practiced in an attempt to avoid liability in malpractice lawsuits. Some say that the high cost of the U.S. health care system is the result of a malfunctioning legal system. However, most maintain that the high public profile of malpractice diverts attention from the real problems in the health care system (Frakes, 2015).

Malpractice is of little actual consequence to the total cost of health care, but it did serve as a distraction from examining comprehensive reform of the U.S. health care system for decades. At the same time, any real reform of malpractice must begin with a serious look at it within the context of the largest provider of health care, the federal government, and the government health insurance programs that provide basic coverage for more than 105 million Americans (CMS, 2015 and 2015a; Kaiser, 2013).

Principles of Compassion and Justice

The principles of compassion and justice support the drive toward reducing the risk of malpractice. Compassion focuses on the physician-patient relationship when medical errors occur (Moses, 2007; Sawicki, 2010). Justice includes compassion; there can be no compassion without justice (Held, 2007). Principles of justice are used as a backdrop to consider questions about the law and its impact on patient care.

Today, the principle of compassion may be more capable than the principle of justice of determining how malpractice should be determined and what other values, besides financial values, should prevail. Compassion should also consider the limits appropriate for patient rights and how expansive the legal system should be, or not be. Compassion and justice are ideal for a perfect world, but neither principle provides precise guidelines for living in an imperfect world in which the choices and decisions that must be made about medical errors are seldom clear-cut. *See generally* Held, 2007.

The principles of justice and compassion balance competing interests. On one side there is a health care system that demands fair payments for the medical products it provides and the health care services it renders. On the other side are the human rights of patients and consumers who are demanding access to the U.S. health care system. The principle of justice seeks a fair resolution between these competing interests. Principles of compassion are intertwined as opposed to simply competing. *See generally* Held, 2007.

Defining Three Types of Medical Errors

Medical errors that should not happen occur in more than one-third of hospital admissions (Hyman & Silver, 2012; Levinson, 2010). When these medical errors are seriously harmful to patients, they are termed **serious adverse events**. Serious adverse events are either expected from the underlying medical condition or are unexpected; unexpected serious adverse events are termed **serious reportable events**. Nearly half of the serious reportable events are clearly or likely preventable and are termed **preventable adverse events** (Levinson, 2010).

Serious Adverse Events

Serious adverse events are further defined as any expected or unexpected occurrence related or unrelated to a medical intervention that results in any of the following outcomes: death, a life-threatening event, inpatient hospitalization or extension of existing hospitalization, or a persistent or significant disability/incapacity or a congenital anomaly/birth defect. Treatment that may require medical or surgical intervention to prevent one of these outcomes is also considered a serious adverse event.

These serious adverse events shed light on how patients are being harmed while seeking care. Expanding the number of insured, a primary goal of health care reform, will likely reduce the number of patients who use hospital emergency rooms for primary care. This could have significant favorable patient safety implications, as the highest proportion of serious adverse events occurs in emergency rooms (Widman, 2010). Emergency rooms should become more manageable as they are able to become more focused on actual urgent care requiring immediate medical attention.

Serious Reportable Events Are Unexpected

Triggered by unexpected serious adverse events, serious reportable events contribute to as many as 187,000 deaths in hospitals each year (*see, e.g.,* Goodman, et al., 2011), which is an estimated 15,000 deaths every single month (Levinson, 2010; Van Den Bos, et al., 2011). The disclosure of serious reportable events to medical ethics committees is mandatory. Disclosure of serious reportable events is also mandatory to outside regulatory agencies, including state patient safety agencies, the National Institutes of Health for patients in clinical trials, and the U.S. Food and Drug Administration for instances involving medical products, as well as the **Joint Commission**, the nation's predominant standards-setting and accrediting body in health care. Accreditation is required for Medicare and Medicaid certification and licensing in many states. Yet, it is estimated that only one-tenth of the serious reportable events that occur in hospitals are reported to outside regulatory agencies or the Joint Commission, because there is no standardized definition of serious or unexpected (Classen, et al., 2011).

While few would defend the legal system as a cost-effective method of either malpractice compensation or quality improvement, serious reportable events are an even more troubling problem for the U.S. health care system than frivolous lawsuits (Studdert, et al., 2006). The annual social costs of serious reportable events are estimated to be $393 to $958 billion in lost productivity to the U.S. economy (Goodman, et al., 2011).

Preventable Adverse Events

Preventable adverse events, as illustrated in **FEATURE BOX 9-1**, are hospital-acquired conditions that result in serious harm to patients. Almost 14 percent of the patients hospitalized with Medicare health insurance coverage experience preventable adverse events during their hospitalization (Levinson, 2010). When this percentage is translated into the actual number of Medicare-insured patients harmed, 1.7 million patients experience preventable

Preventable Adverse Events (*Serious Reportable Events*)

- Bed sores and stage III and IV pressure ulcers that develop after patients are hospitalized
- Blood and urinary tract infections from catheters placed in hospitalized patients
- Blood transfusion with incompatible blood
- Burns, electric shocks, and other injuries received during hospital stays
- Falls and trauma resulting in broken bones and other injuries
- Injuries and complications from air or gas bubbles entering blood vessels
- Poor control of blood sugar for patients with diabetes
- Sponges, surgical instruments, or other foreign objects left in patients after surgery
- Vascular infections from catheters placed in hospitalized patients

— Sources: Classen, et al., 2011; CMS, 2015; Hyman & Silver, 2012; NQF, 2011; Van Den Bos, et al., 2011.

adverse events during their hospitalization every year (OIG, 2010). Prior to 2012, when the federal government stopped paying for the additional costs of preventable adverse events as part of the nation's health care reform, the annual cost of these events to the Medicare program alone exceeded $4.4 billion (Levinson, 2010).

While some of these preventable adverse events are attributable to incompetence and inattention by individual health care professionals, many more events result from system-level failings (Hyman & Silver, 2012). Comprehensive research consistently documents that institutional practices drive preventable adverse events more than individual failings of providers (IOM, 2006; Levinson, 2010). For instance, whether patients are having the right surgery on the right part of their bodies is not dependent solely on the skills of the surgeons. The total health care costs of these preventable adverse events exceed $17.1 billion annually (Van Den Bos, et al., 2011). Today, for the first time, this information is now public.

Lack of Disruptive Innovation in the Insurance Market

The health care system, the legal system, and the insurance industry have been inhibited from innovating to reduce the risk of malpractice out of fear of disrupting the insurance market (Van Detta, 2009). Until recently, attention was not directed to patient safety or achieving just compensation for victims of malpractice (Timm, 2010). The concept of **disruptive innovation** that displaces existing technologies or ideas altogether, or when new entrants arrive in the marketplace that are a better fit for what consumers actually need and are willing to pay, were not evident in the traditional insurance market for malpractice (Schumpeter, 1942/2008). For better or worse, anything established today is now vulnerable to being overturned by a technology or idea that is then called disruptive. Today's health care reform disruptions, however, allow insurance products to be provided in a more suitable fashion than traditional insurance. In contrast to the negative implication associated with disruptions, disruptive innovations are generally beneficial to patients and the U.S. health care system.

The history of medical innovation teaches that when a disruptive innovation is first introduced to a market, it meets resistance from the established players who have a vested interest in the existing way of doing business (Schumpeter, 1942/2008). Evidence-based medicine, clinical practice guidelines, and telemedicine are examples of such disruptive innovations to the practice of medicine. Over time, the efficiencies associated with the disruptive innovation ultimately displace the older and more established way of doing things (Gupta & Sao, 2011). New methodologies for providing malpractice insurance that is cheaper must be developed if health care costs are to be lowered (Nelson, et al., 2011). Cheap, no-frills malpractice insurance products, however, are rarely offered, and when they are offered, they are subject to intense criticism and resistance from the established malpractice insurance carriers, which have a vested interest in maintaining their hold on higher-priced insurance products (Epstein & Hyman, 2013; Marzen, 2014).

How Malpractice Occurs

Malpractice occurs when a health care provider engages in negligence or commits an intentional injury of a patient (Restatement, 2013). The damages due to medical errors or the duties arising from medical errors are generally the responsibility of the hospitals and physicians who injured the patient. **Damages**, or injuries, are the economic (such as medical bills) and non-economic (such as pain and suffering) consequences of malpractice suffered by the patient. The core of a malpractice claim is that a health care provider failed to administer the care and skill ordinarily exercised under similar circumstances and that such negligent conduct resulted in damages to the patient and possibly also the patient's family. Today, evidence-based clinical practice guidelines increasingly help define and establish the standards of care for hospitals and health care professionals.

ETHICS CASE
Patient Non-Compliance

Torres-Lazarini v. United States
[Patient v. Veterans Administration Hospital]
523 F.3d 69 (U.S. Court of Appeals for the 1st Circuit 2008)

Facts: After Torres-Lazarini, a 71-year-old retired Marine, injured his shoulder in a fall, he went to the Veterans Health Administration (VA) hospital's emergency room complaining of pain and limited range of motion and was treated by Dr. Rodriguez. Rodriguez examined his shoulder and ordered x-rays of the area. The x-rays revealed no damage from the fall, but did reveal a mild degenerative bone condition indicative of a precursor to osteoporosis. Torres-Lazarini was offered anti-inflammatory medication, but refused it. Rodriguez suggested that he apply ice to the shoulder and told him to return in two weeks if there was no improvement.

Torres-Lazarini returned to the VA with complaints of shoulder pain two months later. Dr. Rodriguez reexamined the shoulder and concluded that its condition had worsened. She offered to refer Torres-Lazarini to a physiatrist, a specialist who could determine if an MRI study was required and would recommend physical therapy, if appropriate. The patient turned down these suggestions. Three months later, he returned to the VA, again complaining of shoulder pain, but refused Rodriguez's offer to reevaluate his shoulder.

Eighteen months following his last appointment, Torres-Lazarini had his fourth appointment with Rodriguez, still complaining of shoulder pain. Rodriguez recommended that Torres-Lazarini undergo an MRI, receive physical therapy, and schedule follow-up appointments. Torres-Lazarini underwent an MRI a few weeks later. The MRI revealed osteoarthritis and tearing of several tendons in the shoulder. The VA offered him surgery. Torres-Lazarini was told that although surgery would not necessarily help restore his range of motion, it would ease his pain. He declined the surgery and sued the VA for malpractice.

At trial, an orthopedic surgeon who had never examined Torres-Lazarini testified that the VA breached its duty of care by failing to conduct an orthopedic evaluation shortly after the fall and by waiting two years before conducting an MRI. He also testified that surgery soon after the accident would have restored the patient's range of motion and alleviated his pain.

The VA presented the testimony of its expert, an orthopedic surgeon who physically examined Torres-Lazarini, asserting that severe osteoarthritis was causing the shoulder pain. He stated that Rodriguez's recommendation of physical therapy was the proper treatment for loss of motion due to a dislocated shoulder. In addition, he testified that there was no breach of care because it was not standard practice to refer a patient with negative x-rays to an orthopedist. Rather, standard procedures were followed by immediately ordering x-rays, recommending a course of anti-inflammatory medication, and scheduling follow-up appointments. Finally, he stated that Rodriguez's recommendation that Torres-Lazarini receive evaluation from a physiatrist was proper.

Legal Analysis: *Negligence* is defined as conduct "which falls below the standard established by law for the protection of others against unreasonable risk of harm" (Restatement, 2013). It generally arises from a failure to exercise the proper standard of care. The court found that the care Torres-Lazarini received for his shoulder was in full compliance with the standards of care for the type of soft tissue injury he had suffered. While health care providers may still be found to have imposed an unreasonable risk on a patient even when they apply the standard diagnoses and carefully evaluate all possible medical treatments, the court found that Torres-Lazarini refused the conservative treatment offered to him: he missed appointments, rejected physical therapy, and refused to cooperate with the VA in assessing and treating his shoulder injury.

Rule of Law: When a malpractice claim alleges negligence against a health care professional who has a duty to provide care, four elements must be demonstrated: (1) a generally recognized medical standard of care exists; (2) deviation from that standard occurred; (3) the deviation was the cause of any damage the patient suffered; and (4) the patient actually suffered some form of damage.

Ethics Issue: Should noncompliant patients be given the opportunity to sue their health care providers for malpractice?

Ethics Analysis: Answers to this ethical dilemma are part of the effort to hold patients responsible for managing their illnesses, diseases, and preventable conditions. Patients have an obligation to adhere to the treatment regimen recommended by their physicians and other health care professionals. **Treatment adherence** (or noncompliance) plays a significant role in the resolution of most malpractice lawsuits, including whether the patient: obtained diagnostic procedures; accepted responsibility to follow up on referrals to other specialists; followed prescribed treatment and therapy actions, including surgery as needed; modified lifestyle choices as directed (such as not smoking, diet modifications and exercise, and weight management); and took prescribed medications as directed with regular monitoring.

The problem physicians face is ensuring that their patients genuinely understand how to follow the orders. Today, the health care industry is struggling to determine the appropriate status of patient responsibility. Under the legal system, the issue is whether noncompliance with prescribed treatment plans should establish a complete defense against malpractice or whether treatment adherence should serve as a prerequisite to malpractice.

The health insurance industry has already taken a side on this debate. Health insurance will not provide coverage for subsequent treatments when the patient was not compliant with the treatment regimen. Insurers require treatment adherence to initial recommended treatments before authorizing coverage for additional treatments or more invasive, higher-cost procedures (Wong, 2010). For instance, lung transplants are rarely available to smokers, and elective surgeries are increasingly unavailable to smokers and overweight patients.

Although the quality of health care affects treatment adherence, imperfections in the diagnosis and treatment of patients necessitate caution when access to the malpractice arena is based on adherence to prescribed treatment. Treatment decisions must be made carefully because such decisions inevitably affect patient incentives to accept or refuse treatment options: the familiar dilemma of **moral hazard**.

In this instance, moral hazards arise when patients are insulated from their lifestyle choices. Patients behave differently when they are fully exposed to the health consequences of their behavior. A moral hazard arises when patients take risks they may not otherwise take because they do not bear the consequences of that risk. Moral hazards arise whenever patients do not consider the full consequences and responsibilities of their actions, and therefore act less carefully than they otherwise would, leaving third parties, such as the insurance industry, to hold some responsibility for the consequences of their actions. At the same time, the enormous challenges presented by the risk of noncompliance to prescribed treatment plans should be addressed only through a coordinated, comprehensive system that melds preventive measures and insurance mechanisms into a coherent policy. As is, malpractice insurance pays scant attention to treatment adherence and insufficient attention to the problem of moral hazard.

Court's Holding and Decision: No, Torres-Lazarini failed to prove that the VA committed malpractice; referral to a physiatrist to determine if an MRI was necessary was not a deviation from standard medical practice.

Malpractice Myths

The legal system is often blamed for the lack of access to quality health care due to the rising costs of malpractice insurance (Rodwin, et al., 2015). The public is convinced there is a health care crisis due to excessive malpractice verdicts (CBO, 2006). These

ETHICAL DILEMMAS 9-1

1. Should patients who do not adhere to their treatment regimens be precluded from bringing malpractice claims against the physician or hospital that attempted to treat them?
2. Should treatment adherence be a bar to litigation or a contributing factor to be considered in the settlement of a malpractice claim?

myths must be debunked: malpractice costs are not a significant part of the nation's health care costs and malpractice settlements are not pervasive or irrational (*see e.g.,* Studdert, et al., 2006).

Myth: Malpractice Costs Raise the Nation's Health Care Costs

The American public has focused its attention on malpractice costs, thereby blaming the legal system and insurance industry for the nation's rising health care costs. But in so doing, the public has failed to adequately address the costs associated with health care itself, independent of malpractice insurance and malpractice suits (*see* Perrecone & Fabiano, 2006).

A 25 percent reduction in malpractice costs would lower health care costs by less than half of a percent (about $12.5 billion), which represents a comparably small part of the nation's health care costs (CBO, 2006). Practically speaking, attention should be directed to areas where even greater cost savings can be achieved so that benefits from expenditure of the nation's health dollars can be maximized. As illustrated in **FIGURE 9-1**, the remaining $2.45 trillion in total health care spending should be examined (Keehan, et al., 2008). Malpractice costs are a valid concern, but this does not address the more important issue of how the other 98 percent of health care costs are being spent. Economists generally agree that the principal factor by far in rising costs is medical innovations like new medical products (pharmaceuticals, biologics, and medical devices), new surgical procedures, and new diagnostic techniques, as opposed to malpractice costs (Ostrov, 2012).

Myth: Malpractice Awards Are Pervasive and Irrational

Research at the Harvard School of Public Health found that more than 40 percent of all malpractice claims are not meritorious and most such claims are resolved without any payment of money (Studdert, et al., 2006). Popular opinion, however, has always accepted the myth that malpractice settlements are pervasive and irrational (Baker, 2007). As illustrated in **FEATURE BOX 9-2**, the general public has embraced the myth that the system for malpractice litigation is out of control and U.S. health care is in crisis because of exploding malpractice litigation.

2% Medical Malpractice v. 98% Health Care Industry Costs:
$50 Billion v. $2.6 Trillion

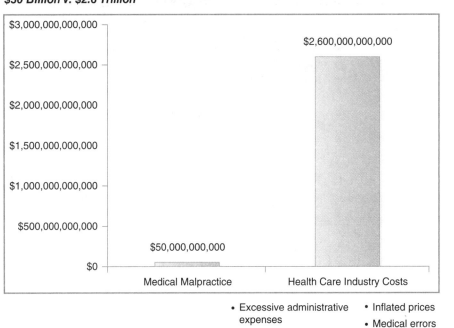

• Excessive administrative   • Inflated prices
  expenses   • Medical errors
• Inappropriate care   • Poor management
• Inefficiencies   • Waste and fraud

FIGURE 9-1 Out-of-Control Bill for Health Care
Sources: Berman, 2012; Buck, 2013; CBO, 2006; Keehan, 2008.

The reality of malpractice could not be more different (Rachlinski, 2011). Empirical research over the past 2 decades shows that malpractice settlements are deliberate and rational (Hyman, et al., 2007). The amounts awarded to injured patients generally correlate to the merits of the underlying claims. Settlement amounts are likely to be lowest when the quality of care was high, higher when care quality was too difficult to determine, and highest when care quality was inadequate (Peters, 2007).

FEATURE BOX 9-2

Malpractice Myths

- Premiums for malpractice insurance are skyrocketing, rendering physicians afraid and unable to afford to practice medicine.
- Encouraged by litigious attorneys, undeserving victims sue seeking enormous awards from the insurance industry, hospitals, and physicians who struggle to pay arbitrary awards.
- Victims of medical errors and attorneys always win; physicians always lose.
- Malpractice litigation forces reasonable physicians to close their medical practices.

— Sources: Baker, 2007; Davis; 2011; Pfeffer & Sutton, 2006; Rachlinski, 2011.

The Ethics of Malpractice Reforms

Reform of the malpractice system centers on 3 highly controversial reforms: restricting non-economic damages for medical errors, limiting liabilities for innovative and experimental medical treatments, and setting compensation benchmarks for malpractice awards. Each reform reflects the dual duty of care between the law and ethics (Mantel, 2015). All the reforms focus on what their proponents believe is the most compassionate and just way to compensate patients who are harmed by medical errors.

Restricting Non-Economic Damages

While the ethics surrounding the issue of **non-economic damages** for pain and suffering or emotional distress remain divisive, caps appear to reduce the cost of malpractice insurance. States that have enacted caps on awards for non-economic damages have had significantly lower rates of premium increases for malpractice insurance than those without caps (Danzon, et al., 2004). Although determining non-economic damages is largely left to the discretion of the courts (which generally rely upon expert testimony to calculate such damages), malpractice awards are often based on ratios of 3:1 (Dunne, 2006); for instance, if someone's past and future medical costs and their lost wages or expected income amounts to $100,000, then they may receive $300,000 in non-economic damages. **Economic damages**, such as medical expenses, lost wages, and rehabilitation costs, are not discretionary, as is often claimed by the public (Cohen, 2006). They must be proven in court, such as with documentation and expert testimony.

Most states limit non-economic damages. Supporters maintain that caps balance the occasional need for lawsuits with the larger public need for affordable health care. Opponents argue that damage caps violate the rights of juries to determine malpractice awards (McBride, 2011). Though this opponents' argument has generally been unsuccessful, the challenges continue (Mello, et al., 2008).

Limiting Liability for Innovative and Experimental Medical Treatments

The increasing pace of medical innovation demands a better definition of malpractice. Fairness and justice suggest that the providers of health care should not be solely liable, absent negligence, if cutting-edge treatments do not meet patient expectations. Some maintain that patients have an obligation to carry disability and life insurances to help cover unexpected events in life, such as the event of premature ill health (Lawrence, 2009). Others contend that this expectation is not reasonable for the average person. In other words, the

ETHICAL DILEMMAS 9-2

3. When complicated medical procedures simply do not work out due to their complexity, is it fair and just that health care providers be held accountable to injured patients, or should patients who consented to high-risk medical procedures share some responsibility?

argument is that when patients assume the risk of receiving innovative medical technologies, providers should be liable for anticipated results even in the absence of medical errors or preventable adverse events.

Setting Compensation Benchmarks for Malpractice Awards

Because malpractice has an impact on health care costs, the ethical issue is determining how to manage this impact so that everyone is treated fairly. Research from the University of Pennsylvania and Stanford University on the value of a quality-adjusted life-year is one benchmark that could be used to set economic and non-economic compensation benchmarks in malpractice claims (Wharton, 2011). The **quality-adjusted life-year** method measures the benefit of health care or years of life gained by receiving medical treatment. For instance, the economic value of each year of life for any given patient is about $129,000; therefore, in a case where malpractice costs a patient 10 years of life, a figure of $1.29 million could be used to begin settlement negotiations (Lee, et al., 2009).

Providing a **benchmark** for awards in malpractice lawsuits is important, as it establishes a precedent for how compensation should be set. Increasing numbers of malpractice lawsuits have ended in higher awards that have set new precedents, thereby harming the U.S. health care system; hospitals and physicians pay these costs, and ultimately all patients pay the bill, as these costs are passed on to them (Lee, et al., 2009). Moreover, to avoid being hit with a malpractice lawsuit, physicians practice defensive medicine, ordering excessive diagnostic tests and treatments but without a benefit in terms of quality of care. Defensive medicine in turn drives up the overall cost and overuse of health care (Avraham, 2011; Clark, 2011). In other words, physicians provide excessive care to adjust for uncertainty in malpractice and are rewarded for such behavior by the health insurance system (Smith, 2011). Yet it is easier to blame malpractice concerns for the unnecessary overtreatment of Americans than to address the reasons for allowing medically unjustifiable defensive practices to continue. Professional norms in medicine reinforce physicians' control over decision-making and support their preference for doing more and using new medical technologies to learn as much as possible regardless of cost (Davis, 2011).

Redefining Malpractice by Focusing on Patient Safety Measures

There is no agreement about who should be involved in assuming responsibility for malpractice or whether the health care industry should be responsible for the social costs of health care. While the health care industry should be responsible for the harm to society caused by medical errors (such as increased health care costs to patients harmed), there are limits to the industry's social responsibility. An ethical medical malpractice scheme should not cost the industry more than $50 billion a year, which is the estimated annual cost of malpractice in the United States (CBO, 2006; Reeves, 2011).

Raising the Standards of Care

The law defines the boundaries of liability; health care professionals define the standards of care. Professionals are liable for negligence only if they cause injury as a result of deviating from their self-imposed standards of care. While the ethics of allowing the health care system to set its own standards of care in malpractice actions are debatable, one way to raise the standards of care is through medical advancement based on examining and correcting medical errors and near-mishaps (Memorandum, 2009). But by failing to acknowledge medical errors because of the fear of litigation, the U.S. health care system has implicitly prevented advancement of patient safety measures (MacCourt & Bernstein, 2009). As a result, the standards of care have been artificially depressed, a result that is an extremely weak incentive to prevent medical errors.

ETHICS CASE
Prescriber Liability

Coombes v. Florio
[Accident Victim v. Patient]
877 N.E.2d 567 (Supreme Court of Massachusetts 2007)

Facts: Lyn-Ann Coombes brought this lawsuit on behalf of her 10-year-old son, Kevin, who was killed while standing on the sidewalk with a friend when David Sacca, a patient of Dr. Roland Florio, lost consciousness while driving and struck the boy when his car left the road. Coombes claimed that the accident was a result of the side effects caused by the 8 different medications Florio prescribed to Sacca. By the date of the accident, Sacca was 75 years old and suffered from several serious health conditions, including asbestosis, chronic bronchitis, emphysema, high blood pressure, and metastatic lung cancer. Potential side effects of the combination of medications Florio had prescribed to Sacca at the time of the accident included drowsiness, dizziness, lightheadedness, fainting, altered consciousness, and sedation.

Moreover, combining multiple medications often causes more severe side effects than the side effects resulting from individual use. The standard of care for a primary care physician includes warning elderly or chronically ill patients about the potential side effects of combination medications, and their effect on a patient's cognition. Florio did not warn Sacca about any potential side effects of the various medications prescribed or the possibility that they could impair Sacca's ability to drive.

Legal Analysis: The court made clear that this was an ordinary negligence claim and not a malpractice claim, which would require a direct physician-patient relationship. Florio was found negligent under ordinary common law negligence principles in prescribing multiple medications without warning of their potential side effects. The duty to warn extended to Coombes because his death was a foreseeable consequence of Florio's negligence.

To bring a negligence claim, Coombes had to show the existence of an act or omission that violated a duty owed to her and her son by Florio. A precondition of the required duty is foreseeability; the risk of the harm that occurred must have been foreseeable to Florio. Physicians have a duty of reasonable care, including the duty to warn their patients about side effects when prescribing medications. When the side effects involved are likely to impair the patient's mental capacity, the foreseeable risk of injury in an automobile accident is not limited to the patient alone but also extends to potential accident victims.

Turning to similar cases outside the medical context, the duty of reasonable care extends to all those involved when there is a foreseeable risk of an automobile accident. In addition, it is relevant whether Florio did foresee, or should have foreseen, the particular circumstances even if Sacca was an intermediary actor.

The duty to warn patients about the effects of medications has generally been limited to medications taken in a physician's presence. This time, however, this distinction was not made. Instead, the court concluded that the risk of potential side effects was foreseeable when the physician issued 8 different prescriptions, regardless of where the medications were taken. Finally, the court determined that public policy favors imposing a duty on physicians under these circumstances, reasoning that the duty will not impose a heavy burden on physicians because physicians are already required to warn their patients of side effects from their medications. Additionally, the benefit of imposing the duty is significant because it protects the public from the foreseeable risk of known side effects impairing a patient's ability to drive.

Florio argued that fear of litigation arising from this duty would affect a physician's decision about course of treatment. In response, the court asserted that the duty only involves warning a patient of side effects and does not imply negligence in choosing a course of medical treatment. Florio also argued that increasing malpractice rates are a strong reason against expanding a physician's duty to non-patients, but the court asserted that limiting physician liability to reduce malpractice rates is a decision best reserved for Congress and state legislatures.

When analyzing the facts of this case, the court said that the number and combination of medications Sacca took increased the potential severity of any side effects and the likelihood that his ability to drive would become impaired. The court further concluded that Florio owed a duty to all those foreseeably put at risk by his failure to warn, including Coombes. Finally, the court clarified that Florio was not the cause of Coombes's injury; Sacca was responsible for knowing how he was reacting to the medications he was taking. The jury must decide what degree of responsibility, if any, was shared by Sacca's prescribing physician.

Rule of Law: The duty to warn patients of the side effects of medications extends to non-patients foreseeably put at risk by a failure to warn.

Ethics Issue: Should the duty of physicians and other prescribers to warn patients of the side effects of their medications be expanded to include non-patients as injured third parties?

Ethics Analysis: The fundamental ethical issue is fairness: whether it is fair to assign responsibility for foreseeable consequences to medical professionals and not their patients. This decision presents several ethical dilemmas to physicians and other prescribers. Prescribers are not, in ordinary circumstances, legally responsible for the safety of others on the highway, or elsewhere, based on medical treatments afforded patients. The duty still resides with patients to know how their medications affect them; under this decision, however, some of that duty of care is shifted to prescribers.

This decision also enhances the duty to warn of the potential side effects of all medications. Physicians and other prescribers are now on notice of the consequences of prescribing **drug cocktails**, a multitude of medications prescribed to patients with compound symptoms, any combination of which could affect the cognition of patients. There is no medical certainty of how multiple medications taken together, and over the course of time, might possibly interact with one another in individual patients. Medications are not generally approved for use in treatments where multiple different medications are prescribed together and taken in combination. While some medications have warnings about specific interactions with other medications, clinical trials are not conducted on the effects of every conceivable combination of medications individually prescribed. In clinical practice, this decision raises the possibility that prescribers may reconsider prescribing multiple medications they believe will be effective but have cognitive side effects. Prescribers may also overwarn patients about every conceivable side effect of medications, thereby deterring patients from taking their prescribed medications.

Court's Holding and Decision: Yes, the duty to warn extends to foreseeable third-party non-patients. Massachusetts is the first state to combine the duty to warn with the duty of care, which enlarges the field of liability in the health care industry.

See, e.g., Rothstein & Siegal, 2012; Schwartz & Appel, 2012 (discussing this court decision).

Combining the Duty to Warn with the Duty of Care

The medical profession prescribes 13 different medications on average to patients over the course of their lifetimes (Epstein, 2011). While there may be justifications for physicians and other prescribers prescribing this level of different medications, prescribers have an ethical responsibility to understand how multiple medications, when taken together, may affect their patients. While patients have an obligation to know how their medications affect them, prescribers also have a special duty to warn patients of the health risks involved in taking this many different medications, including the possibility that their cognitive skills may be impaired (*infra, Coombes v. Florio*, 877 N.E.2d 567 (Supreme Court of Massachusetts 2007); Schwartz & Appel, 2012).

Challenges to the Status Quo: Enterprise Liability

It bears repeating: Hospital practices drive medical errors more than the individual failings of health care providers (IOM, 2015 and 1999; Levinson, 2010). Accordingly, hospitals rather than individuals should bear the responsibility for malpractice (Ballerini, 2010). Liability for malpractice against hospitalized patients should rest on the hospital, regardless of the physician's status as an employee, independent contractor, or holder of admitting privileges.

The benefits of **enterprise liability**, placing liability on hospitals and not individuals, far outweigh its disadvantages (IOM, 1999). In this instance, delivery of care to any one patient involves a variety of complex interlinked systems; different providers are involved who are governed by interwoven regulations from provider groups, facilities, states, and the federal government. Factors at every level of these systems affect the incidence of medical errors and the responses that they provoke (Peters, 2007). Serious adverse events are easy to identify; enabling regulatory agencies to detect such medical errors, to hold hospitals accountable, and to assist hospitals in developing best practices to reduce future errors is much harder (IOM, 2015 and 1999). The only apparent disadvantage of enterprise liability is disruption of the status quo: hospitals are content with shifting liability onto individuals and away from the hospital.

With about 90 percent of the nation's malpractice claims arising out of care given inside hospitals (Peters, 2007), enterprise liability should be an area of ever-expanding legal responsibility. Enterprise liability arises under the common law doctrine of agency. Under this doctrine, hospitals are vicariously liable for the activities of health care professionals

ETHICAL DILEMMAS 9-3

4. Physicians and other prescribers owe a duty of care to patients when prescribing medications. Should this duty be expanded to non-patients as injured third parties?

whose conduct results in a medical error. It is only required that the hospital knew of or should have known of the conduct and failed to take immediate and appropriate corrective action. Hospitals, of course, do not want any additional liability shifted to them and often oppose enterprise liability (Rodwin, et al., 2015).

In the rest of the health care industry, the entity that delivers the medical product is vicariously liable for the errors of its workforce. For instance, manufacturers of medical products are liable for defective products, not the individuals on the team who engineered the medical device or developed the drug. Liability is shifted entirely from individuals to the larger business enterprise. As a practical matter, the medical products industry operates under a system in which the enterprise bears all the costs of legal liability. By contrast, most malpractice claims in hospitals are brought against individuals (Peters, 2007).

Ethically speaking, existing laws should be changed to make hospitals liable for the malpractice of health care professionals; it is unfair to hold individuals responsible for malpractice when most claims are the result of system failures rather than individual errors. In other words, hospitals are more often to blame than individuals. Moreover, enterprise liability is a more ethical policy, since patient safety could improve if hospitals were fully accountable for malpractice costs resulting from medical errors (Nelson, et al., 2011). Hospitals would be more likely to implement changes to improve patient safety and reduce the risk of errors and poor outcomes (Mor & Einy, 2012). Based on the likelihood of improved patient safety, enterprise liability should also be extended to medical errors occurring in outpatient facilities and those caused during office visits following hospitalization (McLean, 2011).

Today the emphasis is on managing risks in health care systems, rather than focusing on the performance of individual professionals (IOM, 2015 and 2006). The greatest improvements in patient safety come from greater attention to the processes by which health care is delivered, because most medical errors are due to system breakdown, not individual error (Epstein, 2011). Greater attention to the system of delivery, rather than individual error, enables risk managers to identify those stages of the process at which medical errors are most common and to redesign those stages to make errors both less common and more swiftly and effectively corrected (IOM, 2015 and 1999). For instance, it could be as simple a procedure as repeatedly identifying patients or body parts, or having multiple nurses check the compatibility of blood products before transfusion. Accomplishing this objective requires both the capacity and the willingness to look at the entire health care delivery system; hospitals are better situated to accomplish this than individuals.

Questioning the Price of Physician Independence

The price of physician independence has, in some sense, become the cost of malpractice. A century ago, when physicians feared that their corporate employment would threaten the prevailing model of private practice, they successfully lobbied for enactment of **corporate practice prohibitions**, laws that preclude non-physicians from interfering with the practice of medicine. Under corporate practice prohibition laws, financial or other arrangements cannot influence the medical judgment of physicians (Robertson, 2014). Physicians have resisted corporate influence since the enactment of these prohibitions, most recently in their alliance with patients to limit the power of managed care organizations (Avraham, 2011).

Private practice physicians have always been different from other highly trained professionals in the medical products industry; physicians have historically been treated as independent contractors, not employees, and have valued the independence associated with this status (Robertson, 2014). Yet there is no ethical justification for imposing **vicarious liability** on hospitals for the conduct of physicians who are exclusively hospital-based, but not on attending physicians who have independent medical practices but attend to their patients in hospitals (Jacobs, 2008). It is not fair for hospitals to escape liability for the medical errors of attending physicians who are generally treated as independent contractors rather than as employees of the hospital (Avraham, 2011). Physician independence has a cost, however, which is the liability of malpractice.

Risk Management of Systems, Not Individuals

The most promising patient safety initiatives are led by hospitals that operate under a system of enterprise liability (IOM, 1999). For instance, Harvard University Health Services, Kaiser Permanente, and the University of Pennsylvania Health System are leading efforts to improve diagnostic accuracy and avoid medical errors. They are employing new tools in the health care industry, like computer decision-support systems, to help order correct tests, institute proper follow-up plans, obtain complete medical histories, and perform adequate physical exams (Fineberg, 2009). Hospitals at the forefront of patient safety voluntarily disclose medical errors and also employ and insure their attending physicians (IOM, 2015 and 1999).

Experience Rating of Malpractice Insurance

Hospitals can be experience-rated, unlike individual physicians (Nelson, et al., 2011). Insurance rates for hospitals are based on actual claims, or their history of malpractice, rather than on the demographics of their geographic community, as is the case for individual physicians. Experience rating creates a powerful incentive to reduce medical errors (*see* Raper, 2013). Health care entails far too many medical errors not to take advantage of this potential to enhance patient safety.

While hospitals have an obvious financial reason to resist the transfer of legal responsibility entirely onto their shoulders, the issue is more complex for physicians. On the one hand, enterprise liability would take physicians out of the front line in malpractice litigation as liabilities shifted to hospitals (Hill, 2010). On the other hand, physicians have traditionally opposed expanding hospital vicarious liability because they fear it will mean greater interference in their medical decision-making. But this objection evokes a health care world that has long since passed. With rare exceptions, physicians already function as part of complex systems (Baker, 2007). Surely, physicians understand

ETHICAL DILEMMAS 9-4

5. Would elimination of individual liability foster more ethical behaviors by making it easier for hospitals to institute a blame-free culture that encourages open discussion of medical errors and near-misses more freely?
6. Could eliminating individual liability dilute the effort individual health care professionals make to avoid medical errors?

the importance of building those systems carefully. Sooner or later, the law must adapt (Dworkin, 2013). In hindsight, it is now obvious that the law's delay in doing so has been harmful for both physicians and patients, keeping individual physicians in the forefront of malpractice litigation and depriving patients of the safety systems that enterprise liability will produce.

The New Ethics of Malpractice

The dysfunctional malpractice system that neither deters medical errors nor consistently recognizes and pays injured patients must be replaced. Ethically speaking, if medical errors and preventable adverse events can be prevented through good organizational design and management, it is unethical not to act. The principles of compassion and justice demand a better allocation of the nation's limited health care resources (Held, 2007). The new health care reform laws are now refusing to pay the $4.4 billion in annual costs that Medicare always paid for adverse events (Levinson, 2010), which is a significant beginning to reform of the U.S. malpractice system.

ETHICAL OR UNETHICAL DECISION

Medical Negligence

Ethics Issue: *Do pharmacies have a duty and ethical obligation to protect the public from customers who may be abusing prescription medications?*

Ethics Analysis: Yes, pharmacies are the designated gatekeepers for the dispensing of prescription medications. Pharmacists have an ethical obligation to take action once they suspect one of their customers may be abusing narcotics. As a matter of public policy, pharmacies should protect the general public from any potential harm that could be caused by a pharmacy customer's narcotic abuse. Dispensing pharmacists have a duty to investigate narcotic prescription abuse, protecting customers and non-customers alike from possible injury.

Ethics Analysis: No, without a mandate from the state legislature requiring that a pharmacy take specific actions when it suspects that one of its customers may be abusing prescription medications, a pharmacy is only obliged to fill valid prescriptions from physicians and other prescribers. There is no special relationship between a pharmacy and the public.

Court's Holding and Decision: Pharmacies do not owe a duty to third parties with whom they have no direct relationship. The act of dispensing prescription medications does not create a legal duty; therefore, the standards of care imposed on pharmacies do not extend to the public and unidentified third parties.

— *Sanchez, et al. v. Wal-Mart Stores, et al.,* 221 P.3d 1276 (Supreme Court of Nevada 2009). *See* Todd, 2010 (discussing this court decision).

CHAPTER SUMMARY

- While the principles of compassion and justice support taking responsibility for reducing the risk of malpractice, the same principles balance the competing interests of individual victims of medical errors and the health care industry that harmed them while seeking to help them.
- Malpractice liability arises when a health care provider engages in negligence or intentionally injures a patient; negligence occurs when the conduct of hospitals or physicians falls below the professional standards of care, established by law, for the protection of patients against unreasonable risk of harm or injury.
- Although the public is convinced that there is a health care crisis due to excessive malpractice verdicts, this belief is not factually supported.
- While the ethics surrounding the issue of non-economic damages caps remain highly controversial, caps appear to reduce premium growth for malpractice insurance.
- The benefits of enterprise liability far outweigh its disadvantages, but there are a number of differing opinions on who should bear responsibility for malpractice.
- With about 90 percent of the nation's malpractice claims arising out of care given inside hospitals, enterprise liability should be an area of ever-expanding legal responsibility.
- A century ago, when physicians feared that their corporate employment would threaten the prevailing model of private practice, they successfully lobbied for enactment of corporate practice prohibitions, laws that preclude non-physicians from interfering with the practice of medicine.
- The most promising patient safety initiatives are led by hospitals that operate under a system of enterprise liability; hospitals at the forefront of patient safety voluntarily disclose medical errors and also employ and insure their attending physicians.

REFERENCES

Avraham, R. (2011). President Obama's first two years: A legal reflection: Private regulation. *Harvard Journal of Law and Public Policy, 34,* 543–637.

Baker, T. (2007). *The medical malpractice myth.* Chicago, IL: University of Chicago Press.

Ballerini, J. E. (2010). The apparent agency doctrine in Connecticut's medical malpractice jurisprudence: Using legal doctrine as a platform for change. *Quinnipiac Health Law Journal, 13,* 317–376.

Berman, M. L. (2012). Improving patient safety and providing fair compensation. *New England Law Review, 46,* 409–415.

Buck, I. D. (2013). Caring too much: Misapplying the False Claims Act to target overtreatment. *Ohio State Law Journal, 74,* 463–513.

CBO (Congressional Budget Office). (2006). *Background paper: Medical malpractice tort limits and health care spending.* Washington, DC: CBO.

Clark, B. (2011). Using law to fight a silent epidemic: The role of health literacy in health care access, quality, and cost. *Annals of Health Law, 20,* 253–327.

Classen, D. C., et al. (2011). Global trigger tool shows that adverse events in hospitals may be ten times greater than previously measured. *Health Affairs, 30*(4), 581–589.

CMS (Centers for Medicare and Medicaid Services). (2015). *Medicaid and CHIP applications, eligibility determinations, and enrollment report.* Baltimore, MD: CMS.

___. (2015a). Medicare enrollment: Hospital insurance and/or supplemental medical insurance programs for total, fee-for-service and managed care enrollees.

Cohen, H. (2006). *Report for Congress: Medical malpractice liability reform: Legal issues and fifty-state survey of caps on punitive damages and noneconomic damages.* Washington, DC: Congressional Research Service.

Danzon, P. M., et al. (2004). *The "crisis" in malpractice insurance.* Research paper prepared for the Seventh Annual Brookings-Wharton Conference on Financial Services: Public Policy Issues Confronting the Insurance Industry, at the Wharton School of the University of Pennsylvania, Philadelphia, PA.

Davis, F. H. (2011). Medical liability and the disclosure-offer approach: Transforming how Arkansans should think about medical malpractice reform. *Arkansas Law Review, 64,* 1057–1093.

Dunne, B. (2006). *Theobald v. University of Cincinnati*: Reforming medical malpractice in Ohio: A survey of state laws and policy impacts. *Journal of Law and Health, 20,* 69–93.

Dworkin, R. (2013). *Justice for hedgehogs.* Cambridge, MA: Belknap Press.

Epstein, R. (2011). President, Advanced Clinical Science & Research and Chief Clinical R&D Officer, Medco Health, Capstone speaker at the 17th Annual Wharton Health Care Business Conference: Leadership in an evolving global market. Philadelphia, PA.

Epstein, R. A., & Hyman, D. A. (2013). Fixing Obamacare: The virtues of choice, competition, and deregulation. *New York University Annual Survey of American Law, 58,* 493–537.

Fineberg, H. V. (2009). President, IOM (Institute of Medicine), President's address at the 2009 Annual Meeting: Health reform: Beyond health insurance. Washington, DC.

Frakes, M. D. (2015). The surprising relevance of medical malpractice law. *University of Chicago Law Review, 82,* 317–391.

Goodman, J. C., et al. (2011). The social cost of adverse medical events, and what we can do about it. *Health Affairs, 30*(4), 590–595.

Grunebaum, A., et al. (2011). Effect of a comprehensive obstetric patient safety program on compensation payments and sentinel events. *American Journal of Obstetrics and Gynecology, 204*(2), 97–195.

Gupta, A., & Sao, D. (2011). The constitutionality of current legal barriers to telemedicine in the United States: Analysis and future directions of its relationship to national and international health care reform. *Health Matrix: The Journal of Law-Medicine, 21,* 385–442.

Held, V. (2007). *The ethics of care: Personal, political, and global.* New York, NY: Oxford University Press.

Hill, J. W. (2010). Law and the healthcare crisis: The impact of medical malpractice and payment systems on physician compensation and workload as antecedents of physician shortages: Analysis, implications, and reform solutions. *University of Illinois Journal of Law, Technology and Policy, 2010,* 91–156.

Hyman, D. A., & Silver, C. (2012). Medical malpractice and compensation in global perspective: How does the United States do it? *Chicago-Kent Law Review, 87,* 163–197.

Hyman, D. A., et al. (2007). Do defendants pay what juries award? Post-verdict haircuts in Texas medical malpractice cases. *Journal of Empirical Legal Studies, 4,* 3–68.

IOM (Institute of Medicine). (2015). *Improving diagnosis in health care.* Washington, DC: IOM.

___. (2006). *Preventing medication errors.*

___. (1999). *To err is human. Building a safer health system.*

Jacobs, A. J. (2008). Duty to third parties in employment references: A possible poisonous potion for the health care industry? *Journal of Contemporary Health Law and Policy, 24,* 312–360.

Kaiser Commission on Medicaid and the Uninsured. (2013). *The Medicaid program at a glance.* Washington, DC: Kaiser Family Foundation.

Keehan, S., et al. (2008). Health spending projections through 2017. *Health Affairs, 27*(2), 146–155.

Lawrence, M. J. B. (2009). In search of an enforceable medical malpractice exculpatory agreement: Introducing confidential contracts as a solution to the doctor-patient relationship problem. *New York University Law Review, 84,* 850–879.

Lee, C. P., et al. (2009). An empiric estimate of the value of life: Updating the renal dialysis cost-effectiveness standard. *Value in Health, 12*(1), 80–87.

Levinson, D. R. (2010). *Adverse events in hospitals: National incidence among Medicare beneficiaries.* Washington, DC: U.S. Department of Health and Human Services, Office of the Inspector General.

MacCourt, D., & Bernstein, J. (2009). Medical error reduction and tort reform through private, contractually-based quality medicine societies. *American Journal of Law and Medicine, 35,* 505–559.

Mantel, J. (2015). A defense of physicians' gatekeeping role: Balancing patients' needs with society's interests. *Pepperdine Law Review, 42,* 633–726.

Marzen, C. G. (2014). Public policy considerations concerning insurance bad faith and residual market mechanisms. *Baylor Law Review, 66,* 388–424.

McBride, G. (2011). Medical malpractice insurance in Illinois: Where we've been and where we're going after *Lebron v. Gottlieb Memorial Hospital,* 930 N.E.2d 895 (Ill. 2010). *Southern Illinois Law Journal, 35,* 517–541.

McLean, T. R. (2011). The schizophrenia of physician extender utilization. *Annals of Health Law, 20,* 205–251.

Mello, M. M., et al. (2008). Policy experimentation with administrative compensation for medical injury: Issues under state constitutional law. *Harvard Journal on Legislation, 45,* 59–105.

Memorandum for the President. (2009, July 1). Information on medical malpractice reform options from Nancy-Ann DeParle, Director, White House Office of Health Reform and Susan Sher, Health-Care Adviser, to President Barack Obama.

Mor, S., & Einy, O. R. (2012). Quality of health care and the role of relationships: Bridging the medico-legal divide. *Health Matrix: The Journal of Law-Medicine, 22*, 123–138.

Moses, S. (2007). A just society for the elderly: The importance of justice as participation. *Notre Dame Journal of Law, Ethics and Public Policy, 21*, 335–362.

Nelson, III, L. J., et al. (2011). Medical liability and health reform. *Health Matrix: The Journal of Law-Medicine, 21*, 443–519.

NQF (National Quality Forum). (2011). *Serious reportable events in healthcare: A consensus report.* Washington, DC: NQF.

OIG (Office of the Inspector General). (2010). *Adverse events in hospitals. National incidence among Medicare beneficiaries.* Washington, DC: U.S. Department of Health and Human Services: OIG.

Ostrov, G. (2012). Former Chief Executive Officer, Bausch + Lomb, Capstone speaker at the 18th Annual Wharton Health Care Business Conference: Innovation in a Changing Health Care Environment. Philadelphia, PA.

Perrecone, F. A., & Fabiano, L. R. (2006). Medical malpractice: Emerging issues and the effect of tort reform: The fleecing of seriously injured medical malpractice victims in Illinois. *Northern Illinois University Law Review, 26*, 527–552.

Peters, P. G. (2007). What we know about malpractice settlements. *Iowa Law Review, 92*, 1783–1833.

Pfeffer, J., & Sutton, R. I. (2006). *Hard facts, dangerous half-truths and total nonsense: Profiting from evidence-based management.* Boston, MA: Harvard Business Review Press.

Rachlinski, J. J. (2011). Evidence-based law. *Cornell Law Review, 96*, 901–922.

Raper, S. E. (2013). Announcing remedies for medical injury: A proposal for medical liability reform based on the Patient Protection and Affordable Care Act. *Journal of Health Care Law and Policy, 16*, 309–351.

Reeves, M. (2011). Senior Partner & Managing Director, The Boston Consulting Group, Capstone speaker at the 17th Annual Wharton Health Care Business Conference: Leadership in an Evolving Global Market. Philadelphia, PA.

Restatement of the Law, Third: Torts. (2013). Negligence: §§ 440–442. Washington, DC: American Law Institute.

Robertson, C. B. (2014). Private ordering in the market for professional services. *Boston University Law Review, 94*, 179–234.

Rodwin, M. A., et al. (2015). Why the medical malpractice crisis persists even when malpractice insurance premiums fall. *Health Matrix: The Journal of Law-Medicine, 25*, 163–225.

Rothstein, M. A., & Siegal, G. (2012). Health information technology and physicians' duty to notify patients of new medical developments. *Houston Journal of Health Law and Policy, 12*, 93–136.

Sawicki, N. N. (2010). Character, competence, and the principles of medical discipline. *Journal of Health Care Law and Policy, 13*, 285–323.

Schumpeter, J. A. (2008). *Capitalism, socialism, and democracy* (3rd ed.). New York, NY: Harper Perennial Modern Classics (Original work published 1942).

Schwartz, V. E., & Appel, C. E. (2012). Reshaping the traditional limits of affirmative duties under the Third Restatement of Torts. *John Marshall Law Review, 4*, 319–351.

Smith, C. (2011). Between the Scylla and Charybdis: Physicians and the clash of liability standards and cost cutting goals within accountable care organizations. *Annals of Health Law, 20*, 165–203.

Studdert, D. M., et al. (2006). Claims, errors, and compensation payments in medical malpractice litigation. *New England Journal of Medicine, 35*(19), 2024–2033.

Tenner, S., & Ringel, L. (2014). A medical complication compensation law: Improving quality healthcare delivery while providing for injury compensation. *Health and Biomedical Law Society, 10*, 55–100.

Timm, N. T. (2010). From damages caps to health courts: Continuing progress in medical malpractice reform. *Michigan State Law Review, 2010*, 1209–1234.

Todd, A. (2010). Scope of Nevada pharmacies' duty of care: Nevada Supreme Court rules that pharmacies have no legal duty to third parties for harm caused by customer misuse of prescription drugs—*Sanchez v. Wal-Mart Stores. American Journal of Law and Medicine, 36*, 277–279.

Van Den Bos, J., et al. (2011). The $17.1 billion problem: The annual cost of measurable medical errors. *Health Affairs, 30*(4), 595–603.

Van Detta, J. A. (2009). Dialogue with a neurosurgeon: Toward a dépeçage approach to achieve tort reform and preserve corrective justice in medical malpractice cases. *University of Pittsburgh Law Review, 71*, 1–70.

Wharton School at the University of Pennsylvania. (2011). Cost-effective medical treatment: Putting an updated dollar value on human life. *Knowledge@Wharton.*

Widman, A. (2010). Liability and the health care bill: An alternative perspective. *California Law Review Circuit, 1*, 57–69.

Wong, M. (2010). Coverage for kidneys: The intersection of insurance and organ transplantation. *Connecticut Insurance Law Journal, 16*, 535–570.

Our Health Care System's Ethical Response to Vulnerable Members of Society

Part V takes a systematic look at the intellectually disabled, people suffering from the effects of Human Immunodeficiency Virus and Acquired Immune Deficiency Syndrome (HIV/AIDS), and victims of gun violence. The emphasis is on the costs of health care for the most vulnerable members of our society.

Courtesy of Peter Blanck

CHAPTER 10

Mental Health

"Over the course of the twenty-first century, our challenge is to strive toward national policies that promote inclusion of all people, with and without disabilities, based on values of individual worth, fairness, and justice."

— **Peter Blanck**, Professor, Syracuse University School of Law, Chairman of the Burton Blatt Institute

LEARNING OBJECTIVES

After completing this chapter, the reader should be able to:

1. Summarize the ethical principles of human dignity and personal autonomy underlying the health care system's response to mental illness and disability.
2. Understand how the epidemiology of mental health reveals the magnitude of severe mental disorders in the United States.
3. Explain disease burdens and understand why depression ranks as more of a burden to the U.S. health care system than any other illness.

KEY TERMS

Best interests standard	Disease burden	Mentally disabled
Competency	Gross negligence	Negligence
Competency standard	Health care costs	Order of conditions
Continuing obligation (principle of)	Intellectually disabled	Severe mental disorders
	Involuntary commitment	Sub-average intellectual
Dangerous mental disorder	Mental disorders	functioning
	Mental health	Substituted judgment
Deinstitutionalization	Mental illness	standard

Abuse and Neglect of the Mentally Disabled

Ethics Issue: *Should state advocates for the mentally disabled be able to sue another state agency for ongoing violations of federal law?*

In Brief: Two **mentally disabled** residents in state-run institutions in Virginia, with impaired capacities to appreciate the nature and consequences of their conduct, died in what the Virginia Office of Protection and Advocacy alleges were examples of extreme abuse and neglect while in the custody of state officials. One resident who had severe mental disorders died 8 days after ingesting 2 latex gloves. A second resident, despite complaining that he was unable to breathe, suffocated while institution staff attempted to place him in restraints. Government advocates were denied access to patients and records in the course of investigating the deaths and injuries. This case has major implications for all agencies that work to protect the rights of people with **mental disorders**, which are defined as biologically based health conditions characterized by alterations in thinking, mood, and behavior.

— *Virginia Office for Protection and Advocacy v. Stewart,* 131 S.Ct. 1632 (U.S. Supreme Court 2011). (*See Ethical or Unethical Decision* at the end of the chapter for discussion of this ethics issue.)

Introduction

People with mental illnesses or diagnosable mental disorders (including, among others, Alzheimer's disease, bipolar disorder, borderline personality disorder, major depression, obsessive compulsive disorder, panic disorder, posttraumatic stress disorder, and schizophrenia) have less access to and receive poorer quality health care than people without such ailments (Horvitz-Lennon, et al., 2006). The limits of psychiatry's understanding of mental illness and its therapeutic abilities have repeatedly distorted care for the mentally disabled (Fish, 2012).

Mental illness is the leading **disease burden** on the U.S. health care system (WHO, 2014) in terms of both mortality and morbidity. This time-based measure quantifies the burden of disease and risk factors based on the years of life lost due to premature death, or mortality, and time lived in states of morbidity, or less than full health. These combined years lost are the result of premature mortality as well as time lost as a result of the presence of disease. Disease burden is a term in health economics, not to be confused with the term **health care costs**, which simply means the amount that is paid or charged for health care. Obesity, smoking, and gun violence often advance the onset and increase the severity of disease burdens and are the nation's leading health care costs.

Yet, it takes tragedies like the Tucson, Arizona, massacre, where 20 people were shot by Jared Lee Loughner, a suspended college student, to focus public attention on the nation's response to mental illness (Brusca & Ram, 2010). Many view mental illness as one of, if not the most, overlooked health issues in the United States. While the National

Institute of Mental Health estimates that only a small percentage of the 44 million Americans suffering from mental illness and disability has a **dangerous mental disorder**, it is this mentally disabled population at imminent risk of causing harm that should concern everyone.

In Tucson, students and faculty at Pima Community College feared for their safety as Loughner's erratic behavior led to a series of encounters with campus police in the months before he was suspended from school and told he could not return without a mental health clearance. Loughner never consulted with a mental health professional to discuss his symptoms and was never diagnosed with a mental disability, and his life abruptly spiraled out of control. Two months after his college suspension, he bought a gun at a supermarket and used it to leave 6 dead and 14 wounded, including U.S. Representative Gabrielle Giffords. Though mass shootings are committed by mentally ill people, a key contributor to this phenomenon is the disconnection in the health care system that provides most of the care for people with severe mental disorders. There was no medical intervention for Loughner; he never received treatment, and no one felt responsible for monitoring his mental health. *See generally* Eaton, et al., 2011.

Defining Mental Illness and Disability

The law has rarely doubted the existence of mental illness and disability, but it has struggled with its definition and its disposition (Erickson, 2008). Mental health and mental illness are points on a continuum of behavior. For instance, erratic behavior may often appear harmless in a vacuum, but if it is brought into the context of a continuum where there is a continuous series of unpredictable erratic actions that depart from expected standards of behavior at any time, it takes on a far more harmful character. Loughner's erratic behavior at Pima Community College months before he shot 20 people at a supermarket is a pertinent example of a continuum.

The first Surgeon General's report ever issued on this topic set forth the most accepted definition. **Mental health** is a condition of successful performance of mental function, resulting in productive activities, fulfilling relationships with other people, and the ability to adapt to change and cope with adversity (U.S. Surgeon General, 2011). **Mental illness**, in contrast to mental health, is less broadly defined.

All diagnosable mental illnesses are defined by the American Psychiatric Association, which developed the *Diagnostic and Statistical Manual of Mental Disorders*, currently in its fifth edition and known by mental health professionals as the *DSM-5*. The *DSM-5* contains diagnostic codes and detailed descriptions for all recognized mental illnesses. Although there may not be biological tests to diagnose every different mental illness, fairly standard methods of diagnosis exist (APA, 2013). Mental health professionals often meet with their patients to discuss their symptoms and to have them describe how they have been feeling and how these feelings have affected their daily lives; after this type of consultation, the mental health professionals consult the *DSM-5* (Nadim, 2009).

The general public may be inclined to think of mental disorders as character flaws, but they are legitimate illnesses that respond to specific treatments, just as other physical health conditions respond to medical interventions (Erickson, 2008). Yet, the unemployment rate of people with mental disorders continues to be 3 to 5 times higher than among those with no mental disorder (Hensel & Jones, 2005). At the same time, people today are more likely to hold stigmatizing attitudes toward the mentally disabled than their counterparts nearly half a century ago because of the lack of community support to address their needs (*see* Blanck, et al., 2007). Simultaneously, there has been a weakening of ethical norms that define society's role in caring for the mentally disabled.

Before the mid-1960s, the mentally disabled were likely to be institutionalized in state psychiatric hospitals when they exhibited erratic behavior. Discoveries of sub-human conditions at large residential state-run psychiatric hospitals, as well as the discovery that many patients were institutionalized who did not require intensive inpatient care, led to the **deinstitutionalization** movement of the 1960s and 1970s. Today, most long-term state psychiatric hospitals have been replaced by community-based care, where people who previously would have been institutionalized are no longer continuously supervised by mental health professionals. The result is that the mentally disabled are now often imprisoned when they do not take their psychotropic medications and their behavior departs from expected standards. In other words, deinstitutionalization has led to criminalization of the mentally ill (Wren, 2010). More recently, the advent of restrictions on the availability of health insurance coverage for inpatient psychiatric treatment has further reduced rates of hospital treatment.

Epidemiology of Mental Disorders

Even though mental disorders are widespread in the population, the main burden of **severe mental disorders** is concentrated in a much smaller proportion (Tovino, 2009). This subpopulation involves people with one or more of the following mental illnesses with acute anxiety, mood, or psychotic symptoms: severe autism, bipolarism, manic depression, schizoaffective disorder or schizophrenia, as well as persistent forms of delusions, major depression, panic, posttraumatic stress disorder, and obsessive-compulsions (Entzeroth, 2011; Johnston, 2012; Riley, 2011; Wasicek, 2010). While the National Alliance on Mental Illness estimates that mental illness affects 1 in 5 families in the United States, only about 6 percent of Americans suffer from a severe and persistent mental disorder (or 1 in 17 Americans). All the same, treatments for severe mental disorders are highly effective; between 70 and 90 percent of the people treated with a combination of medications, psychosocial treatments, and support have significant reduction of symptoms and improved quality of life. Without treatment, as illustrated in **TABLE 10-1**, the consequences of mental illness for the individual and society are staggering.

TABLE 10-1 Consequences of Mental Illness

Homelessness
Inappropriate incarceration
Co-occurring substance abuse
Wasted lives
Unnecessary disability
Unemployment
Suicide

Treatment Shortage for Severe Mental Disorders

Mental health is supposed to be a component of the U.S. health care system, yet people with mental disorders have largely been excluded from the current health care system and rely on public safety net programs (Rosenbaum, et al., 2011). Although federal law mandates that health insurers treat mental illness in the same manner as physical illness, government funds to treat mental disorders are declining and, in many instances, disappearing altogether (Dougherty & Merrick, 2011). In 2013 alone, an estimated 5.1 million adults reported an unmet need for mental health care (CBHSQ, 2014). The United States is increasingly facing a shortage of treatment slots, with mental health facilities generally running at full capacity with growing wait lists (Chorney, 2014). The result of this treatment shortage is that it is now difficult to find a bed for a person with a severe and persistent mental disorder who needs to be hospitalized. In 1955 there was 1 psychiatric bed for every 300 Americans; today, there is 1 psychiatric bed for every 3,000 Americans (Torrey, et al., 2014; Broches, 2013). This situation is the result of American society's increasing embrace of free market ideology over the last generation or so (Wacquant, 2009; Whitman, 2012). Treatment shortages for severe mental disorders are occuring because the United States abandoned policies of government intervention in favor of market solutions (Harcourt, 2012).

Only the most severe cases of mental disorders involving court-mandated **involuntary commitments** are being accepted to receive treatment (Bloom, 2010; Boldt, 2014; House Report, 2007). People with severe mental disorders are committed to hospitals or mental health facilities on an involuntary basis if treatment is essential to their welfare and their judgment is so impaired that they are unable to understand the need for such treatment. Less acute mental disorders and neuroses, including chronic depression, phobias, or any other type of disabling emotional or mental condition, are left to be dealt with by the general health care system, including by health care professionals not trained to treat mental disorders and by the nation's emergency rooms.

Global Burden of Disease Study

The Global Burden of Disease Study, originated in the early 1990s by the World Health Organization in collaboration with the World Bank and Harvard University, was the first effort to look systematically at the magnitude of mental illness and its impact on wellness and productivity (Wren, 2010). The magnitude of mental illness and its treatment shortage points to the need for a mental health system that recognizes society's responsibilities to the mentally disabled. As illustrated in **FEATURE BOX 10-1**, the urgent need to create a system from today's non-system arises from the devastating social impact of mental illness on individuals, society, and the U.S. health care system (Shamash, 2011).

Growing Burden of Depression Disorders

Depression, a common debilitating illness, is the leading mental disorder in the United States, with the rate of this disease state growing every year (WHO, 2014). People with major depression (where feelings of sadness, anger, and frustration interfere with their daily lives) share common psychosocial and environmental factors: alcoholism, bereavement at a young age, insufficient family structure, physical and sexual abuse, and trauma (Shipler, 2005). The question is whether it is ethical for a society to neglect the mental health of such a large portion of its population.

FEATURE BOX 10-1

The Social Impact of a Non-System for Mental Health

- Mental illness is the second leading cause of premature mortality.
- Four of the 10 leading causes of disability in the United States are mental disorders.
- Major depression will be the leading cause of disability from mental illness by 2020.
- Mental disorders account for more than 15 percent of the overall burden of disease from *all* causes and slightly more than the burden associated with all forms of cancer.

— Sources: Bernstein & Koppel, 2008; WHO, 2014.

High Incidence of Severe Mental Disorders among the Homeless

There is a high incidence of mental illness among the homeless, with approximately one-third of the estimated 600,000 homeless suffering from a severe and persistent mental illness (Nadim, 2009; USICH, 2012). Although most homeless people with mental disorders do not need to be institutionalized, and can live in the community with appropriate supportive housing options, many are unable to obtain access to supportive housing or other treatment services (NCH, 2009). Consequently, they are over 10 times more likely to be incarcerated than the general population (Greenberg & Rosenheck, 2008). Many people question the ethicality of jailing people for quality-of-life offenses, including public nuisance offenses such as disorderly conduct, urinating in public, and noise violations (Ali, 2014). Such behaviors are often symptoms of mental illness and disability (Tars, et al., 2014).

Connection between Incarceration and Mental Disorders

The United States has returned to the conditions of the 1840s, where the mentally disabled are incarcerated as opposed to being hospitalized (Torrey, et al., 2014). As illustrated in **FEATURE BOX 10-2**, involuntary commitments by the courts and a safety-conscious society have left the prisons and jails in the United States unable to control their inflow and outflow (Cummings, 2010; Erickson, 2008). For the first time in history, 1 out of every 100 Americans is imprisoned on any given day (Pew, 2009; Vera, 2013). This is a higher percentage of the general population imprisoned than in any other country in the world (Walmsley, 2014).

Regardless of how many people are in prison at any given time, and even if it does so for good reason, the government has an ethical obligation when it imprisons more than 2.2 million Americans (Glaze & Kaeble, 2013). When more than 1.2 million incarcerated people in the United States have a severe and persistent mental disorder, a grave health care problem is being ignored (Osher, et al., 2012). This surge in imprisonment of the mentally disabled appears to be a phenomenon caused by the breakdown of the nation's mental health system. Today, it seems that the nation's largest mental health facilities are urban jails.

It is clear that severe mental disorders among the incarcerated are a significant health problem. This problem is exacerbated when the U.S. health care system encounters

FEATURE BOX 10-2

Mental Disabilities and Incarceration

- There are more than 3 times more mentally ill people in jails and prisons than in hospitals and mental health facilities.
- About 1 out of every 5 prisoners has a severe and persistent mental disorder, a number that has tripled since the mid-1980s.
- An estimated 360,000 people with severe mental disorders are placed in American prisons and jails each year, about three-quarters of whom also have co-occurring substance abuse disorders.
- The incidence of schizophrenia in state prisons is 3 to 5 times higher than in the general population, and 2 to 3 times higher in local jails than in the general population.
- Imprisoned adolescents are about 10 times more likely to suffer from severe mental disorders and psychosis than their peers.

— Sources: Glaze & Kaeble, 2013; NIC, 2012; Osher, et al., 2012; Torrey, et al., 2014.

mentally ill prisoners after they have been released to their communities, many having acquired a variety of sexually transmitted and communicable diseases during their incarceration (Malave, 2014; Quinn, 2009). The potentially devastating effects after incarceration are yet another reason why there is an ethical obligation to mentally disabled prisoners. It is possible that public health arguments have the potential to move society to pay the costs for mental health care in prisons out of clear self-interest, whereas heretofore the public has been unwilling to do so based solely on the values of beneficence, human dignity, and justice (Kohn, 2014).

States facing limited financial resources for social programs prefer to allocate taxpayer funds to the community's economic development, education, or health care, as opposed to their criminal justice systems (Bernstein, 2008). Even when the criminal justice system does receive government funding, when a choice has to be made between allocating funds for law enforcement or corrections, funds generally go to the police, not to jails or prisons (Brink, 2005). Without federal mandates and oversight, the nation's correctional system will continue to deteriorate.

Mental Illness and Disability Within Specific Populations

Two more specific populations merit attention: college-age young adults and returning combat veterans, as illustrated in **FEATURE BOX 10-3**. At issue is whether an ethical society, and the institutions within that society, have a social obligation to address mental illness and disability.

College-Age Adults

With mental illness and disability usually striking during adolescence and young adulthood, free preventive care is now available for this population, including depression screenings to

FEATURE BOX 10-3

The Magnitude of Mental Illness and Disability In College-Age Adults

- One in 5 college-age young adults has a severe and persistent mental disorder that disrupts their daily lives.
- Less than 1 in 4 with severe mental disorders will actually seek treatment.
- Five percent of the total college-age young adult population seeks treatment.

In Returning Combat Veterans

- About 1 in 5, or about 300,000, returning veterans from Iraq and Afghanistan have severe and persistent mental health disorders, generally PTSD or major depression.
- Roughly half of the returning veterans who need treatment for PTSD or depression seek it, but only slightly more than half of those who seek treatment obtain quality, evidence-based care.
- The number of returning veterans diagnosed with PTSD is growing by about 8,000 per year.

— Sources: Bibelhausen, et al., 2015; Blanco, et al., 2008; Brown, et al., 2015; Kern, 2015; Tanielian, et al., 2008.

ensure accurate early diagnosis and treatment (Landro, 2011). While all ages are susceptible to depression and mental illness, college-age young adults are especially vulnerable because their lives are generally characterized by rapid intellectual and social development (Ruan, et al., 2008). Contrary to common perceptions, the overall rate of mental illness and disability is not different between college-attending individuals and their non-college-attending peers (Blanco, et al., 2008). It is just that mental illness may be more recognizable in the college population undergoing a major life transition, as one of the markers of depression is an inability to cope with change. *See* Bernstein & Koppel, 2007.

Some colleges and universities offer student privacy waivers to their students so parents can have more oversight of their children's behavior and health conditions (Waldman, 2015). Other schools continue to encourage parents to take a hands-off approach. Yet, there is no ethical consensus on how much access and influence parents ought to have regarding the mental health records of college-age adults, particularly when parents are paying the tuition (Riggs, 2014).

ETHICAL DILEMMAS 10-1

1. Is it ethical for colleges and universities to offer student privacy waivers to their students so parents can have more oversight and control, or should schools encourage parents to take a hands-off approach by encouraging the independence of college-age students?

Returning Combat Veterans

The stigma attached to mental illness and disability in the military is pervasive and often prevents service members from seeking needed care during their military service (OIG, 2008). The U.S. Department of Veterans Affairs (VA) is overwhelmed by the seriousness of the mental health needs of the veterans returning from Afghanistan, Iraq, and other conflict zones (Bilmes, 2011). Early evidence suggests that the mental toll of these deployments may be disproportionately high compared with the physical injuries of combat, which may be the result of prolonged exposure to combat-related stress over multiple deployments (Tanielian, et al., 2008).

One in 5 returning combat veterans from Iraq and Afghanistan is suffering from posttraumatic stress disorder (PTSD), and approximately 6,600 commit suicide each year (Wilson, 2010). Preventing suicides and treating PTSD and depression among returning veterans is an increasing problem for the VA and the U.S. health care system (CBO, 2010; DOD, 2007). With personnel deployed around the world as part of the U.S. efforts to combat global terrorism, countless thousands have been exposed to traumatic events during combat and many have returned home with a variety of psychological and mental injuries (O'Brien, 2008). Nevertheless, combat veterans who are discharged from the military service for PTSD are not always entitled to disability coverage for treatment of the disorder that led to their discharge.

ETHICS CASE

Liability for Deaths Caused by Mentally Ill Veterans after Discharge from Treatment

DeJesus v. U.S. Department of Veterans Affairs
[Parents of Murder Victims v. VA]
479 F.3d 271 (U.S. Court of Appeals for the 3rd Circuit 2007)

Facts: Alejandro DeJesus, an unemployed, homeless Vietnam veteran with a history of substance abuse and domestic violence, voluntarily entered a VA inpatient program where he was diagnosed with intermittent explosive disorder, a condition characterized by repeated violent outbursts. He was prescribed medications to control his condition. Later, DeJesus was diagnosed with only mild depression. Accordingly, the VA assigned DeJesus to psychotherapy and substance abuse counseling.

After a few months of inpatient treatment, the VA recommended DeJesus for a transitional residence program that provided mental and physical health care to homeless veterans. The VA failed to inform the program about his intermittent explosive disorder and did not release his inpatient records, even though the records would have alerted the transitional program that DeJesus suffered from violent outbursts and suicidal ideations. While in the transitional program, DeJesus threatened another resident with a knife, leading the VA to recommend his discharge.

Before DeJesus left the transitional residence program, he gave away all his possessions and shredded his clothing, common signs of suicidal thoughts and impending suicidal action. Despite his behavior, none of the staff who participated in DeJesus's discharge followed involuntary commitment or emergency psychiatric intervention procedures. Eighteen hours after leaving the transitional program, DeJesus charged into his estranged wife's apartment and shot and killed 2 of their children and 2 other children before turning the gun on himself.

His wife and the mother of the other deceased children filed a claim against the VA, alleging that by negligently discharging and subsequently failing to recommit DeJesus, even when he overtly posed an imminent threat, the VA caused the wrongful deaths of their children. Further, they claimed that the VA negligently failed to warn them about DeJesus's mental state.

Legal Analysis: The court determined the standard of care by analyzing whether the VA had a duty to warn third parties about DeJesus's mental health status. While mental health providers have an affirmative duty to warn an intended victim if a patient poses a severe danger of violence, this duty does not extend to a situation involving no specific threat of immediate harm to readily identifiable victims.

The court also considered whether the VA was grossly negligent. **Gross negligence** is a form of fault-based conduct, where there is substantially more than ordinary carelessness, inadvertence, laxity, or indifference, which falls below the standard of care established by law for the protection of others against unreasonable risk of harm or injury. Here a state mental health law provided immunity to mental health providers for treating and discharging mentally ill patients from treatment in the absence of willful misconduct or gross negligence. While providers are generally protected from liability, they must refrain from gross negligence in the treatment and discharge of mentally ill patients. In this case, DeJesus received inpatient treatment at a VA facility and the VA participated in the decision to discharge him from a transitional residence program for homeless veterans, thus imposing on the VA a duty to refrain from gross negligence in DeJesus's treatment and discharge.

In evaluating the gross negligence standard, the court determined that several actions demonstrated the VA's gross negligence: (1) DeJesus's complete medical history, including his diagnosis as having an intermittent explosive disorder, was never transmitted to his treatment providers; (2) the VA failed to recognize DeJesus's violent outbursts leading up to the shootings as consistent with his particular mental illness and disability; and (3) the VA failed at both preventing DeJesus's release and effecting his recommitment despite his suicidal tendencies. In finding that the VA's actions met the standard for gross negligence, the court held that the VA was liable for breaching its duty and thus was liable for DeJesus's post-discharge actions.

Rule of Law: The VA is liable in the same manner and to the same extent as private parties when gross negligence is involved. In this case, the VA violated its duties by discharging and failing to recommit a severely mentally ill veteran.

Ethics Issue: How should the rights of patients be balanced against the rights of the public when it comes to potentially dangerous mentally ill patients?

Ethics Analysis: If the U.S. health care system is inadequate to meet the needs of people with severe mental disorders, this could threaten the health of both those people and other people who may become victims of crime committed by those people. Ethical dilemmas arise in determining how best to prevent harms from ever occurring to the public when it is not possible to predict with any degree of certainty the dangerousness of people with specific mental disorders. Mental health providers face conflicting demands when trying to respond to the treatment needs of potentially violent and dangerous patients with severe mental disorders while maintaining security in their treatment programs and protecting the public. Mental health providers must take responsibility for their own treatment decisions and discharge actions; problems arise when people with severe mental disorders enter treatment and the providers fail to adequately treat their propensity for violence.

One side of this debate focuses on society's right to be protected from violence. Mental health providers are subject to charges of failing to control patients with severe mental disorders when these patients commit acts of violence. Treatment providers owe an ethical obligation, as well as a broad duty, to exercise reasonable care in the treatment and discharge of mentally disabled patients to protect against reasonably foreseeable events. Restrictions placed on the freedom of violent patients with severe mental disorders must somehow be counterbalanced by providing them with increasing levels of high-quality treatment.

Another side of this debate focuses on the inadequate treatment of people with severe mental disorders resulting from an overburdened system. Various diagnoses (such as intermittent explosive disorder or depression or co-occurring substance abuse) may not always be sufficient to predict a propensity to violence before discharge from treatment. This lack of understanding about a person's mental condition and symptoms means that the mere diagnosis of a disorder is not sufficient to predict dangerousness (Frank & Glied, 2006). Diagnosis of a mental disorder reflects the existence of a harmful abnormality in mental functioning, but it does not always describe how that abnormality will affect individual behavior.

Yet other values come into play on both sides of this debate about the rights of the public versus the rights of individuals. First is the principle of **continuing obligation**; under this ethical principle, once a mental health provider begins a course of treatment for a person with a severe mental disorder, care cannot always be terminated when the patient is discharged or released from an institutional setting (Jones, 2007). There is an ethical obligation for continuity of care to minimize the harshness that can confront the mentally ill from suddenly living outside an institution, which can exacerbate the illness.

Second is the recognition that the purpose of mental health treatment is to make patients better off than they were before treatment. This principle is a progressive step beyond the principle of continuing obligation; it moves to improving the overall situation to the benefit of both patients and society. This shift significantly opens the door to expanding the human right to health to include right to mental health (Wiley, 2014).

A third ethical principle is that there is a right to the highest practicable standards for treatment of people with severe mental disorders, both for those patients and the public at large (Jubilut, 2007). It is different, and far better, to provide people with dangerous mental disorders with treatment in mental health facilities intended for that purpose than to subject them to imprisonment (Whitman, 2012). Many states and providers of mental health care do not even claim to follow this standard, much less actually follow it. If these 3 values were mandatory, patients would have a better chance of success following their treatment.

Court's Holding and Decision: Yes, the VA is liable for the wrongful death of the 4 children. It breached the standard of care for mental health providers and was grossly negligent in deciding that DeJesus should be discharged from a transitional residence program when he should have been involuntarily recommitted.

See Bard, 2005; Martin, 2007 (discussing this court decision).

This decision could potentially affect the mental health sector of the health care system by recognizing an ethical obligation and imposing an affirmative duty to refrain from negligence in treatment and discharge of the mentally disabled. **Negligence**, in this instance, is defined as any fault-based conduct that falls below the standards of care established by law for the protection of the public against unreasonable risk of harm or injury. Mental health providers may be responsible for the actions of patients they release, especially when people with severe mental disorders are a known or foreseeable potential danger not only to themselves but also to others (Martin, 2007).

Intellectually Disabled

Intellectually disabled people with **sub-average intellectual functioning** describes people with significant limitations in adaptive skills (such as communication, self-care, and self-direction) and limitations that affect their ability to understand and process information, to abstract from mistakes and learn from experience, to engage in logical reasoning, to control impulses, and to understand the reactions of others (Pifer, 2010). The intellectually disabled are one of the most socially stigmatized groups mental health providers encounter (Stein & Stein, 2007; Smith, 2014). This is because their disability renders them less able either to assert their human rights or to protect themselves with regard to health care decisions (Frank, 2014; Gostin & Gable, 2004).

Defining Intellectual Disabilities

The term *intellectually disabled* does not define a distinct class of people; in fact, individual abilities may differ widely, and there is no recognized assessment method firmly grounded in scientific evidence (Freedman, 2014). This chapter uses the term *intellectually disabled* to describe what has historically been referred to as *mentally retarded*. The term *intellectually disabled* focuses on intellectual capabilities instead of mental functions and categorizes the condition as a disability as opposed to an illness (Frank & Glied, 2006).

Current clinical definitions of the intellectually disabled require not only sub-average intellectual functioning, but also significant limitations in adaptive skills to care for themselves. Although people who meet this clinical definition are often readily identifiable, significant sub-average intellectual functioning is defined as an IQ standard score of approximately 75 to 70 or below (Schalock & Borthwick-Duffy, 2009). Such intellectual deficiencies diminish the personal culpability of intellectually disabled people for their actions. Intellectual disabilities also lead to confusion when health care providers are facing questions such as informed consent for life-sustaining treatments, end-of-life care, and involuntary commitments and hospitalizations.

Medical Decision-Making

There is a critical shift occurring with the social values and ethical principles regulating intellectual disabilities. There is a shift from values where society is expected to assume responsibility for care of the intellectually disabled to values where adults are expected to modify risks by avoiding unhealthy lifestyle choices, such as drinking alcohol and smoking tobacco during attempts to conceive and pregnancy, by avoiding knowingly passing on genes that carry a high risk of birth defects, and by obtaining early noninvasive prenatal testing and diagnoses that can minimize the possibility of the birth of children with severe intellectual disabilities (Robertson, 2011).

ETHICAL DILEMMAS 10-2

2. If families alone had to bear the costs of caring for children born prematurely with severe intellectual disabilities, would potential parents be more likely to have genetic screening for genes known to cause severe intellectual disabilities or prenatal care that can prevent premature births or diagnose fetal abnormalities early in a pregnancy?

During this transition, courts are struggling with allocating the cost of health care for the intellectually disabled. There are ongoing fierce debates about the ethical obligation and responsibility of parents to be more solicitous about prenatal care and terminating pregnancies where severe disabilities are evident in the fetus (Donley, 2013; Petersen, 2015). Others maintain that respect for the life of an abnormal fetus should be of vital concern to society. One of the most recent cases to tackle the issue of medical decision-making on behalf of the intellectually disabled was a class action lawsuit in the District of Columbia.

ETHICS CASE
Abortion Decisions on Behalf of Intellectually Disabled People

Doe ex rel. Tarlow v. District of Columbia, et al.
[Incompetent Intellectually Disabled People v. District Mental Health Agency]
489 F.3d 376 (U.S. Court of Appeals for the District of Columbia 2007)

Facts: This is a class action lawsuit comprised of a class of intellectually disabled people who live in District of Columbia facilities and receive health care services from the district. The plaintiffs were all subjected to non-emergency surgery; 2 of the plaintiffs received abortions. They never had the mental capacity to make medical decisions for themselves. By definition, the plaintiffs have never had the capacity for personal autonomy or the ability to form values or preferences. The policy at issue was adopted to regulate the health care of intellectually disabled people in the district, including consent for elective surgical procedures such as abortions. For intellectually disabled people who have always lacked the mental capacity to make informed decisions, the policy authorized the District's mental health agency to make health care decisions on behalf of them if: (1) 2 licensed physicians certified that the proposed treatment was in the best interests of the intellectually disabled person (**best interests standard**); (2) attempts were made to provide an explanation of the proposed treatment to the intellectually disabled person; and (3) no guardian, family member, or other close friend or associate was available to consent or withhold consent.

The Health Care Decisions Act is the District of Columbia law claimed to be inconsistent with the policy at issue. It provides that when making a health care decision on behalf of an incompetent person, the decision must be based on the **substituted judgment standard**, or the most ascertainable decision that the patient would have made if the patient were competent. If the wishes of the person are unknown and cannot be at all ascertained, then the decision can be made on a good faith belief as to the best interests of the incompetent person.

Legal Analysis: The court began its analysis by observing that the Health Care Decisions Act implicitly distinguishes between 2 categories of people who lack mental capacity. There are people who once possessed the mental capacity to make decisions (such as those in a coma) and people who have always lacked the mental capacity to make decisions (such as minors and the intellectually disabled). For people who once had the mental capacity to make decisions, health care decisions must be based on the most likely decision people would have made for themselves, if those wishes can be ascertained, or the substituted judgment standard. For patients who have never had the mental capacity to make decisions, health care decisions must be based on the best interests of the patient, or the best interests standard.

The court then held that the policy regulating the health care of intellectually disabled people did not infringe upon their human rights. While acknowledging that the policy did not consider the wishes of people who have never possessed the mental capacity to make decisions, the court held that this does not violate their rights because acting on the wishes of such people could result in erroneous health care decisions, with harmful or even deadly consequences. People who have always lacked the mental capacity to make decisions do not have a right to have their wishes considered.

Rule of Law: The human rights of incompetent people who once possessed the mental capacity to make decisions are distinct from the human rights of intellectually disabled people who never had such capacity.

Ethics Issue: Should the wishes of incompetent intellectually disabled women be considered when abortions are performed?

Ethics Analysis: This decision involves 2 categories of human rights: the rights of intellectually disabled people and the rights of the public by way of the mental health providers who care for the intellectually disabled. The ethical conflict centers on the principles of personal autonomy and human dignity that give intellectually disabled women the same human rights as competent women, specifically the reproductive right to decide whether to carry an unintended pregnancy to term or to terminate the pregnancy. While mental health providers are limited in their ability to infringe upon these protected human rights, they nonetheless retain some ability to control and protect the intellectually disabled women under their care based on the principle of beneficence, including serious consideration of the women's ability to rear and support a child.

One position believes that the human rights of women have to be weighed against the interests of society. For intellectually disabled women, the right to procreate is regarded as a dubious and uncertain right when society will be entrusted to care for their unplanned children. There is also the implicit consideration of genetic impairments being passed on to future generations. When a pregnant woman is so profoundly disabled that she is entirely incapable of making decisions and wholly reliant on others for her care, the best interests standard may restrict her reproductive rights based on the near impossibility of the woman ever being able to fulfill her parental role.

Regardless of societal costs, a second position holds that decision-making for intellectually disabled pregnant women should be guided by the principle of substituted judgment, which is based on the ascertainable wishes of the disabled woman. Societal interests have limits, and invasive medical procedures such as abortions cannot be justified when it would be against the wishes of the woman. For proponents of this viewpoint, this promotes the underlying values of personal autonomy better than the standard of best interests.

A third position sees flexibility in both the best interests and substituted judgment standards. The most humane way you can treat somebody is to treat them appropriately for what their needs are. Greater weight may be given to different considerations depending on the facts of each situation, such as the likelihood that the woman had the **competency** or possessed sufficient mental capacity to understand her sexual situation or whether her pregnancy was the result of rape. Another consideration is the woman's ability to function normally and care for a child on her own or with the father. This position considers what it means to lack capacity to consent to an abortion. Even a low intelligence quotient does not permit the inference that all intellectually disabled women lack the capacity to consent to abortions or to care for a child. In other words, simply because a woman is intellectually disabled, it does not mean that she lacks the capacity to make an abortion decision or to care for a child. The 2 inquiries are separate. What is required is that each intellectually disabled woman understand that an abortion will result in her inability to bear the potential child she is carrying. An abortion must be in the woman's best interests as opposed to for society's benefit, as the first position would have it.

The fallacy of applying the ascertainable wishes standard, which is based on the principle of substituted judgment, lies in the very definition of substituted judgment. Substituted judgment ensures that the decisions made are the decisions based on the values and preferences of the disabled women if they were competent. This does not explain how to deal with women who were never competent to make their wishes known in the first place, since there is no way to determine what they would have chosen had they been competent. If the intellectually disabled women never had prior values and preferences, the substituted judgment standard cannot apply, because the intellectually disabled women never had coherent concepts of self and never developed value systems (Carle, 2005). Where intellectually disabled women are concerned, substituted judgment is a poor choice of words to describe their abortion decisions; whatever is decided based on their ascertainable wishes is pure conjecture or fabrication if they were never competent to make decisions.

It should be noted that the court never needed to take a position on the question of the government paying for the abortions of intellectually disabled pregnant women. While government health insurance programs have no ethical obligation or legal duty to pay for elective abortions, no mention was made as to funding under the circumstances of this case. Thus, the court could base its decision on the less controversial law-based analysis of standards of decision-making for others. But if government insurance will not pay for an abortion, then intellectually disabled women with no money or private insurance for the procedure do not have a true choice of preferences.

Court's Holding and Decision: No, the policy was consistent with the Health Care Decisions Act and the best interests standard is appropriate.

See, e.g., Amar & Strumolo, 2007; Jorgensen, 2009; Ryan, 2008 (discussing this court decision).

While the substituted judgment standard, based on women's ascertainable wishes, and the best interests standard, based on choosing the highest quality care to be administered, almost always result in the same outcome for competent adult women who want the best care possible, this is not always the case for intellectually disabled women. Intellectually disabled women may wish to make decisions that have harmful consequences; they lack the ability to know what is in their best interests. Therefore, pregnant women who never met a **competency standard**, showing that they are capable of functioning normally and possess sufficient mental capacity to make and express informed, autonomous choices on matters of importance, are incapable of knowing what decisions are in their best interests (Lamparello & MacLean, 2014).

Involuntary Commitments

It has been said that the government of a nation can be judged by the way it treats its institutionalized (Churchill, 1949/1986). By this measure, the United States is still in the Middle Ages (Davoli, 2010). Although most mental disorders are thought to be biologically based or due to head trauma, commitment laws are different for mentally ill and physically ill patients. Most mental illnesses and severe mental disorders are no different from physical illnesses, yet the mentally disabled are often subject to mandatory treatment while the physically ill are allowed to decide whether to seek treatment.

The Involuntary Civil Commitment Process

Involuntary civil commitment laws allow mentally ill people to be committed to a hospital or mental health facility for treatment on an involuntary basis. The 2 major phases of the process are the petition and prehearing detention period, and the involuntary civil commitment hearing. Mentally ill people enter the process through an emergency court order requiring that they be taken into custody and examined. Following the evaluation, they are either released or detained for additional evaluation and treatment under a temporary detention order. Courts may order involuntary civil commitments for treatment only if there is clear and convincing evidence that individuals pose a danger to themselves or others and are largely incapable of caring for themselves (Harris, 2015; Pfeffer, 2008).

Expanding Definitions of Dangerousness to Pedophiles and Pregnant Women

The ethics of extending involuntary commitment procedures to convicted pedophiles who have served their criminal sentences (Kaplan, 2015), as well as to pregnant women who smoke or are abusing alcohol or drugs, in order to safeguard their fetuses' interests, are 2 controversial areas currently being debated by Congress, state legislatures, and lower trial courts (Borgmann, 2014; Stutz, 2013). To date, neither issue has been satisfactorily dealt with by the highest federal or state appellate courts, or the U.S. Supreme Court.

Defining Dangerous Mental Disorders

Whereas the mentally disabled with dangerous mental disorders were once ignored by being forced to remain inside mental hospitals, they are now ignored through civil commitment laws and criminal imprisonment (Collins, 2009). As addressed earlier, while the United States incarcerates at a higher rate than any other advanced country, the nation also has fewer beds for the mentally ill than any other advanced country (Harcourt, 2012). Moreover, increased incarceration over the last generation has been directly paralleled by a decline in the institutionalization of the mentally ill (Whitman, 2012). Even as U.S. prisons house people who would be hospitalized in other economically advanced democratic countries (Harcourt, 2012), the law continues to struggle with the underlying involuntary commitment procedures for people who are dangerous to themselves and to society.

ETHICAL DILEMMAS 10-3

3. Like the commitment of the mentally disabled, should pregnant women who smoke or misuse illegal drugs or alcohol retain their independence or face incarceration, detention, or hospital confinement so as to protect the health of their fetuses?

ETHICS CASE
Involuntary Commitment of Mentally Ill People

Ernst J. v. Stone
[Mentally Ill Patient v. State Commissioner of Mental Health]
452 F.3d 186 (U.S. Court of Appeals for the 2nd Circuit 2006)

Facts: Ernst suffered from chronic schizophrenia. During a psychotic episode in which he heard voices and thought an elderly man was the devil, Ernst attacked the man, leaving him with severe bite wounds to his hand and genitalia. Ernst was charged with assault and burglary. Ernst pled guilty to the assault charge. In accordance with criminal procedure, psychiatrists examined Ernst and determined that although he suffered from schizophrenia, at the time of the examination he was not suffering from a dangerous mental disorder. The psychiatrists recommended that Ernst be required to obtain treatment in an outpatient setting. The court agreed with the psychiatrists' recommendation and ordered Ernst to be conditionally discharged, subject to a 5-year order of conditions. One of the conditions was that Ernst was required to remain in outpatient treatment 5 days per week to treat his severe mental disorders.

Two years later, Ernst was arrested for criminal trespass and harassment. He pled guilty to harassment and was sentenced to conditional discharge. The following year, Ernst was arrested again for criminal trespass, although he was not prosecuted for this offense. As time passed, Ernst's behavior became increasingly violent. A year later, and within days of the expiration of his 5-year order of conditions, Ernst, while living in a residential treatment center, took a female social worker hostage and threatened to sexually assault her. After this incident, he was hospitalized on an emergency basis. Soon after, Ernst's order of conditions was extended and his involuntary commitment was extended.

A month later, Ernst was transferred to another psychiatric hospital where he continued his violent behavior. The second hospital requested a 3-month period of retention, based upon clear and convincing evidence that Ernst was mentally ill and posed a substantial threat of harm to himself and others. Additionally, his order of conditions was extended for a second time, this time for an additional 3 years. After 3 months of psychiatric treatment, staff determined that Ernst had developed a dangerous mental disorder and sought a court order for him to be committed to a secure psychiatric facility.

Legal Analysis: Certain protections exist for involuntary civil commitment, such as requiring clear and convincing evidence that mentally ill persons pose a danger to themselves or others. Extensive evidence must be presented to show that the mentally disabled are substantially more likely than not to engage in dangerous behavior. *Mentally disabled*, for purposes of an involuntary commitment, means: (1) a person is currently suffering from a mental disorder; (2) treatment in an in-patient facility is essential to the person's welfare; and (3) the person's judgment is so impaired that he or she is unable to understand the need for such treatment.

Courts must first order a psychiatric examination to determine the person's current mental condition, followed by a hearing to determine the appropriate treatment. Based on the findings at the hearing, the person is placed in one of three tracks based on a preponderance of the evidence. The treatment decision requires a lower standard of proof than the commitment decision. Evidence is merely required to show that a mentally ill person is more likely than not to demonstrate one of three behaviors: (1) track 1 people are determined to suffer from a dangerous mental disorder and must be committed to a secure psychiatric facility; (2) track 2 people are determined not to be suffering from a dangerous mental disorder, but are nonetheless mentally ill; and (3) track 3 people are neither mentally ill nor suffering from a dangerous mental disorder.

Track 2 people are remanded to the custody of a mental health agency subject to an order of conditions. An **order of conditions** means a court order directing a mentally ill person to comply with a prescribed treatment plan, or any other condition the court determines to be reasonably necessary or appropriate. Orders of condition are valid for 5 years, except for good cause shown; the court may extend the period for an additional 5 years.

Track 3 people are either discharged unconditionally or discharged subject to an order of conditions, which generally requires them to enroll in outpatient treatment. State law recognizes the possibility that a person in track 2 or track 3 may, during the course of outpatient care, develop a dangerous mental disorder and require commitment in a secure psychiatric facility or hospital. For a court to order recommitment, the person must have a dangerous mental disorder. *Dangerous mental disorder* means that a person currently suffers from a mental disorder and because of such condition, he or she currently constitutes a physical danger to self or others.

In civil commitment proceedings, states must prove the elements of a mental disorder and dangerousness by no less than clear and convincing evidence. This evidentiary standard concerns only the initial confinement of mentally ill people, and does not specifically address the standard of proof applicable to recommitment or release proceedings. States may not continue to confine people who remain dangerous but who no longer suffer from any mental disorder.

Rule of Law: It is not unreasonable to provide for the recommitment of mentally ill people under the low preponderance of the evidence standard; this policy does not violate their human rights.

Ethics Issue: At what point it is acceptable to violate the human rights of disabled individuals in favor of the rights of the public?

Ethics Analysis: Once individuals become candidates for civil commitment, the decision to commit them depends on whether the magnitude of the danger they pose to society exceeds the deprivation imposed by their involuntary commitment (Frank & Glied, 2006). The ethical dilemma centers on defining the standards as to what constitutes dangerousness and the need for treatment that complements the traditional danger to self standard (Collins, 2009).

One side of this debate relies on determinations of dangerousness to justify involuntary civil commitments by either danger to others or danger to self. For involuntary commitments, it is argued that the government may act as the guardian of people suffering from mental disorders until they are able to take care of themselves.

The other side of this debate objects to civil commitment based on preventive detention because predicting future dangerousness is unreliable by almost any mental health standard. Moreover, the process of involuntary commitment dehumanizes the mentally disabled by depriving them of their liberty based on something they may or may not do in the future. In addition, there is no accepted legal definition of the term *dangerousness* in order to indicate the type of danger a person may pose.

Danger alone has never constituted an offense. Therefore, it seems that if dangerousness is not an offense, or an illness, or even a symptom, dangerousness should not justify involuntary commitments. The ethical dilemma is whether or not involuntary commitments are justified because they benefit people who are mentally ill and they serve to protect society.

A third side to this debate views the involuntary civil commitments process as an issue of economics and the nation's refusal to provide universal health insurance coverage. Most people who are subject to involuntary civil commitment are poor and financially distressed without access to quality mental health care (or lawyers qualified to represent the mentally disabled). While the mentally ill are likely to respond well to treatment, without treatment they are at an increased risk of hospitalization. Although individuals with a mental disorder are likely to experience success with treatment, less than half the adults with a severe and persistent mental disorder actually receive the treatment they need (CBHSQ, 2014). Cost is the number one reason why people do not receive treatment; people with a severe and persistent mental disorders are more likely to be uninsured and less likely to have private insurance (Collins, 2009).

Nothing would do more to close the gap in mental health care than providing appropriate health insurance coverage for this population; some would say there is an ethical imperative to do so. As a society, the underlying social structures that keep the mentally disabled marginalized must be examined. Ultimately, the process of civil commitment needs to recognize the role of economics (Collins, 2009).

Court's Holding and Decision: Yes, a lower standard of proof may be used to involuntarily hospitalize people suffering from a dangerous mental disorder who are determined to be not responsible by reason of their mental disorder, as opposed to the higher standard required for the mentally disabled who are not dangerous.

See, e.g., Halbrook, 2015 (discussing this court decision).

Although the mentally disabled may be recommitted by procedure using a lower standard than required in criminal proceedings, it is not clear that this mental health policy will remain in place indefinitely. Ethically speaking, this issue has not been settled (Erickson, 2008).

Conditional Release of the Mentally Disabled

Mental illness and disability alone cannot justify hospitalization or confinement indefinitely (Frank & Glied, 2006). Nor can people be involuntarily confined because of an antisocial personality absent a showing of dangerousness, because being antisocial is not a recognized mental disorder. Involuntary confinement cannot be justified indefinitely absent public safety concerns or the need for treatment; thus, the mentally disabled can be conditionally released.

ETHICS CASE
Conditional Release from Involuntary Commitment

United States v. Franklin
[Federal Government v. Involuntarily Committed Patient]
435 F.3d 885 (U.S. Court of Appeals for the 8th Circuit 2006)

Facts: Gordon Franklin was involuntarily committed for 12 years due to a mental disorder. When he was released from hospitalization due to improvement in his mental condition, his release was subject to 7 conditions requiring him to comply with a prescribed treatment regimen. In addition, he was required to comply with the standard conditions of probation.

A year following his release, Franklin called the probation office and first spoke to a receptionist, and then to his probation officer, Mark Davy, who told Franklin he should discuss revocation of his conditional release with Davy or Davy's supervisor, not the receptionist. In response, Franklin became agitated and upset with Davy and made death threats directed toward Davy, Davy's supervisor, and the judge who had ordered his commitment.

Franklin's conditional release was immediately revoked on the grounds that he violated the required conditions of his release, and he was recommitted. Franklin then filed a motion for his release and requested a mental examination. A clinical psychologist examined him and concluded that he continued to suffer from bipolar disorder and met the criteria for involuntary commitment. A risk assessment report compiled by a panel of mental health experts found that despite Franklin's reported compliance with his prescribed treatment regimen, his mental condition had deteriorated to a point where his medications were no longer adequate. The report concluded that because Franklin had resisted increasing the dosage level of his medications, his release would pose a substantial safety risk to himself and others. Franklin testified that he regretted his comments to Davy, that he was coping with his mental disorder, and that he would not pose a danger to himself or others as long as he continued taking his prescribed medications. The court determined that although there was no direct evidence that Franklin did not follow his prescribed treatment regimen, his sudden behavioral change supported that conclusion. Franklin's conditional release was revoked and he was involuntarily recommitted.

Legal Analysis: Franklin claimed there was insufficient evidence to conclude that he had violated the requirements of his release by failing to take his prescribed medications. The government maintained that Franklin violated his probation by breaking the law when he threatened the people who had ordered his commitment. Franklin countered that he could not be recommitted on these grounds because the revocation of a conditional release is only allowed when a person fails to comply with the prescribed treatment regimen.

The court held that when a person suffering from mental illness and disability is released from hospitalization, additional non-health conditions, such as probation, may be imposed that are ancillary to the prescribed treatment regimen, as long as the additional conditions are related to the person's mental illness and disability and reasonably necessary to protect the safety of others. In addition, a conditional release may be revoked for violation of non-health conditions, at least when the violation flows from the person's mental illness and disability and demonstrates that continued release presents a danger to others.

A conditional release may be revoked after determining a person's failure to comply with a prescribed treatment regimen if the continued release would create a substantial risk to the safety of others. Although the law does not specifically mention what recourse is available when a released person violates a non-medical condition, the court reasoned that Congress must have contemplated a mechanism for enforcing violations of non-health conditions. Otherwise, released persons could blatantly violate such conditions and courts would be powerless to revoke their release, even if the violations demonstrated that the persons posed a danger to the public.

Applying these principles to this situation, the court found that the condition of probation was related to Franklin's mental illness and disability and was reasonably necessary to ensure his safety and the safety of others, at least as far as it required Franklin to refrain from violating probation standards by threatening the lives of the people who had ordered his commitment. The court revoked Franklin's conditional release, finding that his violation of probation flowed directly from his mental illness and disability and demonstrated a threat to himself and others.

Rule of Law: When people with a mental disorder are released from an involuntary commitment, additional conditions may be imposed on their release that are unrelated to compliance with their prescribed treatment regimens; their release may be subsequently revoked and they may be recommitted for violating such non-medical conditions.

Ethics Issue: Should the release of a mentally ill patient from involuntary confinement be conditioned upon fulfilling requirements, other than the requirement to comply with a prescribed treatment regimen?

Ethics Analysis: Public pressure to confine people with severe mental disorders will probably preclude rational alternatives to recommitment. The mentally disabled are often inextricably trapped in a revolving door of petty crime, involuntary commitment, release, homelessness, and recommitment. People with severe mental disorders generally do not have adequate rehabilitative services available to them during their confinement, and few mental health providers have transition programs to assist with reorientation to the community following lengthy hospitalizations. Fewer yet have access to newer psychiatric medications, because of the costs. This unjust situation results from a paucity of effective humanitarian programs for treating the mentally disabled (Dougherty & Merrick, 2011).

Increasingly, non-medical conditions other than the requirement to follow prescribed treatment regimens are being added to the conditional release of mentally ill patients from involuntary commitment. Good behavior, specified curfews, abstention from drugs or alcohol, as well as employment and education instructions, may be added to conditional releases. Non-medical conditions are almost always added for patients who were found not responsible for their criminal actions by reason of their mental disorder. This decision extends standard conditional release policies and then goes one step further by providing for recommitment as a permissible mechanism for enforcing non-medical conditions—a potentially broad reach.

Court's Holding and Decision: Yes, the conditional release of mentally ill patients from hospitalization may be revoked and patients may be involuntarily recommitted for failure to comply with non-medical conditions other than the requirement to follow prescribed treatment regimens.

No citing references.

Uncertain, Changing, and Competing Social Values

Health care ethics are a reflection of society. The current values of society are reflected in the treatment of people with a mental disability. When there is more than one accepted and forceful social value at work, ethics becomes a complex matrix as society attempts to accommodate competing values in a variety of situations. As a result, some ethical principles may succeed in a given situation and fail in another. Competing values may change over time and may vary on a particular issue as time passes. In perhaps no other area of ethics is this interplay between competing values reflected more clearly than in the laws and ethical principles pertaining to the treatment of mental disorders.

The mentally disabled are the most disadvantaged and misunderstood patient group of our time (Fazel, 2011). Because of their actions, people with a mental disability become a focal point of both the mental health and legal systems. Ordinarily, the processing of criminal actions is routine. However, when mental illness and disability become an issue, either as part of the initial criminal prosecution or subsequent to conviction, involuntary commitment and treatment by mental health providers becomes a matter of great concern. Despite the medical progress in treatment, this disadvantaged group remains worse off than most others in American society (Frank & Glied, 2006). What the future will be depends on stakeholders working together toward a shared vision of inclusion of all people, with and without mental disorders, based on values of individual worth, fairness, and justice (Hill & Blanck, 2009).

ETHICAL OR UNETHICAL DECISION

Abuse and Neglect of the Mentally Disabled

Ethics Issue: *Should state advocates for the mentally disabled be able to sue another state agency for ongoing violations of federal law?*

Ethics Analysis: Yes, states should do away with their exemption from prosecution when residents in the custody of state officials are found to have been abused and neglected. Moreover, vulnerable populations with mental disorders who are abused by state officials should have federal remedies against such abuse and neglect regardless of whether a state consents to be sued. Accordingly, Congress should provide for enforcement of federal laws that seek to protect people who are mentally ill.

Ethics Analysis: No, state advocates should resort to avenues other than litigation, such as administrative challenges, to secure compliance from other state agencies. State advocates seeking to protect abused and neglected residents in the custody of state officials should not have the right to prosecute other state agencies; this is a waste of taxpayer money.

Court's Holding and Decision: The Court determined that federal courts may hear lawsuits against state officials brought by another agency of the same state for abuse and neglect of the mentally disabled. In this instance, the state's refusal to produce requested records violated federal law. State law gave state advocates the power to sue state officials.

— *Virginia Office for Protection and Advocacy v. Stewart*, 131 S.Ct. 1632 (U.S. Supreme Court 2011). *See, e.g.*, Gunn, 2014; Mariner, 2012; Preis, 2013 (discussing this court decision).

CHAPTER SUMMARY

- The state of mental health care in the United States is regressive as opposed to progressive; people with mental disorders have less access to and receive poorer quality health care than people without mental disorders, making mental illness and disability the leading disease burden on the U.S. health care systems.
- Mental disorders are not character flaws; they are legitimate illnesses that respond to specific treatments, just as other physical health conditions respond to medical interventions.
- Mental health is supposed to be a component of the U.S. health care system, yet because of their illnesses, people with mental disorders have largely been excluded from the current health care system and rely on public safety net programs.

- There is a high incidence of mental illness and disability among the homeless, with approximately one-third of the estimated 600,000 homeless suffering from severe and persistent mental disorders.
- The stigma attached to mental illness and disability in the military is pervasive and often prevents service members from seeking needed care during their military service.
- College-aged adolescents are another group among whom mental illness is more prevalent due to the amount of growth and change that typically occurs during that stage of life.
- Intellectually disabled people with sub-average intellectual functioning are one of the most socially stigmatized groups that mental health providers encounter.
- Whether involuntary commitment procedures should be extended to convicted pedophiles who have served their criminal sentences, as well as to pregnant women who choose to smoke or abuse drugs or alcohol during their pregnancy, in order to safeguard their fetuses' interests, are 2 controversial areas currently being debated by Congress, state legislatures, and lower trial courts.
- The mentally disabled with dangerous mental disorders were once ignored by being forced to remain inside mental hospitals, often with limited freedom of movement within the institutions themselves; now they are ignored through civil commitment laws and criminal imprisonment.
- The overarching ethical dilemma in this chapter is about the human rights of mentally disabled patients versus the right of society to be protected from potential danger.

REFERENCES

Ali, F. (2014). Limiting the poor's right to public space: Criminalizing homelessness in California. *Georgetown Journal on Poverty Law and Policy, 21*, 197–249.

Amar, J., & Strumolo, A. R. (2007). Medical decision on behalf of incompetent patients: Federal court upholds law allowing medical decisions for incompetent patients: *Doe ex rel. Tarlow v. District of Columbia. American Journal of Law and Medicine, 33,* 703–708.

American Psychiatric Association. (2013). *Diagnostic and statistical manual of mental disorders* (5th ed.). Arlington, VA: American Psychiatric Publishing.

Bard, J. S. (2005). Re-arranging deck chairs on the Titanic: Why the incarceration of individuals with serious mental illness violates public health, ethical, and constitutional principles and therefore cannot be made right by piecemeal changes to the insanity defense. *Houston Journal of Health Law and Policy, 5,* 1–73.

Bernstein, E. (2008, October 16). How new law boosts coverage of mental care. *Wall Street Journal,* p. A1.

Bernstein, E., & Koppel, N. (2008, August 16). Death in the family: Aided by advocates for the mentally ill and disabled, William Bruce left the hospital only to kill his mother. *Wall Street Journal,* p. A1.

____. (2007, April 27). Delicate balance: Colleges' culture of privacy often overshadows safety, laws allow disclosure of troubling behavior but many schools resist. *Wall Street Journal,* p. A1.

Bibelhausen, J., et al. (2015). Mental health: Reducing the stigma: The deadly effect of untreated mental illness and new strategies for changing outcomes in law students. *William Mitchell Law Review, 41,* 918–947.

Bilmes, L. (2011). *Current and projected future costs of caring for veterans of the Iraq and Afghanistan wars* (Faculty Research Working Papers Series). Cambridge, MA: John F. Kennedy School of Government, Harvard University.

Blanck, P., et al. (2009). *Disability civil rights law and policy* (American Casebook Series, 2nd ed.). Eagan, MN: West Academic Publishing.

____. (2007). Employment of people with disabilities: Twenty-five years back and ahead. *Law and Inequality, 25,* 323–353.

Blanco, C., et al. (2008). Mental health of college students and their non-college-attending peers: Results from the national epidemiologic study on alcohol and related conditions. *Archives of General Psychiatry, 65*(12), 1429–1437.

Bloom, J. D. (2010). Conundrums and controversies in mental health and illness: The incarceration revolution: The abandonment of the seriously mentally ill to our jails and prisons. *Journal of Law, Medicine and Ethics, 38,* 727–733.

Boldt, R. C. (2014). Perspectives on outpatient commitment. *New England Law Review, 49,* 39–81.

Borgmann, C. E. (2014). The constitutionality of government-imposed bodily intrusions. *University of Illinois Law Review, 2014,* 1059–1127.

Brink, J. (2005). Epidemiology of mental illness in a correctional system. *Current Opinion in Psychiatry, 18*(5), 536–541.

Broches, R. S. (2013). Creating continuity: Improving the quality of mental health care provided to justice-involved New Yorkers. *Georgetown Journal on Poverty Law & Policy, 21,* 91–122.

Brown, R. A., et al. (2015). *Access to behavioral health care for geographically remote service members and dependents in the United States.* Santa Monica, CA: RAND Center for Health Policy Research.

Brusca, R., & Ram, C. (2010). A failure to communicate: Did privacy laws contribute to the Virginia Tech tragedy? *Washington and Lee Journal of Civil Rights and Social Justice, 17,* 141–168.

Carle, S. D. (2005). Theorizing agency. *American University Law Review, 55,* 307–393.

CBHSQ (Center for Behavioral Health Statistics and Quality). (2014). *National survey on drug use and health.* Rockville, MD: U.S. Department of Health and Human Services, Substance Abuse and Mental Health Services Administration, CBHSQ.

CBO (Congressional Budget Office). (2010). *Potential costs of veterans health care.* Washington, DC: CBO.

Chorney, D. (2014). A mental health system in crisis and innovative laws to assuage the problem. *Health and Biomedical Law Society, 10,* 215–249.

Churchill, W. (1986). *Their finest hour (Second World War).* New York, NY: Houghton Mifflin Harcourt (Original work published 1949).

Collins, V. L. (2009). Camouflaged legitimacy: Civil commitment, property rights, and legal isolation. *Howard Law Journal, 52,* 407–458.

Cummings, J. E. (2010). The cost of crazy: How therapeutic jurisprudence and mental health courts lower incarceration costs, reduce recidivism, and improve public safety. *Loyola Law Review, 56,* 279–310.

Davoli, J. I. (2010). Physically present, yet mentally absent. *University of Louisville Law Review, 48,* 313–348.

DOD (U.S. Department of Defense) Task Force on Mental Health. (2007). *An achievable vision: Report of the DOD, Task Force on Mental Health.* Washington, DC: DOD.

Donley, G. (2013). Does the Constitution protect abortions based on fetal anomaly? Examining the potential for disability-selective abortion bans in the age of prenatal whole genome sequencing. *Michigan Journal of Gender and Law, 20,* 291–328.

Dougherty, C., & Merrick, A. (2011, February 7). Governors chop spending: Politicians in both parties aim to balance state budgets through cuts, not taxes. *Wall Street Journal,* p. A1.

Eaton, L., et al. (2011, January 13). Suspect's downward spiral: Police records show accused killer growing more erratic before college suspension. *Wall Street Journal,* p. A1.

Entzeroth, L. (2011). The challenge and dilemma of charting a course to constitutionally protect the severely mentally ill capital defendant from the death penalty. *Akron Law Review, 44,* 529–582.

Erickson, S. K. (2008). The myth of mental disorder: Transsubstantive behavior and taxometric psychiatry. *Akron Law Review, 41,* 67–121.

Fazel, S. (2011, January 15). The line between madness and mayhem: What science tells us about the risk of violence, and why treatment in prisons could help. *Wall Street Journal,* p. C3.

Fish, J. (2012). Overcrowding on the ship of fools: Health care reform, psychiatry, and the uncertain future of normality. *Houston Journal of Health Law and Policy, 11,* 181–265.

Frank, R. G., & Glied, S. A. (2006). *Better but not well: Mental health policy in the United States since 1950.* Baltimore, MD: Johns Hopkins University Press.

Frank, S. (2014). Eligibility discrimination of the intellectually disabled in pediatric organ transplantation. *Journal of Health and Biomedical Law, 10,* 101–136.

Freedman, A. (2014). Mental retardation and the death penalty: The need for an international standard defining mental retardation. *Northwestern University Journal of International Human Rights, 12,* 1–21.

Glaze, L. E., & Kaeble, D. (2013). *Correctional populations in the United States.* Washington, DC: U.S. Department of Justice, Bureau of Justice Statistics.

Gostin, L. O., & Gable, L. (2004). The human rights of people with mental disabilities: A global perspective on the application of human rights principles to mental health. *Maryland Law Review, 63,* 20–121.

Greenberg, G. A., & Rosenheck, R. A. (2008). Jail incarceration, homelessness, and mental health: A national study. *Psychiatry Services, 59*(2), 170–177.

Gunn, T. (2014). The Fourteenth Amendment: A structural waiver of state sovereign immunity from constitutional tort suits. *Northern Illinois University Law Review, 35,* 71–117.

Halbrook, W. P. (2015). New York's not so "safe" act: The Second Amendment in an Alice-in-Wonderland world where words have no meaning. *Albany Law Review, 78,* 789–817.

Harcourt, B. E. (2012). *The illusion of free markets: Punishment and the myth of natural order.* Cambridge, MA: Harvard University Press.

Harris, J. E. (2015). Processing disability. *American University Law Review, 64,* 457–533.

Hensel, W. F., & Jones, G. T. (2005). Bridging the physical/mental gap: An empirical look at the impact of mental illness stigma on ADA outcomes. *Tennessee Law Review, 73*, 47–79.

Hill, E., & Blanck, P. (2009). Future of disability rights advocacy and "the right to live in the world." *Texas Journal on Civil Liberties and Civil Rights, 15*, 1–31.

Horvitz-Lennon, M., et al. (2006). From silos to bridges: Meeting the general health care needs of adults with severe mental disorders. *Health Affairs, 25*(3), 659–669.

House Report No. 110-374. (2007). Paul Wellstone Mental Health & Addiction Equity Act of 2007. House Committee on Education and Labor. Washington, DC: U.S. House of Representatives.

Johnston, E. L. (2012). Theorizing mental health courts. *Washington University Law Review, 89*, 519–578.

Jones, D. (2007). Discharge planning for mentally ill inmates in New York City jails: A critical evaluation of the settlement agreement of *Brad H. v. City of New York*. *Pace Law Review, 27*, 305–337.

Jorgensen, M. E. (2009). Is today the day we free electroconvulsive therapy? *Quinnipiac Health Law Journal, 12*, 1–57.

Jubilut, L. L. (2007). Death penalty and mental illness: The challenge of reconciling human rights, criminal law, and psychiatric standards. *Seattle Journal for Social Justice, 6*, 353–380.

Kaplan, M. (2015). Taking pedophilia seriously. *Washington and Lee Law Review, 72*, 75–170.

Kern, B. (2015). Balancing prevention and liability: The use of waiver to limit university liability for student suicide. *Brigham Young University Education and Law Journal, 15*, 227–270.

Kohn, N. A. (2014). Vulnerability theory and the role of government. *Yale Journal of Law and Feminism, 26*, 1–27.

Lamparello, A., & MacLean, C. E. (2014). The separate but unequal constitution. *DePaul Law Review, 64*, 113–183.

Landro, L. (2011, January 18). Unexpected limits of new, free preventive care. *Wall Street Journal*, p. D1.

Malave, E. (2014). Prison health care after the Affordable Care Act: Envisioning an end to the policy of neglect. *New York University Law Review, 89*, 700–738.

Mariner, W. K. (2012). The Affordable Care Act individual coverage requirement: Ways to frame the commerce clause issue. *Annals of Health Law, 21*, 45–62.

Martin, K. R. (2007). Third Circuit holds federal agency liable for deaths mentally-ill patient caused after negligent discharge from treatment program: *DeJesus v. United States Department of Veterans Affairs*. *American Journal of Law and Medicine, 33*, 527–530.

Nadim, S. (2009). The 2008 Mental Health Parity and Addiction Equity Act: An overview of the new legislation and why an amendment should be passed to specifically define mental illness and substance use disorders. *Connecticut Insurance Law Journal, 16*, 297–322.

NCH (National Coalition for the Homeless). (2009). *Why are people homeless?* Washington, DC: NCH.

NIC (National Institute of Corrections). (2012). *Adults with behavioral health needs under correctional supervision: A shared framework for reducing recidivism and promoting recovery*. Washington, DC: NIC.

O'Brien, J. C. (2008). Loose standards, tight lips: Why easy access to client data can undermine homeless management information systems. *Fordham Urban Law Journal, 35*, 673–699.

OIG (Office of the Inspector General). (2008). *Observations and critique of the Department of Defense Task Force on Mental Health*. Washington, DC: Department of Defense.

Osher, F., et al. (2012). *Adults with behavioral health needs under correctional supervision: A shared framework for reducing recidivism and promoting recovery*. New York, NY: Council of State Governments Justice Center.

Petersen, C. J. (2015). Reproductive justice, public policy, and abortion on the basis of fetal impairment: Lessons from international human rights law and the potential impact of the Convention on the Rights of Persons with Disabilities. *Journal of Law and Health, 28*, 121–163.

Pew Center on Governments. (2009). *One in 100: Behind bars in America 2008*. Washington, DC: Pew.

Pfeffer, A. (2008). "Imminent danger" and inconsistency: The need for national reform of the "imminent danger" standard for involuntary civil commitment in the wake of the Virginia Tech tragedy. *Cardozo Law Review, 30*, 277–312.

Pifer, N. (2010). Is life the same as death? Implications of *Graham v. Florida*, *Roper v. Simmons*, and *Atkins v. Virginia* on life without parole sentences for juvenile and mentally retarded offenders. *Loyola of Los Angeles Law Review, 43*, 1495–1532.

Preis, J. F. (2013). In defense of implied injunctive relief in constitutional cases. *William and Mary Bill of Rights Journal, 22*, 1–53.

Quinn, C. (2009). The right to refuse treatment or to direct the course of treatment: Where should inmate autonomy begin and end? *New England Journal on Criminal and Civil Confinement, 35*, 453–488.

Riggs, G. (2014). Taking HIPAA to school: Why the privacy rule has eviscerated FERPA's privacy protections. *John Marshall Law Review, 47*, 1–31.

Riley, G. (2011). The pursuit of integrated living: The Fair Housing Act as a sword for mentally disabled adults residing in group homes. *Columbia Journal of Law and Social Problems, 45*, 177–224.

Robertson, J. A. (2011). Abortion and technology: Sonograms, fetal pain, viability, and early prenatal diagnosis. *University of Pennsylvania Journal of Constitutional Law, 14*, 327–388.

Rosenbaum, S., et al. (2011). Crossing the Rubicon: The impact of the Affordable Care Act on the content of insurance coverage for people with disabilities. *Notre Dame Journal of Law, Ethics and Public Policy, 25,* 527–562.

Ruan, W. J., et al. (2008). The Alcohol Use Disorder and Associated Disabilities Interview Schedule-IV (AUDADIS-IV): Reliability of new psychiatric diagnostic modules and risk factors in a general population sample. *Drug and Alcohol Dependence, 92,* 27–36.

Ryan, C. (2008). Revisiting the legal standards that govern requests to sterilize profoundly incompetent children: In light of the Ashley treatment, is a new standard appropriate? *Fordham Law Review, 77,* 287–326.

Schalock, R. L., & Borthwick-Duffy, S. A. (2009). *Mental retardation: Definition, classification, and systems of supports* (11th ed.). Washington, DC: American Association on Intellectual and Developmental Disabilities.

Shamash, A. (2011). A piecemeal, step-by-step approach toward mental health parity. *Journal of Health and Biomedical Law, 7,* 273–324.

Shipler, D. K. (2005). *The working poor: Invisible in America.* Stony Point, NY: Vintage Book.

Smith, C. (2014). Fit through unfairness: The termination of parental rights due to a parent's mental challenges. *Charlotte Law Review, 5,* 377–403.

Stein, M. A., & Stein, P. J. S. (2007). Beyond disability civil rights. *Hastings Law Journal, 58,* 1203–1240.

Stutz, L. (2013). Myth of protection: Florida courts permitting involuntary medical treatment of pregnant women. *University of Miami Law Review, 67,* 1039–1069.

Tanielian, T., et al. (2008*). Invisible wounds of war: Psychological and cognitive injuries, their consequences, and services to assist recovery.* Santa Monica, CA: RAND Center for Health Policy Research.

Tars, E. S., et al. (2014). The right to adequate housing in the United States: Can I get some remedy? Criminalization of homelessness and the obligation to provide an effective remedy. *Columbia Human Rights Law Review, 45,* 738–771.

Torrey, E. F., et al. (2014). *The treatment of persons with mental illness in prisons and jails: A state survey.* Arlington, VA: Treatment Advocacy Center and Alexandria, VA: National Sheriffs' Association.

Tovino, S. A. (2009). Neuroscience and health law: An integrative approach? *Akron Law Review, 42,* 469–517.

U.S. Surgeon General. (2011). *Mental health: A report of the Surgeon General.* Rockville, MD: U.S. Department of Health and Human Services, Office of the Surgeon General.

USICH (U.S. Interagency Council on Homelessness). (2012). *Searching out solutions: Constructive alternatives to criminalization.* Washington, DC: USICH.

Vera Institute of Justice. (2013). *The potential of community corrections to improve communities and reduce incarceration.* New York, NY: Vera Institute of Justice, Center for Sentencing and Corrections.

Wacquant, L. (2009). *Punishing the poor: The neoliberal government of social insecurity.* Durham, NC: Duke University Press Books.

Waldman, E. G. (2015). Show and tell? Students' personal lives, schools, and parents. *Connecticut Law Review, 47,* 699–740.

Walmsley, R. (2014). World prison population list (11th ed.). London: King's College International Centre for Prison Studies.

Wasicek, A. (2010). Palliative exceptions: Substance abuse, mental illness, and drug courts. *Connecticut Public Interest Law Journal, 10,* 199–232.

Whitman, J. Q. (2012). The free market and the prison. *Harvard Law Review, 125,* 1212–1233.

WHO (World Health Organization). (2014). *The global burden of disease.* Geneva, Switzerland: WHO.

Wiley, L. F. (2014). Health law as social justice. *Cornell Journal of Law and Public Policy, 24,* 47–105.

Wilson, C. M. (2010). Saving money, not lives: Why the VA's claims adjudication system denies due process to veterans with post-traumatic stress disorder and how the VA can avoid judicial intervention. *Indiana Health Law Review, 7,* 157–186.

Wren, G. L. (2010). Mental health courts: Serving justice and promoting recovery. *Annals of Health Law, 19,* 577–593.

CHAPTER 11

The HIV/AIDS Pandemic

"HIV has exposed the vulnerability of humanity: poverty, greed, xenophobia, and stigma threaten our survival more than microbes. Human rights and personal dignity of every human being must be the battle cry."

— **Marshall Forstein, MD**, Interim Chair, Department of Psychiatry, Director of Adult Psychiatry Training, Cambridge Health Alliance; Associate Professor of Psychiatry, Harvard Medical School

LEARNING OBJECTIVES

After completing this chapter, the reader should be able to:

1. Understand that lack of access to testing and prophylactic care is the major driver of the Human Immunodeficiency Virus (HIV)/Acquired Immune Deficiency Syndrome (AIDS) pandemic in the United States and that the primary factor behind the spread of HIV is not reckless human behavior, but restricted access to prevention, diagnosis, and treatment.

2. Assess the intensified call to address the long-term health needs of the chronically ill in the United States, including people living with HIV.

3. Understand why economically vulnerable populations in the United States do not always have access to antiretroviral and other prophylactic medications until they are disabled and become eligible for government health insurance.

4. Describe why debate about HIV/AIDS elicits highly charged opinions, emotions, and reactions about human dignity, sexual behavior, the right to self-determination, and access to health care.

5. List the ethical issues surrounding debate over the role and responsibility of the pharmaceutical industry in addressing the HIV/AIDS pandemic.

6. Explain the conflicting ethical principles the pharmaceutical industry must contend with as it offers essential HIV/AIDS medications to the uninsured, underinsured, and Americans with government health insurance at prices far below market prices.

7. Understand why HIV/AIDS has led to a critical examination of the government's regulatory system for oversight of new medical products in the United States.

KEY TERMS

Acquired Immune Defi-
    ciency Syndrome (AIDS)
Americans with
    Disabilities Act of 1990
Antiretroviral medications
    (ARVs)
Entitlements
Epidemic

Human Immunodeficiency
    Virus (HIV)
Human rights
Kaposi's sarcoma
Medically needed care
Opportunistic diseases
Opt-out testing
Pandemic

Per se disability
Principle of least
    infringement
Retrovirus
Social determinants
    of health
Tuberculosis (TB)
Unmet medical need

ETHICAL OR UNETHICAL DECISION

Criminalization of Exposure to HIV Infection

Ethics Issue: *Should people living with HIV be subject to imprisonment or other criminal penalties for engaging in voluntary, protected sexual encounters without first disclosing their HIV status to prospective sex partners?*

In Brief: While RD was never infected with HIV, Adam Donald Musser was convicted
under Iowa's HIV criminal transmission law for engaging in sexual encounters (using
a condom) 3 times with RD, without informing RD that he was HIV-infected. At
the time of the voluntary and otherwise consensual encounters, Musser was
receiving medical treatment for his condition and had a suppressed viral load of
less than 200 copies of the HIV virus per milliliter of blood. In other words, his infection was under control and at a level that he was considered healthy. Months later,
when RD learned that Musser was HIV-positive, she contacted the police. Musser
was charged with criminal transmission of HIV. Knowing consent to exposure would
have been an affirmative defense under Iowa law:

> It is an affirmative defense that the person exposed to the human immuno-
> deficiency virus knew that the infected person had a positive human immu-
> nodeficiency virus status at the time of the action of exposure, knew that the
> action of exposure could result in transmission of the human immunodefi-
> ciency virus, and consented to the action of exposure with that knowledge.

Iowa Code § 709C.1(5)

Scientists have shown that successful treatment for HIV significantly lowers the
risk of transmitting the disease. Despite its notorious reputation, HIV does not infect the
human body easily, and only a fraction of unprotected sexual encounters result in passing the virus from one person to another (Winslow, 2010). When the viral load of someone living with HIV is undetectable and that person engages in protected sexual activity,
transmission of the disease can generally be prevented 96% of the time (Currie, 2012).
    Condoms help prevent and close off HIV transmission from one partner to an-
other during sexual encounters, if used correctly and no mishaps occur (Vernazza,
et al., 2008). Musser claimed that RD, who was HIV-negative, was as responsible as
he was for taking measures to reduce or avoid sexual behavior that could lead to HIV
transmission. Musser's defense to this criminal action was that he used a condom.

— *State v. Musser*, 721 N.W.2d 734 (Iowa Supreme Court 2006). (*See Ethical or Unethical Decision* at the end of the chapter for
discussion of this ethics issue.)

Introduction

The **Human Immunodeficiency Virus (HIV)** and its resulting **Acquired Immunodeficiency Syndrome (AIDS)**, as defined in **FEATURE BOX 11-1**, have profoundly affected medicine, health care ethics, and adult mortality (Corey, 2011). Almost half of all Americans know someone living with HIV, and with a new HIV infection happening every 10 minutes, the HIV/AIDS pandemic affects all Americans (ICASO, 2015; The White House, 2014).

An **epidemic** is defined as a communicable disease outbreak that infects at least 1% of the general population (CDC, 2014a). Epidemics become **pandemics** when a communicable disease (like the HIV that causes AIDS) occurs over widespread geographic areas and affects large numbers of people. Although the highest number of deaths from the HIV/AIDS pandemic occurred in the early 1990s, the pandemic is not in decline in the United States (CDC, 2015a-c). In fact, the incidence of HIV infections is higher than ever before, with more than 1.2 million Americans living with the infection (CDC, 2014).

Addressing Human Rights and Entitlements

The HIV/AIDS pandemic highlights how **human rights**, derived from the commitment to treating people as equals, became the centerpiece of health care reform in the United States (IOM, 2013; ICASO, 2015). How and why this human rights phenomenon occurred for HIV/AIDS is worth considering, for it has a bearing on whether the positive rights to health, more generally, will be judicially enforceable in the United States (Novogrodsky, 2014).

FEATURE BOX 11-1

Defining HIV and AIDS

By definition, HIV and AIDS are simply two different stages of the same retroviral infection. Basically, HIV destroys certain white blood cells critical to the normal functioning of the human immune system that defends the body against illness. When HIV weakens the immune system, a person becomes more susceptible to developing a variety of cancers and infections from viruses, bacteria, and parasites. People who test positive for HIV are diagnosed with AIDS when laboratory tests show that their immune systems are severely weakened by the virus or when **opportunistic diseases** develop (these are infections that might not affect people with normal immune systems but that take advantage of damaged immune systems).

While HIV is treatable but incurable, AIDS is preventable. Once someone is infected with HIV, they either control the damaging progression of the virus with **antiretroviral medications (ARVs)** before infections appear, or they become symptomatic with AIDS and face imminent death from multiple cancers and infections. ARVs can slow down the rate at which HIV weakens the immune system to the point of being diagnosed with full-blown AIDS. There are also other treatments that can prevent or treat infections associated with AIDS, but not cure AIDS itself.

— Sources: CDC, 2015; Kaiser Family Foundation, 2014; WHO, 2010.

While all people must be given the unfettered opportunity to achieve and maintain a secure sense of independent wellbeing and human dignity, society has a special ethical obligation to assist vulnerable populations, in this instance, people infected with HIV (Burris, et al., 2010). Yet while litigation was an effective trigger for access to AIDS medications, judicial activism to enforce social and economic quality of life issues remains a rarity (Farmer, 2005).

Inadequate health resources, unequal and uneven access to affordable health insurance, poverty, and social injustice have fueled the HIV/AIDS pandemic in the United States (CDC, 2014; Winslow & McKay, 2010). **Entitlements**, or the individual right to opportunities like achieving a healthy wellbeing and maintaining one's health (Burris, et al., 2010), are sometimes different from what the law, properly interpreted, actually offers to people (Kruse, 2011). Such entitlements are not always available to people infected with HIV who are uninsured or are covered by government health insurance (Burris, et al., 2010).

This failure to treat everyone as equals has severely constrained what the government can do to respect, protect, and fulfill the right to health care (Mikkonen & Raphael, 2010), including medications required to treat HIV infections. The nation is at a crossroads as to what reasonable actions it will continue to take with the HIV/AIDS pandemic to ensure that people infected with HIV are able to maintain their health and prevent the onset of AIDS. Providing health care to HIV/AIDS patients is one of the nation's continuing challenges and one of the nation's moral imperatives, regardless of opposition or difficulty incurred in providing care to people infected with HIV (Novogrodsky, 2009).

Our Crossroads Challenge

AIDS, one of the most pressing threats to public health in the present day, is a preventable disease (Kaiser Family Foundation, 2014). By 1996, within 12 years of HIV's identification as the cause of AIDS, medical innovation produced ARVs. ARVs slow down the rate at which HIV weakens the human immune system to the point of full-blown AIDS; ARVs suppress the **retrovirus**, a virus with genetic information in its RNA as opposed to DNA and that causes HIV infections and certain cancers. ARVs are transforming the HIV infection into a treatable, non-fatal medical condition (Purcell, 2010).

Nevertheless, with a resurgence in unsafe sex among young adults, who casually engage in one-night sexual encounters or short sexually-focused relationships, there has been an increase in transmission of HIV in 20- to 24-year-olds (Helmink, 2010). In addition, the nation's lack of commitment to addressing poverty and social inequality has played a powerful role in impacting the HIV/AIDS pandemic (Wilkinson & Pickett, 2011; Burris, et al., 2010). As a consequence of these two social forces (unsafe sex and poverty), the number of people living with HIV infection in the United States is higher than ever before (CDC, 2014). AIDS diagnoses have returned to the levels last seen at the height of the pandemic in the early 1990s (Winslow & McKay, 2010); deaths of people with an AIDS diagnosis are at the highest levels since HIV first hit the United States (CDC, 2011a). Still, the simple but essential fact is that most of these infections and deaths could be prevented if everyone had access to information and medical treatment for preventing and treating HIV (Tramont & Boyajian, 2010).

The Chronic Nature of HIV Infections

As explained in Feature Box 11-1, once a person is infected with HIV, they remain infected for life. It is important to understand that HIV can be managed as a lifelong chronic disease if it is detected early enough and if people have access to medical treatment to successfully care for and manage the disease. It is these two "ifs" that make the HIV/AIDS pandemic such a tragedy in the United States. *See* Fagan, et al., 2010.

HIV does not have to lead to AIDS if people who are infected have access to ARVs while their immune systems are still strong. With access to health care, opportunistic diseases need not occur. Opportunistic diseases, as noted above, are cancers and infections from viruses, bacteria, and parasites that might not affect people with normal immune systems but that take advantage of HIV-infected people with damaged immune systems. **Kaposi's sarcoma**, a secondary cancer of the connective tissue associated with AIDS, should not be as common a death as it is.

Tumorous lesions appear under the skin and in the lining of the mouth, nose, throat, and other organs, making breathing difficult and often resulting in internal bleeding. Americans die from HIV/AIDS every year because they needed care but did not get it because they could not afford it (CDC, 2015a-c; Venkatapuram & Marmot, 2009), or were too socially disorganized to use offered care.

The extent of this continuing pandemic is illustrated in **FEATURE BOX 11-2**. In the end, ethical policies should be guided by simple answers to a complex question: how does the nation provide affordable access to health insurance for everyone, and how does the nation provide health care to individuals living with HIV? As scientific consensus continues to move toward earlier and earlier treatment of HIV, the nation will be forced to determine how to pay for early treatment that could costs billions of dollars at a time when funding for everything has tightened (Southerland, 2011).

The Emerging Threat of HIV/TB Co-Infections

There is no need to look further than the airborne infectious disease of **tuberculosis (TB)** to fully grasp the impact of HIV/AIDS on the nation's public health (Price, 2014). TB is a bacterial disease that primarily affects the lungs, but can attack any organ in the body (CDC, 2014a). Approximately 13 million people are infected with active and latent TB infections in the United States (CDC, 2014a), compared to the 1.2 million living with HIV in the United States (CDC, 2015b). HIV weakens the ability of the immune system to fight TB infections; consequently, up to half of all those living with HIV and latent

---

FEATURE BOX 11-2

Key U.S. Public Health Statistics

- Almost 1 in 7 Americans infected with HIV are unaware of their infection.
- 1.2 million are living with HIV in the United States.
- More than 50,000 new HIV infections occur annually.
- One out of 4 new HIV infections occurs among adolescents 13–24 years old.
- Casual sexual encounters by people diagnosed as HIV-positive are widespread.
- 13,500 deaths from AIDS and related illnesses occur each year (more than 658,000 have died from AIDS since the pandemic reached the United States).
- HIV prevention efforts saved more than $130 billion in health care costs over the past decade.

— Sources: CDC, 2015a-c, 2014, and 2013b; Helmink, 2010; Kaiser, 2015, 2014, and 2011a; The White House, 2014.

TB infections eventually develop active TB (CDC, 2011). The seriousness of emerging communicable disease threats to people not infected with HIV becomes obvious when the epidemiological data of TB infections is analyzed, as illustrated in **FEATURE BOX 11-3**. *See generally* CDC, 2011.

Multi-drug-resistant TB first appeared in the United States in 2007; the fear is that more latent TB infections will become active and multi-drug-resistant (McKay, 2013). The single biggest factor driving up resistance to treatment of TB infections is the irregular use of antibiotics, often a result of patients being non-compliant with their prescribed medications (CDC, 2014a). Moreover, HIV is aggravating and contributing to the spread of the TB resistance problem to people not infected with HIV (CDC, 2014a and 2013; WHO, 2014a).

Although ARVs can treat HIV as a chronic disease, treatment for multi-drug-resistant TB works for only about a third of those infected, when care is even available (CDC, 2011). With highly contagious diseases like TB, bacteria are spread from person to person through the air; someone can speak or cough and the bacteria contaminate whoever is nearby (Sinclair, 1905/2015). This second wave of the HIV/AIDS pandemic combined with multi-drug-resistant TB could easily continue for years until better medications are developed. Undoubtedly, the second wave of HIV-related deaths from multi-drug-resistant TB could exceed the first wave of the HIV/AIDS pandemic (CDC, 2011). Regrettably, one-third of the new TB cases in the United States now have some drug resistance (Tracey & Lange, 2012).

While all health departments are required to track and treat all patients diagnosed with TB for free, the therapy at public health clinics is often inadequate, long-term medication compliance is low, and lower quality generic medications are the norm, all of which leads to recurrent disease (Lin, 2013; Gerwint, 2011). If 33 million Americans remain uninsured as the United States witnesses an increase of multi-drug-resistant TB infections, the consequences could be economically devastating if patients with latent TB are not diagnosed before the disease develops. Moreover, uninsured patients with latent TB are less likely to be diagnosed until the disease becomes overt. The TB epidemic will present itself not only as a secondary disease to people infected with HIV, but people not infected with HIV will also face the financial cost of treatment and the loss of life from highly contagious TB. Additionally, the effects on economic interests will be just as palpable, since those quarantined or isolated with TB infections would be unable to participate normally in daily life costing employers productive workers (Price, 2014).

FEATURE BOX 11-3

Connectivity of HIV/TB Co-Infections

- People who have both HIV infection and latent TB infection are 20 to 30 times as likely to develop active TB disease as those who do not have HIV infection.
- 250,000 to 400,000 of active TB cases will most likely be multidrug-resistant TB.
- There are 75,000 to 120,000 multidrug-resistant TB deaths annually, compared to 13,500 AIDS deaths annually.

— Source: CDC, 2014a.

Personal Interdependence and Collective Interests

Human rights in the context of HIV/AIDS resonated across the world and resulted in a powerful call for access to essential medications (Kagan, 2007). As illustrated in **FEATURE BOX 11-4**, this commitment to treating people as equals contributed to important changes in the ethical principles and rules of law underlying U.S. health care reform (George, 2011). Clearly, infectious disease waves are not constrained by boundaries. Viruses like HIV defy understanding mainly because they are invisible and unpredictable (Wong, 2010). Today, no one exists in isolation as diseases spread farther and faster. HIV and its high-cost co-infections are a global phenomenon that is expected to become increasingly severe in a more integrated world economy (Wharton, 2006a).

The Dual Role of Government and the Pharmaceutical Industry

There are suggestions that the HIV/AIDS pandemic is a special disease state, one so serious that government and the pharmaceutical industry have an ethical obligation to simultaneously address both equitable access and optimal innovation (Outterson, 2008). The Access to Medicines movement, an informal coalition of organizations such as Medecins Sans Frontieres, HealthRight, Oxfam, and Knowledge Ecology maintain that essential ARVs and other AIDS medications should be provided to ameliorate the preventable disease of AIDS and decrease the possibility of a second wave of highly contagious co-infections from arising that could be communicated to people without HIV infections. Given the gravity of the

---

FEATURE BOX 11-4

Ethical Principles and Rules of Law Underlying the Nation's Response to the HIV/AIDS Pandemic

By enacting the Affordable Care Act (ACA), the nation has recognized its fundamental responsibilities and duties in ensuring that all Americans have:

- Affordable access to basic health insurance
- Access to health care so everyone has the opportunity to achieve and maintain high levels of health, which are necessary for a lifetime of well-being and human dignity
- Reasonable access to necessary life-prolonging medical interventions based on scientific evidence as opposed to ideology
- Rights to personal autonomy, human dignity, and self-determination arising from their common humanity

— Sources: Patient Protection and Affordable Care Act, 42 U.S.C. § 18001, *et seq.* (2010) *as amended by* Health Care and Education Reconciliation Act of 2010, Pub. L. No. 111-152, 124 Stat. 1029 through 124. Stat. 1084; The White House, 2014 and 2010.

ETHICAL DILEMMAS 11-1

1. What arguments can counter opponents of the ACA, who ask why people infected with HIV should be provided access to government health insurance before they are symptomatic or why HIV infections should not be considered a preexisting health condition that will not be covered by insurance for anyone who is uninsured when they discover they are HIV-positive?

HIV/AIDS pandemic, this role should come before many other government demands and industry profits (Emilio, 2011). Calls for the government and the pharmaceutical industry to do more to meet the needs of people living with HIV are not limited to AIDS activists. Almost every advocate of health care reform is demanding more action from the government (Gostin, et al., 2011).

While most social and economic rights reforms do not involve litigation, the struggle for essential ARVs and other HIV/AIDS medications and the use of the legal system as a tool to vindicate the human right to health offers one possible path to success for promoting justice in environments of poverty and deprivation. HIV/AIDS set a precedent in health care; the legacy of the effort to deliver care to people in need is present in a number of situations concerning human dignity and a measurable quality of life, institutional responsiveness, and the expanded use of the philosophies of human rights to promote justice (Novogrodsky, 2014). It may be hubris to reconceive health care ethics in this fashion, but it is consistent with the tradition of bringing previously unenforceable demands to the forefront of the nation's collective imagination. For the next generation who choose to promote the human right to health, the HIV/AIDS pandemic is a powerful symbol of what once was and what still could be (Baxi, 2012).

Access to Medical Coverage

Closely related to this issue of entitlement to essential ARVs and other AIDS medications are the minimum obligations of government to its citizens. One obligation which the United States recently accepted is the provision of access to affordable health insurance. The debate over what constitutes access (who has the right to make use of what medical innovations) and what comprises basic medical coverage is far from over.

One argument is that lack of early access to ARVs to slow down the rate at which HIV weakens the immune system is the difference between life and death. When people living with HIV cannot benefit from available treatment, their chances for survival are lowered (IOM, 2010). Therefore, because people have a right to good health and well-being, there

ETHICAL DILEMMAS 11-2

2. Ethically speaking, if everyone infected with HIV has the right to make use of advanced medical innovations, does this also mean that all innovations, including the newest medications for other illnesses and diseases, should be covered by basic health insurance?

is a right of affordable access to ARVs. In this instance, the issue is whether the right to benefit from medical progress applies to the provision of ARVs and other essential AIDS medications. How these dual ethical obligations, the right to affordable health insurance and the right of access to health care, are being addressed is the focus of the remainder of this chapter.

Prevention, Detection, and Treatment of HIV/AIDS

Today, there are 2 prongs of the approach to the HIV/AIDS pandemic in the United States. The first prong is prevention, early detection, and treatment of HIV. The second prong is containment (CDC, 2013a). Considering the stigmatized status of people with HIV, some of the greatest issues facing people living with HIV are social inequality, poverty, and lack of protection from disability-based discrimination, not simply lack of access to health care (Basas, 2010; Wilkinson & Pickett, 2011).

Social Determinants Impacting the Incidence of HIV/AIDS

HIV testing rates have been flat for the past decade, including among higher risk populations (Kaiser Family Foundation, 2014a). A systematic review of sexual abstinence and monogamy programs for HIV prevention finds no evidence that this approach has resulted in a reduction of the incidence of HIV infections (Scott, 2009). In fact, the nation's concentrated attention on sexual abstinence and monogamy as opposed to attention about safe sex and the use of condoms may have inadvertently caused the decline of HIV detection (MMWR, 2011).

A second factor contributing to flat HIV infection rates is the fact that most people in the United States are tested only after HIV/AIDS symptoms appear, which may be 10 years or more after being infected (Kaiser Family Foundation, 2014a). These late testers are more likely to have contracted HIV through heterosexual contact than any other method (Kaiser Family Foundation, 2014a; MMWR, 2011). Regrettably, more than one third of the late testers receive an AIDS diagnosis within 1 year of testing HIV-positive (Kaiser Family Foundation, 2014a), meaning their HIV infection is diagnosed too late in its course to prevent the onset of AIDS.

One of the most important factors linking poverty to AIDS in the United States is the lack of access to affordable health insurance as illustrated in **FIGURE 11-1**. In part because of barriers to affordable basic coverage, economically vulnerable populations often postpone treatment until they are late in their illness (CDC, 2015c). Even when they are aware of their HIV status during the early stages of infection, many do not have access to comprehensive treatment to manage or monitor medical complications associated with HIV (Kaiser Family Foundation, 2014c). This lack of access inevitably fuels a downward cycle of poverty and premature death as illustrated in **FEATURE BOX 11-5** (Wilkinson & Pickett, 2011).

The total societal benefits derived from treating individuals who are HIV-infected must be considered. While the lifetime treatment cost for each HIV-positive adult is about $380,000 (CDC, 2013a), lifetime access to ARVs to reduce the rate of disease progression and the incidence of opportunistic diseases is far more economical than no testing and subsequent treatment for AIDS. The average lifetime cost-savings is $36,700/year (Schackman, et al., 2008). In other words, every 10 percent increase in spending on ARV therapy of individuals who are HIV-positive could result in societal cost savings of $44 million/year. Societal costs of preventable ill health are one of the hidden savings made possible by providing access to health insurance to almost every member of society (Levine, et al., 2007).

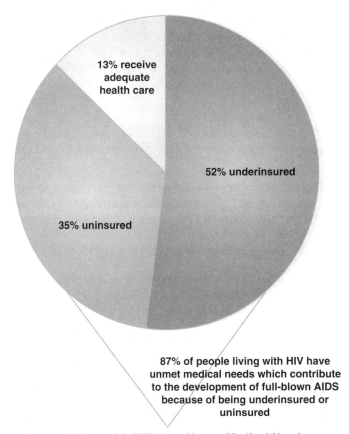

People Living with HIV Have Unmet Medical Needs

FIGURE 11-1 Lack of Access to Affordable Health Insurance: Leading Social Determinant of AIDS

Sources: CDC 2015a, 2015b, 2015c, and 2014; IOM, 2013, 2011, and 2010; The White House, 2014.

When lifetime ARV therapy is more economical, access to health care becomes a major ethical failing (Wynia & Schwab, 2006).

Anti-Discrimination for HIV/AIDS

Ethically speaking, there is a need for greater confidentiality and anti-discrimination protections for people living with HIV/AIDS (UCSF & National HIV/AIDS Clinicians' Consultation Center, 2011). Federal legislation and a few states afford adequate protection against disability-based discrimination and social exclusion for people with HIV (Selmi, 2006). While enactment of the federal **Americans with Disabilities Act of 1990** represented a consensus in the United States that there should be a comprehensive national mandate for the elimination of disability-based discrimination and social exclusion of people with disabilities, there is little demand for extending anti-discrimination laws (Ray, 2007). Thus, although there is generally broad support for protecting people with serious disabilities at the end stage of AIDS, there is little support for extending disability-based

FEATURE BOX 11-5

Downward Cycle of Poverty and HIV Infection
Caused by Lack of Access to Health Care

- Americans living with HIV infections who are unable to obtain health care are forced to abandon the labor force due to illness.
- More than one-third delayed or did not obtain needed health care because of food and housing needs.
- One-third to one-half are either homeless or in imminent danger of losing their homes due to health care costs and limited incomes due to the reduced ability to keep working.

— Sources: HUD, 2015; The White House, 2014 and 2010; Tomaszewski, 2011.

ETHICAL DILEMMAS 11-3

3. While there are current restrictions on disability-based discrimination against people who are HIV-infected, should they differ from the existing social norms for treating anyone differently who is asymptomatic but HIV-positive?

discrimination protections to asymptomatic HIV-infected people (Eisenberg, 2010). In other words, the public consensus is that people with asymptomatic HIV infections should not receive any special accommodations regarding their job application procedures (hiring, advancement, or discharge), compensation, or job training; they should be treated the same as everyone else (Kaiser Family Foundation, 2011).

ETHICS CASE
HIV Infection as a Disability

Waddell v. Valley Forge Dental Associates, Inc.
[Dental Hygienist v. Dental Clinic]
276 F.3d 1275 (U.S. Court of Appeals for the 11th Circuit 2001),
cert. denied, 535 U.S. 1096 (U.S. Supreme Court 2002)

Facts: Spencer Waddell, an HIV-positive dental hygienist, sued Valley Forge Dental Associates, his employer, claiming that he was discriminated against when his employer refused to allow him to continue treating patients due to his HIV-positive status.

Legal Analysis: The court concluded that several factors, when taken together, indicated that the hygienist posed a significant risk to others in the workplace: (1) possibility of an inadvertent bite or other accident during a dental cleaning; (2) risk that hygienists will be stuck or pricked while using an instrument; (3) routine patient bleeding during dental work; (4) statements of the hygienist and his medical experts acknowledging that there was some risk, even if theoretical and small, that blood-to-blood contact between the hygienist and patients could occur; and (5) use of sharp instruments by hygienists.

The court noted that the U.S. Supreme Court declined to address whether asymptomatic HIV is a **per se disability**, where everyone with that impairment would be considered disabled without reference to individualized, case-by-case inquiries. Under current law, individualized inquiries of disability must be made. In other words, the issue of whether someone is disabled and entitled to protection against disability-based discrimination must be made on a case-by-case basis.

Rule of Law: The hygienist, because he was infected with HIV, was a direct threat to his workplace, and therefore was not qualified for protection against disability-based discrimination because of his disease status.

Ethics Issue: Should society permit an HIV-positive dental hygienist to be discriminated against simply because of his disease status?

Ethics Analysis: The courts remain very hesitant to open the door to nontraditional disabilities such as communicable diseases. This lack of comprehensive protection against HIV-based discrimination and social stigma is generally related to accumulated fears regarding the potential costs of accommodating the 1.2 million people living with HIV, especially when such accommodation could occur from the time of their infection (Southerland, 2011). In this instance, misunderstandings about HIV are as handicapping as are the physical limitations that flow from HIV (Mendonsa, 2010). A legal standard that would make acts of discrimination and prejudice wrong is necessary to protect the human rights of people with asymptomatic HIV and achieve equality for everyone with disabilities.

Court's Holding and Decision: No, because the hygienist posed a significant risk of transmitting his disease to patients, he was not entitled to any protection against disability-based discrimination under the Americans with Disabilities Act of 1990.

See, e.g., Mendonsa, 2010; Southerland, 2011 (discussing this court decision).

Routine HIV Testing and Detection

With improvements in treatment and the advent of some confidentiality protection, HIV testing is slowly becoming a constructive tool in the fight against HIV/AIDS (Schalman-Bergen, 2007). In 2006, the federal government revised its guidelines for HIV testing and detection (MMWR, 2006). Now routine testing of everyone between the ages of 13 and 64 is recommended, regardless of individual risk factors.

While HIV testing remains voluntary, it is usually offered on an **opt-out testing** basis. Separate, written informed consent for HIV blood testing is no longer needed. In other words, consent to be tested for HIV is part of any general informed consent to receive routine health care services. Routine screenings identify people with HIV just like screening and diagnostic tests for high cholesterol or some other sexually transmitted diseases. Today, HIV tests are increasingly treated the same as cholesterol tests and Pap smears, like standard diagnostic tests routinely administered. *See generally* Pierce, et al., 2011. Ethically speaking, if HIV/AIDS is treated as a routine communicable and chronic disease, then the ethical **principle of least infringement**, or the least intrusive means of encroaching on personal autonomy and privacy while preventing AIDS, should apply to HIV testing (Yuen, 2007). People should not have to affirmatively agree to HIV tests; rather, HIV testing should be routinely administered as a diagnostic test on an opt-out basis without any requirement for affirmative agreement (Tramont & Boyajian, 2010).

Living in a community necessarily requires giving up certain rights for the common good (Gregg, 2011). Under opt-out testing, self-autonomy would be infringed upon in order to achieve the public health goal of increasing the level of HIV detection, and ultimately controlling its spread. This early HIV diagnosis is crucial because early intervention leads to slower disease progression. When ARVs are taken early and consistently, HIV is a chronic, manageable disease that generally does not develop into full-blown AIDS because of the low maintained level of virus in the bloodstream (HHS, 2014). ARVs also significantly reduce the transmissibility of HIV by lowering the amount of virus in the bloodstream of those infected (Cohen, et al., 2011). Furthermore, someone who is infected can take precautions against infecting others once they are aware of their infection. In this instance, everyone has some obligation for the health of all community members (Gregg, 2011).

Minors' Right to Consent to HIV Testing and Treatment

Controversy also centers on whether states should permit minors to consent to HIV testing and treatment, and whether health care providers should be required to inform parents if a minor is seeking testing or receiving treatment. Alternatively, the question is whether minors should be able to obtain HIV tests without parental consent, though not HIV treatment. Since the first AIDS case was reported in the United States, states have expanded minors' authority to consent to health care without parents taking part in their decisions, including care related to sexual activity (Kaiser Famiy Foundation, 2011a). The age of majority is generally accepted as 18 years, but all states allow most minors, generally beginning around 12 years of age, to consent to HIV testing (Guttmacher, 2015).

Access to Health Care

HIV testing should be an integral component of preventive health care, which raises the ethical issue of the right to access life extending care. Early medical treatment significantly improves the health of people with HIV while also greatly reducing transmissibility of the disease. Therefore, early access to health care is crucial to the success of widespread HIV testing and prevention. Unfortunately, the health insurance industry opposes more widespread HIV testing due to the industry's attempt to minimize short-term costs, resulting in the lack of opportunity to access ARVs early for many insured Americans (IOM, 2010).

While federal funds are available to subsidize ARVs when no other resources are available (Kaiser Family Foundation, 2014c), early access to comprehensive care is unobtainable for many people with HIV, especially those without access to health insurance (Kaiser Family Foundation, 2014). Medicaid insurance represents the largest source of medical coverage for Americans living with HIV. Almost half of the people diagnosed with AIDS are enrolled in Medicaid insurance; an additional one-third are uninsured (Kaiser Family Foundation, 2014b). However, in order to qualify for Medicaid insurance, most people with HIV must be both low income and disabled, or unable to perform some or all of life's basic tasks. Most symptomatic people with AIDS qualify for Medicaid insurance because they are both disabled and low income.

While all states are required to provide Medicaid insurance to the disabled, people with HIV often do not qualify as disabled without an AIDS diagnosis (IOM, 2010). The cruel irony is that this requires people with HIV to manifest symptoms of the disease before they are eligible for Medicaid insurance. This means treatment is often withheld for uninsured

Americans until it is too late for prophylactic care (Montaner, et al., 2006). The ethics of this HIV disability policy are controversial since they do not adequately reflect medical reality of prophylactic care that prevents the occurrence of AIDS. In other words, today, adherence to ARV therapy strongly correlates with HIV-suppression, reduced rates of resistance, increased survival, and an improved quality of life if treatment is received before AIDS symptoms manifest (Robichaud, 2009). *See generally* IOM, 2010.

Containment of HIV

The second prong of the U.S. approach to containment is reporting and contact notification. HIV testing has been expanded such that it is recommended that everyone receive a routine HIV test whenever they come into contact with the health care system (MMWR, 2006). In addition, and in an effort to contain the spread of HIV, the United States has mandatory reporting requirements of people who test positive for HIV and most states have criminal sanctions in place for the knowing transmission of HIV (Klemm, 2010). The United States also had immigration restrictions on people who were HIV-infected until recently (Kysar, 2011).

Partner Notification Requirements

Physicians and testing laboratories are required to report the names of newly diagnosed HIV patients to state communicable disease registries. A controversial issue is whether physicians should also disclose the HIV status of patients to known sexual partners to whom HIV is likely to be transmitted (Pottker-Fishel, 2007). As is, there is tension between the duty of health care professionals to the greater good of their community and their duty towards individual patients (Richards, 2010). Similarly, there is a conflict between the right of confidentiality and privacy of people with HIV and the entitlement of their sexual partners to know about their risks of HIV infection (Johnstone, 2010). Physicians are generally not required to investigate and notify third parties about their risk of contracting HIV (Pottker-Fishel, 2007).

Punitive Criminal Laws

Many states have punitive criminal laws that in effect discourage HIV testing and, therefore, have a corrosive impact on efforts to combat HIV/AIDS (NASTAD, 2011). For instance, most states will prosecute people with HIV who engage in sexual encounters without first disclosing their HIV status to prospective sex partners (Perone, 2013). All states have criminal laws that punish people with HIV for sexual encounters posing some risk of HIV transmission, even if no transmission occurs (Minahan, 2009). While most states find the knowing transmission of HIV to be a felony, not all criminal laws are grounded in public health science (Klemm, 2010). Unfortunately, many states criminalize all exposure to bodily fluids by anyone who is HIV-infected, including saliva (NASTAD, 2011). Whether any of these laws influence high-risk sexual encounters is debatable (Burris, et al., 2007).

Immigration Restrictions

The strict immigration controls against entry into the United States for people with HIV infections have been eliminated (Kysar, 2011). Now, an emerging controversy is the ethicality of deporting HIV-positive non-U.S. citizens who have access to medical treatment in the United States but who are being deported to a country where such treatment is unavailable (Mitchell, 2011). Non-U.S. citizens seeking legal protection from removal that would terminate their HIV/AIDS treatment claim that removal constitutes a death sentence if they are deported to a country where they will not have access to life-sustaining medical treatment (Mooty, 2010). Yet, asylum, the withholding of removal, and the law enacting the United Nations Convention against Torture and Other Cruel, Inhuman or Degrading Treatment or Punishment are too narrow to protect non-U.S. citizens from removal, often terminating HIV/AIDS treatment (Mitchell, 2011).

HIV as a Routine Communicable Disease

HIV is technically treated no differently from other communicable diseases, yet there is disagreement over whether states should report the identities of HIV-infected students to school officials or whether students and their families should decide whether to disclose their health status (Gostin, et al., 2011). There are 2 sides to this debate. One side supports reporting the identities of students with HIV because, according to this line of thinking, the law sufficiently protects people living with HIV. Proponents of this view accept routine HIV testing and do not see any significant existing stigma associated with HIV/AIDS (Fishman, 2013).

The other side maintains that there is ongoing stigma, disability-based discrimination, and distrust of the health care system in many high-risk communities. Proponents of this view are concerned with civil rights and privacy protections of those in society who are at the greatest risk of disability-based discrimination and social exclusion. They want to treat HIV/AIDS differently from other infectious diseases. Despite these differing points of view, both sides of this debate agree on the need for a national, coordinated public health response to the HIV/AIDS pandemic in the United States (MMWR, 2011). *See generally* Schalman-Bergen, 2007.

Adequacy of Protection from Stigma, Discrimination, and Social Exclusion

The HIV/AIDS pandemic in the United States has emerged as a health care crisis with a human rights struggle in an unprecedented way. The most marginalized group in American society is the poor. They were stigmatized and discriminated against before AIDS arrived and gradually they became those at the highest risk of HIV infection (Mann, 1996); they are also largely the uninsured. While disability-based discrimination and social exclusion continues to lead in multiple ways to heightened HIV rates through poverty and its attendant barriers to safer sex, these systemic factors are far from being addressed more than 3 decades after the disease first appeared in the United States (Winslow, 2010).

One central disagreement over routine HIV detection, testing, and reporting is whether laws adequately protect against the stigma of HIV/AIDS. Though protections exist, laws vary widely, many without fully protecting people living with HIV or AIDS (Schalman-Bergen, 2007). Courts, including the U.S. Supreme Court, usually insist that only a narrow set of deserving people who are HIV-infected qualify for protection against disability-based discrimination. Yet, whenever infection risk is defined in terms of individual behavioral choices (such as condom use, sexual abstinence, or using clean needles), disability-based discrimination results and the courts permit it to occur (Frautschi, 2010).

Confidentiality of HIV Status

Public health surveillance of new HIV infections reflects the vision of protecting the public health. Virtually every state collects the names of people who test positive for HIV. Many states also require physicians to report private information, such as medication use and sexual history about anyone who tests positive (ACLU, 2008). The ethics of reporting new cases of HIV by full names as opposed to by codes remains controversial. One side of the debate claims name-based reporting is essential for epidemiological purposes, while the other side claims the practice is unnecessary and dissuades some people from being tested out of concern for their confidentiality (Stoto, 2008).

The HIV/AIDS Pandemic and Health Care Reforms

The search for new health care models to help uninsured Americans has drawn attention to the millions who live without health care. While the HIV/AIDS pandemic has focused largely on essential medications, it raised awareness about the lack of health care systems to deliver care to many Americans (Kaiser Commission, 2008). Because it has highlighted problems with the current health care system, the HIV/AIDS pandemic has helped enable broader health care reform, especially with regards to the need for health information networks and national standards of care (Mukherjee, 2007). Moreover, all the money and attention directed to this particular disease segment has helped build a foundation for near-universal access to primary care and comprehensive high quality continuous care management of chronic conditions (Wharton, 2006).

Early Access and Treatment Adherence

The public perception of HIV/AIDS is that there needs to be affordable medications, but the problem is not necessarily cost as it was in the earlier years of the pandemic (Mukherjee, 2007). Instead, it is now the multifaceted struggle of obtaining early access to medical treatment (IOM, 2011). Access difficulties are intertwined with the willingness of those infected to accept responsibility for adherence to their treatment regimens (Tsai, 2007). HIV treatment requires a high degree of adherence to taking ARVs, and with the advent of combination therapies, regimen compliance is particularly complex. Unfortunately, many people who take ARVs are noncompliant and develop resistance and ultimately fail therapy (Gostin, et al., 2011). There is also the very real danger that non-compliance will lead to transmission of resistant viruses to others, a phenomenon that is already emerging (McArthur, 2009).

Affordable Access as an Insurance Problem, Not Simply a Pricing Problem

In recent years, the pharmaceutical industry's pricing system has come under pressure. The uninsured and those with inadequate prescription plans have discovered they are paying much more for ARVs and AIDS medications than patients in the rest of the world. People living with HIV in the United States complain about being denied access to ARVs

ETHICAL DILEMMAS 11-4

4. Should the private health insurance sector still be able to use coverage exclusions, limitations on treatments, annual and lifetime caps on coverage, and other restrictions to restrict the care of people suffering from HIV/AIDS, or are prohibitions on such restrictions regulatory overreach by the federal government?

that can prevent their immune systems from being weakened to the point where they are disabled by full-blown AIDS (Anderson, 2010). However, this is not simply a pricing problem; the problem of obtaining access to ARVs is also an insurance problem. People living with HIV need affordable health insurance with reasonable prescription coverage, meaning co-payments that are at an affordable level and plans that provide basic coverage for needed medications.

Fair Pricing of Essential Medications

As publicly-traded companies, members of the pharmaceutical industry are obligated to seek profits for shareholders. Yet the pharmaceutical industry is not like other for-profit businesses. Theoretically, the industry is free to charge the highest prices the market will bear. Because they can charge patients $10,000 to $15,000 for medications costing only a few dollars to make, and most patients do not have the option of not buying most essential medications, they either pay the retail price or go without the treatment (Wharton, 2011).

Any debate about profit margins, however, must take into account a complete picture of the pharmaceutical industry. Manufacturing costs alone do not reflect the billions of dollars that go into discovering, testing, and meeting the regulatory hurdles faced by companies in bringing a new medication to market. The pharmaceutical industry works continuously to make treatments for disease less costly (Vagelos, 2014). While the United States does not regulate drug prices, there is debate on whether price regulation would affect pharmaceutical innovation. Most ARVs and AIDS medications under study never make it to market; they turn out to be ineffective, burdened by side effects, or are too expensive to produce and disseminate (Wharton, 2011). Therefore, the few successful medications must recoup the costs of all the failures, not to mention the costs of marketing those successful medications. Again, HIV/AIDS has forced examination of the entire regulatory scheme and how to best price medications.

Ethical Pricing Incentives

At the onset of the HIV/AIDS pandemic, the pharmaceutical industry erred by not quickly reaching an agreement to provide essential ARVs and AIDS medications at affordable prices. It did so only after massive public pressure and as the number of people directly affected by this pandemic approached 90 million worldwide (WHO, 2010). When thousands of Americans die as a direct result of lack of access to available ARVs and AIDS medications, the U.S. pharmaceutical industry suddenly faces different pressures than other industries. Clearly, whenever the balance between public expectations of a fair price and the price set by the industry dramatically differ, the vulnerabilities of the industry come into play.

ETHICAL DILEMMAS 11-5

5. Given the responsibility of the pharmaceutical industry to its shareholders and employees, what would make it easier for the pharmaceutical industry to act in the public interest with regard to the HIV/AIDS pandemic in the United States?

The Ethics of Government Incentives

Trillions of dollars in government incentives for taxpayer-financed research, government provided patent protection, and government insurance payments for its medical products are placed in the hands of the pharmaceutical industry. If incentives to the pharmaceutical industry are too strong, more products are produced than needed and prices are too high. If incentives are too weak, prices are less, but society misses out on medical innovations.

The Unrelenting Stigma of HIV/AIDS

The ethical paradox of our time is that although the HIV/AIDS causes 50 deaths each day in the United States, the pandemic remains hidden in many ways (MMWR, 2011; The White House, 2014). Attempts to quantify the disease fail to reflect the true human struggles and tragedies reflected by each individual. More than 3 decades into the pandemic, HIV/AIDS is not seen as a devastating issue to most Americans (Kaiser Family Foundation, 2011). Most Americans are insufficiently aware of the many human rights that are violated when anyone finds out that they are infected with HIV, the cumulative effect of these violations, and how, all together, they constitute a human rights crisis that will likely exist for some time (Walker, 2007).

Blaming the Disease on the Diseased

With no simple solution for eliminating the HIV/AIDS pandemic, people who are HIV-infected are often blamed for the disease (Barry, 2010). Much of this blame can be traced to the time before HIV/AIDS appeared when there was an American subculture of sexual innocence, experience, and experimentation (Spindelman, 2011). Absent minor sexually-transmitted diseases in this subculture, the sexual behavior was basically free of deadly diseases until 1981 when the first reports of a new immune deficiency syndrome, now known as HIV/AIDS, were reported in homosexual men in New York City, Los Angeles, and San Francisco (Tramont & Boyajian, 2010). Over 650,000 Americans have died from AIDS since the first case was defined in 1981 (CDC, 2015b; Tramont & Boyajian, 2010), but the disease began earlier and was probably imported from Haiti or Africa (WHO, 2014). Now, over 1.2 million people are currently living with the disease in the United States and approximately 57,000 new HIV infections appear each year (MMWR, 2011).

HIV/AIDS is often viewed as a fault-based disease with a general belief that people with the disease were not innocently or inadvertently infected with HIV, but simply made poor lifestyle choices. This view, in turn, results in moral and judgmental attitudes that HIV/AIDS is an impure disease affecting immoral people (UNAIDS, 2013). As a result of these views, many Americans hold attitudes that stigmatize people with HIV/AIDS (Kaiser Family Foundation, 2011). These prejudicial attitudes are strongly correlated with misunderstanding the mechanisms of HIV transmission and overestimating the risks of casual contact (Goldfein & Schalman-Bergen, 2010). Negative attitudes affecting social groups disproportionately affected by the pandemic further stigmatize the disease. Nevertheless, these views and attitudes do not have to remain this way, and they should not be this way 35 years into the pandemic (CSDH, 2015, 2008). As HIV co-infections affect people in the mainstream of society, prejudicial attitudes and behaviors may change in subsequent years. Likewise, ARV treatment may help reduce stigma and discrimination; as people living with HIV stay productive, they may not be viewed as social outcasts.

Social Determinants of Health

As the quote by Marshall Forstein at the beginning of this chapter noted, those populations who, before the HIV/AIDS pandemic arrived, were already socially marginalized or stigmatized, became at greatest risk of HIV infection (Mann, 1996; Novogrodsky, 2009). Blaming the diseased for a disease ignores the **social determinants of health**; the primary factors that shape the health of people are not medical treatments but rather the living conditions they experience—including, but not limited to, the unrelenting stigma, disability-based discrimination, and social exclusion from being HIV-infected. As illustrated in **FEATURE BOX 11-6**,

---

FEATURE BOX 11-6

Social Determinants of Health Complicating Comprehensive Solutions to the HIV/AIDS Pandemic:

- Denial
- Discrimination
- Homelessness
- Homophobia
- Inadequate medical coverage
- Inadequate social safety network
- Lack of education about HIV infections based on public health science
- Limited access to health care
- Misinformation and misunderstanding (or rejection) of science
- Poverty
- Punitive criminalization of HIV status
- Racism
- Restricted access to life-extending care
- Sexism
- Social exclusion
- Stigmatization of HIV
- Unemployment and job insecurity due to infections and opportunistic diseases

— Sources: CSDH, 2015; DOJ & CDC, 2014; Mikkonen & Raphael, 2010; Strangio, 2015; The White House, 2014.

these determinants of health are not substantially different today than from living in the 1980s when the pandemic first appeared in the United States (Mendonsa, 2010).

While a complex set of intertwined forces presents significant challenges to addressing HIV/AIDS, the pandemic is a shared responsibility that necessitates equitable access to health care (WHO, 2010). To an extent, the government is responsible for controlling the social determinants of health that affect the risk of contracting HIV (Walker, 2007). The traditional value of compassion for the least fortunate demands attention to the effects of untreated HIV infection on individuals and families (Levine, et al., 2007). A compassionate society cannot tolerate avoidable suffering.

Our Challenge: At the Crossroads Facing the Second Wave

While more than half of Americans support increased funding for HIV/AIDS (Kaiser Family Foundation, 2011), how the nation chooses to respond determines the manner by which the pandemic will be confronted (Mann, 1996). **FEATURE BOX 11-7** illustrates what could be done, or what ethically should be done, in addition to everything that is already being done.

Today, HIV/AIDS is as much an ethical issue as a medical one. As illustrated in **FEATURE BOX 11-8**, the HIV/AIDS pandemic has taught the nation what human rights are important and necessary (Frautschi, 2010; Novogrodsky, 2009).

The nation has begun to accept responsibility for reforming its health care system to meet the needs of nearly all members of society, but all the same, HIV/AIDS remains a national issue deserving of the highest priority (The White House, 2014). If the second wave of the HIV/AIDS pandemic begins to hit the nation coupled with a wave of co-infections (possibly multi-drug-resistant TB) as is already happening in developing nations worldwide (WHO, 2014b), the question is whether we are taking too long to learn from the lessons of the recent past (Anand, 2012; Tramont & Boyajian, 2010; Wharton, 2006).

FEATURE BOX 11-7

The Nation's Ethical Obligations

- Comprehensively contain communicable diseases acquired from birth, accidents, violence, or lifestyle choices
- Continue funding comprehensive public health programs to address communicable diseases
- Decrease HIV-related health disparities
- Find a way to weigh and then balance civil liberties protections with routine HIV testing
- Increase unfettered access to high-quality life-extending care
- Optimize health outcomes
- Provide affordable access to health insurance
- Provide palliative and hospice care to people experiencing AIDS-related end-stage illnesses
- Reduce HIV incidence

— Sources: IOM, 2011; Kagan, 2007; Mann, 1996; The White House, 2014.

FEATURE BOX 11-8

Human Rights Regardless of Age, Ethnicity, Gender or Gender Identity, Race, Sexual Orientation, or Socioeconomic Circumstances

- Access to affordable health insurance
- Access to health care
- Human dignity and self-determination
- Life-prolonging and quality-of-life-enhancing medical interventions based on scientific evidence as opposed to ideology

— Sources: Mann, 1996; The White House, 2014.

ETHICAL OR UNETHICAL DECISION

Criminalization of Exposure to HIV Infection

Ethics Issue: *Should people living with HIV be subject to imprisonment or other criminal penalties for engaging in voluntary, protected sexual encounters without first disclosing their HIV status to prospective sex partners?*

Ethics Analysis: Yes, people living with HIV have a duty and ethical obligation to inform their sex partners before engaging in any encounters that could transmit the virus to someone else, even if they have an undetectable viral load. It is not ethical for anyone who is HIV-infected to knowingly engage in any type of sexual encounter without informing their partners of their HIV infection, even if a condom is safely used and no transmission of HIV occurs. The unethical act is risking exposing their partners to HIV without their knowledge, and therefore without their fully informed and truly voluntary consent, not the actual HIV transmission. In more legal terms, the sex partner consented to the sexual act, but not to the sexual act with the risk of contracting HIV.

Ethics Analysis: No, people living with HIV cannot generally transmit the disease when their viral load is undetectable and they engage in safe sexual activity. Penalties for claimed nondisclosure and exposure should be proportionate to any actual resulting harm.

Court's Holding and Decision: Transmission of HIV is not required for a criminal conviction that could result in 25 years' imprisonment. The prohibited activity covers all sexual conduct that could possibly expose someone to HIV without informing the partners of the HIV infection, regardless of whether or not their partners contract HIV.

— *State v. Musser*, 721 N.W.2d 734 (Iowa Supreme Court 2006). *See, e.g.,* Lee, 2014; Perone, 2013; Spindelman, 2013 (discussing this court decision). Note: Two years following this decision, peer-reviewed literature began documenting that people who are HIV-positive without any other sexually transmitted infections and who are following an effective ARV treatment regimen are not generally infectious (Langley & Nardi, 2010; Vernazza, et al., 2008). Yet, because there is still a 4% chance of HIV infection during any sexual encounter (including with the use of a condom, due to the possibility of improper usage and breakage), this finding does not affect the duty or ethical obligation to inform sex partners of one's infection status (Currie, 2012). This medical information may, however, help destigmatize the disease in the 32 states where risking the transmission of HIV can be a crime (DOJ & CDC, 2014).

CHAPTER SUMMARY

- The HIV/AIDS pandemic has profoundly affected medicine, the ethics of health care, and adult mortality.
- Early identification and monitoring of HIV is integral to health care; HIV does not have to lead to AIDS if people who are infected have access to ARVs while their immune systems are still strong.
- This public health issue is influential in the reform of the U.S. health care system.
- Thousands are still dying from this preventable disease in the United States; they need prophylactic care but do not get it because of the cost, or they delay HIV testing because of the cost until it is too late, or they are too socially disorganized to use offered care.
- There are suggestions that HIV/AIDS is a special disease state, one so serious that the government and the pharmaceutical industry have an ethical obligation to provide essential ARVs and AIDS medications to ameliorate this preventable disease.
- A systematic review of HIV prevention programs advocating sexual abstinence outside a monogamous marriage finds no evidence that these programs reduced the incidence of HIV infections over the past decade.
- The ethics of reporting new cases of HIV by full names as opposed to by codes remains controversial.
- There are two prongs of the approach to the HIV/AIDS pandemic in the United States: early detection and treatment of the HIV infection before it progresses to full-blown AIDS.
- Testing for HIV is increasingly becoming a routine part of interaction with the health care system in the U.S.
- Minors can consent to testing for HIV in all states and can consent to treatment for HIV/AIDS in many states.
- In the absence of state duty-to-warn laws, a physician's failure to warn known sexual partners of a newly diagnosed HIV patient does not generally give rise to liability.
- All states have criminal laws punishing HIV-positive individuals for behaviors that risk HIV transmission, even if no transmission occurs.
- HIV-infected individuals do not enjoy protection against discrimination under the ADA.
- The second wave of HIV infections is bringing with it the risk of more severe secondary infections, such as TB; this risk is increased even for individuals without HIV because the infections are multi-drug-resistant.
- Most HIV infections and AIDS-related deaths could be prevented if everyone had access to information and medical treatment for preventing and treating HIV.
- Controlling, and ultimately ending, the global HIV/AIDS pandemic is as much an economical responsibility as an ethical one.

REFERENCES

ACLU (American Civil Liberties Union). (2008). *State criminal statutes on HIV transmission*. New York: ACLU.

Anand, G. (2012, June 19). India in race to contain untreatable tuberculosis. *Wall Street Journal*, p. A1.

Anderson, Jr., H. E. (2010). We can work it out: Co-op compulsory licensing as the way forward in improving access to anti-retroviral drugs. *Boston University Journal of Science and Technology Law, 16*, 167–193.

Barry, J. M. (2010). *The great influenza: The story of the deadliest pandemic in history* (Revised). New York, NY: Penguin Books.

Basas, C. G. (2010). The new boys: Women with disabilities and the legal profession. *Berkeley Journal of Gender, Law and Justice, 25*, 32–115.

Baxi, U. (2012). The place of the human right to health and contemporary approaches to global justice: Some impertinent interrogations. In J. Harrington & M. Stuttaford (Eds.), *Global health and human rights: Legal and philosophical perspectives* (pp. 12–27). New York, NY: Routledge, Taylor and Francis Group.

Burris, S., et al. (2010). Racial disparities in injection-related HIV: A case study of toxic law. *Temple Law Review, 82*, 1263–1302.

___. (2007). Do criminal laws influence HIV risk behavior? An empirical trial. *Arizona State Law Journal, 39*, 467–517.

CDC (Centers for Disease Control and Prevention). (2015). *About HIV*. Atlanta, GA: CDC.

___. (2015a). *HIV among youth*.

___. (2015b). *HIV in the United States: At a glance*.

___. (2015c). *HIV surveillance report: Diagnoses of HIV infection in the United States and dependent areas*.

___. (2014). *CDC fact sheet: HIV in the United States: The stages of care*.

___. (2014a). *TB and HIV coinfection*.

___. (2013). *Extensively drug-resistant tuberculosis (XDR TB)*.

___. (2013a). *HIV cost-effectiveness*.

___. (2013b). *Turning the tide on HIV: Division of HIV/AIDS prevention annual report*.

___. (2013c). Mortality slide series.

Cohen, M. S., et al. (2011). Prevention of HIV-1 infection with early antiretroviral therapy. *New England Journal of Medicine, 365*(6), 493–505.

Corey, L. (2011, June 18). Thirty years of fighting AIDS: A progress report. *Wall Street Journal*, p. A15.

CSDH (Commission on the Social Determinants of Health). (2015). *Health in the Americas*. Geneva, Switzerland: World Health Organization.

___. (2008). *Closing the gap in a generation: Health equity through action on the social determinants of health*. Geneva, Switzerland: World Health Organization.

Currie, D. (2012). National fight against HIV/AIDS targets improved care, education. *The Nation's Health*, p. 8.

DOJ (U.S. Department of Justice) & CDC (Centers for Disease Control and Prevention). (2014). *Prevalence and public health implications of state laws that criminalize potential HIV exposure in the United States, AIDS and behavior*. Washington, DC: DOJ and Atlanta, GA: CDC.

Eisenberg, C. B. (2010). Genetic predispositions v. present disabilities: Why genetically predisposed asymptomatic individuals are not protected by the amended ADA. *Boston University Journal of Science and Technology Law, 16*, 130–156.

Emilio, A. B. (2011). Tripping over TRIPS and the global HIV/AIDS epidemic: Legislation and political decisions in Brazil and the United States. *Journal of Contemporary Health Law and Policy, 28*, 57–85.

Fagan, J. L., et al. (2010). Understanding people who have never received HIV care: A population-based approach. *Public Health Reports, 125*, 520–527.

Farmer, P. (2005). *Pathologies of power: Health, human rights, and the new war on the poor*. Oakland, CA: University of California Press.

Fishman, H. R. (2013). HIV confidentiality and stigma: A way forward. *University of Pennsylvania Journal of Constitutional Law, 16*, 199–231.

Frautschi, S. (2010). Understanding HIV-specific laws in Central America. *International Journal of Legal Information, 38*, 43–92.

George, E. (2011). The human right to health and HIV/AIDS: South Africa and South-South cooperation to reframe global intellectual property principles and promote access to essential medications. *Indiana Journal of Global Legal Studies, 18*, 167–197.

Gerwint, L. E. (2011). Planning for pandemic: A new model for governing public health emergencies. *American Journal of Law and Medicine, 37*, 128–171.

Goldfein, R. B., & Schalman-Bergen, S. R. (2010). From the streets of Philadelphia: The AIDS Law Project of Pennsylvania's how-to primer on mitigating health disparities. *Temple Law Review, 82*, 1205–1230.

Gostin, L. O., et al. (2011). Restoring health to health reform: Integrating medicine and public health to advance the population's well-being. *University of Pennsylvania Law Review, 159*, 1777–1822.

Gregg, S. (2011). Health, health care, and rights: A new natural law theory perspective. *Notre Dame Journal of Law, Ethics and Public Policy, 25*, 463–478.

Guttmacher Institute. (2015). *Minors' access to STI services: State policies in brief*. New York, NY: Guttmacher Institute.

Helmink, J. M. (2010). Sexually transmitted identification. *Information Society Journal of Law and Policy, 5*, 569–601.

HHS (U.S. Department of Health and Human Services). (2014). *Guide for HIV/AIDS clinical care*. Rockville, MD: HHS, Health Resources and Services Administration.

HUD (U.S. Department of Housing and Urban Development). (2015). *The annual homeless assessment report to Congress*. Washington, DC: HUD.

ICASO (International Council of AIDS Service Organizations). (2015). *Working together: A community-driven guide to meaningful involvement in national responses to HIV*. Toronto, Canada: ICASO.

IOM (Institute of Medicine). (2013). *Evaluation of the President's Emergency Plan for AIDS Relief (PEPFAR)*. Washington, DC: National Academies Press.

___. (2011). *HIV screening and access to care: System capacity for increased HIV testing and provision of care.*

___. (2010). *HIV screening and access to care: Exploring barriers and facilitators to expanded HIV testing.*

Johnstone, G. L. (2010). A social worker's dilemma when a client has a sexually transmitted disease: The conflict between the duty of confidentiality and the duty to warn sexual partners. *University of Louisville Law Review, 49*, 111–132.

Kagan, E. T. (2007). Morality v. reality: The struggle to effectively fight HIV/AIDS and respect human rights. *Brooklyn Journal of International Law, 32*, 1201–1226.

Kaiser Commission on Medicaid and the Uninsured. (2008). *Approaches to covering the uninsured: A guide.* Washington, DC: Kaiser Commission on Medicaid and the Uninsured.

Kaiser Family Foundation. (2015). *Estimated number of adults and adolescents living with an HIV diagnosis.* Menlo Park, CA: Kaiser.

___. (2014). *The HIV/AIDS epidemic in the United States.*

___. (2014a). *HIV testing in the United States.*

___. (2014b). *State Medicaid coverage of routine HIV screening.*

___. (2014c). *Fact sheet: AIDS drug assistance programs (ADAPs).*

___. (2011). *HIV/AIDS at 30: A public opinion perspective.*

___. (2011a). *Fact sheet: Sexual health of adolescents and young adults in the United States.*

Klemm, S. (2010). Keeping prevention in the crosshairs: A better HIV exposure law for Maryland. *Journal of Health Care Law and Policy, 13*, 495–524.

Kruse, K. R. (2011). The jurisprudential turn in legal ethics. *Arizona Law Review, 53*, 493–531.

Kysar, R. M. (2011). Lasting legislation. *University of Pennsylvania Law Review, 159*, 1007–1068.

Langley, E. E., & Nardi, Jr., D. J. (2010). The irony of outlawing AIDS: A human rights argument against the criminalization of HIV transmission. *Georgetown Journal of Gender and Law, 11*, 743–794.

Lee, S. G. (2014). Criminal law and HIV testing: Empirical analysis of how at-risk individuals respond to the law. *Yale Journal of Health Policy Law and Ethics, 14*, 194–238.

Levine, M. A., et al. (2007). Improving access to health care: A consensus ethical framework to guide proposals for reform. *Hastings Center Report, 9/10*, 14–19.

Lin, S.-R. (2013). A costly illusion? An empirical study of Taiwan's use of isolation to control tuberculosis transmission and its implications for public health law and policymaking. *Asian Pacific Law and Policy Journal, 14*, 107–165.

Mann, J. (1996). Essay: Human rights and AIDS: The future of the pandemic. *John Marshall Law Review, 30*, 195–206.

McArthur, J. B. (2009). As the tide turns: The changing HIV/AIDS epidemic and the criminalization of HIV exposure. *Cornell Law Review, 94*, 707–741.

McKay, B. (2013, March 2). Dangerous TB patient detained on U.S. border. *Wall Street Journal*, p. A9.

Mendonsa, L. R. S. (2010). Dueling causation and the rights of employees with HIV under § 504 of the Rehabilitation Act. *The Scholar: St. Mary's Law Review on Minority Issues, 13*, 273–316.

Mikkonen, J., & Raphael, D. (2010). *Social determinants of health: The Canadian facts.* Toronto, Canada: York University School of Health Policy and Management.

Minahan, W. T. (2009). Disclosure before exposure: A review of Ohio's HIV criminalization statutes. *Ohio Northern University Law Review, 35*, 83–106.

Mitchell, V. K. (2011). Protecting non-U.S. citizens from removal terminating HIV/AIDS treatment. *Fordham International Law Journal, 34*, 1620–1664.

MMWR (*Morbidity and Mortality Weekly Report*). (2011). HIV surveillance. *60*(21), 689–693.

___. (2006). Revised recommendations for HIV testing of adults, adolescents, and pregnant women in health care settings. *55*(14), 1–17.

Montaner, J. S., et al. (2006). The case for expanding access to highly active antiretroviral therapy to curb the growth of the HIV pandemic. *The Lancet, 368*, 531–536.

Mooty, B. M. (2010). Solving the medical crisis for immigration detainees: Is the proposed Detainee Basic Medical Care Act the answer? *Journal of Theory and Practice: Law and Inequality, 28*, 223–252.

Mukherjee, G. N. (2007). Improving the pharmaceutical industry: Optimality inside the framework of the current legal system provides access to medicines for HIV/AIDS patients in sub-saharan Africa. *Journal of Transnational Law and Policy, 17*, 121–150.

NASTAD (National Alliance of State and Territorial AIDS Directors). (2011). *National HIV/AIDS strategy imperative: Fighting stigma and discrimination by repealing HIV-specific criminal statutes.* Washington, DC: NASTAD.

Novogrodsky, N. (2014). After AIDS. *Melbourne Journal of International Law, 14*, 643–669.

___. (2009). The duty of treatment: Human rights and the HIV/AIDS pandemic. *Yale Human Rights and Development Law Journal, 12*, 1–61.

Outterson, K. (2008). Should access to medicines and TRIPS flexibilities be limited to specific diseases? *American Journal of Law and Medicine, 34*, 279–301.

Perone, A. (2013). From punitive to proactive: An alternative approach for responding to HIV criminalization that departs from penalizing marginalized communities. *Hastings Women's Law Journal, 24*(2), 363–406.

Pierce, M. W., et al. (2011). Testing public health ethics: Why the CDC's HIV screening recommendations may violate the least infringement principle. *Journal of Law, Medicine and Ethics, 39*, 263–270.

Pottker-Fishel, C. G. (2007). Improper bedside manner: Why state partner notification laws are ineffective in controlling the proliferation of HIV. *Journal of Law and Medicine, 17*, 147–179.

Price, P. J. (2014). Sovereignty, citizenship, and public health in the United States. *New York University Journal of Legislation and Public Policy, 17*, 919–988.

Purcell, J. (2010). Adverse clinical and public health consequences of limited anti-retroviral licensing. *Berkeley Technology Law Journal, 25*, 103–134.

Ray, J. A. (2007). A social disability? The medical realities and social implications of classifying asymptomatic HIV as a disability under the Americans with Disabilities Act. *Loyola Law Review, 53*, 257–289.

Richards, III, E. P. (2010). The United States smallpox bioterrorism preparedness plan: Rational response or Potemkin planning? *William Mitchell Law Review, 36*, 5179–5220.

Robichaud, S. (2009). Considering innovative alternatives to handling cases of adults with special conditions under the Social Security Act. *Journal of the National Association of Administrative Law Judiciary, 29*, 433–478.

Schackman, B. R., et al. (2008). The cost-effectiveness of HLA-B5701 genetic screening to guide initial antiretroviral therapy for HIV. *AIDS, 22*(15), 2025–2033.

Schalman-Bergen, S. (2007). CDC's call for routine HIV testing raises implementation concerns. *Journal of Law, Medicine and Ethics, 35*, 223–225.

Scott, J. T. (2009). The difficult road to compelling vaccination for sexually transmitted diseases: How Gardasil and those to follow will change the way that states require inoculation. *Kentucky Law Journal, 97*, 697–719.

Selmi, G. (2006). Interpreting the Americans with Disabilities Act: Why the Supreme Court rewrote the statute, and why Congress did not care. *George Washington Law Review, 76*, 522–575.

Sinclair, U. (2015). *The jungle*. New York, NY: Signet (Original work published 1905).

Southerland, A. N. (2011). Stigmatized silence: The exclusion of HIV and AIDS sufferers from the "Obamacare" legal landscape. *Cornell Journal of Law and Public Policy, 20*, 833–853.

Spindelman, M. (2013). Sexuality's law. *Columbia Journal of Gender and the Law, 24*, 87–252.

____. (2011). Sexual freedom's shadows, unlimited intimacy: Reflections on the subculture of barebacking by Tim Dean. *Yale Journal of Law and Feminism, 23*, 179–253.

Stoto, M. A. (2008). Public health surveillance in the twenty-first century: Achieving population health goals while protecting individuals' privacy and confidentiality. *Georgetown Law Journal, 96*, 703–719.

Strangio, C. (2015). *HIV is not a crime*. New York, NY: American Civil Liberties Union.

Tomaszewski, E. O. (2011). *Human rights update: HIV/AIDS and homelessness*. Washington, DC: National Association of Social Workers.

Tracey, E., & Lange, R. (2012). *A medical news roundup from Johns Hopkins: One in three patients had some drug resistance*. Baltimore, MD: Johns Hopkins Medicine.

Tramont, E. C., & Boyajian, S. S. (2010). Learning from history: What the public health response to syphilis teaches us about HIV/AIDS. *Journal of Contemporary Health Law and Policy, 26*, 253–299.

Tsai, J. T. (2007). Not tripping over the pebbles: Focusing on overlooked TRIPS article 66 for technology transfer to solve Africa's AIDS crisis. *Michigan State Journal of Medicine and Law, 11*, 447–478.

UCSF (University of California-San Francisco) & National HIV/AIDS Clinicians' Consultation Center. (2011). *Compendium of state HIV testing laws*. San Francisco, CA: UCSF.

UNAIDS (United Nations Programme on HIV/AIDS). (2013). *Report on the global AIDS epidemic*. Geneva, Switzerland: World Health Organization.

Vagelos, P. R. (2014, February 22). Chairman of the Board, Regeneron Pharmaceuticals, Keynote Address on "Reimaging Health Care: Driving Change in a Patient-Centered World" at the 2014 Wharton Health Care Business Conference, Philadelphia, PA.

Venkatapuram, S., & Marmot, M. (2009). Epidemiology and social justice in light of social determinants of health research. *Bioethics, 23*(2), 79–89.

Vernazza, P., et al. (2008). Sero-positive people that do not have any other STI and are following an effective regime of ARVs are uninfectious through sexual contact. *Swiss Medical Bulletin, 89*, 1–7.

Walker, E. M. (2007). The HIV/AIDS pandemic and human rights: A continuum approach. *Florida Journal of International Law, 19*, 335–419.

Wharton School at the University of Pennsylvania. (2011). What's behind U.S. drug companies' response to the AIDS crisis abroad? *Knowledge@Wharton*.

____. (2006). Pandemics in an integrated global society: An economist's view.

___. (2006a). Raising money to treat the world's sickest people isn't the problem: Spending it is.

White House, The. (2014). *National HIV/AIDS strategy for the United States: Update of 2014 federal actions to achieve national goals and improve outcomes along the HIV care continuum.* Washington, DC: The White House, Office of National AIDS Policy.

___. (2010). *National HIV/AIDS strategy for the United States.*

WHO (World Health Organization). (2014). *HIV/AIDS fact sheet.* Geneva, Switzerland: WHO.

___. (2014a). *Global tuberculosis report.*

___. (2014b). *What is multi-drug resistant tuberculosis and how do we control it?*

___. (2010). *Report on the global AIDS epidemic.*

Wilkinson, R., & Pickett, K. (2011). *The spirit level: Why greater equality makes societies stronger.* New York, NY: Bloomsbury Press.

Winslow, R. (2010, July 23). Crucial window to beat back HIV. *Wall Street Journal*, p. A5.

Winslow, R., & McKay, B. (2010, July 19). Study links HIV to urban poverty. *Wall Street Journal*, p. A2.

Wong, G. (2010). *Research paper: Is SARS a poor man's disease? Socioeconomic status and risk factors for SARS transmission.* Philadelphia, PA: Wharton School at the University of Pennsylvania.

Wynia, M. K., & Schwab, A. P. (2006). *Ensuring fairness in health care coverage: An employer's guide to make good decisions on tough issues.* New York, NY: American Medical Association.

Yuen, M. (2007). HIV testing of pregnant women: Why present approaches fail to reach the desired objective and the unconsidered option. *Cardozo Journal of Law and Gender, 14,* 185–210.

CHAPTER 12

© Keystone Pictures USA/Alamy

Environmental Safety and Gun Injury Prevention

"No society that feeds its children on tales of successful violence can expect them not to believe that violence in the end is rewarded."

— **Margaret Mead** (1901–1978), American cultural anthropologist

LEARNING OBJECTIVES

After completing this chapter, the reader should be able to:

1. Understand that environmental safety and the well-being of the U.S. population should guide the nation's laws and ethical principles with regard to gun injury prevention.
2. Analyze the distinct but similar fundamental legal and ethical principles underlying the individual rights to both self-defense and gun control.
3. Describe the environmental safety issues stemming from homicides and suicides committed with guns, including the medical and financial impact of guns on American society.
4. Evaluate the data and research on decreased life expectancy as a result of gun injuries and how this information might be used to address the gun control controversy.

KEY TERMS

Corrective justice
Environmental safety
Firearms
Handguns

Inattentional blindness
Protection of Lawful Commerce in Arms Act of 2005 (PLCAA)

Risk pools
Substitution effect

ETHICAL OR UNETHICAL DECISION

Firearms on College Campuses

Ethics Issue: *What ethical principles, if any, would justify students and visitors being allowed to carry loaded, concealed guns on university campuses?*

In Brief: The issue of guns on campus gained prominence after senior Seung-Hui Cho murdered 32 and injured 25 students and faculty in 2 related incidents on the campus of Virginia Tech University before committing suicide himself in 2007. While Utah is the only state to allow licensed gun owners to carry concealed weapons on public university campuses, 10 states have introduced legislation to allow guns on campus, according to the National Conference of State Legislatures. *See generally* Campoy, 2011.

Part of this debate is Students for Concealed Carry on Campus, a national advocate for the right to carry concealed firearms on campuses. The University of Colorado bars those who hold a concealed carry permit from carrying on campus. Before Students for Concealed Carry on Campus filed this lawsuit, several students sought permission to carry on campus and all requests were denied.

— *The Regents of the University of Colorado, et al. v. Students for Concealed Carry on Campus, LLC, et al.,* 271 P.3d 496 (Colorado Supreme Court 2012). (*See Ethical or Unethical Decision* at the end of this chapter for discussion of this ethics issue.)

Introduction

The ethics surrounding the gun debate are volatile. Discussions tend to evolve around how things are expressed, as opposed to what is expressed. For instance, because there is no common agreement or generally accepted definition of **environmental safety**, or freedom from being harmed or injured by violence, there is legitimate concern that any discussion on gun injuries could be misleading (Bishop, 2012). In this chapter, the focus of environmental safety is on reasonable regulation of **handguns**, or small, cheap guns that can be fired with one hand (Kendall, 2011), as opposed to **firearms**, which are defined as all guns, including handguns. Gun control proponents decry the inadequacies of regulations that permit relatively free access to handguns and argue that the boundless availability of handguns encourages gun injuries (Buckman, 2010). Advocates of gun rights, for their part, condemn measures that penalize law-abiding citizens, and instead call for more vigorous enforcement of existing laws targeting criminals (Henderson, 2010; NRA, 2012).

This chapter attempts to rationally depict what each side of the gun debate has in common with the other by discussing facts neither side can reasonably disagree with, as illustrated in **FEATURE BOX 12-1**. While no claim can be made to have covered all factual commonalities, this chapter attempts to mitigate differences by using numerous measures of gun injuries. The fundamental principle in this debate is that environmental safety and the well-being of the U.S. population must be the focus of the nation's laws and ethical principles (Selkowitz, 2011). The ethical principles must direct the law to achieve effective prevention strategies and reduce gun injuries.

Despite its status as an advanced, high-income country, the United States has some remarkable characteristics with regard to environmental safety (Wharton, 2005). As illustrated in **FEATURE BOX 12-2**, while the United States is considered among the safest countries

FEATURE BOX 12-1

Environmental Safety Facts: Ethical Intolerance (or Unethical Tolerance) of the Situation at Hand

- Gun injuries kill 44,000 to 55,000 adults and children every year (151 deaths per day).
- Almost 4 times as many people suffer from gun injuries as are killed by guns.
- There are 135,000 to 168,000 non-fatal gun injuries each year (19 every hour).
- Approximately 310 million privately owned guns are in the United States, which is nearly the equivalent of 1 gun per person (including infants and children).
- More than half of the country's 36,000 yearly suicides are committed with firearms.
- For 15- to 24-year olds, firearm homicide rates in the United States are 43 times higher than in the other countries.

— Sources: CDF, 2014; Parks, et al., 2014; Richardson & Hemenway, 2011. Note: The number of privately owned guns in the United States does not include unlicensed guns, guns in the possession of law enforcement, or guns held by other government agents, like the 2.2 million armed service personnel in the U.S. military.

FEATURE BOX 12-2

U.S. Homicide Rates from Gun Violence

- 12 times that of Japan
- 10 times that of France and Germany
- 7 times that of Spain
- 5 times that of Australia and China
- 4 times that of Canada
- 3 times that of Finland

— Source: United Nations, 2015. Note: Homicide rates per 100,000 people in a country's population are from countries' law enforcement and public agency reports to the United Nations Office on Drugs and Crime.

in the world in terms of avoiding personal harm or injury, deaths from gun injuries are astoundingly high (Richardson & Hemenway, 2011).

Environmental Safety Litigation

America's large cities are experiencing an alarming number of homicides, mostly committed with guns (Macinko & Marinho de Souza, 2007). Debate surrounds how to address and apply this fact. New York City decided to attack the so-called iron pipeline of illegal guns on the basis of the community's environmental safety.

ETHICS CASE
Illegal Gun Sales

City of New York v. A-1 Jewelry & Pawn, Inc. (A-1 Jewelry III), et al.
[New York City v. Gun Dealer]
252 F.R.D. 132 (U.S. District Court for the Eastern District of New York 2008)

Facts: More than half of the murders in New York City stem from illegal handguns, and most of the guns confiscated in New York come from outside of the state. Therefore, in 2006, the city sued 27 gun dealers in Georgia, South Carolina, Virginia, Pennsylvania, and Ohio, claiming that their lax screening practices and illegal gun sales created a public nuisance in the city.

Legal Analysis: All but one of the 27 dealers settled with New York City and agreed to court appointment of a federal monitor to oversee firearm sales at their stores. The 27th dealer moved for summary judgment, but this motion was denied in part because extensive discovery revealed that at least 72 firearms sold by this dealer were recovered in connection with criminal activity. This number of illegal guns was determined to be a public nuisance, since illegally possessed firearms interfere with the health and safety of a large number of people within the city.

Rule of Law: The exercise of personal jurisdiction over out-of-state dealers is appropriate and the sales practices of dealers can be considered a public nuisance.

Ethics Issue: Should gun dealers be held responsible for violence resulting from their illegal gun sales?

Ethics Analysis: While a wave of guns acquired from illicit gun traffickers through interstate smuggling pipelines has been breaking over the nation for years, less than 1 percent of the federally licensed gun dealers account for the majority of guns that can be traced to crimes. New York City set out to hold this 1 percent accountable for illegally selling guns to criminal consumers, unlicensed traffickers, or straw purchasers who make sham purchases in their names and then hand the weapons over to prohibited purchasers not entitled to purchase guns, such as minors or felons. As the city's litigation was starting, Congress avoided addressing gun dealers' responsibility by enacting the **Protection of Lawful Commerce in Arms Act of 2005 (PLCAA)**. This legislation shields the firearms industry from any liability for gun injuries. The ethical dilemma of this ongoing litigation is obscured by the issue of whether a high number of certain dealers' guns traced to crimes actually indicate illegal behavior by those licensed gun dealers.

   One side of this debate maintains that the best indicator that a gun has been illegally trafficked is if the gun was sold by a licensed dealer to whom many other crime guns have been traced. The other side maintains that tracking evidence of illegal gun sales by gun dealers is circumstantial at best. Tracking of crime guns to a few dealers is more the result of their high-volume sales as opposed to illegal sales to purchasers prohibited from acquiring guns. In support of this position, opponents of trace counts maintain that most crime guns are acquired by illegal acts of the purchasers, not by illegal acts of the gun dealers. Supporters of trace counts acknowledge that most licensed gun dealers operate within the confines of the law; they simply want to track the 1 percent who are unaccounted for under the current system and hold them responsible for the violence resulting from their illegal gun sales.

Gun control proponents fear that the legislative process in Congress is frustrated by powerful special interest groups who vehemently oppose stricter controls. While strict gun control laws are the first line of defense against illegal gun sales, many gun control laws are being struck down by courts recognizing an individual right to possess guns for self-defense. Given this situation, state and local governments are left on their own to rid their streets of illegal guns. Today, neither side disputes the fact that most crime guns are sold by a small minority of licensed firearms dealers in 10 states with low-control gun laws, but this is where agreement by both sides of this debate ends.

Gun control proponents want gun dealers who fail to take any reasonable measures to mitigate illegal sales to straw purchasers, convicted felons, juveniles, and others prohibited by law from acquiring guns, to be held responsible for the gun injuries ensuing from their sales practices. Such gun dealers are seen as crossing the line of ethics; their reckless behavior too often succeeds in increasing the risk of harm to victims of gun injuries and deaths.

Advocates of gun rights maintain that individual gun dealers should not be forced to bear the social costs of violence (or harms to society, such as health care costs from gun injuries), as a means of achieving environmental safety. In recognition of this need to balance individual rights against social costs, the PLCAA shields gun dealers from civil liabilities arising from gun injuries; gun dealers are not civilly liable for sales of guns to criminal consumers, unlicensed traffickers, or straw purchasers, although they remain criminally liable for such sales.

Court's Holding and Decision: There was enough evidence to go forward with the case; however, most of the gun dealers chose to settle with New York City early on, as opposed to take the risk of litigation; the 1 gun dealer who held out also settled with the city in the end.

— Note that this case was vacated and remanded by *City of New York v. Mickalis Pawn Shop, LLC, et al.*, 645 F.3d 114 (U.S. Court of Appeals for the 2nd Circuit of New York 2011) (holding that injunction granted in *City of New York v. A-1 Jewelry & Pawn, Inc., et al.* was insufficiently specific and overbroad), and eventually dismissed by *City of New York v. Adventure Outdoors*, Inc., 2015 U.S. District LEXIS 75447 (U.S. District Court for the Eastern District of New York 2015) (parties reached settlement). *See, e.g.*, Morley, 2014 (discussing this court decision). *See also* Bridge, 2012; DePalo, 2013 (discussing New York City's handgun laws).

The early evidence indicates that this litigation against gun dealers is having a positive effect on limiting gun injuries in New York City, with a significant drop in illegal guns coming from a sample of the dealers sued (Selkowitz, 2011). While New York City's success may provide a model for other jurisdictions, it may also serve to influence Second Amendment jurisprudence.

ETHICAL DILEMMAS 12-1

1. Should the firearms industry share in the environmental safety and social costs arising from the individual right to gun ownership, or is protection of individual rights a social obligation, the human and financial consequences of which must be shared by all members of society?

Individual Rights and Second Amendment Jurisprudence

The flashpoint in the long-running debate over regulation of guns is the Second Amendment to the U.S. Constitution, which states: "A well regulated militia, being necessary to the security of a free state, the right of the people to keep and bear arms, shall not be infringed." Gun control proponents read this amendment as permitting regulation of gun ownership; advocates of gun rights read it as enshrining in law an individual's unfettered right to own guns (Wharton, 2005).

Although under current law the right to own guns is not absolute, there are ways to achieve common goals without completely sacrificing the Second Amendment (Wershbale, 2010). There is not an absolute trade-off between gun control and gun rights. In 2007, the U.S. Court of Appeals for the District of Columbia entered this debate and made history as the first federal appeals court to strike down a strict gun ban as a violation of the Second Amendment. The U.S. Supreme Court agreed to review this decision on gun ban regulations and issued its first ruling on the Second Amendment in nearly 70 years in *District of Columbia, et al. v. Heller.*

ETHICS CASE
Federal Regulation of Firearms

District of Columbia, et al. v. Heller
[Nation's Capitol v. Special Police Officer]
554 U.S. 570 [U.S. Supreme Court 2008]

Facts: The District of Columbia's gun ban prohibited ownership of handguns without a license and required all registered guns to be kept in an inoperable condition. District residents were required to keep lawfully owned firearms unloaded and disassembled or bound by a trigger lock or similar device in their homes. Dick Heller, a special police officer, was denied a license to keep a semi-automatic handgun at his home based on the District's handgun ban because the 7-clip bottom-loading weapon was characterized as a machine gun. Heller claimed he had a Second Amendment right to possess guns for self-defense in his home.

Legal Analysis: Heller, who had no association with any militia, challenged the District's gun ban; he did not assert a right to carry firearms outside his home, nor did he challenge the District's authority to require the registration of guns. As a special police officer, he was authorized to carry a handgun while on duty, but he also wanted to keep a handgun in his home for self-defense.

The Court extensively analyzed the precedent, text, and history of the Second Amendment and held that it granted individuals the right to possess guns, subject to reasonable restrictions. The District's complete gun ban was struck down as unconstitutional. It was found to reduce some modern-day categories of guns to the point of being useless, and unconstitutionally prohibited the lawful use of handguns for self-defense.

Rule of Law: When overly broad, general bans on private ownership of handguns for self-defense violate the Second Amendment; gun control laws prohibiting felons or the mentally ill from owning firearms, prohibiting possession in sensitive areas such as schools and government buildings, and regulating sales of guns remain permissible.

Ethics Issue: Should the ban on handguns have priority over the right of individuals to keep guns for private use in their homes?

Ethics Analysis: The essential goal of the gun ban was to reduce the total number of handguns in the District, which would reduce gun injuries and the number of gun-related deaths and accidents. Any restrictions that limit the availability of guns, however, also limit their availability for self-protection. Thus, important interests were at stake on each side of this equation.

There was a sharp division among the U.S. Supreme Court Justices on the question of whether those who ratified the Second Amendment would have prohibited gun bans based on the social impact of gun injuries in the District. Because court decisions interpret the U.S. Constitution, or make decisions based on what those who ratified the Second Amendment meant, sides with very different ethical principles are able to make authoritative claims about who Americans are and what they owe one another from the perspectives of advocating for gun control and gun rights.

Gun control proponents maintain that the Second Amendment was ratified to prevent the federal government from disbanding state militias. This side reads the Second Amendment as protecting only a right to possess arms in conjunction with service in a well-regulated militia; they do not acknowledge the individual right to possess guns for non-military purposes like self-defense. Advocates of gun rights, on the other hand, read the Second Amendment to preserve the militia as codifying the common law right of self-defense. This side elevates the individual right to use firearms in self-defense above the interests of the community.

This ruling may help move the gun debate forward. While the concept of the public good is often used to justify gun control, trade-offs involving Second Amendment rights are rarely simple. Gun control laws continue to remain controversial globally. While the assertion of an absolute right to guns often creates deadlock, this stalemate changed slightly in favor of gun rights advocates with this decision.

Court's Holding and Decision: The District's gun ban violated the human rights bestowed on individuals under the Second Amendment.

See, e.g., Adams, 2013; Bindbeutel, 2014; Bridge, 2012; Burns, 2013; Castiglione, 2012; Colvin, 2014; Crane, 2014; Curtis, 2015; Daniels, 2013; DeMitchell, 2014; DePalo, 2013; Dulan, 2014; Duquette, 2014; Fair, 2014; Foody, 2013; Forsey, 2013; Fox & DeLateur, 2014; Giles, 2014; Hardy, 2014; Hubbard, 2014; Lamartina, 2013; McNamara, 2014; Moeller, 2014; Moran, 2013; O'Shea, 2012; Pelaez, 2014; Pinals, 2014; Record & Gostin, 2014; Renneker, 2015; Rose, 2014; Ruebsamen, 2013; Salvin, 2014; Stidham, 2015; Stowell, 2014; Sturzenegger, 2013; Vasek, 2014; Wahl, 2014; West, 2013; Whitney, 2014 (discussing this court decision).

Heller is the first ruling by the U.S. Supreme Court to recognize an individual right to possess guns (Wyrick, 2011). The ruling explained and made clear that individuals bore arms before the Second Amendment was ever adopted (Hatt, 2011; NRA, 2012). While the decision ruled that the complete ban of handguns in the District of Columbia was unconstitutional, it stressed that certain regulations are legitimate. In addition to limiting the type of firearms that can be owned, the decision also upheld restrictions on the possession of firearms by felons and laws imposing conditions on the commercial sale of firearms.

Social Costs: Important or Unimportant?

As the gun injuries in America and their attendant health care costs continue to escalate, one side of this debate maintains that the individual right to possess guns should be balanced against the costs to society arising from exercise of that right. The other side maintains that social costs should never influence individual rights (Blackman, 2011). The debate after *Heller* is whether states and local governments should be permitted to place reasonable restrictions on the individual right to possess guns. While gun restrictions should not depend exclusively on their effects on individuals' welfare (Zamir & Medina, 2008), the next battleground is determining how the environmental safety of local communities can be emphasized so as to restore balance with the present emphasis on the right to possess guns.

ETHICS CASE
State and Local Regulation of Guns

McDonald, et al. v. City of Chicago, et al.
[Residents of Chicago v. City of Chicago]
561 U.S. 742 (U.S. Supreme Court 2010)

Facts: Otis McDonald, Adam Orlov, Colleen Lawson, and David Lawson are Chicago residents who would like to keep handguns in their homes for self-defense but are prohibited from doing so by Chicago's firearms laws. In 2008, in *District of Columbia, et al. v. Heller,* the U.S. Supreme Court held that the Second Amendment protected the right to possess guns for the purpose of self-defense and struck down a similar District of Columbia law that banned the possession of handguns in the home. Chicago and the village of Oak Park, a Chicago suburb, have laws effectively banning handgun possession by almost all private citizens. Chicago and Oak Park maintained that their municipal laws were constitutional because the Second Amendment has no application to the states. After *Heller*, McDonald filed this federal lawsuit alleging that Chicago's handgun ban has left them vulnerable to criminals.

Legal Analysis: The challenged ordinances effectively banned ownership of handguns by law-abiding private citizens. The U.S. Supreme Court held that the Second Amendment protected the right to possess guns for self-defense and that the Second Amendment was fully applicable to the states. Self-defense is a basic right and the central component of the Second Amendment. This Second Amendment right applies to handguns, which are the preferred firearm to keep and use for protection of one's home and family.

Rule of Law: The Second Amendment gives individuals the right to possess firearms for self-defense, a right implicit in the concept of ordered liberty.

Ethics Issue: Should the newly confirmed right of individuals to possess guns be a limitation on states when addressing local communities' needs to ban handguns?

Ethics Analysis: According to the individual rights approach of this U.S. Supreme Court decision, the community's right to environmental safety does not have priority over the right of individuals who wish to keep guns in their homes for self-defense.

Gun control proponents maintain that increased gun controls will improve environmental safety and reduce the incidence of gun injuries. In contrast, advocates of gun rights argue that law-abiding citizens will be made less safe by their inability to defend themselves against criminal violence. Both sides perceive risks associated with gun control: either too little gun control that inevitably leads to intentional shootings and accidents involving guns, or too much gun control that disarms responsible, law-abiding citizens and leaves them subject to violence.

Court's Holding and Decision: The Second Amendment right to own and possess handguns applies at the state and local level; state and local governments may not improperly restrict the human rights granted by the Second Amendment.

See, e.g., Bindbeutel, 2014; Bridge, 2012; Burns, 2013; Campbell, 2013; Colvin, 2014; Crane, 2014; Curtis, 2015, Daniels, 2013; DePalo, 2013; Fair, 2014; Forsey, 2013; Fox & DeLateur, 2014; Graham, 2010; Golimowski, 2012; Hubbard, 2014; Moeller, 2014; Moran, 2013; O'Shea, 2012; Pelaez, 2014; Perry, 2012; Pratt, 2014; Record & Gostin, 2014; Renneker, 2015; Ruebsamen, 2013; Stidham, 2015; Stowell, 2014; Styles, 2012; Tomei, 2012; Vasek, 2014; Wagner, 2012 (discussing this court decision).

The Epidemiology of Gun Injuries

While gun injury prevention is an ethical imperative, it also makes economic sense. Between $2.0 and $2.3 billion in preventable health care costs could be saved by reducing gun injuries (Selkowitz, 2011; AMA, 2007; Lemaire, 2005). Paradoxically, this cost of gun injuries is nearly the same cost that the nation's health care system spends on obesity, and with it diabetes, annually (Browne, et al., 2010; CDC, 2015). Put another way, gun injuries cost every man, woman, and child in the United States more than $320 each, annually. Over a lifetime, gun injuries cost each individual taxpayer more than $20,000 in preventable health care costs. Certainly this is an instance of **inattentional blindness** where the nation's thinking is being adapted at different rates by different groups. As illustrated in FEATURE BOX 12-3, these costs are a real tax that affects people on both sides of this debate.

While the cost of firearm fatalities is the highest of any injury-related deaths (Nance, et al., 2010), other gun injury costs, such as the social costs of fear, are difficult to quantify. Advocates of gun rights claim that preventable health care costs are a false model for decision-making on gun injury prevention, since health care costs should not entirely influence the individual right to possess guns. For gun rights advocates, the preventable health care costs of gun ownership should not outweigh the individual right to possess a gun. In other words, legal rights (such as the individual right to gun ownership) should be defended regardless of cost (Pound, 1911; Tidmarsh, 2010). In this instance, both sides are right. In

---

FEATURE BOX 12-3

Inattentional Blindness: Aggregate Costs of Gun Injuries

- Cost of public resources devoted to emergency transport, law enforcement, and criminal justice
- Emotional costs to the forced adaptation to increased risk
- Health care costs ($2 to $2.3 billion/year)
- Limits on freedom to live or work in certain places
- Limitations in hours of operation of retail establishments
- Lost productivity of victims and changes in the quality of life
- Private investments by business and individuals in protection and avoidance
- Restrictions on residential and commercial location decisions
- Toll on family and friends of gun injury and death victims

— Sources: CDF, 2014; WHO, 2014.

ETHICAL DILEMMAS 12-2

2. Does the individual right to bear arms outweigh the preventable health care costs from gun injuries?
3. Can individual rights and social costs be reconciled?

other words, preventable health care costs are a factor in environmental safety and must be considered in any strategies to prevent gun injuries, but health care costs are not the only factor that should be considered.

Cultural War Phenomenon over Facts

Environmental safety researchers note that federal databases on gun injuries suddenly became severely restricted leading up to the litigation for the U.S. Supreme Court's *Heller* decision (GAO, 2008). *Heller* left the door open for accepting reasonable gun control legislation if supported by findings of fact regarding the epidemiology of gun injuries. Debates about this epidemiology are just beginning to emerge as the clashes between gun control proponents and advocates of gun rights become more polarized (Kahan, et al., 2011). According to the Cultural Cognition Project at Yale Law School, when conclusions about gun injury prevention conflict with cultural values, people do not accept the consensus of environmental safety researchers (Greene, 2010). Yale labels this a "cultural war over facts," unfortunately, a phenomenon not unique to gun control.

Americans' Reduced Life Expectancy

Life expectancy is considered one of the best measures of quality of life when evaluating health care decisions. This measure summarizes in a single number all individual and external damages affecting people's lives (Lemaire, 2005). As illustrated in **FEATURE BOX 12-4**,

FEATURE BOX 12-4

Factors Affecting Life Expectancy

*   Accident history
*   Defective family genes
*   Environmental safety
*   High-risk sexual behavior
*   Limited access to high quality health care
*   Poor social-economic status
*   Proximity to environmental degradation
*   Malnutrition
*   Wars

— Source: Bezruchka, 2012.

while life expectancy is affected by numerous individual and external factors, including limited access to highquality health care, age distribution is not affected by these external factors; thus, life expectancy is an appropriate epidemiological tool for comparing different populations with dissimilar age structures.

Compared to other countries, America does not measure up very well in terms of life expectancy, and especially not when its spending on health care is considered. The life expectancy of Americans, as illustrated in **TABLE 12-1**, is less than other similar, high-income countries around the world. With the world's highest expenditures on health care (16 percent of gross domestic product), the United States ranks 33rd in life expectancy, which is behind almost every other industrialized nation in the world (WHO, 2014). Every country in the world spends significantly less on health care than the United States, so similar health care expenditures on a per capita basis do not appear to be the reason for this discrepancy. What creates this difference in life expectancies in the United States? Is there the possibility that gun injuries affect life expectancy in the United States?

Gun Injuries Affect Life Expectancy

Several respected research studies at Harvard University and the University of Pennsylvania have analyzed the impact on typical American life expectancy due to violent behavior, specifically violence from guns (Redelings, et al., 2010). They have found that gun homicides and suicides kill mostly young people (Krieger, et al., 2005; Lemaire, 2005). Among all fatal injuries, only motor vehicle accidents have a greater effect on life expectancy than gun deaths (Lemaire, 2005; Miniño, et al., 2010). Although violent injury is a major drain on American society, gun injuries have never been a national priority (Miniño, et al., 2010).

TABLE 12-1 Global Life Expectancies

Average Age of Death	Developed Countries
82	Switzerland
81	Australia, Canada, France, Iceland, Israel, Italy, Norway, Singapore, Sweden
80	Andorra, Austria, Germany, Ireland, Korea, Netherlands, New Zealand, United Kingdom
79	Belgium, Chile, Costa Rica, Cuba, Cyprus, Greece, Finland, Liechtenstein, Luxembourg, Malta, Portugal, Slovenia
78	Denmark, Qatar, **United States**

— Source: WHO, 2014.

The Substitution Effect and Public Health Determinants

One objection to the idea that reducing gun deaths and injuries could reduce health care costs is the argument that guns are simply a means to an end. In other words, people who are intent on violence either toward themselves or others will find a way to achieve that objective with whatever tools are available. This is called the **substitution effect** (Wharton, 2005). The question then becomes whether Americans are necessarily more violent than other nationalities around the world. Certainly history shows that violence is not unique to Americans.

While Japan generated more than its fair share of violence in the 20th century, today it is considered among the safest countries in the world and has some of the world's strictest gun control restrictions. With few handguns in Japan, crimes committed with guns are low (Ajdacic-Gross, et al., 2006). The failure of the substitution effect is apparent in Japan, meaning that the rate of other violent crimes has not increased in Japan in the absence of gun violence there.

Of course, some skeptics argue it is the cultural differences in these two affluent democracies accounting for the difference in violence between Japan and the United States, not simply the lack of accessibility to guns in Japan. Japan is very much a paternalistic, collective society, and American society is much more individualistic, with a deeply ingrained sense of a right to self-defense and ethical obligation to protect property. No gun control policies are going to change this cultural difference. While there is empirical support for many economic and social factors (demographics, ethnic diversity, education, income, inequality, deterrence, and the like) that determine gun violence, it is not clear why such factors alone would explain the large difference in violence between the United States and Japan, nor is it clear how these factors explain the existing patterns of gun availability, gun control, and violence (Ajdacic-Gross, et al., 2006).

The Substitution Effect Does Not Affect Gun Homicides

Comparative research has found that the rate of gun crimes is not subject to the substitution effect; that is, the rates of other violent crimes do not increase when access to guns is reduced or limited (Macinko & Marinho de Souza, 2007; Wharton, 2005). While there is little or no substitution effect in gun homicides, there is a positive correlation between the rate of household gun ownership and the rate of homicides, as well as the rate of homicides committed with a gun (Lemaire, 2005). Moreover, as illustrated in **FEATURE BOX 12-5**, environmental safety researchers found that gun injuries generally decline after implementation of strict gun control laws.

The Substitution Effect Does Not Affect Life Expectancy

National life expectancy increases with better gun control (Wharton, 2005). Yet, when debates about extending life expectancy center on gun injury prevention, emotional debates about the Second Amendment keep Americans from seeking common ground on the question of how to best address this public health problem (Blackman, 2011). Regardless, the evidence on life expectancies should stimulate further debate over whether regulation of guns can be an effective strategy in reducing gun injuries in the United States.

FEATURE BOX 12-5

Gun Homicides and Environmental Safety Research

- A significant portion of the declines in gun-related deaths and hospitalizations are reasonably attributed to measures reducing the availability of guns.
- Strengthening the capacity of local law enforcement to enforce gun control measures affects the decline in gun injuries.
- Declines in gun injuries are not offset by homicides committed using other weapons.

— Sources: Macinko & Marinho de Souza, 2007; Wharton, 2005; WISQARS, 2015.

Given the over 300 million privately owned guns in the country, it is extremely unlikely that anyone would try to confiscate privately owned guns, nor should the United States necessarily ban guns. Public health officials must decide how the United States can responsibly control the use of all these guns. Perhaps gun control proponents and advocates of gun rights should consider exploring particular conceptions of corrective justice to best regulate these millions of privately owned guns. **Corrective justice** is defined as undoing a wrong or as giving rise to specific reasons for rectifying wrongs such as individual and social losses from gun injuries (Dorfman, 2010). Two examples of this principle follow in the next section.

Applying the Principle of Corrective Justice

The parties responsible for introducing products into the marketplace should assume responsibility for any injuries caused by their products (Rustad, 2011). Here, this means applying the principle of corrective justice in order to hold the firearms industry responsible for the social costs of its products.

Balancing Social Costs with Social Benefits

In any ethical policy, the costs incurred by the firearms industry to control the distribution of guns should equal the social costs of the gun injuries that the gun control policies prevent. For instance, an ethical gun control policy should not cost the firearms industry more than $100 billion a year (the annual cost of gun violence in the United States), including $2.0 to $2.3 billion in health care costs plus $4.9 billion in life insurance costs, in addition to the public law enforcement costs, private security costs, $43 billion in criminal justice system costs including incarceration, lost productivity of victims, limits on freedoms to live or work in certain places, restrictions on residential and commercial location decisions, limitations in hours of operations of retail establishments, emotional costs of the forced adaptation to increased risk, and the cost of pain and fear (Lemaire, 2005; McWhirter & Fields, 2012; Wharton, 2005). The corollary to this statement is that the firearms industry has an ethical obligation to spend $100 billion a year in prevention of injuries caused by their products. In other words, the social cost for gun rights adherents should be compared with the social benefit of gun control proponents, ultimately striking a balance between the 2 distinct but similar social values (Harel & Porat, 2011).

Premium Adjustments for Health Insurance

Researchers at the Firearm and Injury Center at the University of Pennsylvania's Department of Surgery analyzed how much more Americans pay for their health insurance as a result of their reduced life expectancy from gun injuries (Lemaire, 2005). Victims of gun injuries are more likely to need medical treatment requiring high payouts from the health insurance industry; this, in turn, raises the costs of the state **risk pools**, thereby raising costs for everyone participating in the pools (Wharton, 2005). By definition, risk pools broadly distribute the costs of poor health among both healthy and sick people with health insurance coverage. There may be potential opportunities for the health insurance industry to better price and perhaps more equitably distribute the cost of the risks associated with guns. Just owning a handgun significantly increases the chance of dying from gun injuries (Forell, 2010; Graham, 2010), mainly through suicides and accidental shootings (Hemenway, 2011; Record & Gostin, 2012).

One logical thread to pursue is the risk calculations the insurance industry makes in pricing health insurance. Demographics and lifestyle choices are the bread and butter of risk calculations, but gun ownership is not currently a factor (Wharton, 2005). One University of Pennsylvania study estimated that the increased insurance premiums paid by Americans as a result of gun injuries are probably $2.0 billion to $2.3 billion, which is the same amount of health care costs due to gun injuries (Lemaire, 2005).

The Environmental Safety Problem of Gun Injuries

From an ethical perspective, individual obligations and responsibilities should be emphasized along with rights and privileges. There are no rights to gun ownership without responsibilities for environmental safety; at the same time, environmental safety cannot override the individual right to gun ownership. There is a need to restore this common ethic that emphasizes obligations and responsibilities as well as individual rights and privileges (Rawls, 1971/2005). With recognition of the individual rights and privileges of gun ownership, there must be an acceptance of the need to address the responsibilities of ensuring environmental safety and minimizing the problem of gun injuries. This realignment would create a restored symmetry in which lawful behavior is rewarded and illegal behavior is not. Most people agree that the United States is not doing everything it can to keep guns away from people not allowed to have them, resulting in thousands of gun injuries that could be prevented (Jenkins, 2011; Kendall, 2011; O'Connell & Fields, 2011). This chapter has attempted to present the best available evidence on the social consequences of gun injuries. As illustrated in **FEATURE BOX 12-6**, the facts from each side of the gun debate have been focused on 5 questions.

The Second Amendment right to possess guns comes with a price; someone must pay the multibillion-dollar cost of gun injuries. The question is how to best balance this cost in the controversy between gun rights adherents and gun control proponents within the national debate on health care reform. Gun injuries are a public health problem that can be largely resolved; the question is how. This is one national debate that will ideally continue until it is satisfactorily resolved.

FEATURE BOX 12-6

The Debate: Individual Gun Rights v. Community Gun Control

- How can reasonable restrictions be placed on the individual right to possess guns?
- How do Americans compare to other countries in terms of life expectancy?
- Are Americans necessarily more violent than people in the rest of the world?
- How should the public health problem of reduced life expectancies be addressed?
- How can regulation of handguns become an effective public health strategy to reduce gun injuries and increase life expectancies?

— Sources: Blackman, 2011; CDF, 2014; Chemerinsky, 2009; Record & Gostin, 2014; Richardson & Hemenway, 2011.

ETHICAL OR UNETHICAL DECISION

Firearms on College Campuses

Ethics Issue: *What ethical principles, if any, would justify students and visitors being allowed to carry loaded, concealed guns on university campuses?*

Ethics Analysis: No, the presence of guns on campus threatens the tranquility of the academic environment and contributes in an offensive manner to an unacceptable climate of violence. Virginia Tech University showed the danger of guns on campus; allowing concealed carrying on campus could lead to more shootings. Moreover, every year about 1,100 college students commit suicide, and another 24,000 attempt to do so on U.S. campuses. Given that 90 percent of attempted suicides with guns are successful, easy access to guns on campus could also likely lead to an increase in suicides (Brady Center, 2010; Parks, et al., 2014).

Ethics Analysis: Yes, holders of state-issued concealed handgun licenses should be allowed the same measure of personal protection on college campuses that current laws afford them virtually everywhere else. Gun-free zones serve to disarm only those law-abiding citizens who might otherwise be able to protect themselves.

Court's Holding and Decision: Residents of Colorado have a right to carry concealed handguns; this right to bear arms in self-defense may not be restricted on college campuses.

— *The Regents of the University of Colorado, et al. v. Students for Concealed Carry on Campus, LLC, et al.*, 271 P.3d 496 (Colorado Supreme Court 2012). *See, e.g.,* de Leeuw, 2013; Eden, 2014; Oblinger, 2013; Smith, 2013; Vasek, 2014 (discussing this decision).

CHAPTER SUMMARY

- There is a need to restore the ethics of health care that emphasizes, or at least balances, societal obligations and responsibilities over individual rights and privileges.
- While gun injury prevention may be an ethical imperative, it also makes economic sense, since gun injuries account for $2.0 and $2.3 billion in preventable health care costs.
- Because conclusions about gun injury prevention conflict with cultural values, namely individual rights, people do not accept the consensus of environmental safety researchers that gun injuries generally decline after implementation of strict gun control laws.
- One objection to the principle that reducing gun deaths would increase life expectancy is the argument that guns are simply a means to an end, but this substitution effect argument does not pass scientific muster.
- Victims of gun injuries are likely to need medical treatment requiring high insurance payouts; this, in turn, raises the costs of the risk pools, thereby raising health insurance costs for everyone else. Inevitably, a large proportion of the financial burden from gun injuries falls on society through government health insurance programs and higher premiums for all insureds, not to mention the social costs.

REFERENCES

Adams, C.-M. (2013). Grandparents, guns, and guardianship: Incapacity and the right to bear arms. *The Florida Bar Journal, 87*, 48–51.

Ajdacic-Gross, V., et al. (2006). Changing times: A longitudinal analysis of international firearm suicide data. *American Journal of Public Health, 96*(10), 1752–1755.

AMA (American Medical Association). (2007). *Report of the Council on Science and Public Health.* Chicago, IL: AMA.

Bezruchka, S. S. (2012). The hurrier I go the behinder I get: The deteriorating international ranking of U.S. health status. *Annual Review of Public Health, 33*, 157–173.

Bindbeutel, B. (2014). Domestic tranquility: The goals of home protection. *Southern Illinois University Law Journal, 39*, 1–21.

Bishop, J. (2012). Hidden or on the hip: The right(s) to carry after *Heller. Cornell Law Review, 97*(4), 907–929.

Blackman, J. (2011). The constitutionality of social cost. *Harvard Journal of Law and Public Policy, 34*, 951–1042.

Brady Center to Prevent Gun Violence. (2010). *No gun left behind: The gun lobby's campaign to push guns into colleges and schools.* Washington, DC: Brady Center to Prevent Gun Violence.

Bridge, M. (2012). Exit, pursued by a "bear"? New York City's handgun laws in the wake of *Heller* and *McDonald. Columbia Journal of Law and Social Problems, 46*, 145–206.

Browne, M. N., et al. (2010). Overweight/obesity as a protected category: The complexity of personal responsibility for physical attributes. *Michigan State Journal of Medicine and Law, 14*, 1–69.

Buckman, E. (2010). Just a soul whose intentions are good? The relevance of a defendant's subjective intent in defining a "destructive device" under the National Firearms Act. *Fordham Law Review, 79*, 563–603.

Burns, B. (2013). Holding fire: Why long waiting periods to buy a gun violate the Second Amendment. *Charleston Law Review, 7*, 379–410.

Campbell, K. M. (2013). Can rights be different? Justice Stevens' dissent in *McDonald v. City of Chicago. Texas Wesleyan Law Review, 19*, 733–759.

Campoy, A. (2011, March 3). Texans divide over guns on campus: Backers say weapons would bolster safety, but opponents argue colleges are better off. *Wall Street Journal*, p. A3.

Castiglione, J. D. (2012). *Heller* conundrum: Is it a Fourth Amendment "exigent circumstance" to keep a legal firearm in your home? *UCLA Law Review Discourse, 59*, 230–243.

CDC (Centers for Disease Control and Prevention). (2015). *Chronic diseases: The leading causes of death and disability in the United States.* Atlanta, GA: U.S. Department of Health and Human Services: CDC.

CDF (Children's Defense Fund). (2014). *State of America's children 2014 report: Gun violence.* Washington, DC: CDF.

Chemerinsky, E. (2009). The Second Amendment and gun control. *Touro Law Review, 25*, 695–702.

Colvin, L. (2014). History, *Heller*, and high-capacity magazines: What is the proper standard of review for Second Amendment challenges? *Fordham Urban Law Journal, 41*, 1041–1083.

Crane, Jr., K. T. (2014). Replacing the Second Amendment is the only way to preserve the individual right to self-defense while reducing gun violence. *New England Journal on Criminal and Civil Confinement, 40*, 427–454.

Curtis, K. (2015). A wiki weapon solution: Firearm regulation for the management of 3D printing in the American household. *Rutgers Computer and Technology Law Journal, 41*, 74–107.

Daniels, K. L. (2013). Keys, wallet, and pistol: The Seventh Circuit establishes a constitutional right to carry firearms outside of the home. *The Seventh Circuit Review, 8*, 339–373.

de Leeuw, M. B. (2012). The (new) new judicial federalism: State constitutions and the protection of the individual right to bear arms. *Fordham Urban Law Journal, 39*, 1449–1502.

DeMitchell, T. A. (2014). Locked down and armed: Security responses to violence in our schools. *Connecticut Public Interest Law Journal, 13*, 275–299.

DePalo, A. C. (2013). The doctor will see you now: An argument for amending the licensing process for handguns in New York City. *Touro Law Review, 29*, 867–902.

Dorfman, A. (2010).What is the point of the tort remedy? *American Journal of Jurisprudence, 55*, 105–161.

Dulan, S. W. (2014). State of madness: Mental health and gun regulations. *Thomas M. Cooley Law Review, 31*, 1–14.

Duquette, M. (2014). The RX and the AR [Automatic/Assault Rifles]: A products liability approach to the mass shooting problem. *Nova Law Review, 38*, 359–385.

Eden, J. W. (2014). Don't take your guns to school (in Nebraska): Assessing the constitutionality of the private universities' exemption from the Concealed Handgun Permit Act. *Creighton Law Review, 48*, 113–144.

Fair, M. (2014). Dare defend: Standing for stand your ground. *Law and Psychology Review, 38*, 153–176.

Foody, M. (2013). Docs versus Glocks: N.R.A. takes aim at Florida physicians' freedom of speech: Leaving patients' health, safety, and welfare at risk. *Cardozo Law Review de novo, 2013*, 228–257.

Forell, C. (2010). Who is the reasonable person? What's reasonable? Self-defense and mistake in criminal and tort law. *Lewis and Clark Law Review, 14*, 1401–1434.

Forsey, L. A. (2013). State legislatures stand up for Second Amendment gun rights while the U.S. Supreme Court refuses to order a cease fire on the issue. *Seton Hall Legislative Journal, 37*, 411–436.

Fox, J. A., & DeLateur, M. J. (2014). Weapons of mass (murder) destruction. *New England Journal on Criminal & Civil Confinement, 40*, 313–343.

GAO (U.S. Government Accounting Office). (2008). *Centers for Disease Control and Prevention: Changes in obligations and activities before and after fiscal year 2005 budget reorganization.* Washington, DC: GAO.

Giles, M. G. (2014). The path to full incorporation of the Second Amendment: An individual right. *Nevada Lawyer, 22*, 18–20.

Golimowski, J. (2012). Pulling the trigger: Evaluating criminal gun laws in a post-*Heller* world. *American Criminal Law Review, 49*, 1599–1622.

Graham, D. L. (2010). Statutory marksmanship: Enacting laws that reduce gun-related crime and accidents. *Phoenix Law Review, 4*, 461–488.

Greene, J. (2010). Guns, originalism, and cultural cognition. *University of Pennsylvania Journal of Constitutional Law, 13*, 511–528.

Hardy, D. T. (2014). Gun owners, gun legislation, and compromise. *Thomas M. Cooley Law Review, 31*, 33–50.

Harel, A., & Porat, A. (2011). Commensurability and agency: Two yet-to-be-met challenges for law and economics. *Cornell Law Review, 96*, 749–787.

Hatt, K. (2011). Gun-shy originalism: The Second Amendment's original purpose in *District of Columbia v. Heller*. *Suffolk University Law Review, 44*, 505–523.

Hemenway, D. (2011). Risks and benefits of a gun in the home. *American Journal of Lifestyle Medicine, 5*, 502–511.

Henderson, I. W. (2010). Rights, regulations, and revolvers: Baltimore City's complex constitutional challenge following *District of Columbia v. Heller*. *The University of Baltimore Law Review, 39*, 423–465.

Hubbard, F. P. (2014). The value of life: Constitutional limits on citizens' use of deadly force. *University of South Carolina Law Review, 21*, 1–34.

Jenkins, H. W. (2011, January 12). The Jared Loughner problem. *Wall Street Journal*, p. A13.

Kahan, D., et al. (2011). Cultural cognition of scientific consensus. *Journal of Risk Research, 14*, 147–174.

Kaufman, E. (2009). The Second Amendment: An analysis of *District of Columbia v. Heller*. *Touro Law Review, 25*, 703–724.

Kendall, B. (2011, January 10). The Arizona shootings: Massacre renews focus on gun buys. *Wall Street Journal*, p. A4.

Krieger, N., et al. (2005). Painting a truer picture of U.S. socioeconomic and racial/ethnic health inequalities: The Public Health Disparities Geocoding Project. *American Journal of Public Health, 95*, 312–323.

Lamartina, D. (2013). The Firearms Safety Act and the future of Second Amendment debate. *University of Baltimore Law Forum, 44*, 75–84.

Lemaire, J. (2005). The cost of firearm deaths in the United States: Reduced life expectancies and increased insurance costs. *Journal of Risk and Insurance, 72*(3), 359–374.

Macinko, J., & Marinho de Souza, M. (2007). *Reducing firearm injury: Lessons from Brazil. Leonard Davis Institute Issue Brief.* Philadelphia, PA: Wharton School at the University of Pennsylvania.

McNamara, C. (2014). Finally, actually saying "no": A call for reform of gun rights legislation and policies to protect domestic violence survivors. *Seattle Journal for Social Justice, 13*, 649–689.

McWhirter, C., & Fields, G. (2012, August 18–19). Communities struggle to break a grim cycle of killing. *Wall Street Journal*, p. A1.

Mead, M. (1964). Continuities in cultural evolution (the Terry lectures). Cambridge, MA: Yale University Press (Lectures given at Yale 1957).

Miniño, A. M., et al. (2010). Deaths: Preliminary data for 2008. *National Vital Statistics Reports, 59*(2). Hyattsville, MD: National Center for Health Statistics.

Moeller, N. (2014). The Second Amendment beyond the doorstep: Concealed carry post-*Heller. University of Illinois Law Review, 2014*(4), 1401–1430.

Moran, C. L. (2013). Under the gun: Will states' one-gun-per-month laws pass constitutional muster after *Heller* and *McDonald? Seton Hall Legislative Journal, 38*, 163–188.

Morley, M. T. (2014). Consent of the governed or consent of the government? The problems with consent decrees in government-defendant cases. *University of Pennsylvania Journal of Constitutional Law, 16*, 637–696.

Nance, M. L., et al. (2010). Variation in pediatric and adolescent firearm mortality rates in rural and urban U.S. counties. *Pediatrics, 125*(6), 1112–1118.

NRA (National Rifle Association). (2012). *Right-to-carry 2012.* Fairfax, VA: NRA.

Oblinger, L. H. (2013). The wild, wild west of higher education: Keeping the campus carry decision in the university's holster. *Washburn Law Journal, 53*, 87–117.

O'Connell, V., & Fields, G. (2011, January 12). The Arizona shootings: Many mentally ill can buy guns, federal law prohibits sales only to people declared unfit by judge; States slow to update database. *Wall Street Journal*, p. A5.

O'Shea, M. P. (2012). Modeling the Second Amendment right to carry arms: Judicial tradition and the scope of "bearing arms" for self-defense. *American University Law Review, 61*, 585–676.

Parks, S. E., et al. (2014). Surveillance for violent deaths: National violent deaths: National violent death reporting system, 16 states. *Morbidity and Mortality Weekly Report (MMWR), 63*(SS01), 1–33.

Pelaez, D. D. (2014). Second Amendment right to bear arms: The cost to carry: New York State's regulation on firearm registration. *Touro Law Review, 30*, 1007–1025.

Perry, R. P. (2012). Second Amendment: Guns and ammo: For convicted Americans viewing pictures of others enjoying their fundamental constitutional right to bear arms in a magazine is the closest they will ever get to seeing the Second Amendment at work. *Touro Law Review, 28*, 665–685.

Pinals, D. A. (2014). Firearms and mental illness: Preventing fear and stigma from overtaking reason and rationality. *New England Journal on Criminal and Civil Confinement, 40*, 379–402.

Pound, R. (1911). The scope and purpose of sociological jurisprudence. *Harvard Law Review, 25*, 140–147.

Pratt, J. E. (2014). Uncommon firearms as obscenity. *Tennessee Law Review, 81*, 1–40.

Rawls, J. (2005). *A theory of justice.* Boston, MA: Belknap Press (Original work published 1971).

Record, K. L., & Gostin, L. O. (2014). What will it take? Terrorism, mass murder, gang violence, and suicides: The American way, or do we strive for a better way? *University of Michigan Journal of Law Reform, 47*, 555–574.

___. (2012). A robust individual right to bear arms versus the public's health: The court's reliance on firearm restrictions on the mentally ill. *Charleston Law Review, 6*, 371–384.

Redelings, M., et al. (2010). Years off your life? The effects of homicide on life expectancy by neighborhood and race/ethnicity in Los Angeles County. *Journal of Urban Health: Bulletin of the New York Academy of Medicine, 87*(4), 670–676.

Renneker, A. (2015). Chalk talks: Packing more than just a backpack. *Journal of Law and Education, 44*, 273–282.

Richardson, E. G., & Hemenway, D. (2011). Homicide, suicide, and unintentional firearm fatality: Comparing the United States with other high-income countries. *Journal of Trauma, Injury, Infection, and Critical Care, 70*(1), 238–243.

Rose, L. A. (2014). Constitutional law—don't take your guns to town: Maryland's good-and-substantial-reason requirement for handgun permits passes intermediate scrutiny—*Woollard v. Gallagher*, 712 F.3d 865 (4th Cir. 2013). *Suffolk Journal of Trial and Appellate Advocacy, 19*, 245–260.

Ruebsamen, M. (2013). The gun-shy commonwealth: Self-defense and concealed carry in post-*Heller* Massachusetts. *Suffolk Journal of Trial and Appellate Advocacy, 18*, 55–83.

Rustad, M. L. (2011). Torts as public wrongs. *Pepperdine Law Review, 38*, 433–550.

Salvin, D. J. (2014). Landmark change in California firearms law. *Orange County Lawyer, 56*, 32–36.

Selkowitz, J. E. (2011). Guns, public nuisance, and the Protection of Lawful Commerce in Arms Act: A public health-inspired legal analysis of the predicate exception. *Temple Law Review, 83*, 793–828.

Smith, M. L. (2013). Second Amendment challenges to student housing firearms bans: The strength of the home analogy. *UCLA Law Review, 60,* 1046–1080.

Stidham, D. A. (2015). You have the right to bear arms, but not the ability? The evanescence of the Second Amendment. *New England Journal on Criminal and Civil Confinement, 41,* 137–158.

Stowell, E. T. (2014). Top gun: The Second Amendment, self-defense, and private property exclusion. *Regent University Law Review, 26,* 521–555.

Sturzenegger, T. L. B. (2013). The Second Amendment's fixed meaning and multiple purposes. *Southern Illinois University Law Journal, 37,* 337–393.

Styles, J. J. (2012). The right to bear arms and the abominable snowman: How six inches of snow swallowed a fundamental right. *North Carolina Law Review Addendum, 90,* 84–105.

Tidmarsh, J. (2010). Resolving cases "on the merits." *Denver University Law Review, 87,* 407–436.

Tiefer, C. (2011). Can Congress make a president step up a war? *Louisiana Law Review, 71,* 391–449.

Tomei, R. J., Jr. (2012). Watching the watchmen: The people's attempt to hold on-duty law enforcement officers accountable for misconduct and the Illinois law that stands in their way. *Northern Illinois University Law Review, 32,* 385–418.

United Nations Office on Drugs and Crime. (2015). *Homicide statistics, rate for 100,000 population.* New York, NY: United Nations.

Vasek, B. (2014). Rethinking the Nevada Campus Protection Act: Future challenges & reaching a legislative compromise. *Nevada Law Journal, 15,* 389–430.

Wagner, D. M. (2012). Thomas v. Scalia on the constitutional rights of parents: Privileges and immunities, or just "spinach"? *Regent University Law Review, 24,* 49–82.

Wahl, C. J. (2013). Keeping *Heller* out of the home: Homeowners associations and the right to keep and bear arms. *University of Pennsylvania Journal of Constitutional Law, 15,* 1003–1036.

Wershbale, J. L. (2010). The Second Amendment under a government landlord: Is there a right to keep and bear legal firearms in public housing? *St. John's Law Review, 84,* 995–1055.

West, R. (2014). Has the constitution fostered a pathological rights culture? The right to bear arms: A tale of two rights. *Boston University Law Review, 94,* 893–912.

Wharton School at the University of Pennsylvania. (2005). Insurance, life expectancy and the cost of firearm deaths in the United States. *Knowledge@Wharton.*

Whitney, C. R. (2014). A liberal's case for the Second Amendment. *Thomas M. Cooley Law Review, 31,* 15–31.

WHO (World Health Organization). (2014). *World health statistics.* Geneva, Switzerland: WHO.

WISQARS. (2015). National Center for Injury Prevention and Control Web-based Injury Statistics Query and Reporting System. *Fatal and nonfatal injury, violent death, and cost of injury data.* Atlanta, GA: Centers for Disease Control, Division of Violence Prevention.

Wyrick, J. A. (2011). A right to a gun. *Michigan Bar Journal, 90,* 34–35.

Zamir, E., & Medina, B. (2008). Law, morality, and economics: Integrating moral constraints with economic analysis of law. *California Law Review, 96,* 323–391.

PART VI

Pressing Issues Facing Our Health Care System

Part VI is comprised of chapters describing pivotal ethical issues and real-world pitfalls the United States is confronting.

Courtesy of Albert Johnson

CHAPTER 13

Women's Reproductive Health

"Ethics bears most stringently on those who have the ability to dominate and exploit [others]. The structured responsibility that underlies the concept of ethics also implies power. Ethics is, then, the moral limitation placed on power."

— **Albert R. Jonsen**, Emeritus Professor of Ethics in Medicine at the University of Washington School of Medicine

LEARNING OBJECTIVES

After completing this chapter, the reader should be able to:

1. Summarize, in terms of ethical principles, why the provision of health care related to procreation is different from the provision of health care for other health conditions.
2. Evaluate the ethical issues surrounding women's reproductive care in light of the increasing inaccessibility of contraception and prenatal care.
3. Describe the ethical principles underlying state regulations that limit access to abortion, including partial-birth abortion bans.
4. Explain sexual privacy issues and be familiar with the ethical principles surrounding refusal or conscience legislation and emergency contraception provisions in the law.
5. Understand how the U.S. health care system's ethical foundation has created disparities in the treatment of health conditions that affect both men and women.

KEY TERMS

Abortifacient	Fetus	Partial-birth abortion
Abortion	Gender-based	Personal autonomy
Beneficence	discrimination	Pregnancy Discrimination
Cases of first impression	Health exception	Act of 1978
Conception	Implantation	Pre-viability
Conscience legislation	Inattentional blindness	Preterm
Contraception	Intact dilation and	Principle of least
Contraceptives	extraction	infringement
Dilation and evacuation	Judicial bypass	Refusal clause
Embryo	Large fraction test	legislation
Emergency contraceptives	Maternity coverage	Religious exemptions
Enjoin	Off-label use	Viability
Fertilization	Over-the-counter (OTC)	

ETHICAL OR UNETHICAL DECISION

Access to Emergency Contraception

Ethics Issue: *Should emergency contraception be made available over-the-counter to women of all ages, without any restrictions for minors?*

In Brief: The U.S. Food and Drug Administration (FDA) approved **emergency contraceptives** (ECs), also known as the morning-after pill or Plan B, for prescription use in 1998. While this medication prevents sperm from fertilizing an egg that has been released, if **fertilization** has already occurred (it takes five to seven days to fertilize an egg), ECs block implantation of the resulting fertilized egg in the uterus. ECs have no abortive effect on a developing human embryo once **implantation** occurs (once an embryo becomes embedded in the lining of the uterus). An **embryo** is what the human organism is generally known as during the gestation period from conception to about eight weeks, though there is no single scientific or legal definition of this term.

Moreover, ECs will not interrupt or harm an established pregnancy after implantation (NWLC, 2011). ECs have no known serious or long-term side effects, though they may have some mild and short-term side effects, such as nausea or abdominal pain, in some women. However, because there is a chance that ECs could prevent implantation of a fertilized egg, some consider it a method of **abortion** to end a pregnancy by getting rid of a fertilized egg, as opposed to **contraception** to prevent fertilization of an egg or implantation of an egg that has been fertilized. As a result, the Family Research Council and Concerned Women for America pushed for limited access to ECs.

In 2001, the Association of Reproductive Health Professionals and 65 other organizations filed a Citizen's Petition, asking the FDA to switch ECs, which then required a prescription, to **over-the-counter** (OTC) status. OTC status would make ECs available without a prescription and without seeing a physician. Because ECs are time sensitive, meaning they lose their efficacy as time elapses after the need for them first arises, women's ability to easily obtain this medication OTC would reduce delays in access and thereby make it easier to prevent an unwanted pregnancy. The American Medical Association, the American Academy of Family Physicians, the American College of Obstetricians and Gynecologists, and the American College of Pediatrics all supported OTC access for ECs.

In 2003, after preliminary meetings with the FDA suggested that ECs would be approved for OTC status, Barr Pharmaceuticals requested that ECs not only be switched to OTC status but also be made available to women of all ages without restrictions for minors. The FDA scientific review staff and the FDA advisory committees voted overwhelmingly in favor of granting OTC status to ECs without restriction for minors. However, in response to criticism by several committee members, Barr sought non-prescription access only for women 16 and older.

For the first time, the FDA ignored the recommendations of its scientific staff and advisory committees. The FDA concluded that the lack of data on adolescent use of ECs rendered Barr's application for OTC status incomplete. After receiving additional data from Barr, the FDA indicated that the scientific evidence was only sufficient to support ECs as an OTC product for women 17 or older. The change from OTC for all ages to OTC only for women over the age of 17 was notable because, for other drug applications, lack of data on adolescent use is not considered a barrier to OTC status for all ages.

Seven years after receipt of a Citizen's Petition to switch ECs from prescription to OTC status, the FDA issued a decision that made ECs available without a prescription for minors (defined as women under 18) (FDA, 2006). The OTC status was restricted to behind-the-counter venues with a licensed pharmacist on staff.

— *Tummino v. Torti*, 603 F.Supp.2d 519 (U.S. District Court for the Eastern District of New York 2009), *reconsideration denied*, *Tummino v. Hamburg*, 260 F.R.D. 27 (U.S. District Court for the Eastern District of New York 2009). (*See Ethical or Unethical Decision* at the end of this chapter for discussion of this ethics issue.)

Introduction

During the last half century the human rights of women have improved, yet **gender-based discrimination** remains (Ginsberg, 2008; Siegel, 2013).[a] Men and women do not have the same earnings, employment opportunities, health insurance benefits, or reproductive rights (Sepper, 2014; Shriver, et al., 2009). Moreover, as illustrated in **FEATURE BOX 13-1**, many human rights women have come to take for granted in health care are not secure.

Since the passage of the Civil Rights Act in the mid-1960s, the battle for women's rights has shifted its form. Now, instead of fighting for laws that grant human rights to women, women's rights advocates must fight *against* laws that impose limitations to women's rights. In this chapter, there are more **cases of first impression**, where there was no prior binding legal authority existing on the matter presented to the highest federal and state courts, than on any other topic in this text. Most of the decisions affecting women's health have involved

FEATURE BOX 13-1

Gender-Based Discrimination

- Women's health is increasingly jeopardized by limited access to health care.
- Women's health insurance plans often cost more than men's for the same basic coverage with the same insurer in disregard of laws prohibiting this practice.
- Reproductive rights of women are under assault.
- Women's health needs are often overlooked and understudied compared to those of men.
- Disparities continue to widen in the treatment outcomes of men and women with the same health conditions.

— Sources: Kaiser, 2014a; NWLC, 2009; Savitsky, 2010.

[a]*Cf. Shelby County, Alabama v. Holder, et al.*, 133 S.Ct. 2612, 2632 (U.S. Supreme Court 2013) (Ginsberg, J., dissenting) ("Recognizing that large progress has been made, Congress determined, based on a voluminous record, that the scourge of discrimination was not yet extirpated."); *Fisher v. University of Texas, et al.*, 133 S.Ct. 2411, 2434 n.4 (U.S. Supreme Court 2013) (Ginsburg, J., dissenting) ("Actions designed to burden groups long denied full citizenship stature are not sensibly ranked with measures taken to hasten the day when entrenched discrimination and its aftereffects have been extirpated." (quoting *Gratz v. Bollinger*, 539 U.S. 244, 301 (U.S. Supreme Court 2003) (Ginsburg, J., dissenting))).

disputes over attempts to restrict, as opposed to expand, application of antidiscrimination laws and the human rights of women to health care.

Women's Reproductive Rights

There is no universal ethic regarding health care issues for women. The human rights of women seeking health care are incomplete (Savitsky, 2010), with a dynamic and often unexpected evolution of social relationships regarding the role of women in American society. Few ethical principles match the complexity or volatility of women's reproductive care. As opposed to avoiding the most critical ethical dilemmas, this chapter is directed to the real reasons why certain human rights of women are opposed and not others; every attempt is made to see whether these reasons might yield some common ground.

Other Health Interests Confronting Women

U.S. courts are reactive institutions; they do not create the controversies that come to them, but rather respond to disputes emerging in society. Women must bring their controversies to the U.S. Supreme Court and the nation's appellate courts when lower trial court decisions are unfavorable. While there are a myriad of female-specific issues that could be addressed in any chapter on women's health, if the nation's highest appellate courts have not recently reviewed the issue, this chapter excluded discussion of the topic (such as the struggle to have premenstrual syndrome recognized as a diagnosis, single motherhood, treatments for menopause, domestic and relationship violence, and elder care for women). As a consequence, much of this chapter is about health care for women of childbearing age. This necessarily excludes a large percentage of women who are not of childbearing age but are nonetheless discriminated against by health care policies.

This chapter focuses on the disparate provision of health care for procreation (and noncreation) concerns, and addresses reproductive issues against the backdrop of how the newer forms of contraception and prenatal care are falling out of reach for more and more women in the United States. While discussion regarding abortion is emphasized, with a focus on partial-birth abortions and state regulations that attempt to limit access to abortions, this chapter also concentrates on related sexual privacy issues such as ECs and pharmacists' **conscience legislation**, which allows pharmacists to refuse to fill contraceptive prescriptions.

Health Risks for Women and Children

Women and children may face unnecessary health risks because they lack basic coverage for prenatal care and childbirth (Kaiser, 2014b); half of American women and children fail to receive adequate prenatal care (Annie E. Casey Foundation, 2014). Many states refuse to allow basic coverage for prenatal treatment while pregnant women are waiting for approval of their government insurance applications (Hammell, 2011). If the United States is to assist children in becoming healthy adults who are able to embrace life's opportunities and contribute meaningfully to society (rather than detract from it), new ways of thinking about the health of children and the women who bear and raise them must be adopted (Fentiman, 2006). Although the United States acknowledged that high infant mortality was inextricably tied to the health of women at the beginning of the 20th century (Meigs, 1917), nearly a century later infant mortality is still intractably high. Yet, the best guarantee of ensuring healthy American children remains the same: providing access to quality health care across the life span of women (Sepper, 2014; Callaghan, 2010).

The Ethics of High Infant Mortality

There are more than 23,000 infant deaths each year in the United States; that is an average of 64 infant deaths each day (NCHS, 2015). The U.S. rate of infant mortality and morbidity is high compared to other industrialized countries, and research indicates that these rates are high because infants are born prematurely and without proper prenatal care (Gregory, et al., 2014; Law, 2008). In 2013, 55 nations had lower infant mortality rates than the United States, including virtually all European countries and Japan (CIA, 2013).

The Ethics of High Rates of Premature Births

Each year in the United States, more than half a million infants (or 1 in 8) are **preterm**, at less than 37 weeks' gestation, due to unintended pregnancies and consequent lack of prenatal care (Callaghan, 2010). This high rate of premature births constitutes a public health concern that costs almost 20 times more than the average full term birth (Behrman & Butler, 2007; Fleischman, 2008). It costs, on average, about $2,800 to provide health care to infants who are carried to term (Fleischman, 2008), while the estimated cost for every infant born prematurely is $51,600 (Behrman & Butler, 2007). As illustrated in **FEATURE BOX 13-2**, prolonging pregnancy by weeks or even days can dramatically affect both health and cost. With proper prenatal care, most of what would otherwise be premature births can be carried to term.

Reproductive Health: When Exactly Does Human Life Begin?

Many ethical controversies over reproductive health evolve over this one question: when does human life begin? Is it the moment of **conception**, at the moment of fetal **viability** (when a human **fetus** can naturally survive outside a women's uterus), or somewhere in between,

---

FEATURE BOX 13-2

Costs of Prematurity Exceed $26 Billion: Annual Cost Burden

- Cerebral palsy
- Chronic illnesses (such as lung disease)
- Developmental problems
- Ductus arteriosus (leading to heart failure)
- Intracranial hemorrhage (brain damage)
- Intellectual disabilities
- Neurodevelopmental disabilities
- Necrotizing enterocolitis (potentially dangerous intestinal problem)
- Physical disabilities
- Respiratory Distress Syndrome
- Retinopathy (untreated, leads to vision loss)

— Sources: AAP, 2015; ACOG, 2011; Callaghan, 2010.

perhaps at implantation? Complicating this controversy, is the fact that there is no universally accepted definition of conception (Olson, 2013).

Whereas the law is clear that neither Congress nor state legislatures may adopt one theory of when human life begins (*see City of Akron v. Akron Center for Reproductive Health, Inc.*, 462 U.S. 416 (U.S. Supreme Court 1983), *overruled, Planned Parenthood v. Casey*, 505 U.S. 833 (U.S. Supreme Court 1992)), arguments over health insurance coverage for contraceptives, **maternity coverage** (for prenatal physician visits, lab tests, ultrasounds, and childbirth), conscience legislation by pharmacists, and the use of ECs are the latest issues regarding women's reproductive rights that directly result from that controversial question. The U.S. Supreme Court, even as it upheld women's constitutional right to abortion, avoided answering the ethical dilemma of when life begins, stating: "When those trained in the respective disciplines of medicine, philosophy, and theology are unable to arrive at any consensus, the judiciary, at this point in the development of man's knowledge, is not in a position to speculate as to the answer" (*Roe v. Wade*, 410 U.S. 113, 159 (U.S. Supreme Court 1973); *see also* Olson, 2013).

Restricted Access to Emergency Contraception Pills

Emergency contraception medications are concentrated doses of hormones found in many regular birth control pills that can prevent pregnancy when taken within 120 hours after unprotected sex (consensual or otherwise) or when protection was faulty. The use and regulation of ECs are filled with ethical controversy (FDA, 2010). The ethics of using ECs has been complicated by the question of whether ECs should be classified as **abortifacients** (devices that induce abortion) as opposed to as **contraceptives** (devices that act to prevent fertilization and/or implantation). As a result of this complication, the right to access ECs has become entangled with the nation's abortion debate. However, if pregnancy occurs when a fertilized egg implants in a woman's uterine lining, the ethical controversy ostensibly tied to abortion disappears.

The other side of this ethical controversy reflects the dichotomy between religion and science. The position that ECs are abortifacients is based on philosophical and theological definitions of conception, not scientific understandings of reproductive biology. While some dismiss this as being a simple misunderstanding of the purpose of ECs, clearly the issue is more complicated than that. Science holds that pregnancy does not occur before implantation, so the argument is that it is okay to use ECs because they prevent pregnancy; they do not end it once it occurs. The philosophical and theological argument is that life begins when an egg is fertilized. The ethical contradiction is that ECs can prevent both fertilization and implantation (Hrobak & Wilson, 2014; LaSpina, et al., 2010).

Fabricated Entanglements

While the debate over ECs is distinguishable from the ethics of whether abortion should remain legal, access to ECs was delayed by being entangled with abortion for more than a decade. The effect has been unplanned and unwanted pregnancies for many women who chose not to or could not prevent a pregnancy (NWLC, 2011b). Nearly half the pregnancies in the United States are unintended, due to contraception failures, having sex without using or without properly using contraception, or being forced to have unprotected sex; yet emergency contraception is 81–90 percent effective at preventing pregnancy (Kaiser, 2014). The ethics of such delay tactics are debatable; the rightness or wrongness of the tactics against ECs depends on one's position of whether women should have a second chance to avoid an unintended and unwanted pregnancy (Hrobak & Wilson, 2014), particularly in the case of sexual assault. The EC controversy becomes further entangled when states attempt to prevent women from having access to health insurance plans that cover abortion and access to ECs is limited.

Logistical Barriers to Access

ECs were first approved by the FDA as a prescription form of emergency contraception for women in 1998. While only a small share of American women has used ECs over the past decade, nearly half of the pregnancies in the United States are unintended (Kaiser, 2014; IOM, 2011). Given that ECs are highly effective at preventing pregnancy, the high rate of unintended pregnancies constitutes an anomaly.

One reason for this anomaly is that many women did not have access to ECs from 1998 when the pills were first approved, until 2006, when the FDA finally permitted OTC sales (Broekhuizen, 2009). Because a woman's right to use ECs was dependent upon the aid and compliance of pharmacists in accessing the pills before 2006, pharmacists who opposed dispensing ECs imposed a logistical barrier for many women (LaSpina, et al., 2010). Since 2006, however, the rate of unintended pregnancies has declined (Ventura, et al., 2011; Guttmacher Institute, 2014).

Pharmacists' Conscience Legislation

The combination of the words *pharmacist* and *conscience,* especially where it involves issues of contraception and reproduction, evokes passionate positions in most discussions (Mau, 2009). Since pharmacists are now on the front line of the women's reproductive issue, as medical technology expands and social values change, the number of potential conflicts of conscience is likely to increase (Miller, 2006; Schlueter, 2013). Pharmacists, however, are not the only providers who might refuse to dispense ECs; some hospitals and other health care professionals also refuse to dispense ECs (Kaiser, 2014). The ethical controversy surrounding contraception makes enacting any legislation protecting access to ECs an especially controversial and politically precarious undertaking (LaSpina, et al., 2010).

ETHICAL DILEMMAS 13-1

1. Could women's need to obtain ECs on a timely basis outweigh the rights of licensed pharmacists who object to dispensing them?
2. Is there some common ground that can be identified among Congress, state legislatures, and the courts that are dealing with competing ethical interests involving the sale of ECs?

Point: The Ethical Obligation to Fill *All* Prescriptions

Consideration of ethical convictions is not limited to pharmacists who oppose ECs; many others have a sense of obligation to provide ECs. Supporters of ECs object to conscience laws because they say pharmacists have an ethical obligation to fill all prescriptions. The refusal to provide ECs violates women's freedom of conscience (Kaiser, 2014; Sax, 2010). In other words, refusal to provide ECs violates women's right not to be deprived of the use of contraception. State laws generally agree and mandate that pharmacists must dispense all safe, legal prescriptions and put the best interests of their customers ahead of their own (Duvall, 2007).

Counterpoint: The Right to Conscientious Objection

Health care providers who oppose ECs have had some success in urging state legislatures to pass **refusal clause legislation**. Refusal clause legislation protects a health care provider's perceived right to conscientiously object to dispensing ECs, but such refusal clauses often do little to protect the opposing right of a patient to access ECs (Drahan, 2011). Generally, it results in federal-state conflicts between the FDA and the states, both of which regulate access to ECs. Some pharmacists, whose beliefs prohibit abortion and the use of birth control, claim that dispensing ECs to women is an infringement on their conscience, since they view ECs as a form of abortion (Davidson, et al., 2010). The American Pharmacists Association supports a pharmacist's right of conscience (Mau, 2009).

Pharmacist refusals began when the FDA approved ECs in 1998 and intensified in 2006 after opponents lost their battle to restrict OTC access. These refusals have occurred, regardless of state law and company policy, at outlets of large drugstore chains such as Walgreens, Osco, K-Mart, CVS, and Eckerd, as well as at small independent pharmacies (NWLC, 2011a). Complicating the controversy surrounding ECs is access to emergency contraception without a prescription for minors. Opponents of ECs maintain that teenagers are not able to make rational decisions about their reproductive health, claiming that expanded access would jeopardize the ability of parents to care for their daughters' physical and emotional well-being. Despite this opposition, nine states allow all women (including minors) to obtain ECs directly from a pharmacist without a prescription (Kaiser, 2014).

ETHICAL DILEMMAS 13-2

3. What ethical principles direct the action of pharmacists who refuse to fill prescriptions for contraceptives for women while filling prescriptions for Viagra and other medications targeting male reproductive health?

4. Distinguish the ethical considerations that underlie the conflict between the rights of health care professionals not to provide certain health care services to women, and the considerations underlying the human rights of women to receive these legal health care services.

Inadequate Education about Family Planning and Restricted Access to Contraceptives

At the same time as women in the United States do not have adequate access to contraception, neither women nor men have adequate access to education about family planning (Sepper, 2014a; Schwarz, 2007). In some communities, public schools teach that if you use condoms, you are more likely to contract HIV (Alvare, 2011), which is in direct contradiction to scientific studies on the subject. Other public schools only teach abstinence (Phillis, 2011), which has been proven to have no effect on the rate of unintended pregnancy. Providing education and better access to contraception is necessary to reduce the number of unintended pregnancies and, as a result, the number of abortions. While Planned Parenthood offers women affordable contraceptives at its health centers nationwide, only 1 in 5 childbearing-age women has timely access to such services near their homes or work (Motro, 2010). There are even fewer family planning services that serve communities where English is a second language (Alvare, 2011).

Restricted Health Insurance Coverage for Contraceptives

As illustrated in **FEATURE BOX 13-3**, too many women face financial barriers in accessing ECs and other contraceptives because their health insurance plans do not cover them. Since women have (for the most part) won the right to health insurance coverage for birth control, under the Affordable Care Act the debate has shifted to attempts to carve out exceptions to the mandate that health insurers must provide coverage for contraceptives. Health insurers and employers continue to face increased litigation pressure as new legal theories are unleashed.

FEATURE BOX 13-3

Gender-Based Barriers to Health Care Access

- Government health insurance is no longer required to cover ECs since the pills have acquired non-prescription status by the FDA.
- Employers are not always required to provide coverage for ECs or other contraceptives.
- Some employers can choose not to cover ECs or other contraceptives that go against their beliefs.

— Source: Rutledge, 2014.

ETHICS CASE
Inclusion or Exclusion of Contraception Coverage

Standridge, et al. v. Union Pacific Railroad Company, et al.
[Employee v. Employer]
479 F.3d 936 (U.S. Court of Appeals for the 8th Circuit 2007)

Facts: Union Pacific Railroad Company provided health insurance to its employees through several different insurance plans. These plans provided coverage for services such as routine physician visits and tetanus shots. The plans excluded all coverage for contraceptives unless the medication was medically necessary for a non-contraceptive purpose, such as treating skin problems. Two female employees, Brandi Standridge and Kenya Phillips, brought suit against Union Pacific for gender-based discrimination under the federal **Pregnancy Discrimination Act of 1978** (PDA). Standridge and Phillips claimed that Union Pacific discriminated against its female employees by failing to cover prescription contraception. The PDA provides that employers cannot discriminate against any person regarding compensation, terms, conditions, or privileges of employment because of the person's gender. Women affected by pregnancy, childbirth, or related health conditions must be treated the same, including receipt of health insurance benefits.

Legal Analysis: The court distinguished between preventing conception and health conditions that occur only after conception, without defining when conception occurs. Applying this distinction, the court held that the PDA does not apply to contraception because contraceptives are used prior to pregnancy. Contraception is not a medical treatment related to pregnancy but a treatment to prevent pregnancy, and therefore, it is not covered by the PDA.

The court also considered whether the health insurance plan discriminated on the basis of gender. Under a claim of disparate treatment, female employees have to establish that they were treated less favorably than similarly situated male employees. Rather than address this issue, the court held that comparing the coverage provided to each gender by the health plan was too broad. The proper comparative was the medical benefit of contraceptives. Because the health insurance plan did not cover men's contraceptives (condoms and vasectomies), the court held that the plan did not treat men more favorably than women. Because contraception is a gender-neutral term that applies to men and women equally, health insurance plans that deny coverage to contraceptives to everyone do not violate the PDA. Thus, the denial of contraceptive coverage did not discriminate against women.

Rule of Law: Since the PDA does not require employers to cover contraceptives as part of their health insurance plans, employers may exclude contraceptives from their health care benefit plans.

Ethics Issue: Should employers be required to provide contraception coverage in their health insurance plans?

Ethics Analysis: The court considered several ethical issues. The first issue addressed was the effect of employers not providing contraception coverage for women in their health insurance plans. One argument was that it is inequitable to deny health insurance coverage for contraception. The failure to offer coverage only affects women, as they bear all the health consequences of unintended pregnancies.

Health insurance plans that provide coverage for preventive health care, but fail to cover contraceptives used to prevent pregnancies exclusively in women, are not equal.

In the counterargument, the effects of not providing contraception coverage are not considered under the ethical **principle of least infringement**, whereby the least intrusive means should always be used. Absent a clear mandate from Congress, the courts should not determine what health insurance coverage employers should provide to their employees. If Congress intends for employers to provide contraception coverage, then it should amend federal law to conform to this intent.

The second ethical issue centered on what should constitute comparable health insurance coverage. One argument was that comparable health insurance coverage should compare the preventive medical coverage provided to women and men. Congress enacted the PDA to overrule a decision by the U.S. Supreme Court that did not require employers to cover pregnancy in their short-term disability plans. Congress found that it was discriminatory for employers to offer protection against all risks except pregnancy. Comparable health insurance coverage should compare women who face a risk of pregnancy with men who do not. On this basis, it is discriminatory to offer health insurance that, but for pregnancy, offers protection for all risks. Health insurance plans must treat contraceptives aimed at preventing pregnancy the same as all other types of preventive health care.

The counterargument examined the benefit of contraception. If a health insurance plan does not cover men's contraception, then the plan is not required to cover women's contraception (birth control pills, sponges, diaphragms, intrauterine devices, or tubal ligations). If there is no contraception coverage for men, health insurance plans may treat women the same and cover the same risks.

Court's Holding and Decision: Yes, employers may exclude contraception coverage from their health insurance plans.

See Hill, 2012; Melone, 2015; Rudary, 2013; Rutledge, 2014; Siegel, 2013 (discussing this court decision).

While the *Standridge* decision allows some employers, such as large employers that are self-funded, to drop coverage for prescription contraception, contraceptive coverage has become a standard practice for most employers, especially since the Affordable Care Act was enacted. Employers, including Union Pacific, find that it costs far less to cover contraceptives than to cover a pregnancy (Sepper, 2014a; Golub & Gartner, 2007), both in terms of health care costs as well as the cost of lost productivity when new parents take extended time off from work, and sometimes do not return, forcing employers to incur the cost of recruiting and training new employees..

Mandated Pelvic Exams as a Condition of Access to Contraceptives

Federally funded family planning programs, such as Planned Parenthood and Medicaid insurance, must require all women to undergo pelvic exams as a condition of access to oral contraceptives and sometimes other hormonal methods of birth control (Dixon, 2004). There is vigorous debate on whether this invasive procedure is ethical (Noah, 2007). Opponents of the policy argue that the practice violates women's reproductive **personal autonomy** and treats women unequally based on their socioeconomic position in society; mandatory exams unnecessarily burden impoverished women. Exam proponents maintain that the requirement helps to educate women about safe sex, pregnancy, and sexually transmitted diseases, and ensures that women are healthy enough for hormonal birth control (Phillis, 2011).

The pelvic exam requirements not only increase the cost of providing contraceptives, but also result in decreased use of publicly funded health care clinics and deter minors from seeking contraception (Goyal, et al., 2009). Incongruously, women seeking the same birth control from private providers or those with the ability to pay for contraception are not subject to this pelvic exam mandate.

In other areas of health care, it is not appropriate to withhold a prescription from someone who has been informed of the risks involved and chooses to forego screening for an unrelated condition. Yet for the past 50 years, pelvic exams have been required for women seeking birth control at health clinics receiving federal funding. The justification for the government mandate is that FDA-approved package inserts accompanying oral contraceptives recommend pelvic exams if women are using the pill. Still, oral contraceptives are dispensed OTC without a prescription and without pelvic exams in Europe and much of the rest of the world (Phillis, 2011).

Conscientious Objections to Contraception

While restrictions based on conscientious objections to contraception may limit women's access to reproductive care (Melone, 2015; NWLC, 2009), the ethical principles of personal autonomy and **beneficence** weigh in favor of the human rights of women to unrestricted access to contraception. On the one hand, beneficence requires restrictions on birth control to be balanced against the costs of unintended pregnancies; on the other hand, beneficence may also extend not only to women but also to potential human life. Restrictions on access to contraception have a potentially devastating effect on women's reproductive health, as well as their overall status in society, and disproportionately affect women in rural or underserved populations (IOM, 2011). The interests of women facing the possibility of unintended pregnancies due to restricted access to ECs and other contraception may outweigh the interests of pharmacists and other health care professionals whose views are opposed to birth control (Weisberg & Frazer, 2009). In contrast, proponents of restrictions stress the fundamental right of pharmacists and other health care professionals to express their convictions and to live in accordance with these beliefs (Rudary, 2013). The problems for women seeking ECs and other forms of contraception begin when these opposing values collide (IOM, 2011).

Religious Exemptions from Mandated Contraception Coverage

Religious exemptions are becoming a divisive ethical issue for many states with mandated contraception coverage. States must determine whether employers' requests for exemptions from providing state-mandated health insurance coverage for contraception are conscientious objections or calculated obstruction. When employers choose not to cover contraceptives because of their opposition to birth control, women claim that denying health insurance coverage for contraceptives impinges on their right to be free from gender-based discrimination in the workplace. It also perpetuates the notion that women's needs and desires are subservient to others' and that women require guidance and supervision, both in the workplace and beyond (Calabresi & Rickert, 2011).

Lack of All-Inclusive Federal Legislation

Half the states have passed laws requiring health insurers to cover prescription contraception under most circumstances (NCSL, 2012). While additional states are considering

ETHICAL DILEMMAS 13-3

5. Should employers with religious exemptions, who are exempt from providing mandated health insurance coverage for contraception, be required to contribute added taxes or assessments to pay for the additional social and economic costs that states incur from unplanned and unwanted pregnancies arising from women's lack of access to contraception or from acts of sexual violence against women? In other words, who should share in the added social and economic costs arising from philosophical and theological expressions of faith, or should these added costs always be equally shared?

similar legislation, the reach of the legislation is limited to state-regulated plans; most large employers are self-funded and not subject to state mandates (Kaiser & HRET, 2014a) or are exempt from the federal mandate to provide no-cost contraceptives (Rutledge, 2014). If state laws are not working as extensively as originally hoped, federal legislation could broaden the scope of coverage to reach employees whose plans are not bound by state mandates. Yet federal legislation requiring contraceptive coverage has repeatedly failed in Congress (Carlson, 2006). The Equity in Prescription Insurance and Contraceptive Coverage Act was first considered in 1997 but was never enacted (Lee, 2011).

When health insurers are required to cover contraceptives, women's access to contraception has significantly expanded (NWLC, 2009; Pillard, 2007). Abortion rates and unintended pregnancies are much lower once contraceptives are more available (Carlson, 2006). If prevention of unintended pregnancies and lower rates of infant mortality and premature births are common goals for the U.S. health care system, then it is logical to strive for widespread coverage for and accessibility to birth control that could lead to a major reduction in infant mortality, premature births, and abortions.

Narrowly tailored conscience clauses in federal legislation mandating contraceptive coverage could create a bridge between the competing sides, if the two sides came together to effect a common goal: reduced abortion rates and significantly fewer unintended pregnancies. In an age when the United States has the most scientifically advanced medical institutions in the world, with elaborate systems of specialized knowledge and advanced technologies, it bears repeating that almost half the nation's pregnancies are still unintended (Kaiser, 2014; IOM, 2011). As illustrated in **FEATURE BOX 13-4**, certainly this is one of the instances of widespread **inattentional blindness**, where the nation's thinking is being adapted at different rates by different groups.

Inadequate Maternity Coverage

With approximately 4 million births in the United States each year, pregnancy- and childbirth-related conditions are the leading causes for hospital stays and account for almost 11 percent of the nation's hospitalizations (Law, 2008). Yet prenatal care is increasingly out of reach for women in the United States. Women, including many with otherwise comprehensive health insurance, are finding themselves uncovered for one of their biggest health care costs: comprehensive maternity care. One reason is that health insurers are failing to provide women reproductive services mandated by the Affordable Care Act, a problem that appears to be systemic nationwide (NWLC, 2015). Even women with no

Contraception's Inattentional Blindness

Without contraception:

- Women are likely to become pregnant 12 to 15 times over the course of their reproductive lives.
- 85 out of 100 sexually active women of childbearing age will become pregnant each year.
- 500,000 infants per year would be born preterm.
- 3 infants die every hour due to unintended pregnancies and consequent lack of prenatal care (over 28,000 deaths/year).

— Sources: AAP, 2015; ACOG, 2011; *Standridge v. Union Pacific Railroad Company*, 479 F.3d 936 (U.S. Court of Appeals for the 8th Circuit 2007).

history of complicated births have a hard time getting affordable access to maternity coverage that covers monthly prenatal physician visits, lab tests, ultrasounds, and childbirth (Davidoff, 2010). In this instance, the average cost-sharing deductible for families is between $6,000 and $10,600 (Armour, 2015).The insurance industry argues that to include maternity coverage with more affordable cost-sharing, they have to increase costs to their other customers, which in turn would result in a loss of profits, as the cost of maternity care is too high for them to cover (Radnofsky, 2015). Yet the insurance industry's argument does not factor in the increased cost of care resulting from no maternity coverage, such as emergency deliveries or health problems after birth for mothers and children without prenatal care (Callaghan, 2010; IOM, 2011).

Individual Insurance Restrictions

By law, employers that offer a group health insurance plan must include access to maternity coverage. But for childbearing-age women who do not have employer-provided health insurance benefits or Medicaid insurance coverage, there are few, if any, affordable options (Law, 2008). While the Pregnancy Discrimination Act requires maternity coverage

6. What ethical principles should guide the U.S. health care system as it attempts to deal with childbearing-age women who do not have maternity coverage and do not qualify for Medicaid insurance?

7. Should the United States become more hospitable toward women and provide universal access to prenatal care to better protect women and their newborn children? Pregnancy is given special, generous protection in other high-income countries like Australia, Canada, Europe, and New Zealand (Cogan, 2011).

if employers offer group health insurance as an employee benefit, individual health insurance plans that provide some sort of maternity coverage do so at a high premium (Kaiser, 2014a). In many states, once a woman is pregnant, it is impossible to obtain affordable individual health insurance. While the idea of purchasing health insurance across state lines in the individual market as part of health care reform has supporters, states would be powerless to stop out-of-state insurance companies from selling coverage in their state which did not include maternity coverage, unless it continues to be mandated at the federal level (Kanwit, 2009).

The Ethics of High Caesarean Deliveries

The United States has the highest rates of caesarean surgeries of any nation in the world (CIA, 2013). Prior to the ACA, most state insurance laws required unexpected complications during delivery, such as those requiring an emergency caesarean, to be covered by health insurance, while standard vaginal deliveries were not covered without explicit maternity coverage for childbirth. Although the correlation between the U.S. failure to provide basic prenatal and maternity coverage for childbirth to all women and the nation's high rate of caesarean surgeries may be coincidental, this cause and effect may not be pure coincidence (CIA, 2013). The actual effect is much more nuanced. While the requirement to cover caesarean births is well justified, universal insurance coverage protects women by helping to limit the occurrence rate of this negative health outcome (Baker, 2010) and at the same time it is more cost-effective (Laufer-Ukeles, 2011). Universal maternity coverage for childbirth is justified, not simply as a fundamental issue of the justice principles, but also from the standpoint of clinical effectiveness (Law, 2008).

Right to and Permissible Abortion Regulations

Abortion is, for the most part, one of America's most divisive issues. It involves competing cultural values: pro-life and pro-choice. While both sides in the nation's cultural war may ask what kind of country the United States might be if society encouraged its families and supported women when they made the decision to become a parent, the family values of the two sides are polarized (Huntington, 2011). While the pro-life forces originally emphasized the importance of conventional gender roles with women as stay-at-home mothers and housewives, their agenda has come to depend on the belief that abortion constitutes murder because fetuses and embryos are considered people (Carbone & Cahn, 2010). Pro-choice forces define abortion as a choice-based issue centered on women's human rights

ETHICAL DILEMMAS 13-5

8. How does the federal mandate that health insurance plans provide some sort of maternity coverage for prenatal care and childbirth impact the abortion and conscience clause controversies?

(Ziegler, 2011). It is important to note that the term *pro-choice* is not a synonym for pro-abortion: pro-choice advocates support women's right to choose; they do not favor or encourage abortion over other options.

Several states are considering bans on abortion in anticipation that the U.S. Supreme Court may overrule the court decision holding that a woman has a constitutional right to have an abortion during the first two trimesters of pregnancy (*Roe v. Wade*, 410 U.S. 113 (U.S. Supreme Court 1973)). The *Roe v. Wade* decision affirms the basic right of women to terminate their pregnancies in the early stages (*Planned Parenthood of Southeastern Pennsylvania v. Casey*, 505 U.S. 833, 844 (U.S. Supreme Court 1992) (affirming and refusing to overturn *Roe v. Wade*)).

Several states are considering sharply limiting or banning coverage of abortion by health plans offered in the new insurance exchanges. Now that women have the right to an abortion, the debate is over defining that right and permissible abortion regulations. Abortion-related laws passed at the state level are increasing, most including new restrictions or bolstering limits on the procedure already embedded in federal law (Mathews, 2011). While some argue the United States should remove the impediments to access and financing for contraception, so as to prevent a pregnancy in the first place, this position does not address the women who do find themselves pregnant and are faced with the choice of an adoption or a baby if abortion is not an available option.

The number of abortions in the United States has begun to rise slightly following a downward trend that began in 1990; based on the most recent statistics available, abortions now stand at about 1.2 million a year (Mathews, 2011). While the stalled decline may be tied to several factors, such as the economic recession that started in 2007, teenage pregnancy rates appear to have stopped falling, and there has been an absence of any gains in contraceptive use in recent years (Gold, 2011). Regardless of the rise, more than one-third of American women live in counties with no health care professional who performs abortions (Mathews, 2011). Lost in the abortion debate is the fact that more than one-third of the teen pregnancies in the United States resulted in abortions (Kaiser, 2014c).

Dilation and Extraction Abortion Bans

Abortions performed very late in pregnancy are rare and tend to occur due to a potentially fatal condition diagnosed in the fetus or the mother (Brin, 2011).

ETHICAL DILEMMAS 13-6

9. Even for those who maintain that the choice to have an abortion belongs to women, when almost half of the unintended pregnancies result in abortions, is the ratio of unintended pregnancies to abortions ethically acceptable? For some, would any ratio be acceptable?

10. Does the value of developing human life justify restricting the basic right of pregnant women of the choice to have an abortion during the first two trimesters of their pregnancies? What about the third trimester?

ETHICS CASE
Dilation and Extraction Abortions

Gonzales v. Carhart
[Federal Government v. Physician]
550 U.S. 124 (U.S. Supreme Court 2007)

Facts: States are prohibited from outright banning abortion before the human fetus develops to the point where it could live independently of the mother, a period known as **pre-viability**. During pre-viability, states cannot impose an undue burden on women seeking to exercise their legal right to abortion. In the period after viability, known as post-viability, states may regulate abortion as long as the restrictions do not endanger the life or health of pregnant women.

After the U.S. Supreme Court struck down Nebraska's **intact dilation and extraction** (D&X) abortion ban in 2000, Congress enacted a federal version of the Nebraska law which contained no exception for when the mother's health was at risk. Congress specifically banned D&Xs in the second trimester of pregnancy. Most D&Xs involve delivering the fetus intact until part of it passes through the vagina, where it is then aborted. This is also referred to as a **partial-birth abortion**, although this term is neither recognized nor used in medical literature. Congress maintained that D&X abortions are never medically necessary; however, the federal law includes an exception when a woman's life is in danger, but not if her health is merely at risk.

Legal Analysis: The U.S. Supreme Court found that in D&Xs, a **health exception** was unnecessary based on congressional findings that this procedure was never medically necessary. Additionally, because medical alternatives to the banned procedure exist that do not violate federal law, the Court found that there was no undue burden on pregnant women.

The Court stated that challenges to the federal partial-birth abortion law require a showing that the law would be unconstitutional in a large fraction of relevant cases. The Court found that the law applied to any and all situations in which physicians would choose to perform D&Xs, not merely those where the women are suffering from medical complications, and therefore the law is not unconstitutional in the large fraction of relevant cases.

Rule of Law: People are prohibited from intentionally partially delivering a viable fetus and then performing an overt act that the person knows will kill the partially delivered fetus.

Ethics Issue: How are D&X abortions ethically different from "regular" abortions during the first two trimesters?

Ethics Analysis: This decision has significant implications for the future of women's right to terminate their pregnancies. As the current state of these laws illustrates, abortion is subject to increasing restrictions that depart greatly from *Roe v. Wade*. The Court was clear in the ethicality of prohibiting anyone from intentionally partially delivering a viable fetus and then knowingly performing an overt act to kill the partially delivered fetus. The line between pre-viability and post-viability abortions in the second trimester, however, was blurred by a focus on how and where

D&Xs occur, as opposed to addressing the ethical principles underlying the *Roe* trimester framework based on fetal age and viability.

For the first time since *Roe v. Wade*, the Court prohibited a medical procedure with no exception for safeguarding women's health—a significant change in the ethics of abortion law. The ethical dilemma centered on the perceived need to safeguard women's health when regulating abortions. One argument for prohibiting D&Xs is that the government has an interest in preserving the *potential life* of a fetus (without regard to viability). Because alternative abortion procedures, such as a **dilation and evacuation** (D&E), where the contents of the uterus are surgically evacuated, are still available if D&Xs are banned, a ban would not necessarily prevent the safeguarding women's lives. The counterargument centered on avoiding subjecting women to health risk when states ban D&Xs, thereby forcing women to resort to less safe methods of abortion. The ethicality of D&X bans was considered in terms of the ban's impact on vulnerable populations. Minors and indigent women were found to be more likely than other women to have difficulty obtaining an abortion during the first trimester of pregnancy. While minors are often unaware they are pregnant until relatively late in pregnancy, financial constraints are an obstacle to timely receipt of reproductive services for both groups of women. The potential effect of a ban on one type of late-term abortions for minors and indigent women is not having access to lawful abortions. The issue is whether this outcome is ethical even if it is legal.

The second ethical dilemma centered on the ethics of obfuscating facts in legislative hearings on D&Xs. While one side acknowledged this obfuscation of facts, it supplied no reason to reject those findings in upholding the ban on D&Xs. The other side focused on the impact of forcing women to undergo two alternative procedures to D&Xs. First, while an injection to kill the fetus was seen as an alternative to D&Xs, the counterargument is that inducing fetal death by injection poses tangible risks and provides no benefits to women. Second, while medical induction of labor is an alternative to D&Xs, this requires a hospital stay, rendering it inaccessible to women who lack financial resources, and it too is considered less safe for many women and impermissible for others.

The last ethical dilemma focused on the right to abort when serious disabilities are found in a fetus. Women's right to decide whether such pregnancies should be brought to term was not considered, but the counterargument noted that severe fetal anomalies are also causes of second-trimester abortions; many such conditions cannot be diagnosed or do not develop until the second trimester. Nearly all women carrying fetuses with serious disabilities choose to abort their pregnancies.

Court's Holding and Decision: Yes, intact D&Xs are never medically necessary and women have alternatives to the banned procedure.

See, e.g., Abrams, 2013; Anderson, 2015; Bakelaar, 2014; Benedict, 2013; Bonner & Sheriff, 2013; Cahill, 2013; Cheu, 2012; Dolgin & Dieterich, 2012; Donley, 2013; Duane, 2013; Franzonello, 2013; Forsythe, 2014; Friedman, 2013; Gray & Holden, 2014; Huberfeld, 2013; Jayadevan, 2015; Johnsen, 2015; Koss, 2014; Lang, 2014; Madeira, 2014; Malinowski, 2012; Melling, 2014; Pergament, 2013; Prior, 2014; Samuels, 2014; Scaldo, 2013; Shainwald, 2013; Siegel & Siegel, 2013; Stam, 2012; Suter, 2013; Toscano & Reiter, 2014; Vandewalker, 2012; Vargo, 2012; Wardle, 2013; Will, 2013; Young, 2014 (discussing this court decision).

The federal government has made it a crime to perform D&X abortions during the second trimester, marking the *Carhart* decision as the first time the U.S. Supreme Court has held that physicians can be prohibited from using a medical procedure deemed necessary to benefit a patient's health (Ginsburg, 2008). Though the time of fetal viability varies for legally performing D&Xs, before 24 weeks is average; 24 weeks is usually considered the earliest a human fetus can survive outside the womb, and is therefore the point in time at which performing a D&X becomes illegal (Brin, 2011).

Following the *Carhart* decision, the health exception that had always been required in the past is no longer a strict requirement (Helling & Nam, 2010). Now, there is concern that health care professionals will not perform legal D&Xs out of fear that they might be investigated for criminal wrongdoing (Drazen, 2007). A Nebraska law bans abortions after 20 weeks; the law is built on research indicating that 20 weeks is the point at which a fetus may begin to experience pain (Stahle, 2007). Nebraska is the first state law banning abortions so early in a pregnancy, without a medical exception for the health of pregnant women.

The impact of *Carhart* expands beyond the issue of abortion and intrudes into the practice of medicine. Legislative judgment was allowed to trump medical judgment by preventing physicians from performing a medical procedure they believe to be in the best interests of their patients (Annas, 2007). *Carhart* marks a significant change in the U.S. Supreme Court's abortion jurisprudence. Future cases will have to further define a state's power to restrict the right to abortion and the human rights of physicians to treat their patients. Many fear that *Carhart* will cause physicians to avoid similar legal medical procedures, possibly even when a woman's life is in jeopardy (Greene, 2007).

Parental Notification Limitations

Greater regulation of abortion access for minors has consistently been allowed because of the lesser rights of minors and parental interests. Regulations that require parental consent are constitutional, provided they contain a **judicial bypass** for minors who do not want to inform their parents (Helling & Nam, 2010). Minors who want abortions without notifying or getting consent from a parent must first go to court and convince a judge that they are sufficiently mature and competent enough to make the decision themselves. As illustrated in **FEATURE BOX 13-5**, many states have parental notification requirements before abortions may be performed on minors that generally require young women to wait at least 48 hours after written notice of the pending abortion has been delivered.

FEATURE BOX 13-5

Exceptions to the 48-Hour Parental Notification Rule

Physicians may perform abortions on minors without the 48-hour parental notification when one or more of the following conditions are met:

- An abortion is necessary to save a minor's life (medical emergencies) and there is insufficient time for parental notification.
- A parent certifies they have already been notified.
- The court grants approval after being petitioned.

— Sources: *Ayotte v. Planned Parenthood of Northern New England,* 546 U.S. 320 (U.S. Supreme Court 2006); Manian, 2012; Pedagno, 2011.

ETHICS CASE
Parental Notification for Abortions

Ayotte v. Planned Parenthood of Northern New England
[New Hampshire v. Reproductive Clinic]
546 U.S. 320 (U.S. Supreme Court 2006)

Facts: New Hampshire enacted a parental notification law prohibiting abortions upon minors until at least 48 hours after written notice of the pending abortion had been delivered to their parents or guardians. The law allowed for three exceptions where a physician could perform an abortion on a minor without notification: (1) abortion was necessary to prevent the minor's death and there was insufficient time to provide the required notice; (2) people entitled to receive notice provided written certification that they had been notified; or (3) minor petitioned a judge to authorize an abortion and the judge found that the minor was mature and capable of giving her informed consent, or that an abortion without parental notification served the minor's best interests.

This judicial bypass measure was confidential and courts had to rule on bypass petitions within 7 days. Though the exceptions to parental notification were to be acknowledged prior to a minor's abortion, abortions could not be performed in a medical emergency involving serious and often irreversible damage to the minor's health without parental notification unless it was a matter of life and death for the minor.

An obstetrician/gynecologist and 3 clinics that offer reproductive health care and abortions for pregnant minors brought this lawsuit, claiming that New Hampshire's parental notification law was unconstitutional because it did not include an exception allowing a physician to perform an abortion on a minor in any and all medical emergencies.

Legal Analysis: The U.S. Supreme Court began by stating that it was not revisiting its abortion precedents, but rather addressing a question of remedy. The Court carefully sidestepped the opportunity to confront its controversial abortion precedents by framing the question around the issue of whether the lower courts erred by invalidating the New Hampshire parental notification law in its entirety because it failed to provide an emergency health exception.

When confronted with a constitutional flaw in any law, the Court noted that it preferred to **enjoin**, meaning to bar the enforcement of only the unconstitutional applications of a law while leaving other applications in force; in other words, to sever its problematic portion(s) while leaving the remainder intact whenever possible. The Court outlined 3 principles that should inform a court's approach to remedies: (1) courts must not invalidate any more of a legislature's work than is necessary, because invalidating an entire law as unconstitutional frustrates the intent of the people's elected representatives; (2) courts must avoid rewriting state law to conform to federal constitutional requirements even while the courts attempt to salvage the law, since making distinctions in constitutional contexts may involve an invasion of the legislative field; and (3) courts cannot use their remedial powers to skirt a legislature's intent since once a court finds an application or portion of a law unconstitutional, the court must ask whether the legislature would prefer what is left of its law to no law at all.

The Court found that the lower courts improperly chose the bluntest remedy by invalidating the parental notification law in its entirety. The Court agreed with New

Hampshire's position that such a wholesale invalidation of the parental notification law was unnecessary. Therefore, the Court concluded, as long as the lower courts remain faithful to legislative intent, the lower courts could issue a more narrowly drawn injunction preventing enforcement of only the law's unconstitutional applications while leaving the rest of the law in force. Or, if the lower courts found that they could not issue an injunction preventing the enforcement of the unconstitutional applications of the law, then they could invalidate the law in its entirety. The crucial question is legislative intent: whether a state legislature would have preferred a law with an exception for pregnant minors in medical emergencies or the striking of the law in its entirety, meaning there would no longer be any requirement for parental notification at all.

Rule of Law: Portions of New Hampshire's parental notification law could not be applied constitutionally and thus required revision.

Ethics Issue: Should state legislatures be permitted to restrict abortions in a manner that exposes minors to significant, but perhaps not fatal, health risks?

Ethics Analysis: The Court considered whether parental involvement should be required when a minor considers terminating her pregnancy. There is no dispute that state legislatures have the right to require parental involvement. The argument is that parents have a strong and legitimate interest in the welfare of their daughters, whose immaturity, inexperience, and lack of judgment may sometimes impair their ability to decide wisely, as in the case of an unintended pregnancy. The counterargument considers those instances where parents are not supportive or capable of helping their daughters make the best decision for their futures, and instances in which parental notification might place the minor in danger. Usually, this situation occurs when one or both parents inflict domestic violence and notification would only provoke further battering and abuse.

Court's Holding and Decision: Remanded to determine whether the court could, consistent with legislative intent, formulate a narrower remedy than a permanent injunction against enforcement of the parental notification law in its entirety.

See, e.g., Fore, 2014; Forsythe, 2014; Gray & Holden, 2014; Jayadevan, 2015; Manian, 2012; Pruitt & Vanegas, 2015; Scaldo, 2013; Wardle, 2013; Young, 2014 (discussing this court decision).

In deciding *Ayotte*, the U.S. Supreme Court reaffirmed that state legislatures may require parental involvement in abortion decisions involving minors. Following *Ayotte*, if parental notification laws lack health exceptions and states willingly refrain from applying criminal penalties for medically necessary abortions, courts do not have to invalidate the law (Helling & Nam, 2010). While *Ayotte* has made courts less likely to invalidate entire abortion laws, another consequence of this decision has been an increase in abortion litigation.

Informed Consent Restrictions

There is growing controversy over the ethics of state-mandated abortion counseling (Corbin, 2009). The progression of the informed consent doctrine was addressed in the New Jersey Supreme Court ruling in the *Acuna v. Turkish* decision, which held that health care professionals do not have an ethical obligation to inform pregnant women about the ethics of abortions and are only required to disclose medical information.

ETHICS CASE
Informed Consent for Abortion

Acuna v. Turkish
[Pregnant Woman v. Gynecologist]
930 A.2d 416 (Supreme Court of New Jersey 2007),
certiorari denied, 555 U.S. 813 (U.S. Supreme Court 2008)

Facts: Rosa Acuna, a married mother of two children under three years of age, consulted her gynecologist, Dr. Sheldon Turkish, about abdominal pains and headaches. After Turkish informed her that she was six to eight weeks pregnant, Acuna decided to terminate her unintended pregnancy. Turkish performed the abortion, but after complications developed, Acuna was sent to a local hospital. When she asked a nurse why a further procedure had been performed, the nurse responded that Turkish had left parts of the baby inside of her. It was only at this point, Acuna claims, that she started to realize there was a baby inside her and not just blood. This realization led to a decline in her mental health and a diagnosis of post traumatic stress disorder.

The facts of the information exchange prior to the decision to terminate her pregnancy were disputed. Acuna maintained that Turkish told her that due to a complication with her kidneys, she would have to terminate the pregnancy or die in three months. Acuna further claimed she asked Turkish if it was the baby in there, to which Turkish replied, it is only blood. Turkish, in contrast, asserted that Acuna suggested the option of abortion and that he had never encouraged her to terminate her pregnancy to preserve her health. Turkish could not remember the conversation, but believed he would have told her that a seven-week pregnancy is not a living human being, but merely tissue at that time.

Acuna filed this action alleging a lack of informed consent. She claimed that had Turkish provided her with the necessary medical and factual information surrounding the nature of abortion and the fact that her child was a complete, separate, and unique human being, she would not have terminated her pregnancy.

Legal Analysis: The court dismissed Acuna's informed consent claim and ruled that there was no common law duty for physicians to inform patients that an abortion would kill an actual existing human being. According to the court, the instructions sought were opinion and not medical fact; they were, therefore, a departure from the doctrine of informed consent. The court emphasized it would only ever compel physicians to provide medical information, not information based on philosophy or theology.

Negligence actions predicated on lack of informed consent must demonstrate that a physician withheld medical information that a reasonably prudent pregnant woman would have considered material before consenting to a termination of pregnancy. The knowledge Acuna sought cannot be compelled from a physician who may have a different viewpoint on the issue of when life begins. Physicians might be required to convey medical information that reflects a consensus opinion in the medical community. However, without such a consensus, instructions cannot be required.

The court also found that the instructions were at odds with current abortion law, suggesting that both the physician and the patient would be complicit in committing the equivalent of murder. This in turn would have contradicted the state legislature's choice to exclude a fetus from the definition of a person in the state's wrongful death act.

Rule of Law: While potential parents should be provided sufficient medical information to make an informed decision whether or not to continue an unplanned pregnancy to term, physicians have no duty to provide ethical guidance.

Ethics Issue: Should health care professionals be required to inform pregnant women that their seven- to eight-week-old embryos are complete and separate human beings, given that these embryos cannot survive outside the woman's uterus during the time when legal abortions may occur?

Ethics Analysis: This case centers on whether informed consent for abortions must include provisions to advise pregnant women that their embryos are living human beings. While there is agreement that embryos are biological entities belonging to the human species, it is not at all obvious if embryos are human beings in a distinct sense, or whether embryos are members of the community of human entities whose existence possesses human dignity and warrants respect. One argument is that health care professionals have an ethical obligation to inform pregnant women that abortions kill an existing human being. The counterargument is that this is a philosophical and theological statement with no broad support in the medical community or society as a whole. The law leaves the decision of whether to abort or go to term with a non-viable embryo for women to decide for themselves, since there is a lack of national consensus on the beginning-of-life question.

Court's Holding and Decision: No, physicians are not required to inform patients seeking abortions that the procedure will kill an actual existing human being.

See, e.g., Olson, 2013; Rebouche & Rothenberg, 2012; Schlueter, 2013 (discussing this court decision).

Some states require health care professionals to give pregnant women seeking abortions a written statement containing information similar to that requested in the *Acuna* case (Sanger, 2009). Whether such disclosures will expand existing informed consent laws to require the provision of ethical guidance and advice remains to be seen (Borgmann, 2009).

Mandatory In-Person, Informed Consent Requirements

The *Carhart* decision supports laws that expand informed consent requirements for abortions. The U.S. Supreme Court signaled its willingness to accept requirements aimed at informing women's reproductive decisions. Whether the expanding restrictions on abortion represent new emerging values in society as a whole is not clear.

ETHICS CASE
Judicial Bypass of Parental Consent Requirement and Mandatory In-Person, Informed Consent Meetings

Cincinnati Women's Services, Inc. v. Taft
[Reproductive Clinic v. Governor]
468 F.3d 361 (U.S. Court of Appeals for the 6th Circuit 2006)

Facts: Prior to 1998, Ohio law required that minors receive the informed consent of a parent or guardian before receiving an abortion. The law, however, allowed minors to petition a juvenile court for a judicial bypass of the parental consent requirement; the court could determine whether the minor was sufficiently mature and well informed enough to decide whether to have an abortion or whether notification of her parents was not in her best interest. The law did not impose any limitations on the number of times a minor could petition a court for such a bypass.

Ohio law also mandated that women seeking an abortion receive information about the procedure from a physician prior to the abortion. The informed consent provision required that a physician inform the pregnant woman, verbally or by other non-written means of communication, about abortion. This was interpreted to mean that videotaped or audiotaped physician statements would be an adequate means of imparting the necessary information to women seeking abortions. In 1998, the state legislature amended the judicial bypass and informed consent provisions of its abortion regulations with two regulations: the single-petition rule that limited minors to only one attempt to obtain a judicial bypass during the term of each pregnancy, and the in-person rule that required informed consent meetings to take place in person.

Legal Analysis: The court began its analysis by determining that the proper standard to apply to challenges of abortion restrictions is the **large fraction test**. The large fraction test requires a reviewing court to determine whether a large fraction of the women for whom the law is a restriction will be deterred from procuring an abortion as surely as if the government had outlawed abortion in all cases.

Applying the large fraction test to the single-petition rule, the court held that the regulation created an undue burden to a large fraction of minors who are initially refused a bypass but later experience changes entitling them to a bypass. The court reasoned that the single-petition rule affected minors who were denied a bypass at first, but who would be bypass-eligible if they were to reapply because of changed circumstances in their life (for instance, increased maturity or discovery of medical anomalies with the fetus). The court concluded that because the single-petition rule would form a substantial obstacle to obtaining an abortion for *most* minors who had experienced changes in their circumstances, it was unconstitutional.

Next, the court upheld the in-person rule, holding that the number of abortion seekers likely to be frustrated by the regulation was not large enough to justify overturning the provision. In determining the number of women who would be unduly burdened by the in-person rule, the court noted that 25 percent of the women excused from the in-person meetings were in abusive relationships. Of this 25 percent, only half would be completely unable to obtain an abortion if they were forced to have a separate in-person meeting prior to an abortion, for reasons ranging from geographic and financial constraints to fear of repercussion given their abusive relationships. The court held that an undue burden on 12 percent was not enough to consider the law unconstitutional.

Rule of Law: In-person informed consent meetings may be required before abortions may be performed and minors may petition for judicial bypass of the parental notification rule more than once per pregnancy.

Ethics Issue: Do the single-petition and in-person rules unduly burden pregnant women?

Ethics Analysis: The court faced several ethical dilemmas when tasked with protecting the best interests of minors and assuring that all women, including minors, make informed decisions about their pregnancies. In seeking to uphold the abortion law, the impact of the restrictions was evaluated to determine whether the restrictions unduly burdened pregnant women.

One side assumed that women make abortion decisions impulsively. If women were forced to delay deciding by 24 hours and given more information in person, it was assumed that they would not consent to aborting their pregnancies.

The counterargument assumed that women, even minors, understand abortions and unintended pregnancy, and that women are able and best positioned to decide what is at stake. The counterargument, in essence, supports the right of women to self-determination.

The second ethical dilemma centered on regulating women's decisions. Since women are perceived to require protection, attention must be directed to providing information so that women understand what they could suffer by virtue of consenting to an abortion. The counterargument focused on the decision-making process itself. Women have a right to make their own decisions about terminating their pregnancies. Is the decision process fair, and are the obstacles to making the decision intended or incidental? Respect is owed to the decision-making process as well as the actual decisions. When women have no choice but to comply with in-person counseling laws, those laws may unfairly burden women in the form of delay or interference in the physician–patient relationship and the decision-making arising from that relationship.

The third ethical dilemma, although not considered by the court, involves balancing parental rights and the competing interests and human rights of pregnant minors. Judicial bypass laws attempt to both assist minors as autonomous adults and protect them as children. Judicial bypass is based on concerns about minors' inability to make important life decisions without parental support. Though judicial bypass procedures exist to allow minors to make abortion decisions independently, no consideration was given to parents' traditional rights to raise and control their minor children when the judicial bypass procedure was reviewed, nor was any consideration given to the possible rights of the father of the unborn child.

Court's Holding and Decision: Yes, limiting minors to only one petition for judicial bypass of a parental consent requirement for an abortion is an unconstitutionally undue burden; and yes, minors may be required to attend an in-person meeting with a physician prior to receiving an abortion.

See, e.g., Duane, 2013; Gray & Holden, 2014; King, 2012; Spindelman, 2012; Toscano & Reiter, 2014 (discussing this court decision).

One aspect of the current abortion debate centers on the question of whether minors have the maturity to independently make decisions about unintended pregnancies. It may be logically inconsistent to maintain that minors lack the maturity to make decisions about abortion while considering the same minors mature enough to raise children on their own. However, this part of the abortion debate may indicate that some discussion is moving away from the focus on whether abortion should be legal to a more economic discussion of whether minors are prepared to accept responsibility for raising children (Cahn & Carbone, 2015).

Per Se Medical Exceptions

In 2000, the FDA approved mifepristone, an artificial steroid also known as RU-486, which can be used as a contraceptive, as well as to induce abortions. As such, RU-486 blurs the distinction between contraception and abortion, suggesting that there is no ethical distinction between preventing pregnancy and terminating it in its early stages (Helling & Nam, 2010). Four years after approval of RU-486, Ohio became the first state to restrict the **off-label use** of RU-486. The medication could only be prescribed within the first 7 weeks of a pregnancy, as expressly approved on its package insert. Off-label use of the medication past the first 7 weeks of pregnancy was prohibited. Litigation on different aspects of RU-486 has been ongoing ever since.

ETHICS CASE
Per Se **Medical Exceptions**

Planned Parenthood Cincinnati Region v. Taft
[Reproductive Clinic v. Governor]
444 F.3d 502 (U.S. Court of Appeals for the 6th Circuit 2006)

Facts: In 2000, the FDA approved the use and manufacture of RU-486, a medication that medically induces abortion without surgical intervention. The treatment regimen the FDA approved was to be taken within the first 7 weeks of a pregnancy: oral administration of RU-486 followed 2 days later by the oral administration of misoprostol. Referred to as the *abortion medication*, RU-486 terminates a pregnancy by detaching the gestational sac from the uterine wall; misoprostol is a prostaglandin which induces the contractions necessary to expel the fetus and other products of conception from the uterus, essentially resulting in a miscarriage.

Generally, once the FDA has approved a medication, physicians have the legal authority to prescribe it for off-label uses, unless state regulations require otherwise. An off-label use of RU-486 was the so-called *Schaff protocol* (named after the physician whose research led to its development), which allowed for the administration of RU-486 within up to the first 9 weeks of a pregnancy. The Schaff protocol provided for the oral administration of RU-486 followed 1 to 3 days later by misoprostol administered vaginally. The American Medical Association and the American College of Obstetricians encourages the Schaff protocol because of its high rate of effectiveness (98 percent) with few side effects.

The Ohio legislature prohibited the off-label use of RU-486 in Ohio. Various Ohio chapters of Planned Parenthood and two physicians challenged the constitutionality of this law. The federal Sixth Circuit Court enjoined Ohio from regulating RU-486, because the law lacked a health exception that might pose significant risks to the health of pregnant women.

Legal Analysis: The court explained that the role of the judiciary is to construe legislative intent. The provisions of the state law are not ambiguous. It allows physicians to provide RU-486 to induce an abortion only in accordance with the FDA's approval letter. Accordingly, the state's law that restricted physicians from using RU-486 after the seventh week of pregnancy and vaginal administration was not ambiguous. While Planned Parenthood argued that physicians have the authority to prescribe medications for off-label use in the practice of medicine, the Ohio legislature specifically restricted the use of RU-486 to physicians who provide the medication in accordance with the prescribing information outlined in the FDA approval letter and the final printed labeling.

Rule of Law: The Schaff protocol, allowing for administration of RU-486 through a patient's ninth week of pregnancy, is prohibited under Ohio state law.

Ethics Issue: Should the use of abortion-inducing medications be restricted to the first 7 weeks of a pregnancy, if the only alternative for women after the first 7 weeks but before the ninth week of a pregnancy is a surgical abortion (such as a dilation and evacuation procedure)?

Ethics Analysis: The ethical dilemma is whether the use of abortion-inducing medications that force women to surgically terminate their pregnancies after

7 weeks of a pregnancy should be banned. Women's choice to terminate a pregnancy can be restricted due to the state interest in human life, a principle with important consequences for women's health and procreative freedom.

One argument de-emphasizes women's health by maintaining the position that curtailing non-surgical abortions will not harm the health of pregnant women, as long as alternatives are available to terminate a pregnancy. With no non-surgical abortion alternatives available after week 7 of a pregnancy, pregnant women themselves are culpable for failing to access the abortion-inducing medications before the 7 weeks. This argument focused on the ends desired (women may still terminate a pregnancy even if surgery is required after 7 weeks of pregnancy) and neglects the importance of the means (whether a surgical abortion is as safe, or safer, than using abortion-inducing medications). How this ban would impact women's health was not a consideration; women were seen as having voluntarily waived their previously available options by not seeking abortions within 7 weeks of their pregnancy.

The counterargument focuses on protecting women's personal autonomy and their reproductive health. The lack of non-surgical alternatives to terminating pregnancies after 7 weeks is detrimental to women's health and threatens the availability of abortions for some women. The ban of abortion-inducing medications does not value women's health, since it poses unnecessary risks to the health of pregnant women seeking abortions after 7 weeks of a pregnancy. Restricted access to and the limited availability of reproductive care generally contribute to delays and the inability to receive abortions in a timely manner, not the unsound decisions of pregnant women.

Court's Holding and Decision: Yes, physicians may provide RU-486 to induce an abortion only through a patient's seventh week of pregnancy and only by using the oral method of administration approved by the FDA in the final printed labeling.

See, e.g., Jayadevan, 2015; Manian, 2012; Wardle, 2013 (discussing this court decision).

The implication of the *Taft* decision is that states may restrict off-label uses of abortion-inducing medications if a medical exception is included in the restriction. The personal autonomy of physicians and other health care professionals involved in women's reproductive care could be inhibited since RU-486 can be used as emergency contraception (LaSpina, et al., 2010). This rationale leads down a slippery slope that could even be expanded to prevent off-label use of birth control pills, which are often prescribed as ECs and to treat acne as well as irregular periods and severe premenstrual syndrome symptoms. This in turn could leave women and their ability to exercise their right to access contraception at the mercy of individual states (LaSpina, 2011).

Women's reproductive rights are meaningless if access to contraception cannot be freely exercised. The right to access contraception free from governmental interference has been firmly established in the law for almost 50 years (*see Griswold v. Connecticut*, 381 U.S. 479 (U.S. Supreme Court 1965); *Carey v. Population Services International*, 431 U.S. 678 (U.S. Supreme Court 1977); *Roe v. Wade, supra*; *Eisenstadt v. Baird*, 405 U.S. 438 (U.S. Supreme Court 1972); *but see Burwell, et al. v. Hobby Lobby Stores, Inc., et al.*, 134 S.Ct. 2751 (U.S. Supreme Court 2014) (holding that closely held corporations with sincerely held religious beliefs against contraception are not required to provide health insurance coverage for contraceptives because there are other ways for women to access contraception cost-free)). However, even though established law gives women the right to access contraception, limits and bans, such as the off-label uses of RU-486, create a law-based barrier between women and their established legal right to access contraception. *See generally* LaSpina, 2011. Women who work for employers that do not provide health insurance coverage for contraception can still, in theory, access free contraceptives (Howell, 2015); this right to access just may not always be what is medically necessary or desirable, or easily available.

Values That Impact Women's Reproductive Health

This chapter has demonstrated that it is necessary to understand the values that impact women's reproductive health. Human dignity and respect are values that are taken quite seriously in other health care situations, but some argue that they have been subjugated with regard to women's reproductive care (Sanger, 2009). Yet, failing to value reproductive care is costly to the U.S. health care system. For instance, women's contraception has the potential to significantly reduce public health spending; for every 1 dollar spent on providing contraceptives, an estimated 4 dollars is saved in Medicaid insurance expenditures for unintended pregnancy-related and newborn care (Slaughter, 2007). Moreover, women's health rights are truly human health rights (Wiley, 2014), as it can be argued that some reproductive rights of men are also desecrated when their partners are not permitted to freely exercise the reproductive rights that only women can physically exercise (Strout, 2014).

Many American women—half a century after the U.S. Supreme Court stated that women have the right to access contraception—still cannot choose whether or when to become pregnant, or how many children to have, because they lack access to reproductive care. The human rights and freedoms of women are limited by strict controls on pregnancies, while at the same time little is done to ensure that unintended pregnancies do not occur in the first place. On the one hand, while it may be necessary to begin effectively addressing the values that are the root causes of unintended pregnancies, the other side of this ethical debate maintains that the lives of fetuses and embryos need to be protected at all costs.

E pluribus unum (one from many), a phrase on the Great Seal of the United States, refers to the nation as one people out of many. There are many philosophies about the value of human life, as the United States is comprised of many individuals and families from many nations, yet these many individuals and families are one when it comes to the need to protect human life as well as the need to lead lives as each sees fit. The polarizing ethics of contraception and abortion discussion may not be as illogical when viewed through this set of lenses.

ETHICAL OR UNETHICAL DECISION

Access to Emergency Contraception

Ethics Issue: *Should emergency contraception be made available over-the-counter to women of all ages, without any restrictions for minors?*

Ethics Analysis: Yes, women have a right to access emergency contraceptives OTC based on the conclusions of the FDA scientific staff and advisory committees; ECs should be allowed to meet the same agency criteria and be subject to the same level of scrutiny as other OTC products. Access to contraception is part of women's right to privacy. As such, women must be free of unwarranted intrusion into matters affecting their pregnancies. Women are unfairly burdened if they are only allowed to receive ECs for use as contraception from licensed pharmacists.

Ethics Analysis: No; although ECs may be safe according to the FDA scientific staff and advisory committees, ECs may be used as an abortion-inducing medication. As such ECs may not always be medically safe for OTC distribution to all women, especially to minors.

Court's Holding and Decision: The court found that the FDA repeatedly delayed issuing a decision on ECs for suspect reasons. Political considerations, delays, and implausible justifications for decision-making evidenced a lack of good faith and reasoned agency decision-making. Indeed, the FDA's conduct regarding ECs departed from the agency's normal procedures regarding similar applications to switch products from prescription to non-prescription use. The FDA was ordered to reconsider denial of the Citizen Petition from the Association of Reproductive Health Professionals and 65 other organizations to make ECs available to women 17 and older without a prescription; point-of-sale restrictions to minors were permitted.

— *Tummino v. Torti,* 603 F.Supp.2d 519 (U.S. District Court for the Eastern District of New York 2009), *reconsideration denied, Tummino v. Hamburg,* 260 F.R.D. 27 (U.S. District Court for the Eastern District of New York 2009). *See* Brandt, 2010; LaSpina, et al., 2010; Termini & Lee, 2011 (discussing this court decision).

CHAPTER SUMMARY

- Women's rights to reproductive care are insecure, with limited, costly access to comprehensive maternity care and constant attack on their reproductive choices.
- The conscience of women is rendered less important by pharmacists' conscience legislation that exempts pharmacists from dispensing contraceptive pills if doing so is against their personal beliefs.
- Better access to contraception is necessary to reduce the number of unintended pregnancies and the resulting number of abortions; too many women face financial barriers in accessing ECs and other contraceptives because their right to have health insurance coverage for contraceptives is not guaranteed.
- Where states require health insurers to cover contraceptives, women's access to contraception has significantly expanded; as a consequence, unintended pregnancies and abortion rates are much lower once contraceptives are more available.
- The U.S. Supreme Court, even as it upheld women's constitutional right to abortion, has avoided answering the ethical dilemma of when human life begins.
- With approximately 4 million births in the United States each year, pregnancy- and childbirth-related conditions account for almost 11 percent of the nation's hospitalizations; yet, comprehensive prenatal care and maternity coverage are falling out of reach for more women.
- States generally require unexpected complications during delivery, such as emergency caesareans, to be covered by health insurance, whereas standard vaginal deliveries are not covered without explicit maternity coverage. As a result, the United States has the highest rates of caesarean surgeries of any nation in the world.
- Abortion is one of America's most divisive issues, involving competing human rights and pro-life and pro-choice arguments, but the rate of abortion also begs the question of what kind of country the United States might be if society encouraged its families and supported women when they made the decision to become parents.

- Greater regulation of abortion access for minors has consistently been allowed because of parental interests and the lesser rights of minors.
- It is necessary to understand how human dignity and respect—values that in other health care situations are taken quite seriously—affect women's reproductive health.

REFERENCES

AAP (American Academy of Pediatrics). (2015). Caring for your baby and young child: Birth to age 5. Washington, DC: AAP.

Abrams, P. (2013). The scarlet letter: The Supreme Court and the language of abortion stigma. *Michigan Journal of Gender and Law, 19*, 293–337.

ACOG (American College of Obstetricians and Gynecologists). (2011). *Frequently asked questions.* Washington, DC: ACOG.

Alvare, H. M. (2011). Beyond the sex-ed wars: Addressing disadvantaged single mothers' search for community. *Akron Law Review, 44*, 167–220.

Anderson, B. J. (2015). Litigating abortion access cases in the post-*Windsor* world. *Columbia Journal of Gender and Law, 29*, 143–155.

Annas, G. J. (2007). The Supreme Court and abortion rights. *New England Journal of Medicine, 356*(21), 2201–2207.

Annie E. Casey Foundation, The. (2014). *The kids count data book.* Baltimore, MD: The Annie E. Casey Foundation Kids Count Data Center.

Armour, S. (2015). Health care costs hinge on high court ruling: Subsidies that made insurance plans affordable face crucial test. *Wall Street Journal*, p. A1.

Baker, H. J. (2010). "We don't want to scare the ladies:" An investigation of maternal rights and informed consent throughout the birth process. *Women's Rights Law Reporter, 31*, 538–593.

Behrman, R. E., & Butler, A. S. (2007). *Preterm birth: Causes, consequences, and prevention.* Washington, DC: National Academies of Science.

Bakelaar, R. (2014). The North Carolina Woman's Right to Know Act: An unconstitutional infringement on a physician's First Amendment right to free speech. *Michigan Journal of Gender and Law, 20*, 187–223.

Benedict, K. S. (2013). When might does not create religious rights: For-profit corporations' employees and the contraceptive coverage mandate. *Columbia Journal of Gender and Law, 26*, 58–122.

Bonner, M. H., & Sheriff, J. A. (2013). A child needs a champion: Guardian ad litem representation for prenatal children. *William and Mary Journal of Women and the Law, 19*, 511–584.

Borgmann, C. E. (2009). The meaning of "life": Belief and reason in the abortion debate. *Columbia Journal of Gender and Law, 18*, 551–608.

Brandt, S. C. (2010). The availability of Plan B to minors in the aftermath of *Tummino v. Torti. Journal of Gender, Race and Justice, 14*, 199–232.

Brin, D. W. (2011, January 20). Abortion doctor charged with murder. *Wall Street Journal*, p. A23.

Broekhuizen, F. (2009). Emergency contraception, efficacy and public health impact. *Current Opinion in Obstetrics and Gynecology, 21*(4), 309–312.

Cahill, C. M. (2013). Abortion and disgust. *Harvard Civil Rights-Civil Liberties Law Review, 48*, 409–456.

Cahn, N., & Carbone, J. (2015). Growing inequality and children. *American University Journal of Gender, Social Policy and the Law, 23*, 282–317.

Calabresi, S. G., & Rickert, J. T. (2011). Originalism and sex discrimination. *Texas Law Review, 90*, 1–101.

Callaghan, W. M. (2010, May, 12). Acting Chief, Maternal and Infant Health Branch, Centers for Disease Control and Prevention, CDC congressional testimony: Prematurity and infant mortality: What happens when infants are born too early? Hearing before the Committee on Energy and Commerce Subcommittee on Health, U.S. House of Representatives, Washington, DC.

Carbone, J., & Cahn, N. (2010). Families, fundamentalism, and the First Amendment: Embryo fundamentalism. *William and Mary Bill of Rights Journal, 18*, 1015–1052.

Carlson, K. E. (2006). A study of the effectiveness of mandated state contraceptive coverage in Iowa and Missouri and the case for a federal law. *Drake Law Review, 54*, 509–534.

Cheu, M. (2012). Now and then: How coverture ideology informs the rhetoric of abortion. *Texas Journal of Women and the Law, 22*, 113–130.

CIA (Central Intelligence Agency). (2013). *The world factbook.* Washington, DC: CIA.

Cogan, J. A. (2011). Public health reform: Patient Protection and Affordable Care Act implications for the public's health: The Affordable Care Act's preventive services mandate: Breaking down the barriers to nationwide access to preventive services. *The Journal of Law, Medicine and Ethics, 39*, 355–362.

Corbin, C. M. (2009). The First Amendment right against compelled listening. *Boston University Law Review, 89*, 939–1016.

Davidoff, K. (2010). Time to close the gap: Women in the individual health insurance market deserve access to maternity coverage. *Gender and Society, 25*, 391–415.

Davidson, L. A., et al. (2010). Religion and conscientious objection: A survey of pharmacists' willingness to dispense medications. *Social Science and Medicine, 71*(1), 161–165.

Dixon, H. S. (2004). Pelvic exam prerequisite to hormonal contraceptives: Unjustified infringement on constitutional rights, governmental coercion, and bad public policy. *Harvard Women's Law Journal, 27*, 177–233.

Dolgin, J. L., & Dieterich, K. R. (2012). The "other" within: Health care reform, class, and the politics of reproduction. *Seattle University Law Review, 35*, 377–425.

Donley, G. (2013). Does the constitution protect abortions based on fetal anomaly? Examining the potential for disability-selective abortion bans in the age of prenatal whole genome sequencing. *Michigan Journal of Gender and Law, 20*, 291–328.

Drahan, S., for the National Women's Law Center (NWLC). (2011). *HR358 (Protect Life Act) headed to House floor; Health care law and access to contraception at risk.* Washington, DC: NWLC.

Drazen, J. M. (2007). Government in medicine. *New England Journal of Medicine, 356*(21), 2195.

Duane, M. (2013). The disclaimer dichotomy: A First Amendment analysis of compelled speech in disclosure ordinances governing crisis pregnancy centers and laws mandating biased physician counseling. *Cardozo Law Review, 35*, 349–389.

Duvall, M. (2007). Pharmacy conscience clause statutes: Constitutional religious "accommodations" or unconstitutional "substantial burdens" on women? *American University Law Review, 55*, 1485–1522.

FDA, U.S. Food and Drug Administration. (2010). FDA news release: FDA approves Ella tablets for prescription emergency contraceptives. Bethesda, MD: FDA.

___. (2006). FDA news release: FDA approves over-the-counter access for Plan B for women 18 and older; Prescription remains required for those 17 and under.

Fentiman, L. C. (2006). The new "fetal protection": The wrong answer to the crisis of inadequate health care for women and children. *Denver University Law Review, 84*, 537–599.

Fleischman, A. (2008, June 19). President, March of Dimes Foundation, presentation to U.S. Surgeon General's Conference on the Prevention of Preterm Births. Rockville, MD: U.S. Surgeon General's Office.

Fore, W. (2014). A joyful heart is good medicine: Sexuality conversion bans in the courts. *Michigan Journal of Gender and Law, 21*, 311–340.

Forsythe, C. (2014). The medical assumption at the foundation of *Roe v. Wade* and its implications for women's health. *Issues in Law and Medicine, 29*, 183–214.

Franzonello, A. (2013). Reproductive healthcare legislation: Where we've been and where we're going. *Albany Law Journal of Science and Technology, 23*, 519–529.

Friedman, A. D. (2013). Reproductive justice: Bad medicine: Abortion and the battle over who speaks for women's health. *William and Mary Journal of Women and the Law, 20*, 45–72.

Ginsberg, R. B. (2008). Dissent is an "appeal" for the future. *Alaska Bar Rag, 32*, 1–7.

Gold, R. B. (2011). Wise investment: Reducing the steep cost to Medicaid of unintended pregnancy in the United States. *Guttmacher Policy Review, 14*(3), 6–10.

Golub, D., & Gartner, E. C. (2007). *Equity in prescription insurance and contraceptive coverage.* Washington, DC: Planned Parenthood.

Goyal, M., et al. (2009). Exploring emergency contraception knowledge, prescription practices and barriers to prescription for adolescents in the emergency department. *Pediatrics, 123*(3), 765–770.

Gray, S., & Holden, A. (2014). Fifteenth annual gender and sexuality law: Annual review article: Abortion. *Georgetown Journal of Gender and the Law, 15*, 3–36.

Greene, M. F. (2007). The intimidation of American physicians: Banning partial-birth abortion. *New England Journal of Medicine, 356*(21), 2128–2129.

Gregory, E. C. W., et al. (2014). *NCHS data brief: Trends in infant mortality in the United States, 2006–2012.* Hyattsville, MD: Centers for Disease Control and Prevention, National Center for Health Statistics (NCHS).

Guttmacher Institute. (2014). *Fact sheet: Unintended pregnancy in the United States.* New York, NY: Guttmacher Institute.

Hammell, H. (2011). Broadening the lens for reproductive and sexual rights: Is the right to health a necessary precondition for gender equality? *New York University Review of Law and Social Change, 35*, 131–193.

Helling, E., & Nam, J. (2010). Eleventh annual review of gender and sexuality law: Health care law chapter: Abortion. *Georgetown Journal of Gender and the Law, 11*, 341–369.

Hill, B. J. (2012). What is the meaning of health? Constitutional implications of defining "medical necessity" and "essential health benefits" under the Affordable Care Act. *American Journal of Law and Medicine, 38*, 445–470.

Howell, Jr., T. H. (2015). Obama admin's attempt to follow Supreme Court birth-control ruling pleases few. *Washington Times.*

Hrobak, R. M., & Wilson, R. F. (2014). Emergency contraceptives or "abortion-inducing" drugs? Empowering women to make informed decisions. *Washington & Lee Law Review, 71*, 1385–1428.

Huberfeld, N. (2013). With liberty and access for some: The ACA's disconnect for women's health. *Fordham Urban Law Journal, 40*, 1357–1393.

Huntington, C. (2011). Red families v. blue families: Legal polarization and the creation of culture. *Michigan Law Review, 109*, 903–921.

IOM (Institute of Medicine). (2011). Clinical preventive services for women: Closing the gaps. Washington, DC: National Academies of Science.

Jayadevan, V. R. (2015). Dying in original sin vis-à-vis living in disgrace—In defense of the right to socioeugenic abortion as personal liberty. *Hamline Law Review, 38*, 85–125.

Johnsen, D. (2015). State court protection of reproductive rights: The past, the perils, and the promise. *Columbia Journal of Gender and Law, 29*, 41–84.

Jonsen, A. R. (2010). *Clinical ethics: A practical approach to ethical decisions in clinical medicine.* New York, NY: McGraw-Hill.

Kaiser Family Foundation. (2014). *Emergency contraception.* Menlo Park, CA: Kaiser.

____. (2014a). *Employer health benefits: Annual survey.*

____. (2014b). *How does where you work affect your contraceptive coverage?*

____. (2014c). *Sexual health of adolescents and young adults in the United States.*

Kanwit, S. (2009). Legal solutions in health reform: The purchase of insurance across state lines in the individual market. *The Journal of Law, Medicine and Ethics, 37*, 152–161.

King, J. S. (2012). Not this child: Constitutional questions in regulating noninvasive prenatal genetic diagnosis and selective abortion. *UCLA Law Review, 60*, 2–75.

Koss, K. K. (2014). Constitutional law: Judge Posner got it right: Requiring abortion doctors to have hospital admitting privileges places an undue burden on a woman seeking an abortion. *Seventh Circuit Review, 9*, 263–300.

Lang, D. (2014). Truthful but misleading? The precarious balance of autonomy and state interests in *Casey* and second-generation doctor-patient regulation. *University of Pennsylvania Journal of Constitutional Law, 16*, 1353–1416.

LaSpina, T. M. (2011). Eliminating the need for a "plan b" when trying to obtain Plan B: The need for a federal law requiring pharmacists to dispense emergency contraception. *Georgetown Journal of Gender and the Law, 12*, 213–262.

LaSpina, T. M., et al. (2010). Eleventh annual review of gender and sexuality law: Health care law chapter: Access to contraception. *Georgetown Journal of Gender and the Law, 11*, 371–410.

Laufer-Ukeles, P. (2011). Reproductive choices and informed consent: Fetal interests, women's identity, and relational autonomy. *American Journal of Law and Medicine, 37*, 567–623.

Law, S. A. (2008). Childbirth: An opportunity for choice that should be supported. *New York University Review of Law and Social Change, 32*, 345–380.

Lee, J. (2011). A quick fix solution for the morning after: An alternative approach to mandatory contraceptive coverage. *Georgetown Journal of Law and Public Policy, 9*, 189–216.

Madeira, J. L. (2014). Aborted emotions: Regret, relationality, and regulation. *Michigan Journal of Gender and Law, 21*, 1–66.

Malinowski, M. J. (2012). Doctors, patients, and pills—a system popping under too much physician discretion? A law-policy prescription to make drug approval more meaningful in the delivery of health care. *Cardozo Law Review, 33*, 1085–1130.

Manian, M. (2012). Functional parenting and dysfunctional abortion policy: Reforming parental involvement legislation. *Family Court Review, 50*, 241–251.

Mathews, A. W. (2011, January 11). Abortion rate rises after a long decline. *Wall Street Journal*, p. A7.

Mau, J. R. (2009). *Stormans* and the pharmacists: Where have all the conscientious Rx gone? *Penn State Law Review, 114*, 293–320.

Meigs, G. L. (1917). *Infant welfare work in war time.* Chicago, IL: American Medical Association.

Melling, L. (2014). Lift the scarlet letter from abortion. *Cardozo Law Review, 35*, 1715–1727.

Melone, M. A. (2015). Corporations and religious freedom: Hobby Lobby Stores—A missed opportunity to reconcile a flawed law with a flawed health care system. *Indiana Law Review, 48*, 461–508.

Miller, J. (2006). The unconscionability of conscience clauses: Pharmacists' consciences and women's access to contraception. *Health Matrix: The Journal of Law-Medicine, 16*, 237–277.

Motro, S. (2010). The price of pleasure. *Northwestern University Law Review, 104*, 917–977.

NCHS (National Center for Health Statistics). (2015). *National vital statistics report: Deaths: Final data for 2013.* Hyattsville, MD: Centers for Disease Control and Prevention, NCHS.

NCSL (National Conference of State Legislatures). (2012). *Fifty state summary of contraceptive laws.* Washington, DC: NCSL.

Noah, L. (2007). Too high a price for some drugs? The FDA burdens reproductive choice. *San Diego Law Review, 44,* 231–258.

NWLC (National Women's Law Center). (2015). *State of women's coverage: Health plan violations of the Affordable Care Act.* Washington, DC: NWLC.

___. (2011). *Pharmacy access to emergency contraception.*

___. (2011a). *Press release: Contraceptive coverage should be available to all women, says NWLC.*

___. (2011b). *Pharmacy refusals 101.*

___. (2009). *Fact sheet: Ensuring that the government helps women meet their reproductive health needs.*

Olson, J. R. (2013). Defining fetal life: An Establishment Clause analysis of religiously motivated informed consent provisions. *Indiana Law Journal, 88,* 1113–1145.

Pedagno, A. T. (2011). Who are the parents? In loco parentis, parens patriae, and abortion decision-making for pregnant girls in foster care. *Ave Maria Law Review, 10,* 171–202.

Pergament, D. (2013). What does choice really mean? Prenatal testing, disability, and special education without illusions. *Health Matrix: The Journal of Law-Medicine, 23,* 55–117.

Phillis, N. (2011). When sixteen ain't so sweet: Rethinking the regulation of adolescent sexuality. *Michigan Journal of Gender and Law, 17,* 271–312.

Pillard, C. T. L. (2007). Our other reproductive choices: Equality in sex education, contraceptive access, and work-family policy. *Emory Law Journal, 56,* 941–991.

Prior, K. A. (2014). The ultra sound-off: The ultrasound mandate debate and a litigator's guide to overcoming obstacles to a woman's right to abortion. *Suffolk Journal of Trial and Appellate Advocacy, 19,* 155–175.

Pruitt, L. R., & Vanegas, M. R. (2015). Urbanormativity, spatial privilege, and judicial blind spots in abortion law. *Berkeley Journal of Gender, Law and Justice, 30,* 76–153.

Radnofsky, L. (2015). Health insurers seek big increases. *Wall Street Journal,* p. A1.

Rebouche, R., & Rothenberg, K. (2012). Mixed messages: The intersection of prenatal genetic testing and abortion. *Howard Law Journal, 55,* 983–1023.

Rudary, D. J. (2013). Drafting a "sensible" conscience clause: A proposal for meaningful conscience protections for religious employers objecting to the mandated coverage of prescription contraceptives. *Health Matrix: The Journal of Law-Medicine, 23,* 353–394.

Rutledge, T. E. (2014). A corporation has no soul—the business entity law response to challenges to the PPACA contraceptive mandate. *William and Mary Business Law Review, 5,* 1–53.

Samuels, L. J. (2014). Mifepristone protocol legislation—the anti-choice movement's disingenuous method of attack on the reproductive rights of women and how courts should respond. *Columbia Journal of Gender and Law, 26,* 316–342.

Sanger, C. (2009). New scholarship on reproductive rights: Decisional dignity: Teenage abortion, bypass hearings, and the misuse of law. *Columbia Journal of Gender and Law, 18,* 409–499.

Savitsky, A. (2010). Inertia and change: Findings of the Shriver report and next steps. *Berkeley Journal of Gender, Law and Justice, 25,* 172–198.

Sax, J. K. (2010). Access to prescription drugs: A normative economic approach to pharmacist conscience clause legislation. *Maine Law Review, 62,* 89–129.

Scaldo, S. A. (2013). Deadly dicta: *Roe's* "unwanted motherhood," *Carhart II's* "women's regret," and the shifting narrative of abortion jurisprudence. *Drexel Law Review, 6,* 87–131.

Schlueter, L. L. (2013). 40th anniversary of *Roe v. Wade*: Reflections past, present and future. *Ohio Northern University Law Review, 40,* 105–249.

Schwarz, A. (2007). Comprehensive sex education: Why America's youth deserve the truth about sex. *Hamline Journal of Public Law and Policy, 29,* 115–160.

Sepper, E. (2014). Gendering corporate conscience. *Harvard Journal of Law and Gender, 38,* 193–239.

___. (2014a, December 9). Associate Professor, Washington University School of Law, Remarks at the Harvard Law School Symposium on Religious Accommodation in the Age of Civil Rights: Gendering Corporate Conscience, Cambridge, MA.

Shainwald, S. (2013). Reproductive justice: Reproductive injustice in the new millennium. *William and Mary Journal of Women and the Law, 20,* 123–171.

Shriver, M., et al. (2009). *The Shriver report: A woman's nation changes everything.* H. Boushey & A. O'Leary (Eds.). Washington, DC: Center for American Progress.

Siegel, N. S., & Siegel, R. B. (2013). Equality arguments for abortion rights. *UCLA Law Review Discourse, 60,* 160–170.

Siegel, R. B. (2013). Equality and choice: Sex equality perspectives on reproductive rights in the work of Ruth Bader Ginsburg. *Columbia Journal of Gender and Law, 25,* 63–80.

Slaughter, L. M. (2007). Introduction of the Prevention-First Act to the 110th Congress. *Congressional Record, 110*, 259–260.

Spindelman, M. (2012). On the constitutionality of Ohio's proposed "heartbeat bill." *Ohio State Law Journal, 74*, 149–188.

Stahle, H. (2007). Fetal pain legislation: Protection against pain is an undue burden. *Quinnipiac Health Law Journal, 10*, 251–278.

Stam, P. (2012). Woman's right to know act: A legislative history. *Issues in Law and Medicine, 28*, 3–67.

Strout, J. (2014). Dads and dicta: The values of acknowledging fathers' interests. *Cardozo Journal of Law and Gender, 21*, 135–167.

Suter, S. M. (2013). The politics of information: Informed consent in abortion and end-of-life decision making. *American Journal of Law and Medicine, 39*, 7–61.

Termini, R. B., & Lee, M. (2011). Sex, politics, and lessons learned from Plan B: A review of the FDA's actions and future direction. *Oklahoma City University Law Review, 36*, 351–373.

Toscano, V., & Reiter, E. (2014). Upholding a 40-year-old promise: Why the Texas sonogram act is unlawful according to *Planned Parenthood v. Casey*. *Pace Law Review, 34*, 128–184.

Vandewalker, I. (2012). Abortion and informed consent: How biased counseling laws mandate violations of medical ethics. *Michigan Journal of Gender and Law, 19*, 1–70.

Vargo, M. P. (2012). The right to informed choice: A defense of the Texas sonogram law. *Journal of Medicine and Law, 16*, 457–501.

Ventura, S. J., et al. (2011, January 14). Adolescent pregnancy and childbirth. *Morbidity and Mortality Weekly Report (MMWR), 60*(1), 105–108. Hyattsville, MD: National Center for Health Statistics.

Wardle, L. D. (2013). Instilling pro-life moral principles in difficult times: The experience of one faith community. *Ave Maria Law Review, 11*, 299–363.

Weisberg, E., & Frazer, I. (2009). Rights to emergency contraception. *International Journal of Gynecology and Obstetrics, 106*(2), 160–163.

Wiley, L. F. (2014). Health law as social justice. *Cornell Journal of Law and Public Policy, 24*, 47–105.

Will, J. F. (2013). Beyond abortion: Why the personhood movement implicates reproductive choice. *American Journal of Law and Medicine*, 573–616.

Young, L. (2014). Falling into the TRAP: The ineffectiveness of "undue burden" analysis in protecting women's right to choose. *Pace Law Review, 34*, 947–981.

Ziegler, M. (2011). *Edelin*: The remaking of the headline abortion trial. *Saint Louis University Law Journal, 55*, 1379–1403.

Courtesy of Thomas McGarity

CHAPTER 14

Nutrition and Food Safety

"The free market economy is predicated on the informed consumer. It is the fundamental assumption about how markets work."

— **Thomas O. McGarity**, Professor, University of Texas at Austin School of Law

LEARNING OBJECTIVES

After completing this chapter, the reader should be able to:

1. Evaluate the ethical positions in the debate between the food industry and public health advocates over production of high fructose, corn syrup-based, high-Calorie, high-fat, low-nutrient foods, advertising of non-nutritious foods, and problems with food safety.
2. Assess how government subsidies of commodities like corn and sugar are affecting the nation's food supply.
3. Understand the ethical principles underlying the Food Safety Modernization Act of 2011, the nation's most comprehensive food legislation in almost a century.
4. Explain the food safety controversy of deciding whether genetically modified foods (such as alfalfa, canola, corn, soybean, and sugar beets) should be subjected to a mandatory approval process that would ensure such food is safe, as opposed to assuming that such food is safe unless a hazard is proven to exist.

KEY TERMS

Asymmetric information
Behavioral addiction
Bioequivalent
Consumer
  autonomy
Diet- and weight-related
  diseases
Dietary supplement
Disinformation
Epigenetic risks
Food addiction
Food additives

Food Safety Modernization
  Act of 2011
Food-borne illnesses
Generally recognized as
  safe (GRAS)
Genetically
  modified (GM) foods
Grocery gap
Health foods
High-fructose corn syrup
  (HFCS)
Hydrogenation

Nutrition
Obesity epidemic
Personal responsibility
  legislation
Principle of
  proportionality
Processed
  foods
Safe tolerance
Subsidies
Trans-fat-free
Trans-fats

ETHICAL OR UNETHICAL DECISION

Consumers' Right to Nutritional Information

Ethics Issue: *Should restaurants be required to disclose accurate nutritional information on their menus?*

In Brief: Seeking to combat rising rates of obesity, and with it diabetes, the New York City Board of Health proposed the nation's first menu labeling law mandating that certain restaurants provide nutritional information to their customers. The mandate carried fines ranging from $200 to $2,000 for non compliance. In doing so, the city sought a new regulatory approach that aimed to curb obesity and diabetes by helping consumers make better-informed decisions at the point of purchase. However, the city's efforts were met with strong resistance from the restaurant industry and this litigation from the food retail sector followed.

The New York State Restaurant Association, a trade group of over 7,000 restaurants, challenged the constitutionality of the labeling law, which required about 10 percent of the restaurants in the city, including chains such as McDonald's, Burger King, and Kentucky Fried Chicken, to post Calorie content information on their menus and menu boards. The Association claimed that the posting requirement compelled them to engage in commercial speech in violation of their First Amendment rights.

— *New York State Restaurant Association v. New York City Board of Health, et al.,* 556 F.3d 114 (U.S. Court of Appeals for the 2nd Circuit 2009). (*See Ethical or Unethical Decision* at the end of the chapter for discussion of this ethics issue.)

Introduction

The risks of obesity, and subsequent diabetes, have emerged as critical health care issues (Trexler, 2011). At the same time, over consumption of **food additives** (such as dyes and chemical preservatives), food with **high-fructose corn syrup** (HFCS), sugar, and **trans-fats** is costing the nation billions of dollars in preventable health care costs (Strauss, 2011). For instance, HFCS is an inexpensive, corn-based starch thickener and sweetener added to most U.S. foods to add volume, enhance flavor, soften texture, and maintain freshness. Trans-fats or unsaturated fats are inexpensively created by the processed food industry as a side effect of partially hydrogenating unsaturated plant fats (generally vegetable oils) to increase shelf life and decrease refrigeration requirements (FDA, 2015a). While some people take **epigenetic risks** that manifest in disease causation seriously and would like to impose preventive regulations on the food industry, others resist such measures (Khan, 2010). By definition, epigenetic risks are harms caused to the human body that are not of genetic origin, such as ingesting high-fat foods with little nutritional value. The difficulty is that the health risks from HFCS-based, high-Calorie, high-fat, low-nutrient foods and beverages, as illustrated in **FEATURE BOX 14-1**, are fervently disputed (Barnes, 2011; Foster, 2011).

This chapter considers the ethical principles underlying recent developments in the debate over the nutritional value of food and beverages advertised by the food industry, the production and marketing of non-nutritious foods, and problems with food safety. Faced with public sentiment that the current food safety system is a hazard to public health,

---

FEATURE BOX 14-1

HFCS-Based, High-Calorie, High-Fat, Low-Nutrient Food and Beverages

- **HFCS-based food (high-fructose corn syrup)** = almost all U.S. prepackaged and prepared meals, processed meats, baked goods, breads, breakfast bars, candies, cereals, condiments, fruit drinks, soft drinks, soups, and yogurts
- **High-Calorie food** = animal fats (lards), breads and refined grains, cakes and pies, cheese, chocolate, condiments (especially butter and mayonnaise), corn syrup-based products (which includes almost all prepackaged and prepared meals and processed meats), crackers, dates, nuts and seeds, ice cream and milk shakes, peanut butter, raisins, some salad dressings, sugar-based products, sugar-sweetened beverages (including soda, fruit juices, and sports drinks), trail mix, pasta, potatoes, rice, many canned soups, vegetable oils, and most fast foods
- **High-fat food** = biscuits, muffins, scones, rolls, cakes and pies, chips and crackers, many prepackaged and prepared meals and processed meats, vegetable shortenings and stick margarines, most desserts, frozen pies, other baked goods, and most fast foods
- **Low-nutrient Food** = almost all of the above and almost all prepackaged prepared meals and processed meats

— Sources: FDA, 2015 and 2015a; HHS, 2010. Note: There are no generally accepted definitions for descriptive terms like *high-fat*, *high-Calorie*, or *low-nutrient* (Lytton, 2010).

---

as well as the possibility of consumer litigation and regulatory actions, members of the food industry are seeking to demonstrate that they are concerned about consumer health (Zhang, 2009).

Both the food industry and public health advocates agree that the problem of nutrition and food safety is critical (Wharton, 2005). Consumer health is an issue that has long occupied the brightest minds in the food industry. Every company involved in food production and marketing is looking at its complete product portfolio to develop lower-Calorie, lower-fat, and more natural products. By using healthier ingredients and careful marketing, the food industry is trying to avoid consumer litigation and questions about the industry's ethics.

Setting the Stage: Ethical Issues Shaping the Food Industry

The food industry promotes the principle of **consumer autonomy**, the idea that consumers should have the capacity to make independent selections of their foods and beverages. Consumers are responsible for purchasing healthy, as well as unhealthy, food and beverages for their personal consumption based upon the knowledge available to them; the food industry simply provides the products consumers demand. Public health advocates, in

ETHICAL DILEMMAS 14-1

1. Are the traditional American beliefs in free markets and respect for personal autonomy contributing to diet-related public health crises such as obesity, heart disease, and diabetes?
2. Is obesity, and with it diabetes, an individual and family responsibility, or do governments and public health agencies have a role in preventing diet- and weight-related diseases?

contrast, highlight the presumption that the food industry has the better means of knowledge of the nutritional content of the food and beverages which are offered for sale (Spahn, 2011). With 1 in 5 deaths directly attributable to obesity-related health concerns from high blood pressure, heart disease, and cancers (excluding deaths caused by diabetes) (Masters, et al., 2013), the ethics of the food industry come into question. Perhaps the line needs to be drawn between free choice and consumer protection (Liu, 2012).

Contributing Element of America's Obesity Epidemic

The **obesity epidemic** is connected to the food industry, an industry that controls almost everything the average American eats (Cardello & Garr, 2010). While the quantifying threshold for an epidemic is 1 percent of the general population, more than one-third of American adults are obese (Fryar, et al., 2014; HHS, 2010). How to strike the proper balance between health concerns, costs, and privacy interests is a real ethical problem when addressing the nation's obesity and diabetes rates. Public health officials warn of the health crises from obesity and diabetes in a health care system overburdened by patients with **diet- and weight-related diseases** directly attributable to being overweight or obese (Banker, 2010). If the food industry has an ethical obligation to do no harm to the consumers who eat their food and drink their beverage products, then food producers and retailers should manufacture and retail high-quality products that are safe and healthy (Ahmed, 2009). At the same time, Americans should arguably take more responsibility for their own health.

The United States has the highest rate of obesity in the world (OECD, 2014), with 1 in 3 children overweight or obese (HHS, 2010). America's increase in diet- and weight-related diseases cannot be attributed to genetics alone, as illustrated in **FEATURE BOX 14-2**. Rather, what has changed over the past decades is that Americans are now eating more than half their Calories outside the home (Guthrie, et al., 2013; Wharton, 2005). Moreover, with frozen prepackaged and prepared meals being the fastest growing categories of food in American supermarkets over the past decade (OECD, 2014), it is not surprising that today only about 5 percent of the meals eaten inside the home consist of fresh food (HHS, 2010). Americans' diet quality is declining, as more than half of their daily intake is from highly processed, prepackaged, and prepared food high in carbohydrates and sodium (FDA, 2015). This raises the question of whether consumers have suddenly become less responsible about their health over the past decade, or if the food that is available and affordable for consumers, which is often high in fat and contains little nutritional value, is a contributing factor to obesity, and with it diabetes. Today, fast-food and chain restaurants serving HFCS-based, high-Calorie, high-fat, and low-nutrient food, account for three-fourths of the total restaurant visits (HHS, 2010).

FEATURE BOX 14-2

Who is Responsible for Obesity?

- Parents, who relinquish their responsibilities to their children to provide healthy, nutritional meals and promote exercise?
- Schools that fail to offer healthy eating alternatives in cafeterias and vending machines?
- The fast-food sector, with its high-Calorie, low-nutrient offerings and advertising that seems to be everywhere at once?
- Powerful lobbies that have kept the federal corn and sugar subsidy programs in place since the Great Depression in the 1920s?
- Overweight and obese individuals who feed themselves unhealthy foods in large portions?
- Food manufacturers that add (sometimes hidden) sugar to their products?
- All of the above?

— Sources: Andreyeva, et al., 2011; Hodge, 2012.

Consumer Behavior Shapes Fast-Food and Restaurant Choices

In some ways, the food industry is faced with a choice between two adverse and contrary alternatives toward **nutrition**, the science that deals with food and its effects on human health. Consumers say they want healthier foods, but if one looks at consumer behavior, many consumers choose non-nutritious foods over healthy ones. Indeed, fast-food and restaurant chains that have tried to reduce the size of their meal portions and corresponding prices have been criticized and often reinstate their original serving sizes and return to their original pricing in response to consumer demand (Wharton, 2005). When restaurants try to reduce the size of their portions, consumers soundly criticize the moves (Wharton, 2007). At the same time, consumers say they want healthy options that are just as fast and cheap as the non-nutritious ones. The food industry in general wants to offer healthier alternatives, in part because of all the dire warnings about the relationship between food safety and health. It claims, however, that it simply does not have many other choices. But does it?

ETHICAL DILEMMAS 14-2

3. Does the food industry have an ethical obligation to respect consumers' autonomy and offer the unhealthy food people desire, or should the food industry protect its consumers by eliminating or restricting the types and amounts of unhealthy food available?
4. How should the food industry navigate its way through the nutritional maze of consumers saying that they want healthy foods while instead choosing unhealthy foods?

The Grocery Gap

For decades, communities with high concentrations of poor and financially distressed consumers have had poor availability of healthy foods, fewer supermarkets, and a higher density of unhealthy food outlets (Kotwani & Danis, 2009). Unfortunately, as illustrated in **FEATURE BOX 14-3**, the consequences of what has been termed the **grocery gap** are clear. Decreased access to healthy food means that people in underserved communities suffer more from obesity and diabetes than people residing in communities with easy access to healthy food, particularly fresh fruits and vegetables (Treuhaft & Karpyn, 2010). On one side of the debate, advice about food safety and protection from unhealthy foods by the food industry should give way to individual choice and personal responsibility for food choices (Glover, 2008). Alternatively, health care advocates pose the question of whether personal responsibility is used as a scapegoat to cover up the nation's grocery gap and lack of affordable healthy food in underprivileged communities (Kotwani & Danis, 2009).

U.S. Regulatory System: Does It Protect the Food Industry?

Nutrition and food safety regulation in the United States is fragmented; some health care advocates even characterize the fragmented regulatory system as broken by complexity and conflicting regulations. More than a dozen expert panels inside and outside the government have called for the consolidation of the federal agencies that exercise and share food safety responsibility over an industry whose revenue exceeds $800 billion annually (Pasquinelli, 2010). Apart from the U.S. Food and Drug Administration (FDA) and the U.S. Department of Agriculture (USDA), about 14 more federal agencies have elements of food safety

---

FEATURE BOX 14-3

America's Grocery Gap

Communities with full-service supermarkets and farmers' markets that sell fresh fruits, vegetables, and other healthy food high in nutrients

Versus

Underserved communities with fast-food restaurants and corner convenience stores that sell high-fat, high-sugar, highly-processed foodstuffs and other unhealthy foods low in nutrients

- 24 million Americans lack access to a supermarket within a mile of their home.
- 8 in 10 people living in communities with high concentrations of consumers at the bottom of the socioeconomic pyramid cannot find low-fat milk or whole wheat bread in their neighborhoods.
- Communities with the highest obesity rates have few transportation options to reach supermarkets selling affordable high-quality food.
- Over 70 percent of the nation's food stamp-eligible households travel more than 30 miles to reach a supermarket.
- Residents living in underserved communities have significantly higher rates of premature deaths from diabetes and other diet- and weight-related illnesses.

— Sources: Leib, 2013; Owley & Lewis, 2014; Treuhaft & Karpyn, 2010.

responsibility under 35 assorted federal laws (Fortin, 2015). This federal oversight is in addition to the 50 separate state agricultural agencies and 50 intersecting state environmental protection agencies, with all their overlapping state laws and related agencies (GAO, 2005a). Some agencies and laws have similar regulations, others are contradictory, but all have responsibility for food safety.

Yet the food industry supports this fragmented regulatory system and opposes the creation of a single, unified food safety agency at the federal level (Hoffmann & Harder, 2010). When food safety is regulated by multiple government agencies, all are tempted to ignore any problems in the food industry and free-ride on the anticipated action of others. The results are regulatory gaps and inaction, evidenced by few regulatory mandates or enforcement actions (Liu, 2011).

The Ethics of Subsidizing Unhealthy Foods

For decades, the federal government has been providing multibillion-dollar **subsidies**, or government contributions, to agribusinesses that produce corn and sugar (Peck, 2010). Subsidized commodity crops, such as corn syrup and sugar, translate into low-cost **processed foods** for consumers (Kwan, 2009), with little nutrient value compared to fresh fare. The corn and sugar sectors have long been the most protected sectors in industrial agriculture (Coplan, 2009). Ethically speaking, if public health is a fundamental part of a government's duty of care to its citizens, does the government have the duty and ethical obligation to regulate the nutritional value of the food available to most Americans? Similarly, should the food industry be held responsible by consumers and the government for its unhealthy products (Spahn, 2011)?

Regardless of ethical obligation, the government has created unhealthy incentives for the food industry and consumers. For instance, low prices for sugar derived from corn have been created through government subsidies, thus allowing the food industry to receive price incentives to replace cane sugar with subsidized HFCS, making food high in corn-derived sugar less expensive to make and ultimately to purchase (Harris, 2009). Following decades of corn subsidies of over $5.6 billion annually (Seur & Abelkop, 2010), the U.S. food supply is flooded with HFCS-based products (Spahn, 2011). HFCS is virtually unavoidable in food and directly contributes to serious health threats such as obesity and diabetes (Schreiner, 2009). At the same time, domestic producers, processors, and refiners of sugar receive an additional $2.0 billion in government subsidies (Hitt, 2008). Government support to some of the wealthiest Americans includes special loans to producers and a USDA program designed to prop up prices by controlling the amount of corn and sugar put on the market through import limits and production allotments granted to farmers with gross incomes of up to $2.5 million (Wallinga, 2010). Food subsidies do, however, provide U.S. consumers with necessary protection against food scarcity and high food prices (Goodman, 2015).

Ethical Marketing and Advertising

There may be a joint responsibility between the food industry and consumers. If so, this makes it harder to determine what should be done when marketing and advertising food products. The ethical distinction between consumers' and the food industry's responsibilities is quite blurred (Ahmed, 2009).

The food industry is a business. It sells products that consumers are willing to pay for. The industry maintains that it is delivering foods consumers want; it is not making consumers eat less healthy foods frequently or in large quantities (Wharton, 2005). The counterargument is that consumers never know what they want until it has been marketed and advertised toward them. Food products are not about needs, but about consumer desires. Marketing, as the term itself implies, responds to the free market to increase desired responses from its intended audiences. The food nutrition debate centers on whether marketers have an ethical obligation to consumers to help them make healthy responses through their marketing campaigns. One side of the debate contends that the food industry has an ethical obligation to promote healthier products, and reduce or eliminate less healthy foods regardless of consumer demand. The other side contends that consumers must take personal responsibility for their food choices and thereby control their diet, their exercise, their weight, and their health. Both sides must take responsibility: the food industry in offering healthier foods and consumers in choosing healthier foods (Liu, 2012).

Advertising to Children

Whether food advertising targeted to children should be restricted is controversial (FTC, 2012). The food industry maintains that attempts to restrict advertising violate the right to free commercial speech. Others differ and ask that the industry adhere to nutrition-based standards for marketing food products to children.

Critics of non-nutritious foods find as much to criticize in the food industry's advertisements as in the products themselves. The food industry develops multibillion-dollar marketing strategies aimed specifically at children (Foster, 2011; Kaplin, 2011). Food advertising is not only on television but increasingly on the Internet, in video games, and on cell phones. Many nutritionists claim there is ample evidence linking food advertising to childhood obesity and juvenile-onset diabetes (Fehn, 2012; Kaplin, 2011). Others call on the media and entertainment industries to restrict licensing of their characters to healthy foods and sugar-free beverages that are marketed to children, so that cross-promotions with popular children's movies and television characters will favor more nutritious foods and drinks (FTC, 2012). For instance, Burger King has included Scooby-Doo toys in its kids' meals and McDonald's has used the Minions in its advertising.

Members of the fast-food sector claim that healthy options are on their menus and that they provide nutritional information about food items, all in order to inform consumers about what is available. They say they are not in the business of taking away individual choice and point to the fact that fat levels in food have declined since the 1970s. The trouble is that too many advertisements of non-nutritious foods are still targeted at children (Andreyeva, et al., 2011; Kaplin, 2011). In fact, many of the emerging lawsuits against the fast-food sector have been brought by parents because of the health effects of food on their children and the potentially misleading labeling that prevents making educated food decisions. For instance, parents cannot access accurate ingredient labels that clearly establish the presence of HFCS or genetically modified ingredients in food products (Federici, 2010). Nor can parents always find accurate nutritional information in restaurants or on websites. Most restaurants separate nutritional information from their standard menu items (Cusick, 2011). Fast-food restaurants generally give nutritional information to consumers on a wall poster covered in tiny print, while full service restaurants often post their information only on websites, if at all, making it difficult to compare items in price and Calories in the moment (Bernell, 2010).

Misleading Advertising: Are Healthy Options Really Healthy?

As illustrated by the case at the start of this chapter under the *Ethical or Unethical Decision* section, further complicating marketing strategies of the food industry are the ethics of advertising seemingly healthy options that are in reality nutritionally worse or as equally unhealthy for consumers as traditionally less healthy options (Badilas, 2011). Salads can be drowned in dressing with processed carbohydrates and fats; many granola bars are glorified candy bars. This contributes to consumers' confusion and lack of knowledge about what they are eating. They are choosing the salad, but over-looking the dressing added to it; they are choosing the granola bar, but overlooking the layer of chocolate enrobing it. A lot of packaged goods are guilty of this as well by trying to make products seem healthier than they really are (Wharton, 2005). For instance, those packaged fresh salads on grocery store shelves and fast-food counters make claims of freshness as to particular ingredients, as opposed to the salad as a whole. While chicken or grilled fast foods are considered healthier, those terms do not reflect the actual relative nutritional content of the listed products (Banker, 2010). For inst-ance, the McDonald's Grilled Chicken Club Sandwich actually has ten *more* Calories than a traditional red meat-based Big Mac.

While the current trend shows an increase in healthier food alternatives, processed foods that are high in fat, sugar, and sodium still dominate the nation's food supply (Angelo, 2011; Lytton, 2010). What may be advertised as a healthy alternative to traditional fast-food options, like choosing a salad over a hamburger, may in fact be misleading marketing and promotion of nutritionally inferior food choices. At the same time, the quality and nutri-tional value of fresh fruits and vegetables has declined in recent decades as the agricultural industry plants crops designed to yield higher volumes (Davis, 2009). Half the nutrients in a recent study declined by more than a third, with the average fresh food product declining from between 5 and 40 percent in nutrients compared to those harvested just 50 years ago (Ehrenreich & Lyon, 2011).

Marketing Impacts Food Quality and Availability

The dominance of non-nutritious food in the nation's food supply and the discordant rela-tionship between the food industry and consumers' knowledge of nutrition are accelerating the availability of unhealthy food products on the market (Stearns, 2010). This economic phenomenon occurs whenever there is insufficient or **asymmetric information** between sell-ers and buyers, or when producers of a product always know more than the consumers of a product. In this instance, food producers have more information about the nutritional value of food products than the consumers who consume the products (Wharton, 2005). More specifically, informational asymmetries give rise to adverse selection in markets. Due to imperfect knowledge of nutritional information on the part of consumers, sellers of sub-sidized non-nutritious foods crowd out everyone else from the market. *See generally* Vane & Mulhearn, 2010.

Because consumers do not know the ins and outs of higher-quality foods, lower-quality foods with low prices have a marketing advantage. The resulting marketing behavior is that the food industry tries to create demand for its non-nutritious products, at the expense of healthier options (Harris, et al., 2012). Providers of any low-quality products have little in-centive to reveal the quality of their products, and this gives rise to asymmetric information in the market (Stearns, 2010).

The Impact of Food Industry Marketing

There is clearly some inherent tension between the food industry and its critics, as illustrated in **FEATURE BOX 14-4**. While the food industry claims that marketing is intended to simply move customers from one brand to another, this is not always the case (Wharton, 2005). Marketing works. That is why the food industry spends billions of dollars doing it and why health advocates are concerned about it. While no single practice is causing the obesity epidemic, restaurants that serve meals without any readily available nutrition information at the point of sale contribute to weight-related chronic illnesses by not providing the public with full disclosure of their products' nutritional statistics. At the same time, research shows that most consumers do not completely read the available nutrition information (Lukits, 2011).

While consumers themselves and the food industry are both responsible for nutrition, there are instances where the food industry deliberately markets non-nutritious foods to children. For instance, General Mills Reese's Puffs, Kellogg's Froot Loops, and Post's Pebbles brands rank among the lowest for nutrition and the highest for added sugar—and yet all three cereals are aggressively marketed to children every year. If children eat these presweetened cereals before leaving their houses in the morning, they have consumed as much sugar as they should eat in an entire day. At the same time, General Mills Cheerios and Kellogg's Frosted Mini-Wheats, two cereals with the highest nutrition scores from Yale University's Rudd Center for Food Policy and Obesity, are marketed primarily to adults. *See generally* Harris, et al., 2012.

FEATURE BOX 14-4

Self-Regulation of the Food Industry

For decades, the food industry has:

- Created false impressions that their food products were nutritious and part of a healthy lifestyle
- Deceptively sold fatty, addictive foods
- Declined to disclose that the manner of processing food renders it less healthy than represented
- Failed to disclose that consumption of many food products causes obesity and other diet- and weight-related illnesses
- Misrepresented nutritional information
- Not warned consumers of the unhealthy attributes of its food products
- Refused to disclose the use of food additives
- Spent billions of dollars every year marketing and advertising unhealthy food and beverage products to children

— Sources: Cardello & Garr, 2010; Schlosser, 2012; Wharton, 2005.

ETHICAL DILEMMAS 14-3

5. Should the marketing and advertising strategies for food products continue to be self-regulated, or should government place restrictions on food advertising?

Food Industry Marketing Guidelines or Regulation

The Center for Science in the Public Interest developed guidelines for responsible food marketing, calling on the food industry to use its power to create and market healthy foods consumers will ask for and enjoy. Many interested in consumer protection believe industry marketers have the power to influence wants and needs as much as they respond to wants and needs (Wharton, 2005). The assumption is that the food industry's marketing strategies are making consumers unhealthy. If this is so, perhaps it is time to reevaluate whether the food industry should continue to be self-regulated.

For instance, when industry marketers began advertising the link between fiber in cereals and the reduced risk of cancer, there was a consumer shift to high-fiber diets (Jain, 2010). Such changes in food labeling rules could play an important role in consumer education by adding food industry incentives to focus on the nutritional information of their foods (Green, 2010).

Health-Benefit Claims of Dietary Supplements

Dietary supplements provide health benefits, including the prevention and treatment of disease (Badilas, 2011). More than half the American population takes at least one type of dietary supplement, and many take significantly more (Bailey, et al., 2011). Supplements are added to food, such as calcium to chocolate syrup and vitamin C to soda, to make foods more appealing to health-conscious consumers. Makers of children's food are rolling out yogurt and soy milk products enhanced with DHA omega-3 fatty acid, which Beech-Nut and Dannon say can foster brain and vision development, although physicians question their benefits (Muñoz, 2008).

According to the National Nutraceuticals Center, while food supplements are expanding with over $86 billion in annual sales in the United States, there is minimal regulation over which products are allowed to display health claims on their labels (NNC, 2011). This has resulted in a Pandora's Box of false claims, untested products, and unsubstantiated science (Bagchi, 2014). While dietary supplements have varying uses and effectiveness (GAO, 2009), the definition of what constitutes a supplement often depends on the source. Public health advocates want the term to be more clearly established in order to distinguish between the wide varieties of products out there (NNC, 2011).

Packaging of Health Foods

The food industry is refocusing its marketing toward health benefits; healthier foods are now being offered to consumers (Roller & Pippins, 2010). **Health foods**, or foods

ETHICAL DILEMMAS 14-4

6.　Would it be reasonable, or ethical, to require or incentivize the food industry to influence consumer preferences in ways that would favor healthy choices?

that provide health benefits beyond basic nutrition, are increasingly being marketed by the pharmaceutical and food industries (Slive, 2011). The U.S. market for health foods and sugar-free beverages totals more than $30 billion, and economists expect the market to double within several years (Manning, 2010). Yet consumers are presented with and persuaded by insufficiently supported wellness benefits, including claims that foods will boost the immune system, assist with memory and brain function, boost metabolism, protect the heart, or afford other physical or mental health benefits (Roller & Pippins, 2010). While no scientific evidence is required to support such health claims, grocery aisles are stacked with rows of 'whole-grain' breakfast cereals, 'enhanced' salad dressings, and 'fortified' snacks and drinks that promise on their packaging to fight heart disease, osteoporosis, and other ailments. In some cases, health food products are packaged as alternatives to medications. But are the health-benefit claims real? The food industry is permitted to claim a variety of health benefits that science may not be able to support (Hoflander, 2011). For instance, certain health foods with omega-3 fatty acid and probiotic yogurts claim to promote brain function and regulate digestive systems, respectively; however, these claims are not supported by scientific research. Unsubstantiated health claims have the ability to mislead consumers into believing in the existence of health benefits that have not been established, and in fact, may even be harmful (Badilas, 2011). For instance, scientists are now questioning whether following a low-salt diet might be dangerous for some individuals (Winslow, 2014).

Personal versus Social Responsibility: Mutually Exclusive Ethical Principles or Not?

Food itself can hold only part of the blame for the nation's growing rates of obesity and diabetes. Food is an important factor, but not the only factor. The personal responsibility involved in consuming food is equally important.

Congress has debated federal legislation that would protect the food industry from lawsuits, provided the food products are in compliance with existing laws. The proposed 'Hamburger Bill,' or Personal Responsibility in Food Consumption Act, would prohibit consumers from suing the food industry for any weight-related health conditions (Pomeranz, 2013), but it has failed more than once to garner enough support to be passed at the federal level. Similar legislation is being introduced in states as well (Forell, 2011). The aim of **personal responsibility legislation** is to remove social responsibility from food producers and retailers and place it on the consumer alone. As opposed to seeking to encourage responsibility on both sides of the table, this legislation seeks to shift the obesity and diabetes debate to protect the food industry at the expense of consumers (Rothenberg, 2010). Passage of such legislation is an industry priority and proponents are expected to keep pushing for passage (Rothenberg, 2010). Public health advocates disagree and claim that eliminating the threat of consumer litigation against the food industry eliminates one point of pressure that encourages the food industry to take responsibility for its role in combating obesity and diabetes (Manning, 2010; Roller & Pippins, 2010).

ETHICAL DILEMMAS 14-5

7. Should Congress and state legislatures pass personal responsibility legislation regarding food choices?

Déjà Vu: Social Responsibility of the Food Industry

The past of the tobacco industry could well be the future of the food industry (Pennel, 2009). The lawsuits facing the food industry, demanding that they accept responsibility for the health care costs attributed to their products, have already been experienced by the tobacco industry. *Pelman, et al. v. McDonald's Corp., et al.*, the first lawsuit against the fast-food sector, was litigated for over a decade; it is *déjà vu,* the French term for something already seen.

 **ETHICS CASE**
The Obesity Epidemic

Pelman, et al. v. McDonald's Corp., et al.
[Minor Consumers v. Fast-Food Chain]
396 F.3d 508 (U.S. Court of Appeals for the 2nd Circuit 2005)

Facts: Two teenagers tried to hold McDonald's liable for their obesity and diet- and weight-related diseases. McDonald's advertises its food as nutritious and part of a healthy lifestyle, while failing to warn its customers of the health-related risks and adverse health effects associated with consumption of foods high in cholesterol, fat, salt, sugar, and other additives. The teenagers claimed that McDonald's persuades its customers to ingest unhealthy quantities of fattening, highly processed food that is substantially less healthy than represented in advertisements. In addition, the teenagers claimed that McDonald's engages in deceptive marketing that enticed them to eat its food with unhealthy frequency. Therefore, they now face a higher likelihood of developing diabetes and a host of diet- and weight-related diseases as a direct result of eating at McDonald's.

Legal Analysis: The court rejected the argument that McDonald's should have warned consumers about the adverse health effects associated with foods high in fat, salt, and sugar, reasoning that such information is well known to the average consumer. Nothing suggests that McDonald's food is any less nutritious than the average consumer expects it to be. In addition, the court did not find any specific advertisements or public statements to be deceptive. The court also found that McDonald's failure to provide nutritional information could not be considered deceptive because consumers could reasonably obtain such information on their own. Additionally, there was no causal link between McDonald's food and the obesity-related illnesses of its consumers. The court noted that heredity, sedentary lifestyles, and other health-related factors must be eliminated to show that McDonald's food is a substantial factor in consumers' weight gain.

The court did not find that consumers were addicted to McDonald's food, and no causal link was established between the consumption of McDonald's food and obesity. The court conceded that a discrepancy existed between the advertising around McDonald's use of 100-percent vegetable oil and the fact that beef tallow was also used, but dismissed this disparity as irrelevant to obesity-related illnesses. The court found that the plaintiffs did not allege the beef tallow contained cholesterol, and thus there was no evidence to support the claim that McDonald's acted deceptively in stating that its fries were cholesterol-free. The fact that the vegetable oil contained trans-fatty acids responsible for raising detrimental blood cholesterol levels was deemed irrelevant because the contents of food and the effects of food are different. In dismissing the case with prejudice, the court indicated the claims could not be refiled.

Rule of Law: There are substantial obstacles to negligence liability for obesity-related illnesses allegedly brought on by consumption of fast food.

Ethical Issue: If poor diet, high risk for excess weight gain, and diabetes are linked to high consumption of high-Calorie fast foods and soft drinks, should McDonald's and the food industry be responsible for the health care costs attributable to consumers' obesity, and with it, diabetes?

Ethics Analysis: There are two sides to the debate regarding the food industry's social responsibilities. The food industry's ethics are centered on free choice. The argument is that consumers know that eating McDonald's supersized food orders on a regular basis is unhealthy and may result in weight gain. Consumers are responsible for their eating behavior; the food industry bears no ethical obligation to protect people from their own excesses. Moreover, there is no need for McDonald's to warn consumers about the adverse health effects associated with foods high in fat, salt, and sugar, since such information is well known to the average consumer. McDonald's food is no less nutritious than the average consumer expects it to be. Furthermore, how much public health intrusion into personal eating choices are people willing to tolerate? McDonald's french fries may not have much nutritional value, but few people are ready to accept a government ban.

On the other hand, the ethics of public health advocates are centered on consumer protection. Obesity and diabetes are the only major health problems that are getting worse in the United States, and they are getting worse rapidly (CBO, 2011). McDonald's claims that the weight of individual consumers is a result of personal decisions and primarily affects their own lifestyle and has little implication for others. But this claim ignores the annual cost burden of obesity that could be as high as $344 billion per year by 2019 (Browne, 2011). Inevitably, a large proportion of the financial burden of obesity and related health complications falls on society through government health insurance programs (Slive, 2011). Obviously, McDonald's would prefer that this financial responsibility lie with anyone other than itself. For instance, when confronted with part of the blame for childhood obesity, McDonald's claims that parents should bear the responsibility instead. In many instances, however, when consumers believe they are freely exercising informed choice, their decisions are in fact heavily influenced by McDonald's sophisticated marketing and a lack of consumer knowledge, which puts them at risk of overeating (Forell, 2011). Yet marketing shapes consumer desires in order to maximize profits. McDonald's could simply make its food healthier and its contents more transparent.

Court's Holding and Decision: No, if consumers know, or should know, that eating McDonald's supersized food orders regularly is unhealthy and may result in weight gain, it is not the place of the law or McDonald's to protect them from their own excesses.

See, e.g., Faulk & Gray, 2012; Hodge, 2013; Schwartz & Appel, 2014; Wilking & Daynard, 2013 (discussing this court decision).

Ethical Distinction or Similarity between the Food and Tobacco Industries

Obesity and diabetes may be the next tobacco (Diller, 2013a). Public health advocates maintain that this is a realistic possibility, while the food industry claims it is just a quick attempt to address the nation's obesity epidemic (Schwartz & Appel, 2014). Yet the law firms that pursued the successful litigation against the tobacco industry, which led to $10 billion settlements with state attorney generals, are now at the forefront of the consumer litigation against the food industry (Banzhaf, et al., 2010).

TABLE 14-1 Lessons the Food Industry Could Learn from the Tobacco Industry

Food Industry	Tobacco Industry
1990 – Autonomy: Food manufacturers were required to label nearly all packaged food with Caloric, fat, and carbohydrate content.	**1960 to 1986 – Nonmaleficence:** A ban on television and radio advertising of tobacco, restriction of other forms of advertisement, and taxation of cigarettes reduced smoking prevalence by more than a third.
2002 to Present – Assumption of Risk: Lawsuits are increasingly being filed against food manufacturers blaming food and advertising for causing obesity. While food manufacturers have not yet been held responsible for damages caused by their advertising in court, many other cases are settled as opposed to litigated.	**1964 – Transparency:** The U.S. Surgeon General's report showed tobacco smoke to be a significant cause of several pulmonary and non-pulmonary diseases.
2005 – Transparency: The Institute of Medicine report showed that high-Calorie, low-nutrient food is one explanation for the United States maintaining the highest obesity prevalence in the world.	**1966 – Autonomy:** Tobacco manufacturers were required to label cigarette packages with health warnings to inform consumers of the health consequences of smoking.
2006 to Present – Nonmaleficence: Faced with stricter television, radio, and print regulation, many food manufacturers have started using Internet advertising. There is a citizen's movement to ban food advertising to children and tax high-Calorie, low-nutrient food.	**1994 to 2009 – Assumption of Risk:** Despite full risk warning and consumer freedom to smoke, numerous lawsuits were successfully filed against tobacco manufacturers based on the theories of strict product liability and comparative fault. Tobacco manufacturers were held partially responsible for the damages their products caused, irrespective of consumer knowledge or fault, in part because of their deceptive marketing tactics.
Future Actions: To be determined by the food industry. In contrast to the tobacco industry's decrease in smoking, there are no signs that obesity rates are decreasing.	**1998 to 2009 – Result of Unethical Actions:** Major tobacco manufacturers and the Attorneys General of 46 states entered into a Master Settlement Agreement which attributed accountability to the tobacco industry and obligated the industry to pay approximately $10 billion/year to remediate health damages caused by their products.

— Sources: Ahmed, 2009; HHS, 2014; IOM, 2013; NAAG, 2009.

The link between the food industry and the nation's obesity epidemic, as illustrated in **TABLE 14-1**, raises the issue of whether fat, sugar, and cholesterol have addictive qualities similar to the drug nicotine (Hoffman, et al., 2014). Still, one difference between tobacco and food is in the products themselves (Freeman, 2007). Cigarettes are extremely hazardous to health; the only way to completely eliminate the hazard is to eliminate the commodity. With food, the obesity- and diabetes-promoting characteristics involve not just product content but marketing, packaging, labeling, consumers' lifestyles, and genetics (Min, 2013). Foods are not harmful when used in moderation, whereas cigarettes are; food, of course, cannot be completely removed from any consumer's lifestyle the way cigarettes can. Moreover, while it may be possible to prove that smoking caused a particular lung cancer, and even to identify the company that sold the tobacco products, it may be difficult to determine how much of a role a particular food or fast-food company played in a particular individual's obesity or diabetes. It may be nearly impossible (which is not the same as not possible) to assign responsibility to the sources of HFCS-based, high-Calorie, high-fat, low-nutrient food (Pennel, 2009). In order to be held responsible under the law, the connection between the claimed source of the harm and the harm itself must, at a minimum, be more likely to exist than not.

Most importantly, while food advertising usually does not stress the dangers of overeating, tobacco companies went far beyond a mere failure to disclose by deliberately lying and actively concealing evidence of the harmful effects of the use of tobacco (Forell, 2011; Min, 2013). Similar evidence is emerging of the food industry preventing facts about its products from being known. For instance, the restaurant chain Applebee's misrepresented the information on its menus when it teamed up with Weight Watchers to provide nutritional information including fat, Calories, and Weight Watchers Points values; Applebee's food contained a higher Calorie count and up to three times the amount of fat advertised (Cusick, 2011; Slive, 2011). Another form of deception is putting more than one serving inside what looks like a single-serving-size package.

Responsible Use of Genetically Modified Foods

U.S. consumers have spent almost two decades consuming **genetically modified (GM) foods**, defined as plant products derived from organisms that have had specific changes introduced into their DNA by genetic engineering techniques, without any known, proven adverse effects (Wharton-Universia, 2004). Agricultural biotechnology has received both unproven praise and unproven attacks. While supporters admire the enhanced quality and taste, increased yield, lower production costs, heightened pest and drought resistance, and shorter production times of GM foods, opponents fear the yet unknown environmental, social, and health risks that these foods may bring with them (Wilinska, 2012).

Myths on both sides must be debunked before the ethics of responsible use and regulation of GM foods can be debated. Even the definition of GM foods is often misunderstood. For instance, while most people think of GM pork when the topic of GM food is discussed, no GM animal food products are currently on the market (Tai, 2010). Despite the many benefits attributed to genetic engineering of crops, there are deep divisions as to the inherent health risks posed by GM foods. Most consumers are unaware of their high daily and long-term exposure levels to untested GM substances (Van Tassel, 2009). For instance, while consumers who wish to avoid GM foods may limit their purchases to foods bearing the "USDA-Organic" label, consumers cannot assume that foods bearing such labels do not contain GM ingredients (such as HFCS from GM corn) (Federici, 2010; Liu, 2011a).

GM plant seeds isolate genes from organisms and insert them into the genetic material of crops. Examples of such common GM foods are canola, corn, soybean, and sugar beets. The first GM food, a genetically engineered tomato, was sold in the U.S. market in 1995

(Nunziato, 2014). Yet there is political pressure, such as industry lobbying and regulatory capture (Williamson, 2008), not to take a closer look at GM foods (Peck, 2010). GM food and the use of milk and meat from cloned animals and their progeny are allowed under current U.S. law with no labeling, preapprovals, or post market monitoring (Strauss, 2011).

ETHICS CASE
Genetically Modified Plant Seeds

Monsanto Co., et al. v. Geertson Seed Farms, et al.
[Chemical manufacturer of a genetically modified alfalfa seed v. Conventional alfalfa seed farms]
561 U.S. 139 (U.S. Supreme Court 2010)

Facts: In the midst of a deregulation trend in the agricultural sector, Monsanto asked the USDA to deregulate an alfalfa seed that had been genetically modified so it could be sold and planted nationwide. Rather than conducting a detailed analysis and preparing an environmental impact statement as required for every major federal action significantly affecting the quality of the human environment, the USDA conducted an abbreviated assessment. Conventional farmers and scientists feared that the GM seed could contaminate alfalfa that had not been genetically modified, destroying the American export market for conventional alfalfa and potentially contaminating other plants and breeding a new type of pesticide-resistant weed.

Alfalfa, one of the nation's largest cash crops, is grown on approximately 20 million acres of U.S. land for two primary purposes: hay for livestock consumption and seed for future stock. Many farmers who grow organic and commercial alfalfa were concerned about the potential of cross-pollination occurring between the GM alfalfa, designed to withstand a Monsanto herbicide, and non-GM alfalfa.

While the USDA regulates any organism or product altered or created by genetic engineering, Monsanto, the owner and licensee of the GM alfalfa seed, sought to have the seed deregulated so it could be planted without geographical restrictions. Competing seed companies were worried that wide-scale use of Monsanto's alfalfa-resistant herbicide would cause cross-pollination with their conventional alfalfa, which could be problematic because several major importers of U.S. alfalfa will not accept GM alfalfa.

Legal Analysis: The USDA admitted that the GM alfalfa seed was deregulated without a complete environmental impact assessment, but contended that a partial deregulation to allow use of the GM seed in limited circumstances was the proper remedy pending preparation of a complete assessment. The U.S. Supreme Court held that a partial deregulation of the GM seed with sufficient restrictions could have virtually eliminated the harm of gene flow between altered and conventional alfalfa seeds. Preventing a partial deregulation preempted the USDA's lawful process for determining the scope of regulation of the GM alfalfa seed. Further, since it was improper for the trial court to stop partial deregulation, it was equally inappropriate to completely prohibit planting.

Rule of Law: Deregulation and planting of GM seeds cannot occur without a complete environmental assessment, including consideration of biodiversity impacts, even though the USDA determined GM alfalfa was not toxic to humans or livestock.

Ethics Issue: Should GM seeds be introduced into farm plantings without first fully understanding their impact on the environment?

Ethics Analysis: The ethical issues of this case have the courts seeking to balance economic and social interests. On one hand, GM seeds offer tremendous economic benefits, with increased crop yields and reduction in the use of dangerous pesticides. On the other hand, the engineering process must be monitored because the process has the potential to create foods containing new toxins and previously unknown allergens. Two human health risks associated with GM foods are potential allergies to new proteins that appear in GM foods and the risk that resistance to antibiotics could be spread to humans through genetically engineered organisms. In addition, genetically engineered crops protected from insects and herbicides may have unforeseen adverse impacts on wildlife and plants.

Since advocates for greater regulation of GM foods have not been able to point to quantifiable economic or social harms, but only philosophical concerns, the economic and social interests cannot be balanced. At the same time, the complexity of the environmental issues and the risk of errors calls into question the ethics of moving forward simply because no harm from GM foods can be readily demonstrated. Where conflicting policies cannot be balanced, and where equity concerns raise more questions than can be answered, the best course of action is perhaps to adhere to the time-honored tradition of understanding the full impact of any actions before reaching a decision. In other words, the most ethical action is to undertake the risk assessment and move forward based on the best available information at the time. The key, however, is flexibility on both sides of the issue. Assessment and greater public participation should ideally be integrated into the review process before GM foods are permitted to enter the nation's food supply.

Court's Holding and Decision: The USDA failed to complete environmental impact assessments before allowing planting of GM alfalfa seeds; a partial deregulation would have resulted in restricted planting of the GM alfalfa seeds.

See, e.g., Gartland, 2012; Heckman, 2014; Hester, et al., 2015; Leibowitz, 2013; McCabe, 2012; Morathitz, 2013; Redick, 2014 (discussing this court decision).

While the U.S. Supreme Court forbid partial deregulation and planting of GM alfalfa, the United States has still not established GM-specific requirements for the nation's food supply. Labeling of GM ingredients on food packaging is not required by the FDA because GM plant food is presumed to be **bioequivalent** or essentially the same as traditional food. This means that GM food is regulated in the same way as traditional food (Van Tassel, 2009). Currently, the food industry itself determines what constitutes genetically engineered food and decides whether to label the food as GM food. Perhaps GM crops should be subjected to a mandatory approval process that would ensure such food is safe to eat, as opposed to assuming that food is safe unless a hazard is proven to exist.

Regulating Food Products Not Proven Safe

It is debatable whether foods that carry disease-resistant genes should be used if some of the antibiotics used for this purpose are still used to treat human illnesses (FDA, 2015b). For instance, American cattle, sheep, swine, chickens, and turkeys contain antibiotics used as growth promoters and antimicrobial agents that include viruses, fungi, and parasites. It is also debatable whether foods derived from genetically engineered plants should be permitted to flourish without regulatory oversight in the absence of proven hazards (Dragich, 2013). For instance, most corn, soybean, and wheat products are genetically modified. These issues surround the question of whether GM food should be available for human consumption when safety information is either difficult to interpret or unavailable (Nunziato, 2014).

Europe refuses to import U.S. food products that have not been proven to be safe. For instance, most of Europe will not permit meat or poultry imports from the United States containing hormones used to promote growth in cattle or fowl (chickens, turkeys, ducks, or geese raised for meat or eggs). Europe takes the position that where potential health effects are serious and the relevant science is inadequate to draw a conclusion, a ban is warranted until definitive research is performed (Oriola, 2014). Now, the debate is whether or not to require better labeling of food products in the United States. Many question why food products that are free of antibiotics, antimicrobials, and genetic modification are not labeled as such, especially since the FDA already requires food labels to disclose whether food is irradiated, frozen, homogenized, or pasteurized (Linnekin, 2010).

Concerns regarding the use of growth hormones in food range from the onset of early puberty and antibiotic resistance in humans (Dragich, 2013), to whether they contribute to the nation's obesity epidemic. Hospital-acquired bacterial infections cause an estimated 75,000 deaths a year (Magill, et al., 2014) and antimicrobial resistance costs the U.S. health care system $36 to $45 billion annually (Scott, 2009). The question is whether the use of antibiotics in agriculture is increasing the resistance of bacteria, resulting in reduced effectiveness of antibiotics for treating humans.

Different Values: Food Industry versus Public Health Sector

The **Food Safety Modernization Act of 2011** is the nation's most comprehensive food legislation in almost a century. As seen with the popularity and success of high-fiber foods, public health advocates maintain that the food industry should be able to accomplish profitability by retraining consumers to gravitate toward healthy foods. The challenge is developing a concerted effort across disciplines and across fields. The public health sector is skeptical of the food industry promoting healthy foods when its major concern is profits; at the same time, the food industry views public health advocates as unaware of how businesses operate.

A multiple-domain effort is required across the public and private sectors (Wharton, 2005). Public health scholars and physicians have called for a broad system of taxes on non-nutritious foods, possibly combined with subsidies for certain healthy foods (Taylor, et al., 2015). Many U.S. schools have recently removed non-nutritious foods from their vending machines (Fehn, 2012), and the World Health Organization (WHO) recommends bans on advertising targeted to children. The WHO further suggests limits on sugar consumption and encourages governments to promote the consumption of healthy food. The European Union restricted advertising aimed at children when the food industry failed to take action on its own (Reid, 2014).

Excessive Eating of Unhealthy Foods: A Behavioral Addiction

The food industry may have an ethical obligation to warn consumers which foods are non-nutritious, to warn consumers that some foods that are perceived as healthy are actually not, and to protect children from unhealthy foods. But consumers are a large part of the problem by way of purchasing patterns and personal responsibility (Slive, 2011). In terms of explaining overconsumption behaviors, while recent research on the neurological

ETHICAL DILEMMAS 14-6

8. Should free will or the belief that there is no real free will regarding eating behaviors, or some combination of both, be acceptable as the explanation for excessive eating of unhealthy or non-nutritious foods?

effects of food has shown parallels in neural effects produced by food and dependency-inducing medications, there is no significant correlation between food addiction scores and overweight (Gearhardt, et al., 2011; Hector, 2012). **Food addiction** in this instance refers to a chronically relapsing disorder that causes impulse cravings that lead to unhealthy, or non-nutritious, day-to-day food choices. Compulsive eating is characterized by the inability of individuals to limit their excessive food intake.

No one has shown that the food industry manipulates the addictive content of food to encourage dependence (Muroff, 2011). While food research has not disproven the physically addictive properties of food, behavioral research on unhealthy eating habits shows that food can be a **behavioral addiction** (Nair, et al., 2009). That is, eating that is motivated by emotions ranging along the spectrum of food cravings to compulsive eating, which may also include continued excessive eating of unhealthy foods in spite of adverse consequences. Behavioral addiction is characterized in all instances by a loss of control over one's eating habits. *See generally* Colasurdo, 2010.

Mental health standards, like ethical standards, evolve over time. Though many obese people may prefer high-Calorie foods, their food choices are not lifestyle choices to which society need defer or cater to as a whole (Banker, 2010). If behavioral addictions are to have any meaning in the context of ethics and the law, the addictions must be grounded in empirical data and amenable to diagnosis with some measure of reliability. Ethically and legally, society is debating about the need to tolerate what it presently perceives as behavioral, rather than chemical, addictions to tobacco, alcohol, illicit drugs, eating, gambling, the Internet, love, sex, exercise, work, and shopping (Grant, 2011; Sussman, et al., 2011).

Regulation of Trans-Fats

The most dramatic new regulatory change for the food industry occurred when the FDA required food labels to list the amount of trans-fats in their products (Atwell, 2007); all trans-fat will be restricted in 2018 (Tracy & Gasparro, 2015). The food industry was forced to add nutrition labels showing how many grams of trans-fats are included in each serving. Beyond requiring that labels list the amount of trans-fats in food, the term **trans-fat-free** was defined as less than 0.5 grams of trans-fat per labeled serving (Spivey, 2007). In the realm of dietary dangers, hydrogenated trans-fats rank very high.

Though trans-fats are found naturally in meats and some dairy products, Americans ingest large quantities of trans-fats in the form of hydrogenated oils in crackers, cookies, chips, and other snack foods. **Hydrogenation** is a chemical process used to solidify oils, vegetable shortenings, and margarines to increase the shelf life and flavor stability of foods, and it creates hydrogenated trans-fats. Nearly all fried and baked goods have hydrogenated trans-fats, including food labeled as low-fat. Nutritionists claim trans-fats are so harmful that no level is entirely safe (Slive, 2011; Spahn, 2011). Not only do trans-fats raise bad cholesterol, but they also lower the good cholesterol that is helpful in reducing the risk of clogged arteries.

Together, these regulations could affect the food industry as well as consumer eating habits, just as requiring warning labels on tobacco products in the 1960s led some consumers to give up smoking and resulted in the tobacco industry developing lower-nicotine products (Fehn, 2012). While New York City (Kruk, 2010) and California regulate the use of trans-fats (Linnekin, 2010), the first restrictions at the national level will not occur until 2018, 15 years after the action was first proposed. Critics of trans-fat bans contend that the laws have no impact on the obesity epidemic, and may instead be counterproductive.

Safety of Food Additives and Contaminants

Over the past decade, Congress and the FDA have increasingly turned to labeling regulations on food safety (Barnhill, 2014). A dangerous precedent has been set, however, with federal recognition and acceptance of food that is less than pure (Spahn, 2011). After all, a **safe tolerance** still means that food contains additives and contaminants. While it is now possible to detect harmful additives in the parts per trillion and further advances will allow for detection of even lower levels in food, other additives are introduced through environmental contamination, changes in food processing, sourcing of ingredients from different countries, and a myriad of other reasons (Hahn, 2010). Beginning in the 1980s, the FDA banned sulfite preservatives from fresh fruits and vegetables and required better, more informative labeling on packaged foods. Sodium nitrites, dyes, and other chemical preservatives are more clearly labeled or more restricted than ever (CFSAN, 2013). Still, as illustrated in **FEATURE BOX 14-5**, other harmful levels of additives remain in processed foods without monitoring for potential long-term chemical toxicity, albeit with warnings (Beyranevand, 2013).

As illustrated in **FEATURE BOX 14-6**, some food additives are **generally recognized as safe** (GRAS) and excluded from lists of harmful additives, even though public health advocates maintain that they are harmful and question their long-term safety. The FDA and international food regulatory authorities have designated GRAS food additives as not likely to

---

FEATURE BOX 14-5

The Ethics of Additives in Processed Foods Despite Warnings

There is no monitoring for the potential long-term chemical toxicity of:

- Acrylamid: probable carcinogen found in many processed foods that forms in carbohydrate-containing foods baked, fried, or broiled, like breads, cereals, potato chips, and coffee
- Growth hormones and antibiotics: contribute to antibiotic-resistant bacteria and to overweight and obesity, found in meat products from over crowded slaughterhouses
- Bisphenol A: toxic endocrine-disrupting chemical that comes into contact with food in plastic containers and the lining of aluminum food and drink cans
- Olestra: fat substitute that can cause diarrhea and stomach cramps
- Quorn: fungus-based meat substitute that can cause severe vomiting and anaphylactic reactions

— Sources: Carra, 2011; Stathopoulous, 2010.

GRAS Foods: Safe or Harmful Long-Term?

- Acesulfame-k (artificial sweetener often used in combination with other artificial sweeteners in order to mask each other's bitter aftertaste)
- Aspartame (artificial sweetener also sold under the brand names NutraSweet and Equal)
- Phenylketonurics (denotes the presence of saccharine or NutraSweet, an artificial sweetener used in diet drinks, fruit juices, and alcoholic beverages)
- Potassium bromate (banned by many countries, used in bread)

— Source: Beyranevand, 2013.

cause harm if used as intended. The problem is that it is not clear and definitive what use is intended. What may be considered safe for a full-grown man may not be safe for women, adults with compromised immune systems, or children (Spahn, 2011). Moreover, there is no consensus on what should happen when advances in analytical technology reveal the presence of trace levels of known or potentially harmful additives in food that may always have been present in the food supply, but escaped detection. For instance, it is debatable whether there are acceptable levels of methyl mercury in seafood or lead in candies consumed frequently by children (Hahn, 2010).

Food-Borne Pathogens and Contaminants

The Food Safety Modernization Act of 2011 could not have been enacted at a more critical time. Prior to 2011, the FDA could only respond to outbreaks of food contamination as illustrated in **FEATURE BOX 14-7**, having lacked the authority to prevent food-borne pathogens and contaminants from entering the nation's food supply. Yet, consumers are ethically entitled to have the peace of mind knowing that the foods they eat are safe, wholesome, nutritious, and meet all health expectations (Negowetti, 2014).

Unnecessary Drain on the U.S. Health Care System

Food-borne diseases account for up to 76 million bouts of illness and up to 9,000 deaths every year:

- Bovine spongiform encephalopathy contaminations or mad cow disease in meat products
- Crop fields contaminated with animal waste
- Food additive adulterations
- Meat and egg products infected with salmonella bacteria
- Ready-to-eat foods infected with *E. coli* bacteria and the hepatitis virus
- Residual contagions on food from carcinogenic fungicides, insecticides, pesticides, and rodenticides

— Sources: CFSAN, 2014; GAO, 2005 and 2005a; Mead, 2011; Sinclair, 1905/2015; Spahn, 2011.

This piece of health care reform combats these preventable health care costs by focusing on preventing food-borne illnesses and deaths, improving detection of pathogens and contaminants, and enhancing the safety of imported foods (Preston, 2011). With this health care reform, the FDA is now empowered to order mandatory recalls of contaminated food and has greater oversight of imported food products. The question now is whether the FDA will have the funding to hire the staff needed to conduct the inspections it is required by law to conduct, or whether the food industry will succeed in having food safety inspections delegated to itself (Powell & Menendian, 2012).

Most **food-borne illnesses** are preventable (Trexler, 2011), yet the direct health care costs from food-borne illnesses and premature death are about $164 billion per year. This figure does not include the costs of the chronic diseases triggered by food-borne illnesses listed in **FEATURE BOX 14-8** (Spahn, 2011; USDA, 2010).

The Ethics of Disinformation

Nutrition and food safety are inherently parts of the debate over health care. President Franklin D. Roosevelt, even at a time of war, recognized this important fact: "The total defense which this nation seeks involves a great deal more than building airplanes, ships, guns and bombs. We cannot be a strong nation unless we are a healthy nation" (Dier, 2011). The issue in the food safety debate is identifying who profits by and who pays for self-regulation of the nation's food supply in an age of unprecedented **disinformation**, where false and misleading information is deliberately put out as half-truths, such as the safety of our food supply and the nutritional value, or lack thereof, of our food. Disingenuous low-fat claims and healthy option labels are of dubious value to consumers (Schlosser, 2012).

For decades, everyone has known that some food products contribute to obesity and other diet- and weight-related diseases, yet the food industry chooses to protect non-nutritious products. Food-borne illnesses also raise questions about the processing techniques of industrial agriculture (Trexler, 2011). Until recently, the food industry has successfully manufactured uncertainty by questioning every study by consumer advocates, and by dissecting every method and disputing every conclusion of regulators with regard to the obesity epidemic. In doing so, the food industry has delayed regulation for decades. *See generally* Michaels, 2008.

FEATURE BOX 14-8

Chronic Diseases Caused by Food-Borne Pathogens and Contaminants

Two to three percent of all food-borne illnesses lead to secondary long-term illnesses (660,000 to 990,000 total cases per year), causing additional billions of dollars in health care costs:

- Certain strains of *E. coli* can cause kidney failure in young children and infants.
- Salmonella can lead to reactive arthritis and serious infections.
- Listeria can cause meningitis and stillbirths.
- Campylobacter may be the most common precipitating factor for Guillain-Barré syndrome (inflammatory disorder leading to paralysis).

— Sources: FDA, 2015b; Kilman, 2011; Landro, 2011.

As the quote at the beginning of this section indicates, President Roosevelt recognized that when it comes to ensuring nutrition and safety in the nation's food supply, the federal government must protect consumers. President Obama echoed this same sentiment more than 70 years later, as stated in **FEATURE BOX 14-9**. The passage of time illustrates that the nation has not completely ensured that its food supply is safe (Trexler, 2011). The question is whether the **principle of proportionality**, or the mutual toleration of competing interests, can balance the interests of the food industry and those of public health with regard to nutrition (Hoffmann, 2014), or whether any sense of ethics will be trumped by a political economy that prevents regulatory agencies from adequately considering legitimate food safety concerns (Steinzor, 2010).

FEATURE BOX 14-9

Protecting Consumers: Food Safety Modernization Act

"We are a nation built on the strength of individual initiative. But there are certain things that we cannot do on our own. There are certain things that only a government can do. And one of those things is ensuring that the foods we eat . . . are safe and do not cause us harm."

— **Barack H. Obama** (1961–), 44th President of the United States

— Source: Obama, 2011.

ETHICAL OR UNETHICAL DECISION

Consumers' Right to Nutritional Information

Ethics Issue: *Should restaurants be required to disclose accurate nutritional information on their menus?*

Ethics Analysis: Yes, simple factual disclosure of caloric information on restaurant menus is reasonably related to the goals of combating obesity, and with it diabetes. Even if there was a correlation between menu labeling and consumer behavior, it is still reasonable to believe that providing Calorie information at the point of sale will result in a change in consumer attitudes. Menu labeling is one means to increase consumer awareness, decrease Calories consumed, pressure restaurants to offer healthier choices, and ultimately halt, or at least slow, national weight gain.

Ethics Analysis: No, there is no relationship between menu labeling and consumer behavior that could reduce the obesity epidemic. Such laws unnecessarily burden the restaurant sector and confuse consumers with too much information.

Court's Holding and Decision: The disclosure of factual and uncontroversial nutritional information in order to facilitate responsible decision-making by consumers is not the same as commercial speech that facilitates public discussion, which is protected by the First Amendment. Less than 2 years after this court decision, an industry-approved mandate requiring all food restaurant chains with 20 or more locations to prominently post the Calorie content of their menu items directly on menus and menu boards became law.

— *New York State Restaurant Association v. New York City Board of Health, et al.*, 556 F.3d 114 (U.S. Court of Appeals for the 2nd Circuit 2009). *See, e.g.,* Bennett, 2012; Card, 2013; Dhooge, 2014; Diller, 2013; Fairhurst, 2013; Hodge & Scanlon, 2014; Hodge, 2012; Jacobs, 2014; Keighley, 2012; Norton, 2012; Nunes, 2014; Pomeranz, 2012; Rauer, 2012; Rutkow, 2013; Straub, 2013; Sugarman, 2014 (discussing this court decision).

CHAPTER SUMMARY

- With one-third of Americans suffering from obesity, government as well as the public must recognize that the United States cannot be a strong nation unless it is a healthy nation.
- It is questionable whether individuals alone are responsible for overweight and obesity, when the major corresponding factors to Americans' increased weight over the past few decades are the facts that more meals than ever are eaten outside the home and their diets consist largely of processed food.
- The ethics of nutrition and food safety center on the personal responsibility of consumers in consuming foods and beverage products, as well as the food industry's social responsibility to help consumers make responsible and healthy choices when selecting food and beverages, or to at least not hinder those choices through deceptive marketing.
- The ethical distinction between consumers' and the food industry's responsibilities for the nation's obesity epidemic is blurred, representing the tension between consumer protection and free choice.
- Americans living in food deserts (where there is little access to high quality, fresh nutritious food, but plentiful access to processed and fast food) are at especially high risk for overweight, obesity, and related conditions; this problem has been termed the grocery gap.
- Regulation of the food industry is highly fragmented, which allows the food industry to take advantage of inconsistencies, loopholes, and lax oversight.
- The federal government continues to subsidize some of the least nutritious crops produced by wealthy American farmers, such as corn and sugar, which results in foods containing these ingredients being more affordable, and therefore more likely to be chosen than fresh fare by low income individuals and families.
- The ethics of whether food advertising targeted to children should be restricted are controversial, given the responsibility of parents to determine what children eat and to teach children that they cannot always have everything they might want.
- The food industry actively misleads consumers, by advertising certain options as 'healthy,' when in fact they are often devoid of any nutritional value, and other options may be healthier; in other words, the food industry creates demand for non-nutritious products at the expense of more nutritious options, even going as far as advertising unsubstantiated health benefits in certain foods that may actually be harmful.

- So far, the food industry has not been held liable for its transgressions in the same way as the tobacco industry was.
- The risks of genetically modified foods have yet to be determined, but many countries ban them from import, unlike the U.S.; the U.S. has adopted a policy of authorizing food additives until such time as they are proven unsafe, as has been the recent case with trans-fats.
- Food-borne pathogens and contaminants continue to be a dangerous, even deadly, concern in the U.S.; until 2011, the federal government was not authorized to issue mandatory recalls.
- Given the dominance of non-nutritious processed food in the nation's food supply, the discordant relationship between the food industry and consumers is actually accelerating the decline in food quality.

REFERENCES

Ahmed, H. M. (2009). Obesity, fast food manufacture, and regulation: Revisiting opportunities for reform. *Food and Drug Law Journal, 64,* 565–575.

Andreyeva, T., et al. (2011). *Exposure to food advertising on television: Associations with children's fast food and soft drink consumption and obesity.* New York, NY: National Bureau of Economic Research.

Angelo, M. J. (2011). Building a more sustainable and local food system: Small, slow, and local. *Vermont Journal of Environmental Law, 12,* 354–372.

Atwell, B. L. (2007). Obesity, public health, and the food supply. *Indiana Health Law Review, 4,* 1–27.

Badilas, A. (2011). Food taxes: A palatable solution to the obesity epidemic? *McGeorge Global Business and Development Law Journal, 23,* 255–283.

Bagchi, D. (Ed.). (2014). *Nutraceutical and functional food regulations in the United States and around the world* (2nd ed.). Philadelphia, PA: Elsevier-Academic Press.

Bailey, R. L., et al. (2011). Dietary supplement use in the United States. *Nutrition Journal, 141*(2), 261–266.

Banker, M. (2010). I saw the sign: The new federal menu-labeling law and lessons from local experience. *Food and Drug Law Journal, 65,* 901–928.

Banzhaf, J. F., III, et al. (2010). Protecting the public health: Litigation and obesity. *Journal of Law, Economics and Policy, 7,* 259–279.

Barnes, S. (2011). Labeling our way to a leaner America. *Journal of Law in Society, 12,* 116–155.

Barnhill, A. (2014). Choice, respect and value: The ethics of healthy eating policy. *Wake Forest Journal of Law and Policy, 5,* 1–37.

Bennett, S. J. (2012). Paternalistic manipulation through pictorial warnings: The First Amendment, commercial speech, and the Family Smoking Prevention and Tobacco Control Act. *Mississippi Law Journal, 81,* 1909–1939.

Bernell, B. (2010). The history and impact of the New York City menu labeling law. *Food and Drug Law Journal, 65,* 839–872.

Beyranevand, L. J. (2013). Generally recognized as safe? Analyzing flaws in the FDA's approach to GRAS additives. *Vermont Law Review, 37,* 887–922.

Browne, V. B. (2011). The rules of consumption: The promise and peril of federal emulation of the Big Apple's food laws. *Brooklyn Law Review, 76,* 1049–1092.

Card, M. M. (2013). America, you are digging your grave with your spoon—Should the FDA tell you that on food labels? *Food and Drug Law Journal, 68,* 309–327.

Cardello, H., & Garr, D. (2010). *Stuffed: An insider's look at who's (really) making America fat and how the food industry can fix it.* London, England: Ecco.

Carra, R. J. (2011). It's in our blood: A critique of the FDA's reluctance to regulate the use of bisphenol A in the food supply. *Journal of Health Care Law and Policy, 14,* 153–176.

CBO (Congressional Budget Office). (2011). *How does obesity in adults affect spending on health care?* Washington, DC: CBO.

CFSAN (Center for Food Safety and Applied Nutrition). (2014). *Bad bug book: Food borne pathogenic microorganisms and natural toxins handbook.* Silver Spring, MD: U.S. Food and Drug Administration, CFSAN.

___. (2013). *Approaches to establish thresholds for major food allergens and for gluten in food.*

Colasurdo, B. S. (2010). Behavioral addictions and the law. *Southern California Law Review, 84,* 161–199.

Coplan, K. S. (2009). Ideological plaintiffs, administrative lawmaking, standing, and the Petition Clause. *Maine Law Review, 61*, 377–466.

Cusick, C. (2011). Menu-labeling laws: A move from local to national regulation. *Santa Clara Law Review, 51*, 989–1023.

Davis, D. R. (2009). Declining fruit and vegetable nutrient composition: What is the evidence? *Hortscience, 44*, 15–20.

Dhooge, L. J. (2014). The First Amendment and disclosure regulations: Compelled speech or corporate opportunism? *American Business Law Journal, 51*, 559–659.

Dier, J. K. (2011). S.O.S. from the FDA: A cry for help in the world of unregulated dietary supplements. *Albany Law Review, 74*, 385–418.

Diller, P. A. (2013). Local health agencies, the Bloomberg soda rule, and the ghost of Woodrow Wilson. *Fordham Urban Law Journal, 40*, 1859–1901.

___. (2013a). Do we have what it takes to reinvent the U.S. food system? Obesity prevention policies at the local level: Tobacco's lessons. *Maine Law Review, 65*, 459–464.

Dragich, M. (2013). Do you know what's on your plate? The importance of regulating the processes of food production. *Journal of Environmental Law and Litigation, 28*, 385–445.

Ehrenreich, N., & Lyon, B. (2011). LatCrit South-North Exchange: The global politics of food: Sustainability and subordination: The global politics of food: A critical overview. *University of Miami Inter-American Law Review, 43*, 1–41.

Fairhurst, M. P. (2013). Traffic light labeling on restaurant menus: A call for the communication of nutrition information through color-coded prices. *Quinnipiac Health Law Journal, 16*, 1–41.

Faulk, R. O., & Gray, J. S. (2012). Public nuisance at the crossroads: Policing the intersection between statutory primacy and common law. *Chapman Law Review, 15*, 495–535.

FDA (Food and Drug Administration). (2015). *FDA targets trans fat in processed foods.* Silver Spring, MD: FDA.

___. (2015a). *Talking about trans fat: What you need to know.*

___. (2015b). *Fighting the impact of antibiotic-resistant bacteria.*

Federici, V. (2010). Genetically modified food and informed consumer choice: Comparing U.S. and E.U. labeling laws. *Brooklyn Journal of International Law, 35*, 515–561.

Fehn, J. J. (2012). The assault on bad food: Tobacco-style litigation as an element of the comprehensive scheme to fight obesity. *Food and Drug Law Journal, 67*, 65–81.

Forell, C. (2011). McTorts: The social and legal impact of McDonald's role in tort suits. *Loyola Consumer Law Review, 24*, 105–154.

Fortin, N. (2015). *Food regulation: Law, science, policy, and practice* (2nd ed.). New York, NY: Wiley.

Foster, J. (2011). Subsidizing fat: How the 2012 Farm Bill can address America's obesity epidemic. *University of Pennsylvania Law Review, 160*, 235–276.

Freeman, A. (2007). Fast food: Oppression through poor nutrition. *California Law Review, 95*, 2221–2259.

Fryar, C. D., et al. (2014). *Prevalence of overweight, obesity, and extreme obesity among adults: United States.* Hyattsville, MD: Centers for Disease Control and Prevention, National Center for Health Statistics.

FTC (Federal Trade Commission). (2012). *A review of food marketing food to children and adolescents: Follow-up report.* Washington, DC: FTC.

GAO (General Accounting Office). (2009). *Dietary supplements: FDA should take further actions to improve oversight and consumer understanding.* Washington, DC: GAO.

___. (2005). *Overseeing the U.S. food supply: Steps should be taken to reduce overlapping inspections and related activities.*

___. (2005a). *Food safety: Experiences of seven countries in consolidating their food safety systems.*

Gartland, C. J. (2012). At war and peace with the National Environmental Policy Act: When political questions and the environment collide. *Air Force Law Review, 68*, 27–72.

Gearhardt, A. N., et al. (2011). Neural correlates of food addiction. *Archives of General Psychiatry, 68*(8), 808–816.

Glover, M. A. (2008). Americans with Disabilities Act of 1990, the weight of personal responsibility: Obesity, causation, and protected physical impairments. *University of Arkansas Little Rock Law Review, 30*, 381–411.

Goodman, W. R. (2015, July 13). Should Washington end agriculture subsidies? *Wall Street Journal*, p. R1.

Grant, J. E. (2011). Introduction to behavioral addictions. *American Journal of Drug and Alcohol Abuse, 36*(5), 233–241.

Green, J. S. (2010). Cheeseburger in paradise? An analysis of how *New York State Restaurant Association v. New York City Board of Health* may reform our fast food nation. *DePaul Law Review, 59*, 733–774.

Guthrie, J., et al. (2013). *Americans' food choices at home and away: How do they compare with recommendations?* Washington, DC: U.S. Department of Agriculture, Economic Research Service.

Hahn, M. J. (2010). FDA has the legal authority to adopt a threshold of toxicological concern (TTC) for substances in food at trace levels. *Food and Drug Law Journal, 65*, 217–230.

Harris, J. L., et al. (2012). *Cereal FACTS 2012: Limited progress in the nutrition quality and marketing of children's cereals.* New Haven, CN: Yale Rudd Center for Food Policy and Obesity.

Harris, P. N. (2009). Undoing the damage of the Dew. *Appalachian Journal of Law, 9,* 53–119.

Heckman, C. (2014). Tying its own hands: APHIS's inability to regulate genetically modified crops. *Ecology Law Quarterly, 41,* 325–347.

Hector, C. (2012). Nudging towards nutrition? Soft paternalism and obesity-related reform. *Food and Drug Law Journal, 67,* 103–122.

Hester, T., et al. (2015). Restating environmental law. *Columbia Journal of Environmental Law, 40,* 1–37.

HHS (U.S. Department of Health and Human Services). (2014). *The health consequences of smoking—50 years of progress: A report of the Surgeon General.* Rockville, MD: HHS, Public Health Service, Office of the Surgeon General.

___. (2010). *The Surgeon General's vision for a healthy and fit America.*

Hitt, G. (2008, May 5). Farm bill stuck on sugar-support proposal. *Wall Street Journal,* p. A3.

Hodge, J. G., Jr. (2013). New frontiers in obesity control: Innovative public health legal interventions. *Duke Forum for Law and Social Change, 5,* 1–37.

___. (2012). Food fight! The legal debate over the obesity epidemic, food labeling, and the government's involvement in what you eat: Alternative models to supplement menu labeling. *Nexus: Chapman's Journal of Law and Policy, 17,* 79–95.

Hodge, J. G., Jr., & Scanlon, M. (2014). The legal anatomy of product bans to protect the public's health. *Annals of Health Law, 23,* 161–182.

Hoffman, L. (2014). Cigarettes vs. soda? The argument for similar public health regulation of smoking and obesity. *Connecticut Law Review, 46,* 1889–1901.

Hoffmann, D. E., et al. (2014). Achieving a better regulatory fit. *Food and Drug Law Journal, 69,* 237–272.

Hoffmann, S., & Harder, W. (2010). The future of food regulation: Food safety and risk governance in globalized markets. *Health Matrix: The Journal of Law-Medicine, 20,* 5–54.

Hoflander, J. G. (2011). A Red Bull instead of a cigarette: Should the FDA regulate energy drinks? *Valparaiso University Law Review, 45,* 689–740.

IOM (Institute of Medicine). (2013). *Challenges and opportunities for change in food marketing to children and youth: Workshop summary.* Washington, DC: National Academies Press.

Jacobs, L. G. (2014). Compelled commercial speech as compelled consent speech. *Journal of Law and Politics, 29,* 517–533.

Jain, S. L. (2010). Injuries without remedies: Fear of cancer. *Loyola of Los Angeles Law Review, 44,* 233–252.

Kaplin, L. (2011). A national strategy to combat the childhood obesity epidemic. *University of California-Davis Journal of Juvenile Law and Policy, 15,* 347–399.

Keighley, J. M. (2012). Can you handle the truth? Compelled commercial speech and the first amendment. *University of Pennsylvania Journal of Constitutional Law, 15,* 539–616.

Khan, F. (2010). Preserving human potential as freedom: A framework for regulating epigenetic harms. *Health Matrix: The Journal of Law-Medicine, 20,* 259–323.

Kilman, S. (2011, June 13). Pesticide residue taints apples. *Wall Street Journal,* p. B1.

Kotwani, B. A., & Danis, M. (2009). Ethics of health care law reform: Expanding the current health care reform debate: Making the case for socio-economic interventions for low income young adults. *Journal of Health Care Law and Policy, 12,* 17–45.

Kruk, K. (2010). Of fat people and fundamental rights: The constitutionality of the New York City trans-fat ban. *William and Mary Bill of Rights Journal, 18*(3), 857–882.

Kwan, C. C. (2009). 20-ton canaries: The great whales of the North Atlantic: Fixing the Farm Bill: Using the "permanent provisions" in agricultural law to achieve WTO [World Trade Organization] compliance. *Boston College Environmental Affairs Law Review, 36,* 571–606.

Landro, L. (2011, June 14). Food illness and the kitchen: Salmonella infections rose last year; Home cooks fail to act safely, studies say. *Wall Street Journal,* p. B1.

Leib, E. M. B. (2013). All (food) politics is local: Increasing food access through local government action. *Harvard Law and Policy Review, 7,* 321–341.

Leibowitz, H. (2013). Harmony with nature and genetically modified seeds: A contradictory concept in the United States and Brazil? *Pace Environmental Law Review, 30,* 558–579.

Linnekin, B. J. (2010). The "California effect" & the future of American food: How California's growing crackdown on food & agriculture harms the state & the nation. *Chapman Law Review, 13,* 357–389.

Liu, C.-F. (2011). Global food safety: Exploring key elements for an international regulatory strategy. *Virginia Journal of International Law, 51,* 637–695.

___. (2011a). Is "USDA organic" a seal of deceit? The pitfalls of USDA certified organics produced in the United States, China and beyond. *Stanford Journal of International Law, 47,* 333–378.

Liu, L. (2012). Reshaping the American concept of consumer interest in the food policy debate. *Yale Journal of Health Policy, Law, and Ethics, 12*, 171–206.

Lukits, A. (2011, December 13). The research report: Low readership of nutrition labels. *Wall Street Journal*, p. D2.

Lytton, T. D. (2010). An educational approach to school food: Using nutrition standards to promote healthy dietary habits. *Utah Law Review, 2010*, 1189–1221.

Magill, S. S., et al. (2014). Multistate point-prevalence survey of health care–associated infections. *New England Journal of Medicine, 370*, 1198–1208.

Manning, L. E. (2010). The skinny on the FOP flop: Why the FDA must tighten the belt on FOP labeling in light of the obesity crisis. *Hofstra Law Review, 38*, 1227–1260.

Masters, R. K., et al. (2013). The impact of obesity on U.S. mortality levels: The importance of age and cohort factors in population estimates. *American Journal of Public Health, 103*(10), 1895–1901.

McCabe, M. S. (2012). Superweeds and suspect seeds: Does the genetically-engineered crop deregulation process put American agriculture at risk? *University of Baltimore Journal of Land and Development, 1*, 109–155.

McGarity, T. O. (2013). *Freedom to harm: The lasting legacy of the laissez faire revival.* Cambridge, MA: Yale University Press.

Mead, P. S. (2011). *Food-related death and illness in the United States.* Atlanta, GA: Centers for Disease Control.

Michaels, D. (2008). *Doubt is their product: How industry's assault on science threatens your health.* New York, NY: Oxford University Press.

Min, H (M). (2013). Large-sized soda ban as an alternative to soda tax. *Cornell Journal of Law and Public Policy, 23*, 187–232.

Morathitz, S. J. (2013). A mild winter: The status of environmental preliminary injunctions. *Seattle University Law Review, 37*, 155–200.

Muñoz, S. S. (2008, March 27). Fortified yogurt, soy milk. *Wall Street Journal*, p. D2.

Muroff, J. A. (2011). Policing willpower: Obesity as a test case for state empowerment of integrated health care. *Houston Journal of Health Law and Policy, 11*, 47–77.

NAAG (National Association of Attorneys General). (2009). *Tobacco master settlement agreement.* Washington, DC: NAAG.

Nair, S. G., et al. (2009). The neuropharmacology of relapse to food seeking: Methodology, main findings, and comparison with relapse to drug seeking. *Progress in Neurobiology, 89*(1), 18–45.

Negowetti, N. E. (2014). Defining natural foods: The search for a natural law. *Regent University Law Review, 26*, 329–365.

NNC (National Nutraceutical Center). (2011). *What are nutraceuticals?* Clemson, SC: Clemson University.

Norton, H. (2012). Secrets, lies, and disclosure. *Journal of Law and Politics, 27*, 641–654.

Nunes, B. (2014). The future of government-mandated health warnings after *R.J. Reynolds* and *American Meat Institute. University of Pennsylvania Law Review Online, 163*, 177–213.

Nunziato, T. (2014). "You say tomato, I say solanum lycopersicum containing beta-ionone and phenylacetaldehyde": An analysis of Connecticut's GMO labeling legislation. *Food and Drug Law Journal, 69*, 471–490.

Obama, B. H. (2011). Remarks by President Barack Obama at the signing of the Food Safety Modernization Act of 2011. Washington, DC: White House Office of the Press Secretary.

OECD (Organization for Economic Cooperation and Development). (2014). *Obesity update: Risk factors: Obesity, percentage of females, males and adult population with a BMI>30 kg/m2, based on measures of height and weight.* Paris, France: OECD Directorate Employment, Labor & Social Affairs.

Oriola, T. A. (2014). The limits of regulatory science in transnational governance of transgenic plant agriculture and food systems. *North Carolina Journal of International Law & Commercial Regulation, 39*, 757–883.

Owley, J., & Lewis, T. (2014). From vacant lots to full pantries: Urban agriculture programs and the American city. *University of Detroit Mercy Law Review, 91*, 233–257.

Pasquinelli, S. N. (2010). One false move: The history of organic agriculture and consequences of non-compliance with the governing laws and regulations. *Golden Gate University Environmental Law Journal, 3*, 365–382.

Peck, A. (2010). Leveling the playing field in GMO risk assessment: Importers, exporters and the limits of science. *Boston University International Law Journal, 28*, 241–280.

Pennel, J. L. (2009). Big food's trip down tobacco road: What tobacco's past can indicate about food's future. *Buffalo Public Interest Law Journal, 27*, 101–130.

Pomeranz, J. L. (2013). A conditional funding strategy to address the modern food environment: From public health prevention to state and local preemption. *Duke Forum for Law and Social Change, 5*, 39–63.

___. (2012). No need to break new ground: A response to the Supreme Court's threat to overhaul the Commercial Speech Doctrine. *Loyola of Los Angeles Law Review, 45*, 389–434.

Powell, J. A., & Menendian, S. (2012). Beyond public/private: Understanding excessive corporate prerogative. *Kentucky Law Journal, 100*, 83–164.

Preston, C. (2011). *The Food Modernization Act, another critical piece of health reform*. Washington, DC: Doctors for America.

Rauer, S. (2012). When the First Amendment and public health collide: The court's increasingly strict constitutional scrutiny of health regulations that restrict commercial speech. *American Journal of Law and Medicine, 38*, 690–712.

Redick, T. P. (2014). Coexistence of biotech and non-GMO or organic crops. *Drake Journal of Agricultural Law, 19*, 39–79.

Reid, R.-M. C. (2014). Embedded advertising to children: A tactic that requires a new regulatory approach. *American Business Law Journal, 51*, 721–777.

Roller, S. T., & Pippins, R. (2010). Marketing nutrition & health-related benefits of food & beverage products. *Food and Drug Law Journal, 65*, 447–469.

Rothenberg, J. R. (2010). In search of the silver bullet: Regulatory models to address childhood obesity. *Food and Drug Law Journal, 65*, 185–216.

Rutkow, L., et al. (2013). Local governments and the food system: Innovative approaches to public health law and policy. *Annals of Health Law, 22*, 355–372.

Schlosser, E. (2012). *Fast food nation: The dark side of the all-American meal*. New York, NY: Harper Collins Publishers-Harper Perennial.

Schreiner, Z. R. F. (2009). Genetically modified corn, ethanol, and crop diversity. *Energy Law Journal, 30*, 169–188.

Schwartz, V. E., & Appel, C. E. (2014). Government regulation and private litigation: The law should enhance harmony, not war. *Boston University Public Interest Law Journal, 23*, 185–218.

Scott, II, R. D. (2009). *The direct medical costs of healthcare-associated infections in U.S. hospitals and the benefits of prevention*. Atlanta, GA: Centers for Disease Control and Prevention.

Seur, C. L. L., & Abelkop, A. D. K. (2010). Forty years after NEPA's [National Environmental Policy Act of 1969] enactment, it is time for a comprehensive Farm Bill environmental impact statement. *Harvard Law and Policy Review, 4*, 201–227.

Sinclair, U. (2015). *The jungle*. New York, NY: Signet (Original work published 1905).

Slive, L. (2011). Closing the kitchen? Digesting the impact of the federal menu labeling law in the Affordable Care Act. *Florida Journal of Law and Public Policy, 22*, 255–297.

Spahn, E. (2011). Keep away from mouth: How the American system of food regulation is killing us. *University of Miami Law Review, 65*, 669–715.

Spivey, E. Y. (2007). Trans fat: Can New York City save its citizens from this "metabolic poison"? *Georgia Law Review, 42*, 273–306.

Stathopoulos, A. S. (2010). You are what your food eats: How regulation of factory farm conditions could improve human health and animal welfare alike. *New York University Journal of Legislation and Public Policy, 13*, 407–444.

Stearns, D. W. (2010). On (cr)edibility: Why food in the United States may never be safe. *Stanford Law and Policy Review, 21*, 245–275.

Steinzor, R. (2010). The future of food regulation: High crimes, not misdemeanors: Deterring the production of unsafe food. *Health Matrix: The Journal of Law-Medicine, 20*, 175–201.

Straub, T. J. (2013). Fair warning? The First Amendment, compelled commercial disclosures, and cigarette warning labels. *Fordham Urban Law Journal, 40*, 1201–1264.

Strauss, D. M. (2011). An analysis of the FDA Food Safety Modernization Act: Protection for consumers and boon for business. *Food and Drug Law Journal, 66*, 353–375.

Sugarman, S. D. (2014). Compelling product sellers to transmit government public health messages. *Journal of Law and Politics, 29*, 557–575.

Sussman, S., et al. (2011). Prevalence of the addictions: A problem of the majority or the minority? *Evaluation and the Health Professions, 34*(1), 3–56.

Tai, S. (2010). Comparing approaches towards governing scientific advisory bodies on food safety in the United States and the European Union. *Wisconsin Law Review, 2010*, 627–671.

Taylor, A. L., et al. (2015). The increasing weight of regulation: Countries combat the global obesity epidemic. *Indiana Law Journal, 90*, 257–291.

Tracy, T., & Gasparro, A. (June 17, 2015). Food firms ordered to cut all trans-fat in three years. *Wall Street Journal*, p. B2.

Treuhaft, S., & Karpyn, A. (2010). *The grocery gap: Who has access to healthy foods and why it matters*. Philadelphia, PA: The Food Trust.

Trexler, N. M. (2011). "Market" regulation: Confronting industrial agriculture's food safety failures. *Widener Law Review, 17*, 311–345.

USDA (U.S. Department of Agriculture). (2010). *Food borne illness cost calculator.* Washington, DC: Economic Research Service, USDA.

Van Tassel, K. A. (2009). Genetically modified plants used for food, risk assessment and uncertainty principles: Does the transition from ignorance to indeterminacy trigger the need for post-market surveillance? *Boston University Journal of Science and Technology Law, 15*, 220–251.

Vane, H. R., & Mulhearn, C. (Eds.). (2010). *James A. Mirrlees, William S. Vickrey, George A. Akerlof, A. Michael Spence and Joseph E. Stiglitz* (*Pioneering papers of the Nobel Memorial Laureates in economics*). Northampton, MA: Edward Elgar Publishing.

Wallinga, D. (2010). Agricultural policy and childhood obesity: A food systems and public health commentary. *Health Affairs, 29*(3), 405–410.

Wharton School of the University of Pennsylvania. (2007). Serving up smaller restaurant portions: Will consumers bite? *Knowledge@Wharton.*

___. (2005). Food fight: Obesity raises difficult marketing questions.

___. (2004). Biotechnology in Chile: Looking for a boost from copper and fruits. Universia.

Wilinska, K. (2012). Aquadvantage is not real advantage: European biotechnology regulations and the United States' September 2010 FDA review of genetically modified salmon. *Minnesota Journal of International Law, 21*, 145–176.

Wilking, C. L., & Daynard, R. A. (2013). Beyond cheeseburgers: The impact of commonsense consumption acts on future obesity-related lawsuits. *Food and Drug Law Journal, 68*, 229–239.

Williamson, E. (2008, April 30). Farming critics fault industry's influence. *Wall Street Journal*, p. A4.

Winslow, R. (August 14, 2014). Low-salt diets may pose health risks, study finds. *Wall Street Journal*, p. A1.

Zhang, J. (2009, May 16). Obama sets steps to toughen food safety regulation. *Wall Street Journal*, p. D1.

CHAPTER 15

© Classic Vision/age fotostock/age fotostock

End-of-Life Care

"It hath been often said that it is not death, but dying which is terrible."

—**Henry Fielding** (1707–1754), English novelist and dramatist

LEARNING OBJECTIVES

After completing this chapter, the reader should be able to:

1. Understand the ethical principles underlying the question of whether human beings have a right to die at a time and place of their own choosing.
2. Explain the distinction between palliative sedation and physician-assisted dying.
3. Describe how hospice has been demonstrated to improve quality of life for patients with a terminal prognosis as well as for patients with an untreatable or physically debilitating disease.
4. Analyze the ethical principles surrounding the question of whether mature minors have the right to refuse life-sustaining treatment.

KEY TERMS

Advance directive
Artificial nutrition and hydration
Best interests standard
Bodily integrity
Controlled Substances Act of 1970 (CSA)
Dignified death
Donation after cardiac death
Double effect principle

Euthanasia
Hospice
Human dignity
Legally competent
Life-sustaining treatment
Mature minor
Mature minor doctrine
Medical futility
Non-hospice palliative care
Palliative care

Palliative sedation
Permanent vegetative state (PVS)
Personal autonomy
Physician-assisted dying
Substituted judgment standard
Terminal prognosis
Uniform Determination of Death Act of 1981

ETHICAL OR UNETHICAL DECISION

Defining Death

Ethics Issue: *Should brain-dead donors for heart transplant surgery be declared dead using the irreversible cardio-circulatory death definition if the hearts can be (and are) successfully restarted in the bodies of other recipients?*

In Brief: A medical team at Denver Children's Hospital performed 3 infant heart transplants in a clinical trial using hearts from infant donors who had suffered severe birth asphyxia and who were not technically brain-dead, but who had been removed from tube feeding, or **artificial nutrition and hydration**. The infants all experienced cardiac death within minutes after removal from life support, and organ procurement began within seconds of cardiac death. This was the first time heart transplants using donors who were not declared brain-dead were challenged. This practice is known as **donation after cardiac death**, but it was controversial in this instance - without the corresponding brain deaths - because prior to being removed from life support, the infants were not suffering an irreversible loss of cardiac function. The **Uniform Determination of Death Act of 1981** adopted by Colorado and most other states provides a comprehensive basis for defining death. Colorado's law states that individuals can be declared biologically dead if they have sustained irreversible cessation of either their circulatory and respiratory functions or of their entire brain.

— *Colorado Revised Statutes Annotated* § 12-36-136 (1981); *Uniform Determination of Death Act of 1981*, § 1, 12 U.L.A. 777 (Supp. 2008) (providing guidance as to the determination of death). (*See Ethical or Unethical Decision* at the end of the chapter for discussion of this ethics issue.)

Introduction

Ethical principles are needed to effectively respond to today's unprecedented and unforeseen medical advancements (Callahan, 2011). The personal decision regarding how and when to die is one of the most intimate choices a person may make in a lifetime. As illustrated in **FEATURE BOX 15-1**, during the past century, advances in health care have led to dramatic changes in the life expectancy and death processes of Americans (Critser, 2010). The ethics of health care have struggled to respond to this shifting paradigm of dying. That we die is certain; how we die is not.

Human Dignity and the Right to a Dignified Death

Human dignity and the right to a dignified death are two sides of the same coin (Smith, 2014). **Human dignity** suggests that every individual has the right to determine what self-respect means to them; thus, recognizing human dignity requires recognition of each individual's value and self-worth. The right to a **dignified death** includes the individual right to ask others to respect them and refrain from violating their human dignity; it is the idea that

---

Demographics of Death

While Americans live longer lives, many spend their last few years living with disabilities or chronic illnesses. Relatively few Americans die of acute causes or accidents anymore. Instead, most Americans die from lingering and often complex or combined illnesses that eventually prove fatal. Dementia and frailty shape the last years of life for a large part of the population. This increase in longevity is accompanied by the emergence of long-term, chronic disease as the major pattern of death. Unlike earlier times, most Americans will die slowly.

— Sources: Callahan, 2011; Kochanek, et al., 2014.

---

everyone has an individual right to control the time and manner of their own death and to be free from any unwanted medical intervention (*e.g.*, *Washington, et al. v. Glucksberg, et al.*, 521 U.S. 702 (U.S. Supreme Court 1997); *see also* Kübler-Ross & Byock, 1969/2014; Smith, 2011). The right to a dignified death is equivalent in expression to the right to refuse treatment when the refusal may hasten death. For instance, competent adults have a right to refuse to be connected to dialysis or respirators and to be disconnected from such artificial means, even if they cannot live without such mechanical assistance.

Challenges to the right to a dignified death generally focus on the concept of bodily integrity in need of protection (Miller, 2007). **Bodily integrity** is defined as the right to control one's body without restraint or interference from others. The notion of bodily integrity has its origin in informed consent for medical treatment (Paterick, 2008). The requirement of informed consent leads to the corollary that patients will protect the body and consent to treatment. Informed consent and its corollary rights often lead to conflicts between patients who want to be free from unwanted treatments and health care professionals and families who want them to accept treatment in order to prolong life.

Defining Hospice and Palliative Care

Hospice is not a place; rather, it is a philosophy of palliative care that provides pain management, symptom control, psychosocial support, and spiritual care to patients facing the end of their lives and their families. **Palliative care** is a specialized area of health care that focuses on relieving and preventing the pain and suffering of patients in all disease stages, including those undergoing treatment for curable and chronic diseases, as well as patients nearing the end of their lives (Faull & de Caestecker, 2012). In most cases, palliative care is provided in the patient's home, but care can also be given in freestanding centers, hospitals, nursing homes, and other long-term care facilities. While 3 out of every 4 Americans intend to use hospice to cope with the dying process, only 1 out of every 4 actually does so (NHPCO, 2010).

The term *hospice* is restricted by law to patients who have a **terminal prognosis** of 6 months or less to live and agree to forgo curative or life-prolonging treatments. The term *terminal prognosis* is a medical opinion as to the likely course of a disease or injury that cannot be cured or adequately treated and that is reasonably expected to result in death within a relatively short period of time, usually 6 months.

Non-hospice palliative care, which provides pain management, symptom control, psychosocial support, and spiritual care, is also appropriate for people who are living with serious and complex life-threatening illnesses but who are not facing imminent death. While the two terms, *hospice* and *non-hospice palliative care*, are often confused, this chapter focuses on hospice palliative care for patients who are facing death within 6 months or less. Non-hospice palliative care, as distinguished from hospice care, may be offered simultaneously with life-prolonging and curative therapies (Unroe & Meier, 2011). In essence, all care is palliative; health care is aimed at staving off pain and suffering, and cannot ultimately cure patients of their path to death at some time in the future (McGregor, 2013).

The Philosophy of Hospice Palliative Care

While the commercialization of hospice raises ethical concerns about the movement toward market-driven medicine at the end of life, American medicine has always been a commercial activity and has always presented various ethical problems (Perry & Stone, 2011). Notwithstanding this concern, much of the growth in the hospice industry has been driven by for-profit providers who selectively recruit patients from nursing homes (Pope, 2012). Yet the movement toward hospice is being stymied by the need to predict death within 6 months or less for basic coverage by insurers, particularly when medical technology holds out the promise of dying another day. Today, patients can forestall the moment of their deaths and mechanically preserve permanent unconsciousness with total dependence on intensive care and the use of mechanical devices, such as feeding tubes to provide artificial nutrition and hydration, dialysis, intravenous medications that maintain blood pressure, and mechanical ventilators and respirators.

When 3 of every 5 Americans with terminal prognoses, such as widely metastatic cancer or multi-organ system failure or sepsis, are dying in intensive and critical care settings and are reduced at the end of their existence to a childlike state of helplessness—diapered, sedated, and incontinent—as opposed to a dignified hospice setting, there is a systemic failure in meeting patients' needs and expectations to die naturally (Perry & Stone, 2011). Despite the high value that many Americans place on rational self-determination at the end of life, few actually have their end-of-life desires fulfilled (Nachman, 2011). There is a national disconnect when 75 percent of Americans indicate they want to die with human dignity in hospice, while 60 percent find themselves dying in hospitals (NHPCO, 2010). There is no indication that the 25 percent who do not want hospice care want to die naturally or of how they wish to die when faced with a terminal disease. For the 60 percent dying in hospitals but who indicated they wanted to die in hospice, it is presumed that they thought they would survive longer than their hospice benefits, which fund hospice care instead of curative treatment, would last (Thiess, 2010). In other words, health insurance requirements shaped the care received for 60 percent of the patients in the final stages of life who died in hospitals.

While hospice is gaining public acceptance, including acceptance by the insurance industry, its growth remains hampered by physicians who are reluctant to recommend hospice palliative care (Landro, 2010). Physicians are trained to do all they can to prolong life even where survival is rare, if not actually unprecedented (Smith, 2011). There is a fundamental, almost philosophical, conflict in the way physicians are trained to prolong life, often to the point of overtreatment, and the goals of hospice to offer a dignified death (Callahan, 2011; Wharton, 2006). A physician must concede that a patient's illness is terminal and that the patient will not recover before the patient can use hospice. Many physicians find that difficult to do (CMS, 2013). Advocates for hospice maintain that palliative care is primarily a compassionate way to make it easier for people to die (Bomba, 2011; Cerminara, 2011).

Personal Autonomy and Rational Self-Determination

While the principle of **personal autonomy** is a hallmark of hospice, the concept cannot be divorced from notions of interdependence and care for those who cannot be cured. When pain is unmanageable and unremitting, and suffering follows despite efforts to palliate patients' health condition, terminal sedation and the voluntary refusal of nutrition and hydration, are valid changes in the treatment plan and have the ultimate effect of enhancing patients' personal autonomy (Smith, 2011). One of the most basic values that supports and guides all health care decision-making is respecting the right to patient self-determination (Bollman, 2011). This value is rooted in respect for the right of patients to make independent decisions about their health care. Personal autonomy is also a general indicator of health. Many illnesses at the end of life are characterized by the loss of personal autonomy. This loss of personal autonomy has implications for the ethics of end-of-life care. End-of-life care should be linked to the ethical obligation to minimize pain, suffering, and indignity during the dying process, thereby respecting personal autonomy until death occurs naturally (Smith, 2011). At the same time, if patients want to endure unrelenting pain as they die based on a secular or religious perspective that death must not be hastened, these preferences must also be respected.

The Principle of Informed Consent

Hospice brings various ethical issues to the forefront. Informed consent for hospice is one of the most important concerns. **Advance directives** provide instructions about what health care actions should be taken in the event of the illness or incapacity of patients who are no longer able to make decisions. If patients are competent, or have signed an advance directive giving someone else the authority to make their medical decisions, the patients' wishes about their care at the end of their lives should be determined prior to admission to hospice (Casarett & Quill, 2007).

While the principle of informed consent favors a patient's right of preference, ethical issues arise when patients have no advance directive and are not **legally competent**, meaning they lack the capacity to make decisions. This also includes minors 17 years of age or less. Every hospice struggles with what to do with patients who, at the time of potential entry to hospice, lack the capacity to make end-of-life decisions (Callahan, 2011).

When making decisions about entry to hospice for patients who are dying and lack decision-making capacity and have no discernable preferences, the **best interests standard** is generally used (Kopelman, 2007). Under this standard, the care that will most likely promote patients' well-being at the end stages of life will be administered; it excludes, by definition, curative treatment that is futile and will only prolong the dying process (Webley, 2011). This standard sometimes includes no treatment except for hospice palliative care. While the presumption for the best interests standard is in favor of maintenance of life, because almost everyone wants to continue living, the standard is also the principle that extreme suffering is unacceptable, given nearly everyone's aversion to extreme pain (Webley, 2011).

ETHICAL DILEMMAS 15-1

1. Is it ethical to allow people to decide whether they should live or die, or does the ethic of preserving life outweigh a person's right to make that decision?

Hospice is not for the purpose of extending biological life for the longest time, but to offer comfort and pain control at the end of life (Cherny, et al., 2015).

The Ethics of Withdrawing Nutrition and Hydration

Prolonged life-sustaining treatments often impose undue burdens or serve as futile road-blocks to patients in the end-stage of life, thereby preventing as comfortable a death as possible (Smith, 2011). Accordingly, hospice programs have an ethical mandate to prevent pain and suffering; reasonable steps must be taken to relieve unremitting pain and unmanageable discomfort. While the advantages and disadvantages of withholding or withdrawing nutrition and hydration should be balanced with patients' rights to personal autonomy and rational self-determination at the end of life, the Terri Schiavo case illustrates what hospices face when they accept patients who cannot make their own end-of-life decisions.

The *Schiavo* case was one of the most bitter and protracted civil actions regarding palliative care ever in U.S. jurisprudence (Caplan, et al., 2006). The debate centered on the right to die in accordance with the true wishes of a patient. Family members simply disagreed about what the true wishes of Schiavo were and had differing levels of understanding about her health condition. One side was not allowed to make a decision to withdraw her artificial nutrition and hydration, while the other side was not allowed to make a decision to maintain nutrition and hydration. As it turned out, after Schiavo's cardiac arrest stopped her heart and killed her brain, she received life support and artificial nutrition and hydration for 15 years before she died. The *Schiavo ex rel. Schindler v. Schiavo* decision from the U.S. Court of Appeals for the Eleventh Circuit finally resolved this controversy.

ETHICS CASE
Discontinuance of Life-Sustaining Treatment

Schiavo ex rel. Schindler v. Schiavo
[Parents of Daughter v. Hospice and Husband/Son-in-Law]
403 F.3d 1289 (U.S. Court of Appeals for the 11th Circuit 2005),
rehearing denied, 404 F.3d 1223 (U.S. Court of Appeals for the 11th Circuit 2005)

Facts: This is the highly publicized court battle between Terri Schiavo's parents and her husband and legal guardian regarding the removal of feeding tubes. A young woman, Schiavo did not have an advance directive when she fell into a **permanent vegetative state** (PVS), after collapsing and suffering cardiac arrest at the age of 26. Schiavo's husband claimed that his wife would have refused feeding tubes to provide artificial nutrition and hydration, while her parents, the Schindlers, claimed their daughter would have wanted treatment continued.

PVS is a disorder of consciousness in which patients with severe brain damage have cycles of apparent wakefulness and apparent sleep without any cognition or awareness. As Schiavo breathed, she often moaned, and her hands, elbows, knees, and feet were severely contracted. Over the span of 15 years, her brain deteriorated to the point where CAT scans showed that most of her cerebral cortex was gone and had been replaced by cerebral spinal fluid.

Legal Analysis: The court addressed each of the counts of the parents' complaint. The first count claimed that Schiavo's husband was acting in violation of federal disability laws. The court found that Schiavo's husband was neither a public entity nor a public accommodation, nor was he acting under color of state law, as required for this claim under federal law to proceed.

The second count claimed that hospice care violated federal disability laws by denying Schiavo treatment on the basis of her disability. Turning to the claim against the hospice providers, the court noted that if hospice were a place of public accommodation, the withholding of nutrition and hydration was not done on the basis of Schiavo's disability, but in compliance with a valid court order. The court further observed that federal disability law was never intended to provide an avenue for challenging judicial orders in termination-of-care cases. The court found that the case was not within the scope of disability laws because Schiavo would not have had any need for a feeding tube to deliver nutrition and hydration but for her health condition. The court noted that disability laws were not meant to deal with end-of-life medical treatment.

The third count claimed that an incapacitated patient's wishes must be clearly proven prior to admission to hospice and termination of **life-sustaining treatment** that forestalls the moment of the patient's death. The court found this argument to be without merit because the state courts did make this determination in this case. Stated differently, the requirement of clear proof does not guarantee a particular result.

Fourth, the court held that the count claiming cruel and unusual punishment was without merit. This constitutional provision applies only to punishments inflicted after conviction for crimes, not to life support or medical treatment decisions.

The fifth and final count was that hospice harmed Schiavo and deprived her of her due process rights by not providing artificial nutrition and hydration against her wishes. However, the court noted that hospice's refusal to provide artificial nutrition and hydration was not about due process, since eight years of litigation was enough to ensure that Schiavo's rights were respected in accordance with her due process rights. The court noted that due process does not require a state to protect its citizens against injury by non-state actors; therefore, since neither the husband nor the hospice providers were state actors, the claim of violation of due process was also without merit.

Rule of Law: Palliative care does not violate federal disability laws, nor is it considered cruel and unusual punishment.

Ethics Issues: Should hospices withhold artificial nutrition and hydration from PVS patients? If so, what ethical principles should influence decisions to withhold life-sustaining treatment and accept incapacitated patients to hospice, especially severely brain-damaged patients who have already had their artificial nutrition and hydration withdrawn?

Ethics Analysis: This case was really about the ethics of whether the lives of PVS patients should be preserved at all costs. The ethical issue is when and how decisions should be made to end medical treatment at the end of life, and whether those decisions should be made at all. Society, most health care ethicists, and courts and legislatures have decided that people should largely determine for themselves what medical treatments they receive. This freedom to determine treatment means people may also refuse treatment if they wish, even if such refusal hastens their death.

Complications arise when patients lack the capacity to make end-of-life decisions. This situation arises most harshly in cases of PVS patients who lack the mental capacity to make decisions, but it also arises where patients suffer from various forms of dementia, severe mental illness, and in situations where the disease itself interferes with mental capacity, such as with Lou Gehrig's disease,

Parkinson's disease, or Huntington's disease. Debate centers on whether anyone should presume that incapacitated, terminally ill patients either refuse or consent to life-sustaining treatment, and if so, whether this principle should extend to artificial nutrition and hydration. Some advocate creating no presumptions as to patient intent for end-of-life care and letting incapacitated patients die naturally without any medical interventions. Nevertheless, the most ethical action must be chosen. Choices of immediate life and death are often involved where decisions not to choose artificial nutrition and hydration are considered a failure to meet one's ethical obligations to patients with a terminal prognosis who may want to be kept alive with life-sustaining treatments.

Court's Holding and Decision: Withholding artificial nutrition and hydration was proper where the parents of a severely brain-damaged patient sought to restore feeding tubes that had been removed in compliance with a court order following eight years of litigation.

See, e.g., Jacobson & Mathur, 2010; Webley, 2011 (discussing this court decision).

The Right to Refuse Life-Sustaining Treatment

In order to understand the controversy about withdrawing nutrition and hydration, it is crucial to further define *life-sustaining treatment*. By definition, life-sustaining treatment can only sustain life (Pope & Anderson, 2011). It cannot save a life or improve a health condition. This is a crucial distinction because such treatment at the end of life can, at best, only prolong a slow deterioration to an inevitable and predictable death (Smith, 2011). Its potential benefit can only be measured in relation to personal values (Gordy, 2011). The right to be free from unwanted medical intervention is the right to evaluate the potential benefits and consequences of treatment and to make a personal decision whether to subject oneself to bodily intrusion (Levine & Wolf, 2012). The decision to accept or refuse life-sustaining treatment affects not only the time of one's death, but also the manner in which death occurs (Smith, 2011). Thus, denying a person the autonomy to refuse life-sustaining treatment is the same as denying them the right to decide whether the biological prolongation of life, as it transforms into a prolongation of death, is worth the burdens that one will have to endure.

ETHICAL DILEMMAS 15-2

2. What ethical principles should guide decisions about continuing palliative care for patients who are in a PVS, or suffer from various forms of dementia, or are in situations where curative treatment itself interferes with mental capacity?
3. Should protection of patient populations who cannot protect themselves be paramount, or should the principle of informed consent serve patient populations who are too cognitively impaired to make decisions about end-of-life care?

ETHICAL DILEMMAS 15-3

4. Should human rights inherent to the right to a dignified death, including the
    right to refuse medical intervention or the right to use hospice to ease pain
    and increase comfort level, be limited at the end of life?

Difficulties in Defining Medical Futility

Considering medical technology's ability to prolong near-death life, economic factors are considered in withholding or withdrawing aggressive curative treatment if end-of-life decisions are not guided by ethical reasoning (Perry, 2010). One could argue that if it were possible to make relatively accurate judgments about when an illness is terminal, hospice should be provided as opposed to futile curative treatments (Schuck, 2010).

If patients are terminally ill, it is debatable whether measures to prolong their lives for only a short and often painful period of time are ethical. Given the medical (and sometimes familial) culture of trying to save patients no matter what, hospice is a way to signal that a patient is ready to let go as opposed to continuing treatments that have a small probability of success and can cause excessive pain and suffering (Solomon, 2010). For instance, a meta-analysis of more than 95,000 cases of cardiopulmonary resuscitation (CPR) found that only 8 percent of patients survived for more than 1 month; of these, only about 3 percent could lead a mostly normal life (Ebell & Afonso, 2011).

It is undecided whether the use of curative treatment deprives patients of their fundamental rights to human dignity and humane health care. On one side of this debate are those who maintain that keeping the terminally ill alive by extraordinary medical means may be tantamount to torture that degrades the person's dignity (Tucker, 2011). On the other side are those who maintain that all life is worth preserving no matter the personal cost or the cost to society (Lim, 2015).

Today, the advent of new life-sustaining treatments has made it more difficult than ever for physicians to resist attempting to save patients with a terminal prognosis (Wharton, 2006). Advanced medical technologies, including dialysis, artificial nutrition and hydration through a surgically inserted tube in the stomach, intravenous medications that maintain blood pressure, and mechanical ventilators and respirators, can often forestall the moment of death. Because the medical technology exists, it tends to be used (Smith, 2014).

Medical futility, however, may be a legitimate reason for withholding or withdrawing curative care that will not affect the patient's prognosis but will inflict severe pain (Smith, 2011). Continued curative care is medically futile when medical treatment fails to end dependence on intensive care or preserves permanent unconsciousness; physicians may have an ethical obligation to shift to palliative care as opposed to continuing life-sustaining treatment once it becomes futile (Smith, 2014).

Medical management of the dying process has been a reality at least since the 1950s, when medicine developed the technologies to extend life beyond the point most patients wish to live (Goodwin, 2009). Despite the popular misconception that people try everything when faced with death, patients and their families generally accept death when the time actually arrives (Kübler-Ross & Kessler, 1969/2014). Hospice patients are distinctly less likely to have surgery, hospitalization, resuscitation, or other technological interventions (CMS, 2015). Perhaps the growing interest in hospice versus high-technology

---

ETHICAL DILEMMAS 15-4

5. Should patients and their families be required to pay for medically unnecessary and futile care when such treatment is contrary to the prevailing standard of health care, and should this determination be made by the insurance industry, the government, a patient's medical team, or some combination thereof?

6. If the medical team decides what the standard of care should be, what should occur if everyone does not agree that curative care is futile? Does this question come down to the fundamental ethics of what constitutes a human life worth saving?

---

curative care for an additional few weeks of living with a terminal or life-threatening illness may demonstrate a growing recognition and a return to the acknowledgment that death is part of life and should not to be resisted at every turn by modern medicine (Waldman, 2014).

Despite the fact that medically futile care is not the most compassionate care, some patients and their families still want to do everything possible to prolong life (Shore, 2007). While **medical futility** has generally been defined as treatment that fails to end total dependence on intensive health care (Nachman, 2011), there is no consensus as to what this means in practice. There is no generally agreed-upon definition of what constitutes medical futility or what ethical principles should define this treatment concept. Debate about this concept will continue until a social consensus is reached about what treatments are clearly physiologically and psychologically useless as opposed to treatments where there are simple differences of opinion about how worthwhile a particular intervention is.

Palliative Sedation: Continuation of Palliative Care

As illustrated in **FEATURE BOX 15-2**, **palliative sedation** is defined as the induction of an unconscious state through the use of an opioid infusion or morphine drip to relieve otherwise intractable suffering, and is frequently accompanied by the withdrawal of any life-sustaining means. When less aggressive means fail for patients suffering from severe pain, dyspnea (difficulty in breathing), or other debilitating deterioration resistant to treatment, palliative sedation becomes an option (VHA, 2007). In terms of ethicality, palliative sedation is a similar type of option as withholding or withdrawal of life-sustaining treatment; both are means of accelerating the dying process and enabling a dignified death (Pope & Anderson, 2011). Regardless of whether the decision to withhold or withdraw life-sustaining treatment occurs at the same time as the decision to sedate or the decision to sedate is made separately, once patients exercise their prerogative to withhold or withdraw life-sustaining treatment, there is an ethical obligation to minimize suffering (Pope & Anderson, 2011). At the end-stage of life, the ethics of adjusted care require recognition of the fundamental right to avoid cruel and unusual suffering from terminal illness (Smith, 2011).

FEATURE BOX 15-2

Benefits of Palliative Sedation

- Compassionately alleviates physical discomfort and pain
- Produces an unconscious state before the withdrawal of nutrition and hydration
- Relieves non-physical suffering
- Changes the timing of death in only a minor way

— Sources: *Washington, et al. v. Glucksberg, et al.*, 521 U.S. 702 (U.S. Supreme Court 1997); *Vacco, et al. v. Quill, et al.*, 521 U.S. 793 (U.S. Supreme Court 1997); Smith, 2011; Tucker, 2008.

Most terminally ill patients reach a point where the goal of their care changes from prolonging life to maximizing the quality of remaining life (VHA, 2007). Palliative sedation is a routine continuation of palliative care enabling competent patients with advanced terminal diseases to maintain a sense of self-direction and human dignity in their final days and hours. Continued intimate involvement of the patient's medical team in each of the stages of death is central to palliative care. When palliative sedation is viewed as a continuum of effective health care, it grants control to patients under the principles of respect for personal autonomy and rational self-determination (Griffiths, et al., 2008).

Rational self-determination affects end-of-life decisions. Most terminally ill patients, faced with the prospect of a painful and debilitating death, choose to finish their lives in a peaceful and dignified manner (Tucker, 2008). Hospice and other patient studies report that the average time from palliative sedation to natural death is between 7 and 10 days (Bailey, et al., 2015). Palliative sedation gives patients power over death in a socially approved way (Tucker, 2008); it reflects human compassion and mercy by families and health care providers in a major way (Smith, 2011).

The Ethical Principles of Informed Consent and Double Effect

The compassionate administration of life-shortening analgesics in palliative care is considered to be an ethical act (Pope & Anderson, 2011; Smith, 2011). In other words, medications that hasten death may be compassionately administered so long as the intent is solely to relieve suffering and debilitating symptoms (Smith, 2011). This is what differentiates it from euthanasia. This **double effect principle**, that the good effect of relief from suffering and debilitating symptoms is intended, despite the fact that death is foreseen, is a legitimate line of ethical reasoning (Quill, 2012; Pope & Anderson, 2011). The double effect could be illustrated by the familiar analogy of ordering dinner at a fashionable restaurant: when diners do not intend to order the most expensive item on the menu, but they order their favorite surf-and-turf dish consisting of lobster tail and filet mignon, their selection is one and the same thing. Arbitrarily selecting the most expensive item on the menu is unacceptable; ordering a favorite meal, however, is acceptable. The actions are the same; the intent is different. In this instance, when medications are not intended to hasten death, but do hasten death, the actions are one and the same although the intent is entirely different. Administering the medications to hasten death is unacceptable; administering the same medications to relieve intractable suffering is acceptable even though they may somewhat hasten death.

By definition, under certain circumstances, it is permissible to unintentionally cause harm that would not be permissible to cause intentionally. In this instance, relieving a terminally ill patient's pain may also hasten the patient's death, an effect one would normally be obliged to avoid. Palliative sedation is justified by the principles of informed consent and double effect as an alternative to what otherwise could be a prolonged, painful, and graceless death (Tucker, 2008). When terminally ill patients request analgesics to relieve pain with full knowledge that the medications will shorten their lives, the foreseen harmful effects of death are inseparable from the good effect of relieving pain. The act of prescribing pain analgesics is ethical or at least ethically neutral; the prescriber intends to relieve patients' chronic or intractable pain and not cause their death. The relief from severe suffering, the cause of which cannot be removed or otherwise treated, and no relief or cure can be found, outweighs the risk of imminent death in terminally ill patients (Bailey, et al., 2015).

Consequences that would be wrong if caused intentionally become acceptable (in this instance, the death of a terminally ill patient), even when foreseen, if the actions creating those consequences (relieving the pain and suffering of a terminally ill patient) are intended for a permissible purpose, as illustrated in **FEATURE BOX 15-3**. Critics of the double effect principle maintain that when a result is foreseen as certain, it is the same as if it were desired or intended (Lyons, 2005). If opioid infusions and morphine drips are generally fatal for terminally ill patients, then prescribing this pain relief is the same as intentionally causing a patient's death, the argument goes.

Intractable Pain and Severe Suffering

Regrettably, the emphasis against intentionally causing death encourages health care professionals to be overly apprehensive about providing appropriate palliative care. This apprehension often leads to conflicts between prescribers and patients when patients wish to withdraw nutrition and hydration, a patient request that physicians often ignore (Stern & DiFonzo, 2007). Another risk is that pain medications are often under prescribed (Gray, 2010; Hardjasa, 2008). Up to 50 percent of terminal patients die in severe pain (Pope, 2011); in other words, every year 1.3 million patients die while suffering intractable pain (NCHS, 2015).

FEATURE BOX 15-3

Principle of Double Effect

Reliance on the principle of double effect generally requires four conditions:

- Act creating the risk of adverse consequences should be good, or at least ethically neutral
- Actor should intend the good effect and not the bad effect, although the bad effect may be foreseen
- Bad effect should not be a means to the good effect

— Sources: *Washington, et al. v. Glucksberg, et al.*, 521 U.S. 702 (U.S. Supreme Court 1997); *Vacco, et al. v. Quill, et al.*, 521 U.S. 793 (U.S. Supreme Court 1997); Lyons, 2005.

The alternatives to the informed consent and double effect principles are to accept the intent to cause death, or forbid conduct with the foreseeable effect of not prolonging life. The former alternative directly contradicts the law of almost every state, and the latter alternative leaves some patients (those who are incapacitated before sedation, yet who have previously clearly stated their desire to not prolong their lives at some point) without the ability to obtain palliative sedation.

Even with excellent pain and symptom management, nearly 430,000 dying patients will face a dying process so prolonged and marked by such extreme suffering and debilitating deterioration that palliative sedation is the best alternative (Stern & DiFonzo, 2007; Tucker, 2008). Thus, palliative sedation might be the most ethical option for relieving severe and continuing pain. In other words, competent terminally ill patients have the right to choose a dignified and humane death as opposed to being reduced at the end of their existence to a state of tortured helplessness (Pope & Anderson, 2011; Tucker, 2012).

The Ethics of Palliative Sedation

The palliative sedation debate is often confused by focusing on whether sedation constitutes **euthanasia**, the intentional causing of death (Secara, 2011). There is a range of opinions, ranging from those inflexibly opposed to palliative sedation to advocates of the practice. Some opponents of palliative sedation compare it to euthanasia, viewing the induction of unconsciousness and the withdrawal or withholding of life-sustaining intervention as continuous acts that cause death.

Combining the induction of unconsciousness with the withdrawal of life-sustaining measures, however, confuses the ethical issues raised by palliative sedation. The induction of unconsciousness and the withdrawal of life-sustaining medical interventions are two separate acts supported by two different ethical principles. The induction of unconsciousness builds upon the long-standing and accepted ethics of palliative care (Bailey, et al., 2015); the withdrawal of life-sustaining interventions relies upon the principle of personal autonomy in competent adults (Pope & Anderson, 2011; Tucker, 2012). Despite the U.S. Supreme Court's endorsement of palliative sedation in *Washington, et al. v. Glucksberg, et al.*, 521 U.S. 702 (U.S. Supreme Court 1997) and *Vacco, et al. v. Quill, et al.*, 521 U.S. 793 (U.S. Supreme Court 1997), the debate about its ethicality continues.

Most Americans, including physicians, support palliative sedation (Pew, 2006; Smith, 2014), yet some oppose hastening death. The American Medical Association views palliative sedation as a medically proper way to assure a modicum of human dignity at death. It is a form of patient affirmation of human existence and self-esteem when properly understood (Tucker, 2008). Proponents of palliative sedation maintain that the practice is best understood as a continuum of palliative care to which everyone should be entitled; it validates personal autonomy and rational self-determination (Battin, et al., 2008).

Justification for Palliative Sedation

Ethically speaking, palliative sedation is justifiable palliative care. As long as the compassionate intent is not to cause death, death is a justifiable possibility in palliative care. Under the double effect principle, one may not justify an intended harm with good consequences, but one may justify, with such good consequences, a harm that is only foreseen (Ferzan, 2008).

The principle of double effect guides the provision of palliative care; it is not some fabrication to shield the truth, but rather a highly useful ethical construct guiding care at the bedside (Tucker, 2012). Of course, licensed prescribers know that the use of an opioid infusion, morphine drip, or other interventions may shorten life in those imminently dying. Under Justice Holmes's approach to the law, law is not a science founded on abstract legal or ethical principles but a body of practices that responds to particular situations. This theme is announced in the famous quote at the beginning of his first lecture on the common law: "the life of the law has not been logic; it has been experience" (Holmes, 1881/2015).

The debate over palliative sedation revolves largely around the validity of the double effect principle as a viable ethical construct. Opponents tend to view palliative sedation as one continuous act (Pew, 2006). Supporters, in contrast, view palliative sedation as an extension of sound palliative care, fully justified by the double effect principle and the doctrine of informed consent. Logic and experience need not always be different in end-of-life debates. In other words, end-of-life palliative care is not scientific logic; it is a compassionate continuum of care in the real world of clinical medicine. Palliative sedation is the logical response to cruel death experiences (Smith, 2011), a practical strategy that is not blind to the advanced medical technologies of today (Pope & Anderson, 2011; Stern & DiFonzo, 2007).

End-of-life palliative care is challenging, presenting the potential for clinical ambiguities. Health care professionals often struggle with the conflicting imperatives they face. But struggling with concerns about hastened death is not the same as inaction. Palliative sedation is a topic almost everyone will eventually have to confront, because nearly everyone either faces a terminal illness themselves or has a family member, friend, or significant other who eventually will (Pope & Anderson, 2011). The alternative is the arguably inhumane undertreatment of pain and suffering.

Opposition to Palliative Sedation

Opponents of palliative sedation often focus on its comparison to euthanasia. Unfortunately, anecdotal evidence indicates that health care professionals are not always informing patients about their end-of-life options, including palliative sedation (Curlin, et al., 2007). As a result, patients are not always given the opportunity to make fully informed decisions at the end of their lives.

Opponents of palliative sedation refuse to distinguish between withdrawal of medical treatment and euthanasia, the actual killing of patients. Opponents argue that the process of withholding nutrition and hydration to induce unconsciousness actively and intentionally causes death (compared to the intent to order the most expensive item on the menu); as opposed to sedation that causes unconsciousness when patients cannot eat or drink (compared to the intent to order a (pricey) favorite meal) (Nunziato, 2010; Quill, 2012). This refusal to legitimize the underlying compassionate intent in palliative care is like the failure to distinguish between conduct that is intentionally criminal and merely irresponsible conduct that results in unintended harm (Nunziato, 2010).

In addition, opponents do not distinguish between death from palliative sedation and death resulting from the withdrawal of nutrition and hydration without the induction of unconsciousness. Opponents of palliative sedation claim that the induced state of unconsciousness is responsible for the inability to eat and drink (Parker, 2015). Proponents, in contrast, claim that the inability to eat and drink is a result of the underlying disease (Tucker, 2014).

Opponents of palliative sedation also reject the doctrine of double effect (Smith, 2011). They maintain that because the doctrine of double effect justifies hastened death, it justifies only sedation; the withdrawal of nutrition and hydration does nothing to relieve pain and suffering, but serves only to bring about death. In other words, opponents of palliative sedation would prefer to have unconscious patients indefinitely connected to feeding tubes and other artificial means of prolonging human existence, even when patients cannot exist without such mechanical assistance (Perlmutter, 2011). In contrast, proponents claim that the withdrawing of life-sustaining treatment is premised on the doctrine of informed consent (Pope & Anderson, 2011; Smith, 2011). Thus, while opponents' view of palliative sedation as a single act is not unreasonable, it does not incorporate the principle of personal autonomy and patients' free will to rationally choose to be free of intolerable pain and suffering. Whether palliative sedation is an alternative to assisted dying is a separate issue from whether it is an ethical and appropriate continuation of palliative care (Smith, 2011).

Physician-Assisted Dying

Physician-assisted dying has emerged as one of the most controversial cultural issues in the United States, with Americans almost evenly divided over whether it is ethically acceptable or ethically wrong (Saad, 2011). The action is best defined as the ending of one's life through the voluntary self-administration of lethal medications prescribed by a physician for that purpose (Secara, 2011). Although the unease about assisted dying has been tempered by a greater focus on palliative care to manage the treatment of patients with terminal or life-threatening illnesses, recent developments regarding end-of-life issues may indicate that closer attention will be paid to palliative care (Reynolds, 2014).

There is no real consensus on whether the requirement for a terminal prognosis should be eliminated from physician-assisted dying laws and life-threatening and chronic illnesses added. At the center of this intersection is the discussion on the right to a dignified death. Assisted dying permits patients to actively choose to end their lives before their disease would most likely do so (Tucker, 2011).

ETHICS CASE
Physician-Assisted Dying

Gonzales, et al. v. Oregon, et al.
[U.S. Attorney General v. State of Oregon]
546 U.S. 243 (U.S. Supreme Court 2006)

Facts: Voters approved a ballot initiative making Oregon the first state in the nation to legalize physician-assisted dying. Three years later, voters affirmed the measure. The Oregon Death with Dignity Act of 1997 exempts licensed prescribers who, in compliance with specific safeguards, prescribe a lethal dose of medications upon the request of patients with a terminal prognosis, from civil or criminal liability. The law requires that patients seeking clinical assistance in dying receive a diagnosis that they suffer from an incurable and irreversible disease that, within reasonable medical judgment, will cause death within 6 months. They must also have 2 separate physicians review their request in order to determine that it was made voluntarily and the decision was informed, and that they are not simply suffering from depression.

The Oregon law, however, encountered resistance from the U.S. Department of Justice (DOJ). The controlled substances used during assisted dying are federally regulated under a law whose main objective is combating drug abuse. Controlled substances used in assisted dying require that patients receive a written, non-refillable prescription before gaining access to life-shortening analgesic medications.

The DOJ grants licensed prescribers a registration so that controlled substances can be lawfully prescribed. Federal law also provides that the DOJ may deny, suspend, or revoke this registration if prescriber registrations are inconsistent with the public interest. Federal regulation requires that prescribers issue prescriptions for a legitimate medical purpose. The DOJ issued an interpretive rule declaring that the use of controlled substances in assisted dying was not legitimate health care, thus making such prescriptions under the Oregon law a federal offense. This interpretive rule, making access to life-shortening analgesic medications a non-legitimate medical practice, was termed "the Ashcroft rule," since it was issued under Attorney General Ashcroft, who served in the second Bush Administration.

Accordingly, anyone who prescribed a lethal dose of a controlled substance under the Oregon law would render their prescribing registration inconsistent with the public interest and could have their registration suspended or revoked. Because prescribers could not prescribe medications without a registration, this ruling effectively blocked assisted dying. The state of Oregon, along with a physician, a pharmacist, and several patients with terminal prognoses, sought to prevent enforcement of the DOJ ruling.

Legal Analysis: The Court held that an interpretive rule by the DOJ, which declared that the use of life-shortening analgesic medications in assisted dying was not for a legitimate medical purpose, was not entitled to the deference to which interpretive rules are generally entitled. The Ashcroft rule would have made prescription of the medications used in assisted dying under Oregon law a criminal offense under the federal **Controlled Substances Act of 1970 (CSA)**. Interpretive rules may receive substantial deference if they interpret an issuing agency's ambiguous regulation. Unlike regulations that give specificity to laws and reflect the expertise of the agency interpreting the regulations, the Ashcroft rule merely restated the terms of the CSA. The DOJ does not acquire special authority to interpret the CSA when, instead of using its expertise to formulate a regulation, it merely paraphrases the law.

The Court also held that the Ashcroft rule was not entitled to deference as an interpretation of an ambiguous law. The Court held that the term "legitimate medical purpose" was indeed ambiguous and that the DOJ did not have the authority to declare state laws illegitimate on that basis, because state law sets medical standards for patient care and treatment. According to the Court, the Ashcroft rule was an interpretation of the CSA requirements for valid prescriptions and went well beyond the DOJ's power. In addition, the Court held that the DOJ was not entitled to define state standards of health care, as it did in promulgating the Ashcroft rule.

After finding that the Ashcroft rule did not deserve deference, the Court held that the DOJ's interpretation of the CSA was not persuasive. The Court found that Congress intended to regulate the care given by physicians insofar as it barred physicians from using their prescription-writing powers as a means to engage in illicit dealing of prescribed medications and trafficking, but not to regulate medicine generally. The law presumed that the regulation of medicine was otherwise a function of state police powers. In addition, the CSA included a provision stating that it should not be construed as congressional intent to occupy the medical field to the exclusion of the authority of any state. In the Court's analysis, the treatment regimen under Oregon law was precisely the type of state regulation the law had presupposed not to regulate. In the face of CSA's silence on palliative care and its recognition of state regulation of the medical profession, the Court found it difficult to defend the DOJ's declaration that the CSA criminalized state-sanctioned assisted dying.

The Court went on to address the DOJ's claim that an interpretation of what constituted "legitimate medical purpose" was required. The DOJ argued that "legitimate medical purpose" refers to a healing art and cannot embrace the intentional causing of a patient's death. The Court, however, rejected the argument that the CSA's prescription requirement allowed the DOJ to ban the prescribing of controlled substances for state-sanctioned assisted dying. While the Court recognized that the DOJ's interpretation was reasonable, it held that the CSA undermined any assertion of an expansive federal authority to regulate medicine in the states.

Rule of Law: The regulation of licensed prescribing has traditionally been under the states' power; the federal government lacks the authority to prohibit physicians from prescribing lethal doses of certain medications under the CSA.

Ethics Issue: Is physician-assisted dying ethical or unethical?

Ethics Analysis: One of the primary reasons to ban physician-assisted dying is the compelling interest in preserving human life. The U.S. Supreme Court cited 3 ethical principles that either are not violated or do not apply to physician-assisted dying in its analysis. First, the interest in preserving human life is the most compelling of all interests; all other interests assume the preservation of human life. Second, there is no right to coerce physicians to administer lethal medications to patients; therefore there can be no absolute right to physician-assisted dying. Third, while patients have a protected interest in their own personal autonomy, including the rational right to determine whether they want to refuse unwanted medical treatment, the principles of personal autonomy and the rational right to self-determination give way to the interest in preserving human life.

Because the Court upheld the right to physician-assisted dying, the ethical principle of personal autonomy was recognized. This implies a different outcome where personal autonomy may be violated with no plausible interest in preserving life. Whatever the interest in preserving life, it is diminished in the case of deeply comatose patients whose lives of permanent unconsciousness are being preserved mechanically or terminally ill patients who are totally dependent on intensive care; death is being prolonged, not life.

Court's Holding and Decision: No, the federal government cannot ban the use of medications for assisted dying in this manner.

See, e.g., Copeland, 2012; Donley, 2013 (discussing this court decision).

More Compassionate Palliative Care

One of the unexpected, yet undeniable, consequences of permitting physician-assisted dying is that many improvements in palliative care have occurred following implementation of physician-assisted dying legislation (Tucker, 2008). As opposed to states becoming the brutal slaughterhouse for unfortunate patients as some opponents predicted, the states that permit physician-assisted dying have become national leaders in providing compassionate palliative care and sedation (Schneiderman, 2005). They have helped the nation create medical environments where end-of-life issues can be openly discussed (GAO, 2007).

In turn, specialists in palliative care have developed guidelines for the pharmacological management of intractable symptoms in dying patients, including sedation for those near death (VHA, 2007). As illustrated in **FEATURE BOX 15-4**, palliative sedation is more likely to alleviate concerns if safeguards exist to address opponents' concerns (Warnock & Macdonald, 2009).

Mature Minor Rights to Refuse Life-Sustaining Treatment

While mature minors have the decision-making capacity to make health care decisions and have the right to refuse life-sustaining treatment without prior parental consent, this right

FEATURE BOX 15-4

Safeguards for Palliative Sedation

- Requirements for at least 2 medical opinions by physicians on the need for palliative sedation
- Rigorous informed consent
- Room for conscientious objection by health care providers and pharmacists, while still maintaining safeguards to protect patients' rights and health
- Strict documentation and review of diagnostic and prognostic actions
- Mental health evaluations to ensure that patients' decisions are not guided by depression
- Time delays between requests for palliative sedation and the actual sedation

— Sources: Quill, 2012; Warnock & Macdonald, 2009.

is not exclusive. By definition, a **mature minor** is any child, generally an adolescent, who has decision-making capacity to make health care decisions. Mature minor rights must be balanced against parental interests in the minor child's health choices. When there is a controversy between mature minors and their parents, the state's interest in preserving life often has a role in this decision-making.

Emerging Exception to Parental Autonomy

As a rule, only parents or guardians can grant or decline permission for medical treatment of their minor children (AAP, 2007). The exception is that a state may seek to override parental choices that jeopardize a child's health (Williams, 2011). The power of parents to make decisions regarding treatment of their children does not require any assessment of the child's level of maturity, nor does it allow for any degree of personal autonomy for the minor (Gordy, 2011). The emerging exception, however, is for mature minors (Hill, 2015).

Ethically speaking, there is no justification for a medical team to withhold individualized prognosis or treatment plan information from a mature minor. The consensus is that some minors have sufficient maturity to understand and appreciate the benefits and risks

ETHICAL DILEMMAS 15-5

7. Does the government have a fiscal obligation to pay for a mature minor's medical treatment of a life-threatening condition when a parent withholds consent to treatment that jeopardizes the minor's health?
8. In other words, if mature minors are allowed to make their own decisions regarding life-sustaining treatment, should they be exempt from the associated health care costs?

of proposed medical treatment of all kinds, and thus those mature minors should have the right to give or decline to give informed consent regarding all health care decisions (Laskin, et al., 2014). Since the 1960s, mature minors have had the same rights as adults with regard to informed consent.

The Rational Self-Determination of Mature Minors

The personal autonomy of minors is not unfettered freedom to exercise their wishes, but freedom to exercise wishes that are in their best interests (Iyioha & Akorede, 2010). Hence, the ethical principle of rational self-determination helps define the proper balance between the human rights of mature minors and parental rights when a minor requests protection of the government to withhold or withdraw life-sustaining treatment (Warshak, 2011). The **mature minor doctrine** extends the principle of personal autonomy to mature minors in recognition that the capacity for rational decision-making increases with age and life experience (Hill, 2015). There is no chronological age of consent for health care decision-making, but rather a prerequisite condition to consent, meaning the capacity for understanding (Hill, 2012).

Even though parents or guardians may authorize do-not-resuscitate (DNR) orders for minors, health care professionals should, from an ethical perspective, obtain the consent of mature minors before administering or withholding treatment. Professionals have an ethical obligation to find out whether minors are mature enough to consent to DNR orders and, by implication, other kinds of protocols before authorizing them (Gordy, 2011).

Withholding Life-Sustaining Treatment

The ethical issues raised by life-sustaining treatment of mature minors are significant and in many respects unresolved; indeed, this area of medical decision-making is sorely in need of analytic clarity (Hill, 2011). State interests may be greater than the interests of mature minors or their parents in refusing to consent to medical treatments if the risks or side effects are medically negligible (such as is often the case when refusing blood transfusions for religious reasons). In these situations, parents who support their child's right to refuse life-sustaining treatment risk being charged with neglect if death results from the minor's refusal of treatment. Still, mature minors have a right to consent to or refuse medical treatment. Like adults, mature minors enjoy the right to treatment according to their wishes as opposed to their best interests. Minors capable of rational self-determination may grant or deny assent to treatment regardless of whether parents or guardians provide consent (Hill, 2012).

Since most states do not have absolute age barriers prohibiting minors from consenting to medical treatment, age is not a barrier that necessarily precludes minors from exercising medical rights normally associated with adulthood (Gordy, 2011). Thus, mature minors may refuse medical treatment, even if this refusal results in their death. The mature minor doctrine, however, is not absolute; as with adults, the right to refuse life-sustaining treatment must be balanced against state interests, as illustrated in **FEATURE BOX 15-5**.

The most significant interest is the preservation of life, which is particularly compelling when dealing with minors. If parents or guardians oppose a mature minor's refusal to consent to life-sustaining treatment, this opposition weighs heavily against the minor's right to refuse.

FEATURE BOX 15-5

Balancing the Right to Refuse Life-Sustaining Treatment Against Legitimate Interests of the State

- Maintaining the ethical integrity of health care professionals
- Preserving human life
- Preventing suicides or euthanasia
- Protecting the interests of vulnerable parties from coercion and abuse

— Source: *Vacco, et al. v. Quill, et al.*, 521 U.S. 793 (U.S. Supreme Court 1997).

ETHICAL DILEMMAS 15-6

9. Should mature minors have the sole right to refuse relatively minor medical procedures, such as life-saving blood transfusions, based on sincerely held religious beliefs, or should the parents, medical team, and state, or some combination thereof, have veto power in this decision?

Withdrawal of Life-Sustaining Treatment

When deciding whether to withdraw life-sustaining treatment, the best interest of minors is given priority, as opposed to the substituted judgment standard that applies to adults. A **substituted judgment standard** permits a surrogate to make a decision regarding care based on what a reasonable adult would have chosen had he or she been competent (Hartman, 2012).

Confronting the End of Life

While a social consensus on what constitutes death is unclear, most agree that death involving considerable prolonged pain and impairment of capacities is always the least desirable option. As Hungarian author Arthur Koestler (1905–1983) stated in his essay *Dialogue with Death*, "Most of us were not afraid of death, only of the act of dying; and there were times when we overcame even this fear. At such moments we were free . . . it was the most complete experience of freedom that can be granted a man" (Koestler, 2013).

As stated at the beginning of this chapter, everyone is eventually forced to confront the end of life (Theiss, 2010). Although death cannot be avoided, not everyone agrees that the nation needs to step closer to becoming a society whose belief in personal autonomy and rational self-determination is manifested in opportunities for dying with human dignity (Nachman, 2011); some people instead want death to take its own course, regardless of the forms that death takes under modern medicine.

ETHICAL OR UNETHICAL DECISION

Defining Death

Ethics Issue: *Should brain-dead donors for heart transplant surgery be declared dead using the irreversible cardio-circulatory death definition if their hearts can be (and are) successfully restarted in the bodies of other recipients?*

Ethics Analysis: Yes, there is a need to increase the quality of organs for transplant by pronouncing death as soon as possible. There is no need to wait the standard 3 to 5 minutes after the cessation of both cardiac and respiratory functions to begin the organ retrieval process. Organs can therefore be removed after brain death occurs but before the heart stops, because the closer to life the donor is, the more useful the organs will be to the organ recipients.

Ethics Analysis: No, organs should not be removed from donors who are only mostly dead. Death should only be pronounced when there is no chance of recovery. The physicians in this instance caused the death of three infants who were not dead.

Statutory Law: To date, there has been no litigation and little discussion to decide whether brain death must occur before recognizing permission to remove organs for donation after cardiac death. There remains uncertainty about what it means to be dead and, however death is defined, whether death is a necessary condition for organ donation.

— *Colorado Revised Statute Annotated* § 12-36-136 (1981); *Uniform Determination of Death Act,* § 1, 12 U.L.A. 777 (Supp. 2008) (providing guidance as to the determination of death). *See, e.g.,* AAP, 2013; Cerutti, 2012; Gilman, 2012; Orenstein & Bettini, 2014; Pope, 2012; Robertson, 2013 (discussing this case).

CHAPTER SUMMARY

- Ethical principles are needed to respond effectively to today's unprecedented medical advancements, one of which is the ability to decide whether, how, and when to die with human dignity.
- There are serious economic and moral implications to the fact that the largest portion of health care costs are incurred during the last few weeks of a patient's life; there is a clear possibility that if end-of-life decisions are not guided by ethical reasoning, they will ultimately be made for economic ones.
- Hospice brings various ethical issues to the forefront, including informed consent for hospice; palliative sedation as justified by the principles of informed consent and double effect; and personal autonomy as supporting the refusal or withdrawal of life-sustaining care.
- Ethically speaking, palliative sedation is on the continuum of palliative care; as long as the compassionate intent is to relieve pain and not to cause death, the risk of death is justifiable in palliative care.

- While a denial of a mature minor's personal autonomy to refuse life-sustaining treatment is a denial of the right to decide whether the biological prolongation of life, as it transforms into a prolongation of death, is worth the burdens that will have to be endured, the ethical issues raised are significant and in many respects unresolved; indeed, this area of medical decision-making is sorely in need of analytic clarity.

REFERENCES

AAP (American Academy of Pediatrics). (2013). *Pediatric clinical practice guidelines & policies* (13th ed.). Media, PA: AAP.

AAP, Committee on Bioethics. (2007). Guidelines on forgoing life-sustaining treatment. *Pediatrics, 119*(2), 405.

Bailey, F. A., et al. (2015). *Palliative care: The last hours and days of life.* Philadelphia, PA: Wolters Kluwer.

Battin, M. P., et al. (2008). Physician-assisted dying and the slippery slope: The challenge of empirical evidence. *Willamette Law Review, 45*, 91–136.

Bollman, C. (2011). A dignified death? Don't forget about the physically disabled and those not terminally ill: An analysis of physician-assisted dying laws. *Southern Illinois University Law Journal, 34*, 395–415.

Bomba, P. (2011). Landmark legislation in New York affirms benefits of a two-step approach to advance care planning including MOLST [Medical Orders for Life-Sustaining Treatment]: A model of shared, informed medical decision-making and honoring patient preferences for care at the end of life. *Widener Law Review, 17*, 475–500.

Callahan, D. (2011). Palliative care: A philosophical or management problem? *Journal of Law, Medicine and Ethics, 39*, 114–120.

Caplan, A., et al. (Eds.). (2006). *The case of Terri Schiavo: Ethics at the end of life.* Amherst, NY: Prometheus Books.

Casarett, D. J., & Quill, T. E. (2007). I'm not ready for hospice: Strategies for timely and effective hospice discussions. *Annals of Internal Medicine, 146*, 443–449.

Cerminara, K. L. (2011). Hospice and health care reform: Improving care at the end of life. *Widener Law Review, 17*, 443–472.

Cerutti, C. A. (2012). Donation after cardiac death: Respecting patient autonomy and guaranteeing donation with guidance from Oregon's Death With Dignity Act. *Albany Law Review, 75*, 2199–2222.

Cherny, N., et al. (2015). *Oxford textbook of palliative medicine* (5th ed.). New York, NY: Oxford University Press.

CMS (Centers for Medicare and Medicaid Services). (2015). Coverage of palliative care under hospital insurance. In *Medicare benefit policy manual* (ch. 9, § 10). Washington, DC: U.S. Department of Health and Human Services, CMS.

___. (2013) *Hospice payment system.*

Copeland, C. C. (2012). FDR and Obama: Are there constitutional law lessons from the new deal for the Obama administration? Beyond separation in federalism enforcement: Medicaid expansion, coercion, and the norm of engagement. *University of Pennsylvania Journal of Constitutional Law, 15*, 91–182.

Critser, G. (2010). *Eternity soup: Inside the quest to end aging.* Boston, MA: Little, Brown.

Curlin, F. A., et al. (2007). Religion, conscience, and controversial clinical practices. *New England Journal of Medicine, 356*, 593–600.

Donley, G. (2013). Does the constitution protect abortions based on fetal anomaly? Examining the potential for disability-selective abortion bans in the age of prenatal whole genome sequencing. *Michigan Journal of Gender and Law, 20*, 291–328.

Ebell, M. H., & Afonso, A. M. (2011). Pre-arrest predictors of failure to survive after in-hospital cardiopulmonary resuscitation: A meta-analysis. *Family Practice, 28*(5), 505–515.

Faull, C., & de Caestecker, S. (2012). *Handbook of palliative care* (3rd ed.). Hoboken, NJ: Wiley-Blackwell.

Ferzan, K. K. (2008). Beyond intention. *Cardozo Law Review, 29*, 1147–1190.

Fielding, H. (1987). *Amelia.* New York, NY: Penguin Classics-Random House (Original work published 1923).

GAO (Government Accountability Office). (2007). *Palliative care: Key components provided by programs in four states.* Washington, DC: GAO.

Gilman, S. J. (2012). The use of anencephalic infants as an organ source: An on-going question. *Elon Law Review, 4*, 71–92.

Goodwin, M. (2009). Who owns your body? Expressive minimalism and fuzzy signals: The judiciary and the role of law. *Chicago-Kent Law Review, 84*, 19–53.

Gordy, K. (2011). Adding life to the adolescent's years, not simply years to the adolescent's life: The integration of the individualized care planning & coordination model and a statutory fallback provision. *Yale Journal of Health Policy, Law, and Ethics, 11*, 169–221.

Gray, J. P. (2010). The hopelessness of drug prohibition. *Chapman Law Review, 13*, 521–554.

Griffiths, J., et al. (2008). *Euthanasia and law in Europe* (2nd ed.). Oxford, England: Hart.

Hardjasa, C. (2008). Liberty or death: Federalism, the DEA, and the war on the suffering. *Georgetown Journal of Law and Public Policy, 6*, 669–692.

Hartman, R. G. (2012). Noblesse oblige: States' obligations to minors living with life-limiting conditions. *Duquesne Law Review, 50*, 333–409.

Hill, B. J. (2015). Constituting children's bodily integrity. *Duke Law Journal, 64*, 1295–1362.

___. (2012). Medical decision making by and on behalf of adolescents: Reconsidering first principles. *Journal of Health Care Law and Policy, 15*, 37–73.

___. (2011). Whose body? Whose soul? Medical decision-making on behalf of children and the Free Exercise Clause before and after *Employment Division v. Smith. Cardozo Law Review, 32*, 1857–1878.

Holmes, Jr., O. W. (2015). *The common law.* Boston, MA: Little, Brown (Original work published 1881).

Iyioha, I., & Akorede, Y. A. O. (2010). You give me welfare but take my freedom: Understanding the mature minor's autonomy in the face of the court's *parens patriae* jurisdiction. *Quinnipiac Health Law Journal, 13*, 279–314.

Jacobson, P. D., & Mathur, S. K. (2010). Health law 2010: It's not all about the money. *American Journal of Law and Medicine, 36*, 389–404.

Kochanek, K. D., et al. (2014). *Mortality in the United States.* Hyattsville, MD: National Center for Health Statistics.

Koestler, A. (2011). *Dialogue with death: The journal of a prisoner of the fascists in the Spanish civil war.* Chicago, ILL: University of Chicago Press (Original work published 1938).

Kopelman, L. M. (2007). The best interests standard for incompetent or incapacitated persons of all ages. *Journal of Law, Medicine and Ethics, 35*, 187–194.

Kübler-Ross, E., & Byock, I. (2014). *On death and dying: What the dying have to teach doctors, nurses, clergy and their own families.* New York, NY: Simon and Schuster-Scribner (Original work published 1969).

Kübler-Ross, E., & Kessler, D. (2014). *On grief and grieving: Finding the meaning of grief through the five stages of loss.* New York, NY: Simon and Schuster-Scribner (Original work published 2004).

Landro, L. (2010, November 22). CEO Council (A special report): Health care: Change the incentives. *Wall Street Journal,* p. R6.

Laskin, A., et al. (2014). Beyond autonomy? A transnational comparison of end-of-life decision making by mature minors. *Michigan State University Journal of Medicine and Law, 18*, 139–159.

Levine, A. D., & Wolf, L. E. (2012). The roles and responsibilities of physicians in patients' decisions about unproven stem cell therapies. *Journal of Law, Medicine and Ethics, 40*, 122–133.

Lim, M. (2015). A new approach to the ethics of life: The "will to live" in lieu of inherent dignity or autonomy-based approaches. *Southern California Interdisciplinary Law Journal, 24*, 27–145.

Lyons, E. C. (2005). In incognito: The principle of double effect in American constitutional law. *Florida Law Review, 57*, 469–562.

McGregor, R. R. (2013). Emeritus Professor of Medicine, Penn Medicine Division of Infectious Disease at the University of Pennsylvania and Past Section Chief in Penn's AIDS Clinical Trials Unit, remarks to the Authors.

Miller, R. A. (2007). On freedom and feeding tubes: Reviving Terri Schiavo and trying Saddam Hussein. *Law and Literature, 19*, 161–183.

Nachman, D. D. (2011). Advance directives: Is it time to pull the plug? *Elder Law Journal, 18*, 289–333.

NCHS (National Center for Health Statistics). (2015). Deaths and mortality. Hyattsville, MD: Centers for Disease Control and Prevention, NCHS.

NHPCO (National Hospice and Palliative Care Organization). (2010). *NHPCO facts and figures: Hospice care in America.* Arlington, VA: NHPCO.

Nunziato, D. M. (2010). Preventing prescription drug overdose in the twenty-first century: Is the Controlled Substances Act enough? *Hofstra Law Review, 38*, 1261–1298.

Orenstein, D. G., & Bettini, L. M. (2014). Flipping the light switch: New perspectives on default to donation for organs and tissues. *Annals of Health Law, 23*, 141–159.

Parker, F. R., Jr. (2015). Law, bioethics, and medical futility: Defining patient rights at the end of life. *University of Arkansas at Little Rock Law Review, 37*, 185–234.

Paterick, T. J. (2008). Medical informed consent: General considerations for physicians. *Mayo Clinical Proceedings, 83*(3), 313–319.

Perlmutter, S. (2011). Physician-assisted suicide: A medicolegal inquiry. *Michigan State Journal of Medicine and Law, 15*, 203–226.

Perry, J. E. (2010). A missed opportunity: Health care reform, rhetoric, ethics and economics at the end-of-life. *Mississippi College Law Review, 29*, 409–426.

Perry, J. E., & Stone, R. C. (2011). In the business of dying: Questioning the commercialization of hospice. *Journal of Law, Medicine, and Ethics, 39*, 224–231.

Pew Research Center for the People and the Press. (2006). *Strong public support for right to die.* Washington, DC: Pew.

Pope, T. M. (2012). Physicians and safe harbor legal immunity. *Annals of Health Law, 21*, 121–135.

___. (2011). Managing risk at the end of life. *Widener Law Review, 17*, 1–10.

Pope, T. M., & Anderson, L. E. (2011). Voluntarily stopping eating and drinking: A legal treatment option at the end of life. *Widener Law Review, 17*, 363–427.

Quill, T. E. (2012). Physicians should "assist in suicide" when it is appropriate. *Journal of Law, Medicine and Ethics, 40*, 57–64.

Reynolds, L. (2014). Losing the quality of life: The move toward society's understanding and acceptance of physician aid-in-dying and the Death with Dignity Act. *New England Law Review, 48*, 343–370.

Robertson, J. A. (2013). Paid organ donations and the constitutionality of the National Organ Transplant Act. *Hastings Constitutional Law Quarterly, 40*, 221–275.

Saad, L. (2011, May 31). Doctor-assisted suicide is moral issue dividing Americans most. Washington, DC: Gallup Politics.

Schneiderman, L. J. (2005). Physician-assisted dying. *Journal of the American Medical Association, 293*, 501.

Schuck, P. H. (2010). The golden age of aging, and its discontents. *Elder Law Journal, 18*, 25–70.

Secara, N. A. (2011). Has Italy discovered Virgil? Utilizing the British archetype to create end-of-life legislation in Italy. *Cardozo Journal of International and Comparative Law, 19*, 127–170.

Shore, D. A. (2007). *The trust crisis in healthcare: Causes, consequences, and cures.* New York, NY: Oxford University Press.

Smith, G. P., II. (2014). The future of health law: Exemplary insight into trending topics: Cura personalis: A healthcare delivery quandary at the end of life. *Saint Louis University Journal of Health Law and Policy, 7*, 311–329.

___. (2011). Refractory pain, existential suffering, and palliative care: Releasing an unbearable lightness of being. *Cornell Journal of Law and Public Policy, 20*(3), 469–532.

Solomon, J. (2010, December 27). Medicare set to reimburse doctors for end-of-life talks. *Wall Street Journal*, p. A4.

Stern, R. C., & DiFonzo, H. (2007). Terminal ambiguity: Law, ethics and policy in the assisted dying debate. *Boston University Public Interest Law Journal, 17*, 99–140.

Theiss, D. E. (2010). The Medicare hospice benefit after health reform: Cost controls, expanded access, and system-induced pressures. *Journal of Health and Life Sciences Law, 3*(4), 39–82.

Tucker, K. L. (2014). Freedom of choice at the end of life: Patients' rights in a shifting legal and political landscape: Give me liberty at my death: Expanding end-of-life choice in Massachusetts. *New York Law School Law Review, 58*, 259–276.

___. (2012). Aid in dying: An end of life option governed by best practices. *Journal of Health and Biomedical Law, 8*, 9–26.

___. (2011). When dying takes too long: Activism for social change to protect and expand choice at the end of life. *Whittier Law Review, 33*, 109–160.

___. (2008). In the laboratory of the states: The progress of *Glucksberg's* invitation to states to address end-of-life choice. *Michigan Law Review, 106*, 1593–1611.

Unroe, K. T., & Meier, D. E. (2011). Palliative care and hospice: Opportunities to improve care for the sickest patients. *Notre Dame Journal of Law, Ethics and Public Policy, 25*, 413–427.

VHA (Veterans Health Administration), National Ethics Committee. (2007). The ethics of palliative sedation as a therapy of last resort. *American Journal of Hospice and Palliative Care, 23*(6), 483–491.

Waldman, E. (2014). Bioethics mediation at the end of life: Opportunities and limitations. *Cardozo Journal of Conflict Resolution, 15*, 449–471.

Warnock, M., & Macdonald, E. (2009). *Easeful death: Is there a case for assisted dying?* New York, NY: Oxford University Press.

Warshak, R. A. (2011). Parenting by the clock: The best interest of the child standard, judicial discretion, and the American Law Institute's "approximation rule." *University of Baltimore Law Review, 41*, 83–161.

Webley, E. (2011). Law, insouciance, and death in the emergency room. *Elder Law Journal, 19*, 257–287.

Wharton School at the University of Pennsylvania. (2006). The business of palliative care. *Knowledge@Wharton.*

Williams, Z. (2011). When the physician says you have to get the shot, but mommy says no: The cases of Taige Mueller and Daniel Hauser, and how the state may force parents to accept unwanted medical treatment for their children. *Indiana Health Law Review, 8*, 199–228.

Our Future Health Care System

Part VII, "Our Future Health Care System," briefly overviews health care ethics within the context of health care reforms in the United States.

© jopelka/iStock/Getty Images Plus/Thinkstock

CHAPTER 16

Our Future: A New Kind of Health Care Ethics

"Knowing is not enough; we must apply. Willing is not enough; we must do."

— **Johann Wolfgang von Goethe** (1749–1832), German diplomat, civil servant, novelist, philosopher, playwright, and poet

LEARNING OBJECTIVES

After completing this chapter, the reader should be able to:

1. Predict how the U.S. health care system may change in a way that is more compassionate, fair, and just.
2. Describe the most challenging ethical issues and topical concerns facing health care professionals.
3. Understand the ethical principles underlying the new frameworks that are being developed in each of the major health care sectors: life sciences, health care delivery, and medical products.

KEY TERMS

Altman's law
Average group
    member risk
Common public ethic
Conformity
Consistency
Cross-subsidization
Decency

Ethic of common
    humanity
Ideals
Macroeconomics
Market distortion
Microeconomics
Minimum coverage
    provision

Moral imperative
Redistribution
Shared responsibility
    payment
Social determinants
    of health
Status quo

ETHICAL OR UNETHICAL DECISION

Social Advocates' Fidelity or Infidelity to the Law

Ethical Issue: *Is it ethical for critics of health care reform to obstruct reforms by repeatedly challenging the validity of the Affordable Care Act of 2010 (ACA) and is such social movement advocacy compatible with fidelity and devotion to the law?*

In Brief: The subject of significant bipartisan debate for more than a year, the day after the ACA was signed into law, opposition to its implementation began. Phil Gramm, a former Texas senator, advocated in an opinion-editorial in the *Wall Street Journal* that "Republicans should take the unequivocal position that if they are given a majority in Congress…, they will stop the implementation of the government takeover. And if a Republican is elected president…, they will do with… [the] health care bill what the American voters will have done to the Democrats: Throw it out." Since then, a majority of the states have filed and lost lawsuits in federal court challenging the validity of the law. The reasons underlying this policy obstruction are threefold.

First, every dollar of the $2.6 trillion spent by consumers and the government on health care every year is the income of a recipient stakeholder as payment for work, services, or medical products in each of the major health care sectors (CMS, 2015). Thus, the most feared effect of health care reform is **redistribution** of this $2.6 trillion pie. The health care professionals working and delivering health care services fear the changes required to switch from focusing on medical treatments to focusing on prevention of disease. The hospitals, nursing homes, and other institutional facilities are concerned about how the community-based approach to health care will affect them, while everyone working to supply the medical products industry worries about the evidence-based approach to medicine where cost-effectiveness is a concern. Caught in the middle of all this is the health insurance industry that is working to pay for everything under new cost constraints. Everyone fears the process of apportioning health care resources differently. There is anxiety whenever the **status quo** is changed by distributing something differently from the way it was previously distributed or the current way of doing something is altered. Stakeholders who are receiving any part of the $2.6 trillion pie tend not to want to share their piece of the pie in more equal proportions or among a wider range of different recipients. Every time a dollar is taken from any stakeholder and given to someone else, the loser claims that the status quo was more equitable.

The second obstacle to implementation is **Altman's law**: the status quo is every stakeholder's second choice for health care reform. In other words, when no one can agree on a change, nothing changes, which is where the United States has been in health care since the passage of Medicare and Medicaid in 1965, at least in terms of broad, comprehensive changes.

Third, the emotions and prejudices of the public have been manipulated in a way that is dangerous. For instance, clinical practice guidelines have been described as death panels, while the dreaded concept *rationing* arises whenever a medical product is denied approval by regulatory agencies. Clearly, implementation of health care reform is complicated by the absence of simple solutions; no one completely understands all the reforms because no one person completely understands the complexity of all parts of the health care system as it exists today. Furthermore, as with virtually all comprehensive health legislation, which is generally complicated to explain and easy to misunderstand, nearly everyone in the health care industry is able to manipulate opposition to reform of their vested interests.

— Patient Protection and Affordable Care Act, 42 U.S.C. § 18001, *et seq.* (2010), *as amended by* Health Care and Education Reconciliation Act of 2010, Pub.L.No. 111-152, 124 Stat. 1029 through 124. Stat. 1084. (*See Ethical or Unethical Decision* at the end of the chapter for discussion of this ethics issue.)

Introduction

This chapter concludes by asking whether the real crisis with U.S. health care could be the result of different perceptions about ethics in health care. Since the Roosevelt era's New Deal, U.S. health policy has balanced two concerns: access to affordable health insurance and control of costs (Phelps, 2012). Now, over the past decade, total health care spending has increased more than eightfold and the comparable increase for medications almost tenfold (Siegel, 2012), but there has not been a corresponding increase in the health of the nation. The United States has the world's highest expenditures on health care and yet its life expectancy remains behind that of other industrialized nations in the world (WHO, 2014). Today, more than 16 million U.S. residents have unmet medical needs and need health care but do not get it because they cannot afford it, or delay care because of the cost (Kaiser, 2014). While these numbers are half of what they were before the ACA reforms, obviously, when 1 in 20 people in any society has unmet medical needs, everyone has at least a financial stake in continuing to reform that nation's health care system, if not a moral or jurisprudential one (Siegel, 2012). Yet, policy debates are driven by widely divergent ethical principles or by a lack of coherent ethical grounding that is the result of different perceptions (Levine, et al., 2007).

Today, there appears to be no political consensus on how to best cultivate a higher-quality, more efficient, and more equitable health care system. Many people perceive that access to near-universal health insurance coverage is going to cost the government too much money, but they do not take into account all the cost recovery the U.S. health care system will see when health conditions are treated that prevent people from working or when money is spent on preventive care as opposed to the more expensive treatment of diseases.

The goal of this text was to embark on a journey toward discovering the nation's shared values. Shared values are intertwined with the perennial values of compassion, fairness, justice, and individual and social responsibility in a way that has always been uniquely American. Yet today, different perceptions about fairness may be one of the biggest obstacles to identifying a **common public ethic** of compassion and justice. Progress regarding the role of government and how to balance individual and social responsibilities will be hindered until Americans accept responsibility for understanding and reconciling their common perceptions about fairness.

ETHICAL DILEMMAS 16-1

1. What values and ethical principles are holding back implementation of U.S. health care reforms? Specifically, if it is impossible for any government to finance health care commensurate with its demand, because the potential demand (the desire) for care is virtually unlimited, what values and ethical principles should guide allocation decisions for the $2.6 trillion spent on health care each year?
2. While the ongoing calls for health care reforms exist, what is it that makes ethical issues involving health care so difficult to resolve?
3. Would the health care system be sustainable if every member of society were equally entitled to access basic health insurance for their care, or should everyone only be equally entitled to medically necessary care based on their ability to pay for such care?

Common Public Ethic of Compassion, Fairness, and Justice

The acceptance of some values and the rejection of others have created divergent streams of public ethics that are distinct only in their predicted outcomes rather than on the basis of any principled theory (Staman & Brougher, 2012). Indeed, it was not until the U.S. health care system was calculated to be unsustainable that the nation's governing principles of what is fair now require the health care system to incorporate a common public ethic of justice and compassion.

The principles of compassion, fairness, and justice ultimately define the American system of law and the notions of uniformity and **consistency** under the law (*Straight v. Wainwright, et al.*, 476 U.S. 1132 (U.S. Supreme Court 1986)). This means the law should be logically fair and coherent with no contradictions (Jimenez, 2011); in other words, the law should try to find common opportunities for people to seek like outcomes (Atkinson, 2014). This principle is especially relevant for vulnerable members of society with socioeconomic inequalities who present themselves to the nation's health care providers for care. The primary character of justice has always been compassion and fairness for all, including the most vulnerable members of society, such as low-wage workers and those with adverse or preexisting health conditions, disability, or mental illness (Gilman, 2014). For this reason, to deny access to affordable health insurance could threaten the time-honored traditions of American decency, compassion, and reverence for the **ethic of common humanity**, which are contained altogether within the notions of uniformity and consistency (Yamin, 2008).

Decency in this respect is defined as conformity with ethical principles and accepted standards of what Americans consider as right and fair, whereas *compassion* is the **moral imperative** to assist the most vulnerable members of society (Hagen, 2013), or in this instance, paying attention to the effects of unaffordable access to health insurance and the inadequate health care that results from being uninsured or underinsured. The right and ethical thing for the nation to do is to ensure that every member of society has access to affordable health insurance, regardless of opposition to this legal principle or difficulty in implementing this moral obligation (AMA, 2012; Noush, 2014). Every member of American society must have access to basic health insurance that provides medically needed care (AMA, 2012). This moral obligation is derived from the ethical principles of justice and equality of opportunity (Levine, et al., 2007).

Conformity implies uniform and consistent agreement and following of what is socially acceptable at all levels of society (Wiley, 2014). In this instance, the most vulnerable members of society should receive the greatest assistance from their government and society (Tsai, 2014). Without adherence to the ethical principle of compassion, the policy of justice underlying the law would be undermined by the lack of conformity (Gilman, 2014).

Core Values of Common Ideals

Pursuing common **ideals**, or the ethical principles to which most people aspire, nourishes both a national identity and the sense of national community (Tsai, 2014). Agreement on the core values by individuals or a group, in turn, enables nations to pursue their common ideals (Rawls, 1971/2005). Compassion, courage, diligence, education, fairness, fidelity, generosity, honesty, integrity, justice, self-control, tolerance, and truthfulness are common virtues most people from leading nations in the international community have already adopted (AMA, 2012; Levine, et al., 2007). One need only examine the United Nations International Conventions as proof of the international community's acceptance of these common ideals (Tsai, 2014).

Most Americans will agree that the traditional values of compassion, fairness, and justice should be part of our nation's public health care ethic (AMA, 2012). Accordingly, health care reforms are expected to be compassionate, fair, and just. Together, as illustrated in **FEATURE BOX 16-1**, these traditional values and the nucleus of common virtues could develop the nation's highest potential (Holmes, 1897; Rawls, 1971/2005).

FEATURE BOX 16-1

A New Kind of Health Care Ethics
Focused on Individual and Social Responsibility

Shared values of compassion, fairness, and justice, guided by universally-accepted virtues:

- Compassion
- Courage
- Decency
- Diligence
- Education
- Fairness
- Generosity
- Honesty
- Integrity
- Justice
- Self-control
- Tolerance
- Truthfulness

— Sources: AMA, 2012; Green, 2012; Holmes, 1897; Levin, et al., 2007.

Different Perceptions but Shared Values

The U.S. economy has created an environment in which comprehensive reforms and dramatic changes are happening in the health care industry no matter what laws Congress passes or what the U.S. Supreme Court upholds or overturns (Wharton, 2012a). The rightness or wrongness of each step on the road to reform will, however, be judged by the public's perception of how the journey conforms to the nation's shared values of compassion, fairness, and justice.

Admitting the current inability to agree on what constitutes compassion, fairness, and justice for each of the different measures in **FEATURE BOX 16-2** could be the beginning of newfound wisdom with regard to health care reform. In other words, comprehensive reform of the U.S. health care system first requires acknowledging that Americans have different perceptions of what will benefit them, and at whose expense, and what it means to give others their appropriate due or what they are properly owed (Levine, et al., 2007).

Mind and Market Distortions

People often think the world is how they perceive it and that everyone shares their values. The U.S. health care system cannot be easily explained or understood. It appears to everyone that the market does not work efficiently, when in fact, the health care market has been distorted by regulatory forces (Wharton, 2010).

One of the biggest obstacles to realization of reform is **market distortion** of the U.S. health care system. Today, the U.S. health care system is so complex and so distorted in the way it operates that comprehensive reform is required from top to bottom (Wharton, 2012). Market distortions occur when health services and medical products are not freely available because the forces of supply and demand have been altered; health care costs have become so high that many Americans are uninsured or underinsured as regulatory forces have distorted the market (Christensen, 2009). Tax

---

FEATURE BOX 16-2

How Morally Right or Wrong Are the Following Reform Measures?

- Providing access to affordable health insurance for everyone residing in the United States
- Requiring everyone to be a member of one of the nation's risk pools for health insurance, so the costs from catastrophic sickness and accidents are shared by everyone
- Only paying for medical treatments that have been shown to work, in other words, treatments that conform to evidence-based standards of care
- Systematically learning from the health information about the millions of patients being treated, and the lessons from their experiences
- Conditioning the market approval of new medical products on scientific measures of the products' comparative effectiveness

— Sources: Levine, et al., 2007; Wharton, 2012a.

subsidies and government-financed health insurance have brought the nation to the point where rapidly escalating costs make the delivery of health care unsustainable (Levine, et al., 2007). It is a cautionary tale about the dangers of regulatory interference (Wharton, 2010). The result of market distortions is that the U.S. health care system has become an American enigma; no one person completely understands the entire system.

Compassion, Fairness, and Justice in a Distorted Market

What has become of the traditional values of compassion, fairness, and justice in this distorted market is a critical question in any reform of the health care system. Over the years, health care has become distorted by employment-based health insurance and the consequences of government-financed health insurance. Tax subsidies to help employers pay for the expense of employer-sponsored health insurance and financing of government health insurance exceed $1.1 trillion each year (Klees, et al., 2009; Kleinbard, 2008). These market distortions are perpetuated and worsened by the adverse consequences of **cross-subsidization**, or the shifting of $43 billion in costs by insurers (*Florida, et al. v. U.S. Department of Health and Human Services, et al.,* 648 F.3d 1235 (U.S. Court of Appeals for the 11th Circuit 2011), *affirmed in part and reversed in part*, 132 S.Ct. 2566 (U.S. Supreme Court 2012)). The inevitable result of all three powerful forces (tax subsidies for employer-provided health insurance, government health insurance, and cost-shifting) is that it is now impossible to determine the true cost of health care. Government regulations attempting to allocate costs only result in increasing costs and corresponding increasing prices for health care.

The market distortions in the U.S. health care system, however, have changed fundamentally since the ACA was signed into law (Green, 2010). By starting in the direction of universal access to health care, the United States has committed to making major changes, and there is tremendous potential to create a more sustainable health care system that will be better able to be maintained by the nation in the long term (Wharton, 2010). There is common recognition that a more just and comprehensive system of regulation is required to ensure equitable access to affordable health insurance. In answering the questions outlined in **FEATURE BOX 16-3**, the nation must decide if this is the time to reach a workable consensus about what constitutes compassion, fairness, and justice under the law. The United States is a long way from agreeing to the solutions to these issues, much less making ethical decisions about implementing very many health care reforms.

Reform within the New Ethics of Health Care

The nation's health care laws and regulations must be reworked in order to create a more ethical system that works as intended, especially since the many reforms are changing the laws and regulations already in place (Levine, et al., 2007). Laws and regulations must be reworked to create a more ethical system, as health care is not only increasingly seen as a human right, but also appears to make good economic sense. Health care corporations from different sectors are merging, and new medical products and technologies are emerging that do not fall under any existing regulatory schemes (Christensen, 2009).

FEATURE BOX 16-3

Ethical Dilemmas Now Facing the Nation: Choosing between Moral Imperatives

- Can a national consensus be reached about the role government should play in implementing health care reforms, or should the private sector take the leadership role in making changes to the U.S. health care system?
- Are Americans willing to replace the current system of inequalities and injustices for the common good of everyone, or are individual liberty and the freedom to choose whatever health care one wants greater values than equality and justice?
- Will Americans support health care reforms if the guarantee of universal access to health care is found to cost more money in the short term, despite long-term savings in the future?
- Will businesses and the insurance industry succeed in maintaining the status quo with their $1.1 trillion in government subsidies and shifting of costs, or will opposition to disruption of current conditions decrease as comprehensive health care reforms continue to be implemented?
- Will the traditional values of fairness and justice prevail within the new ethics of health care reform, or will new concepts of what is fair and just emerge?

— Sources: Green, 2010; Klees, et al., 2009; Wharton, 2010.

As costs continue to increase, health care ethics will be used to set limits on available health care (AMA, 2012). People with preventable health conditions arising from lifestyle choices, such as smoking and being overweight, may face higher deductibles, co-pays, and premiums for health insurance to better reflect the higher-than-average risk insurers assume for insuring enrollees who make poor behavioral choices. This is especially true now that the country has decided that everyone should be entitled to affordable health insurance. As a consequence, the present struggles are over how much basic coverage everyone is entitled to and how it should be funded (Wharton, 2012).

Our Future: A New Kind of Health Care Ethics

The health care overhaul—including the minimum coverage provision, expansion of government-financed health insurance programs, state and federal health insurance exchanges, changes to private insurance (community rating, guaranteed issue of basic coverage, no underwriting for adverse or preexisting conditions), and employer requirements—raises many questions about the costs, effectiveness, and political viability of reform. The **minimum coverage provision** requires nearly all adults to buy health insurance either through their employers or independently. The idea for the minimum coverage provision, which came from the Heritage Foundation initially in 1989, was endorsed early on by the Republican congressional leadership, was adopted in Massachusetts under Republican Governor Romney in 2006, and became part of the compromise to get the ACA passed in Congress (Wharton, 2012). Basic coverage is required to be made available so nearly everyone can choose between purchasing affordable insurance during their lifetimes or facing an annual **shared responsibility payment** that must be paid if they fail to maintain their health insurance.

ETHICS CASE
Comprehensive Reform of Health Care

Florida, et al. v. U.S. Department of Health and Human Services, et al.
[State Government v. Federal Government]
648 F.3d 1235 (U.S. Court of Appeals for the 11th Circuit 2011), *affirmed in part and reversed in part*, *National Federation of Independent Business, et al. v. Sebelius, et al.*, 132 S.Ct. 2566 (U.S. Supreme Court 2012)

Facts: The U.S. Supreme Court decided that the ACA is constitutional in this decision where 26 states lost their argument before the 11th Circuit Court to have the entire health care reform law declared unconstitutional. This dispute concerned the role of the federal government in reforming the U.S. health care system. The U.S. Constitution limits the power of the federal government by granting Congress authority in certain defined areas, such as the regulation of commerce. Powers not expressly vested in the federal government by the Constitution are reserved to the states.

Legal Analysis: Debate before the U.S. Supreme Court centered on the issue of whether the ACA's minimum coverage provision requiring almost every member of society to have health insurance was constitutional. While Congress imposed the provision in accordance with its constitutional power to regulate interstate commerce, the mandate is not limited to those who engage in any economic activity. Rather, the mandate applies to every U.S. resident who does not fall within one of the law's limited exclusions. Under the U.S. Constitution, only states have the authority to impose health and safety regulations on individuals; the federal government does not have general police power. Federal legislation must be grounded in one of the enumerated powers the Constitution grants to Congress, such as the power to regulate interstate commerce. Although the U.S. Supreme Court has interpreted the Commerce Clause powers broadly since the Roosevelt era's New Deal, this power is still limited.

In addition to the minimum coverage provision, the ACA also expanded the Medicaid insurance program. Since its inception, Medicaid insurance has been a cooperative federal/state health insurance program with the states contributing funds and having discretion in operating their own programs. Under the ACA, as a means of ensuring near-universal health insurance coverage, Medicaid insurance was expanded to cover anyone unable to access affordable private health insurance. Although states can always choose whether to accept federal funds, the U.S. Supreme Court clearly stated that federal funding conditions had become coercive under the ACA; they violated the U.S. Constitution's principle of limited self-government.

Rule of Law: The minimum coverage provision compelling almost all U.S. residents to purchase and maintain a certain level of health insurance from private insurers unless covered by government health insurance does not exceed Congress' powers; however, mandatory state expansion of Medicaid does exceed Congress' powers.

Ethics Issue: Should Congress have the right to compel almost all U.S. residents to accept individual responsibility for shared societal resources?

Ethics Analysis: This debate concerned the nature of individual liberty and the proper role of government. The legitimacy of the ACA was determined by analyzing the limitations on how Congress may set social policy and allocate resources to address age and illness. With the ACA, Congress attempted to address a complex market failure by addressing the sustainability problems of cost-shifting and adverse selection in the health care and insurance industries. In its legislative findings, Congress acknowledged that the ethical and legal obligations to provide emergency care to the uninsured result in over $49 billion in uncompensated consumption of health care services annually and that this translates into an average cost-shifting of $1,000 in health insurance premiums to families that are insured (Thide, 2012).

On one side of this debate, opponents of the ACA stressed the slippery-slope argument that if Congress can require almost everyone to purchase and maintain health insurance during their lifetimes, without regard to any particular activity in which they have chosen to engage, then there is no limit on federal power. Opponents argued that if Congress can mandate that everyone purchase health insurance because their lack of insurance may, at some point in the future, impose costs on the wider economy, then on the same theory, future federal mandates can require the purchase of virtually any other product, since the failure to have any product can always be said to have some economic impact.

On the other side of the debate, proponents of the ACA maintained that Congress recognized the existence of a fundamental economic right to essential health care and simply expanded federal protection of that right. The ACA does not only expand access to basic health insurance; more importantly, it creates a presumption in favor of near-universal access to affordable health insurance (Zietlow, 2011). In addressing opponents' arguments, proponents of the ACA maintained that society can rely on individual resources, private bargains, or the government to address age and illness needs (Maher, 2011). The ACA mandates that virtually every adult member of society make insurance bargains. Decisions by the uninsured to not buy health insurance affect commerce by materially increasing the costs for the insured. The health care industry is unique and therefore can be regulated in ways other markets cannot. The purpose of the ACA is to avoid such extreme cost-shifting and underwriting costs, two forces that distort the health care market and disrespect state borders. By eliminating wasteful forms of competition, the efficiency of the health and insurance markets can be improved.

Court's Holding and Decision: While the ACA's minimum coverage provision does not exceed Congress's powers, the forced expansion of Medicaid insurance is unconstitutional because Congress could not discontinue federal funding to the states that they had always previously been entitled to for failure to follow new Medicaid expansion requirements; this provision can be severed, however, in order to preserve the rest of the health care reform law.

See, e.g., Adler & Cannon, 2013; Auerbach, 2014; Biebl, 2013; Blumstein, 2014; Bryant, 2013; Cannan, 2013; Carr, 2014; Coogan, 2014; Copeland, 2012; Desantis, 2014; Faizer, 2013; Georgakopoulos, 2013; Gewirtzman, 2012; Gould, 2014; Grusin, 2015; Hall, 2014; Hansen & Newman, 2015; Hartz, 2013; Hasen, 2013; Hewitt, 2013; Hoffmann, 2014; Huberfeld, 2013; Huberfeld & Roberts, 2014; Jones, 2015; LaRocca, 2014; Maher, 2011; Manheim, 2015; Mariner, 2014; McCullough, 2013; Moncrieff, 2013; Nicholson, 2013; Noush, 2014; Nussbaum, 2012; Pantelaki & White, 2014; Pasquale, 2014; Perella & Swartzfage, 2012; Perkins & Singh, 2014; Reynolds & Denning, 2013; Segall, 2015; Siegel, 2012; Sohoni, 2012; Solomon, 2013; Somin, 2014; Sullivan & Gershon, 2014; Tahk, 2013; Thide, 2012; Thomas & Molk, 2013; Tovino, 2012; Underhill, 2012; Weeden, 2013; Widener, 2015 (discussing this court decision).

This overhaul for the allocation of shared societal responsibilities raises questions about a new kind of health care ethics. This is what the health care reforms are working out at the moment. The old frameworks that supported the status quo are being replaced with new ones coming into existence. The ACA is not something that should be opposed; rather, it is something that the nation needs to work with and find strategies to deal with (Wharton, 2010). By pairing two cases (*Florida, et al. v. U.S. Department of Health and Human Services, et al., infra* with *National Federation of Independent Business, et al. v. Sebelius, et al., supra*), the U.S. Supreme Court sent a strong message: no one wants to perpetuate the inequalities and unsustainability of what existed before the first comprehensive reform of health care in decades, when 50 million Americans were uninsured (Kaiser Commission, 2014) and another 106 million were underinsured (Felland, et al., 2010). With the right kind of policies and a new approach to health care, the U.S. health care system may well be more equitable and able to offer higher-quality medical treatments after going through a period of uncertainty and change.

ETHICS CASE
Ethics of the Affordable Care Act

National Federation of Independent Business, et al. v. Sebelius, et al., together with Florida, et al. v. U.S. Department of Health and Human Services, et al. [Nation's Small Businesses and 26 State Governments v. Federal Government] 132 S.Ct. 2566 (U.S. Supreme Court 2012)

Facts: In 2010, Congress enacted the ACA in order to increase the number of Americans covered by health insurance and decrease the cost of health care. One key provision of the law is the minimum coverage provision, which requires most Americans to maintain minimum coverage for essential health care. Individuals who do not receive health insurance through their employer or the government must purchase insurance from a private company. Those who do not comply with the minimum coverage provision must make a shared responsibility payment to the federal government. This penalty must be paid to the Internal Revenue Service when individual tax returns are filed. A second key provision of the ACA is expansion of the Medicaid insurance program. Medicaid currently offers federal funding to states to assist pregnant women, children, needy families, the blind, the elderly, and the disabled in obtaining health care. The ACA expanded the Medicaid program and increased federal funding to the states for this expansion. If a state did not comply with the new ACA coverage requirements, it stood to lose all of its federal Medicaid funds.

Twenty-six states and the National Federation of Independent Business challenged the constitutionality of the minimum coverage provision and the Medicaid expansion in federal court. The U.S. Court of Appeals for the 11th Circuit upheld the Medicaid expansion as a valid exercise of Congress's spending power, but concluded that Congress lacked authority to enact the minimum coverage provision.

Legal Analysis: The Court's analysis was fourfold. First, the Court considered whether to hear and decide this case because of the Anti-Injunction Act, a federal law requiring taxpayers to pay their assessments before they can challenge the legality of their tax. Here, the Court found that Congress did not intend the penalty payment for failure to maintain health insurance to be treated as a tax. The ACA described the payment as a penalty, not a tax. While this label did not determine whether the penalty payment is a tax under the U.S. Constitution, it did determine that the Anti-Injunction law did not apply to this case.

Second, the Court decided whether the minimum coverage provision that required most Americans to carry health insurance or pay a penalty was constitutional. Here, the Court preserved the coverage provision as a form of personal responsibility tax. While Congress labeled the mandate a penalty under provisions of the Anti-Injunction Act, the Court analyzed the mandate as a form of tax in its constitutional analysis.

Third, the Court was also asked whether the ACA should remain in effect without the minimum coverage provision. The federal government maintained that most of the law could stand, while the states argued that the entire law must go. There was no need to answer this question, because the Court upheld the provision.

Lastly, the Court considered whether the law's expansion of the federal–state Medicaid program unlawfully required states to grow the program. Here, the Court found that the Medicaid expansion violated the U.S. Constitution by threatening states with the loss of their existing Medicaid funding if they declined to comply with the expansion. The federal government cannot withdraw existing Medicaid funds from the states for failure to expand the Medicaid program under new requirements.

Rule of Law: The ACA's minimum coverage provision is constitutional as a form of taxation, but the required Medicaid expansion was unconstitutional.

Ethics Issue: Is comprehensive reform of the U.S. health care system constitutional, when that reform requires nearly every member of society to obtain and maintain health insurance or pay a tax penalty for not doing so?

Ethics Analysis: The ACA expands the role of the federal government in health care because improvement of the enduring and complex problems of the U.S. health care system is virtually impossible without a federal response (Gostin, 2008). Moreover, federal action for health care benefits everyone by diminishing state and local vulnerabilities to reform. The Court found that research is now persuasive that the least healthy Americans affect the nation economically. Helping the most vulnerable members of U.S. society makes everyone safer and more secure, in addition to simply being ethical and the right thing to do.

The alternative to the ACA is that nearly everyone would be worse off, particularly those who suffer a mix of health care disadvantages. The ACA focuses on access to affordable health insurance for nearly every member of society, as opposed to the broader vision of the connections between **social determinants of health** and shared responsibility for health. Yet, the ACA acknowledges that social determinants are the primary factors that shape the health of individuals, not medical treatments. The living conditions that individual Americans experience (access to health care; early childhood development; education; employment and working conditions; food security; housing; income and income distribution; social exclusion; social safety network; unemployment and job security; and gender, race, and disability status) are the true determinants of health outcomes.

Nevertheless, as important as expansion of the social determinant of access to health care is, a fuller understanding of the role of social justice in health is needed, particularly as research increasingly links the role of living conditions in health outcomes (Tyler, 2012). Health is special and foundational in that its effects on human capacities impact the opportunities of individual Americans; health must be preserved to ensure equality of opportunity in the United States (Gostin, 2008).

Court's Holding and Decision: Yes, the ACA is constitutional; nearly every member of society is required to obtain and maintain health insurance, but the states may not be forced to expand their Medicaid programs or face losing all federal Medicaid funds.

See, e.g., Adler & Cannon, 2013; Atwell, 2015; Auerbach, 2014; Avraham, 2014 and 2013; Bahrenburg & Robert, 2013; Benedict, 2013; Bisi & Horan, 2013; Bolin, 2014; Bowser, 2015; Carr, 2014; Connell, et al., 2013; Dolgin, 2013; Fischer & Kasper, 2014; Gedicks & Van Tassell, 2014; Glen, 2013; Gould, 2014; Greene, 2012; Grusin, 2015; Hall, 2014; Hansen & Newman, 2015; Hawkes & Seidenfeld, 2014; Hetrick, 2015; Hodge & Scanlon, 2014; Hoffmann, 2014; Huberfeld, 2013a; Hulkower & Wolf, 2013; Kessler, 2014; Kitchen, 2013; Lee, et al., 2013; Manheim, 2015; Mariner, 2014; Marino, et al., 2015; Milhizer, 2013; Moncrieff, 2013; Morley, 2014; Neyarapally, 2013; Noush, 2014; Ogolla, 2015; Pantelaki & White, 2014; Parks, 2014; Perkins & Singh, 2014; Ravel & DeSantis, 2014; Reynolds & Denning, 2013; Robertson, 2013; Roth, 2013; Rudary, 2013; Schwartz, 2013; Solomon, 2013; Sullivan & Gershon, 2014; Teitelbaum & Hoffman, 2013; Thomas & Molk, 2013; Underhill, 2012; Vermeule, 2014; Wriggins, 2013.

Ethical Regulatory Reforms Across the Board

Today, after decades of cat-and-mouse games between the regulated parts of the health care industry and the regulators, a dramatic overhaul of the U.S. health care system has occurred. The historic 900-plus-page ACA is much like what the nation experienced from the Roosevelt era's New Deal, as opposed to the incremental reforms of the past century. Reform of every government agency involved in health care is now needed across the board. Implementation of any meaningful reforms will be enormously complex and require long and careful consideration by all stakeholders, including consumers of health care from all socioeconomic backgrounds.

The ethics of health care concern the ways in which stakeholders ought to treat one another as comprehensive regulatory reforms are implemented. Passage of the ACA by no means ended the health care debate; it just splintered one massive question mark into a lot of new big ones (Wharton, 2010).

Transparency and Protections for Consumers of Health Care

Americans want a better health care system than currently exists. The ACA does not envision a pure single-payer government-run system, nor does it envision a free market private industry program. It is a hybrid, and only time will tell what kind of hybrid it may be. One principle, however, is inviolate: any new health regulations should provide transparency and protections for all consumers of health care (Relman, 2010). Often, enacted health care regulations create more problems than they solve. The nation could easily adopt regulations that would create a more orderly health care system, but those changes could also stifle innovation. Any changes should occur in a carefully considered way. Reforms should be more likely to have a positive impact over the long term, as opposed to immediately dousing the multiple fires that are now burning.

Consolidating Congressional Oversight

Although it may be challenging, there should be some consolidation in oversight of the U.S. health care system in order to improve the delivery of health care to Americans. Politically, it will be very difficult to consolidate, because power in congressional committees is at stake. Health regulation remains fragmented because separate committees in Congress control different regulatory bodies, and no congressional committee is likely to give up power easily (Daschle, et al., 2009). While the House Science and Technology Standing Committee and the Senate Health, Education, Labor, and Pensions Standing Committee most affect the health care industry, there are two select committees in each House and various congressional commissions and joint committees composed of members of both Houses that regulate and oversee the health care industry. Whether decisions can be made that look beyond the power of congressional committees to the benefit of all Americans remains to be seen.

There are many examples of how the health care industry and regulators currently interact, with the largest providers leading and regulators one step behind (Christensen, 2009). Today's fragmented regulatory environment often allows shrewd industry players to choose an oversight venue where government agencies are more likely to approach their role with a narrow focus that prevents them from considering larger, harmful trends shaping the U.S. health care system (Wharton, 2012). For instance, the convergence of many health care sectors is rapidly changing the laws governing provider competition and regulation. Pharmaceutical conglomerates are coupling with biotechnology corporations, while emerging biopharmaceutical products are developing that do not fit into any existing regulatory schemes. Separate regulatory schemes made sense when medications were pharmaceuticals and the biotechnology industry was practically nonexistent. Today, providers of medical products learn how to package a product so that they may choose its regulators (Christensen, 2009). Again, all sorts of improper things can, and do, take place when no single regulatory scheme is comprehensively managing medical products or health care services (Wharton, 2012a).

Redefining the Balance between Regulation and Medical Innovations

While the nation now understands the benefits of preventive care and has begun to think more about the social stakes involved in providing affordable access to every resident in the United States (Golec & DiMasi, 2008), opposition to changing the status quo must continue to be met head-on. There is a paradigm shift as the health care industry changes from treating diseases to preventing or delaying the onset and severity of diseases. At the same time, quality health care depends on safe and effective medicine (Parasidis, 2011). If the nation wants to enjoy the benefits of medical innovation, Americans must continue to support policies that encourage investments in the providers of medical products.

Developing a Comprehensive Regulatory Infrastructure

A careful approach to new regulations must be taken as the nation goes about setting up a better health care system (Wharton, 2012a). The current regulatory infrastructure was created in a fragmented, piecemeal fashion over almost a century. In the wake of the ACA, there is a once-in-a-lifetime opportunity to start over with a comprehensive approach to providing coordinated, accountable health care. In the end, the most pressing thing that nearly everyone agrees on is that the time to make changes in the U.S. health care system is now (Wharton, 2012).

Fair and Consistent Implementation of the Affordable Care Act

Fairness and consistency have sometimes been called the hallmarks of health care ethics (Beauchamp & Childress, 2012). Ethics is supposed to provide principles for decision-making, and in order for it to do so, ethical standards must be rational; to be rational, they must be fair and free of contradiction and conflicts (Rawls, 1971/2005). For instance, if the law says that criminal intent is required before health care providers can be charged with health care fraud, and also asserts that deliberate and planned acts do not necessarily require criminal intent, these standards are ambiguous and conflicting. In the same way, if ethical practices are not fair and lack consistency, rational health care providers will find themselves at a loss as to what they should do and divided about how they should act. Health care ethics requires fairness and consistency in the sense that ethical standards should be fair and not be contradictory or in conflict with societal values or politically realistic trade-offs (AMA, 2012). Uncovering unfairness and inconsistencies and then modifying standards so that they are equitable and consistent are an important part of ethics (Beauchamp & Childress, 2012).

Equitable Standards for Preexisting Health Conditions

Where is inconsistency likely to be uncovered? First, ethical standards may be inconsistent with each other. These inconsistencies are discovered by examining situations in which standards require incompatible behaviors (Rawls, 1971/2005). For instance, the health insurance industry can go from being a partner to an antagonist. It is wrong to refuse to comply with insurance policies, and the law makes it wrong to deny basic coverage for preexisting health conditions or to increase insurance rates exorbitantly if someone uses too much health care in comparison to others. However, suppose that a health insurer denies treatment on other grounds that result in denial of care for a preexisting health condition, such as denial of basic coverage altogether to the extent allowed by state laws. This situation reveals an inconsistency between ethical standards and the law. Either health insurers act in compliance with what health conditions are specifically excluded in their underwriting policies, or they can avoid harming innocent people by providing basic coverage to preexisting conditions, but they cannot do both. To be consistent, one or both of these standards must be modified by examining the reasons for accepting them and weighing these reasons to see which standard is more important and worth retaining, or which is less important and in need of modification (Beauchamp & Childress, 2012).

Fair Fragmentation of Health Insurance Markets

Macroeconomics may have to give way to **microeconomics** for individual American households struggling with health insurance. In other words, the dynamics of health care in terms of growth, inflation, and price levels at the state and national policy level (macroeconomics) may have to succumb to the perspective of individual consumers of health care with a focus on the interaction between providers and consumers and the factors that influence consumer decisions: supply and demand (microeconomics). Small groups and individual health insurance markets may have to be consolidated into larger groups through federal and state exchanges, where insurers are able to price premiums in accordance with overall risk as opposed to individual risk. For instance, all people within large geographic area or employer groups pay the same premium for health insurance based on **average group member risk**; that is, the cost of health care for the group is pooled and shared equally among all members. This is in contrast to the situation before the ACA, where the premiums of individuals and people in small groups were based on an individual or a family's own expected risk rather than the pooled risk of a larger community.

Public policies now preclude the health insurance industry from looking for opportunities to individualize basic coverage at the microeconomic level. People with adverse or preexisting health conditions can no longer be excluded from access to affordable health insurance as a method used to restrain cost (Levine, et al., 2007). In current allocations of risk, large group markets share the risk of poor health equally with individual and small group health markets, causing fair distribution of health risks. Individual and small group markets are no longer charged higher health insurance premiums and treated as a means to manage costs to advance the self-interests of the insurance industry. All insurance markets are now treated the same unless they differ in ways that are relevant to the management of risks, as opposed to avoidance of risks (Mariner, 2010).

Fair and Consistent Application of Ethical Principles

Another kind of injustice and inconsistency emerges when ethical principles are applied to one situation but not applied to another (Beauchamp & Childress, 2012). Processes for designing and administering health insurance should result in similar coverage decisions under similar circumstances (Wynia & Schwab, 2015). For instance, to be just and consistent, the same ethical principle of fairness must be applied to one situation that is applied to another unless the two situations differ in material, relevant ways. In this situation, some people believe they have the right to whatever health care they want, and they claim they are entitled to the latest medical innovations, and that they should be free to decide whatever care they choose, even if the care they demand is still experimental or involves unapproved treatments. In other words, they should receive the health care that they believe will benefit them (Tsai, 2014). Yet the same people often oppose providing this level of access to health care for every member of society. What is the difference between the two situations that would justify this difference in access to health care, if any? What is the difference that makes it all right for some people to have access to the latest medical technologies, while others can be denied access to all but emergency care?

Fairness and Consistency Imply Integrity

There is another sense in which the need for fairness and consistency enters into health care ethics. Ethical standards may be fairly and consistently applied, but some people may fail to be truthful and honest. Integrity characterizes people who act in ways that are consistent with their values. Polonius, a character in Shakespeare's *Hamlet*, points out how critical such integrity is to the moral life when he says to his son, Laertes: "This above all: to thine own self be true, And it must follow, as the night the day, Thou canst not then be false to any man."

Fairness and consistency imply integrity, yet desires may conflict with each other. For instance, the nation's political desire to provide universal access to high-quality, affordable health care by requiring nearly everyone to purchase health insurance is contradicted by the desire to avoid the social costs this mandate may require. Allowing such contradictions when implementing health care reform could become self-defeating, because these desires are contradictory. To achieve fairness and consistency in implementing massive changes to the health care system, the nation's political desires to provide universal access must be realistically traded off to produce a national consensus on what the United States is willing to pay for health care (Christensen, 2009).

As Justice Oliver Wendell Holmes said, the law "has the final title to respect that it exists, that it is not a Hegelian dream, but a part of the lives of men" (Holmes, 1897). Ethical behavior is a matter of being fair and consistent by extending to all people the same regard and consideration that one claims for oneself. One way to summarize health care ethics is the requirement to avoid contradictions between what one thinks is appropriate for others and what one thinks is appropriate for oneself. In other words, morality must be infused into any legal discourse of health care reform.

Ethical Principles and Perennial Issues

Are fairness and consistency all there is to health care ethics? The objective of this text was to identify the perennial issues confronting a health care industry in the midst of flux and change. Rather than advocating that everyone choose for themselves what principles will guide them in making ethical decisions, this text asks that important principles guide important decisions rather than the other way around. The ethical principles of compassion, equality of opportunity, personal autonomy, and beneficence are intertwined with the core American values of justice and individual and social responsibility (Levine, et al., 2007). Focus on the obligation to be ethical must guide reforms to improve the quality and equality of health care for all members of society.

The decision-making process advocated in this text has substance and structure and is guided by a consistent rationale. Ethical principles must be fundamental to the health care industry if it is to be effective and trusted; hence, all stakeholders must be accountable for their ethics and all stakeholders must work together to ensure that shared ethical principles are widely promoted, understood, and followed (Wynia, et al., 1999). There is a moral imperative that is intrinsic in the nation's ongoing health care reform efforts. As was paraphrased from Archbishop Desmond Tutu of South Africa in the preface to this text: "It is time we come to learn we are not our brother or sister's keeper, we are our brother's brother and our sister's sister." While fairness and consistency are not the only features of health care ethics, they are two of the most necessary. Ethics requires fairness and consistency among ethical standards and how these standards are applied. Ethics also requires fairness and consistency between ethical standards and actions. Finally, ethics requires fairness and consistency between how we care for ourselves and how, as a nation, we choose to care for *all* of our brothers and sisters.

ETHICAL OR UNETHICAL DECISION

Social Advocates' Fidelity or Infidelity to the Law

Ethics Issue: *Is it ethical for critics of health care reform to obstruct reforms by repeatedly challenging the validity of the ACA and is such social movement advocacy compatible with fidelity and devotion to the law?*

Ethics Analysis: Yes, critics of the ACA have little recourse other than lawsuits to challenge what they perceive as federal intrusions on state sovereignty and individual rights. A traditional litigation strategy is to approach an issue from as many different angles as possible in the hopes that at least one will succeed. Such a strategy is designed to reveal any splits of opinion on critical issues. In this instance, during the bipartisan debate on health care reform, proponents of reform insisted that the minimum coverage provision was not a tax. But when states began challenging the constitutionality of the law, the U.S. Justice Department defended the law as the exercise of Congress's power to lay and collect taxes. Contradictions in the law to buy health insurance had to be challenged. This is not obstruction; it is an opportunity to clarify and strengthen the law.

Ethics Analysis: No, obstruction is the wrong approach. Instead of obstructing the ACA, critics should look at all the ways the nation can meet the challenge to deliver high-quality health care to all Americans. The minimum coverage provision for health insurance coverage has brought about substantive discussions about cost containment. This is a transformative mandate that calls for a dramatic change toward more equitable health care. The starting point is no longer whether to expand basic coverage. Policy debates going forward are about how to expand access to affordable coverage and contain misallocated spending (Wharton, 2010).

Change brings pain to people who are too heavily invested in the status quo, but it brings opportunity to everybody else (Wharton, 2010). While adding formerly uninsured Americans will put stresses on the U.S. health care system (Cohen & Martinez, 2010), more health care professionals can be trained and tasks can be reoriented. By starting in the direction of universal health care, the nation has committed to making major changes to achieve a higher-quality and more equitable health care system consistent with a focus on what is best in science and modern medicine.

Court Holdings and Decisions: One federal judge in Florida struck down the entire ACA because it requires almost all individuals to buy health insurance or pay a penalty, a provision the judge ruled both unconstitutional and inseparable from the rest of the law. On appeal to the U.S. Supreme Court, the court was found to have erred in its decision to invalidate the entire law. Though more federal courts have upheld the law than struck it down, the U.S. Supreme Court took up this issue and upheld the entire ACA, with the exception of the portion that allowed the federal government to withdraw previously authorized federal funding for Medicaid if a state failed to comply with the ACA's expanded Medicaid requirements.

— Patient Protection and Affordable Care Act, 42 U.S.C. § 18001, *et seq.* (2010), *as amended by* Health Care and Education Reconciliation Act of 2010, Pub.L.No. 111-152, 124 Stat. 1029 through 124. Stat. 1084. *See also Seven-Sky, et al. v. Holder, et al.,* 661 F.3d 1 (U.S. Court of Appeals for the District of Columbia Circuit 2011), *cert. denied,* 133 S.Ct. 63 (U.S. Supreme Court 2012); *Commonwealth of Virginia ex rel. Cuccinelli v. Sebelius, et al.,* 656 F.3d 253 (U.S. Court of Appeals for the 4th Circuit 2011), *cert. denied,* 133 S.Ct. 59 (U.S. Supreme Court 2012); *Liberty University, et al. v. Geithner, et al.,* 671 F.3d 391 (U.S. Court of Appeals for the 4th Circuit 2011), *cert. denied,* 133 S.Ct. 60 (U.S. Supreme Court 2012); *Thomas More Law Center, et al. v. Obama, et al.,* 651 F.3d 529 (U.S. Court of Appeals for the 6th Circuit 2011), *cert. denied,* 133 S.Ct. 61 (U.S. Supreme Court 2012); *Florida, et al. v. U.S. Department of Health and Human Services,* 648 F.3d 1235 (U.S. Court of Appeals for the 11th Circuit 2011), *affirmed in part and reversed in part,* 132 S.Ct. 2566 (U.S. Supreme Court 2012).

CHAPTER SUMMARY

- Critics seek to block changes contained in the ACA because of its threat of redistributing over $2.6 trillion in health care costs, disturbing the status quo, and bringing uncertainty into an already complex situation.
- The motives behind opposition to the ACA require ethical evaluation, because the goal of health care reform is greater fairness and justice in the U.S. health care system.
- The goal of this text is to embark on a journey toward discovering America's shared values and a common public ethic so as to develop a fair and just health care system, thereby promoting the highest potential for the nation.
- Comprehensive reform of the U.S. health care system requires acknowledging that Americans have different perceptions of what will benefit them and what it means to give others their just due.
- Market distortion through tax subsidies and unrestrained government-financed health insurance programs has escalated costs and created such complexities that the true dynamics of the U.S. health care system have become a social enigma.
- As the nation seeks to develop a more just and comprehensive health care system, Americans must decide what role government should play in implementing health care reform.

REFERENCES

Adler, J. H., & Cannon, M. F. (2013). Taxation without representation: The illegal IRS rule to expand tax credits under the PPACA. *Health Matrix: The Journal of Law-Medicine, 23*, 119–195.

AMA (American Medical Association). (2012). *The ethical force program: Advancing ethics in health care.* Chicago, IL: AMA.

Atkinson, R. (2014). An elevation of neo-classical professionalism in law and business. *Georgetown Journal of Law and Public Policy, 12*, 621–730.

Atwell, B. L. (2015). Rethinking the childhood-adult divide: Meeting the mental health needs of emerging adults. *Albany Law Journal of Science and Technology, 25,* 1–37.

Auerbach, D. (2014). Assessing the true impact of the ACA: Revisiting the CBO's initial predictions. *American Journal of Law and Medicine, 40,* 231–236.

Avraham, R. (2014). Overlooked and underused: Clinical practice guidelines and malpractice liability for independent physicians. *Connecticut Insurance Law Journal, 20,* 273–332.

___. (2013). The economics of insurance law: A primer. *Connecticut Insurance Law Journal, 19,* 29–112.

Bahrenburg, R., & Robert, M. (2013). Health care access: Access after health care reform. *The Georgetown Journal of Gender and the Law, 14,* 489–515.

Beauchamp, T. L., & Childress, J. F. (2012). *Principles of biomedical ethics* (7th ed.). New York, NY: Oxford University Press.

Benedict, K. S. (2013). When might does not create religious rights: For-profit corporations' employees and the contraceptive coverage mandate. *Columbia Journal of Gender and Law, 26,* 58–122.

Biebl, H. (2013). Re-thinking health insurance. *University of Michigan Journal of Law Reform Online, 2,* 62A–66A.

Bisi, R., & Horan, P. (2013). Access to contraception. *The Georgetown Journal of Gender and the Law, 14,* 245–279.

Blumstein, J. F. (2014). Understanding the faulty predictions regarding the challenges to health reform. *University of Illinois Law Review, 2014,* 1251–1263.

Bolin, M. (2014). The Affordable Care Act and people living with HIV/AIDS: A roadmap to better health outcomes. *Annals of Health Law, 23,* 28–60.

Bowser, R. (2015). Race and rationing. *Health Matrix: The Journal of Law-Medicine, 25,* 87–106.

Bryant, A. C. (2013). Institutional newspeak: Learning to love the Affordable Care Act decision. *Journal of Legislation, 39,* 15–42.

Cannan, J. C. (2013). A legislative history of the Affordable Care Act: How legislative procedure shapes legislative history. *Law Library Journal, 105,* 131–173.

Carr, M. (2014). Arkansas's section 1115 waiver and expansion of Medicaid: A path toward equal care. *Annals of Health Law, 24,* 43–51.

Christensen, C. M. (2009). *The innovator's prescription: A disruptive solution for health care.* New York, NY: McGraw Hill.

Cohen, R. A., & Martinez, M. E. (2010). *Health insurance coverage: Early release of estimates from the National Health Interview Survey.* Atlanta, GA: Centers for Disease Control, National Center for Health Statistics.

Connell, C., et al. (2013). Religious refusals under the Affordable Care Act: Contraception as essential health care. *DePaul Journal of Health Care Law, 15,* 1–14.

Coogan, L. A. (2014). A few for-profit businesses' battle over the Affordable Care Act's preventative services mandate. *Journal of Law and Commerce, 32,* 381–399.

Copeland, C. C. (2012). FDR and Obama: Are there constitutional law lessons from the New Deal for the Obama administration? Beyond separation in federalism enforcement: Medicaid expansion, coercion, and the norm of engagement. *University of Pennsylvania Journal of Constitutional Law, 15,* 91–182.

Daschle, T., et al. (2009). *Critical: What we can do about the health-care crisis.* New York, NY: Macmillan/Thomas Dunne Books.

Desantis, J. A. (2014). The thin red federal poverty line: How rejecting the Medicaid expansion affects those with exchange coverage. *John Marshall Law Review, 47,* 1–23.

Dolgin, J. L. (2013). Who's smiling now? Disparities in American dental health. *Fordham Urban Law Journal, 40,* 1395–1446.

Faizer, A. (2013). Chief Justice John "Marshall" Roberts—How the Chief Justice's majority opinion upholding the federal Patient Protection and Affordable Care Act of 2010 evokes Chief Justice Marshall's decision in *Marbury v. Madison. University of New Hampshire Law Review, 11,* 1–26.

Felland, L. E., et al. (2010). *The economic recession: Early impacts on health-care safety net providers.* Washington, DC: Center for Studying Health System Change.

Fischer, C., & Kasper, J. (2014). Access to contraception. *The Georgetown Journal of Gender and the Law, 15,* 37–55.

Gedicks, F. M., & Van Tassell, R. G. (2014). RFRA exemptions from the contraception mandate: An unconstitutional accommodation of religion. *Harvard Civil Rights-Civil Liberties Law Review, 49,* 343–384.

Georgakopoulos, N. (2013). An insurance structure to encourage investment in preventive health care. *University of Michigan Journal of Law Reform, 46,* 477–493.

Gewirtzman, D. (2012). Lower court constitutionalism: Circuit court discretion in a complex adaptive system. *American University Law Review, 61,* 457–520.

Gilman, M. (2014). A court for the one percent: How the Supreme Court contributes to economic inequality. *Utah Law Review, 2014,* 389–463.

Glen, P. (2013). Health care and the illegal immigrant. *Health Matrix: The Journal of Law-Medicine, 23,* 197–236.

Golec, V. J., & DiMasi, J. (2008). *Drug development costs when financial risk is measured using the Fama-French three factor model.* Unpublished paper, Tufts University, Boston, MA.

Gostin, L. O. (2008). Meeting basic survival needs of the world's least healthy people: Toward a framework convention on global health. *Georgetown Law Journal, 96*, 331–392.

Gould, B. (2014). How the countervailing power of insurers can resolve the tradeoff between market power and health care integration in accountable care organizations. *George Mason Law Review, 22*, 159–199.

Green, S. (2010). *Good value: Reflections on money, ethicality and an uncertain world.* Berkeley, CA: Atlantic Monthly Press.

Greene, J. (2012). Panel III: The limits of authority: Thirteenth Amendment optimism. *Columbia Law Review, 112*, 1733–1767.

Grusin, S. L. (2015). Holding health insurance marketplaces accountable: The unheralded rise and imminent demise of structural reform litigation in health care. *Annals of Health Law, 24*, 337–409.

Hagen, E. (2013). The moral judiciary: Restoring morality as a basis of judicial decision-making. *New England Law Review, 48*, 139–170.

Hall, M. J. (2014). A fiduciary theory of health entitlements. *Cardozo Law Review, 35*, 1729–1779.

Hansen, R., & Newman, R. (2015). Health care: Access after health care reform. *The Georgetown Journal of Gender and the Law, 16*, 191–227.

Hartz, N. M. (2013). Adequate assurance or medical mediocrity: An analysis of the limits on the Affordable Care Act's application to women's health. *William and Mary Journal of Women and the Law, 20*, 245–269.

Hasen, R. L. (2013). End of the dialogue? Political polarization, the Supreme Court, and Congress. *Southern California Law Review, 86*, 205–251.

Hawkes, J., & Seidenfeld, M. (2014). A positive defense of administrative preemption. *George Mason Law Review, 22*, 63–102.

Hetrick, M. (2015). Medicaid and migrant farmworkers: Why the state residency requirement presents a significant access barrier and what states should do about it. *Health Matrix: The Journal of Law-Medicine, 25*, 437–484.

Hewitt, S. (2013). A time to heal: Eliminating barriers to coverage for patients with eating disorders under the Affordable Care Act. *Law and Inequality, 31*, 411–436.

Hodge, Jr., G., & Scanlon, M. (2014). The legal anatomy of product bans to protect the public's health. *Annals of Health Law, 23*, 161–182.

Hoffmann, J. (2014). Preemption and the MLR [Medical Loss Ratio] provision of the Affordable Care Act. *American Journal of Law and Medicine, 40*, 280–297.

Holmes, O. W. (1897). The path of the law. *Harvard Law Review, 10*, 457–478.

Huberfeld, N. (2013). Heed not the umpire (Justice Ginsburg called NFIB). *University of Pennsylvania Journal of Constitutional Law Heightened Scrutiny, 15*, 43A–55A.

____. (2013a). With liberty and access for some: The ACA's disconnect for women's health. *Fordham Urban Law Journal, 40*, 1357–1393.

Huberfeld, N., & Roberts, J. L. (2014). Medicaid expansion as completion of the great society. *University of Illinois Law Review, 2014*, 1–8.

Hulkower, R. L., & Wolf, L. E. (2013). Federal funds for syringe exchange programs: A necessary component toward achieving an AIDS-free generation. *Annals of Health Law, 22*, 307–341.

Jimenez, M. (2011). Finding the good in Holmes's bad man. *Fordham Law Review, 79*, 2069–2126.

Jones, J. (2015). National Federation of Independent Business's impact on state Medicaid programs and the rise of federalism by waiver. *University of Pennsylvania Journal of Constitutional Law, 17*, 1225–1253.

Kaiser Commission on Medicaid and the Uninsured. (2014). *The uninsured: A primer—Key facts about Americans without health insurance.* Washington, DC: Kaiser.

Kessler, S. (2014). Mental health parity: The Patient Protection and Affordable Care Act and the parity definition implications. *Hastings Science and Technology Law Journal, 6*, 145–164.

Kitchen, R. C. (2013). Negative lawmaking delegations: Constitutional structure and delegations to the executive of discretionary authority to amend, waive, and cancel statutory text. *Hastings Constitutional Law Quarterly, 40*, 525–610.

Klees, B. S., et al. (2009). *Brief summaries of Medicare and Medicaid.* Washington, DC: U.S. Department of Health and Human Services, Centers for Medicare and Medicaid Services.

Kleinbard, E. (2008, July 31). Chief Economist for the Joint Tax Committee in Congress, Tax expenditures for health care. [Testimony before the U.S. Senate Committee on Finance], Washington, DC.

LaRocca, R. M. (2014). A tale of litigation past, present, and future: The Patient Protection and Affordable Care Act. *Rhode Island Bar Journal, 62*, 23–38.

Lee, C. J., et al. (2013). Enhancing communication between scientists, government officials, and the lay public: Advancing science and protecting the public's welfare through better multi-stakeholder interfacing. *Annals of Health Law, 22*, 246–279.

Levine, M. A., et al. (2007). Improving access to health care: A consensus ethical framework to guide proposals for reform. *Hastings Center Report, 37*(5), 14–19.

Maher, B. S. (2011). The benefits of opt-in federalism. *Boston College Law Review, 52*, 1733–1793.

Manheim, K. (2015). The health insurance mandate—A tax or a taking? *Hastings Constitutional Law Quarterly, 42*, 323–391.

Mariner, W. K. (2014). Health insurance is dead; Long live health insurance. *American Journal of Law and Medicine, 40*, 195–214.

___. (2010). Health reform: What's insurance got to do with it? Recognizing health insurance as a separate species of insurance. *American Journal of Law and Medicine, 36*, 436–451.

Marino, B., et al. (2015). A case for federal regulation of telemedicine in the wake of the Affordable Care Act. *Columbia Science and Technology Law Review, 16*, 274–347.

McCullough, R. L. (2013). What is all the fuss about? The United States Congress may impose a tax (it's called the "individual mandate"). *Southern California Interdisciplinary Law Journal, 22*, 729–780.

Milhizer, E. R. (2013). The morality and legality of the HHS mandate and the "accommodations". *Ave Maria Law Review, 11*, 211–225.

Moncrieff, A. R. (2013). The individual mandate as healthcare regulation: What the Obama administration should have said in *NFIB v. Sebelius. American Journal of Law and Medicine, 39*, 539–572.

Morley, M. T. (2014). Public law at the cathedral: Enjoining the government. *Cardozo Law Review, 35*, 2453–2503.

Neyarapally, G. A. (2013). A review of recent federal legislative and policy initiatives to enhance the development and evaluation of high value drugs in the United States. *DePaul Journal of Health Care Law, 14*, 503–556.

Nicholson, C. (2013). Access to Medicaid: Recognizing rights to ensure access to care and services. *University of Michigan Journal of Law Reform Online, 2*, 22A–25A.

Noush, (2014). A storied past demands greater access to health care now and into the future. *Annals of Health Law, 24*, 53–70.

Nussbaum, A. (2012). Can Congress make you buy health insurance? The Affordable Care Act, national health care reform, and the constitutionality of the individual mandate. *Duquesne Law Review, 50*, 411–467.

Ogolla, C. (2015). The public health implications of religious exemptions: A balance between public safety and personal choice, or religion gone too far? *Health Matrix: The Journal of Law-Medicine, 25*, 257–307.

Pantelaki, M. I., & White, C. (2014). Health care: Access after health care reform. *The Georgetown Journal of Gender and the Law, 15*, 95–121.

Parasidis, E. (2011). Patients over politics: Addressing legislative failure in the regulation of medical products. *Wisconsin Law Review, 2011*, 929–1001.

Parks, J. R. (2014). A new theory of taxpayer standing. *Columbia Journal of Tax Law, 6*, 118–146.

Pasquale, F. (2014). The hidden costs of health care cost-cutting: Toward a post-neoliberal health-reform agenda. *Law and Contemporary Problems, 77*, 171–193.

Perella, D. F., & Swartzfage, L. K. (2012). Healthy decision or unhealthy oversight? A legal debate on the Patient Protection and Affordable Care Act and the impact of the Supreme Court's recent decision: "Freestanding conceptions of state sovereignty": The *Sebelius* decision's necessary-and-proper holding and its jurisprudential impacts. *Nexus: Chapman's Journal of Law and Policy, 18*, 57–79.

Perkins, J., & Singh, D. (2014). ACA implementation: The court challenges continue. *Annals of Health Law, 23*, 200–214.

Phelps, C. E. (2012). *Health economics* (5th ed.). New York, NY: Pearson Education.

Ravel, G., & DeSantis, A. (2014). Crossing 138: Two approaches to churn under the Affordable Care Act. *Health Matrix: The Journal of Law-Medicine, 24*, 109–141.

Rawls, J. (2005). A theory of justice. Boston, MA: Belknap Press (Original work published 1971).

Relman, A. (2010). *A second opinion: Rescuing America's health care plan for universal coverage serving patients over profit.* New York, NY: Perseus Books Group, Public Affairs.

Reynolds, G. H., & Denning, B. P. (2013). *National Federation of Independent Business v. Sebelius*: Five takes. *Hastings Constitutional Law Quarterly, 40*, 807–832.

Robertson, J. A. (2013). Paid organ donations and the constitutionality of the National Organ Transplant Act. *Hastings Constitutional Law Quarterly, 40*, 221–275.

Roth, V. J. (2013). Will FDA data exclusivity make biologic patents passe? *Santa Clara Computer and High Technology Law Journal, 29*, 249–304.

Rudary, D. J. (2013). Drafting a "sensible" conscience clause: A proposal for meaningful conscience protections for religious employers objecting to the mandated coverage of prescription contraceptives. *Health Matrix: The Journal of Law-Medicine, 23*, 353–394.

Schwartz, R. (2013). Bearing the burden of contraception: Why for-profit businesses must comply with the "contraceptive mandate." *Fordham Journal of Corporate and Financial Law, 18*, 1049–1088.

Segall, E. J. (2015). Making law out of nothing at all: Why the government should win the latest Obamacare challenge. *University of Pennsylvania Law Review Online, 163*, 216–223.

Siegel, N. S. (2012). The constitutionality of the Affordable Care Act: Ideas from the academy. *Law and Contemporary Problems, 74*, 1–6.

Sohoni, M. (2012). The idea of "too much law." *Fordham Law Review, 80*, 1585–1632.

Solomon, S. (2013). Health exchange federalism: Striking the balance between state flexibility and consumer protection in ACA implementation. *Cardozo Law Review, 34*, 2073–2110.

Somin, I. (2014). *NFIB v. Sebelius* and the constitutional debate over federalism. *Oklahoma City University Law Review, 39*, 415–439.

Staman, J., & Brougher, C. (2012). *Requiring individuals to obtain health insurance: A constitutional analysis*. Washington, DC: Congressional Research Service.

Sullivan, J. C., & Gershon, R. (2014). State fiscal considerations and research opportunities emerging from the Affordable Care Act's Medicaid expansion. *American Journal of Law and Medicine, 40*, 247–252.

Tahk, S. C. (2013). Everything is tax: Evaluating the structural transformation of U.S. policymaking. *Harvard Journal on Legislation, 50*, 67–107.

Teitelbaum, J. B., & Hoffman, L. G. (2013). Health reform and correctional health care: How the Affordable Care Act can improve the health of ex-offenders and their communities. *Fordham Urban Law Journal, 40*, 1323–1355.

Thide, F. (2012). In search of limiting principles: The Eleventh Circuit invalidates the individual mandate in *Florida v. U.S. Department of Health and Human Services*. *Boston College Law Review, 53*, 359–372.

Thomas, S. A., & Molk, P. (2013). Employer costs and conflicts under the Affordable Care Act. *Cornell Law Review Online. 99*, 50–63.

Tovino, S. A. (2012). All illnesses are (not) created equal: Reforming federal mental health insurance law. *Harvard Journal on Legislation, 59*, 1–51.

Tsai, R. L. (2014). *The many American constitutions: America's forgotten constitutions*. Cambridge, MA: Harvard University Press.

Tyler, E. T. (2012). Aligning public health, health care, law and policy: Medical-legal partnership as a multilevel response to the social determinants of health. *Health and Biomedical Law Society, 8*, 211–247.

Underhill, K. (2012). Paying for prevention: Challenges to health insurance coverage for biomedical HIV prevention in the United States. *American Journal of Law and Medicine, 38*, 607–666.

Vermeule, A. (2014). One-hundred years later—Revisiting Charles Beard's *An Economic Interpretation of the Constitution of the United States*: Beard and Holmes on constitutional adjudication. *Constitutional Commentary, 29*, 457–473.

von Goethe, J. W. (1998). *Faust: A tragedy*. New York, NY: W. W. Norton (Original work published 1604).

Weeden, L. D. (2013). The Commerce Clause implications of the individual mandate under the Patient Protection and Affordable Care Act. *Journal of Law and Health, 26*, 29–49.

Wharton School at the University of Pennsylvania. (2012). Health care reform: Life after the Supreme Court debate. *Knowledge@Wharton*.

____. (2012a). Looking for solutions in a rapidly changing health care environment.

____. (2010). Health care reform: Not ready to be discharged yet.

WHO (World Health Organization. (2014). *World health statistics*. Geneva, Switzerland: WHO.

Widener, M. J. (2015). The presentment clause meets the suspension power: The Affordable Care Act's long and winding road to implementation. *The Boston University Public Interest Law Journal, 24*, 109–141.

Wiley, L. F. (2014). Health law as social justice. *Cornell Journal of Law and Public Policy, 24*, 47–105.

Wriggins, J. B. (2013). Mandates, markets, and risk: Auto insurance and the Affordable Care Act. *Connecticut Insurance Law Journal, 19*, 275–322.

Wynia, M. K., et al. (1999). Medical professionalism in society. *New England Journal of Medicine, 341*, 1612–1616.

Wynia, M. K., & Schwab, A. P. (2015). *Ensuring fairness in health care coverage: An employer's guide to make good decisions on tough issues*. New York, NY: American Medical Association.

Yamin, A. E. (2008). Will we take suffering seriously? Reflections on what applying a human rights framework to health means and why we should care. *Health and Human Rights, 10*, 45–63.

Zietlow, R. E. (2011). Democratic constitutionalism and the Affordable Care Act. *Ohio State Law Journal, 72*, 1367–1405.

Glossary

Abortifacient: medication or medical device that causes an abortion.

Abortion: medical intervention to end a pregnancy by removing an implanted embryo or fetus from a woman's womb.

Acquired Immune Deficiency Syndrome (AIDS): last stage of Human Immunodeficiency Virus, which destroys certain white blood cells critical to the normal functioning of the human immune system; once people become symptomatic and their immune systems are severely compromised or opportunistic infections develop, they face imminent death from multiple cancers and infections. *See* **Human Immunodeficiency Virus** (HIV) *and* **opportunistic diseases**.

Actual price: one of two charges used by hospitals for payment; insurers negotiate this discounted charge from the list price for health care services rendered. *Compare* **list price**.

Actuarial fairness: creates segmented risk pools based on the health risks of specific individuals. The social consequences of health insurance and the allocation of health resources are not considered under this principle; instead, premiums are adjusted according to expected future costs.

Acute care: short-term care for serious diseases or trauma.

Advance directive (*aka* advance decision or living will): provides instructions about what health care actions should be taken in the event of a patient's illness or incapacity and he or she is no longer able to make decisions. *Compare* **health care proxy** (that part of the advance directive appointing someone, other than the patient, to make health care decisions).

Adverse event: potentially avoidable occurrence that harms patients; including patient falls, medication administration errors, pressure ulcers, hospital infections, and mortality

in health care settings. *Compare* **serious adverse event** (unexpected) *and* **serious reportable event** (harm that should have been prevented).

Adverse selection: the tendency of people who are poorer risks to seek health insurance to a greater extent than do healthier people who are better risks; situation that occurs when price increases or reduced benefits make insurance no longer price-effective, taking those who make fewer and less expensive claims out of the risk pool, leaving only higher-risk individuals.

Affordable Care Act of 2010 (ACA) (*aka* colloquially by opponents of the law as Obamacare): a new legal framework for health care overhaul designed to expand health insurance coverage to nearly everyone, mainly by giving lower earners subsidies to purchase private insurance, expanding Medicaid insurance, and creating new marketplaces where consumers of health care can shop for policies; includes hundreds of provisions to remake the health care system, from payment changes for providers to a requirement that chain restaurants list Calorie counts.

Altman's law: the principle that when no one can agree on a change, nothing changes; holds that every stakeholder's second choice for health care reform is the status quo. Named for Brandeis University health policy professor, Stewart Altman.

American ethic (*aka* common public ethic): more than simply a collection of individuals with similar personal values, it is a combination of the customs, norms, and traditions of individual citizens in the United States; the common ethical standards essential for a just law and civil society; guards against governmental and business abuses. *See* **universal values**.

Americans with Disabilities Act of 1990 (ADA): federal law that prohibits employers from discriminating against disabled people on the basis of their disability in regard to job application procedures (hiring, advancement, or discharge), compensation, or job training.

Anti retroviral medications (ARVs)**:** can slow down the rate at which the Human Immunodeficiency Virus weakens the human immune system to the point of full-blown Acquired Immune Deficiency Syndrome. *See* **Acquired Immune Deficiency Syndrome** (AIDS) and **Human Immunodeficiency Virus** (HIV).

Artificial nutrition and hydration (*aka* extraordinary life support)**:** a death-prolonging medical procedure (also identified as a life-sustaining procedure) whereby patients are fed nutrients or fluids by a tube inserted in a vein, under the skin in the subcutaneous tissues, or in the stomach.

Asymmetric information: in consumer and business relationships, refers to situations in which sellers always know more than the buyers; for instance, food producers have more information about the nutritional value of food products than the consumers who consume the products.

Authority-based medicine: traditional philosophy of care where individual clinical experience provides the foundation for diagnosis, treatment, and prognosis; clinical training relies on expert medical opinion and common sense. *Compare* **evidence-based medicine** (opposite of authority-based medicine; relies on scientific information, not individual expert medical opinions).

Autonomy: capacity for self-determination; ethical value which ensures that individuals that have the right to make independent, legitimate decisions about their own health care based on their own value systems. Burdens all stakeholders (patients, physicians, nurses, and other health care professionals alike) to be well-informed regarding treatment decisions. Involves more than simply protecting individuals' freedom to decide within the existing health care system; assumes that freedom in self-governance is always informed by moral preferences that are relevant considerations as opposed to transient arguments. *Compare* **personal autonomy** (prohibiting paternalism or interference with the decisions of patients for their own good) *with* **autonomy from government** (individual freedom from non-interference or unreasonable involvement and control; interference requires justification).

Autonomy from government (*aka* political autonomy)**:** the right of individuals and corporate organizations to make legitimate decisions and act on them as free and independent moral agents absent government interference; the right to have individual and private-sector decisions respected, honored, and heeded. *Compare* **corporate autonomy** (the right to pursue one's interests without undue restriction; interference requires justification).

Average group member risk: within large group insurance markets, the cost of health care for the group is pooled and shared equally among all members; in contrast to small group and individual insurance markets where the cost of health care is based on the individual's (or family's) own expected risk.

Bad debt: accounts written off as unpaid by health care providers even though patients have the ability to pay; extraordinary billing and collection practices against charitable care patients are restricted under the APA. *Compare* **charitable care** (excludes bad debt as a component of charitable care) *and* **uncompensated care** (sum of charitable care and bad debt).

Basic health insurance: provides necessary coverage for medically necessary care services that support the goals of prevention, traditional diagnosis, and treatment; does not extend coverage to long-term critical care or extensive hospitalizations for acute care. *See* **medically necessary care**.

Behavioral addiction: generally refers to eating that is motivated by emotions ranging along the spectrum of food cravings to compulsive eating; continued excessive eating of unhealthy foods in spite of adverse consequences; loss of control over one's eating habits. *See* **food addiction**.

Benchmark: precedent for how malpractice compensation should be set. *See* **quality-adjusted life year**.

Beneficence: ethical value that promotes the well-being of others in ways that serve their best interests and are beneficial to them, all the while seeking to achieve the highest-quality (not just high-quality) results on their behalf. Implies that one does not inflict harm but rather seeks to prevent harm; principle for providing benefits; balances benefits against risks and costs.

Best interests standard: refers to the highest-quality care that will be administered to a terminally ill and suffering patient at the end of life, not necessarily for the purpose of extending biological life for the longest time, but to offer compassion and pain control; often applied to minors. *Compare* **substituted judgment standard** (decisions based on what the patient would have chosen).

Bioequivalent: the assumption that genetically modified food ingredients are the same as traditional food; criteria are determined by the food industry.

Bodily integrity: the right to control one's body free from the restraint or interference of others; generally used in abortion and end-of-life discussions.

Care coordination (*aka* integrative care)**:** manages health care interventions for patients with chronic health conditions, such as diabetes, heart disease, and asthma; reduces health care costs through improved patient compliance with treatment plans. Referred to as *disease management* before the focus of health care became prevention or delay of disease as opposed to treatment of disease.

Cases of first impression: involve questions of law which have been presented for the first time and which have never been decided before in any reported court decisions. *See* **first impression** (cases or issues of).

Certification: recognition that labor unions are the sole representative of employees in bargaining with employers; refers to an employer's recognition of a labor union as the representative of its employees. *Compare* **decertification petition** (opposite of certification).

Chargemaster rates (*aka* undiscounted or list charges)**:** a uniform set of charges and codes that health care providers can bill to patients or insurers. Codes are developed by the American Medical Association to assist individual providers in developing their own financial management systems; rates only apply to the insured and individuals who qualify for charitable care (*i.e.*, can still bill list charges to patients who do not qualify for free or discounted care).

Charitable care: discounted or free necessary and reasonable care for financially distressed patients who meet the eligibility criteria set by a health care provider; includes costs not charged, but excludes bad debt. *Compare* **uncompensated care** (the sum of free and discounted care plus bad debt).

Charitable care standard: criterion used to measure tax-exemption status; requires tax-exempt hospitals to provide access to emergency and medically necessary care regardless of patients' ability to pay for such care. *Compare* **community benefit standard** (requires hospitals to provide emergency care, financial assistance for medically necessary care [not just emergency care], health education, and community-building activities that directly address the social determinants of health).

Choices model (of decision-making)**:** focuses attention on how decisions to choose among moral rights are made; emphasis on the importance of respect for the human dignity of everyone; concerned with the conditions or rules the action can meet. *Compare* **exceptions model** *and* **utility model** (that focus on results and outcomes).

Chronic pain: pain lasting longer than 3 to 6 months, the usual time period expected for tissue healing; has no adaptive purpose (unlike acute pain); it serves no other purpose than suffering.

Civil Rights Act of 1964: federal legislation that prohibits discrimination in employment based on race, color, national origin, sex, or religion.

Class action lawsuit: legal term describing a lawsuit brought by a large group of plaintiffs or in which a large number of defendants are sued; the court must grant permission (certify the class) for this kind of lawsuit to proceed.

Common good: achieved when the burdens and benefits of life function together to achieve a sustainable society; includes the things Americans commit to do as a society that benefit all U.S. residents.

Common good model (of decision-making)**:** considers more than just those affected by a decision; rather society is the priority. Focuses on whether a decision contributes to or burdens a particular aspect of the common good; considers system functions and the impact of decisions on the wellbeing of all members of society. *Compare* **utility model** (that focuses on the total benefits and burdens or total net effects for everyone affected by a decision).

Common public ethic (aka public ethic *and* American ethic)**:** ethical principles and beliefs of a nation with shared general interests and historical traditions. *Compare* **universal values** (that may also apply to a person or a group or a community of people within a nation rather than just a nation).

Community benefit standard: criteria for determining the tax-exempt status of hospitals as opposed to the provision of charitable care. Hospitals qualify for exemption status by providing emergency care, health education, and community-building activities that directly address the social determinants of health. *Compare* **charitable care** (provision of medically necessary care regardless of the ability to pay) *and* **uncompensated care** (sum of charitable care and bad debt even though patients have the ability to pay).

Comparative effectiveness: compares 2 or more medical treatments or medications to measure their relative benefits or harms for prevention, diagnosis, treatment, and monitoring of health conditions. The purpose of this evidence-based analysis is to improve health outcomes by determining which interventions are most effective for which patients and under what circumstances.

Compassion: 1 of the 3 foundational principles of the newly emerging ethics of health care (in addition to justice and equality of opportunity); requires physicians, nurses, and other health care professionals to respond to those suffering from disease or injuries with a deep awareness of patients' human dignity. Arises from the common humanity of every member of society, especially the relationship between providers of health care and their patients. This ethical obligation is supported by economic and social considerations; the moral imperative to assist the most vulnerable members of society (for instance, paying attention to the effects of unaffordable access to health insurance coverage and the inadequate health care that results from being uninsured or underinsured). *See* **justice** *and* **equality of opportunity**.

Compensatory justice: refers to the extent to which individuals and institutions are fairly compensated for their injuries by those who have injured them. Just compensation is proportional to the harm inflicted; redresses harms caused by misconduct of the health or insurance industries, the government, or some other third party; focuses on a systems-oriented, problem-solving, collaborative model of decision-making. For instance, this ethical principle would resolve successful malpractice claims through a compensation fund instead of requiring resort to the legal system.

Competency: sufficient mental capacity to understand and make voluntary, informed decisions; in minors, a certain level of maturity can denote competency to make important medical decisions regarding their own care.

Competency standard: presenting as being capable of functioning normally and possessing sufficient mental capacity to make and express self-directed choices on matters of importance.

Conception: occurs during implantation of the fertilized egg five to seven days after sexual intercourse; also equated with fertilization or the union of the male sperm and the female egg, which occurs within 120 hours after sexual intercourse. This definition is often a source of dispute between science and religion. *Compare* **fertilization** (cellular fusion of male sperm and female egg).

Conflictss of interest: interdependence between scientific and commercial interests that arises from the commercialization of medical research through federal legislation and the need for subsidization of scientific progress by the medical products industry. Conflicting interests are generally undefined, but imply that improper influence or bias may be unavoidable, even if subconscious or unintended; can sometimes be remedied by voluntary disclosure of any source of bias or influence.

Conformity: uniform and consistent agreement and following of what is socially acceptable and expected.

Conscience legislation (aka refusal clause legislation)**:** allows health care providers to conscientiously object to performing certain medical procedures (for instance, pharmacists filling contraceptive prescriptions or physicians performing abortions).

Consent: the freedom to think and act without being constrained by government; citizens agree to transfer some of their fundamental freedoms to the government in order to protect their rights and promote the common good. *Compare* **liberty** (the right to be free, independent of any laws).

Consistency: logically coherent with no contradictions in the law; having common outcomes, especially for vulnerable populations with socioeconomic inequalities who present themselves for care.

Consumer autonomy: philosophy that maintains consumers should have the capacity to make independent selections of their food and beverages.

Contingent employees: employment is dependent on future circumstances and as yet unknown need for their continued work.

Contingent work: any job in which an employee does not have an explicit or implicit expectation of long-term employment; includes

part-time and temporary employees, independent contractors, and outsourced employees of subcontracting employers or temporary job agencies. *See* **outsourced employees**.

Continuing obligation (principle of)**:** once a provider begins a course of treatment for a person with a severe mental disorder, care cannot always be terminated when the patient is discharged or released from an institutional setting without making arrangements for the patient's continued care elsewhere.

Contraception: the prevention of pregnancy using natural methods such as avoiding sex during a woman's known fertile periods or using artificial methods such as birth control pills or condoms.

Contraceptives: devices that act to prevent fertilization and/or implantation.

Controlled Substances Act of 1970 (CSA)**:** defines and regulates the unlawful distribution and use of controlled substances (which includes the distribution and use of prescribed medications). Sets out a criminal law enforcement function performed by the U.S. Drug Enforcement Administration.

Corporate autonomy: the right of the private sector to freely make ethical business decisions without government or political interference; for instance, providers of health care (such as hospitals and physician practices) are free to choose whom to serve in non-life-threatening medical situations. *See* **personal autonomy** and **autonomy from government**.

Corporate practice of medicine doctrine: seeks to keep the economic and business incentives of corporate organizations from interfering with the professional duties of licensed physicians. *Compare* **enterprise liability** (shifts liability away from individuals to hospitals or other corporate organizations).

Corporate practice prohibition: common law that precludes non-physicians from interfering with the practice of medicine; financial or other arrangements cannot control or influence the medical judgment of physicians.

Corporate well-being: long-term financial health or survival of a health care organization.

Corrective justice: defined in terms of undoing a wrong or as giving rise to specific reasons for rectifying wrongs, such as individual and social losses from gun injuries.

Cost avoider: the party who could most lessen the social costs arising from illegal gun sales.

Cost-sharing: payment of deductibles and co-payments in health insurance plans.

Cost-shifting: occurs when the insurance industry charges more for certain medical products and health care services in order to subsidize products and services that are provided at or below cost.

Cross-subsidization: the transfer of costs from regulated parts of the health care system to unregulated parts; results in overuse and unfair allocations of the nation's health care resources.

Damages (*aka* injuries): the economic (actual costs) and non-economic (pain and suffering) injuries caused by a breach of a legal duty, such as medical malpractice.

Dangerous mental disorder: whenever a person's mental condition is a physical danger to self or others. *See* **mental disability**.

Death: general term of law whereby individuals can be declared biologically dead if they have sustained irreversible cessation of either their circulatory and respiratory functions or of the entire brain; this uniform definition may vary by state.

Decency: conformity with ethical principles and commonly accepted standards of what is right.

Decertification petition: request from employees represented by a labor union stating that the union no longer represents their work interests and requesting that the union's representation be terminated. *Compare* **certification** (opposite of decertification).

Decision-making models (*aka* mental models): eight theoretical ways to make an ethical decision, as explained in this text; includes only those philosophies and works of theoretical philosophers that have been recognized and recurrently cited by the U.S. Supreme Court, the U.S. Courts of Appeals,

and highest state courts since 2010. *See* **choices model**, **common good model**, **exceptions model**, **justice model**, **rights model**, **social media model**, **utility model**, and **virtue model**.

Defensive medicine: refers to detailed record-keeping, the performance of more diagnostic procedures than are necessary or beneficial, and assuring that patients are fully informed before any treatment decisions are made; also includes avoidance of diagnostic procedures perceived as too risky.

Deinstitutionalization: the process of replacing in patient psychiatric hospitals with community-based, outpatient mental health care.

Detailing: industry marketing term; refers to face-to-face conversations between sales representatives in the medical products industry and physicians or other prescribers and decision-makers who may influence prescribers.

Diabetes: chronic metabolic disorder characterized by high blood sugar, either because the body does not produce enough insulin or because cells do not respond to the insulin that is produced.

Diet- and weight-related diseases: include high blood pressure, heart disease, and other chronic illnesses and cancers directly attributable to being overweight or obese.

Dietary supplement: contains nutrients derived from food products; includes vitamins, minerals, herbs or other botanicals, amino acids, and substances such as enzymes, organ tissues, glandulars, and metabolites. *Compare* **health foods** (conventional foods that are not dietary supplements but supplement the diet by providing health benefits beyond basic nutrition).

Dignified death: includes all the individual rights everyone has in controlling the timing and circumstances of the process of their own death; the right to choose a dignified and humane death as opposed to being reduced at the end of one's human existence to a graceless state of helplessness by being.

Dilation and evacuation (*aka* D&E): medical procedure where the contents of the uterus (including the fetus and other products of conception) are surgically removed after the cervix is dilated; common surgical procedure for second-trimester pregnancy terminations for fetal anomalies or fetal death.

Disease burden: time-based measure used by the World Health Organization that combines years of life lost due to premature death and years of life lost due to time lived in states of less than full health.

Disinformation: occurs when false and misleading information is deliberately put out as half-truths.

Disruptive innovation (*aka* transformative innovation): allows health care to be provided cheaper and in a more convenient fashion than traditional care; ultimately displaces older and more established products and practices.

Distributive justice: the extent to which government ensures that the benefits and burdens of life are distributed among members of society in ways that are fair and just; requires that the needs and resources of the entire society be taken into account when distributing health risks or resolving compensation claims of patients injured by medical errors.

Donation after cardiac death: the act of performing transplants using donors who are not declared brain dead; in other words, the donors are not legally dead at the time organ procurement begins. *Compare* **death** (generally when there is sustained irreversible cessation of either the circulatory and respiratory functions [*i.e.*, both functions must cease] or of the entire brain [*i.e.*, either alternative], but varies by state).

Double effect (principle of): generally applies to end-of-life circumstances under which it is permissible to cause foreseeable harm that would otherwise not be permissible to cause intentionally (imminent death), but which is permissible because the intent is to serve a good purpose (alleviation of intractable pain and distress) rather than to cause death.

Drug cocktails: the practice of prescribing a multitude of approved medications for patients in combinations that have never been clinically tested for their interactions together; also used to describe HIV/AIDS medication regimens and lethal injections of drug combinations in criminal executions.

Drug Effectiveness Review Project (DERP): collaboration of 15 states that systematically reviews scientific studies to inform agency purchasing decisions in an effort to compare the effectiveness of different medications.

Duties: obligations that are undertaken for legal, if not also ethical, reasons. Government health insurance was established to provide medical coverage to the most vulnerable populations in American society (the people at the bottom of the nation's socioeconomic pyramid, such as children, the disabled, and the elderly).

Dynamic pricing: rating of premiums for health insurance based on lifestyle choices such as smoking, weight status, or medication and treatment adherence behaviors.

Economic damages: non-discretionary medical expenses, lost wages, and rehabilitation costs.

Economic fairness: while there is no set formula to define this broad term, it is equated with efficiency. Charging health insurance premiums that reflect expected health risks increases efficiency because it discourages the purchase of additional basic coverage when it would be cheaper to invest in preventive care; in this instance, everyone has the incentive to optimize their overall cost of protecting against health risks.

Economic utility: the difference between what buyers are willing to pay and the price they actually pay; seeks to ensure that health insurance coverage is worth more to the public than the cost of the insurance.

Egalitarianism: belief in human equality and dignity that everyone is, in principle, equal and should enjoy equal access to medical coverage.

Embryo (human): covers the gestation period of the human organism from conception to about eight weeks; there is no single scientific or legal definition of this term.

Emergency care: care rendered in a situation that poses an immediate threat to health, or that might have serious implications for continued health and well-being.

Emergency contraceptives: a concentrated dose of hormone found in many regular birth control pills that can prevent pregnancy when taken within 120 hours after unprotected sex, but ideally within 72 hours.

Emergency Medical Treatment and Active Labor Act of 1986 (EMTALA)**:** federal law that ensures access to emergency services regardless of ability to pay; hospitals that offer emergency services must provide a medical screening examination when a request is made for an emergency health condition; hospitals are then required to provide stabilizing treatment if needed before transferring the patient to another hospital; if a pregnant woman presents in active labor, she must be admitted and treated until delivery is completed, including the afterbirth.

Employee Retirement Income Security Act of 1974 (ERISA)**:** federal law that establishes minimum standards for employer-sponsored health insurance plans.

Enjoin: to bar the enforcement of one application of a statutory law while leaving other applications in force, in other words, to sever the problematic portions of a law while leaving the remainder intact.

Enterprise liability: shifting of liability away from individual physicians, nurses, and other health care professionals on to hospitals or other corporate health care organizations.

Entitlement spending: tax expenditures, such as tax deductions for employer-provided health insurance, government loans and grants, home mortgage interest deductions, failure to tax the earnings of qualified pension plans, and government health insurance expenditures. *Compare* **Medicare** (health insurance benefits for anyone aged 65 or older or who is permanently disabled or has end-stage renal disease) *and* **Medicaid** (health insurance benefits for anyone with limited income and assets). *See* **entitlements**.

Entitlements: the right to have opportunities, such as the chance to achieve healthy well-being and maintain one's health; arise

from the common humanity of people in ethics, which may be different from what the law, properly interpreted, actually provides to many people.

Environmental safety: there is no common agreement or generally accepted definition of this term; generally refers to freedom from being harmed or injured by violence.

Epidemic (aka generally seasonal outbreaks)**:** communicable disease outbreak that spreads more quickly and more extensively than expected; threshold is 1 percent infection prevalence in a general population. *Compare* **pandemic** (global epidemic).

Epigenetic risks: health hazards that manifest in disease causation, causing damage and injury to the human body that is not of genetic origin; for instance, the dangers resulting from HFCS-based, high-Calorie, high-fat, low-nutrient food and beverages.

Equality: refers to the state of being equal in terms of human rights or treatment; 1 of the 4 foundations of justice (in addition to social stability, interdependence, and human dignity). *See* **justice, social stability**, **interdependence**, *and* **human dignity**.

Equality of opportunity: 1 of the 3 foundational principles of the newly emerging ethics of health care (in addition to compassion and justice); ensures that nearly all members of society have an equal claim to medically necessary health care; requires society to provide legitimate subsidies to help cover the health insurance costs in support of anyone who faces disproportionate health burdens. *Compare* **compassion** (meets individual needs) *and* **justice** (confronts system changes that encourage self-sufficiency).

Equitable access to health care: provision of health care that is necessary and reasonable, based on medical needs that if not provided might have serious implications for continued health and well-being. *Compare* **emergency care** (care in response to an immediate threat to health).

Ethic of common humanity: emphasizes human dignity and self-reliance; includes the traditions of decency, compassion, and reverence for self in the same manner as others; the focus is on improving the quality of life of vulnerable populations. *See* **decency, compassion** and **reverence for self**. *Compare* **ethics of care** (that also focuses on caring for vulnerable populations).

Ethical: actions that are consistent with and conform to accepted moral principles of fair, just, and compassionate conduct. *Compare* **unethical** (opposite of ethical).

Ethical dilemmas: situations or policy choices in which there are 2 or more valid decisions or policies to choose from, but 1 or more of the alternatives is more satisfactory and leads to more desirable outcome, or at least a less unethical result.

Ethical health care system: where medicine's ethical foundations of honesty, competence, and compassion are married to commerce in the delivery of high-quality care and where respect for patient needs has the highest priority.

Ethical judgment: required when actions involve an actual or a potential burden or harm to someone or to the health care system itself, or there is a violation of lawful behavior. *See* **ethical** *and* **unethical**.

Ethics of care: health care is a unique industry whose success is not measured simply by financial returns; the vulnerability of patients and the suffering caused by illness create an industry that compels an ethic comprised of compassion, justice, and equality of opportunity. *See* **compassion, justice,** and **equality of opportunity**.

Euthanasia: intentionally causing the death of someone suffering from a severe and incurable disease, in order to put an end to that person's pain and distress.

Evidence-based guidelines: systematically developed statements to assist physician and patient decisions about appropriate health care.

Evidence-based medicine: current philosophy of care that uses reason and mathematics, and relies on scientific evidence to assess the risks and benefits of medical treatments,

including lack of treatment. *Compare* **authority-based medicine** (which relies on individual expert medical opinions and common sense).

Exception: someone or something that is not included in or does not fit into the normative standards of conduct or ethical principles.

Exceptions model (of decision-making)**:** focuses on how decisions are made; an exception claims that in any given situation, an action may be ethical if done by one person but unethical if done by a different person; asks what would happen if the individual exception became the ethical principle for everyone; concerned with the conditions or rules the action can meet. *Compare* **rights model** (that is often used this decision-making model) *and* **utility model** (Prior to opposite of this decision-making model).

Exempt employees: salaried employees who are not subject to overtime compensation (unlike hourly workers who perform the same job functions); presumption is that employees making over a certain threshold in compensation are not in need of additional overtime pay.

Existentialist: a philosophy formulated in the 19th century that requires people to take responsibility for their own actions and shape their own destinies.

Experimental treatments: care within a clinical trial context using unapproved medications or unapproved medical devices that have not been proven to be safe or effective for the indicated use; usually employed when all other medically sound options have been exhausted, as medications could be potentially toxic and medical devices potentially dangerous. *Compare* **off-label prescribing** (experimental use of approved medications with no proven therapeutic benefit for the indicated use; occurs outside a clinical trial context).

Extrinsic value: in the health care space, the value of a person as determined by the status of his or her health attributes or health insurance.

Fair Labor Standards Act of 1938 (FLSA)**:** federal law that provides the protection of minimum wage and maximum hour rules.

Fair value: reasonable cost; generally determined by comparing how much similar health care products and services are paid for or how much is offered for payment in the ordinary course of business.

Fairness: ethical value that promotes giving to others what they are due. Requires that there be freedom of bias and injustice in the U.S. health care system so that patients in distress may receive the care they medically need while requiring that those entrusted with governance of limited health resources act in a trustworthy and ethical manner; also refers to objective judgments in which individuals and institutions have the habit or virtue of giving to others what they are due; value comes into play when attending to the human rights and interests of stakeholders in the health care industry.

Federal poverty level: poverty guidelines from the U.S. Department of Health and Human Services, which defined poverty as $11,770 for a household comprised of one individual and $24,250 for a family of four in 2015.

Federal preemption: legal rule stating that federal law supersedes state or local laws where such laws are in direct conflict with each other.

Fee-for-service: payment system that pays for whatever health care a physician recommends.

Fertilization: the process whereby a female egg and male sperm unite to form a zygote in one of the fallopian tubes (fertilized egg). *See* **conception**. *Compare* **implantation** (the zygote travels down the fallopian tube, where it becomes a morula; the morula becomes a blastocyst once it reaches the uterus; blastocyst then burrows into the uterine wall where it continues to grow into a human fetus).

Fetal viability: 24 weeks is generally considered the earliest a human fetus can naturally survive outside a women's uterus; there is no single legal definition of this term; each state defines the term differently.

Fetus (human)**:** individual organism when all the rudimentary human organs are in place, from about 8 weeks after fertilization until the moment of birth; there is no single scientific or legal definition of this term.

Fidelity: loyalty to a promise or accuracy in reporting facts.

Firearms: generally includes handguns and other guns.

First impression (cases or issues of)**:** lawsuits that raise completely original questions of law for decision by the courts, where there is no prior binding legal authority existing on the matter presented to the court. This text analyzes only those cases of first impression from the U.S. Supreme Court, the U.S. Courts of Appeal, and highest state courts.

Food addiction: a chronically relapsing disorder or habit that is characterized by a physical or psychological loss of control to freely make healthy food choices, such as in compulsive eating characterized by the inability to limit the intake of food. There is no consensus definition of this term other than that the day-to-day choices cause adverse consequences for individuals and are harmful to society.

Food additives: natural (such as antioxidants like Vitamin C) and artificial (such as preservatives and food colorings) substances added to processed food to preserve flavor or enhance its taste and appearance; must be non-carcinogenic. *Compare* **generally recognized as safe** (not likely to cause harm if used as intended).

Food-borne illnesses: diseases caused by pathogens and contaminants in food; certain strains of *E. coli* can cause kidney failure in young children and infants; Salmonella can lead to reactive arthritis and serious infections; listeria can cause meningitis and stillbirths; and *Campylobacter* may be the most common precipitating factor for Guillain-Barré syndrome (inflammatory disorder leading to paralysis).

Food Safety Modernization Act of 2011: the most comprehensive federal legislation regulating the food and beverage industry in a generation; empowers the federal government to order mandatory recalls of contaminated food and grants greater oversight of imported food products.

For-profit subsidiaries: companies that are controlled and owned by tax-exempt, nonprofit hospitals to fulfill key hospital functions, such as emergency physician groups, the hospital pharmacy, and a cafeteria.

Free-riders: individuals and institutions who take the benefits the ethic of the common good provides, but refuse to do their part to support the common good of their community; anyone who does not contribute their fair share but receives an equal share of benefits. For instance, the term refers to the economic problem of people taking advantage of government health insurance and exploiting the U.S. health care system without due compensation. *Compare* **social loafers** (who reduce their fair share contribution efforts, whereas free-riders do not contribute at all).

Fundamental rights: human entitlements that are deeply rooted in the nation's history and traditions, and implicit in the principles of justice and liberty (*i.e.*, the right to personal autonomy and self-determination; equal protection and due process of law; First Amendment right to freedom of expression; Second Amendment right to bear arms for self-defense; the rights to freedom of religion and privacy).

Gender-based discrimination: usually refers to situations in which women do not have the same earnings equality, employment opportunities, health insurance equity, or reproductive rights as men. *Compare* **reverse discrimination** (where men do not have the same gender equality as women).

General well-being: insurance analysis term; management of the health risks of insured patient populations to minimize their risks of disease or injury. *Compare* **health-related well-being** (management of individual insured patients).

Generally recognized as safe (*aka* GRAS)**:** a designation used by the FDA to designate food additives that may be put on the market because they are not likely to cause harm if used as intended.

Genetically modified foods (*aka* GM foods)**:** plant products derived from organisms that have had specific changes introduced into their DNA by genetic engineering techniques; includes alfalfa, canola, corn, soybean, and sugar beets. No genetically modified animal products are currently on the market. *See* **food additives**.

Geographic rating (*aka* community rating**:** risk classification for individuals and small nongroups that sets health insurance premiums at the same price for everyone based on the average costs of providing health care in a geographic community based on gender and age.

Government health insurance: includes public-provided insurance plans such as the Children's Health Insurance Program (CHIP), Medicaid, Medicare (including Medicare disability), state-sponsored or other government-sponsored health plans, and military plans.

Great Recession: economic term referring to a period beginning in early 2007 when losses on subprime mortgages battered the U.S. housing market and burst the U.S. housing bubble, leading to a period of worldwide bank collapses, extreme volatility in the global financial markets, international credit freezes, burgeoning unemployment, bank takeovers and government monitoring of formerly venerable Wall Street investment firms, a universal decline in stock market averages, and billions in economic stimulus packages and bailouts by the federal government.

Grocery gap: communities where there is poor availability of healthy foods, few supermarkets, and a high density of unhealthy food outlets.

Gross negligence: a form of fault-based conduct where there is substantially more than ordinary carelessness, inadvertence, laxity, or indifference which falls below the standard of care established by law for the protection of others against unreasonable risk of harm or injury.

Guaranteed issue: prohibits the health insurance industry from denying basic coverage to individuals with preexisting health conditions and bars insurers from charging higher rates to individuals based on their medical history.

Habits: personal characteristics and attitudes acquired from one's values (*i.e.*, compassionate, courageous, diligent, educated, fair, generous, honest, high ethical principles, self-controlled, and tolerant). *See* **values** *and* **virtues**.

Handguns (*aka* junk guns)**:** small, compact, inexpensive pistols, revolvers, and other short-barreled hand-held guns.

Harms: burdens or duties that are the responsibility of others for someone else; setback to the interests of people who are burdened; also includes damages, discomfort, injuries, or losses (for instance, the injuries of patients caused by medical errors in malpractice claims). *See* **duties**.

Health-based comparative effectiveness: *see* comparative effectiveness.

Health capital: financial burden associated with the loss of income and quality of life that people (especially the uninsured and other vulnerable populations) experience because of poorer health and shorter life spans.

Health care costs: the amount that is paid or charged for health care.

Health care proxy (*aka* durable power of attorney for health care, medical power of attorney, health care agent, or authorized surrogate)**:** that part of the advance health care directive that allows individuals to appoint someone to make health care decisions on their behalf if they cannot speak for themselves.

Health exception: constitutionally required provision that very precisely defines the contours of certain medical procedures, such as defining a woman's right to control her body in seeking an abortion when her health is jeopardized.

Health foods: provide health benefits beyond basic nutrition.

Health insurance exchanges: geographic statewide risk pools, established by the Affordable Care Act, that allow individuals and small businesses to leverage their collective buying power to obtain competitively priced health insurance; operated by the states or the federal government for the states.

Health outcomes: evaluates the effect of health care interventions on patient health status; often referred to as *health economics*.

Health risks: the likelihood of serious illness or injury adversely affecting the health of human populations, as well as individuals.

Health status: what makes people healthy or unhealthy. Determined by four attributes: access to the health care delivery system, environmental factors, genetics, and lifestyle choices.

Health-based comparative effectiveness: compares two or more treatments or medications to determine which medical interventions are most effective for which patients and under what circumstances.

Health-related well-being: insurance analysis term; management of the health risks of individual insured patients to minimize their risks of disease or injury. Used in determining whether the medical needs of individual patients will receive medical coverage as compared to deciding whether insurance will be provided for treatment of specific diseases. *Compare* **general well-being** (management of patient populations).

High-Calorie food: no standardized definition; generally more than 250 Calories for snacks and 400 Calories for a single entrée serving, but term is subjective and varies; includes processed meals, meats, and many canned soups; animal fats (lards); some breads and refined grains; cakes and pies; cheese; chocolate; condiments (especially butter and mayonnaise); corn syrup products; crackers; dried fruits; nuts and seeds; ice cream and milk shakes; peanut butter; many salad dressings; sugar-sweetened beverages, including soda, fruit juices, and sports drinks; trail mix; pasta, potatoes, and rice; vegetable oils, most fast foods (hamburgers, sandwiches, tacos, and French fries). Most adults need a diet of 2,200 (women) to 2,700 (men) Calories per day.

High-fat food: no standardized definition. Generally 6 or more grams of saturated fat per serving, but term is subjective and varies; includes processed meals and meats; biscuits, muffins, scones, and rolls; cakes and pies; many dairy products; chips and crackers; and most desserts.

High-frutose corn syrup (HFSC)**:** inexpensive corn-based starch thickener and sweetener with little nutritional value but added to most U.S. foods to add volume, enhance flavor, soften texture, and maintain freshness. Health risks are disputed.

High-fructose corn syrup-based foods (aka HFCS-based foods)**:** almost all U.S. prepackaged and prepared meals and processed meats and beverages; baked goods, breads, breakfast bars, candies, cereals, condiments, fruit drinks, soft drinks, soups, and yogurts.

Hospice: a philosophy of palliative care that provides pain management, symptom control, psychosocial support, and spiritual care to patients and their families facing death; a term restricted by law to patients who have a terminal prognosis of 6 months or less and agree to forego curative or life-prolonging treatments. *See* **palliative care**.

Human dignity: ethical value that respects the inherent worth of every member of society; all people are entitled to respect as people of full human stature and must not be treated as lesser beings; concept requires recognition of each individual's unique value to the common humanity of people and suggests that everyone has their own definition of self-respect and worthiness as a human being; requires a commitment to respond to everyone with mutual affinity, respect, and stateliness 1 of the 4 foundations of justice (in addition to social stability, equality, and interdependence); the driving ethical value underlying health care reforms. *See* **justice**.

Human Immunodeficiency Virus (HIV)**:** retrovirus that destroys certain white blood cells critical to the formal functioning of the human immune system; as the immune system weakens, a person becomes susceptible to developing cancers and infections from viruses, bacteria, and parasites resulting in diseases like hepatitis and tuberculosis. When the immune system is severely weakened or when opportunistic infections develop, patients are diagnosed with full-blown AIDS. *See* **Acquired Immune Deficiency Syndrome** (AIDS) and **opportunistic diseases**.

Human rights: claimed entitlements arising from the nature of humanity, by means of which everyone is given the unfettered opportunity to achieve and maintain a secure sense of independent well-being and human dignity; fundamental responsibilities and duties of society that can be exercised in an ethical or unethical manner; derived from a commitment to individual autonomy and treating people as equals.

Human solidarity: the recognition that human interests and responsibilities are mutually shared.

Hyde Amendment: amended the Medicaid insurance law to deny federal funding for abortions, except when the mother's health is in jeopardy or the pregnancy resulted from sexual assault. In other words, there is no entitlement to federal funds to realize women's right to abortions.

Hydrogenation: used to process vegetable oils and animal fats by converting unsaturated fatty acids to saturated ones; implicated in circulatory diseases. *See* **trans-fats**.

Idealist: views ethics as essentially social; believes ethical duties are founded on people's need to aspire to goodness and high ethical principles as opposed to acting badly and being unethical. *Compare* **utilitarianism** (the pursuit of basic happiness).

Ideals: the ethical principles to which most people aspire.

Implantation: the stage at which an embryo becomes embedded in the lining of a woman's uterus. *See* **conception** *and* **fertilization**.

Inattentional blindness (aka cognitive dissonance)**:** result of different people or groups adapting their thinking at different rates.

Indemnity health insurance: risk-spreading product that assumes the risk-taking for all health care costs on a fee-for-service basis and that allows the insured an unlimited choice of providers. *Compare* **managed care** (minimizes premium costs by restricting provider choices; lesser out-of-pocket charges for deductibles and co-payments).

Individual mandate (*aka* minimum coverage provision)**:** term used for the provision in the Affordable Care Act for the basic coverage required to be made available to almost all adult U.S. residents so everyone can access affordable health insurance during their lifetimes or face an annual shared responsibility payment based on household income, which the law calls a penalty, if someone does not maintain their health insurance.

Individual responsibility: ethical value which emphasizes personal accountability for healthy lifestyles and preventable ill health. This obligation is both a free choice and a personal and shared duty; assumes that avoidance of unhealthy day-to-day choices will help avoid preventable ill health from occurring or delay the onset of and the severity of symptoms from unpreventable aging, illness, and death.

Informed consent: shared decision-making process between physicians and patients, especially when scientific evidence alone does not identify a favored course of medical treatment.

Insurance analysis: management of the health risks of disease in populations; decision-making based on the general well-being of a population comprised of the insured versus the individual insureds.

Insurance risk pools: describes the pooling of similar health risks by health insurers to help pay for health care expenses; subsidies are required to voluntarily pool dissimilar risks. Ideally, the costs of illness and disease are spread across an entire society; health care reform would automatically enroll nearly all U.S. adult residents in risk pools for medical coverage financed through broad-based premiums and subsidies for those unable to pay the premium costs.

Compare **Medicare** (federal risk pool comprised of the eligible disabled and those 65 years of age and older). *See* **health insurance exchanges**.

Intact dilation and **extraction** (*aka* intact D&X)**:** method of late-term abortion where the mother's cervix is dilated and the fetus is partially delivered before being destroyed; although not a medically-recognized term, this is the procedure often referred to as a "partial birth abortion." *See* **partial birth abortion**.

Intellectually disabled: person with sub-average intelligence or intellectual functioning. There is no single legal definition of this term and, thus, each state defines the term differently.

Interdependence: 1 of the 4 foundations of justice (in addition to social stability, equality, and human dignity); every member of society retains their voluntary social unit only to the extent that their institutions and their laws are just. *See* **justice, social stability**, **equality**, and **human dignity**.

Intrinsic value: human beings are recognized as valuable in and of themselves without regard to the status of their health or their health insurance in the health care space.

Involuntary commitment: a process governed by state law that allows for people with severe mental disorders to be committed to a hospital or mental health facility without their consent if treatment is essential to their welfare and their judgment is so impaired that they are unable to understand the need for such treatment.

Joint Commission on Accreditation of Healthcare Organizations (JCAHO)**:** the nation's predominant standards-setting and accrediting body in health care; accreditation is required for Medicare and Medicaid certification and licensing in many states.

Judicial bypass: requires pregnant minors who want abortions, without notifying or getting consent from a parent, to first go to court and convince a judge that they are sufficiently mature and informed to make the decision themselves.

Junk food: foods that are high in Calories, saturated fat, and sodium while being low in nutritional value; refers to foods with no to low nutritional value (containing empty Calories) or unhealthy ingredients when eaten regularly or at all; includes processed foods with high levels of saturated fats, salt, or sugar, and little or no fruit, vegetables, or dietary fiber.

Justice: the foundational principle of traditional ethics defined more than 2,000 years ago, whereby equals should be treated equally and like things treated alike; 1 of the 3 foundational principles of the emerging new ethics of health care (in addition to compassion and equality of opportunity). Ethical value requiring fairness and equality in the way every member of society is treated and decisions are made; ensures access to affordable health insurance and the kinds of medically necessary care that are owed; depends on society's notion of what is right and fair and the allocation of shared societal resources for health care (which should incorporate precise measures of the total societal costs of preventable ill health and total societal benefits from health care); means reasonableness, especially in the way ethical decisions are made and whether people are treated fairly and given their appropriate due or what they are properly owed. *See* **compassion** and **equality of opportunity**.

Justice model (of decision-making)**:** puts human dignity at the center of the decision-making process; focuses on giving people their appropriate due or what they are properly and rightfully owed; adapts decisions to respond to the needs and interests of everyone affected. *Compare* **common good model** (considers more than just those directly affected).

Justification: a reason that validates an ethical decision or action.

Kaposi's sarcoma: secondary cancer of the connective tissue caused by a herpes virus and associated with AIDS; tumors generally appear as bluish-red or purple lesions under the skin and in the lining of the mouth, nose, throat, and other organs making breathing difficult and often resulting in internal bleeding. *See* **Acquired Immune Deficiency Syndrome** (AIDS) *and* **opportunistic diseases**.

Labor: the collective term for the employees in the health care industry.

Labor-management relations: a collaborative relationship between labor unions (representing employees) and supervisory or managerial employees (representing employers); addresses mutual interests regarding the terms of employment (grievances, wages, hours of employment, and other working conditions), protection from discrimination, and guarantees of employee health and safety; dealings that protect the interests of shareholders, owners of capital, and management with regard to the shared interests of employees working in the health care industry.

Labor Management Relations Act of 1947 (LMRA) (*aka* Taft-Hartley Act)**:** amends the National Labor Relations Act (NLRA) of 1935; mitigates the power of labor unions that had increased since passage of the NLRA. *See* **National Labor Relations Act of 1935**.

Labor unions: corporate organizations that support employees and advance their interests in terms of wages, benefits, working hours and conditions.

Large fraction test: requires a court to determine whether a significant number of people for whom a particular law is a restriction will face increased obstacles as a result of the law; parties in litigation often argue over defining the denominator of people affected; for instance, in abortion cases, precedent holds that the denominator is the total number of pregnant women who seek an abortion in all cases and the numerator is the number of pregnant women who would be unduly burdened by a specific restriction to abortion, which is a fraction of all cases; the closer in size the numerator and denominator are (in other words, the closer the two numbers are to being equal), the larger the fraction, and thus the higher proportion of people who are unduly burdened.

Least infringement (principle of)**:** the least intrusive means should always be used when encroaching on somebody's human rights or privileges, especially in minor ways.

Legal rights: human constructs created by society, enforced by governments, and subject to change; they constitute the claims that some people have against others.

Legally competent: the capacity to make informed and voluntary decisions.

Liberty: the freedom to think and act without being constrained by the government; fundamental right of all U.S. citizens independent of any laws. *Compare* **consent** (governments exist as a result of a social contract whereby citizens consent to transfer some of their powers to the government in order to protect their rights and promote the common good) *and* **social contract** (the U.S. Constitution).

Lifestyle discrimination: policies that protect employers from employees attempting to pursue legal action related to their engaging in lawful, private off-duty conduct which the employer prohibits.

Life-sustaining treatment (*aka* life-sustaining medical treatment or LMST)**:** refers to advanced medical technologies that forestall the moment of death, such as dialysis, feeding tubes to provide artificial nutrition and hydration, intravenous medications that maintain blood pressure, and mechanical ventilators and respirators.

Limited-benefit health insurance: low-premium plans with high out-of-pocket expenses for medical services not covered by the limited benefit plan; sold as dread disease, specific disease (such as cancer), or accident-only policies to supplement comprehensive health insurance. Sometimes referred to as mini-med or McDonald plans (because this is the health insurance plan offered to employees of the fast-food restaurant chain); banned under the Affordable Care Act.

List price: one of two charges used by hospitals for payment; undiscounted real cost for health care services rendered. *Compare* **actual price** (discounted cost).

Living wages: the employment earnings on which employees and their familyies can live according to minimum customary standards; does not reflect a middle-class standard of living but instead a minimum estimate of the cost of living. Definition may be based on the cost of food and minimum dietary requirements or the cost of housing (according to the federal Housing and Urban Development standard, 30 percent of a person's gross monthly income should be spent on housing) or the federal poverty level (poverty guidelines from the U.S. Department of Health and Human Services define poverty as $24,250 for a family of four in 2015).

Low-wage employees: the most vulnerable group of workers in the health care industry who are earning minimum wages or less have minimal benefits if any.

Macroeconomics: examines the dynamics of health care from the state or national perspective, such as the rate of growth, inflation, and price levels.

Malpractice, medical: improper and negligent health care that causes injury to patients for which physicians, nurses, and other health care professionals may be sued for damages.

Managed care: cost-sharing health insurance product; applies utilization review techniques to control the health risks for the care the insurance covers and the providers used. *Compare* **indemnity health insurance** (less cost-effective but maximum flexibility in selection of providers).

Management: the collective term for senior executives who control managerial responsibilities and determine corporate policies in the health care industry.

Mandated health insurance: laws designed to ensure that all U.S. residents have basic coverage for medically necessary care. Americans have a duty to be insured and employers have a duty to contribute to the costs of their employees' health insurance; includes required preventive care and coverage for specific health conditions (*e.g.,* contraceptives, mental health treatment).

Marginal utility: this prediction of short-term and long-term outcomes considers the relative value of the outcomes for different people.

Market distortion: occurs when medical products or health care services are not freely available because the market forces of supply and demand have been disrupted. Health care costs have become so high that many Americans are uninsured or underinsured as regulatory forces have distorted the market (*e.g.*, tax subsidies for employer-provided health insurance, tax credits for individual health insurance, tax-exemptions for hospitals, government health insurance programs) making it impossible to calculate how much the provision of health care actually costs.

Maternity coverage: covers monthly prenatal physician visits, lab tests, ultrasounds, and childbirth under health insurance plans that include it.

Mature minor: a child, generally an adolescent, who has decision-making capacity to make health care decisions. There is no set age whereby a minor is deemed mature; rather, the determination is based upon an analysis of several factors to assess the minor's competency.

Mature minor doctrine: extends the principle of personal autonomy to minors determined to be sufficiently mature in recognition that the capacity for rational decision-making increases with age.

Means-tested discounts: the price for health care based on the income and other resources patients have to pay their medical bills.

Medicaid: federal-state health insurance program for people at the bottom of the nation's socioeconomic pyramid or who face high out-of-pocket health care expenses; this welfare program is needs-based. *Compare* **Medicare** (health insurance entitlement based on age or disability criteria).

Medical ethics committees: forum where many ethical dilemmas are resolved by multidisciplinary teams comprised of health care professionals from medicine, nursing, law, chaplaincy, and social work.

Medical futility: medical treatment that fails to end total dependence on intensive care or that mechanically preserves permanent unconsciousness.

Medical monitoring: form of long-term public health surveillance based on repetitive use of the same diagnostic tests to detect a specified change in health conditions that indicates a need for medical treatment; people being screened are not necessarily at an enhanced risk for future illness.

Medical negligence: conduct that falls below the professional standard of care established by law for the protection of others against unreasonable risk of harm or injury; by definition, appropriate conduct is measured in comparison to what reasonable professionals either do or should do in similar circumstances.

Medical triage: clinical screening of patients to determine their health condition and corresponding needs: those who need treatment in order to survive (life-threatening), those who cannot be expected to survive even with treatment (urgent), and those who will recover without treatment (semi-urgent or in need of no care).

Medically necessary care: basic minimum level of primary health care (including medications) to treat the most common injuries and diseases that should be, ethically speaking, universally accessible and affordable to every member of society so they have the unfettered opportunity to achieve and maintain high levels of health which are necessary for a lifetime of well-being, human dignity, and meaningful contribution to society. Does not necessarily include advanced care or access to highly specialized physicians; minimum core obligations of basic health insurance (public and private); no uniform definition of this term exists at this time. *Compare* **medically needed care** (highest attainable standard of medically necessary care) *and* **reasonable and necessary care** (legitimate expectation for medically needed diagnosis and appropriate treatment).

Medically needed care: refers to the highest attainable standard of necessary health care and medical treatments (including advanced medications and medical devices) that are needed but not received because they are unaffordable or delayed because of costs. *Compare* **medically necessary care** (basic minimum level of primary care).

Medicare: federal health insurance program for people over 65 years of age and the disabled. This entitlement program is partially funded by payroll taxes; people are entitled to receive this insurance coverage when they meet its age or disability criteria for eligibility. *Compare* **Medicaid** (need-based program).

Mental disability [*aka* mental disorder]**:** any mental disorder that significantly impairs a person's capacity to appreciate the nature and consequences of his or her conduct, exercise rational judgment, or conform conduct to the requirements of the law and general ethical principles. Conduct attributable solely to the acute effects of alcohol or other drugs does not, standing alone, constitute a mental disability. *See also* **mental disorders** (term used interchangeably with mental disability).

Mental disorders: biologically based health conditions characterized by alterations in thinking, mood, and behavior; clinical diagnosis of a mental disability.

Mental health: successful performance of mental functions, resulting in productive activities, satisfactory relationships with other people, and the ability to adapt to change and cope with adversity; not just lack of a mental disability or mental disorder.

Mental illness: diagnosable mental disorders, including, among others Alzheimer's disease, bipolar disorder, borderline personality disorder, major depression, obsessive compulsive disorder, panic disorder, post traumatic stress disorder, and schizophrenia.

Mentally disabled: individuals with psychiatric disorders or impaired capacities to appreciate the nature and consequences of their conduct.

Microeconomics: examines the dynamics of health care from the perspective of individual consumers of health care; focuses on the models of decision-making and the interaction between the providers and consumers of health care and the factors that influence their decisions, such as supply and demand.

Minimum coverage provision: clause in the ACA providing for the core coverage required to be made available to almost all U.S. residents so everyone can purchase and maintain affordable health insurance during their lifetimes or face an annual shared responsibility payment, which the ACA calls a penalty, if they do not. *See* **individual mandate**.

Moral hazard: occurs when patients, insulated from their lifestyle choices, behave differently than they would have if they were fully exposed to the health consequences of their behavior. Moral hazards arise whenever hospitals and physicians do not consider the full consequences and responsibilities of their actions, and therefore act less carefully than they otherwise would, leaving third parties (such as the insurance industry) to hold some responsibility for the consequences of their actions (for instance, physicians with malpractice insurance might be less cautious about medical errors because the negative consequences of such errors are partially the responsibility of the insurance industry).

Moral imperative: actions that are the right and ethical thing to do, regardless of opposition or difficulty.

Moral preferences: the subjective spiritual, irrational, and emotional preferences of each member of society.

Moral rights: universal rights not easily subject to change in that they apply to everyone in similar situations; empowers every member of society to engage in conduct that does not violate the legitimate human rights of others; justified by acknowledged ethical principles which are not necessarily clearly codified in law (*e.g.*, the moral right to health care). *See* **choices model**.

National Fair Labor Standards Act of 1938: federal law regulating minimum wage, maximum hours, and overtime pay.

National Labor Relations Act of 1935 (NLRA): regulates labor union activities; legal framework for management-labor relations created out of the distress, dislocation, and turmoil of the Great Depression.

National Labor Relations Board (NLRB): federal agency that administers processes for designating a union as a representative of employees to protect their work interests.

Natural rights: The U.S. Declaration of Independence lists 3 fundamental and inherent human rights: life, liberty, and the pursuit of happiness (meaning a life lived to its full potential); basic rights to which all humans are equally entitled.

Necessary and reasonable care: individualized evaluation and assessment of a patient's unique health conditions and individual needs to determine care and health insurance coverage. Everyone has a legitimate expectation for appropriate diagnosis and treatment to improve health outcomes; sometimes includes the best that modern medicine has to offer, which involves decisions that are part medical and part economic (what necessary care is reasonable for society or members of an insurance risk pool to pay; what necessary care should reasonably be an individual responsibility versus a societal responsibility); rarely defined, largely unexamined, generally misunderstood, and idiosyncratically applied by the health insurance industry. *See* **medically needed care** and **unmet medical need**.

Negative law: what an individual or corporation cannot do; restrains and limits actions. *Compare* **positive law** (rights and privileges granted by the U.S. Constitution).

Negative moral rights: permit inaction; one may refrain from acting or others may refrain from acting. *Compare* **positive moral rights** (requires action, obligation to act).

Negligence: conduct that falls below the professional standard of care established by law for the protection of others against unreasonable risk of harm or injury; fault-based; consists of duty (to act or not act), a breach of that duty, and damages resulting from the breach of that duty.

New federalism: an emerging constitutional paradigm of two competing visions of the value of personal autonomy from government; this converging philosophy of government empowers Congress to address any problem that the states are unable to address separately.

No-fault insurance: alternative to the current litigation system; the central premise of this model is that patients need not prove negligence to access compensation; they must prove only that they have suffered an injury, that it was caused by their medical treatment, and that it meets whatever severity or other threshold criteria apply; like workers compensation.

Non-economic damages: pain and suffering; other examples include emotional distress and loss of consortium.

Non-hospice palliative care: appropriate treatment for people who are living with serious and complex, sometimes life-threatening, illnesses with symptoms of severe pain; may be offered simultaneously with life-prolonging and curative therapies.

Non-malfeasance: avoidance of harm; the opposite of beneficence. Requires physicians and other health care professionals to first do no harm, or if no good can be done without causing harm, then actions that have no curative effect or result should not be undertaken.

Nutrition: the science that deals with food and its effects on human health; also refers to the minerals, vitamins, and other nutrient substances in food that are absorbed and processed by the human body in order to maintain its nourishment and avoid disease.

Obese: weight that endangers health because of its high body fat relative to lean body mass; for adults, a weight 20 to 30 percent above one's ideal weight.

Obesity epidemic: the threshold for an epidemic is 1 percent of the general population; over 35 percent of Americans were obese in 2015. *See* **obese**.

Off-label: absent state regulation, approved medical products may be prescribed for indications and in dosages other than those expressly approved on package inserts; practice does not violate federal law or Food and Drug Administration (FDA) regulations because the FDA regulates the marketing and distribution of medications and medical devices, not the practice of medicine, which is generally the responsibility of individual states.

Off-label prescribing (*aka* off-label use)**:** the practice of using approved medications or medical devices for unapproved purposes or unapproved patient groups or at unapproved dosage levels or by unapproved forms of administration outside the clinical trial context; prescribing with no proven therapeutic benefit and that has not been proven to be safe or effective for the indicated use. *Compare* **experimental treatments** (use of unapproved medications or treatments).

Off-label use: treatment with unapproved medications with no proven safety or effectiveness.

Opportunistic diseases: cancers and infections from viruses, bacteria, and parasites that might not affect people with normal immune systems but that take advantage of HIV-infected persons who have compromised immune systems.

Opt-out testing: does not require separate, written informed consent, meaning a diagnostic test or medical procedure is part of any general informed consent to receive routine health care services; patients must specifically decline to have particular tests or procedures administered.

Order of conditions: court order that directs a mentally ill person to comply with a prescribed treatment regimen, or any other condition the court determines to be reasonably necessary or appropriate to protect the person as well as other people.

Outsourced employees: independent contractors of subcontracting employers or temporary job agencies with no formal employment relationship with their employers or with employers' outside contractors and no expectation of long-term employment. *See* **contingent work**.

Over-the-counter (OTC)**:** includes non-prescription treatments and medications other than food.

Overweight: includes people who have more body weight than is considered healthy for their height, build, and age; 7 out of 10 American adults are overweight in 2015, which includes those who are also obese.

Palliative care: specialized area of health care that focuses on relieving and preventing the pain and suffering of patients in all disease stages, including those undergoing treatment for curable and chronic diseases, as well as patients nearing the end of life. *Compare* **hospice** (specific type of palliative care for patients with six months or less to live).

Palliative sedation (*aka* palliative sedation to unconsciousness, terminal sedation, continuous deep sedation, primary deep continuous sedation, pharmacological oblivion)**:** induction of an unconscious state to relieve otherwise intractable distress and pain in palliative care.

Pandemic: widespread communicable disease epidemic, such as HIV/AIDS, that spreads very quickly over a wide geographic area in many different countries and affects large numbers of people. *See* **epidemic**.

Partial-birth abortion: political term for intact dilation and extraction which is neither recognized in the medical literature nor used by physicians who perform late-term abortions.

Per se disability: a specific impairment for which everyone with that impairment would be considered disabled without reference to any number of additional factors or individualized, case-by-case inquiries; the impairment is, on its face, considered a disability without any further analysis.

Permanent vegetative state (PVS)**:** disorder of consciousness in which patients with severe brain damage have cycles of apparent wakefulness and apparent sleep without any cognition or awareness.

Personal autonomy (*aka* rational self-determination)**:** the freedom to exercise one's individual wishes. Minors and mentally disabled people are non-autonomous because of their inability to make decisions due to social and relational constraints; at the center of controversies arise over the level of freedom and accommodations required when health care policies are established. *See* **autonomy**.

Personal responsibility legislation: protects food industry manufacturers from lawsuits when their products are in compliance with existing laws. The (as-yet-unpassed) federal Cheeseburger Bill or Personal Responsibility in Food Consumption Act prohibits consumers from suing the food industry for any weight-related health conditions.

Personalized prevention: getting people involved in their own health care while preventable diseases can still be prevented; includes smoking cessation, weight reduction, and medicine and treatment regimen adherence programs.

Physician-assisted dying (*aka* physician-assisted suicide)**:** a value-neutral term for the process of dying with medical assistance that extends up to just before the point of biological death; in 2015, this practice was legal in Oregon, Washington, Vermont, Montana, and one county in New Mexico; multiple safeguards are required under physician-assisted dying laws to ensure that patients are not abused and that they have made a voluntary, informed, and competent choice to request assistance in dying.

Pluralism: existence of different nationalities and minorities with an underlying and unifying national consensus about standards of justice and what constitutes right and wrong; unique characteristic of the United States.

Pluralistic society: community where cultural differences are encouraged and political and economic powers are shared by different nationalities and minorities.

Positive law: rights and privileges granted to the federal government or reserved to the states by the U.S. Constitution; corporate organizations only have the rights and privileges granted to them by the government, which means they are subject to legitimate regulation of their corporate self-interests by the government.

Positive moral rights: require action; one must act or others are obliged to act. *Compare* **negative moral rights** (permit inaction; no obligation to act).

Potentially avoidable events (*aka* avoidable hospital acquired-conditions and preventable adverse events)**:** includes foreign objects retained after surgery, air embolisms, blood incompatibilities, stage III and IV pressure ulcers, falls and traumas, vascular catheter-associated infections, catheter-associated urinary tract infections, and manifestations of poor glycemic control. See preventable adverse events.

Poverty wages: wages less than a living wage. *Compare* **living wages** (generally $8–12/hour with benefits).

Pregnancy Discrimination Act of 1978 (PDA)**:** provides that employers cannot discriminate against any person regarding compensation, terms, conditions, or privileges of employment because of gender; women affected by pregnancy, childbirth, or related health conditions must be treated the same as men and other non-similarly situated women, including receipt of health insurance benefits.

Preterm: infants born at less than 37 weeks' gestation.

Preventable adverse events: hospital acquired-conditions; includes foreign object retained after surgery, air embolism, blood incompatibility, stage III and IV pressure ulcers, falls and trauma, vascular catheter-associated infection, catheter-associated urinary tract infection, and manifestations of poor glycemic control.

Preventable behaviors: include smoking, overeating, and failure to take medications or follow treatment regimens as prescribed; behaviors that often advance the onset and increase the severity of diseases.

Preventable diseases: tobacco-related illnesses, overweight and obesity, and chronic conditions such as arthritis, circulatory disorders, and diabetes; diseases that are preventable or that can be delayed from occurring or decreased in severity by changes in behavior.

Preventive care: delays the onset and decreases the severity of illness and disease; blocks preventable diseases from ever arising or minimizes or delays the severity of their symptoms.

Pre-viability: before the human fetus develops to the point where it could live independently of the mother. *Compare* **viability** (at 24 weeks).

Price discrimination: the common practice of charging different prices to different patients for identical health care even when the actual costs are identical.

Principles (*aka* values): accepted norms that define ethical decision-making of an individual or group; define what is ethical and right to do. Used to morally evaluate any action or corporate organization; used interchangeably with the term *values*, although defined differently; the assumption in this textbook is that Western philosophical principles are universal in the U.S. health care industry, if not always the only suitable or most superior in a liberal democracy. *See* **universal values**.

Privilege: restricted right or benefit; there is an ethical obligation to do something or refrain from doing something in order to exercise it (*e.g.*, right to access medically necessary health care. *Compare* **rights** (opposite of privilege; no obligation do anything for the claimed entitlement, *i.e.*, the right to affordable health insurance).

Processed foods: convenience foods overloaded with saturated fats, sodium, and sugar with little to no nutritional value.

Proportionality (principle of): refers to mutual toleration of competing interests.

Prospective medicine: tailors medications and other treatments to individual needs so patients can develop healthy lifestyles and block preventable diseases from ever arising, or minimize their deleterious effects once developed.

Protection of Lawful Commerce in Arms Act of 2005 (PLCAA)**:** federal legislation that shields the firearms industry from any liability for gun injuries.

Public ethic (*aka* common public ethic *and* American ethic)**:** refers to the State, its government and its policies. *See* **universal values** (synonymous term).

Public legitimacy: respect for the authority of laws from a democratic government.

Quality-adjusted life-year: method used to measure the benefit of health care or years of life gained by receiving medical treatment.

Quid pro quo: (Latin) meaning something is equally exchanged for something else.

Rationing: the withholding of limited resources from specific individuals so the resources will be available for others in the future. *Compare* **health-based comparative effectiveness** (allocates resources based upon what is most effective for which patients and under what circumstances).

Reasonable and necessary care: legitimate expectation for appropriate diagnosis and treatment to improve patient outcomes; sometimes includes the best that modern medicine has to offer; part medical and part economic decision (what necessary care is reasonable for society or members of an insurance risk pool to pay); rarely defined, largely unexamined, generally misunderstood, and idiosyncratically applied by the health care and health insurance industries. *Compare* **medically necessary care** (basic minimum standard of primary care) *and* **medically needed care** (highest attainable standard of medically necessary care).

Redistribution: the process of apportioning health care resources differently; changing the status quo by distributing more or less of something previously distributed.

Refusal clause legislation (*aka* conscience legislation)**:** protects health care providers' right to conscientiously object to dispensing or providing medical treatments, such as contraception and abortions.

Religious exemptions: provisions that alleviate the burden state laws place on the abilities of pharmacists and other health care professionals to practice their religious beliefs while maintaining their profession. Generally applies to employers who oppose birth control and are excused from providing state-mandated health insurance coverage for contraception and from any financial obligation to contribute to the social costs of refusing to sponsor contraception coverage.

Research bias: non-retracted misinformation that arises when scientific impropriety results in false research findings that are distorted; not always fraudulent (which is the intentional use of misinformation); can be unintentional. *See* **retractions**. *Compare* **research fraud** (deliberate, intentional misinformation).

Research error: unintentional plagiarism, scientific mistake, or ethical problems as a result of poor judgment or lack of care; the most common reason for retractions.

Research fraud: intentional data fabrication, including data plagiarism or falsification. *Compare* **research bias** (unintentional misinformation).

Research impropriety: earnest errors or statistical naiveté arising from experimental design, data collection, data analysis, or data presentation.

Responsible corporate officer doctrine: legal doctrine holding that there is no need to prove that a corporate officer actually knew that certain conduct violated the law; rather, the test is whether that officer was aware of the offensive conduct.

Retractions: when published scientific studies are repudiated, misinformation is removed because the studies have been found to be unreliable, cannot be replicated, or are simply wrong, but the article, with an accompanying retraction notice, remains available. *See* **research bias**.

Retrovirus: has genetic information in its RNA as opposed to DNA; generally causes HIV and cancers.

Reverence for self (principle of)**:** principle of respect for oneself must exist in the same manner as respect for the dignity of others. *See* **decency** *and* **compassion**.

Rights (*aka* benefits)**:** claimed entitlements arising from the nature of humanity and freely granted by law without the obligation to do anything; the rule of law and principles of ethics about what is owed to people based on certain principles that are accepted by society to be legitimate; classified as natural (fundamental), legal, claim/privilege, positive/negative, or individual/group. *Compare* **privilege** (restricted right; opposite of rights).

Rights model (of decision-making)**:** based on the belief that every human being is valuable in and of themselves; the intrinsic human value of everyone means every human being needs to aspire to goodness and high ethical principles; focuses attention on the importance of respect for everyone's human dignity and self-determination; everyone has rights that empower them to engage in conduct that does not violate the rights of others. *Compare* **exceptions model** (for use after this decision-making model).

Risk classification: insurers underwrite health insurance in accordance with the risk factors known to affect the health of the insured (actual claims or demographics).

Risk pooling: describes the pooling of similar health risks by insurance companies to help pay for health care expenses; government subsidies are required to voluntarily pool dissimilar risks; special programs created by most state legislatures to provide a safety net for the medically uninsurable population, which often includes victims of gun injuries.

Risk pooling: broadly distribute the costs of poor health among both healthy and sick people with health insurance coverage.

Risk-spreading: health insurance term; the insurance provider assumes the risk-taking for all health care costs of the insured.

Safe tolerance: reasonable certainty of no harm from food containing additives and contaminants, including pesticide chemical residue.

Safety net hospital: delivers a significant level of uncompensated care to the uninsured and patients with government insurance. *See* **uncompensated care**.

Self-insured: employers carry their own risks for health care costs rather than purchasing health insurance from an insurer; insurers often administer self-insured health insurance plans.

Serious adverse event (*aka* potentially avoidable event)**:** any expected or unexpected occurrence related or unrelated to a medical intervention that results in any of the following potentially avoidable outcomes: death, a life-threatening event, in patient hospitalization or extensions of existing hospitalization, a persistent or significant disability/incapacity or a congenital anomaly/birth defect, as well as important medical events that may require medical or surgical intervention to prevent one of these outcomes. *Compare* **serious reportable event** (unexpected harm to patients).

Serious reportable event: triggered by unexpected serious adverse events and precursor events and near misses, whatever their cause, that may not ultimately result in serious harm (such as loss of limb or function) because of medical or surgical interventions; includes patient falls, medication administration errors, pressure ulcers, hospital infections, and unexpected mortality in health care settings. Mandatory reporting required to medical ethics committees, the Joint Commission, state patient safety agencies, the National Institutes of Health (NIH) for patients in clinical trials, and the U.S. Food and Drug Administration (FDA) for instances involving medical products. No standardized definition of *serious* or *unexpected* exists. *See* **serious adverse event** (potentially avoidable harm to patients that should have been prevented).

Service Employees International Union (SEIU)**:** largest corporate labor organization in the health care industry.

Severe mental disorders: disorders involving one or more of the following mental illnesses with acute anxiety, mood, or psychotic symptoms: autism, bipolarism, manic depression, schizoaffective disorder or schizophrenia, as well as persistent forms of delusions, major depression, panic, posttraumatic stress, and obsessive-compulsive disorders.

Shared responsibility payment: annual penalty that will be assessed on U.S. residents who do not purchase and maintain a certain level of health insurance coverage based on household income. *See* **minimum coverage provision**.

Shared values: accepted ethical principles of what constitutes compassion, fairness, and justice for all members of society. *See* **American ethic**.

Smell test (*aka* the Twitter Model or the front-page-of-the-newspaper test)**:** part of the social media model of decision-making, a common-sense and intuitive tool to help decide if an action or situation is ethical; asks whether an action or situation seems dishonest or whether something is troubling or seems wrong, bad, or dangerous; if one would not want the action or inaction publicized, it is probably unethical. *See* **social media model**.

Social contract: defines the scope of the U.S. Constitution; in 2012, the constitutional validity of the Affordable Care Act rested on whether Congress could mandate that nearly all U.S. residents obtain and maintain health insurance; in 1965, the constitutional validity of Medicare and Medicaid insurance rested on whether Congress possessed the right to expand its Social Security legislation to include Medicare and Medicaid insurance.

Social costs: harm to society, such as the health care costs arising from preventable gun injuries; misallocated health care costs caused by disregard for clinical practice guidelines; and costs resulting from non-enforcement of Affordable Care Act mandates or food safety regulations and guidelines.

Social determinants of health: the primary factors that shape the health of people are not medical treatments but rather the living conditions they experience (access to health care; early childhood development; education; employment and working conditions; food security; housing; income and income distribution; social exclusion; social safety network; unemployment and job security; gender, race, and disability status).

Social justice: refers to the idea of creating a society based on the principles of equality and social solidarity, that understands and values human rights, and that recognizes the dignity of every human being; the health care industry, by and large, strives to be an expression of this ideal.

Social loafers: people who have health insurance but who fail to avail themselves of the prophylactic treatments which have been shown to reduce the risk of further disease; a medical phenomenon that is often the result of family and social environments that do not support healthy lifestyles; for instance, overweight and obese people often exert less effort to achieve weight goals when they are around other overweight people. *Compare* **free-riders** (who make no contributions at all, as opposed to social loafers, who reduce their fair share contribution efforts because they believe they would not obtain their fair share of benefits in return).

Social media model (of decision-making *aka* the Twitter Model, the front-page-of-the-newspaper test, or the smell test): helps determine whether application of any of the other seven different decision-making models is necessary; the most common form of decision-making; where most discussion of ethical issues begins. Asks how one would feel having one's actions go viral, and if that level of public scrutiny is undesirable, the action is probably unethical. *See* **choices model, common good model, exceptions model, justice model, rights model, smell test,utility model,** and **virtue model**.

Social responsibility: an ethical framework mandating actions for the benefit of society; health care systems must not be focused solely on the bottom line or maximizing financial profits.

Social risks (*aka* the social determinants of health): economic and community conditions that shape people's health, such as the ability to access affordable health insurance.

Social solidarity: refers to the harmony of interests and responsibilities among U.S. citizens. This principle means that health care should be financed by individuals on the basis of their ability to pay, but should be available to all who need it on more or less equal terms.

Social stability: depends upon the extent to which the members of a society feel that they are being treated justly; one of the four foundations of justice (in addition to equality, interdependence, and human dignity). *See* **justice, equality, interdependence,** and **human dignity**.

Socioeconomic pyramid: economic term first used by President Franklin D. Roosevelt; the more current usage refers to a global economy that has a small wealthy populace at the top of the social order, while gradually expanding to a large less wealthy populace at the bottom of the social order.

Stakeholder: a person or group with a direct interest in something; an approach to health care that asks everyone—government, academics, patients, and the health care industry—To address and balance the multiple claims of shared interests and concerns.

Stakeholder society: where legal rights enjoyed are intricately linked to responsibilities and ethical obligations of people or groups with a direct interest, involvement, or investment in a community that is bound together by similar traditions, institutions, or nationality.

Standards of care: appropriate conduct of physicians, nurses, and other health care professionals in comparison to what reasonable professionals either do, or should do, in similar circumstances with similar resources; legal standards vary from state to state.

Status quo: the way things are now; conditions that currently exist. In this textbook, the term generally refers to the U.S. health care system before comprehensive health care reform was enacted in 2010 and the Patient Protection and Affordable Care Act became the law of the land.

Sub-average intellectual functioning: clinically describes people with significant limitations in adaptive skills (such as communication, self-care, and self-direction), limitations that affect their ability to understand and process information, to communicate, to abstract from mistakes and learn from experience, to engage in logical reasoning, to control impulses, and to understand the reactions of others.

Subsidies: usually refers to government contributions to private industry to help them continue to function.

Substituted judgment standard: permits a surrogate to make a decision regarding health care based on what the patient would have chosen had he or she been competent; should approximate the patient's preferences and values. *Compare* **best interests standard** for minors and for patients whose wishes are not known (highest-quality, optimal care for the patient).

Substitution effect: theory that guns are the preferred tool of violence, but people who are intent on harming themselves or others will find a way to achieve their objective of harm, with whatever tools are available; this theory has not been proven with regard to gun violence.

Supplemental health insurance: provides coverage for unrestricted access to advanced care, including access to highly specialized physicians over and above the basic needs for medically necessary prevention, traditional diagnosis, and treatment of diseases and health conditions; health insurance deductibles and co-payments may still restrict access. *Compare* **medically needed care** (the standard of necessary health care and medical treatments, which sometimes includes advanced medications and medical devices) *and* **universal coverage** (includes the option of buying supplemental coverage).

Tax-exempt: health care systems that have this status do not have to pay federal, state, or local taxes, can access the bond market on a tax-free basis, and are able to solicit charitable donations.

Terminal prognosis: an opinion as to the likely course of a disease or injury that cannot be cured or adequately treated and that is reasonably expected to result in the death of the patient within a relatively short period of time (generally 6 months); usually used for progressive diseases such as cancer or advanced heart disease, rather than trauma.

Trans-fat-free: defined as less than 0.5 grams of trans-fat per labeled serving (equivalent to half of a small paper clip); note that some experts believe no amount of trans-fat is safe to consume.

Trans-fats: substances inexpensively created by the processed food industry as a side effect of partially hydrogenating unsaturated plant fats (generally vegetable oils); increase product shelf life and decrease refrigeration requirements; increase the risk of cardiovascular disease, depression, and obesity. *See* **trans-fat-free**.

Treatment adherence: the good faith effort by patients to comply with the treatment regimens recommended by their physicians and other health care professionals; includes obtaining diagnostic procedures, taking prescribed medication as directed with regular monitoring, modification of lifestyle choices as directed (such as not smoking, healthy diet and exercise, and weight management), accepting responsibility to follow up on referrals to other specialists, and following all other recommended treatment and therapy actions, including surgery as needed.

Truthfulness: ethical value which is an overriding component at all levels of the U.S. health care system; takes an ongoing commitment to build and maintain with all stakeholders; requires the medical products industry, physicians, nurses, and other health care professionals to honestly and accurately report health information to patients; recognizes patients' right to know the truth of their health status. Personal autonomy is compromised by withholding truth from patients.

Tuberculosis (TB): communicable disease that generally affects the lungs causing pulmonary mucous membranes to swell; currently categorized as an epidemic in the U.S.

Uncompensated care: the sum of charitable care and bad debt. *Compare* **charitable care** and **bad debt** (accounts written off as unpaid by health care providers even though patients have the ability to pay).

Underinsured: included the insured with restricted health insurance plans that were banned under the Affordable Care Act (such plans only paid for accidents or specific catastrophic diseases like cancer, or had low-annual caps with $500 or $1,000 of coverage and low-lifetime caps).

Unethical: conduct that does not conform to agreed-upon moral standards, especially within a particular profession; immoral principles of people. *Compare* **ethical** (opposite of unethical).

Unhealthy behaviors: harmful lifestyle choices that are not good for human health, such as smoking, overeating, or failing to take medications or follow treatment regimens as prescribed.

Uniform Determination of Death Act of 1981: model law that may be adopted by state legislatures that provides for individuals to be declared biologically dead if they have sustained irreversible cessation of either their circulatory and respiratory functions or of their entire brain.

Universal coverage: a payment system that provides access to basic health insurance for nearly everyone with the option of buying additional coverage. The Affordable Care Act requires everyone to have health insurance coverage for medically necessary care with government subsidies to the economically disadvantaged as needed. *See* **supplemental health insurance** (option to purchase additional coverage to access the highest attainable standard of necessary health care and medical treatments; provides access to advanced medications and medical devices).

Universal values (aka American ethic): ethical principles and beliefs of a person or a group or a nation. In this textbook, the assumption is that a liberal democracy is the most suitable political system for the United States and that Western political principles are universal in the U.S. health care industry, especially the ideals of compassion, fairness, justice, and individual and social responsibility. Used interchangeably with the term *principles*, though defined differently. *Compare* **common public ethic** (which only applies to communities of people within a nation who share common beliefs, general interests, and historical traditions). *See* **principles**.

Unmet medical need: situations where people needed care but did not get it because they could not afford it or delayed care because of worry about the cost.

Utilitarianism: a philosophy of ethics whose ethical component argues that the ends justify the means.

Utility model (of decision-making): focuses on the benefits or total net effects for the people affected by a decision; concerned with results and consequences; actions that provide the greatest benefit to the most people are the most ethical course of action under this model where everyone counts the same; ends justify the means, in other words, actions are ethical if they result in the best overall outcome (regardless of who is affected); often claims that an action must be ethical because everyone else is doing it. *Compare* **exceptions model** and **choices model** (that focus on how decisions are made and concerned with the conditions or rules the action can meet) *with* **common good model** (that considers more than just those affected) and **exceptions model** (that is the opposite of this decision-making model). *See* **utilitarianism**.

Values (aka principles): character traits developed through learning and through practice that enable people to be and to act in ways that develop their human potential; common attitudes that enable a nation to pursue the ideals and ethics its people have adopted; the accepted standards toward which everyone in a nation or particular health care system or group within the health care industry strives; the core beliefs that allow for the full development of every member of society; used interchangeably with the term *principles*, although defined differently. The importance of compassion, equality of opportunity, and justice are 3 common principles of the newly emerging ethics of health care. *Compare* **virtue ethics** (where everyone strives toward common values). *See* **habits** (values become habits) and **principles**.

Viability: when a human fetus can naturally survive outside a women's uterus, generally after 24 weeks. *Compare* **pre-viability** (before 24 weeks).

Vicarious liability: the legal responsibility of individuals or institutions that have the right, ability, or duty to control the activities of someone whose conduct injures a patient or other third party.

Virtue ethics: a philosophy of ethics that believes there are certain common ideals (*i.e.*, commitment to excellence) toward which everyone should strive and which allow the full development of humanity; with this approach to ethics, one strives to grasp the core values of common ideals and then bring them to bear on everyday decision-making.

Virtue model (of decision-making): focuses primarily on core values and the kind of person almost everyone aspires to be and secondarily on judging individual actions; believes

people must take responsibility for their own actions and shape their own destinies.

Virtues: habits of acting in certain ways that correspond to the core values most people aspire to; character traits that enable people to be and to act in ways that develop their human potential (*i.e.*, compassion, courage, diligence, education, fairness, generosity, honesty, integrity, self-control, and tolerance); attitudes that enable nations to pursue values that most of their citizens have adopted based on national tradition. *See* **compassion** and **fairness**.

Vulnerable populations: social groups that experience health disparities as a result of lack of access to health care and therefore face increased exposure to health risks. The most vulnerable populations in American society are minorities, underprivileged people, people who are marginalized by societal norms, such as sexual orientation or immigrant status, high-risk mothers (defined as unmarried, low-income women), children, people with HIV/AIDS, and homeless families.

Wellness rules: require all employees covered under the same employer-sponsored health insurance plan to pay the same insurance premiums regardless of their health, with wellness programs being the exception; employers can offer incentives of as much as 50 percent off the cost of insurance premiums to employees participating in risk assessment programs.

List of Boxes

List of Figures

List of Tables

Index

Note: Page numbers followed by *b*, *f*, or *t* indicate material in boxes, figures, or tables, respectively.